Macroeconomics

Prentice Hall Series in Economics

Macroeconomics

DAVID C. COLANDER
Middlebury College

EDWARD N. GAMBER
Lafayette College

Prentice
Hall

Upper Saddle River, New Jersey 07458

Library of Congress Cataloging-in-Publication Data

Colander, David C.
    Macroeconomcis / David C. Colander, Edward N. Gamber.
        p. cm.—(Prentice-Hall series in economics)
    Includes index.
    ISBN 0-13-030372-0
    1. Macroeconomics. I. Title. II. Series.

HB172.5 .C638 2001b
339—dc21   2001036876

Executive Editor: Rod Banister
Development Editor: Audrey Regan
Editor-in-Chief: PJ Boardman
Managing Editor (Editorial): Gladys Soto
Assistant Editor: Marie McHale
Editorial Assistant: Lisa Amato
Media Project Manager: Nancy Welcher
Marketing Manager: Joshua P. McClary
Marketing Assistant: Christopher Bath
Managing Editor (Production): Cynthia Regan
Senior Production Editor: Richard DeLorenzo
Production Assistant: Dianne Falcone
Permissions Coordinator: Suzanne Grappi
Associate Director, Manufacturing: Vincent Scelta
Production Manager: Arnold Vila
Design Manager: Pat Smythe
Art Director: Janet Slowik
Interior Design: Karen Quigley
Cover Design: Joan O'Connor
Cover Illustration/Photo: DamanStudio
Illustrator (Interior): Matrix Publication Studios
Manager, Print Production: Christy Mahon
Composition/Full-Service Project Management: Compset Inc.
Print/Binder: Quebecor World Color—Versailles

Credits and acknowledgments borrowed from other sources and reproduced, with permission, in this textbook appear on appropriate page within text.

Pearson Education LTD.
Pearson Education Australia PTY, Limited
Pearson Education Singapore, Pte. Ltd
Pearson Education North Asia Ltd
Pearson Education, Canada, Ltd
Pearson Educación de Mexico, S.A. de C.V.
Pearson Education–Japan
Pearson Education Malaysia, Pte. Ltd

10 9 8 7 6 5 4 3 2 1
ISBN 0-13-030372-0

To our children,
Zach and Kasey Colander
William and Emily Gamber

About the Authors

DAVID C. COLANDER

David C. Colander is the Christian A. Johnson Distinguished Professor of Economics at Middlebury College. In the 2001–2002 academic year, he was the Stanley Kelley Jr. Professor of Distinguished Teaching at Princeton University. He has authored, coauthored, or edited over 30 books and over 80 articles on a wide range of economics topics.

Professor Colander earned his B.A. at Columbia College and his M. Phil and Ph.D. at Columbia University. He also studied in England and Germany. He has previously taught at Columbia University, Vassar College, and the University of Miami, and has been a consultant to Time-Life Films, a consultant to Congress, a Brookings Policy Fellow, and a Visiting Scholar at Nuffield College, Oxford.

He belongs to a variety of professional associations, has served on the Board of Directors, and as Vice President and President of both the History of Economic Thought Society and the Eastern Economic Association. He has also served on the editorial boards of the *Journal of Economic Perspectives,* the *Journal of Economic Methodology,* the *Journal of the History of Economic Thought,* the *Eastern Economic Journal,* and the *Journal of Economic Education.* His current research is on the policy implications of complexity.

EDWARD N. GAMBER

Edward N. Gamber is an Associate Professor of Economics at Lafayette College. He has authored numerous articles on macro and monetary economics. His principal areas of research are on what causes business cycles and how the Federal Reserve reacts to economic fluctuations.

Professor Gamber earned his B.A. at Towson State University and his M.A. and Ph.D. at Virginia Tech. He has taught at Oberlin College and at the University of Missouri, St. Louis. He has worked as a consultant in private industry as well as the Federal Reserve Bank of Cleveland and as principal analyst at the Congressional Budget Office from 1996 to 1998. Professor Gamber received the Omicron Delta Epsilon award for outstanding teaching. He serves on the editorial boards of the *Journal of Economics* and the *Eastern Economic Journal* and is currently author of *The Wall Street Journal Macroeconomic Educator's Review.*

Brief Contents

Contents

Acknowledgments

Economics is a discussion of ideas and policies—an approach we think students will find in this text. We have had the pleasure of such discussions with many reviewers whose insights and criticisms improved the text enormously. We thank them for their careful reading of all or parts of the manuscript at different stages.

Rashid Al-Hmoud, Texas Tech University
Doris Bennett, Jacksonville State University
Yongsung Chang, University of Pennsylvania
Steven Dickey, Eastern Kentucky University
Linda Ghent, East Carolina University
Charles Haase, San Francisco State University
James Hartley, Mount Holyoke College
John S. Irons, Amherst College
John Keating, University of Kansas
Faik Koray, Louisiana State University
Masoud Moghaddam, St. Cloud State University
Ann Owen, Hamilton College
Douglas Pearce, North Carolina State University
Helen Roberts, University of Illinois at Chicago
Willem Thorbecke, George Mason University
Mark Wohar, University of Nebraska, Omaha
Douglas Woolley, Radford University

PEOPLE TO THANK

Writing this book like this is an enormous job, and there are many people to thank. We would first like to thank Gary Nelson, a friend who encouraged us to write it. Next we would like to thank Rod Banister, our editor. He shared our view that the market needs this book, and he provided consistent support to complete the project. He is a great editor. We'd also like to thank Audrey Regan, our Development Editor, whose word-smithing kept us on point and whose humor added levity to the team.

Next, we'd like to thank our students who put up with early drafts of the book, told us what worked and what didn't, caught errors, and in the process improved the book enormously. There are too many to acknowledge individually, but they deserve a lot of thanks.

Many people at Prentice Hall helped bring this book to market: Audrey D'Agostino, Advertising Copywriter; Diane DeCastro, Creative Services Manager; Stephen Deitmer, Director of Development; Nancy D'Urso, Advertising Designer; Rick DeLorenzo, Production Editor; Marie McHale, Assistant Editor; Joshua P. McClary, Marketing Manager; Janet Slowik, Senior Designer; Gladys Soto, Managing Editor. We thank them all.

The typesetting was done by Compset Inc. with Janet Domingo taking the lead. New books are never easy to set, and this was no exception. We thank all who contributed to composition of the book.

Another group who did a great job are the supplements authors: Rashid Al-Hmoud of Texas Tech University who wrote the *Instructor's Manual*; Doris Bennett of Jacksonville State University who wrote the *PowerPoint Presentation*; James DeVault of Lafayette College who wrote the Test Bank; Jonathan Irons of Amherst College who wrote *The Study Guide*; Mary Lesser of Iona College who wrote the *Active Graph CD-ROM*; and Willem Thorbecke of George Mason University who wrote the *On-line Study Guide*. Their contributions are essential to this package. We thank them for their outstanding efforts.

Special thanks go to Jenifer Gamber, who, in many ways, is a coauthor of the book. She edited what we wrote, kept us honest, and added innumerable suggestions. She is one amazing woman, and we both thank her immensely.

We also want to thank Pat Colander, who contributed to the project by refusing to talk economics with her husband, keeping their marriage strong.

Preface

We recently received a call from a reporter who asked us to rate macroeconomic forecasters. Given our reputations, the reporter was expecting a negative rating. We told him that macroeconomic forecasters beat back-of-the-envelope forecasting 5 to 10 percent of the time. He said, "You're really down on macro forecasters, aren't you?" "No, not at all!" we answered. "Given the complicated nature of the macro economy, that's a very impressive record—one that makes it worthwhile for firms and governments to employ economic forecasters."

POLICY IN A COMPLEX ECONOMY

The above story reveals this textbook's approach. We start from the assumption that the economy is a complex system. This means, among other things, that the relationships within the economy are constantly evolving, and that the degree of understanding that we can achieve through deductive models, starting from first principles, is limited. However, we do not teach students the science of complexity, or even introduce it. Studying how a butterfly flapping its wings in Australia affects weather patterns in Vermont is a subject matter for other courses. Our desire is to give students a general understanding of the ideas that guide macro policy, given the complex nature of the macro economy.

Consistent with this view, we present macroeconomics as a set of *policy insights* embodied in simple models that policy makers use to reach decisions. If students want to understand recent debates about Fed policy or about the latest tax cut, they need to understand those macroeconomic models and the rules of thumb that underlie them.

This emphasis on policy is central to our approach to teaching macroeconomics. We teach a policy course that does not require a deep understanding of formal theory but rather a practical type of knowledge—a good sense of terminology, data, institutions, and models. The models provide the frameworks within which macroeconomic policy discussions take place. This, we believe, is the essence of the intermediate macroeconomics course. With our primarily policy-oriented book, we provide frameworks for discussing complicated economic issues. We show how macroeconomists give pragmatic policy advice—based on a combination of models and a sense of history and institutions—that is useful but is far from perfect.

MODELS AS WORKING TOOLS

Consistent with the approach we've taken in this book, we do not present models as simplifications of the Truth, with a capital "T." Instead, we present them as working tools, which, when used with an educated common sense, a good understanding of relevant institutions, and insights gained from considering economic issues deductively, provide a reasonable set of guidelines for policy. We treat models as frameworks for organizing thoughts, not representations of the Truth. For example, Chapters 8 and 9 present the IS/LM model and encourage students to use it as an important first step to understanding the economy in the short run. But they also remind students that, like any model, the IS/LM model cannot fully capture the complexity of the economy. It simply provides an initial framework.

This text provides the components necessary for using models right from the start. Instead of jumping directly into formal models, the first four chapters introduce students to the observed behavior and institutions of the economy, contemporary policy issues, and the short- and long-run frameworks that economists use to organize their thoughts about the economy.

A MODERN ORGANIZATION

We present growth and a discussion of the long run first, before the presentation of the short run. We do this not just because it is the modern approach; we do so because it makes sense. Over decades, long-run growth determines the wealth of nations. The study of growth and the long run gives students a sense of the power of markets, and provides a good starting point for a consideration of business cycles and short run models, which give students a sense of the pain that markets can cause.

We believe it is important for students to have this dual sense of markets. What we present is a story of how markets have delivered the goods better than alternative institutional structures. The markets in our story are not perfectly competitive markets—real world markets are never perfectly competitive. They are part of a broader institutional structure that involves government regulation, and policy that offsets the negative side effects of markets. Policy concerns the nature of that regulation and the institutional structure underlying markets.

A BALANCED PERSPECTIVE

This book is neither Keynesian nor Classical. It is simply a macroeconomics book. The Keynesian/Classical division that characterized earlier textbooks, and that still characterizes some books, is no longer useful in distinguishing modern debates in macro. We do present various viewpoints, but we give each a sympathetic interpretation. We emphasize that most policy makers and businesspeople use a variety of frameworks to help them understand what is happening in the economy, and most of them understand the limitations, as well as the strengths, of those frameworks. This openness to multiple viewpoints comes naturally because our own views of macroeconomic theory and policy differ, as we occasionally point out in the book's running narrative and in some of the boxes called *The Briefing Room*.

POLITICAL REALITIES ARE IMPORTANT

Because of the book's strong policy focus, it covers the political realities and institutions of macroeconomics in greater detail than many competing books. What we mean by political realities and institutions are such things as the budgetary process and the operating procedures of the Fed. It is our belief that political realities limit what economic policy makers can accomplish. If students are to understand macroeconomic policy, they must understand the institutions within which it is implemented and the political realities that influence those institutions. Although we discuss institutions of the economy throughout, Chapters 13 and 14 are devoted exclusively to the institutions of monetary and fiscal policy. These chapters give students a feel for the logistics of how policy makers act within institutions to formulate and ultimately implement policy.

INTERNATIONAL AND OPEN ECONOMY MACRO

In today's global economy, any modern text must consider issues within a global context. International concepts are not just relegated to chapters on exchange rates and trade. They are considered throughout the book. Chapter 1, for example, highlights the fact that policy makers set goals for international economic measures that are consistent with their domestic goals. Chapter 2 compares the U.S. economic experience to other OECD and developing countries, and Chapter 3 discusses the causes and cures of high European unemployment. Just about any chapter one chooses will have some international example or comparison.

PEDAGOGICAL FEATURES

The job of a textbook is not just to present the material clearly, but to help students organize their thoughts, facilitate good study habits, and do well in their courses. We've added a number of features to do just this.

Each chapter begins with *Learning Objectives*, which help guide the student's reading of the chapter. A *Key Points* section revisits these objectives at the end of the chapter.

Although you can find policy discussions within the running narrative of every chapter, to ensure that students understand the policy relevance of the discussion we conclude nearly all chapters with a *Policy Perspective* section that presents real-world policy issues, debates, and events in relation to the chapter's main topic. We have also placed notes in the margin to help students identify key concepts in the text.

POLICY PERSPECTIVE: SOCIAL SECURITY AND THE LONG-TERM BUDGET PROBLEM

One of the primary fiscal issues that policy makers will have to deal with in the future is that of Social Security. Social Security is a partially unfunded retirement system, which means that some current expenditures come out of current revenue. In a funded retirement system, all current payments go into a trust fund, from which future benefits are paid. In a partially unfunded system, the trust fund is insufficient to cover future benefit payments.

The Financial Problem

The financial problem of Social Security is that the Social Security system is a partially unfunded system and the ratio of workers to retirees is declining.

As long as a large number of current workers are contributing for each retiree, an unfunded system presents no financial problem; each individual worker will fund only a small fraction of a retiree's benefits. This was the situation when Social Security was started in 1935—there were about 30 workers for every retiree—but this ratio has changed. The first reason why it has changed is that people are living longer. In 1935, a 65-year-old could be expected to live another 12½ years; today, a 65-year-old

The following are the topics covered in the book's Policy Perspective sections.

Policy Perspectives

Chapter 2   How Long-Term Capital Management's inaccurate Treasury bond forecast nearly pushed the U.S. economy into recession.

Chapter 3   The relationship between inflation and growth.

Chapter 4   The uncertainty about which framework was most applicable to the U.S. economy in the late 1990s.

Chapter 5   The saving and investment policies that follow from the neoclassical growth model.

Chapter 6   Policies that follow from the extended Solow growth and new growth models.

Chapter 7   Adjustment mechanisms under various exchange rate regimes.

Chapter 8   How policy makers can use fiscal and monetary policies to offset shocks to the economy.

Chapter 9   Why the Federal Reserve reversed course twice in three years to keep the U.S. economy on an even keel.

Chapter 10 The Asian and Mexican currency crises.

Chapter 11 Why the increase in the United States' real output went beyond potential output but did not generate increased inflation.

Chapter 12 The importance of expectations in policy that has led economists to consider policy actions within a context of policy regimes and credibility.

Chapter 13 Recent Fed policy actions.

Chapter 14 Social Security and the long-term budget problem.

Periodic *Executive Summaries* provide a way for students to pause within a chapter and review their understanding of the main ideas. Though we expect students to read the entire book, these summaries are similar to the executive summaries many business people see at the top of memos they don't necessarily read entirely.

Executive Summary

- An economy is in internal balance when the government achieves its domestic goals. An economy is in external balance when the government achieves its trade and exchange rate goals.

- A large country with imperfectly mobile capital (upward-sloping BP curve) and flexible exchange rates *can* pursue domestic policy goals without regard for whether the balance of payments is in equilibrium. The exchange rate will adjust to bring the balance of payments into equilibrium.

- A large country with imperfectly mobile capital (upward-sloping BP curve) and fixed exchange rates *cannot* pursue domestic policy goals without regard for whether the balance of payments is in equilibrium. If the policies create a balance of

payments deficit, the country will have to buy up the excess supply of its currency, using its foreign reserves. It will eventually run out of reserves.

- Countries can use capital outflow controls, import controls, tariffs, quotas, or voluntary export restraints to shift the BP curve and achieve external balance.

- The Mundell-Fleming model of the open economy assumes that capital is perfectly mobile. This model is useful for the analysis of small open economies. In this model, the BP curve is horizontal. Countries cannot pursue policies to change their interest rates, because capital flows are so large, they push the interest rate back to the world interest rate.

- A small open economy with perfect capital mobility must use monetary policy and fiscal policy combined. Neither works independently.

Within each chapter there are also two types of boxes—*Q&A* and *The Briefing Room*. These boxes present information that is not central to the narrative but that enhances and reinforces students' understanding of the material in the text.

Q&A boxes pose questions from a student's perspective and provide additional explanation of material in the text. An example is the *Q&A* in Chapter 1, "What exactly is a model?" This box describes the elements of a simple model.

Q & A

QUESTION   What exactly is a model?

ANSWER   Taking our definition further, models are assumed relationships among variables that are used to predict or explain behavior.

You are more familiar with models than you might think. You use informal models every day. For example, you use an informal model to decide whether to carry an umbrella. If there are gray skies, you predict rain and carry an umbrella. Economists' models are generally a lot more formal. In formal models, assumptions, variables, and their interrelationships are more clearly stated than in informal models.

Models generally are composed of three ingredients:

1. Assumptions about how people will behave.
2. Variables that are not affected by the model but do affect variables inside the model. These variables are called exogenous variables. Exogenous means determined outside the model.
3. Variables that are explained by the model. These are called endogenous variables. Endogenous means determined inside the model.

Economists use models to predict endogenous variables on the basis of their measures of exogenous variables. Let's take an example using the standard microeconomic supply-and-demand model. Suppose you observed that Florida had been hit by a hard frost (exogenous variable)

that killed many of the early orange flowers. Using the standard supply-and-demand model, what do you predict would happen to the quantity of oranges sold and their price (endogenous variables)? The standard economist's prediction is shown in the illustration.

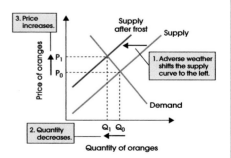

The adverse weather shifts the supply curve to the left, lowering equilibrium quantity and increasing equilibrium price.

The Briefing Room boxes "brief" students about real-world policy and provide commentary on text material. "Strategies To Lower European Unemployment," for example, presents policies European nations have undertaken to address their high unemployment rates.

THE BRIEFING ROOM   Strategies to Lower European Unemployment

In an earlier Briefing Room feature, we discussed how European unemployment rates have been high in recent years. As you can imagine, policies to reduce these high rates have been an important topic of discussion among economists and European policy makers. Most of this discussion has been based on the economists' belief that the high unemployment stems from high natural rates of unemployment, and is not cyclical in nature. The natural rate of unemployment does not respond to demand-side policies, so most of their discussion has been about supply-side and structural policies. Some of the policies that have been recommended include the following:

● Improve labor-force skills through education and training. Higher skilled labor means more productive labor, which makes firms want to hire more workers, reducing unemployment. The problem with these policies is that education and training is often expensive, and the programs can quickly become self-serving for the educators, providing them with income but not providing workers with significant skills.

● Reform (read: reduce) employment security laws. It is very costly to fire workers in much of Europe. Firms must pay large separation payments. This makes firms worried about hiring in the first place. Therefore, paradoxically, these laws have the same effect as a tax on hiring. In the 1990s, many European countries relaxed their stringent labor laws, allowing firms more flexibility with regard to hiring, pay, and work-week hours.

● Reduce regulation of work time and temporary jobs. Firms will only hire workers if they think the workers' production will exceed their wages. Many European countries, however, have strong regulations that limit hours of work and prevent firms from hiring temporary and part-time workers. By reducing these regulations, firms are more able to shift production to meet the varying demands in the market.

● Reform the level and duration of unemployment benefits. Unemployment benefits pay people for not working, so the higher they are, the less likely the unemployed will want to work. By reducing unemployment benefits, you lower the reservation wage and increase the likelihood that workers will accept lower paying jobs.

There are, of course, many other similar types of policies, but these give you a sense of the kind of policies that governments are exploring to reduce their natural rate of unemployment.

It is possible for these policies to work. For example, Ireland's natural rate of unemployment fell by over 6 percentage points in the 1990s. During this time Ireland reduced unemployment benefits, reduced employment taxes, and increased efforts to train workers. It is one of the European Community's major success stories.

You can read more about these policy issues in *Implementing the OECD Jobs Strategy* (www.oecd.org).

We have found that many students have a hard time reading graphs. To help students, we have added call-out boxes to many graphs. These call-out boxes take the students step-by-step through the material that the graphs present. It's like having a tutor within the text.

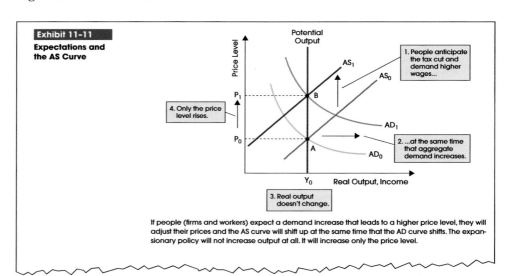

Exhibit 11-11

Expectations and the AS Curve

1. People anticipate the tax cut and demand higher wages...

2. ...at the same time that aggregate demand increases.

3. Real output doesn't change.

4. Only the price level rises.

If people (firms and workers) expect a demand increase that leads to a higher price level, they will adjust their prices and the AS curve will shift up at the same time that the AD curve shifts. The expansionary policy will not increase output at all. It will increase only the price level.

The *Key Points* at the end of each chapter provide a summary of the chapter's main concepts and are based on the chapter's opening learning objectives.

A list of *Key Terms* appears at the end of each chapter, complete with a reference to the page where that term is defined.

Following the *Key Terms* are *Questions for Thought and Review* as well as *Problems and Exercises*. The Questions for Thought and Review help the student master all of the concepts in the chapter. The *Problems and Exercises* tend to be more involved and quantitative in nature, with some of them requiring Internet research. Chapter 15 concludes with a sample final exam. Answers to the even numbered end-of-chapter questions are on the textbook's Web site www.prenhall.com/colander. Answers to all the questions reside in the *Instructor's Manual*.

READABILITY

All the bells and whistles are important, but they don't mean a thing unless the students read the book. Our style of writing isn't the most "professorial" style, but it is one that students (we've been told) find enjoyable. (Actually, we didn't believe the students at first, but they repeated this appraisal after they had received their grade, which gave their statements more credibility.)

ORGANIZATION OF THE BOOK

This book is shorter than most macroeconomic textbooks: 15 chapters divided into five parts. You can use it for a semester-long or quarter-long course. It is appropriate for a policy-oriented intermediate macroeconomics course or a macroeconomics course for MBA students. The following summary on the next page gives you a concise overview of the chapters and their contents to use in designing your course.

Brief Contents

Chapter 1 Presents macro policy's four standard goals—high growth, smooth growth of output, low unemployment and low inflation—and looks at U.S. performance of these four goals.

Chapter 2 Covers the concepts and data of macroeconomics, focusing on international data. Highlights the policy implications of measurement issues.

Chapter 3 Discusses three policy goals—low inflation, low unemployment, and growth. Explains why each is an economic goal and how they may be related.

Chapter 4 Presents the roles of businesses, households, government, and the foreign sector. Differentiates long-run and short-run equilibrium, focusing on saving and investment.

Chapter 5 Explains the importance of growth (through the Solow Model) to policy and asks, What causes growth?

Chapter 6 Extends the basic Solow model to New Growth Theory, which emphasizes the roles of technology and increasing returns to growth.

Chapter 7 Discusses the quantity theory of money as a theory of inflation and purchasing power parity as a theory of changes in exchange rates in the long run.

Chapter 8 Derives the multiplier model and a model of the money market to develop the fixed price IS/LM model.

Chapter 9 Shows how fiscal and monetary policies operate in the IS/LM framework. Discusses the real-world difficulties of using aggregate demand management policies.

Chapter 10 Presents the IS/LM/BP model and the Mundell-Fleming model of the open economy.

Chapter 11 Incorporates price level changes into the IS/LM model and focuses on the role of potential output to inflation. Discusses how expectations affect the impact of policy.

Chapter 12 Completes the short-run model and relates it to the long-run model by looking at the micro foundations of investment and consumption decisions.

Chapter 13 Details the workings of the Fed—its structure, duties, and various targets. Discusses the "rules vs. discretion" debate.

Chapter 15 Reviews major points learned and discusses how policy makers use theory, facts, and judgment to formulate policy. In place of the normal end-of-chapter material, the chapter ends with a collection of exam questions from selected exams.

Chapter 14 Explains in detail how the U.S. budgetary process works.

THE TEACHING AND LEARNING PACKAGE

The book comes with a number of supplements that enhance the learning experience for both instructors and students.

PRINT SUPPLEMENTS

Instructor's Manual

The Instructor's Manual, prepared by Rashid Al-Hmoud of Texas Tech University, takes the instructor carefully through the text's organization by providing an overview and outline of each chapter. It also includes additional case studies, follow-up exercises to those provided in the text, extra questions, and Internet links/exercises. In addition, the manual includes detailed answers to all of the end-of-chapter questions and problems.

Study Guide

The Study Guide, prepared by Jonathan Irons of Amherst College, summarizes the material in each chapter to enhance student comprehension. It provides chapter objectives, an overview, and an explanation of the different sections/topics in the chapter. "Tips and tricks" boxes give students helpful hints and reminders about chapter material.

Test Bank

The Test Bank, prepared by James DeVault of Lafayette College offers approximately 40 multiple-choice and 20 short answer problems per chapter for a total of 900 questions. The testbank provides the answer to each multiple-choice question as well as an explanation for that response.

TECHNOLOGY SUPPLEMENTS

Prentice Hall Test Manager, Version 4.1

This computerized version of the Test Bank allows instructors to design, save, and generate classroom tests. The test program permits instructors to edit, add, or delete questions from the test banks; edit existing graphics and create new graphics; analyze test results; and organize a database of tests and student results.

MyPHLIP Prentice Hall's Learning on the Internet Partnership/myPHLIP

www.prenhall.com/colander

myPHLIP is a content-rich, multidisciplinary Web site with Internet exercises, activities, and resources related specifically to *Macroeconomics*. It includes the following features:

   In the News—Current events related to topics in each chapter, are supported by group activities, critical-thinking exercises, and discussion questions. These articles, from current news publications to economics-related publications, help show students the relevance of economics in today's world.

   Internet Exercises—New Internet resources are added every two weeks by a team of economics professors to provide both the student and the instructor with the most current, up-to-date resources available.

Syllabus Manager—For the instructor, myPHLIP offers resources such as the answers to Current Events and Internet exercises, and a Faculty Lounge area including teaching tools and faculty chat rooms.

The Online Study Guide—prepared by Willem Thorbecke of George Mason University, offers students another opportunity to sharpen their problem-solving skills and to assess their understanding of the text material. The Online Study Guide contains 20 multiple-choice and three short answer questions per chapter. It grades each question submitted by the student, provides immediate feedback for correct and incorrect answers, and allows students to send results to as many as four e-mail addresses.

Downloadable Supplements—From the myPHLIP Web site, instructors can download supplements and lecture aids. Instructors should contact their Prentice Hall sales representative to get the necessary username and password to access the faculty resources on myPHLIP. Downloadable supplements and lecture aids include:

- The PowerPoint Presentation
  This lecture presentation tool, prepared by Doris Bennett of Jacksonville State University, offers outlines and summaries of important text material, tables and graphs that build, and additional exercises.
- Transparency Masters—A complete set of transparency masters for *all* of the figures and tables in the text.

ONLINE COURSE OFFERINGS

WebCT

Developed by educators, WebCT provides faculty with easy-to-use Internet tools to create online courses. Prentice Hall provides the content and enhanced features. For more information, please visit http://www.prenhall.com/webct.

Blackboard

Blackboard's single template and tools make it easy to create, manage, and use online course materials. Instructors can create online courses using Blackboard's capabilities, which include design, communication, testing, and other course management tools. For more information, please visit http://www.prenhall.com/blackboard.

CourseCompass

This customizable, interactive online course management tool powered by Blackboard provides the most intuitive teaching and learning environment available. Instructors can communicate with students, distribute course material, and access student progress online. For further information, please visit http://www.prenhall.com/coursecompass.

CourseCompass with Ebook

This online course package provides the features of CourseCompass along with an electronic version of the textbook. The addition of a digital textbook to CourseCompass gives instructors greater choice and flexibility as they design and build their courses. With this package, students can remain online and have access to their digital textbooks.

SUBSCRIPTION OPTIONS

The Wall Street Journal Print and Interactive Editions Subscription

Prentice Hall has formed a strategic alliance with *The Wall Street Journal*, the most respected and trusted daily source for information on business and economics. For a small charge, Prentice Hall offers students a 10-week subscription to The Wall Street Journal print edition and The Wall Street Journal Interactive Edition. Adopting professors will receive a complimentary one-year subscription of the print and interactive version as well as weekly subject-specific Wall Street Journal educators' lesson plans.

The Financial Times Subscription

We are pleased to announce a special partnership with *The Financial Times*. For a small charge, students will receive a 15-week print subscription when they purchase a package containing the book and subscription supplement. Instructors will receive a complimentary one-year personal subscription. Please contact your Prentice Hall representative for details and ordering information.

Economist.com Subscription

Through a special arrangement with Economist.com, upon adoption of a book and subscription supplement package, professors will receive a six-month subscription and students will get a 12-week subscription to the magazine's online version. Please contact your Prentice Hall representative for details and ordering information.

1

Economics is a science of thinking in terms of models, joined to the art of choosing models which are relevant to the contemporary world.

—*J. M. Keynes*

Introduction

After reading this chapter, you should be able to:

1. Define macroeconomics

2. List four standard policy goals of macroeconomics

3. Summarize the United States' recent experience with output, unemployment, inflation, interest rates, the budget balance, and the trade balance

4. Describe policies designed to affect the demand side and the supply side of the economy

5. Explain why potential output and the natural rate of unemployment are important concepts for macro policy

6. Discuss the relationship between models and vision

Welcome to macroeconomics. Before we begin, let's listen in on some macroeconomic conversations from around the globe.

In a corporate office:

> Looks like we've got a lot of unsold goods piling up. We may have to cut production and lay off some workers. When do you think the Federal Reserve is going to lower interest rates and get this economy going again?

In a Southeast Asian country's Ministry of Finance:

> Our currency is dropping like a stone. Should we keep on trying to support it? Foreign investment has dried up and our foreign reserves are nearly depleted. It looks like we may be in for some inflation and slow growth. Maybe the International Monetary Fund will give us some assistance to avoid a complete economic collapse.

In the European Central Bank office:

> The euro has just gone down another 2 percent against the dollar. Washington will be all over us to raise interest rates. What's the latest forecast on inflation and unemployment, and how is the euro doing against the yen? Call up the economics division at the U.S. Treasury to get their read on the situation.

On a factory floor somewhere in Brazil:

> Darn economists running the country! The government austerity program is killing us. Julio got laid off last week and who knows which of us will be next.
>
> Yeah, I hear you, but at least prices aren't rising 2,000 percent per year—I can afford something.
>
> But you won't be able to buy anything once you lose your job.

In the U.S. Congressional Budget Office:

> Can you believe this? Unemployment has fallen to 4 percent, and inflation has barely risen. Should we adjust our estimate of 5.2 percent for the natural rate of unemployment? You know, the unemployment rate has been below 5.2 for some years now—where's the inflation?

All of these conversations involve various aspects of macroeconomics. The goal of this book is to give you insight into questions such as these—the type policy makers and businesspeople pose. (See The Briefing Room, "Real-World Policy Makers.")

THE POLICY SCIENCE OF MACROECONOMICS

> Macroeconomics is the study of issues that affect the economy as a whole, especially unemployment, inflation, and economic growth.

Macroeconomics is the study of issues that affect the economy as a whole, especially unemployment, inflation, and economic growth. Macroeconomics asks such questions as: Why is there unemployment? Why is there inflation? What causes an economy to grow? What policies will achieve satisfactory rates of unemployment, inflation, and growth?

The general answer to the first three questions appears simple: Somehow, unemployment, inflation, and growth are the collective result of the decisions that the 6 billion people in the world make about such issues as how much to consume, save, work, produce, and invest. The specific answer, however, is more complicated. These decisions involve the interrelationships and interdependencies of trillions of daily decisions. Nevertheless, how they all work out is what macroeconomic theory is all about. The answer to the fourth question—the policy question—is even more complicated because it depends on the answers to the first three questions.

> The market's role in the economy is to coordinate individual decisions to trade goods and services.

When you think about it, the fact that problems such as unemployment and inflation exist should not be surprising; what is surprising is that economies function at all. A central reason why economies function is the **market**—an institution that coordinates individual decisions to trade goods and services. Because we do have functioning economies, the market clearly is doing something remarkable to coordinate those decisions. Macroeconomics studies how the coordination of those decisions affects the aggregate, or whole, economy.

> The macro policy question: Do current institutions coordinate the decisions of individuals in society sufficiently well, or should we modify the institutions and adjust the market results in some way?

To put it another way, macroeconomics studies (1) how the market coordinates individual decisions, so that they do not lead to "undesirable" levels of unemployment, inflation, and growth; and (2) whether additional policies can be implemented to achieve the macroeconomic goals of society. These two issues form the **macro policy question:** Do current institutions coordinate the decisions of individuals in society sufficiently well, or should we modify the institutions and adjust the market results in some way?

Precisely what macroeconomists study depends on what events are currently affecting an economy. For example, an important U.S. policy question in the late

1990s and in early 2000 was: Would rapidly rising stock prices lead consumers to spend more than the economy could produce, and result in accelerating inflation? If so, should policy makers implement policies to curb rising spending? In the early 1980s, a central U.S. policy question was: How can inflation be lowered without causing too much unemployment? The policy question in the mid-2000s may be something different.

This focus on policy may make you think that macroeconomics is not a science. However, if you broadly define science, as we do, as the systematic examination of ideas in reference to empirical observation, macroeconomics is indisputably a science. The macroeconomics that you will find in this book is a *policy science*—the systematic examination of ideas in reference to empirical observation that is intricately concerned with policies needed to achieve stated goals.

Policy science uses abstract theory, but does not dwell on it.

Why point this out? It is necessary to do so because, for some students, the word *science* means formal models and abstract thinking quite removed from their lives. That's not true of a policy science. Policy science concerns actions government can take; it deals with abstract theory only to the degree that the theory helps us understand policy debates.

There are, of course, other aspects of the science of macroeconomics. The *pure science* branch of economics, sometimes called **positive economics,** is the study of the economy and how it works. Positive macroeconomics is often highly abstract and, quite frankly, pretty challenging mathematically. We'll talk about issues inherent in this branch of macroeconomics as backdrops to policy, but we won't dwell on them. Our goal is to help you understand current macroeconomic policy debates. To accomplish this, we have to give you a glimpse of some of the positive economics that underlie these debates, but only a glimpse.

THE STANDARD GOALS OF MACROECONOMICS

Because policy concerns achieving goals, let's talk a bit about the goals of macroeconomics. What are the goals? Who decides what they are? How are they chosen? The general goal economists use is to improve the welfare of individuals in society. We use the term society to refer to the collective group of individuals who make up an economy. To improve welfare, the improvement must be sustainable. In terms of macroeconomic variables, improving welfare is usually translated into these four standard goals:

- High growth
- Smooth growth of output
- Low unemployment
- Low inflation

Positive economics = what is. Normative economics = what should be.

Economists did not choose these goals—governments, as representatives of individuals in society, did. Determining the appropriate goals of society is part of **normative economics**—the study of what society's goals for the economy should be. Normative economics necessarily involves value judgments. Although a policy science requires making normative judgments, economists try to keep their own judgments out of their study of the economy. Economists try to remain objective and use the normative goals determined by government.

Policy Is Dependent on Normative Goals

Despite the importance of normative goals to policy discussions, we will not carefully discuss the normative dimensions of the four standard macroeconomic goals. Such a discussion is beyond what is generally considered in macroeconomics at this level. We will focus on the policy science of macroeconomics: how the macroeconomy works in reference to the standard goals.

We do, however, want to point out that the macroeconomic policy discussion would change considerably if the goals changed. Here's an example. Say society decides that one of its goals should be to hurt no living thing. Much economic activity and economic growth inevitably kills living things. In this case, society might want to drop the growth goal and judge the economy on how it *decreases* economic activity. As an alternative, and more realistically, say society thinks it needs to develop stronger family relationships. To achieve this end, one of its goals might be that people spend more time at home, which would decrease economic activity. Put simply, increasing economic activity is not the be-all and end-all goal. As are all goals, it's debatable.

Politics and Economics

Another point about goals is that political leaders, because they determine the laws that govern society, ultimately determine which goals to target. We must rely on our analysis of the political structure to determine whether the goals our government aims for are the goals that represent the goals that society would choose. If the political structure is a dictatorship, goals of society and the dictator's goals can differ significantly. In that case, economists may look elsewhere than government to find the goals of society. In a democracy, in which the political leaders are elected, there is a stronger argument that policy makers will take actions that are consistent with the goals of society.

Feasible Goals

One final comment concerning goals: The goals that policy makers pursue must be feasible. Often they are not, and it's up to economists to identify which goals are realistic and which are not. Society's goals often conflict, and society seldom wants to face the difficult trade-offs in choosing among goals.

Most governments want no inflation, high growth, 2 percent unemployment, and a trade surplus. This is equivalent to someone wanting to run a 4-minute mile; high jump 6 feet, 6 inches; and bench press 450 pounds without training. It's highly unlikely. So one job for macroeconomists is to explain to policy makers what can and cannot be done—spell out what goals can and cannot be achieved simultaneously—and to explain the trade-offs in achieving various goals.

IMPORTANT CONCEPTS AND MEASURES IN MACROECONOMICS

To be able to discuss these normative goals and to determine what is feasible, economists have developed a variety of measures of economic performance and policy. We discuss these throughout the book, so we provide only a quick introduction here.

Measures of Feasible Goals

Exhibit 1–1 shows output in the United States since 1947. By output, we mean total production of final goods and services in an economy. The shaded regions in this exhibit and in Exhibits 1–2 through Exhibit 1–6 indicate periods during which output declined. The blue solid line in Exhibit 1–1 shows that output has both risen and fallen but has followed a general upward trend, shown by the red dotted line. This trend rise in output is called the underlying growth rate. The underlying growth rate in the United States has averaged about 3.5 percent per year since 1947. Based on this history, economists usually define 3.5 percent growth as a feasible goal for annual growth in output for the United States. When economists talk about growth, they generally are referring to growth in potential output. **Potential output** is the amount of goods and services an economy is capable of producing for a sustainable period of time. Economists usually argue that the U.S. economy's potential output can increase at a rate of 3.5 percent per year (give or take 1 percent, depending on population growth, capital accumulation, and technological progress).

Output growth fluctuates. Sometimes it exceeds trend, sometimes it falls below trend, and sometimes it actually declines. Economists call these fluctuations in output **business cycles.** Policy makers would like to eliminate or reduce these cycles, but their ability to do so is limited.

Exhibit 1–1 gives us some sense of how much output has fluctuated around its growth trend since 1947. The small inset shows a close-up of a business cycle in the 1970s to give you a sense of how much output fluctuates each quarter (3 months) of a year above and below its trend. Output rose over 4 percent above its trend in 1973 and declined by over 4 percent below its trend in 1975. Some business cycles

> Potential output means maximum sustainable output.

Exhibit 1–1

Output in the United States

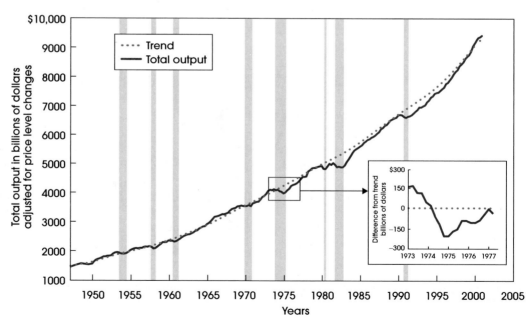

The *dotted red line* shows the trend rise in economic output, or growth. The *blue line* shows how economic output has fluctuated around that trend. The *shaded bars* indicate periods during which output declined. The inset highlights how output fluctuated around its trend in the 1970s. The exact measure of output shown in the graph is real GDP, which we introduce in Chapter 2. Source: Department of Commerce, Bureau of Economic Analysis (www.bea.doc.gov).

have been much larger. The largest decline in output since 1947 was in 1982, when output fell 8 percent below its trend. The largest increase in output above its trend was in 1966, when output rose 6 percent above its trend for one quarter of the year.

On average, since 1947 output has fluctuated roughly 1 percent to 2 percent above or below its trend. Based on that history, economists define preventing downward fluctuations of more than 2 percent as a feasible goal. Recently, the U.S. economy has done better; output has risen steadily for the last 11 years, and in 2000, output was almost 3 percent above its trend. Some economists are now arguing that a new economy with a higher trend has arrived and decreases in output will no longer occur. (Most economists remain dubious.)

A measure that is related to fluctuations in output is the **unemployment rate**—the percentage of people who want a paying job but do not have one. Unemployment generally rises when output falls, and falls when output rises. Exhibit 1–2 shows the U.S. unemployment rate since 1948. The unemployment rate has fluctuated between 3 percent and 11 percent, averaging 5.6 percent. When it has gone below that, inflation has tended to accelerate. So, a key focus of policy is the unemployment rate below which inflation tends to accelerate. This is called the **natural rate of unemployment.** (See the Q&A feature for a discussion of this term.)

Until the 1990s, economists thought that 5.5 percent to 6.0 percent was the lowest unemployment could go without generating accelerating inflation, so their policies targeted 5.5 percent to 6.0 percent unemployment. But in the mid-1990s, the unemployment rate fell significantly below 5.5 percent, and inflation actually declined, so economists have had to reexamine what is feasible. In the early 2000s, the unemployment rate fell to about 4 percent, and inflation still had not risen, causing many economists to argue that the goal for unemployment should be lowered.

The natural rate of unemployment means normal unemployment. There will be a tendency for the economy to gravitate to the natural rate of unemployment.

Exhibit 1–2

U.S. Unemployment

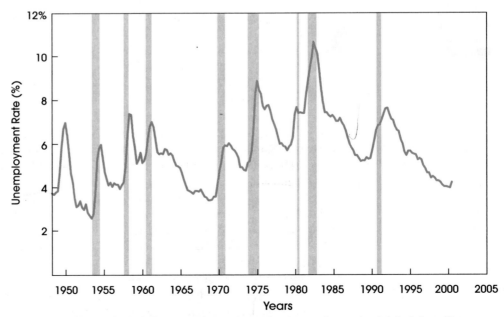

The unemployment rate is the percentage of people who want a paying job but do not have one. The *shaded regions* indicate periods during which output declined. The unemployment rate tends to rise when output declines and fall when output rises. Source: Department of Labor, Bureau of Labor Statistics (stats.bls.gov).

Exhibit 1-3

U.S. Inflation

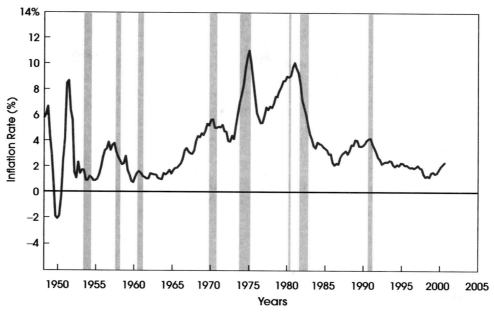

Inflation has been a fact of U.S. life since 1950. In the 1970s, inflation rose to over 11 percent. In the 1990s and early 2000s, inflation has subsided to about 2 percent to 3 percent. The *shaded regions* indicate periods during which output declined. Source: Department of Commerce, Bureau of Labor Statistics (stats.bls.gov).

Inflation is a continual rise in the price level.

A fourth measure of economic performance is inflation. **Inflation** is a continual rise in the average price of goods and services in an economy. Exhibit 1–3 shows inflation since 1948. As you can see, inflation has fluctuated from as little as 1.5 percent to as much as 11 percent per year and has, at times, been quite volatile. As a general rule, inflation rises as economic output rises above its potential (and unemployment falls below its natural rate). Similarly, inflation declines as economic output falls below its potential (and unemployment rises above its natural rate). This observation provides policy makers with a perceived short-run trade-off. If increases in output above potential and low unemployment are associated with inflation, policy makers must sometimes either accept high inflation to achieve high output and low unemployment, or accept low output and high unemployment to achieve low inflation. But trade-offs can also be fleeting, and one of economists' jobs is to point this out. Today, most economists believe that the trade-off between inflation and unemployment is, in the long run, an illusion.

Policymaking is made even more difficult by exceptions to the short-run trade-off. Exceptions include two oil price hikes in the 1970s, during which consumer prices rose at double-digit annual rates even though output was below potential, and the low inflation in the late 1990s and early 2000s, even though the economy was above potential and experiencing its longest postwar rise in output.

What is the lowest inflation rate possible with an economy growing at 3.5 percent a year and an unemployment rate at the natural rate? This is a question economists have not answered completely. Currently, a majority of economists believe that 2 percent to 3 percent annual inflation is achievable, although a significant minority argue that zero to 1 percent annual inflation could be achieved without giving up the other goals. (You'll read more about this issue later.)

Q & A

QUESTION   Is the "natural rate of unemployment" the desirable level of unemployment that the economy should accept because it is natural?

ANSWER   No. Society determines what is desirable. The natural rate of unemployment is simply the normal rate that the economy tends toward given its institutions, history, and structure. It is not immutable.

Good economists attempt to remain neutral and objective in their empirical and theoretical work. It isn't always easy, especially because the language we use is often biased. This problem has proved to be a difficult one for economists in their attempt to find a term to describe that level of unemployment that is consistent with potential output. This rate is generally called the *natural rate of unemployment*. Economists have often used the term *natural* to describe economic concepts. For example, they've talked about the "natural rate of interest."

The problem with this use is that what's natural to one person isn't necessarily natural to another. The term *natural* often conveys a sense of "that's the way it should be." However, in calling the rate of unemployment associated with potential output the *natural rate*, economists aren't making value judgments about whether 5.5 percent unemployment is what should, or should not, be.

They simply are saying that, given the institutions in the economy, that is what is achievable without causing accelerating inflation.

A number of economists have objected to the use of the phrase *natural rate of unemployment*. As an alternative, some economists started to use the term *nonaccelerating inflation rate of unemployment* (NAIRU), but even users of this term agreed it was horrendous. Therefore, most economists avoided using NAIRU. Another term for the natural rate is the *target rate of unemployment*. All three terms indicate the rate of unemployment that is attainable without causing accelerating inflation. We use the term *natural rate* because, by convention, it is the term generally used. Remember, however, that NAIRU, the target rate of unemployment, and the natural rate all mean the same thing and that *natural* carries no normative connotation.

Measures of Intermediate Goals

Much of the policy discussion in macroeconomics is not about these four measures of standard goals; instead, it is about intermediate measures that affect the goals. Some important intermediate measures are the interest rate, the budget balance, and the trade balance.

The first intermediate measure we will consider is interest rates. The **nominal interest rate** is the interest rate lenders charge borrowers for the use of funds, stated as a percent of each dollar loaned at annual rates. If you borrowed $1 for a year from a bank and at the end of the year repaid the $1 loan plus 7 cents interest, the interest rate would be 7 percent.

The purple line in Exhibit 1–4 shows a representative nominal interest rate for the economy—the 3-month Treasury bill rate.[1] There are many other interest rates—for example, one for mortgages and another for long-term bonds—but we'll

---

[1] Many of you will notice that the data presented in this book begin at different years. Many students think that data are absolute. Any practicing economist knows better. Individuals and groups construct the data for a variety of purposes and make decisions about definitions, data collection, and sampling to fit their purposes. When the groups collecting the data change, the choices, and consequently the data series, change, which makes comparisons difficult. It has only been since World War II that the U.S. government has tackled the enormous task of making consistent data series. Some foreign countries have even less reliable and consistent data. In this book, we try to use generally available data series and avoid taking you through the intricacies of linking various data sets. As a result, the data we present will begin in different years. Whenever possible, we give you a URL for the Web so that you can update the data presented in the book.

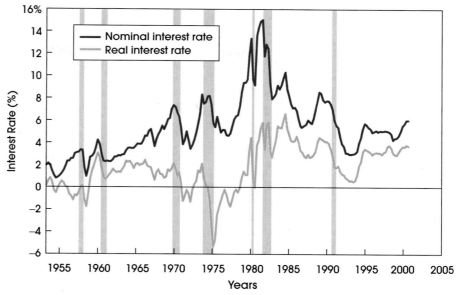

Exhibit 1-4

Interest Rate in the United States

The nominal interest rate (shown in purple) is the amount lenders charge borrowers for the use of funds. The real interest rate (shown in green) is the nominal interest rate adjusted for inflation. There are many interest rates in the economy. The nominal interest rate in this exhibit is the 3-month Treasury bill. The *shaded regions* indicate periods during which output declined. Source: Board of Governors, the Federal Reserve (www.federalreserve.gov).

Real interest rate—the nominal interest rate adjusted for inflation.

hold off discussing these until later. One interest rate concept, however, is so central to macroeconomics that we present it here—that is, the **real interest rate.** The real interest rate is the nominal interest rate, adjusted for inflation. It is the amount lenders actually receive from borrowers after the effect of inflation on the repayment is taken into account. Because inflation reduces the value of the dollars with which the loan is repaid, the real interest rate is calculated by subtracting inflation from the nominal interest rate. For example, if the nominal interest rate is 7 percent and inflation is 3 percent, the real interest rate is 4 percent (7 percent − 3 percent).

The green line in Exhibit 1–4 shows a real interest rate. Real interest rates generally rise when output rises, and fall when output falls. Short-term interest rates, such as the 3-month T-bill, are important indicators of **monetary policy**— deliberate government action to affect the amount of money available for borrowing. Interest rates are important intermediate goals because they affect the level of borrowing, spending, and, ultimately, output. Higher interest rates tend to lower output, while lower interest rates tend to raise output.

Two key macro policies are monetary policy and fiscal policy.

A second intermediate measure is the federal government's **budget balance**—the difference between the taxes government collects and the expenditures government makes. Exhibit 1–5 shows the U.S. budget balance as a percent of gross domestic product (GDP) since 1947. For most years since 1947, the U.S. government has spent more than it has collected in revenue; that is, it has had a budget deficit. Beginning in 1998, however, revenues have exceeded expenditures, so the government has had a budget surplus. The budget balance is affected by both changes in output and changes in **fiscal policy**—the government's intentional change in taxes or expenditures to affect the level of activity in the economy. When government raises taxes or lowers spending, the budget balance rises; when government lowers taxes or raises spending, the budget balance declines. Higher taxes or lower expenditures will

**U.S. Government
Budget Balance**

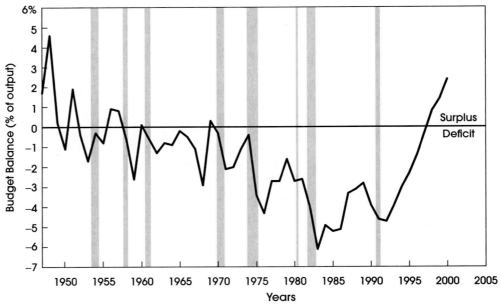

This chart gives you a sense of the size of the U.S. budget balance relative to total output. The vertical bars indicate recessions. The federal government has run deficits most of the time since 1947. In 1998, the budget deficit turned into a budget surplus (source: Congressional Budget Office (www.cbo.gov)). The budget balance shown is the unified budget balance on a fiscal-year basis. Fiscal years start October 1st and end on the following September 30th.

U.S. Trade Balance

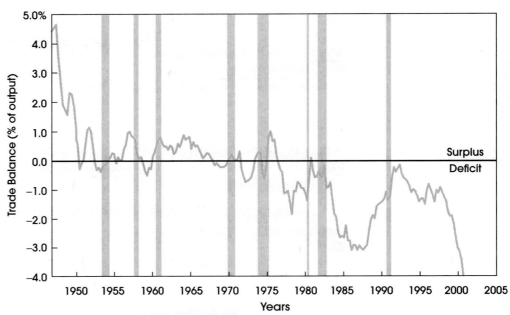

Since the late 1970s, the United States has had a trade deficit. The trade balance is shown as a percent of output to give you a sense of its size relative to total output in the economy. The *shaded bars* indicate periods during which output declined. Source: Department of Commerce, Bureau of Economic Analysis (www.bea.doc.gov).

increase the budget balance, which tends to decrease total spending and output in the economy. Lowering taxes and raising expenditures has the opposite effect.

The U.S. domestic economy is integrally connected to the rest of the world, which leads us to a third intermediate measure—the **trade balance.** A country's trade balance is the difference between the value of goods and services a country sells to the rest of the world (exports) and the value of goods and services it purchases from the rest of the world (imports). Exhibit 1–6 shows the U.S. trade balance since 1947. As you can see, since 1976, the United States has imported more than it has exported. A country that imports more than it exports has a trade deficit. If it exports more than it imports, it has a trade surplus. In the early 2000s, the U.S. trade deficit was at a record high.

The trade balance is a domestic concern because a higher trade balance contributes to greater economic output, while a lower trade balance reduces economic output. That's why in 1998, when Japan wanted to expand its economy, the government urged Japanese firms to produce goods for export. Japan was instituting a **trade policy**—government action to change either imports or exports to affect economic output.

> Trade policy is government action to change either imports or exports to affect economic output.

Executive Summary

- Macroeconomics is the study of issues that affect the economy as a whole.

- The goals of an economy are (1) high growth, (2) smooth growth of output, (3) low unemployment, and (4) low inflation.

- What economists believe to be feasible goals are determined, in part, by the past performance of the economy.

- Growth in the United States has averaged 3.5 percent a year since 1947.

- On average, output fluctuates between 1 percent and 2 percent above and below its growth trend.

- Until recently, economists thought that 5.5 percent to 6.0 percent was the lowest unemployment could be without generating inflation.

- At times, policy makers face a short-run trade-off between low unemployment and low inflation. Most economists, however, believe there is no long-run trade-off.

- Economists use intermediate measures such as interest rates, the budget balance, and the trade balance to measure progress toward society's ultimate goals.

ACHIEVING GOALS: SUPPLY-SIDE AND DEMAND-SIDE POLICIES

Once policy makers have decided what goals are feasible, they must determine what policies to use. When analyzing policies, economists divide their analysis into aggregate demand issues and aggregate supply issues. Short-run analysis focuses on demand—issues affecting aggregate expenditures. Long-run analysis focuses on supply—issues affecting aggregate production. Economists' models tend to highlight either demand or supply issues. In your principles course, you were likely introduced to the AS/AD model. This model allows you to discuss macro policy issues—policies that affect either aggregate demand or aggregate supply.

> Demand-side policies: monetary, fiscal, and trade policies. They work through changing aggregate demand.

The major **demand-side policies** that policy makers use to achieve their goals are monetary policy, fiscal policy, and trade policy. These policies seek to affect

THE BRIEFING ROOM   Real-World Policy Makers

Our focus in this book is on policy. For this reason, we spend a lot of time talking about policy makers—what they do, what they say, and how they see the world. Of course, this raises the following question: Who are these policy makers?

Although a precise definition is impossible, the following will serve as a working proposition: A policy maker is anyone who designs or implements a course of action chosen by government. This definition is very broad and includes a wide range of economists who work for government or in policy think tanks, as well as politicians and other researchers. In fact, it likely includes many of your professors, because many of them are doing research on some governmental policy program.

To understand how policymaking works, think of policy makers as operating within a pyramid. A narrow group of economists is on the top and a broad group of researchers and professors is on the bottom. (Most professors don't just pick up the phone and suggest a policy to the president, but some do.) The work of the people on the bottom is important, however, because it supports the decisions of the people on the top.

We will often use the term policy maker in a narrower sense, and mean by policy makers the people on the top of the pyramid who actually influence policy on a day-to-day basis. This narrower group consists of individuals such as the chairman of the Federal Reserve Bank, members of Congress, the President, and their advisers, heads of international organizations such as the International Monetary Fund and the World Bank. Our list could go on, but this should be sufficient to give you a feel for who the top policy makers are.

For some fun, you might try to determine your "policy-wonk index." Following is a list of ten macroeconomic policy makers on one side, and the positions they held in 2001 on the other. If you can match them all, you are an expert policy wonk. If you can match 7 or more, you are an experienced policy wonk on your way to the major leagues. If you match 5 to 7, you are a novice wonk. If you match fewer than 5, you should spend some time getting familiar with the names of people who set policy in the United States and in the world. (The answers are upside down at the bottom of the box.)

_____ 1. U.S. Chairman of the Federal Reserve Bank
_____ 2. U.S. Secretary of the Treasury
_____ 3. U.S. Chairman of the Council of Economic Advisers
_____ 4. Head of the European Central Bank
_____ 5. Head of the IMF
_____ 6. Head of World Bank
_____ 7. U.S. Director of the National Economic Council
_____ 8. U.S. Director of the Congressional Budget Office
_____ 9. U.S. Chairman of the Senate Finance Committee
_____ 10. Chairman of the Joint Economic Committee

a. James D. Wolfensohn
b. Alan Greenspan
c. Jim Saxton
d. Dan L. Crippen
e. Willem F. Duisenberg
f. Lawrence Lindsey
g. Horst Köhler
h. Paul H. O'Neill
i. R. Glenn Hubbard
j. Max Baucus

Answers: 1-b; 2-h; 3-i; 4-e; 5-g; 6-a; 7-f; 8-d; 9-j; 10-c

aggregate demand, or what economists call aggregate expenditures. Expansionary policy increases aggregate demand and economic output; contractionary policy decreases aggregate demand and economic output.

Policies directed at changing the amount an economy is capable of producing are **supply-side policies.** Supply-side policies seek to change the incentives to work, produce, and innovate by focusing on the labor force, investment in machinery and factories, and advances in technology—all to increase potential output. Major supply-side policies are changing the income tax structure, welfare reform, and deregulation of industries.

> Supply-side policies: policies that work through changing incentives, such as changing tax structure, welfare reform, and deregulation. Supply-side policies affect potential output.

The Central Role of Potential Output and the Natural Rate

The policies economists suggest are highly dependent on their estimate of potential output. If they know how much an economy is producing relative to potential, the appropriate aggregate demand policies to use are clear. If the economy is producing below its potential, expansionary demand-side policies (expansionary monetary, fiscal, or trade policies) will increase output without much danger of rising inflation. If output is above potential, expansionary demand-side policy will ultimately lead only to inflation, and contractionary demand-side policies should be used to bring the economy back to its potential. If the economy is producing at its potential, and the goal is for a still higher output, then policies that increase potential—expansionary supply-side policies—are needed.

Unfortunately, economists cannot measure potential output directly. They must estimate it. A common method of estimating potential output is to observe the level of output at which inflation begins to rise. Economists often judge this level in reference to the natural rate of unemployment—the unemployment rate that exists when the economy is at potential output and, as mentioned earlier, below which inflation increases. Therefore, underlying policy makers' concept of potential output and the natural rate is a theory of inflation.

The Problem of Forecasting

In the mid- to late-1990s economists argued considerably about feasible potential output, the feasible natural rate, and just how far the U.S. economy could expand without generating rising inflation. Some economists argued that output had exceeded the inflation threshold; other economists argued that further expansion in output was possible. No economist knew for sure, and those who suggested they did know generally ended up with egg on their faces.

Consider the following discussion of statements by leading economists in 1994, when the unemployment rate fell from 6.7 percent to 5.4 percent without generating significant inflation. (By 2000, it had fallen to about 4 percent, without generating much additional inflation.) The quotations are from *Business and Academia Clash over a Concept: "Natural" Jobless Rate,* by Amanda Bennett, *The Wall Street Journal,* January 24, 1995.

Economists' record of predicting inflation was not good in the late 1990s.

Are too many Americans at work these days for the economy's own good?

Absolutely, says Martin Feldstein, a Harvard University professor and former head of the Council of Economic Advisers under President Reagan. By Mr. Feldstein's calculations, unemployment already has fallen way below the level he believes is sure to trigger steadily rising inflation—even if the economy begins slowing soon on its own. "We are . . . into the danger zone," he says. . . .

"The danger zone for unemployment seems . . . to be lower than I had been previously estimating," says Robert Gordon, a professor of economics at Northwestern University. As recently as last month, Prof. Gordon advised the Federal Reserve Board that the inflation trigger was an unemployment rate that was probably 6% and possibly as high as 6.5%. "I am the guy who sold 6% to the world," he says. Today, he thinks that trigger point is probably closer to 5.5% and could be as low as 5%.

By Prof. Gordon's earlier reckoning, the economy tripped the inflation switch as early as last March; according to his new calculations, trouble could still be a way off, and hundreds of thousands more people could go back to work before serious inflation rears its ugly head. "I've just created 600,000 jobs," he quips.

Frederic S. Mishkin, executive vice president and director of research at the Federal Reserve Bank of New York, says businesspeople are indulging in wishful thinking (that inflation won't significantly increase in a year or two). "There really is no evidence that [they] can point to except to say 'Gee, we haven't seen inflation yet,' and that's no evidence at all. People keep on making this mistake over and over again," he says.

How can famous economists make such significant forecasting errors? Because the economy is highly complex. Most economists, having made their share of errors, have become far less sure of the models, and far more cautious in their predictions. As Milton Friedman, one of the creators of the term natural rate of unemployment, said when asked to define the natural rate, "I don't know what the natural rate is, neither do you, and neither does anyone else. I don't try to forecast short-term changes in the economy. The record of economists in doing that justifies only humility." We agree, and the macroeconomics presented in this book will be of a humble sort. Real-world policy options are never certain, and economists have found that determining the level of potential output is an art, not a science.

THE ROLE OF MODELS IN ECONOMICS

> Economists look at the economy through models—simplified representations of relationships within an economy.

It isn't only by looking at history that we determine what goals are feasible and what policies are desirable; we also look at models. Models in macroeconomics are important because economic knowledge, like all knowledge, is conjecture and there are many different ways of looking at the world.[2] Models are a way of looking at the world and thinking about it. Much of our knowledge about the economy is embodied in **models**—simplified representations of relationships within an economy—which means that models are fundamentally important in macroeconomics. Indeed, a good portion of this book is concerned with introducing you to standard macroeconomic models. It is important, therefore, that you understand the uses, as well as the limitations, of models.

The development of models comes naturally. By studying the economy, economists begin to recognize certain patterns in the data. These patterns usually take the form of relationships among two or more data series. For example, when productivity rises, real output also tends to rise. Economists then formulate ideas about what causes these patterns and formalize these relationships in a model.

Economists have developed models of how the economy behaves and how policy makers can affect the economy that are simple enough to present to students and to discuss with non-economists. The need for such simplified models is obvious. Working through the aggregate economy's trillions of interactions would be mind-boggling. To arrive at any policy conclusion, the macroeconomist must find a mechanism with which to cut through the confusion. A model is such a mechanism.

Formal and Informal Models

Models can be formal or informal. Formal models explicitly state all assumptions and reduce the economy to simple relationships among various measures. Informal models do not explicitly state all assumptions behind the relationships among measures. The models in this book are a lot more formal than the informal models you generally have in the back of your mind when you think about the economy. The advantage of these formal models is that they make the logic of the model clear. The

---

[2]One group of philosophers, postmodernists, take this view to the extreme and argue that one way of looking at the world is no better than another; it's all rhetoric. Most economists don't go that far. They agree that one's vision of reality has a subjective element, but they argue that some ways of looking at the economy are more insightful than others—specifically, the way economists look at the economy is much preferred to the way individuals who are not trained in economics look at the economy. We certainly believe so, or we wouldn't be writing an economics text.

QUESTION	What exactly is a model?
ANSWER	Taking our definition further, models are assumed relationships among variables that are used to predict or explain behavior.

You are more familiar with models than you might think. You use informal models every day. For example, you use an informal model to decide whether to carry an umbrella. If there are gray skies, you predict rain and carry an umbrella. Economists' models are generally a lot more formal. In formal models, assumptions, variables, and their interrelationships are more clearly stated than in informal models.

Models generally are composed of three ingredients:

1. Assumptions about how people will behave.
2. Variables that are not affected by the model but do affect variables inside the model. These variables are called exogenous variables. Exogenous means determined outside the model.
3. Variables that are explained by the model. These are called endogenous variables. Endogenous means determined inside the model.

Economists use models to predict endogenous variables on the basis of their measures of exogenous variables. Let's take an example using the standard microeconomic supply-and-demand model. Suppose you observed that Florida had been hit by a hard frost (exogenous variable)

that killed many of the early orange flowers. Using the standard supply-and-demand model, what do you predict would happen to the quantity of oranges sold and their price (endogenous variables)? The standard economist's prediction is shown in the illustration.

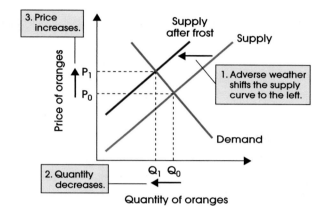

The adverse weather shifts the supply curve to the left, lowering equilibrium quantity and increasing equilibrium price.

disadvantage is that they force you to make assumptions that don't fit all circumstances, and which must be modified when the formal model is applied to the real world. This is why, to understand a model, you must understand both the model and the assumptions on which it is based.

As a businessperson, voting citizen, or consumer of information about the economy, you hear forecasts of the state of the economy, interest rates, or inflation all the time. These forecasts appear in the news, at business meetings, or in internal business reports prepared for management meetings. Forecasts are central to business and personal planning. The prices businesses set, how hard workers fight for an increase in wages, and whether you buy a bond or a stock, all depend on such forecasts. Economic forecasts are constructed using macroeconomic models, so these models affect many aspects of your life.

Models and Visions

The simplification process in modeling is enormous. For example, economists have to make assumptions about the world's underlying economic structure. Is the economy a wildly unstable structure that is continually in the process of changing? Does the economy have a life, and an evolution, of its own, unless it is somehow controlled by the institutions that people develop? Or is it a stable structure that will

Exhibit 1-7

Two Faces or an Urn?

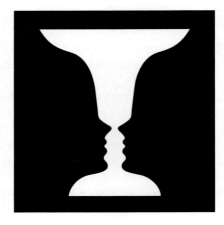

naturally settle down to an equilibrium? The answers to these questions reflect the model maker's underlying world vision and form the basis for the simplifying assumptions in the model.

It's for that reason that vision plays a fundamental role in how economists think about the macroeconomy, and in the metaphors they use. Vision affects how models are constructed, interpreted, and used to analyze various policies; behind every model is a vision. Therefore, an understanding of economists' alternative visions becomes important to understanding the policy debates.

One way of seeing how visions can differ is to look at Exhibit 1–7. What do you see? Some people see two people looking at each other; others see a goblet or vase. Which vision is right? The answer is: Both are. What you see depends on how your mind frames the picture. The same is true for economics. How one frames an issue is based on one's vision.

> Behind every model is a vision. That vision guides how a model is constructed and interpreted.

Visions, however, are usually vague and rarely thought about. Moreover, people often assume their visions are the correct ones. If you share a vision with another person, that person's explanations will tend to make a lot of sense. If you don't, that person's explanations often don't make sense.

Two Visions of the Economy

Understanding differences in vision can illuminate how economists see economic issues differently, because differences in vision underlie some current, ongoing debates. Some economists have a competitive market-clearing vision—a view of the economy that sees a perfectly competitive market as solving the economy's complex coordination problems in a highly effective manner.

In the perfectly competitive model of an economy, all prices adjust instantaneously to achieve equilibrium. Economists who subscribe to this vision know that real markets do not always behave this way, but argue that the perfectly competitive model is a useful guide to thinking about, and understanding, macroeconomic issues. For example, in the competitive market–clearing vision, wages adjust so that the quantity of labor demanded always equals the quantity of labor supplied. Any unemployment, therefore, is voluntary. Those who hold the competitive market–clearing vision know that this isn't true, but feel that this view of the world is a more useful guide to policy than other views that miss this voluntary perspective of unemployment.

> Two economists' visions are the competitive market-clearing vision and the complexity vision.

Another set of economists leans more toward a complexity vision—a view that sees the problems of an economy as too complicated to be solved instantaneously by perfectly competitive markets. According to this vision, thinking of the aggregate economy in reference to perfectly competitive markets is not especially useful. They use a variety of models that build existing institutional structures into the assumptions of the model. The resulting models are less general, but conform better to the particular issues being considered. In these institutional models, markets do coordinate, but that coordination takes time, works imperfectly, and is subject to coordination failures. Within the complexity vision, the economy is coordinated by a system of layered institutions and by historically determined, society-specific patterns of behavior. All analyses of the economy must take institutions and history into account.

Classical economists tend toward the competitive market-clearing vision; Keynesian economists tend toward the complexity vision.

Traditionally, the competitive market-clearing vision has been associated with Classical economists and the complexity vision with Keynesian economists (named for J.M. Keynes whose book *The General Theory of Employment, Interest, and Money* was the beginning of what we now call short-run macroeconomic analysis). (We discuss these two schools of thought later in the text.) However, the distinctions between these two schools of thought have become so blurred over time that we've decided that describing visions is more meaningful than describing schools of thought. This book reflects a double vision—combined into a single composite vision. The reason is that one of the authors of this book leans toward the complexity vision and the other toward a competitive market-clearing vision. This book presents the common ground between these two visions as well as the areas of disagreement.

To illustrate one of the areas of disagreement, let's think about growth. According to the competitive market-clearing view, a relatively simple formal model of growth can explain a significant part of the growth process. In such a model, the steady march of technological innovation combined with the available labor and capital in the economy fully describes the trend of output, and any departure from that trend is temporary.

According to the complexity vision, the growth process is more complicated. As economic events unfold, new institutions develop and the trend changes. According to this vision, it is difficult, if not impossible, to predict, using simple formal growth models, where the economy will go in the long run. The best we can do with the formal model is gain some insight into short-run issues, and even this is difficult. Long-run issues must be dealt with informally.

Executive Summary

- Supply-side policies seek to change potential output. Supply-side policies focus on the incentives to work, produce, and innovate.

- Demand-side policies seek to change aggregate expenditures. Demand-side policies include fiscal policy, monetary policy and trade policy.

- Underlying potential output is the natural rate of unemployment.

- Models are simplified representations of the economy.

- Formal models explicitly state all assumptions and, by nature, reduce the economy to simple relationships among various measures.

- Informal models do not explicitly state all assumptions. They are the models one has at the back of one's mind.

- The competitive market-clearing vision sees a perfectly competitive market as solving the economy's complex coordination problems in a highly effective manner. The complexity vision sees the problems of an economy as too complicated to be solved instantaneously by perfectly competitive markets.

- Behind every model is a vision.

CONCLUSION

One of the many old jokes about economists is the one about the student who returns to her professor of 25 years ago, and sees that he is giving the same exams. She asks, "How can you give the same exam for 25 years?" He responds, "In economics, the questions are always the same; it's the answers that change." It's a good joke, and it says a lot about how we present macroeconomics in this book. In our view, if the answers are likely to change it is inappropriate to present them as immutable, and in this book we won't. Where most economists currently agree, we present that agreement, not as the truth, but as a tentative judgment. Where they don't agree, we try to give you a sense of why, and we point out the judgments behind what we present.

The economy is highly complex. When analyzing something as complex as the economy, there's nothing wrong with saying that we cannot precisely predict what it is going to do. We can, however, say something, and we can make issues clearer. We cannot, however, make them clearer than they are.

KEY POINTS

- Macroeconomics is the study of issues that affect the economy as a whole, especially unemployment, inflation, and growth.

- The fundamental macroeconomic policy question is: Do current institutions coordinate the decisions of individuals in society sufficiently well, or should we modify institutions and adjust the market results in some way?

- The four normative goals of macroeconomics are high growth, smooth growth of output, low unemployment, and low inflation.

- Output has grown an average of 3.5 percent per year in the United States since 1947.

- Output in the United States fluctuates around its long-run trend.

- Unemployment and inflation in the United States were uncharacteristically low in the late 1990s and early 2000s.

- Interest rates are important indicators of monetary policy. Higher interest rates tend to lower output, while lower interest rates tend to raise output.

- For most years until 1998 the U.S. government has had budget deficits.

- Since 1976 the United States had has trade deficits.

- Monetary and fiscal policies are demand-side policies. They are designed to affect aggregate expenditures. Policies aimed at changing the incentives to work, produce, and innovate are supply-side policies.

- Policy makers need to know the economy's potential output when deciding whether to use expansionary or contractionary policies because pushing an economy beyond its potential (and pushing the unemployment rate below its natural rate) will lead to inflation. Unfortunately, they are difficult to predict.

- Much of our knowledge about the economy is embodied in simplified representations of the economy, called models. The assumptions used to create a model depend on one's underlying vision of the economy.

- The competitive market-clearing vision sees the problems of an economy as being solved by the perfectly competitive market. The complexity vision sees the economy as too complicated to be solved by perfectly competitive markets. Markets play a role, but these markets are embedded in institutions.

KEY TERMS

budget balance 9
business cycle 5
demand-side policy 11
fiscal policy 9
inflation 7
macro policy question 2
macroeconomics 2

market 2
model 14
monetary policy 9
natural rate of unemployment 6
nominal interest rate 8
normative economics 3
positive economics 3

potential output 5
real interest rate 9
supply-side policy 12
trade balance 11
trade policy 11
unemployment rate 6

QUESTIONS FOR THOUGHT AND REVIEW

1. Define *macroeconomics*.
2. What is the macro policy question?
3. What are the four standard goals of macroeconomics, and how do they relate to the economist's general goal of improving individual's welfare in society?
4. Suppose society decides on a normative goal of reducing air pollution. How might this impact the four standard goals stated in the text? Will this necessarily mean an individual's welfare falls?
5. Who decides what are the goals of macroeconomics? Do the chosen goals always reflect a society's desires? Explain.
6. Describe a macroeconomic goal that might be desirable but not feasible.
7. Define *potential output*. What has been the average growth rate of potential output in the United States since 1947?
8. What is a business cycle? Is U.S. output (as measured by real GDP) currently rising or falling? You can get this information from the Bureau of Economic Analysis (www.bea.doc.gov).
9. Define the *natural rate of unemployment*.
10. What is inflation? What generally happens to inflation when output rises above its potential?
11. What is the difference between the nominal interest rate and the real interest rate?

12. Describe how each of the three intermediate goals is related to the four standard goals of macroeconomics.
13. What is the difference between the demand and supply sides of the economy? What types of policies are designed to affect the demand side? What types of policies are designed to affect the supply side?
14. Suppose the economy is above potential and policy makers want to reduce the threat of inflation. What demand-side policies could they use?
15. Suppose the economy is above potential and policy makers want to increase potential output. What supply-side policies could they use?
16. Does economists' poor track record of forecasting the economy mean that they shouldn't bother trying? Comment briefly.
17. Why do economists build models?
18. What is the difference between formal and informal models in economics?
19. What is the relationship between models and visions? Is it possible to have a model that is independent of vision?
20. How does the competitive market-clearing vision differ from the complexity vision?
21. What different answers do you think the competitive market-clearing vision economists and the complexity vision economists give to the macro policy question?

PROBLEMS AND EXERCISES

1. Find the following information for the most recent period:
   a. Growth rate of real output (quarter)
   b. Unemployment rate (month)
   c. Inflation rate (quarter)

   d. Describe how each, (a) through (c), compares to its historical values. (You can either find this information in the publication *Economic Indicators* in your library or go to the White House Economic Statistics Briefing Room on the Internet [www.whitehouse.gov/fsbr/esbr. html].)

2. Find the current interest rate on 3-month Treasury bills. (You can find this information on the front page of section C of *The Wall Street Journal*.) Use the most recent inflation rate you found for problem 1 to calculate the real interest rate.

3. Look through recent newspaper articles and other publications and list three macroeconomic questions facing economic policy makers today.
   a. What are the names of the policy makers who are concerned about each question you listed?
   b. What has made the questions you listed concerns for policy makers?
   c. What actions (if any) are policy makers taking to deal with these concerns? Are these actions demand-side or supply-side policies?

4. Find a forecast of the economy for the upcoming quarter.
   a. What is the forecast for inflation and output? How do they compare to their recent performance?
   b. What are the major factors that contributed to their forecast? (One source for this information is on the Internet at www.phil.frb.org/econ/spf/index.html. Then click on the most recent survey of professional forecasters.)

5. Find out whether the economy is currently above or below estimated potential by reading Chapter 2 of the *Economic Outlook* in the most recent *Budget and Economic Outlook* at www.cbo.gov. According to the CBO, what are the consequences of the economy being in this position relative to potential output? What policies can policy makers use to try to move the economy back toward potential output?

2

Measuring the Economy

After reading this chapter you should be able to:

1. Define both real and nominal GDP and state the components of GDP

2. Distinguish between the various measures of inflation

3. Explain how the unemployment rate is calculated and describe its shortcomings

4. Recount the U.S. and world experience with growth, business cycles, unemployment, and inflation

5. Describe how the U.S. trade balance and the exchange rate have changed over time

One of our colleagues from graduate school is now the chief economist at a major U.S. financial institution. He's one of the talking heads you see on the evening news and is one of the economists whose forecasts influence high-level financial decisions. His predictions are rated among the top ten most accurate forecasts. (Yes, forecasters are tracked and graded.) We asked him the secret to his success. His answer was, "I know the numbers—where they come from, how they're gathered and how they are put together. I collect data on my own that are similar to those collected by the agencies that report official numbers. I use my data to predict the economy's future. The theory I learned in graduate school plays only a small role in my forecasting." As you can see from this story, knowing how the economy is measured is important to businesspeople and policy makers.

This chapter begins with an introduction to how output, inflation, and unemployment are measured. It then elaborates on the measures of the four standard goals presented in Chapter 1.

Although learning about how the economy is measured and becoming familiar with the data aren't always fun, they are necessary background work. Think of this chapter as the mandatory calisthenics you do when training for a sport, or the memorization of vocabulary when learning a foreign language.

CENTRAL MEASURES OF THE ECONOMY

In the last chapter, we introduced you to some central measures of the economy: output, inflation, and unemployment. We now consider these measures more carefully. Specifically, we consider how they are constructed and what their importance is to forecasting and policy.

Total Output: Gross Domestic Product

In Chapter 1, we said that total output is the amount of final goods and services produced in an economy. Total output (or production) in a year is measured by **gross domestic product (GDP)**—the market value of all final goods and services produced within a country within a year. GDP can be calculated in two ways:

> *Two ways to calculate GDP: Add up output or add up income.*

1. Add up the *output* of (or expenditures on) final goods and services.
2. Add up the *income* earned in the production of goods and services.

Calculating GDP. The first method of measuring GDP is to add up the output of final goods and services. In this method, final goods are separated from *intermediate goods* (goods used in the production of other goods). Only those goods sold to their ultimate end-users are counted. Goods sold from one firm to another to make other goods are intermediate goods and do not count because their value is already included in the value of final goods. Counting intermediate goods in addition to final goods would be double counting GDP.

There are two ways to add up output: The first way is to add up the value each firm contributes to the production of final goods and services. Economists call this the firm's **value added.** It is calculated by subtracting the cost of intermediate goods from the firm's revenue. Not surprisingly, this method is called the *value-added approach.* The second way is to add up all of firms', individuals', governments', and foreigners' expenditures on final goods and services. This method is called the *expenditures approach.*

> *Value added: Subtract cost of intermediate goods from revenue.*

Let's begin with the value-added approach. Suppose a firm makes a computer and sells it to a consumer for $1,000. To produce the computer, the firm buys components from a chip-making company for $300, pays workers $500 to assemble the computer, and earns a profit of $200. The chip-making company pays workers $200 to produce the chips, giving it a profit of $100. (To keep things simple, we're assuming the chip-making company has no other costs.) Here is the information in table form.

Chip-making Company		Computer Company	
Revenue from sales: $300		Revenue from sales: $1,000	
Costs		**Costs**	
Wages:	$200	Wages:	$500
Parts:	—	Parts:	$300
Profit:	$100	Profit:	$200

Counting all production (both intermediate and final goods) in the economy would suggest that GDP is $1,300. The error of this method becomes clear if you suppose the two firms merged—measured GDP declines by $300, but no fewer goods are produced.

What is the correct measure of GDP? Using the value-added approach, we can see that it is $1,000. That $1,000 consists of $300 of value added by the chip-making company and $700 of value added by the computer-making company. To get value added from total sales of all firms, subtract the cost of the intermediate goods (parts), or $300. The $300 has already been included in the $1,000 of final sales by the computer company. Counting revenues from both firms would be double counting the production of computer chips.

The second method of adding up output is straightforward in principle but hard to do in practice. This second method is simply to add all expenditures by consumers, government, businesses, and foreigners on final goods. In our example, a consumer purchases the computer for $1,000. Because total expenditures on the final product are $1,000, GDP equals $1,000. Why is it hard to do in practice? The reason is that the data collected to calculate GDP does not come from final end-users. They are collected from the firms that sell the goods. No one—or agency—tracks whether the goods firms sold will be consumed or used to produce additional products.

Now let's turn to the income approach. When firms produce goods, they also produce an equal amount of income. By adding up the income that is paid out to those who supply the factors of production (resources firms use to produce goods and services, such as labor, capital, and raw materials), economists can calculate the value of that production. Our example has two types of income: wages paid to laborers and profit paid to the owners of the firm, or proprietors. Wages and profit paid by the chip-making company equal $300, and wages and profit paid by the computer company equal $700. Their sum is $1,000.

> Remember: Total output = total income.

The Income-Output Identity. Notice that both the production and income approaches lead to the same result. This illustrates an important accounting identity that economists use:

$$total\ output = total\ income \qquad (2\text{-}1)$$

Exhibit 2–1 shows this identity in a circular flow diagram. The *bottom arrows* show that firms pay households income in exchange for factors of production. The *top arrows* show that households use that income to buy goods and services from firms.

Exhibit 2–1

Income Equals Output: Circular Flow Diagram

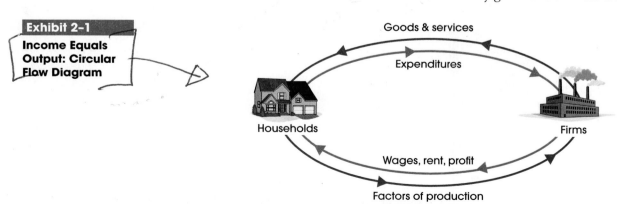

The circular flow diagram shows that total output in the economy equals total income earned from the production of that output. Firms sell goods and services to households in exchange for their expenditures, as the *top arrows* show. The *bottom arrows* show that households sell factors of production to firms in exchange for wages, rent, and profit.

The flow of expenditures from households to firms creates an equal flow of income from firms back to households.

This equality is true for every stage of production. In our example, the chip company's contribution to GDP exactly equals the income earned to produce its output: $200 in wages and $100 in profits. The same is true for the computer company. Its contribution to GDP, $700, is equal to the income earned in producing its output: the $500 in wages and $200 in profit. Economists often use the terms *production, output*, and *income* interchangeably because these terms are all equal to each other. So when you see one, think of the others, until it is imprinted on your mind that output equals production equals income.

National Income and Product Accounts. The accounting identity (output equals income) is the basis of the **National Income and Product Accounts (NIPAs),** the U.S. federal government's official report of GDP and related measures. The Bureau of Economic Analysis (BEA) is the government agency that estimates and reports the NIPAs. The NIPAs report the most widely used measures of production and income in the United States. In these accounts, output is measured in two ways. On the product side of the accounts, output is measured by adding up expenditures by U.S. firms, individuals, government, and foreigners on domestic final goods and services and is reported as GDP. On the income side of the accounts, output is measured by adding up all income earned by the owners of the factors of production and is reported as national income. Table 2–1 shows the primary components on the product side.

As you can see, the primary expenditure components of output on the product side are personal consumption, gross private investment, net exports of goods and services, and government expenditures. **Personal consumption** is payments by households for goods and services. **Gross private investment** is business spending on equipment, structures, and inventories and household spending on owner-occupied housing. **Net exports** is the difference between the value of goods and services a country *sells* to the rest of the world (exports) and the value of goods and services it *purchases* from the rest of the world (imports). Finally, **government expenditures** are government payments for goods and services and investment in equipment and structures.

Gross domestic product encompasses all expenditures, whether for consumption or investment goods. Some of that investment is simply a replacement of capital that has worn out, and is not really a final output, but is instead an intermediate

NIPAs: the U.S. government's official report of GDP and related measures.

Table 2-1		Billions of Dollars	% of GDP
Output and Its Components, 2000			
	Personal consumption expenditures	6,757.3	68
	Gross private investment	1,832.7	18
	Net exports of goods and services	−370.7	−4
	Government consumption expenditures and gross investment	1,743.7	18
	Gross domestic product	9,963.1	100
	Depreciation	1,257.1	—
	Net domestic product	8,706.0	—

Source: Commerce Department, Bureau of Economic Analysis **(www.bea.doc.gov).**

Gross domestic product –
Depreciation = Net domes-
tic product.

good. To take this into account, economists subtract **depreciation** (the wear and tear of capital during production) from gross domestic product to arrive at **net domestic product.** Actually measuring depreciation is extraordinarily difficult, and usually depreciation is estimated as a percentage of existing capital. Recognizing the difficulties of measuring depreciation, economists generally talk about gross domestic product rather than net domestic product, even though the *net* concept is the theoretically more accurate measure.

Table 2–2 shows the primary components on the income side: wages (compensation to employees), profits (proprietor's income and profits of the firm), interest, and rent. Wages plus profits plus interest plus rent in a country equal national income. So, **national income (NI)** is the total income that a country's businesses and individuals earn in the economy in a year.

As you can see, the actual numbers the BEA reports for national income and GDP are not exactly equal. This is due to the accounting conventions the BEA follows for each. We know, however, from the circular flow diagram that output must equal income. The bottom half of Table 2–2 shows how national income and GDP are related in the NIPAs.

NI – net foreign factor
income + depreciation +
indirect business taxes +
statistical discrepancy =
GDP.

We must make three definitional adjustments to national income to get to GDP. First, national income includes payments to domestic owners of all factors of production, regardless of whether those factors are used to produce goods and services domestically or abroad. GDP includes only payments to owners of factors of production used to produce goods and services domestically. To adjust for this difference, we must subtract **net foreign factor income** (income earned abroad by domestic factors of production less income earned in a country by foreign factors of production) from national income. Second, depreciation is a cost of doing business and as such is counted as an expenditure, but is not paid out as income. We must add depreciation to national income. Third, indirect businesses taxes, such as sales taxes, are included in expenditures (product side) but are not counted as income. We must add indirect business taxes to national income.

Net foreign factor income:
income earned abroad
by domestic factors of
production less income
earned in a country by foreign factors of production.

As you can imagine, measuring $10 trillion of output and income is complicated, leaving room for errors. In a single quarter, the income and product

Table 2-2

National Income and Its Components, 2000

	Billions of Dollars	% of National Income
Employee compensation (wages)	5,638.2	70
Proprietor's income	710.4	9
Profits	946.2	12
Net Interest	567.2	7
Rent	140.0	2
National Income	8,002.0	100
– net foreign factor income	– (– 4.4)	—
+ depreciation	1,257.1	—
+ indirect business taxes	769.6	—
+ statistical discrepancy	– 70.0	—
= gross domestic product	9,963.1	—

Note: Two other minor adjustments—subsidies less surplus and business transfer payments—are included in the statistical discrepancy.

Source: *Economic Report of the President,* 2001, Table B-1 (**www.gpo.gov/eop**).

measures can sometimes differ by 1 percent or 2 percent ($100 to $200 billion), although the two typically differ by less than 0.5 percent. The statistical discrepancy arises because the BEA collects the data for each side of the accounts from different sources and estimates each measure separately. These statistical discrepancies account for a fourth difference between national income and GDP. After accounting for these definitional and statistical differences, income equals output. (The Briefing Room feature illustrates the extent to which the data are revised.)

Which measure of total output should people use? As with most policy questions in economics, the answer is, "It depends." The popular press emphasizes estimates based on the product side because those estimates are available on a more timely basis (the first estimate is released the first month after the quarter ends) and because the BEA, which collects the data, claims expenditures are more accurately measured than is income. However, the federal government is often interested in national income because federal tax revenue and expenditures for some federal government programs, such as unemployment insurance benefits, are closely related to national income. For this same reason, policy makers use income estimates to track the federal budget balance.

Even if the numbers accurately measure production, GDP is limited as a measure of the welfare of society. It misses nonmarket activities such as home production, the value of leisure, and counts goods that may be of dubious value (such as goods that cause pollution.) These issues, along with the details of GDP accounting, are discussed in detail in Appendix A at the end of this chapter.

Real versus Nominal GDP. So far, we have discussed what economists call **nominal GDP**—the production of all final goods and services *valued at current market prices*. Although nominal GDP is useful when describing current economic performance, it can be misleading when making comparisons of production over time. If price levels change over time, you are not able to tell whether a rise in nominal GDP is the result of increasing market prices or an increase in the physical quantity of goods and services produced.

For example, suppose the economy had just one firm—a computer company that sold 500 computers for 2 years in a row. If the price of computers were $1,000 apiece the first year and $1,200 the second year, GDP would rise from $500,000 to $600,000, but the physical number of computers produced would not have risen.

Policy makers are interested in the change in the quantity of total output over time, because individuals' welfare is related to the quantity of physical goods and services produced. To measure changes in the quantity of output alone, economists have developed a measure called **real GDP**—the market value of all final goods and services produced in a country within a year, keeping the market price of those goods and services constant. Put another way, real GDP is nominal GDP adjusted for inflation. By keeping the price level constant, any change in real GDP is the result of a change in the quantity of goods and services produced, not in the price level.

Real GDP is nominal GDP adjusted for inflation.

Exhibit 2–2 shows U.S. nominal GDP and real GDP since 1947. Nominal GDP, shown by the red line, rose more than 40-fold since 1947, while real GDP, shown by the blue line, rose by only sixfold. The difference between the two, shown by the light gray shaded region in Exhibit 2–2, is accounted for by changes in the price level. To fully understand this exhibit, however, you need to learn how real GDP is calculated and compared from year to year.

Exhibit 2-2

**U.S. Real GDP
and Nominal GDP,
1947-2000**

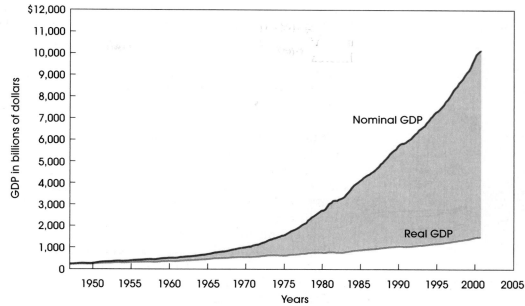

Nominal GDP measures output in current-year prices. Real GDP measures output at base-year prices. In this exhibit, real GDP is shown in constant 1947 prices. Since 1947, nominal GDP has risen 40- fold, while real GDP has risen only sixfold. Changes in the price level account for the difference. Source: Commerce Department, Bureau of Economic Analysis (www.bea.doc.gov).

To calculate real GDP, multiply current quantities by base-year prices.

Calculating Real GDP. In practice, distinguishing between changes in GDP due to changes in prices and those due to changes in the quantity of goods and services produced is not an easy task. To arrive at a measure of real GDP, the BEA tracks the prices of thousands of goods and services and adjusts its measurement of nominal GDP for 20,000 detailed categories of goods and services.

To see how to calculate real GDP and nominal GDP, we'll consider a numerical example for an economy that produces just two final goods: oranges and apples. Table 2–3 shows production during 2001 and 2002. First, let's calculate nominal GDP. Multiplying quantity by price (expenditures) for each good, and adding, we see that nominal GDP was $5 in 2001 and $9 in 2002. Nominal GDP rose 80 percent from 2001 to 2002 ($9 − $5 = $4 and $4/$5 × 100 = 80 percent).

Now, let's calculate real GDP. Real GDP equals the quantities of goods in each time period, keeping prices constant throughout time. We must first choose which year's prices to use, in this case 2001 or 2002. The year of the common prices is called the *base year*. Using 2001 as the base year, real GDP in 2001 is $5, as you can see in the last column of the table. Real GDP in 2002 is calculated by multiplying quantities in 2002 by their 2001 prices:

$$20 \times 0.10 + 20 \times 0.20 = \$6$$

In this example, you can see that real and nominal output measures can differ. While nominal GDP rose 80 percent from 2001 to 2002, real GDP rose only 20 percent ($6 − $5 = $1 and $1/$5 × 100 = 20 percent).

Table 2-3

Calculating Real GDP

			Nominal GDP	Real GDP
base yr.				
2001	Quantity	Price	$P_{01} \times Q_{01}$	$P_{01} \times Q_{01}$
Oranges	30	$.10	$3	$3
Apples	10	$.20	$2	$2
Total			$5	$5
2002	Quantity	Price	$P_{02} \times Q_{02}$	$P_{01} \times Q_{02}$
Oranges	20	$.20	$4	$2
Apples	20	$.25	$5	$4
Total			$9	$6

This table shows how to calculate nominal GDP and real GDP for an economy that produces only two goods—oranges and apples. To calculate nominal GDP, multiply the quantity of oranges and apples by their respective prices in each year and sum the values. Calculating real GDP is more complicated. One must select which year's prices to value production. Here we've chosen to value production using 2001 prices. Doing so gives us one measure of real GDP.

This exercise demonstrates the basic idea of how real GDP is calculated—the calculation adjusts for price level changes, so that we are left with values for the quantities of real output that can be compared over time. The problem with calculating real GDP as described here is the effect that changing relative prices (changes in prices of one or more goods compared with the prices of other goods) and quantities has on the accuracy of one's measure of real GDP. In our example, using 2001 prices means we are weighting apples twice as much as oranges. If we used 2002 prices, we would be weighting them only 25 percent more. Because of the difference in weights, if we had used 2002 as our base year, we would have calculated the percent change in real GDP to be 5.9 percent, quite a bit different from the 20 percent rise using 2001 prices. Relative prices generally change much more slowly than in this example, but it does illustrate an important point: Because relative prices and quantities change more as time progresses, measures of real GDP that are further away from the base year are less accurate than measures of real GDP that are closer to the base year.

Until 1995, the United States dealt with this problem by moving the base year forward every 4 to 5 years: Economic history was rewritten every 4 to 5 years to account for relative price changes. However, when relative prices and quantities are changing quickly, even 4-year updates are problematic. This is exactly what happened when the price of computers fell dramatically in the 1990s. Between 1992 and 1996, the price of computers fell by about 25 percent each year, while the average price of most other goods rose by about 3 percent each year. At that same time, the quantity of computers produced rose dramatically. In calculating real GDP, the BEA was multiplying the quantity of computers produced by their high base-year (1992) prices. When the BEA changed the base year to 1996, the measured contribution of computer production to GDP growth fell. This approach meant that major revisions occurred every 4 to 5 years when the BEA changed the base.

In 1995, the BEA began using a *chain-type method* that changes the base-year prices used to estimate real GDP each year. The chain-type method calculates the

Currently, the BEA uses a chain-type method to calculate real GDP. It averages the price changes in consecutive years.

THE BRIEFING ROOM Data Revisions

Policy makers want to know GDP as soon as they can, so the BEA provides early estimates of annual GDP for each quarter, using the information it has and making assumptions about data that aren't yet available. (A quarter is a 3-month period, which is the period for which GDP figures are tallied. The quarterly GDP figures are reported at annual production rates. GDP during a year, therefore, is the average of GDP figures for the four quarters in that year.) The BEA then revises the initial estimate as more complete data become available.

The first month of every quarter (January, April, July, October) the BEA reports what is called the *advanced estimate* of GDP for the most recent quarter completed. It then publishes two more estimates the following 2 months, called *preliminary* and *final estimates,* respectively. Every July, the BEA revises the GDP data, going back 3 years. In addition, every 5 years or so, the BEA revises the entire set of GDP estimates (GDP and its component parts) going back to 1947.

This figure, from a study by Federal Reserve Bank of Minneapolis economist David Runkle, shows the difference in annual growth rates between the BEA's preliminary estimate of GDP growth and its final (most recent) estimate.

As you can see, the BEA's estimates for the mid-1970s were revised by as much as 7.5 percentage points. Such a revision can mean that a reported deep recession is really a mild recession.

Data revisions are important for two reasons. First, the size of past revisions indicates that policy makers should interpret the BEA's estimates of the economy's current state with caution. The economy may be doing better or worse than the BEA reports. Second, when looking at the currently published data of past years, keep

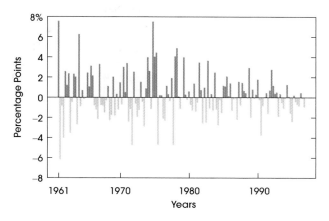

Differences Between Preliminary and Final GDP Estimates

in mind that policy makers at that time probably had different numbers with which to work. For example, the BEA reported in January 1975 that real GDP declined 9.1 percent in the fourth quarter of 1974, but reported in December 2000, after a series of revisions, that real GDP declined by only 2.2 percent. Policy makers in 1975 could have been seriously led astray by the BEA's initial estimate.

This is not to say that the BEA does a bad job of measuring the U.S. economy. The U.S. economy is huge and complicated, and it takes thousands of calculations to construct estimates of GDP. As more information becomes available, the BEA incorporates that information.

---

percent change in real GDP from one year to the next, using the average price of goods in both years. By averaging price levels in the current and previous year, the adjustments are made every year and are smoothed out.

Once the BEA calculates annual percent changes by this method, it creates an index for real GDP equal to 100 in a chosen year, currently 1996. The BEA then uses the annual percent changes in real GDP to construct a chain of indexes for real GDP. For example, because the index was set at 100 in 1996 and real GDP rose by 4.4 percent in 1997, the index in 1997 was 104.4 (100 × [1 + .044]). The index in 1998 is constructed by augmenting the 1997 index by the percentage increase in real GDP in 1998. Table 2–4 shows the index for 1996 through 2000. The chain-type quantity index equaled 119.27 in 2000, meaning that real output was 19.27 percent higher than in 1996.

Sometimes, you will find that only the index for real GDP is reported. However, if you know the base-year GDP in dollars, you can convert those indexes to levels

Table 2–4	Real GDP (Chain Index)	Real GDP (Billions of Chained 1996 Dollars)
Chain-weighted GDP		
1996	100.00	7,813.2
1997	104.40	8,159.5
1998	108.99	8,515.7
1999	113.60	8,875.8
2000	119.27	9,318.5

Note: Some values not exact due to rounding.

Source: Bureau of Economic Analysis (www.bea.doc.gov).

> To convert the index into levels for real GDP, multiply the index by GDP in the base year and divide by 100.

of real GDP by multiplying the index by GDP in the base year and dividing by 100. For example, real GDP in 2000 was (119.27 × 7813.2)/100, or $9,318.5. This value represents real GDP for 2000 stated in chained 1996 dollars. The second column in Table 2–4 shows real GDP in dollars associated with the index numbers. Both the index for real GDP and real GDP in chained 1996 dollars are reported in the *Economic Report of the President.*

This continual updating of base-year prices reduces the distortions that big movements in relative prices and quantities can cause and eliminates the large adjustments in measured real GDP when BEA changes the base years.

The Price Level

A second measure central to macroeconomic policy discussions is the **price level**—the average price of goods and services produced in an economy, stated as an index. The economy produces many goods and services, so the agencies that calculate the various price indexes (the BEA and the Bureau of Labor Statistics [BLS]) must weight, and average, the prices into a single price index. Because inflation is a continual rise in the average price level, to understand inflation, you must understand how the price level is measured. Appendix B treats the issues of price indexes and their measurement in some detail. Here we will present the basics.

Economists, the popular press, and politicians talk about a variety of price measures. We'll talk about three: the GDP deflator, the consumer price index (CPI), and the producer price index (PPI). Each measure is designed for different purposes. The GDP deflator measures prices of goods and services that consumers, government, and firms purchase. It includes prices of all goods and services produced in a country. The CPI measures prices the average consumer faces and is the most commonly reported price measure. The PPI measures the prices of goods producers purchase.

All price-level measures are reported as indexes—average price levels in the current year stated relative to the average price levels in a base year. An index is constructed by dividing the price level of a basket (collection) of goods and services in the current year by the price level of a basket of goods in the base year and multiplying by 100. For example, if the average price of a basket of goods is $30 in the base year and $35 the following year, the price index is 100 (30/30 × 100) in the base year and 117 (35/30 × 100) the next year. Because current and base-year prices are the same, an index always equals 100 in its base year. Indexes are tools for comparison.

THE BRIEFING ROOM   Sources of U.S. Macroeconomic Data

Most economic data are collected and published by government sources and agencies. Each source and agency reports data in its own publication and Internet site. We list here some publications and Web sites, but many more sources of data exist. (Links to these and other sites can be found on our Web site at www. prenhall.com/colander.)

The White House

The White House provides a summary of economic statistics in its Economic Statistics Briefing Room on the Internet at www.whitehouse.gov/fsbr/esbr.html. The Council of Economic Advisers to the President publishes the *Economic Report of the President* each year. The latest is available at www.access. gpo.gov/eop. It summarizes the performance of the economy and provides the President with advice on domestic and international economic policy matters. The back pages of the Report have a number of tables listing a lot of data, including the full NIPAs; population, employment, wage, and productivity data; price data; money supply data; and international statistics.

The Commerce Department

The Commerce Department sponsors a number of data-collecting agencies that publish data themselves. The Commerce Department's web site provides a good starting point to find numerous data series. It is at www.doc. gov. One important agency is the Bureau of Economic Analysis (BEA) (www.bea.doc.gov). It publishes the NIPAs and international accounts. The *Survey of Current Business* is its main print publication. Another is the Census Bureau (www.census.gov). Its main statistical function is to gather population statistics. Its Web site provides a variety of statistics produced by other agencies, including a list of links to statistical sites of foreign countries.

The Bureau of Labor Statistics

The Bureau of Labor Statistics (BLS) provides data on employment, unemployment, wages, the CPI, and the PPI at stats.bls.gov. This site also includes documents that describe the methodology of data collection. The *Monthly Labor Review* is its major print publication.

The Federal Reserve System

The Board of Governors Web site (www.federalreserve. gov) is the central site for the entire Federal Reserve System. Along with a complete list of Internet locations for all U.S. regional banks, it posts speeches by Fed governors, minutes of the Federal Open Market Committee (the monetary-policy decision-making committee of the Federal Reserve), and data for exchange rates, interest rates, and monetary aggregates. The Board also publishes the *Federal Reserve Bulletin*.

Individually Federal Reserve Banks also have their own publications and Web sites. The Minneapolis Federal Reserve bank Web site (woodrow.mpls.frb.fed.us) reviews monetary policy. The Federal Reserve Bank of Cleveland Web site (www.clev.frb.org) publishes "Economic Trends," a monthly pamphlet that summarizes the economy's current status.

The National Bureau of Economic Research

The National Bureau of Economic Research (NBER) is a private nonprofit organization that promotes studies of how the U.S. economy works. The NBER houses the committee that officially dates U.S. business cycles. Its Web site (www.nber.org) lists the dates for U.S. business cycles and provides a number of statistics online.

International Monetary Fund

A number of international agencies collect and publish economic data for foreign countries. The International Monetary Fund, a multinational financial institution concerned with international monetary issues, publishes financial statistics in *International Financial Statistics*, trade statistics in *Direction of Trade Statistics*, and economic indicators in *World Economic Outlook*. Some of its publications are available at its Web site (www.imf.org).

There are many other sources of economic statistics, including magazines and newspapers. We don't list such magazines or periodicals here because they usually require a subscription.

If you can't find a federal agency, try Fedstats (www.fedstats.gov), which provides easy access to the full range of federal statistics and links to federal agencies.

GDP Deflator = nominal (GDP/real GDP) × 100.

The GDP Deflator. The **GDP price deflator**—a measure of the market prices of all final goods and services produced in an economy stated as an index of base-year prices—is the price index most economists favor because, of the three measures, it reflects the broadest range of prices. The BEA reports the GDP deflator quarterly, along with GDP.

The GDP deflator can be calculated by using nominal and real GDP. Remember, nominal GDP is GDP calculated at current prices, while real GDP is GDP calculated at base-year prices. The ratio of nominal to real GDP, therefore, represents the rat of prices of the goods and services produced in the current year to prices of the goods and services produced in the base year. This ratio is the GDP deflator.

$$GDP\ deflator = \frac{nominal\ GDP}{real\ GDP} \times 100 \qquad (2\text{-}2)$$

Because nominal GDP and real GDP are the same in the base year, the GDP deflator is 100 in the base year.

Let's return to Table 2–3 and calculate the GDP price deflator. In Year 2001, the base year, the GDP price deflator is $5/$5 × 100 = 100. In year 2002, the GDP price deflator is $9/$6 × 100 = 150. So, in this example, the GDP price deflator has risen by 50 percent. That is, the average price of goods and services produced has risen by 50 percent.

The Consumer Price Index. The price index that you will hear mentioned most often in the news is the **consumer price index (CPI)**—a measure of the prices of goods and services consumers pay, stated as an index of base-year prices. The BLS collects data on the prices of goods facing consumers, and calculates and reports a monthly CPI. The CPI is calculated using a fixed market basket of goods and services that make up a "typical" individual's consumption in a base year. So, the CPI is calculated as follows:

> CPI = (a specific year's price of a base-year market basket of goods)/(the base-year price of a base-year market basket of goods) × 100.

$$\frac{a\ specific\ year's\ price\ of\ a\ base\text{-}year\ market\ basket\ of\ goods}{the\ base\text{-}year\ price\ of\ a\ base\text{-}year\ market\ basket\ of\ goods} \times 100 \qquad (2\text{-}3)$$

In 2001, the base period for the basket of goods was 1993 to 1995, and the base-year index period was 1982 to 1984. Beginning in 2002, the BLS will update the basket of goods every 2 years with a survey taken from a sample of U.S. consumers.

Differences Between the CPI and the GDP Deflator. Because the CPI measures the cost of living for a typical consumer, while the GDP deflator measures the price of all goods and services produced, the two are constructed quite differently. One major difference is that they cover the prices of different items. The typical consumer buys goods produced in foreign countries, so the CPI includes the prices of imported goods. The GDP deflator includes only domestically produced goods. At the same time, the GDP deflator includes the prices of goods and services, such as industrial machinery and exports, that a typical domestic consumer would not buy and, as such, are not included in the calculation of the CPI.

Another major difference is that the CPI's basket of goods is fixed for a number of years, while the GDP deflator's basket of goods and services reflects the ever-changing composition of domestic production. This means that if consumers change their buying habits quickly, the CPI will not reflect true consumer inflation as accurately until the basket of goods is updated. This is not as much of a problem with the GDP deflator, because its basket of goods is updated quarterly.

While changes in both the CPI and the GDP deflator are measures of inflation, the composition and differences in relative importance of goods and services included give slightly different pictures of inflation. Which measure a businessperson, policy maker, or forecaster uses depends on their purpose. If they are looking for a broad-based measure of inflation, the GDP deflator is appropriate. If they are looking for a measure of consumer inflation and increases in the cost of living only, they use the CPI.

Biases in the CPI. In the 1990s, the government's measure of consumer inflation, the CPI, came under scrutiny from government economists and policy makers. Their concern was that the CPI overstates cost-of-living increases. This was of concern to them because measuring inflation is not just an academic exercise—it affects policy and business decisions. For example, about one-fourth of all labor union contracts use the CPI to compensate workers' wages for inflation. Many nonunion employers do the same. The government increases Social Security payments to the elderly and food stamp payments to those with low incomes based on rises in the CPI. In fact, the CPI affects one-third of the U.S. federal government expenditures. The U.S. government also uses the CPI to adjust income tax brackets and standard tax deductions each year.

In 1996, the Senate brought together a panel of economists to look into the accuracy of the CPI. The panel found areas where the CPI estimated inflation on the high side. They argued that the CPI does not recognize that consumers change their behavior when relative prices of goods and services change. For example, when the price of oil skyrocketed in 1973, automobile drivers switched to more fuel-efficient cars and homeowners switched to cheaper sources of energy; the consumption of oil fell, but the weight that oil had in the CPI did not.

The panel also identified three specific measurement issues that the CPI does not take into account: (1) improvements in the quality of products, (2) the introduction of new products, and (3) the discount buying habits of consumers. (We discuss each issue in more detail in Appendix B of this chapter.) Because of these issues, the panel suggested that the CPI overstates the prices that people actually pay for the goods they buy, and that the CPI overstates inflation by as much as 1.1 percentage points per year—enough to affect policy.

How big are the problems that the CPI's shortcomings create? Overestimating consumer inflation raises government spending by raising expenditures for programs, such as Social Security, that are based on the CPI. It also lowers tax revenues by raising tax brackets and standard deductions people use to calculate their federal income taxes. Economists forecasted that correcting the overestimation problems would raise the U.S. government budget surplus by about $148 billion in 2006 and lower the government debt by $691 billion by 2006.

The response by various lobby groups to these findings shows how political this issue got. The United Auto Workers Union and the American Association of Retired Persons attacked the Commission's findings as an easy way for the government to raise taxes and lower spending without having to enact legislation. Congress did not address the CPI problem with legislation. The BLS did, however, institute changes based on its own research to improve its measure of consumer prices, even before the panel began looking into these issues. Those changes have reduced measured inflation by 0.7 percentage point per year. Because of the changes that the BLS made to the CPI, direct comparisons of the CPI before and after 1996 are difficult.

To avoid some of the measurement problems of the CPI, the Federal Reserve (the federal agency responsible for formulating and implementing monetary policy) started using another measure—the **personal consumption expenditure (PCE) deflator**—to gauge consumer prices. The PCE deflator is a measure of prices of

Three measurement problems with the CPI are product improvements, new products, and discount buying habits.

PCE deflator: measure of prices of goods and services that only consumers purchase.

goods and services that only consumers purchase that, like the GDP deflator, allows the basket of goods to change over time as people's buying habits change. It, therefore, smooths out some of the problems associated with the fixed-basket CPI.

The Producer Price Index. The **producer price index (PPI)**—a measure of the prices domestic firms pay for intermediate goods and services, stated as an index of base-year prices—is also widely reported. Intermediate goods include things such as steel, gas, oil, and financial services. Although the PPI does not measure prices consumers face, it does give an early indication of the likely direction of prices at the consumer level, because it tracks the prices of raw materials used to produce consumer goods. In late 1999 and early 2000, when the PPI began rising, most economists predicted higher consumer price inflation for the near future—and they were right.

PPI: measure of prices domestic firms pay for intermediate goods, stated as an index of base-year prices.

Executive Summary

- Gross domestic product measures the value of final goods and services produced in a country within a year. It can be measured by adding up either expenditures or income.

- Real GDP is a better measure than nominal GDP of the change in the physical quantity of goods and services produced. It keeps the prices of goods and services produced constant.

- The price level is the average price of a basket of goods and services. The GDP deflator measures market prices of all final goods and services produced in an economy. It is the most general measure of the price level for the economy.

- Remember this formula:

$$\text{GDP deflator} = \frac{\text{nominal GDP}}{\text{real GDP}} \times 100.$$

- The CPI measures the prices of selected goods and services typical consumers purchase.

- Remember this formula: CPI =

$$\frac{\text{a specific year's price of a base-year market basket of goods}}{\text{the base-year price of a base-year market basket of goods}} \times 100$$

- The PPI measures the prices of goods businesses purchase to produce final goods and services.

- The PCE deflator measures prices consumers face but, unlike the CPI, allows the basket of goods to change each quarter.

Unemployment

Another central measure of economic performance is unemployment. Our modern U.S. economy has always had, and always will have, some unemployment. Unemployment is not necessarily bad. In fact, a certain amount is inevitable as people make career moves and firms change production to meet new demand and integrate new technology. If government guaranteed a permanent job for everyone, firms would have difficulty finding new workers for new enterprises, and workers would have little incentive to adapt to a changing economy. Still, unemployment presents problems for those who are unemployed and their families. The real policy issues are how much unemployment an economy needs to accommodate growth and change, and how that unemployment should be distributed among the population.

The Employed and the Unemployed. Every month, the BLS reports estimates of the number of people who are employed and unemployed—and various characteristics of people in each category. These estimates are based on a survey of 60,000 randomly selected households. Each member of the household who is 16 years old or older is asked a series of questions. Depending on their answers to those questions, each survey respondent is placed into one of three categories: (1) employed, (2) unemployed, or (3) not in the labor force.

The **employed** are people who are working for pay for at least 15 hours during the survey week, including both part-time and temporary workers. People who have a job but are absent due to bad weather, illness, vacation, or other personal reasons, and those in a labor-management dispute are also counted as employed. The **unemployed** are people who are actively seeking work but do not currently have a job. The **labor force** is comprised of the unemployed and the employed. People who are not employed, or unemployed, are said to be "not in the labor force." People not in the labor force include individuals who do not work due to a disability, people who are retired, homemakers, full-time students who do not work, and individuals who are too discouraged to look for jobs.

The statistic most often cited from this survey is the unemployment rate—the number of unemployed as a percent of the labor force. It is calculated as follows:

Unemployment rate = (number of unemployed/labor force) × 100.

$$unemployment\ rate = \frac{number\ of\ unemployed}{labor\ force} \times 100 \qquad (2\text{-}4)$$

The unemployment rate is affected by both the number of unemployed and the labor force. For most months, a rise in the number of unemployed results in a higher unemployment rate. If a rise in unemployment occurs during a month in which the labor force rises by a greater proportion, however, the unemployment rate will *fall*. This points to another employment measure: the **labor force participation rate**—the labor force as a percent of the all people capable of working, which the BLS calls the "noninstitutional population." It is calculated as follows:

Labor force participation rate = (labor force/noninstitutional population) × 100.

$$labor\ force\ participation\ rate = \frac{labor\ force}{noninstitutional\ population} \times 100 \qquad (2\text{-}5)$$

The BLS considers children under age 16 and individuals in institutions, such as those in prisons, as incapable of working and excludes them from the noninstitutional population.

Exhibit 2–3 shows the breakdown of the civilian population into the various categories used in the BLS survey. (Members of the armed forces are excluded from the BEA's employment and unemployment measures, so these statistics, including

Exhibit 2–3

The Labor Force in 2000

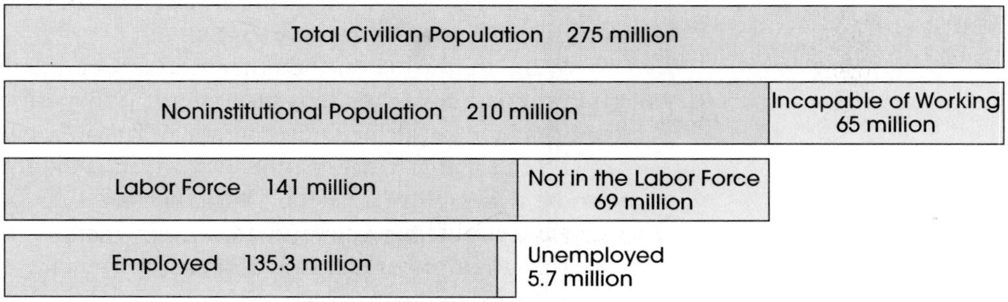

Total Civilian Population 275 million	
Noninstitutional Population 210 million	Incapable of Working 65 million
Labor Force 141 million	Not in the Labor Force 69 million
Employed 135.3 million	Unemployed 5.7 million

The labor force is comprised of the employed and the unemployed. To calculate the labor force, the BLS first subtracts from the civilian population all people incapable of working, such as prisoners and children under 16 years of age. It then subtracts people who are not actively searching for work, such as students, homemakers, and discouraged workers. Source: Department of Labor, Bureau of Labor Statistics (stats.bls.gov).

the labor force, cover only the civilian population.) From this exhibit, the unemployment rate and the labor force participation rate are as follows:

$$unemployment\ rate = \frac{unemployed}{labor\ force} \times 100 = \frac{5.7\ million}{141\ million} \times 100 = 4\ percent \quad (2\text{-}6)$$

$$labor\ force\ participation\ rate = \frac{labor\ force}{non\text{-}institutional\ population} \times 100$$

$$= \frac{141\ million}{210\ million} \times 100 = 67.1\ percent \quad (2\text{-}7)$$

Policy makers watch both of the preceding numbers carefully. Too high an unemployment rate means a loss of production and presents hardships for families and individuals. Too low an unemployment rate puts upward pressure on wages, which may mean building inflationary pressures. An increase in the labor force participation rate, by increasing the supply of labor, lowers the danger of inflation resulting from increased production.

Judgment in Definitions. Determining who is and who is not unemployed is complicated and includes aspects of judgment. The assumptions the BLS uses to decide whom to include as employed and unemployed have been a source of debate. Some economists argue that measured unemployment underestimates true unemployment.

For example, although some people are not in the labor force by choice, others are not because they believe that they do not have a chance of finding a job. These workers are called **discouraged workers.** Should the BLS count discouraged workers as unemployed because they would prefer work? Some economists think so, and argue that true unemployment is higher than the BLS reports.

The official employment statistics also ignore the fact that some people counted as employed are **underemployed**—either working at jobs that don't use their skills fully or have part-time jobs when they would like full-time jobs. Even if the economy is operating at potential output, it is still possible that the economy is not providing enough of the right kinds of jobs and that underemployment exists. Perhaps these people should also be included among the unemployed. Including both discouraged workers and the underemployed as part of the unemployed would raise measured unemployment.

There are arguments on the other side as well. Some people who say they are unemployed may not actually want to work. Why count people as unemployed if they can get a job at the mall, for example, but won't because such a job is "beneath them"? The choice to work or not to work in such an instance is considered by some to be a voluntary decision. Not counting such voluntarily unemployed as unemployed would lower measured unemployment.

So, the unemployment rate is an approximate measure of unused labor resources. It misses many of the people we might want to count as unemployed, and it counts some people we might not want to count. Because of these problems, policy makers are careful to interpret unemployment numbers and to use them only in conjunction with other economic data. Using statistics for economic policy is an art.

The unemployment rate does not count discouraged workers or the underemployed.

Executive Summary

- Remember these three formulas related to employment:

  labor force = employed + unemployed

  unemployment rate = (unemployed/ labor force) × 100

  labor force participation rate = (labor force/ noninstitutional population) × 100

- The unemployment rate can change when either the number of unemployed or the labor force changes.

- Unemployment figures can under- and overstate true unemployment.

THE DATA OF MACROECONOMIC GOALS

In Chapter 1, we listed the four standard domestic goals of macroeconomic policy:

> The standard four goals: high growth, smooth growth of output, low unemployment, and low inflation.

- High growth
- Smooth growth of output
- Low unemployment
- Low inflation

In this part of the chapter, we continue to discuss the performance of the U.S. economy in relation to those goals, but add a global perspective to our presentation. Each section begins with a summary of what we discussed in Chapter 1 and then briefly reviews the historical data pertaining to each of these goals for the U.S. economy. Finally, we discuss other industrialized market economies and some developing economies, whose experience often differs substantially from that of the United States. Combined, the components of this discussion should give you some perspective about what is high and what is low and, in general, what is meant by these goals. (See the Q&A feature, which discusses why the United States collects economic data.)

High Growth

> Economic growth means the average percentage change in real GDP in an economy over long periods of time. It is often adjusted to refer to per-person growth.

In Chapter 1, we talked about growth in terms of trend output. With the terminology learned in this chapter, we can discuss growth more precisely. **Economic growth** is the average percentage change in real GDP in an economy over long periods of time.[1] Most economists use growth in real GDP or growth in real GDP per person as a summary measure of economic performance. Growth in real GDP per person, or economic growth per person, is the average percentage change in real GDP per person (real GDP divided by the population) in an economy over long periods of time. An increase in real GDP per person means that, on average, more goods and services are available for each person to consume.

---

[1]To calculate the percent change in a variable, divide the change in the variable's level by the variable's level in the initial year and multiply by 100. For example, real output was $9,318.5 billion in 2000 and $8,875.8 billion in 1999. The percent change in real output from 1999 to 2000 is (9,318.5 − 8,875.8)/8,875.8 × 100 = 5.0 percent.

Q & A	QUESTION	Why does the U.S. government collect data?
	ANSWER	The U.S. government collects data because, after the Great Depression of the 1930s, government decided that it should take responsibility for steering the economy. To know where to steer it, government needed some measurement of the economy's performance. Before then, it had little reason to collect many data.

After the 1930s, the U.S. government decided to take responsibility for steering the economy. To know where to steer it, government needed some measure of the economy's direction, so it began to develop measures of the economy and collect data. Before then, the prevailing thought among economists and policy makers was that the economy was self-correcting. Left to its own devices, the market was self-adjusting. It didn't need to be steered.

The Great Depression of the 1930s, however, marked a significant change in U.S. economic institutions and ideology. Unemployment rose to over 25 percent. Banks crumbled. Production plummeted. To avoid another Depression, government policy makers wanted to direct the national economy. Statistics play a vital role in policy today.

In the Employment Act of 1946, the U.S. government specifically took responsibility for preventing large fluctuations in the level of economic activity, maintaining a relatively constant price level, and providing an economic environment conducive to economic growth. Knowing what the appropriate action is, however, requires (1) an understanding of how an economy works and (2) a knowledge of the health of the economy, so economists and policy makers seek a scientific and systematic set of data that describes the economy. Thus, government collects data to help achieve the four goals of the economy that we discuss in the chapter.

Another way to calculate economic growth per person is to subtract the growth rate of the population from the growth rate of real GDP. Since 1947, real GDP has risen at an average rate of about 3.5 percent per year and the U.S. population has grown 1.2 percent per year. So, real GDP per person has risen by about 2.3 percent per year. Specifically, this means that real income per person has doubled every 30 years.[2]

Growth is very complicated, and we will discuss it more in a later chapter. However, we'll mention one concept, **labor productivity**—total output per worker—that plays an important part in the measurement of growth. Changes in labor productivity and growth are highly correlated. When the rate of productivity growth rises, economists expect economic growth per person to rise, and when it declines, economists expect economic growth per person to decline.

Looking at average economic growth per person since 1947 hides the fact that it slowed in the mid 1970s—real GDP per person rose by 2.5 percent per year from 1947 to 1973 but by only 1.9 percent per year from 1973 to 1991. A 0.6-percentage-point difference might not sound like a lot, but at a 2.5 annual rate of increase, real GDP per person would have doubled every 28 years. With 1.9 percent, it would take 37 years for real GDP per person to double. The decline in economic growth per person has made growth a focus of policy debate since the mid-1970s, and has given renewed interest to growth in the United States. Since 1991, however, economic growth per person accelerated to a 2.7 percent annual rate, raising the

---

[2]To calculate the number of years it takes any variable to double, use the rule of 70, which states: The number of years it takes an amount to double in value equals 70 divided by the annual rate of increase.

Q & A	QUESTION	Why has productivity growth fluctuated over the past 50 years?
	ANSWER	Economists aren't sure but have suggested labor use in business cycles, oil price fluctuations, changes in labor force composition, changes in the composition of production, and changing technology as possible explanations.

From 1950 to the early 1970s, growth in labor productivity averaged 2.6 percent per year. Beginning in the 1970s, productivity growth fell to 1.2 percent per year. In the late 1990s, it accelerated to 2.5 percent per year. The question of why these fluctuations in productivity have occurred is one that economists have looked at carefully, because labor productivity growth is directly related to growth rates of GDP.

Despite much research into the question, economists still aren't sure of the answer to the productivity puzzle. One suggestion is that much of the fluctuation involves the business cycle. In a recession, firms keep extra labor on hand, which lowers average labor productivity, while, in a boom, firms use their labor more efficiently. This is clearly part of the explanation, but it is not the whole explanation, because the fluctuations in productivity do not match the economy's business cycles.

A second suggestion is that increases in oil prices during the 1970s and early 1980s caused productivity to decrease. This explanation seemed reasonable; after all, oil is an important input to the production of many goods and services. When oil prices fell in the mid-1980s, however, productivity growth did not immediately return to its pre-1970s' trend, suggesting that rising oil prices may not have been the reason that productivity growth slowed in the earlier period.

A third suggestion involves changes in the composition of the labor force. In the 1970s, many Baby Boomers entered the labor market. This large influx of inexperienced workers likely contributed to the slowdown in productivity growth. If this were the explanation, then productivity should have increased in the 1980s or early 1990s as those workers became experienced. It didn't, which casts doubt on this explanation. (Productivity did, however, increase in the late 1990s.)

A fourth suggestion involves changes in the composition of production. Beginning in the mid-1970s, the U.S. economy began shifting away from producing manufactured goods and toward producing services. Because service-sector productivity increases are harder to measure than those in the manufacturing-sector, the slowdown may have been due to an undercounting of service production. In the late 1990s, however, output from services kept increasing, but productivity growth rose, casting doubt on this explanation as well.

A fifth suggestion involves changing technology. In the 1970s, firms were investing in new technology but were not seeing the returns. This overestimated inputs going into production, and hence decreased measured productivity. Then, in the late 1990s, these investments came to fruition and productivity growth increased. Unfortunately, when economists explored this explanation, they found that the sectors that invested in new technologies did not match the sectors that experienced the increase in productivity growth, casting doubt on these explanations also.

So what can we conclude about the productivity puzzle? Productivity is not well understood, and the explanation for the shifts is probably a mix of many different explanations.

question of whether we have entered a new era of prosperity. (Related to these changes in growth are changes in productivity. See the Q&A feature for a discussion of possible reasons for changes in productivity over the past 50 years.)

OECD Countries. The United States usually compares itself with similar industrial countries, most of which are in the Organization for Economic Cooperation and Development (OECD). Members of the OECD include the countries of Europe and North America, Japan, Australia, New Zealand, Mexico, the Czech Republic, Hungary, Poland, and South Korea. (You can learn more about the OECD at its web site: www.oecd.org.)

OECD countries include most industrialized countries.

Table 2-5

Growth in Real Output,
Output per Person in
OECD Countries

	% Change in Real Output		% Change in Real Output per Person	
	1960-1973	1974-1999	1960-1973	1974-1999
United States	3.9	3.0	2.6	2.0
OECD less United States	5.6	2.9	4.3	2.1
Japan	9.6	2.9	8.3	2.3
Germany	4.3	2.0	3.7	1.9
United Kingdom	3.1	1.9	2.6	1.8

Source: *Historical Statistics*, OECD.

As you can see in Table 2–5, economic growth since 1973 has slowed in all OECD countries. However, OECD growth outside the United States has exceeded the U.S. average throughout both periods, and, until recently, average growth in Japan has exceeded growth in all other OECD nations since 1960. Growth in real GDP per person tells a similar story.

Developing Countries. Developing countries are countries that have low levels of income per person and relatively undeveloped market structures. Average income per person in some developing countries in 2000 was only $500 per year. These countries struggle to provide the basic needs to survive. Because their income levels are so low, growth is more important to these countries than to developed countries.

Table 2–6 summarizes growth statistics for groups of developing countries from 1969 to 2000. In Table 2–6, we see that since 1969 certain groups of developing countries grew at a rapid pace while others hardly grew at all. For example, African countries had growth rates of less than 1. One African country, Niger (individual countries not shown), has had extremely low, and sometimes negative, growth rates. In the 1980s and early 1990s, real GDP per person in Niger declined an average of 4.1 percent per year.

Looking at Table 2–6 you'll notice that Asia's developing countries outperformed all the others. For example, South Korea's growth in income per person had been a phenomenal 8.2 percent a year in the 1980s and early 1990s. It belongs to a group of countries referred to as the Asian Tiger economies. Income levels in some

Table 2-6

Real Growth per Person in
Developing Nations

	Average Annual % Change in Real GDP per Person			
	1969-1978	1979-1988	1989-1994	1995-2000
All developing	3.4	2.0	3.6	4.0
Africa	2.2	− 0.6	0.3	2.0
Asia	3.5	5.1	5.9	5.4
Middle East and Europe	4.4	− 1.2	0.8	2.0
Western Hemisphere	3.3	0.5	1.3	2.0

Note: Developing countries include about 160 countries.
Source: *World Economic Outlook*, International Monetary Fund **(www.imf.org)** and author estimates.

of the Asian Tigers—South Korea, Taiwan, Singapore, and Hong Kong—have risen so high that some economists no longer consider them developing countries.

At one point, economists predicted that these economies would grow forever. In the late 1990s, however, many of the Asian economies faltered, raising the question of whether the previously high rates of growth were ever sustainable.

In general, economists talk about economic growth much differently than do policy makers. Economists study growth over decades. Although economic growth over long periods of time can have a dramatic impact on income levels, policy makers, because their success is rated over shorter time periods, are usually much more interested in growth over the next few years. Later in the text you'll see how the recommendations by economists to promote growth sometimes conflict with policies that affect growth over the short term.

Smooth Growth of Output

Another policy goal is smooth growth of output. Most individuals and firms would prefer a steady growth rate of 3.5 percent a year, as compared with 8 percent one year and −1 percent the next. Stable growth makes it easier for firms to make plans, manage inventories, and keep employees. Despite people's desires, the reality is that most countries experience fluctuations in output.

Exhibit 2–4 shows the fluctuations of the U.S. economy since 1875 as deviations of real GDP from its long-run growth trend, which, as you recall from Chapter 1, are called business cycles. As you can see, the U.S. economy has experienced frequent and sometimes large business cycles. The largest and longest decline in output below trend was the Great Depression during the 1930s. The largest increase in GDP above trend was during the 1940s and was caused by increased government expenditures to fight World War II.

Recession: two or more consecutive quarters of declining real GDP.

The Anatomy of a Business Cycle. Business cycles are composed of **recessions,** two or more consecutive quarters of declining real GDP, and **expansions,** periods of

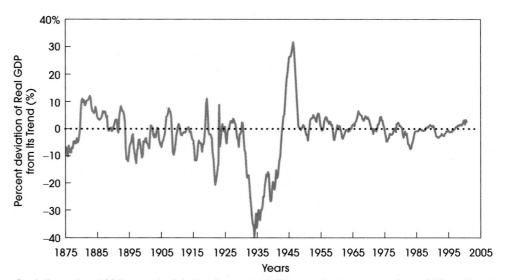

Exhibit 2-4

U.S. Fluctuations in Real GDP Around Its Trend

Deviations of real GDP are calculated as the percent difference between actual real GDP and trend real GDP. Source: Commerce Department, Bureau of Economic Analysis (www.bea.doc.gov) and N. Balke and R. Gordon, in *The American Business Cycle.*

Table 2-7

**Business Cycles
Since 1948**

Dates			Duration in Months	
I Peak	II Trough	III Peak	IV Recession	V Expansion
1. November 1948	October 1949	July 1953	11	45
2. July 1953	May 1954	August 1957	10	39
3. August 1957	April 1958	April 1960	8	24
4. April 1960	February 1961	December 1969	10	106
5. December 1969	November 1970	November 1973	11	36
6. November 1973	March 1975	January 1980	16	58
7. January 1980	July 1980	July 1981	6	12
8. July 1981	November 1982	July 1990	16	92
9. July 1990	March 1991		8	?
Average			*11*	*59*

rising real GDP. The National Bureau of Economic Research (NBER) announces the official dates of recessions and expansions. (Although the NBER looks at hundreds of data series to decide on these dates, recessions have corresponded to two or more consecutive quarters of declining real GDP.) The point at which a recession begins is called the peak, and the point at which real GDP begins to rise is called the trough.

The fluctuations in real GDP, shown in Exhibit 2–4, appear to have lessened since the end of the 1940s. Some economists point to this as evidence that macro-economic policy, which played a more active role in the economy after the 1940s, has succeeded in lessening the severity of economic fluctuations. Other economists disagree with both the evidence and the conclusion. Christina Romer, a Berkeley University economist, has pointed out that the data are ambiguous. She constructed another measure of real GDP that shows that economic fluctuations are about the same before and after the 1940s.

Table 2–7 lists the dates of all U.S. business cycles, beginning in 1948. Each cycle begins with a peak and ends with a peak. As you can see, the United States has had nine recessions since 1948, which have lasted from 6 to 16 months. The duration of a recession is the number of months from the peak (column I) to the trough (column II). The duration of an expansion is the number of months from the trough (column II) to the next peak (column III). At the time this book was written, the U.S. economy was in its longest expansion, which began March 1991. The shortest expansion lasted from July 1980 to July 1981, just 12 months.

The recent ten years of growth slowed in 2000 and 2001, but the economy kept growing. A slowing in the growth rate is technically not a recession, but it sometimes goes under the name growth recession. In 2001 economists were watching carefully to see if the decrease in growth would become a decrease in output for two quarters, at which time it would become an actual recession, and the expansion would be declared over.

As you can see from Table 2–7, expansions have lasted much longer than recessions. This shows that the trend of real GDP is positive. It is difficult, if not impossible, to distinguish the expansionary part of the cycle (a short-term fluctuation) from the trend (economic growth).

Exhibit 2-5

Business Cycles in Japan, the United Kingdom, and Canada

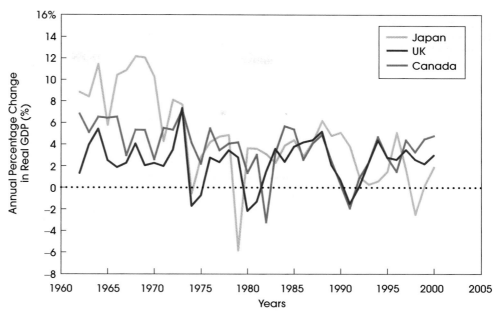

This exhibit shows that economic fluctuations among trading partners are related to one another, although the exact timing of business cycles is different. The economies depicted in the exhibit are all important U.S. trading partners. Source: International Monetary Fund (www.imf.org).

Business Cycles in Other Countries. All economies have business cycles, and, for the most part, countries enter and exit recessions at different times. This is not to say that the timing of business cycles is entirely unrelated. Large economies tend to pull their smaller trading partners in the direction of their own business cycles. The loose correlation between business cycles among three U.S. trading partners— Japan, Canada, and the United Kingdom—is evident in Exhibit 2–5.

Low Unemployment

Let's now consider the policy goal of low unemployment. In the United States since World War II, the unemployment rate has fluctuated from 2.5 percent to over 10 percent. In general unemployment has risen when real GDP has fallen and has fallen when real GDP has risen. The unemployment goal is generally stated in terms of inflation: Keep unemployment low, but not below the point at which inflation will rise. Policy makers today watch the unemployment rate closely. It is the first government statistic about the economy reported each month, and in the late 1990s and in 2000, it was at historic lows, which created a concern about rising inflation.

OECD Countries. Unemployment rates around the world have not mirrored the U.S. experience.[3] In the 1960s, unemployment rates in other OECD countries (especially in Europe) were much lower than in the United States, helped partly by U.S. loans made to rebuild Europe after World War II ended in 1945. Table 2–8 shows unemployment rates for select OECD countries.

---

[3]Methods of calculating unemployment differ from country to country, making comparisons of unemployment difficult. When looking at unemployment rates, it is best to focus on what has happened within a particular country over time.

	1962–1970	1971–1980	1981–1990	1991–1999	2000
OECD	2.7	4.3	7.3	7.4	6.2
OECD-Europe	2.5	4.3	9.3	11.4	7.3
Germany	1.0	3.2	8.1	11.8	7.7
Japan	1.6	2.5	2.9	3.2	4.8
U.S.	4.8	6.4	7.1	5.7	4.0

Note: All column data for years are percentages.

Source: *Historical Statistics* and *OECD Economic Outlook.* OECD Web site: **www.oecd.org**

During the 1980s and 1990s, however, total OECD unemployment rose while unemployment in the United States fell. Unemployment in European countries followed the same pattern. Japan also had low unemployment, about 2 percent to 3 percent since 1947, until the late 1990s when its economy fell into recession and unemployment rose to close to 5 percent.

Developing Countries. Unemployment is difficult to measure in developing countries, where there is both significant unemployment hidden by underemployment and significant nonmarket work. Consider, for example, Niger where most people are subsistence farmers and only a few people have market jobs. An unemployment rate for Niger, measured by U.S. standards would be high, but also a misleading overestimate.

Low Inflation

Deflation: price level falls.

Before 1950, the U.S. price level generally rose, but once in a while it fell. Economists call periods when the price level falls **deflation.** Since 1950, however, the price level has not fallen at all; inflation has been a fact of U.S. economic life, fluctuating from as little as 1.5 percent to as much as 14 percent per year. At times, such as during the mid-1970s and again in the early 1980s, inflation increased. These periods, however, have always been followed by **disinflation**—a decline in the rate of inflation.

Disinflation: rate of inflation falls.

The determination of an appropriate inflation goal is open to debate. Inflation rates of over 11 percent per year during the 1970s dominated political considerations, and policy makers worked hard to bring the rate down. In the late 1990s, policy makers were satisfied when inflation remained at about 2 percent per year. In 2000, policy makers were watching closely *any* uptick in inflation. Their concern was that any increase in inflation would result in even greater inflation, which would be difficult to control. U.S. inflation rates stand in contrast to the inflation rates in the hundreds of percent per year experienced by some developing countries.

OECD Countries. As you can see from Exhibit 2–6, the pattern of rising and falling inflation in OECD countries has followed the pattern in the United States, although inflation in OECD countries has tended to be higher than inflation in the United States.

Developing Countries. Looking at developing countries gives us a much different picture. Developing countries have endured higher, chronic inflation compared with the United States. For example, during the 1970s, prices in developing countries rose an average of nearly 17 percent per year. In the 1980s, prices rose at an even higher rate (45 percent per year). In the late 1980s and early 1990s, prices rose at annual

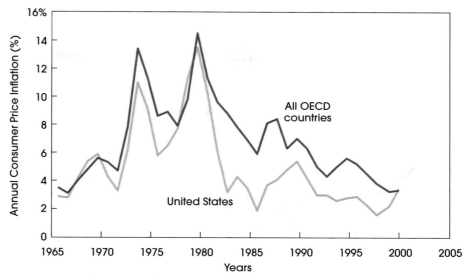

Exhibit 2-6

Inflation in OECD Countries

Inflation in OECD countries has, on average, been higher than in the United States. Source: *Main Economic Indicators,* OECD (www.oecd.org).

rates of about 30 percent per year. Developing countries in the Western Hemisphere, mainly in Latin America, have had particularly high rates of inflation, averaging about 100 percent per year in the 1980s and 1990s. In many developing countries, even the highest U.S. inflation rate wouldn't be seen as inflation at all.

Some developing countries have been periodically hit with very high rates of inflation, called **hyperinflation.** For example, Brazil experienced hyperinflation in 1994, during which prices rose nearly 2,100 percent. That same year, prices rose in the Ukraine by 5,000 percent. Table 2–9 shows some developing countries that have experienced high rates of inflation.

Hyperinflation means very high rates of inflation.

International Considerations for Policy Makers

At one time, the analysis of U.S. macroeconomic issues could ignore the international sector. This is no longer the case. Since 1946, the value of exports has increased approximately 20-fold, and the value of imports has increased 40-fold. In 2000, nearly 20 percent of all goods and services consumed in the United States were imported. Similarly, international flows of assets, both in and out of the

Table 2-9

Inflation in Selected Developing Countries

	Annual Rates of Inflation									
	1980–1991	**1992**	**1993**	**1994**	**1995**	**1996**	**1997**	**1998**	**1999**	**2000**
All developing	45.1	42.8	48.7	54.7	23.2	15.3	9.7	10.1	6.6	6.1
Brazil	384.7	1,022.5	1,927.4	2,075.8	66.0	15.8	6.9	3.2	4.9	7.0
Ghana	34.5	10.1	24.9	24.9	59.5	46.6	27.9	19.3	12.4	25.0
Indonesia	8.3	7.5	9.7	8.5	9.4	7.9	6.6	58.0	20.8	3.8
Turkey	48.5	70.1	66.1	106.3	93.7	82.3	85.7	84.6	64.9	54.9

Note: All column data for years are percentages.

Source: *World Economic Outlook,* International Monetary Fund, various issues (www.imf.org).

United States, have grown tremendously. Today, international considerations permeate most macroeconomic questions. When policy makers think about policies to achieve one or more of the goals of macroeconomics, they now consider the impact that those policies have on international trade and exchange rates, because international considerations themselves affect domestic policy goals.

Ultimately, what matters to policy makers is the domestic economy, so they consider the impact of large trade deficits and large exchange-rate movements in light of how they affect the domestic economy. These effects are uncertain, and, as a result, international goals and considerations are not as clearly defined as domestic macroeconomic goals. International considerations are intermediate goals, not final goals.

Two international considerations in macroeconomic policy are a nation's trade balance and its exchange rate. A nation's trade balance affects the domestic economy. An increase in imports, other things being equal, tends to reduce domestic production and domestic saving, but exports also provide competition to domestic producers by providing domestic consumers and producers with goods at prices either that are cheaper than domestic prices or that are otherwise unavailable. A rise in exports, other things being equal, tends to boost domestic production but may also lead to inflation if the economy is already producing at potential output.

> The exchange rate is the price at which one currency is traded for another.

A country's **exchange rate**—the price at which one currency is traded for another—determines the prices residents must pay for imports and the price of a country's goods to foreigners. The exchange rate also determines prices of international flows of assets and is an important international economic concern.

Let's briefly consider where the U.S. economy stands internationally on the trade balance and the exchange rate value of the dollar.

Trade Balance. For most years until 1976, the United States had a trade surplus (exports exceeded imports). Since then, the United States has consistently had a trade deficit (imports exceeded exports). Exhibit 2–7 shows imports and exports separately. Blue *shaded regions* show trade deficits, while red *shaded regions* indicate

Exhibit 2-7

Exports and Imports in the United States

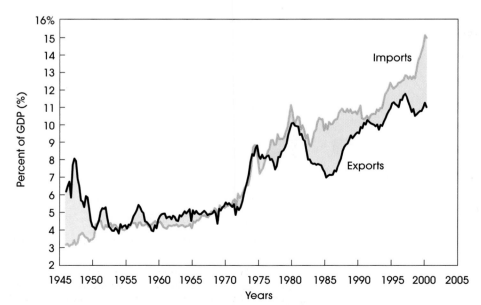

Since 1945, foreign trade has become increasingly important for the United States. Source: Commerce Department, Bureau of Economic Analysis (www.bea.doc.gov).

Table 2-10

Exports and Imports for OECD and Selected Countries, 1999

	Exports (% of GDP)	Imports (% of GDP)
OECD total	22.1	22.4
United States	10.7	13.5
Germany	29.4	28.5
Japan	10.4	8.7
United Kingdom	25.8	27.5
The Netherlands	60.6	55.8

Source: *Main Economic Indicators*, OECD **(www.oecd.org).**

trade surpluses. We show exports and imports separately to demonstrate the increasing importance of trade to the economy. In 1949, the volume of imports and exports equaled about 4 percent of GDP. In 2000, exports equaled 11 percent of GDP and imports equaled 15 percent of GDP.

International trade is an even greater consideration in other economies. Table 2–10 shows exports and imports as a share of GDP for OECD countries as a whole, as well as for selected other countries. Trade tends to be a much larger part of economic activity in smaller countries. In the Netherlands, for example, imports and exports are each about 60 percent of GDP, making international policies much more important to achieving domestic policy goals.

Exchange Rate. The value of the U.S. dollar, compared with other currencies such as the British pound, remained relatively constant through the 1950s and 1960s. After World War II, until 1971, exchange rates were determined by the Bretton Woods

Exhibit 2-8

Trade-weighted Value of the Dollar

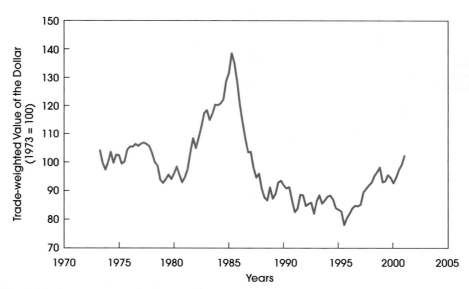

This exhibit shows the multilateral trade-weighted value of the dollar (1973 = 100). This measure of the value of the dollar is an index that weights a group of ten currencies by the volume of trade that each country has with the United States. These countries are Canada, Belgium, France, Germany, Italy, the Netherlands, Japan, Sweden, Switzerland, and the United Kingdom. The index is set to 100 in 1973. Source: Federal Reserve Board (www.federalreserve.gov).

System, a **fixed exchange rate system** in which government buys and sells its own and other currencies to maintain its exchange rate at a constant level. In the 1970s, the United States ended its fixed exchange rate policy and since then has followed a **partially flexible exchange rate system,** in which the government sometimes buys and sells its currency to influence the exchange rate but otherwise lets the market determine its value. In a **flexible exchange rate system,** government never intervenes and lets the market determine its value. After the United States ended its fixed exchange rate system, the U.S. dollar began fluctuating substantially, as you can see in Exhibit 2–8, which shows an index of the value of the dollar that weights currencies of major countries with which the United States trades. (The countries are listed in the caption.) The value of the dollar decreased in the 1970s, increased in the early 1980s, fell in the early 1990s and rose again in the late 1990s and early 2000s.

The effect of fluctuations in a country's exchange rate on an economy is evident in the dramatic declines in the currencies of some Asian countries in the late 1990s. When the baht, Thailand's currency, fell by more than 20 percent in just 2 months, the businesses that received revenue in baht found it impossible to repay loans denominated in U.S. dollars. The price of imports rose to levels unaffordable to many individuals and firms. Companies went bankrupt, the economy fell into a deep recession, and riots broke out. The value of a country's exchange rate is clearly important to domestic policy goals.

Why do such fluctuations occur? How are currencies connected, and what implications do the connections have for macroeconomic policies? Should countries adopt fixed or flexible exchange rates? We'll explore these questions in later chapters.

> Exchange rate systems can be fixed, flexible, or partially flexible. (Most countries have partially flexible systems.)

Executive Summary

- Since 1947, annual economic growth in the United States has averaged 3.5 percent, and annual economic growth per person has averaged 2.3 percent. Labor productivity is a major determinant of growth. In the past decade, growth has been lowest in African countries and highest in Asian countries.

- Since 1947, the United States has experienced nine recessions. At any one time, countries are in different stages of the business cycle.

- Unemployment in the United States has fluctuated from 2.5 percent to over 10 percent. During the 1980s, 1990s and early 2000s, unemployment rose in OECD countries as a whole but fell in the United

States. Unemployment in the United States has recently been lower than in other OECD countries.

- Inflation in the United States has fluctuated between 1.5 percent and 14 percent since 1950. Although inflation has been volatile at times in the United States, we have never experienced the extremely rapid rise in the price level that some developing economies have experienced. Economists call an extremely rapid rise in the price level *hyperinflation.*

- The United States has a partially flexible exchange rate. The U.S. balance of trade has been in deficit since the mid–1970s. Both the exchange rate and the balance of trade affect domestic goals.

POLICY PERSPECTIVE: THE IMPORTANCE OF GOOD FORECASTS

We began this chapter with a discussion of a friend who forecasts the future of the economy for a major financial institution. He bases his forecasts on a knowledge of how statistics are collected. Why do these financial firms pay him big bucks to make those forecasts? The answer is that there are big bucks to be made by accurate forecasts. Financial firms invest in multibillion-dollar funds specializing in stocks and bonds, the values of which fluctuate with movements in the economy. Correctly predicting a change in economic conditions can be worth hundreds of millions of dollars to these firms.

Incorrectly predicting economic conditions can result in great losses. In 1998, Long-Term Capital Management (LTCM)—a U.S. financial investment company—purchased stocks and bonds in the belief that prices that deviate from their norm will, over time, return to their norm. It lost billions of dollars over the course of a few months when its forecast, that the gap between interest rates on U.S. Treasury bonds and other countries' bonds would fall, was wrong.

Policy makers feared that large financial losses by LTCM could create a financial panic, leading other financial institutions to drastically reduce their lending. Such a reduction in lending could lead to lower spending and a recession. Ultimately, the Federal Reserve Bank arranged for an infusion of cash from private companies into LTCM to keep the losses from pushing the U.S. economy into a recession. So, private forecasts are important to firms and to policy makers.

Because government policy actions affect the economy, forecasters spend a lot of time predicting policy. The forecasts themselves, however, affect the decisions of policy makers, which means that *the expectations of policy affect the economy*. This means that what data policy makers look at, their statements about data, and how they interpret them, affect expectations and become part of the policy.

Another economist friend who does forecasting told us he knows each data series that the chairman of the Federal Reserve Bank, Alan Greenspan, looks at. When Greenspan starts looking at a new data series to forecast inflation, as he did when he began to favor the PCE deflator over the CPI, our friend changes his forecast of the economy accordingly.

Knowing the effect that his actions have on forecasters, Greenspan can change policy with words or even tones of voice. For example, when Greenspan began to talk about the rapidly rising stock market prices, people took that as a sign that the Federal Reserve would take action to slow the economy. In response, people began to cut back their spending and the economy slowed on its own. So, the Federal Reserve Bank chairman can conduct policy with his pronouncements. To make sense of those pronouncements, you need to know the data and measures of the economy.

CONCLUSION

We'll stop this chapter here. If you're like us, you need a break from this data grind. However, let us remind you—it is necessary for understanding the economy. You can enhance your understanding outside of this course by listening to the economic news, reading the economic pages of the newspapers, talking about macroeconomic problems, looking at data releases on the Internet, and generally being interested in the economy. Throughout the book, we'll direct you to various sources to sharpen your knowledge of the economy.

KEY POINTS

■ GDP measures the market value of all final goods and services produced within a country in a year. GDP and output equal total income.

■ Expenditure components of GDP are personal consumption expenditures, gross private investment, net exports, and government expenditures.

■ Income components of GDP are employee compensation, rents, interest, and profit. Nominal GDP is a measure of total output at current prices, while real GDP is a measure of total output keeping prices constant.

■ The GDP deflator measures market prices of all final goods and services produced in an economy. GDP Deflator = (nominal GDP/real GDP) × 100

■ The CPI measures the prices of a fixed basket of goods and services typical consumers purchase, stated as an index of base-year prices. CPI = (a specific year's price of a base-year market basket of goods/the base-year price of a base-year market basket of goods) × 100

■ The PPI measures the prices businesses pay for intermediate goods and services, stated as an index of base-year prices.

■ The unemployment rate is the unemployed divided by the labor force. This measure excludes, among others, students, discouraged workers, and homemakers. Depending on how you look at it, the unemployment rate may overestimate or underestimate unemployment.

■ The world experience regarding the four standard macroeconomic goals is varied. Per capita growth in the United States has been somewhat lower than in other OECD countries. Recently, unemployment and inflation have been lower in the United States compared with that of other OECD countries. Although all countries experience business cycles, they generally are not in the same phase at the same time.

■ Countries have experienced vastly different growth rates and have different incomes per person. Developing countries have low incomes per person and are looking to just meet the basic needs of their populations.

■ Appropriate international goals are ambiguous. The value of the dollar has fluctuated following the breakdown in 1971 of a fixed exchange rate system called the Bretton Woods System. Trade has become increasingly important to the United States since 1945.

KEY TERMS

consumer price index (CPI) 32
deflation 44
depreciation 25
disinflation 44
discouraged workers 36
economic growth 37
employed 35
exchange rate 46
expansion 41
fixed exchange rate system 48
flexible exchange rate
   system 48
GDP price deflator 31

government expenditures 24
gross domestic product (GDP) 22
gross private investment 24
hyperinflation 45
labor force 35
labor force participation rate 35
labor productivity 38
national income 25
national income and product
   accounts (NIPAs) 24
net domestic product 25
net exports 24
net foreign factor income 25

nominal GDP 26
partially flexible exchange rate
   system 48
personal consumption expenditure
   (PCE) deflator 33
personal consumption 24
price level 30
producer price index (PPI) 34
real GDP 26
recession 41
underemployed 36
unemployed 35
value added 22

QUESTIONS FOR THOUGHT AND REVIEW

1. Briefly describe the two ways that GDP is calculated.
2. Explain why total output equals total income.
3. What are the four main expenditure categories used to calculate GDP?
4. What is the difference between gross domestic product and net domestic product?
5. What are the five main components of national income?

6. What four adjustments must be made to national income to arrive at GDP?
7. What is the difference between real GDP and nominal GDP, and why is it important?
8. What is the problem with using fixed base-year prices to calculate real GDP when relative prices change? How has the BEA changed its measure of real GDP to account for this problem?

9. How do the GDP deflator, CPI, and PPI differ? Why does the government construct so many different price indexes?

10. How did the CPI overstate inflation? Why is accuracy in the measurement of the CPI important to policy makers?

11. From a macroeconomic perspective, why is some unemployment desirable?

12. How is the unemployment rate calculated in the United States?

13. Who are "discouraged workers," and how do they affect our interpretation of the unemployment rate?

14. How does the growth experience in the United States compare with that in other developed and developing nations?

15. What is a business cycle? How many business cycles has the United States experienced since 1947? Have other countries experienced similar fluctuations in real GDP?

16. How does U.S. experience with unemployment compare with that of other developed countries?

17. How does U.S. experience with inflation compare with that of developing countries?

18. Why are international considerations of growing importance to U.S. policy makers?

19. How does a fixed exchange rate differ from a flexible exchange rate and from a partially flexible exchange rate? What type of exchange rate does the U.S. have?

20. How does Alan Greenspan's choice of data to look at influence forecasts and the economy?

PROBLEMS AND EXERCISES

1. Use the following table to answer the questions:

	Real GDP	Nominal GDP
1990	6138.1	5743.8
1991	6079.0	5916.7
1992	6244.4	6244.4
1993	6383.8	6550.2
1994	6604.2	6931.4

a. Calculate the GDP deflator and the inflation rate for each year.

b. Calculate the growth rate of nominal GDP for each year.

c. Did inflation outpace the growth rate of nominal GDP in any year? If so, what happened to real GDP in that year or years?

2. Suppose the economy is comprised of two firms: a movie production firm and a video store. The production firm hires actors, producers, and directors, paying them $3 million. The firm creates and duplicates the film to video, selling 300,000 copies to individuals for $6 million and 100,000 copies to retail video stores for $300,000. The video store pays $200,000 to store clerks and sells 100,000 videos to customers for $2.5 million. Calculate GDP in the economy using (1) the value-added approach, (2) the income approach, (3) the expenditures approach. Show your work.

3. Calculate real GDP in 2001 and 2002 from Table 2–3, using 2002 as the base year.

4. Assume the GDP chain-weighted GDP index for 2002 is 135 and for 2003 is 140. The base-year is 1996. Nominal GDP in 1996 is $8.5 trillion.

a. By what percent did real GDP rise in 2003?

b. What is the level of real GDP in 2002 and in 2003?

5. The price of oranges goes up 20 percent in a year; the price of apples goes down 20 percent in a year. The consumption of apples and oranges remains constant during this time, with 40 percent of people's income spent on apples and 60 percent spent on oranges.

a. You are called in to determine the rate of inflation. What would your answer be?

b. Your boss tells you that he is unhappy with your answer; he would really like the rate of inflation to be lower than you determined it to be. How would you respond?

6. As part of the USA AID project you have been assigned to set up the NIPA accounts for Asceticland, where all people judge welfare by the degree that they meet the creed of Asceticism—the practice of strict self-denial as a measure of personal and, especially, spiritual discipline. How would you respond to this assignment? Why?

7. The National Bureau of Economic Research Business Cycle Dating Committee is the official body that determines the beginning and end of business cycles. Research the committee (www.nber.org; look under "data" and "business cycle dates") and answer the following questions:

a. How many recessions has the economy experienced since 1945?

b. When was the longest recession since 1945? The shortest since 1945?

c. What is the average length of recessions and expansions since 1945?

d. Is the economy currently in a recession or an expansion? Explain your answer.

8. Use the following table to calculate items (a) through (e):

	In Millions
Noninstitutional Civilian Population over age 16	200
Armed forces	4
Discouraged workers	3
People wanting full-time work, working part-time	2
Unemployed	8
Employed full-time	117
Employed part-time	9

a. The labor force participation rate
b. The employment rate
c. The labor force
d. The unemployment rate
e. Suppose the labor force grows by 4 percent and the number of unemployed grows by 3 percent. Recalculate your answers to (a) through (d). What important property of the unemployment rate does this calculation illustrate?

9. Suppose the unemployment rate is 5 percent and the civilian labor force is 140 million. Calculate the following if 2 million unemployed workers become too discouraged to continue looking for work:
a. The unemployment rate
b. The employment rate

10. Why might the official unemployment rate overestimate true unemployment? Why might it underestimate true unemployment? Using the most recent *Employment Situation Report* (available at stats.bls.gov) under "Employment,"
a. State the current unemployment rate.
b. Construct your own unemployment rate, using information on discouraged workers (Table A–10) and those working part-time but who would like more work (Table A–4). Explain your answer.

c. Construct your own unemployment rate using information on job quitters (Table A–7). Compare your new unemployment rate with the official rate.

11. Look up "How the Government Measures Unemployment" on the Internet (stats.bls.gov/cps_htgm.htm) and answer the following questions:
a. Categorize each member of your family (including yourself) as either employed, unemployed, or not in the labor force. Explain your answer.
b. What is your family labor force participation rate? Its unemployment rate?

12. The Bureau of Labor Statistics maintains an Internet page on frequently asked questions about the CPI. Use that page (stats.bls.gov/cpifaq.htm) to answer the following questions:
a. Whose buying habits does the CPI reflect? Who is excluded?
b. What goods and services are excluded from the CPI?
c. For whom might the CPI be an inappropriate measure of inflation?

13. Go to the White House Briefing Room on the Internet (www.whitehouse.gov/fsbr/esbr.html) and, looking under "prices," answer the following questions:
a. What is the United States' recent experience with inflation? What measure did you use and why?
b. State inflation for the recent past using other measures reported on the Web site. How do they differ? What explanations can you think of for their differences?

14. Go to GPO Gate, which posts the *Economic Report of the President* (www.access.gpo.gov/eop). Use Chapter 2 to answer the following questions:
a. What was real GDP growth in the most recently complete year?
b. List the major components of GDP, and state their contributions to overall real GDP growth in the most recently complete year.
c. What explanations did the report give for the contributions of each component?

Measuring Economic Activity: National Income Accounting

Firms produce millions of products each year, and individuals make millions of economic transactions each and every day. General Motors produces cars, music lovers purchase CDs, the sick purchase medical services, the government purchases defense, you pay tuition—the list goes on. All of these transactions comprise economic activity, which the U.S. government summarizes in the national income and product accounts.

The rules of national income accounting are based on the circular flow shown in the chapter (see Exhibit 2–1). The expenditures (or product) side of the income accounts measures the value of all goods produced by adding up expenditures, while the income side of the domestic income accounts adds up the various components of income. Because every dollar produced creates an equal dollar of income, national product equals national income. Economic output is actually a dynamic flow, which fluctuates up and down. So, the economy is better pictured as a pulsating circular flow, or a spiral. The circular flow diagram is a snapshot of the economy.

Output and income are equal because of accounting conventions. By definition, they have to be equal. Recall the computer firm from the chapter. That firm's contribution to total output equaled the income it paid out. Two "equalizing" concepts—inventory investment and profit—creatively force the accounting equality to be true. **Inventory investment** (unsold goods) is added to the product side and **profit** (revenue less payments to factors of production) is added to the income side to make the two sides equal. For example, say firms produce a lot more than they sell—production exceeds expenditures and the spiral is shrinking. In this case, firms are treated as if they purchase their own inventory. We add "inventory demand" to the firms' demand for their own goods to total expenditures. Similarly, on the income side, the payment for the increased inventory is taken out of firms' profits, and their profits fall.

GROSS DOMESTIC PRODUCT

As you know from the chapter, the product side of the national income accounts is summarized by a single number—gross domestic product. This number summarizes millions of transactions within an economy. We gave the definition of GDP in the chapter; here we look at each component of the definition carefully. First let's restate the definition: GDP is the market value of final goods produced in a country within a year.

Market Value

Of course, you cannot merely add 6 million CDs, 100 heart transplants, 50 million movie tickets, and 8 million McDonald's Extra Value Meals together and expect to have a meaningful concept. Six million CDs, 100 heart transplants, 50 million movie tickets, and 8 million McDonald's Extra Value Meals added together give you 6 million CDs, 100 heart transplants, 50 million movie tickets, and 8 million McDonald's Extra Value meals. To combine them into a single aggregate, each must be valued by a common factor. The common factor that is generally used is a good's market price (the price people actually pay). Multiplying the quantity of each good by its market price converts each good into value terms. For example, 6 million CDs at $15 apiece, 100 heart transplants at $50,000 apiece, 50 million movie tickets at $6 apiece, and 8 million McDonald's Extra Value Meals at $4 apiece equals $427 million.

GDP is calculated by extending this valuing process to all final products in the society. The total value represents a single composite commodity made up of all the goods and services in the economy. Creating this composite allows us to analyze the economy as if it produced only one physical good.

Final Goods

GDP includes only the value of all *final* goods sold. To calculate GDP, you might think that all you have to do is measure the total sales of every firm and add them all together.

This would be wrong for two reasons. First, total sales includes sales of already produced goods—existing assets. The sale of existing assets does not measure new economic activity. Say, for instance, you decide to sell your Mercedes 450 SL to a rich Texan for $40,000. No new production has taken place, and thus the transaction is merely a transfer of an existing asset. We do not want to include transfers in GDP and, therefore, we exclude all such transactions from the aggregate measure.

We introduced the second reason in the chapter. Adding up all transactions would *double-count* production. Consider a one-product economy that makes just ice cream. Say Ben, a dairy farmer, decides to turn the milk he produces into ice cream and sells 100 ice creams for 50 cents apiece at his own ice cream shop. GDP would be the quantity of ice creams × price of ice creams = $50. Now, let's change the process; say that Ben sells Jerry 10 gallons of milk at $1 a gallon to produce Jerry's ice cream. Jerry then sells his 10 gallons of ice cream to Eddy at $2.50 a gallon. Eddy sells 100 ice creams at his shop for 50 cents apiece.

Total market transactions would include the sale of milk from Ben to Jerry at $10, the sale of ice cream to Eddy at $25, and the sale of cones to the public at $50. Total market transactions would be $85. In addition, if, between the ice cream company (Jerry) and the vendor (Eddy), a middleperson bought the ice cream for $25 and sold it for $40, total transactions would rise to $125. In each case, the value of ice cream sold to consumers is its contribution to GDP.

The second method of adding all transactions overstates this value by double-counting the value of inputs at each stage of production. Such a measure is not espe-cially useful in providing us with information about how much ice cream was supplied to consumers, which would be measured only by *final sales*—$50 in this example. The other sales were sales of *intermediate goods*, goods used in the production of other final products. We want to eliminate all these intermediate products from the total to eliminate double-counting. We do this with the value-added method. To see how the value-added method works, consider Table 2–A1, which summarizes our example.

Value added is calculated by subtracting the cost of materials from the value of sales, leaving only the value added at each stage of production. The aggregate value added at each stage of production is, by definition, precisely equal to the value of final sales because it excludes all intermediate products. You can see the equality of the value-added approach and the final-sales approach by comparing the vendor's final sales of $50 in row 4, column II, with the $50 of value added in row 5, column III.

Produced in a Country

As we discussed in Chapter 1, countries are the level at which policy is implemented, but people often cross national boundaries. For example, how should we treat the output of U.S. citizens or firms who reside in Japan? Is it Japanese income because they live in Japan? Or is it U.S. income because they are U.S. citizens? If you answered, "It could be either," you're right. Accountants solve the problem by distinguishing *domestic* income (product) from *national* income (product). GDP is the output that occurs within a country's geographic borders (location matters), regardless of who owns the production. Gross national product (GNP) is the output that is attributable to the citizens of a country (ownership matters), regardless of where production takes place. Of these, GDP is currently the most widely used.

The difference between GNP and GDP is called *net foreign factor income*—the difference between the

Table 2–A1   The Value-added Approach to GDP

	I Cost of Materials ($)	II Value of Sales ($)	III Value Added ($)
1. Farmer Ben	0	10	10
2. Ice cream maker Jerry	10	25	15
3. Middleperson	25	40	15
4. Vendor Eddy	40	50	10
5. Total	**75**	**125**	**50**

The emphasis in domestic income accounting is on income and output, which are flows. This is a different emphasis than what one sees in a firm's accounts. If any of you have had accounting, you know that you generally start by considering a firm's balance statement—a measure of its assets and its liabilities, which are stock concepts. The firm's income statements are only considered later.

What's the difference between the two? The income accounts provide a view of the flow—the value over a specified period of time (a year)—which can be used to see how the country is doing; they are the equivalent to a firm's income statement. The wealth accounts provide a view of a country's stock of wealth—a value at a moment in time; they are the equivalent of the firm's balance statement.

Why do the owners of a business concentrate on the balance statement (stock measure) and economists concentrate on income accounts (flow measure)? In large part, it is because a firm is owned and the owners want to know what the firm is worth, which is closely

related to its assets and liabilities. Countries are not owned by anyone. They belong to the people of the country, so the balance statements are of less direct importance. You don't see anyone going out and making a take-over bid for the shares of a country. Still, countries do collect some information relevant to a balance statement, and this information is found in the domestic wealth accounts.

Although stock concepts and flow concepts are not the same, they are related. If the flow of water into Lake Victoria rises due to heavy rains and the flow of water out of Lake Victoria doesn't change, the stock of water in Lake Victoria will rise. The same principle applies to income and wealth. Your yearly income is a flow, but your wealth is a stock. As you add a portion of your flow of income each month to your bank account, your stock of wealth increases. GDP is a flow concept and must be measured within a specified time period. The Commerce Department reports GDP as the amount the United States produces in a given year.

---

amount that citizens and companies of a country earn abroad and the amount that foreigners and foreign companies earn in that country. GDP plus net foreign factor income equals GNP. For the United States, factor payments to foreigners and factor payments to U.S. citizens are almost equal, so GNP and GDP don't differ by much. In 2000, GDP was $9,963.1 billion and GNP was $9,958.7 billion, and net foreign factor income was −$4.4 billion. GDP differed from GDP by only 0.04 percent. It would, however, make a major difference in a much smaller country such as Ireland, where, in 2000, GDP was 79.7 billion Irish punt and GNP was 66.7 Irish punt. GDP differed from GNP by nearly 20 percent. Income received by foreigners for domestic production exceeded income received by citizens of Ireland for foreign production.

Within a Year

Telling your parents that you have accepted a job that pays $2,000 might not be impressive. They may well think you're going to earn $2,000 per month. However, if you tell them it is $2,000 per week, we suspect they will be impressed. For income to have meaning, it must have a time dimension. The same goes for GDP. It must be expressed per unit of time. Firms produce and people purchase a certain number of items within a period of time. This type of measure is what is called a **flow concept.**

Quantities that are measured at a particular moment in time are called **stock concepts.**

To understand the difference between a flow and a stock, consider Lake Victoria, the world's second largest lake (it's in Africa), and the Kagera River, one of Lake Victoria's water sources. The water in Lake Victoria is a stock. Although its level can rise and fall, the amount of water at any specific time is a stock. The water that flows into Lake Victoria from the Kagera River is a flow. It must be described by an amount per unit of time. Saying 1,000 gallons of water flows into Lake Victoria is much more meaningful when you specified within what period of time.

GROSS DOMESTIC INCOME

You know from the circular flow diagram that another way to measure income is to add up all the payments (income) to the factors of production. When firms produce a good, they hire factors of production (for example, workers) and pay them income. All the goods and services included in GDP have to be produced, and when they are produced, they create income. The income side of the domestic income accounts adds up the various components of income, and, if all income components are measured correctly, according to the definitions, the result is the total income of an economy. It is fundamentally important to remember that GDP, by definition, equals gross domestic income. These two are equal because of the nature of accounting.

COMPONENTS OF GROSS DOMESTIC PRODUCT

GDP is a single value that summarizes numerous transactions in the various sectors of the economy. For policy makers and economists alike, it is helpful to group these transactions into the various sectors of the economy: consumers, business, government, and foreign transactions. At times, the foreign sector will provide the source of growth in income. At other times, consumers will lead economic growth. Knowing which sector is providing the stimulus for growth and which is pulling it down is central to deciding what policies to undertake.

The standard components of GDP are personal consumption, private investment, net exports (exports minus imports), and government spending. Thus, we have the following definitional tautology (a statement that is true by its own definition.)

$$GDP = C + I + X - M + G \qquad (2A-1)$$

where C is personal consumption expenditures, I is gross private domestic investment, X is exports of goods and services, M is imports of goods and services, and G is government purchases.

Table 2–A2 provides a summary measure from the Bureau of Economic Analysis (BEA) of the components of GDP for the United States and OECD countries.

Consumer Sector

As you can see from Table 2–A2, personal consumption expenditures, at 68 percent of GDP, is the largest component of GDP for the United States. Consumption for all OECD countries averages slightly lower than 63 percent of GDP.

The BEA breaks down consumption further into durable goods, nondurable goods, and services. Durable goods include products that last more than 1 year, such as automobiles and appliances. Durable goods industries often experience large cyclical swings in demand. Nondurable goods include goods such as food and clothing. Services include expenditures on items such as medical care, owner-occupied housing, and financial services.

Business Sector

Gross private domestic investment is the second largest component of GDP and is often volatile. In the income

Table 2–A2   Components of GDP, 2000

	United States		OECD
	Billions of Dollars	*% of Total*	*% of Total*
Personal consumption expenditures (C)	6,757.3	67.8	62.6
Durable goods	820.3		
Nondurable goods	2,010.0		
Services	3,927.0		
Gross private domestic investment (I)	1,832.7	18.4	20.6
Fixed investment	1,778.2		
Change in business inventories	54.5		
Net exports of goods and services (X-M)	−370.7	−3.7	0.6
Exports	1,097.3		
Imports	1,468.0		
Government expenditures (G)	1,743.7	17.8	16.3
Federal	595.2		
State and local	1,148.6		
Gross domestic product (GDP)	**9,963.1**	**100.0**	**100.0**

Note: Values for the United States are from 2000. Values do not all sum to total due to statistical discrepancies and rounding errors.

Source: Commerce Department, Bureau of Economic Analysis (**www.bea.doc.gov**); *Main Economic Indicators*, OECD (**www.oecd.org**).

Table 2-A3   Gross Private Domestic Investment, 2000

	Billions of Dollars		% of Total	
Business fixed investment	1,778.2		97	
Nonresidential	1,362.2			74
Structures		324.2		
Equipment and software		1,038.0		
Residential	416.0			23
Change in business inventories	54.5		3	
Gross private domestic investment	**1,832.7**		100	
Depreciation	739.4			
Net private investment	**1,093.3**			

Source: Commerce Department, Bureau of Economic Analysis (www.bea.doc.gov).

accounts, the word *investment* has a specific meaning that is different from the meaning used in everyday conversation. **Investment** in this context is expenditures on fixed assets used to expand productive capacity or to replace machines and buildings that are wearing out, as well as changes in business inventories. Your purchase of securities on the secondary market would not be included as investment expenditures because, although you are gaining an asset, some one else has lost that asset. It is not a new asset. The transactions cancel each other out. Buying stocks and bonds is not an investment according to the economist's definition; these are merely transfers of existing assets. What if Microsoft issues new securities to raise funds to build a new production site? The building of that new factory is counted as business investment. The sale of the securities is not.[1]

To determine whether you've been following the material, answer the following question: Which of the following would be included in investment in 2001?

- In 2001, you purchase a home built in 1947.
- In 2001, a builder constructs a new home for you.

Your purchase of an existing home is not counted as investment because it is not an expenditure on a new asset, but your purchase of a new home is. The BEA further divides investment into two categories, as Table 2-A3 shows.

Business fixed investment includes expenditures on such things as plant and equipment. Machines, factories, and office buildings are examples of fixed investment. Those machines, housing, and factories, however, wear out; they are either used up in the production

process or destroyed merely by the passage of time. That amount of wear is called *depreciation*. Depreciation is a cost of production.

Part of depreciation results from the wear and tear of production, but another part results from a changing economy, changing technology, or changing expectations. Say, for example, you bought a Winnebago for $16,000 and suddenly gas prices tripled. What you might discover is that your motor home is worth only $10,000, not $16,000, because demand for Winnebagos has fallen. It has depreciated $6,000, even if you haven't used it yet. Thus, depreciation is not just a purely physical wear-and-tear phenomenon.

Measuring the value of capital relative to expectations is extremely complicated. Although accounting practices have improved recently, in the NIPAs, as in most business accounts, the BEA depreciates the stock of capital (the value of all machinery, factories, etc.) by a fixed percentage each year. Depreciation remains constant at roughly 10 percent of GDP per year (excluding production by financial firms). **Net investment** is gross investment less depreciation.

Change in business inventories is the difference between what a firm produces and what a firm sells within the accounting time period. An example of inventory investment would be a car dealer who takes delivery of eight cars but sells only six. It has increased its inventory investment by two cars, or by $20,000, if each has a wholesale value of $10,000. This deserves some explanation. Although no market transaction has occurred, a change in inventory is counted as part of production. In this case, the BEA treats firms as if they are purchasing their own goods, and the BEA reduces firms' profits by the amount that inventories increase. If firms sell more than they produce, inventory declines and firms' profits increase. As you can see from Table 2-A3, change in

---

[1]Notice that the economist's concept of investment is different from the layperson's. Buying stocks and bonds is not an investment in the economist's definition; these are merely transfers of existing assets.

Table 2-A4   Net Exports of Goods and Services, 2000

	Billions of Dollars	
Exports	1,097.3	
Goods		788.6
Services		308.7
Imports	1,468.0	
Goods		1,248.6
Services		219.5
Net exports of goods and services −370.7		

Source: Commerce Department, Bureau of Economic Analysis **(www.bea.doc.gov).**

inventory investment is a relatively minor component of GDP, but it can fluctuate significantly over the business cycle. For example, while it was $36.0 billion in 1989, it was −$3.3 billion in 1991.

Foreign Sector

Some goods purchased in the United States are produced in foreign countries (imports), and some goods produced in the United States are sold in foreign countries (exports). Because GDP is the value of production within a country, the BEA removes these components of consumption, investment, and government spending on goods produced in foreign countries. Likewise, the BEA adds spending by foreigners on domestic production. That is, the BEA subtracts imports and adds exports to get domestic production. Although net exports is not a large component of GDP, it provided much of the stimu-

lus for growth in the late 1980s. Table 2–A4 lists exports and imports for the United States in 2000.

Government Sector

The BEA breaks down government purchases into (1) federal and (2) state and local expenditures. It includes items such as the production of defense and nondefense goods and services. Government purchases goods to do business, builds roads and bridges, and turns out thousands of other products and services. The BEA includes all of these purchases in GDP. Because government provides these goods to consumers without a direct sales transaction, the BEA values them at cost. So, if the federal government spends $1 billion to build a bridge, the BEA values the contribution of the bridge to GDP at $1 billion.

The BEA includes in government expenditures only those payments to individuals made in return for a good or a service. The BEA excludes payments to individuals that are not in exchange for goods and services, called **transfer payments** (including Social Security, unemployment compensation, and welfare benefits), from GDP because GDP measures economic activity, not flows of money. A transfer payment creates no economic activity and, thus, is not included in GDP.

In 2000, defense spending made up the largest component of federal government expenditures, as Table 2–A5 shows.

The BEA further divides government expenditures into consumption and investment. This division recognizes government expenditures on equipment and structures such as highways, schools, and computers as government investment. Thus, government

Table 2-A5   Government Consumption and Gross Investment, 2000

	Billions of Dollars		% of Total	
Federal	595.2		34	
National defense		377.0		22
Consumption		319.7		
Gross investment		57.3		
Nondefense		218.2		12
Consumption		169.5		
Gross investment		48.7		
State and local	1,148.6		66	
Consumption		918.0		53
Gross investment		230.6		13
Government purchases	**1,743.8**		**100**	

Source: Commerce Department, Bureau of Economic Analysis **(www.bea.doc.gov).**

investment expenditures are included in gross investment. The BEA also includes a measure of the flow of services government's fixed assets provide. This is added to government consumption expenditures.

COMPONENTS OF NATIONAL INCOME

Let's now consider the details of the income side of domestic accounting. Because the BEA still reports income of the United States as national income, instead of domestic income, we follow that convention and discuss national income. The BEA normally breaks national income into the following categories: compensation to employees, proprietors' income, rental income of persons, corporate profits, and net interest. Table 2–A6 provides the amounts of each of these in 2000.

Compensation to Employees

As you can see from the Table 2–A6, compensation to employees was the largest component of income. It made up 70 percent of total income in 2000. It is composed primarily of wages and salaries paid to individuals, along with employer contributions for social insurance, and to private pension, health, and welfare funds. Because of the importance of wage income, the other sectors often are downplayed, and wage income alone becomes the focus.

Proprietors' Income

Proprietors' income is earnings of individuals and partnerships in unincorporated businesses such as medical practices and sole proprietors. In 2000, proprietor's income composed 9 percent of national income.

Rental Income

Rental income is income from property, received by households. For owner-occupied housing, it is the imputed rent less the cost of maintaining that housing, or depreciation. Rental income in 2000, at 2 percent, was a small portion of national income.

This 2 percent is, in part, an accounting phenomenon. In actual fact rent is combined with various other forms of income—especially proprietors income and profits, so that total rent is a much larger portion of the total than 2 percent. (One economist, Steven Cord, estimated that it was almost 20 percent of total income.)

Net Interest

Net interest is the income private businesses pay to households that have lent businesses money, generally by purchasing bonds issued by businesses. It excludes interest payments from government and households because, by convention, they are assumed not to flow from the production of goods and services. In 2000, net interest composed 7 percent of national income.

Corporate Profits

Profits are the revenue left over after compensation to employees, rents, and interest have been paid out. In 2000, corporate profits composed 12 percent of national income.

Table 2–A6   National Income by Type, 2000

	Billions of Dollars		% of Total
Compensation of employees	5,638.2		70
Wages and salaries		4,769.4	
Supplements to wages and salaries		868.8	
Proprietors' income	710.4		9
Farm		22.6	
Nonfarm		687.8	
Rental income	140.0		2
Corporate profits	946.2		12
Net interest	567.2		7
National income	**8,002.0**		**100**

Source: Commerce Department, Bureau of Economic Analysis (**www.bea.doc.gov**).

Other Important Measures of Income

Two other often-cited measures of income are personal income and disposable personal income.

Personal Income. Personal income measures all income received by individuals. Personal income includes wages and salaries, proprietor's income, rental income, dividend income, personal interest income, and transfer payments by government to individuals. Because national income is a measure of income that is *earned* by individuals from production, while personal income measures all income *received* by individuals, the two income measures differ. Personal income and national income are related in the following way:

$$PI = NI - income\ earned\ but\ not\ received + \quad (2A\text{-}2)$$
$$income\ received\ but\ not\ earned$$

An example of income earned but not received is retained earnings. Retained earnings are profits earned by the firm that are not distributed. They are included in national income because they result from productive work, but because they are not paid to individuals, they are not part of personal income. An example of income received but not earned is transfer payments from government. They are not included in national income because the payments are not the result of productive work, but are part of personal income for individuals.

Table 2–A7 shows the complete relationship between national income and personal income. Lines 2 through 4 represent income that individuals have earned but do not receive; therefore, each is subtracted from national income. We have discussed corporate retained earnings (line 2). Social security taxes (line 3) is subtracted because it is income that is earned by individuals but is not received by individuals. It is paid directly to the government by businesses. Lastly, wage accruals less disburse-

ments (line 4) represent wages that have been earned but still have yet to be paid by firms to individuals.

Lines 5 and 6 represent income that individuals have received but have not earned from productive work. We have discussed government transfer payments (line 5). Business transfer payments (line 6) represent additional income individuals haven't earned but are paid, such as that resulting from personal liability claims.

Line 7 is the final adjustment. The national accounts include all net interest paid by businesses for the use of funds. Because individuals lend funds to other entities, such as government, besides domestic firms, this additional interest income from non-businesses must be added to arrive at personal income.

Disposable Personal Income. Disposable personal income is the amount of income individuals are left with after paying all personal taxes. It is the amount of income individuals have to spend on goods and services. All personal income taxes must be subtracted from personal income to arrive at personal disposable income:

$$PDI = PI - personal\ taxes \quad (2A\text{-}3)$$

WELFARE CONSIDERATIONS OF INCOME ACCOUNTING

Learning any accounting system has a tendency to turn you into an accountant, and accountants are trained to believe that the numbers mean something. In a way, that's good, because numbers do tell you something, but in a way, that's bad, because often the numbers don't tell you what you think they do. Accounting systems lead many people to focus on the numbers, rather than on the broader concepts for which the number serve as a proxy.

Table 2–A7   Relationship of National Income and Personal Income, 2000

		Billions of Dollars
1. National income		= 8,002.0
2. Less:	Corporate retained earnings	− 946.2
3.	Contribution for social insurance	705.6
4.	Wage accruals less disbursements	0.0
5. Plus:	Government transfer payments	+ 1,037.1
6.	Business transfer payments	30.7
7.	Net interest paid to persons	863.7
8. Equals: Personal income		= 8,281.7

Source: Commerce Department, Bureau of Economic Analysis **(www.bea.doc.gov).**

For example, in Chapter 1, we emphasized that the goal of macroeconomics was to maximize welfare. What if a person is happy sitting around playing with her kids, or fishing? What would she contribute to GDP? Nothing. What would she contribute to society? Probably a lot—both in her and her children's well-being. So, it's not necessarily bad if GDP falls because people are choosing activities that do not contribute to GDP but do contribute to their welfare.

As you read it, you will probably agree with the foregoing argument, but you probably won't remember it when you are judging a candidate running for office who makes the argument that GDP falling during his time in office meant he gave people more time for leisure activities. Part of the reason is that government does not include the value of leisure in its accounts and we tend to focus on activities that are easily measured.

Legal Nonmarket Activities

GDP includes only those activities that occur within a marketplace. If a family chooses to pay a house cleaner, that expenditure will be included in GDP. Alternatively, the value of the work a spouse provides the other when he or she cleans house is not included in GDP. Say a doctor marries her housekeeper, whom she was paying $30,000 a year to keep her house. (He was a good housekeeper.) What happens to GDP? If you answer that it decreases because she is now getting services for free for which she had previously paid—a market transaction has been transferred into a nonmarket transaction—you're right.

A number of economists argue that the national income accounts discriminate against women because, historically, homemakers have been women and the accounts do not measure the value of home services. The accountants' response is that the national income accounts only measures market transactions, and is not making any social statement by not measuring domestic household work. However, some economists point out that certain nonmarket activities, such as housing services of owned houses, while a nonmarket activity, are nonetheless estimated and entered into the national income accounts, and they suggest that this inconsistency undermines that answer.

Illegal Nonmarket Activities

National income accounting also excludes illegal activities such as the production and sale of drugs, prostitution, and the production of goods and services "under the table." These goods and services are being produced in what is called the underground economy, but they are not counted as part of GDP. Various studies have been done to estimate the size of the underground economy. The BEA estimates that the underground economy in the United States is about 5.4 percent of GDP. The Internal Revenue Service estimates it to be 8 percent of GDP. Others have estimated it to be as high as 16 percent of GDP.

Resource-depleting Activities

GDP also includes a number of activities that might reduce national well-being. For example, the BEA makes no adjustment for depletion of resources or damage to the environment. Thus, if a manufacturing plant produces output valued at $2 billion and does $4 billion worth of damage to the environment, GDP will rise by $2 billion. A similar problem exists with any activity that is undertaken to avoid an undesirable event, such as crime or war. As a nation prepares for war, GDP will rise substantially as the economy produces more war-related materials. However, does this increase in war-related production increase welfare? Would welfare decrease if the United States could effectively avoid or win a war by spending 50 percent less on defense? GDP would, but welfare would not.

We could go on, but you have probably gotten the idea. Don't consider GDP the Holy Grail; treat it for what it is: a measure of economic activity that is most useful for making comparisons over time when its components do not change much.

KEY TERMS

flow concept 55
inventory investment 53
investment 57

net investment 57
profit 53
stock concept 55

transfer payment 58

B

Price Indexes

As we stated in the chapter, the CPI measures prices of those goods that make up a "normal" individual's consumption, called a *market basket*. The Bureau of Labor Statistics (BLS) changes the weights every few years to reflect changing life styles and expenditure patterns. For example, in the early 1970s, food made up 22.4 percent of the CPI, whereas from 1993 to 1995, the market basket used in 2000, it made up only 16.4 percent. Table 2–B1 shows the relevant percentages in 2000.

By weighting prices by relative expenditures, the CPI produces a more accurate representation of how, on average, the purchasing power of a consumer's dollar changes than if the purchases were not weighted. For example, because entertainment is a smaller portion of most people's budget than housing, a 10 percent rise in the price of entertainment will have much less effect on the purchasing power of a dollar than a 10 percent rise in the cost of housing.

CALCULATION OF THE CONSUMER PRICE INDEX

The CPI calculates the ratio of average prices in the current year to average prices in a base year for a representative basket of consumer goods that is fixed in the base year. In general, the CPI is calculated in the following way:

$$CPI = \frac{\sum_{i=1}^{n}(P_{it} \times Q_{ib})}{\sum_{i=1}^{n}(P_{ib} \times Q_{ib})} \times 100 \qquad (2B\text{-}1)$$

where P_{it} is the price of i in the current time period, P_{ib} is the price of good i in the base period, Q_{ib} is the quantity of good i in the base period, and n is total number of goods in the basket.

To see how to use this formula, let's take an example of two goods and two time periods, time period 0 and time period 1. The standard goods considered in texts are oranges (o) and apples (a), and because we are standard-type people, we will use those goods. Let's consider a numerical example similar to the one in the text:

	Year 0	
	Quantity	*Price*
Oranges	30	$.10
Apples	10	$.20

	Year 1	
	Quantity	*Price*
Oranges	20	$.20
Apples	20	$.25

The denominator is simply the sum of prices times the quantities in the base year, time period 0. The numerator is the sum of prices in time period 1 times the quantities in the base year. Putting the numbers from the table into our formula, we can find the CPI in year 1:

$$CPI = \frac{P_{o1} \times Q_{o0} + P_{a1} \times Q_{a0}}{P_{o0} \times Q_{o0} + P_{a0} \times Q_{a0}} \times 100$$

$$CPI = \frac{.20 \times 30 + .25 \times 10}{.10 \times 30 + .20 \times 10} \times 100$$

$$= \frac{6 + 2.5}{3 + 2} \times 100$$

$$= \frac{8.5}{5} \times 100 = 170$$

Table 2-B1 1993-1995 Market Basket of Goods Composing the CPI in 2000

	% of Total
Food and beverages	16.4
Housing	39.8
Apparel	5.0
Transportation	17.0
Medical care	5.7
Recreation	6.1
Education	5.5
Other goods and services	4.5
All items	100.0

Notice that the denominator and numerator are identical except for the bold terms. Because we know that the CPI in the base year is 100 (if you're not sure why, it is a good exercise to do the calculations), the CPI in year 1 has risen by 70 percent.

MEASUREMENT PROBLEMS OF THE CONSUMER PRICE INDEX

The text indicated that the CPI has a number of measurement problems that lead the CPI to overestimate true inflation. Economists have pinpointed five biases that are inherent in the CPI: the changing market basket bias, the substitution bias, the quality improvement bias, the new product bias, and the discounting bias. Let's consider each in turn.

Changing Market Basket Bias

The first bias is in determining the relevant market basket. We each have our own relevant market basket, and that market basket changes over time. How closely the chosen market basket matches your market basket depends on how close you are to the average when the market basket was chosen. (Students are generally far from it.) The further in time that fixed basket is from the current basket, the worse the CPI is at measuring the true purchasing power of an average current consumer's dollar.

Substitution Bias

As you learned in introductory economics, price changes elicit changes in behavior. If beef becomes cheaper relative to pork, people will tend to buy more beef and less pork. However, because the market basket does not change, the CPI will not capture this change in behavior.

The CPI has a **substitution bias** because it does not take into account the fact that when the price of one good rises, consumers substitute a cheaper item. In our beef example, the CPI will overstate true inflation because beef will be weighted in the price index with the old spending patterns.

New Product Bias

A fixed basket of goods leaves no room for new products. This would not be a problem if the prices of new products changed at about the same rate as prices of other goods in the basket, but in recent history this was not true. For years, the CPI did not include the price of computers, and their prices were declining at a 17 percent annual rate! In this case, increases in the CPI overstated inflation.

Quality Improvement Bias

For most products in the CPI, the fixed basket of goods is assumed to accurately represent similar products in later years. With new technology, however, products improve and increases in the prices of goods, in part, reflect that quality improvement. The result is that price increases due to quality improvements are counted as price increases, not improvements in quality. The CPI does, however, take into account quality changes in cars after model changeovers, computers when more memory and capacity are offered, and apparel to reflect new clothing lines.

Discounting Bias

Ever since World War II (1941–45), consumers have shopped more and more at discount retail stores. The BLS treats products sold at a discount store as different from products sold at retail stores. Products sold at discount stores are assumed to be of lower quality. To the extent they are of equal quality, however, by not including the discount price in the same way as other prices, changes in the CPI overstate inflation.

The BLS has addressed some of these biases. For instance, beginning in 2002, the BLS will update the basket of goods every 2 years. Also, since 1999, it has used a new formula to take into account how people change their consumption based on relative price changes, and will increase the sample rotation to reflect shopping patterns and incorporate new products. Overall changes that the BLS has made, and continues to make, to the CPI from 1995 to 2002 are estimated to have lowered annual CPI inflation by 0.7 percentage point per year.

DIFFERENCES AMONG THE GROSS DOMESTIC PRODUCT DEFLATOR, CONSUMER PRICE INDEX, AND PRODUCER PRICE INDEX

Although the GDP deflator, the CPI, and the PPI are all designed to measure the price level and usually move in the same direction, they differ in two major ways: coverage and weighting. Because of this, at times, they can differ substantially. It is important to remember that one index is not necessarily better than another. All measures have their advantages and disadvantages, depending on their uses. We discussed the differences in coverage in the chapter. Here we discuss the technical differences in weighting.

The CPI and PPI use fixed quantity weights in a base year, while the GDP price deflator allows the weights to change from year to year. For those periods when the base period doesn't change but consumer spending habits change considerably, the CPI is not reliable as a measure of consumer dollar purchasing power. Recall the beef versus pork example. If the price of beef rises significantly, consumers are likely to purchase more pork and less beef. The CPI, however, will weight the prices of beef and pork as if consumption patterns had not changed. The GDP price deflator, by contrast, will reflect the relative consumption changes between beef and pork because its quantity weights are for the current year. In this case, inflation measured by the CPI will be higher than inflation measured by the GDP price deflator.

Changes in the GDP price deflator may reflect either changes in quantities produced or changes in prices. Say that pork costs twice as much as beef. Suppose also that Americans change their taste in meats and switch from buying beef to pork. In this instance, the GDP price deflator will rise by more than the rise in the CPI.

The classic example of a difference between the CPI and the GDP deflator occurred in 1974, when oil prices rose significantly. From 1973 to 1974, the GDP deflator rose by 9.1 percent, while the CPI rose by 13 percent, as you can see in Exhibit 2–B1.

As you also can see in Exhibit 2–B1, the differences in the CPI and the GDP deflator are generally small, and they tend to average out. Thus, exploring the differences makes for wonderful analytic exercises for students, and as we saw earlier, in particular years they can differ substantially, but over a long period, the two tend to move together and one can be replaced with the other.

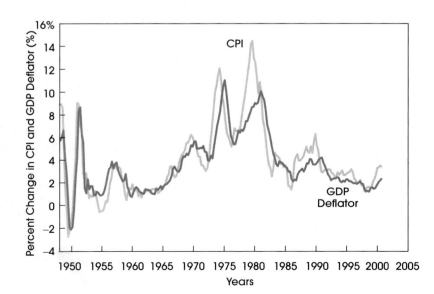

Exhibit 2–B1
The CPI and the GDP Deflator

The CPI and the GDP deflator differ in coverage and weights. The GDP deflator is much more general than the CPI. The CPI is a fixed-weight price index. The GDP deflator's weights are the average of the current and the previous year. Source: The Bureau of Economic Analysis (www.bea.doc.gov) and the Bureau of Labor Statistics (stats.bls.gov).

Laspeyres and Paasche Price Indexes

In the text, you saw the determination of the CPI and the GDP deflator, and we discussed how the new index for real GDP, and, therefore, the GDP deflator, is a chain-weighted index. Here, we briefly expand the discussion, using that index terminology. Economists distinguish two different types of indexes: the Paasche index and the Laspeyres index. A **Laspeyres index** uses base-year quantities to weight the price increase, while the **Paasche index** uses the most-recent-year quantities as weights.

The CPI is a base-year (or Laspeyres) index, which means it uses base-year quantities in calculating the index. Until 1996, the GDP deflator was a present year (or Paasche) index. (*Hint:* A quick way to remember the weights each index uses is to remember L for Laspeyres and L for lagged-year weights; P for Paasche and P for present-year weights.)

Formally, we have the following:

$$Laspeyres\ index = \frac{\sum_{i=1}^{n}(P_{it} \times Q_{ib})}{\sum_{i=1}^{n}(P_{ib} \times Q_{ib})} \times 100 \qquad (2B\text{-}2)$$

$$Paasche\ index = \frac{\sum_{i=1}^{n}(P_{it} \times Q_{it})}{\sum_{i=1}^{n}(P_{ib} \times Q_{it})} \times 100 \qquad (2B\text{-}3)$$

where:

$\sum_{i=1}^{n}$ = *summation of n goods*

P_{it} = *the price of a good in the current year*

P_{ib} = *the price of a good in the base year*

Q_{it} = *the quantity of a good consumed or produced in the current year*

Q_{ib} = *the quantity of a good consumed or produced in the base year*

In 1996, the GDP ceased being a pure Paasche index. It is a chain-weighted price index, which essentially averages the weights of the Paasche and Laspeyres indexes through geometric averaging. It is calculated as the square root of the product of a Paasche index and a Laspeyres index, where the base year is constantly updated to be the most recent year.

When relative prices or quantities aren't changing much, Paasche and Laspeyres indexes move pretty much together. However, when relative prices or quantities change dramatically, the two indexes can diverge substantially. The following example helps to illustrate this.

Numerical Example of Indexes

The following table gives an extreme example. It lists two goods produced in an economy and their associated prices from 1998 to 2002.

	Apples		Oranges	
	Price	Quantity	Price	Quantity
1998	$0.50	10	$1.00	5
1999	1.00	5	1.00	10
2000	1.00	3	1.00	15
2001	1.00	3	1.00	20
2002	1.00	3	0.50	30

The associated levels and percent changes of Laspeyres and Paasche price indexes with base year 1998 are as follows:

	Laspeyres		Paasche	
	Level	% Change from Previous Year	Level	% Change from Previous Year
1998	100	—	100	—
1999	150	50	120	20
2000	150	0	109	−9
2001	150	0	107	−2
2002	125	−17	57	−47

From 1998 to 1999, the price of apples doubled, but consumers substituted away from apples toward oranges. The Paasche index takes into account such substitutions that result from changes in relative prices. The Paasche index shows that the price level rose 20 percent from 1998 to 1999, while the Laspeyres index, which keeps the quantity of goods consumed fixed at the base year, shows a 50 percent price-level increase. From 1999 to 2000, the prices of neither good changed, but for some reason, relatively more oranges were consumed. Because of this, the Paasche index (using a 1998 base) declines, because it is weighted by current-year quantities, but the Laspeyres index doesn't change. We leave it up to you to explain the differences in the remaining 2 years.

An Intuitive Approach to Price Indices

A more intuitive approach to price indices is to consider it as a problem of weighting. When developing an index you have a number of prices going up and you must decide how much weight to give to each increase. In the above example, between 1998 and 2000 the price of apples went up 100 percent and the price of oranges went up 0 percent. The price level must have risen somewhere between the two depending on the importance we give to each. A reasonable way to assign importance is to calculate the percentage of total expenditures on each. But there are a variety of ways that we could view total expenditures and their division.

Let's start by just looking at the price change from 1998 to 1999. Total expenditures in 1998 are $10 and they are equally split—50 percent on each. The Laspeyres index uses those 50 percent weights so we calculate the price increase by multiplying 50 percent times 100 (the amount apples went up) and 50 percent times zero (the amount oranges went up). The result is inflation of 50 percent. If we use 1999 quantities and 1998 prices the total expenditures are $12.50 and the percentage expenditures are 20 percent on apples and 80 percent on oranges. Multiplying the zero increase in the price of oranges by 80 percent and the 100 percent increase in apple prices by 20 percent gives us 20 percent—the Laspeyres index in 1999. (Notice that there are alternative weights. If we used 1999 prices and quantities we would get weights of 33 percent and 66 percent and an inflation rate of 33 percent.) Because quantities have changed it is difficult to say which of these alternatives is preferable.

Now let's look at the price change over more than one year—from 1998 to 2000, which is what the price index allows you to do. Even though from 1999 to 2000 neither price has changed, from 1998 to 2000 they did. To calculate the price index in a year away from a base year one must look back to price changes from that initial year and determine the price index relative to that year. One then calculates the rate of inflation as the change in the price index from one year to the next. In the example, the quantities have changed again. Because the Lasperyes uses base year prices and quantities, this does not matter; the 50 percent weights stay the same and the price level increase remains the same, so inflation—the change in the index—is zero. However, because quantities have changed again the weights in the Paasche index, and hence the Paasche index, are going to change. Specifically, the weights become $(0.5 \times 3)/[(0.5 \times 3) + (1 \times 15)] = 1.5/16.5 = .09$ for the 100 percent price increase and $(1 \times 15)/[(0.5 \times 3) + (1 \times 15)] = 15/16.5 = .91$ for the 0 percent price increase. These weights give us a price index of 109 in 2000. Because the previously calculated price index was 120, the index has fallen by $11/120 = 9$ percent, which is what we got in the above example. So with a Paasche price index, you have to always go back to the initial base year and also to the intermittent years to calculate what the price level change will be from one year to the next.

KEY TERMS

Laspeyres index 65   Paasche index 65   substitution bias 63

3

When more and more people are thrown out of work, unemployment results.

—*Calvin Coolidge*

Grappling with Inflation, Unemployment, and Growth

After reading this chapter you should be able to:

1. Discuss the costs of inflation
2. Explain how inflation can be both grease and sand to an economy
3. Explain why economists focus on the unemployment goal and why some unemployment is necessary
4. Demonstrate the natural rate of unemployment by adjusting the standard labor demand and supply curves for search costs and wage pressures
5. Show the observed short-run relationship between inflation and unemployment using the Phillips curve

Chapter 2 refreshed your memory about the data of macroeconomics. You learned how economists measure the health and performance of the macroeconomy and about the shortcomings of those measurements. This chapter gives you a frame of reference for thinking about those economic barometers. When you read in the newspaper that the unemployment rate is 4 percent, do you think policy makers will seek to raise or lower it? What is a desirable inflation rate? Is the current rate of unemployment too low? How will inflation and unemployment policies affect the economy's rate of growth?

In some ways, trying to answer a policy question such as, "What is the appropriate unemployment rate?" is like trying to answer the question, "What car should I buy?" A reasonable answer would be that it is a matter of personal choice and that individuals make that personal choice after weighing the benefits and costs of a particular car. Policy makers also must weigh the benefits and costs of trying to achieve various goals for inflation, unemployment, and economic growth. In addition, policy makers must make these decisions not for themselves, but for society.

This chapter introduces you to the choices that policy makers face when deciding on the appropriate inflation, unemployment, and growth goals for the economy. For example, lowering the unemployment rate might benefit those who become employed, but it also might raise inflation, which has costs of its own. Lower inflation might benefit retirees on fixed nominal incomes, but it also may raise unemployment. Economists and policy makers continually ask, "Are the benefits of a policy worth the costs of that policy?" In this chapter, we consider that question in relation to the goals of low inflation, low unemployment, and high growth.

Policy is not a zero sum game; well-designed policy choices exploit niches in the market.

Policies to deal with those choices are no simple zero-sum game. Well-designed policies should exploit niches in the market and result in an increase in social welfare. Good policy makers operate in much the same way as do good business people. They look for niches in the market, and exploit them. They are policy entrepreneurs. The difference between the policy entrepreneur and the business entrepreneur is that the goal for the policy entrepreneur is (or at least should be) to increase social welfare, while the goal of the business entrepreneur is to increase profit.

As you can imagine, there is much debate about how many policy opportunities exist; the debates in Congress attest to that. Once in a while, however, there are policy opportunities wherein the benefits exceed the costs by most measures of social welfare. A University of Chicago economist, Mel Reder, put it this way: While there is no such thing as a free lunch, once in a while you can snitch a sandwich—and introduce a policy that improves the workings of the current market institutions.

THE GOALS OF LOW INFLATION, LOW UNEMPLOYMENT, AND GROWTH

We will start with an article from *The Wall Street Journal* that illustrates some of the choices policy makers face. This article reports on the 1994 meeting of the world's central bankers, which is held every year in Jackson Hole, Wyoming.

JACKSON HOLE, Wyo. With budget deficits restraining governments in the United States and Europe from increasing spending or cutting taxes, the task of fighting unemployment in recent years has fallen to the Federal Reserve and other central banks.

Despite uncomfortably high unemployment rates, particularly in Europe, central bankers are now arguing that they have done about as much as they can. Interest rates have already risen substantially in the United States, and they are beginning to rise in Europe, too. Bolstered by arguments from sympathetic economists, the message from most central bankers is: Look elsewhere if you want to cut joblessness further. . . .

Foreshadowing a debate that may produce friction inside the Fed if the U.S. economy slows substantially in the next year or so, Mr. Blinder said here that a central bank "should have a short-run employment objective in addition to its inflation objective." Mr. Greenspan, in contrast, endorsed legislation to make eliminating inflation the Fed's sole mission. Mr. Blinder said that central banks should seek to reduce the unemployment rate until it is just shy of the point where labor shortages begin to push up wages and the inflation rate accelerates. By that standard, he said, "the U.S. is extremely close to on-target. . . ." (David Wessell, *The Wall Street Journal*, August 29, 1994)

The Federal Reserve Bank (the Fed) conducts monetary policy in the U.S.

Let us consider what this article is saying. The first paragraph states that expansionary fiscal policy (increasing spending or cutting taxes) in the early 1990s was not an option for the U.S. government in its fight to reduce unemployment, because policy makers' main concern was reducing the budget deficit. The responsibility for fighting unemployment, therefore, fell on the **Federal Reserve Bank (The Fed),** the agency responsible for monetary policy in the United

States.[1] The second paragraph states that central bankers believe that their policies cannot lower unemployment any further. Although the article does not use the term *natural rate of unemployment,* central bankers are effectively referring to the natural rate when they said that monetary policy cannot reduce unemployment rates any further. The third paragraph centers around two goals of government economic policy: low unemployment and low inflation. Because these goals sometimes conflict in the short run, policy makers must decide which goal has greater priority. As you might suspect, some policy makers give priority to low inflation, while others give priority to low unemployment. Alan Blinder, then Vice-Chairman of the Fed, considered both goals to be equally important. Alan Greenspan, the Chairman of the Fed, supported low inflation as the only appropriate goal for monetary policy.

This particular episode had an important result. Blinder said what most academic economists say—both goals of unemployment and inflation must be considered when formulating policy. However, in saying so, Blinder violated an unstated rule of central bankers today: Central bankers will fight inflation regardless of the consequences on unemployment, because it is believed that inflation hurts long-term growth. If a central banker does not say that, he or she is perceived as soft on inflation. As a result of his policy stance, Blinder lost his inside track to becoming chairman of the Fed (and, shortly thereafter, left the Fed to return to academia); Greenspan kept his job.

The article tells us that the Fed believes the following:

1. There is a natural rate of unemployment that is not affected by monetary policy.
2. Because monetary policy does not affect the natural rate of unemployment, preventing inflation must be the primary goal of monetary policy.

While most economists accept that a natural rate of unemployment exists and that preventing inflation is a key goal of monetary policy, most economists also agree that we have not been very good at measuring the natural rate. For example, at the time the article was written, the unemployment rate in the United States was 6.1 percent. The majority of economists believed that this was the lowest unemployment the economy could achieve before the inflation rate would start rising. They believed that policy makers faced a clear choice: They could achieve either low unemployment or low inflation, but not both.

As the U.S. economy continued to expand through the second half of the 1990s and through 2000, the unemployment rate fell to about 4 percent while inflation remained low. Economists debated whether they had seriously misestimated the natural rate, or whether temporary factors were keeping the inflation rate low, and once those temporary factors disappeared, inflation would rise. Such questions are some of the most challenging questions that policy makers face.

Congress established low unemployment and low inflation as explicit goals for both the Federal Reserve Bank and Congress by the Employment Act of 1946 and the Full Employment and Balanced Growth Act of 1978, also known as the

---

[1]The federal budget deficits of the early 1990s were eliminated; the budget balance turned into a surplus in 1998. Although the budget is expected to continue to be in surplus at least until 2011, this hinges on continual growth in the economy. Furthermore, given commitments such as Social Security benefits, fiscal policy options are still quite constrained.

Q & A	**QUESTION**	What are the Employment Act of 1946 and the Full Employment and Balanced Growth Act of 1978, and how are they related to the goals of the economy?
	ANSWER	These are laws that explicitly set low inflation and low unemployment as goals for policy makers.

After World War II ended in 1945, armed with a new theory of how government could affect the economy, economists and policy makers were ready to tackle U.S. economic problems. Americans knew the toll that high inflation and high unemployment could take on society. Unemployment was very high in the United States between the two world wars, and inflation increased shortly after the end of World War II. In 1946, Congress passed the Employment Act, which required government to use all of its powers to promote "maximum employment, production, and purchasing power." For the first time, the goals of the economy were written into law. These laws were supported further by the Full Employment and Balanced Growth Act of 1978. This Act, by requiring the Federal Reserve Bank chairman to appear before Congress twice a year (in February and July) to present the Fed's forecast for the economy, as well as to announce its targets for growth in the money supply, added a way for Congress to monitor the Fed's progress toward its prescribed goals.

In 1995, Connie Mack (a Republican senator from Florida) introduced a bill to remove the goal of full employment as a priority for the Fed and establish low inflation as its only goal. It didn't pass. Current Fed practice, however, focuses primarily on inflation, if one believes what most Fed officials say. You saw in *The Wall Street Journal* article, for example, how high a priority eliminating inflation was for the Fed in the 1990s. (Other central banks, such as the European Central Bank [ECB], have different legal mandates. The ECB's official mandate is to focus exclusively on the goal of low inflation.)

Humphrey-Hawkins Act. (See the Q&A feature for details.) The goal of low inflation may also help to achieve the goal of high growth over the long term. Let us consider inflation first.

INFLATION AND POLICY

Most people think that inflation makes an economy poorer because the prices they pay for goods and services have risen. They see that a dollar does not buy as much as before. On reflection, however, for society as a whole, that argument does not hold up. Why? Because inflation has two effects: It makes buyers poorer (they must pay higher prices) and it makes sellers richer (they are paid higher prices). Because the average person is both a buyer (as a consumer) and a seller (as an owner of the factors of production), the average person is neither richer nor poorer because of inflation. For example, if all prices doubled, including wages and asset prices, the purchasing power of everyone's average income and wealth would not have changed at all.

Inflation Can Redistribute Income

Inflation redistributes income from those who do not, or cannot, raise their prices to those who can, and do, raise their prices and still sell their goods.

While inflation does not directly make society richer or poorer, inflation can redistribute income among individuals. As a general rule, *inflation redistributes income from those who do not, or cannot, raise their prices to those who can, and do, raise their prices and still sell their goods.* Redistribution due to inflation can occur when it is unanticipated. If inflation is unanticipated, people will not raise their prices simply because they did not expect any inflation to occur. Even those who correctly antic-ipate inflation may not raise their prices: Their prices may be fixed by a contract. That is why inflation redistributes income to those who both expect it and are in a position to adjust their contracts to account for it from those who do not or cannot. That is also why the amount of redistribution associated with inflation depends on whether the inflation is anticipated or unanticipated.

As an example that demonstrates how unanticipated inflation redistributes income, consider mortgages. Suppose you get a 30-year, fixed-rate mortgage with monthly payments of $1,200. The rate at which you borrowed the money was determined by the inflation the mortgage lender expected over the next 30 years and a return the lender wanted to receive. Even though the payment seems like a stretch at first, you borrow so much because you expect that your income will rise by at least the rate of inflation. If inflation is higher than expected you will be bet-ter off. Your income will most likely rise, but your mortgage payments, because they are fixed by contract, will not. The share of income that you will have available to spend on items other than housing will rise. The bank, or the institution that is holding the mortgage, is worse off. (Banks generally sell mortgage loans to other financial institutions.) The income the bank receives has not risen, but the prices it pays, such as salaries to employees, have—hence the general rule: Unanticipated inflation redistributes income from lenders to borrowers.

If, however, the bank had expected the higher inflation, it would likely have increased the mortgage rate by the amount of that expected inflation. If lenders cor-rectly anticipate inflation, and are able to adjust their rates, inflation will not redis-tribute income. For example, if a lender expects 3 percent inflation, it will add that 3 percent to the real interest rate it wants to receive to account for the decline in the value of the dollars the borrower uses to pay back the loan. If the lender wants a 2 percent real return on the money lent when inflation is 3 percent, it will charge a nominal interest rate of 5 percent.

The contract between a borrower and a lender is just one example of a fixed con-tract that is affected by unanticipated inflation. A labor contract is another example. If contracts are designed to change with inflation, there are no redistributional effects, because inflation is built into the contract. Flexible-rate mortgages and esca-lator clauses in labor contracts are examples of contracts that incorporate inflation. Workers who agree to fixed pensions on retirement are hurt if inflation is higher than expected. Their incomes do not purchase as many goods and services as antic-ipated. However, many pensions either are self-controlled (such as 401[k] plans), allowing the person to invest in financial assets, the values of which increase with inflation, or are adjusted for inflation. For example, Social Security pensions are adjusted for inflation. Payments to beneficiaries are increased each year by the annual change in the CPI. Because the redistributional effects of inflation depend on contracts that can be changed, it is difficult to make general statements about whether inflation redistributes income from one particular group to another.

> The real interest rate is the nominal interest rate adjusted for inflation.

Costs of Inflation

Despite the fact that inflation does not make society poorer through price increases alone, it does impose costs on an economy. The costs arise because, with inflation, people have more difficulty making choices, which lowers the efficiency of the economy. People create mechanisms to deal with inflation, which diverts resources

Table 3-1

Costs of Inflation

Informational and uncertainty costs	• Inflation reduces the information contained in prices and makes it more difficult to predict relative price changes.
Institutional and constitutional costs	• Inflation undermines institutions and conventions, such as rules of thumb and contracts. It also undermines the convention of money, which forms the basis of exchange in the economy.
Menu and shoe-leather costs	• Inflation increases the cost of managing cash balances and requires firms to spend more on posting up-to-date prices.

Costs of inflation include informational and uncertainty costs, institutional and constitutional costs, and menu and shoe-leather costs.

away from production. These costs are grouped into three different categories: informational and uncertainty costs, institutional and constitutional costs, and menu and shoe-leather costs, as Table 3–1 shows.

Informational and Uncertainty Costs. In a market economy, market prices convey enormous amounts of information. Individuals store and process this information in their heads every day as they purchase goods and services. Prices facilitate comparison among goods. Inflation reduces the information contained in prices. The knowledge gained from price comparisons that is lost due to inflation is the informational cost of inflation.

Inflation reduces the information contained in prices.

With an idea of the general price of goods, you can tell whether a relative price (the price of one good compared with the price of other goods) is high or low. For example, let's say you know that a Mazda Protégé, costing $15,000, is a good buy; but, if it costs $30,000, it is not. If prices are rising rapidly, that information (that $30,000 is not a good price) would not be so useful in the future. As inflation rises, the time period for which a price maintains its information value shortens. For example, if annual inflation were 3 percent, a year later, that price comparison would still be useful. If, instead, annual inflation were 100 percent, it would not. In this case, using your original comparison, you would not buy a car. You would be hard-pressed to find a $15,000 Protégé, and the $30,000 Protégé would be the good buy.

The larger the rate of inflation, the greater the destruction of information. In a hyperinflation, relative prices can become indecipherable. For example, if prices doubled every month for a year, a reasonably priced 10-cent pencil at the beginning of the year would still be reasonably priced at $204.80 by year's end. When inflation is this high, consumers are not able to store sufficient information about changing prices to update their reference point of the value of one dollar. Without a useful reference point, many consumers will either hold off making purchases or make choices that do not reflect relative prices.

Inflation increases uncertainty about future relative prices.

Closely related to the informational cost of inflation is the uncertainty cost of inflation—the distortion and delay of expenditures caused by the increased difficulty of predicting future relative prices. Typically, when inflation rises, so does its variability. Say you own a business and are making a five-year business plan. You must estimate your future revenue and costs. These estimates are easier if you can count on there being no, or at least predictable, inflation. You would have more difficulty making business plans, entering long-term contracts, and predicting profits if you did not know what the price of your product or costs of production would be in 5 years. Because inflation creates uncertainty, businesses may delay expansions or investments during a period of high inflation. An example is Bulgaria during the early 1990s. Annual inflation was 50 percent and the nominal interest rate was 50 percent, so the real interest rate was 0 percent. Borrowing appeared to be costless, which should have encouraged firms to invest. It did not. Businesses were unwilling to undertake new ventures. When asked why, businesses responded that with such high inflation, any business plan would be highly risky. They did not know whether inflation would stay at 50 percent or come down. If a business took a loan out when annual inflation was 50 percent and inflation came down to 25 percent, the business would not be able to cover its costs. It would go bankrupt, regardless of whether the inherent business plan made sense. Businesses do not like tying their fates so closely to a factor they cannot control directly.

Institutional and Constitutional Costs. A second category of costs of inflation is institutional and constitutional costs. Institutional costs result from inflation's tendency to undermine institutions and conventions that have been based on relatively fixed prices. Many U.S. institutions and conventions, such as rules of thumb and contracts, are based on relatively fixed prices. Businesses base rules of thumb on past experience and use them to make business plans. Inflation destroys those rules of thumb, making business planning difficult.

> Inflation tends to undermine institutions and conventions based on relatively fixed prices.

For example, for years, banks used a rule of thumb that capped monthly mortgage payments at 20 percent of one's monthly gross income. That rule of thumb worked when inflation was low. When inflation soared in the 1970s and early 1980s, an increasing number of consumers could not afford to buy houses based on that rule, because salary increases were not keeping up with rising housing prices. Eventually, banks adjusted the rule to 33 percent, sometimes even 38 percent, allowing banks to lend more. In the process, however, banks turned down many good loans and made many bad loans.

Constitutional costs reflect the erosion of faith in the government and the economy when inflation rises. The very use of money is a convention of society. People accept money from others because they believe others will accept it from them and give them certain things for that money. Inflation undermines the convention of money that forms the basis of exchange in our economy.

> Inflation undermines the convention of money that forms the basis of exchange.

The constitutional cost works as follows: High and variable inflation leads people to lower their faith in the soundness of the economic system based on the use of money, hurting confidence and lowering total expenditures. If inflation is high enough, people will abandon money and resort to barter (the exchange of goods for other goods). The economy will come to a grinding halt. In that sense, you can think of money as oil in an engine. Inflation destroys the function of money, just as the lack of oil destroys the function of the engine. Without oil, the engine blows a piston or seizes.

Menu and Shoe-Leather Costs. A third set of costs of inflation is called menu and shoe-leather costs. This set represents the increased costs of doing business because of inflation. Shoe-leather costs are the costs of having to manage cash holdings more intensively because of inflation. (The name comes from the old

> Inflation increases the costs of doing business.

days, when cash management meant wearing out your shoes when making more frequent trips to the bank.) When inflation is high, consumers change their cash-management procedures, keeping more cash in savings accounts and checking accounts (as long as they pay interest to compensate for the inflation). They withdraw cash only when needed. Businesses also make more frequent deposits of cash sales. They do this because inflation wipes out the value of cash. Therefore, both businesses and people have to pay closer attention to their cash management when there is inflation.

Menu costs also increase the cost of doing business. Menu costs are those that firms incur to change their prices in catalogues, on menus, and on ticketed merchandise. For low inflation, say under 5 percent per year, firms change their prices an average of once or twice a year so that menu costs are relatively small. However, once inflation turns into hyperinflation (extremely high inflation), menu costs can become considerable. With hyperinflation, a firm may have to change its prices daily. During a hyperinflation period in Indonesia in the late 1990s, stores had to close at midday just to take time to change prices.

Low Inflation: Grease or Sand?

Policy makers are concerned about the costs of inflation that may arise when seeking to lower unemployment, because the costs will reduce long-term growth. Inflation lowers long-term growth by diverting resources away from production and toward creating mechanisms to deal with inflation. These mechanisms include information systems that track changing prices, forecasts of inflation prepared by economists, and insurance against price increases. All of these activities divert funds away from what would have been productive uses. As you have read, inflation also distorts and delays expenditures by businesses and consumers. High rates of inflation that destroy institutions and the use of money can greatly reduce an economy's growth.

You might think that economies should avoid inflation at all cost, but it is not quite that simple. While all economists agree that high inflation has negative effects on growth and should be reduced, there is somewhat less agreement about low rates of inflation. The majority of economists believe that inflation of 2 percent or 3 percent per year is not a significant consideration in household and business decisions and does not harm economic growth. Some economists even argue that a 2 percent or 3 percent inflation rate encourages growth. They point to the 2 percent to 3 percent annual inflation during the 1990s though 2000, when the United States was in its longest expansion, and contrast it to deflation and recession in Japan during the same period.

Exhibit 3–1 illustrates how some economists see the relationship between inflation and growth. Below 3 percent, inflation promotes growth, while rates above 3 percent lead to lower rates of growth. Other economists argue that to eliminate all costs of inflation and enjoy high growth requires zero inflation.

The debate about the costs of low inflation is sometimes called the sand versus grease debate. Is a little inflation like grease in a machine, making it easier for relative prices to change, or is it like sand in a machine, causing serious damage? The discussion of the costs of inflation explained why high inflation can be sand. Now let us consider why low inflation can be grease.

The argument goes like this: People do not like to see their wages fall, nor do firms like to reduce their prices. To keep peace in the workplace, businesses often avoid cutting workers' nominal pay, but this presents a problem: In a well-functioning

There is a policy debate about whether low inflation (below 3%) is good or bad for the economy.

Exhibit 3-1

Trade-off Between Inflation and Growth

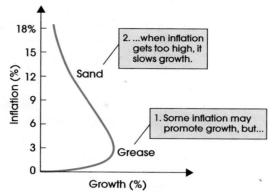

While all economists agree that high inflation has negative effects on growth, there is less agreement about low rates of inflation and growth.

economy, changing market conditions means that some relative wages and prices have to fall; otherwise, other relative wages and prices cannot rise. Relative price changes are important because they determine choices about what to consume and produce. A small amount of inflation allows people to save face—to have their relative wages and prices cut without having to have the wages and prices they actually receive cut. In doing so, inflation eases the necessary relative price changes that an economy must make. It allows the economy to operate more efficiently and at a higher level of output.

This debate is important because, generally, in the short run, stopping inflation has costs. It constrains relative price changes, which results in reduced output, increased unemployment, and slower growth. Policy makers must consider the cost of inflation on growth when making decisions about whether to fight inflation or unemployment. Empirical evidence on the issue is mixed, and the debate will likely continue.

Executive Summary

- The Federal Reserve must balance its goal of low unemployment against its goal of low inflation.

- Unanticipated inflation redistributes income from those who do not or cannot raise their prices to those who can and do raise their prices.

- The costs of inflation are not due to price increases alone. The costs of inflation are also due to informational and uncertainty costs, institutional and constitutional costs, and menu and shoe-leather costs.

- High rates of inflation reduce growth. Whether low rates of inflation promote or deter growth is debated.

UNEMPLOYMENT AND POLICY

Policy makers are concerned with unemployment because of the personal and economy-wide costs it imposes. It is clear, however, that creating jobs is not a goal in and of itself. Consider the following story:

While touring China, [a western businessman] came on a team of nearly 100 workers digging an earthen dam with shovels. The businessman commented to a local official that with an earth-moving machine, a single worker could create the dam in an afternoon. The official's curious response was, "Yes, but think of all the *unemployment* it would create." "Oh," said the businessman, "I thought you were building a dam. If it's *jobs* you want to create, then take away their shovels and give them spoons!" (As told by Jerry Jordan, President of the Cleveland Fed.)

The point of the story is that the real issue for policy makers is how to create high-quality jobs that accomplish useful things for society in the most efficient manner. That goal is much more difficult than simply creating jobs.

Policy makers recognize that some level of unemployment is inevitable, and even beneficial. Before talking about the costs of unemployment, we need to understand the nature of unemployment in a dynamic economy.

Why Is Some Unemployment Necessary?

Wouldn't it be nice if there were no unemployment? Maybe not. Think of what life would be like if everyone were fully employed. You would go to a store and, most likely, wait a long time for clerks, who would be busy with other customers because there would not be enough workers to fill all the needed positions. Or you would go to a restaurant and many items on the menu would not be available because the restaurant supplier could not hire enough workers to meet orders. The point is that the flip side of unemployment (shortages of jobs) is vacancies (shortages of workers). A world with no unemployment would have enormous shortages of workers, which would lead to shortages of goods. A well-functioning economy must balance unemployment with its opposite—vacancies.

> The labor market is a dynamic institution, requiring vacancies and unemployment.

To understand why unemployment and vacancies exist, it is important to view the economy as dynamic and ever-changing. The labor market is not a single market. It is a beehive of markets, with people switching from one market to another all the time. At any moment, people are reassessing their alternatives and changing their work status. Stay-at-home spouses re-enter the job market. Students graduate (they really do) and begin to look for work. People retire. The labor market is busy with the movement of people and jobs. Every month, about 10 million people, 5 percent of those capable of working, are changing their work status.

To function, the economy also needs to allow for changing tastes and technology. Old ways of doing things must make way for new technologies. (If buggy makers had not become unemployed after the automobile was invented, we would still be driving horses and buggies.) Millions of jobs are created and destroyed each year. Fortunately, changes in technology throughout history have created more jobs than they have eliminated.

This is not to say that change in the labor market makes everyone happy. When new technologies change the production process or the very goods an economy produces, many workers have to change careers or upgrade their skills, which sometimes means they must get additional training, or go back to school. Indeed, a number of you may be reading this book for precisely this reason. Some unemployment, therefore, is a necessary result of growth and change.

Flows In and Out of the Labor Market. To show you the dynamic nature of the labor market, let us put some numbers on the flows of people in and out of the workforce, unemployment, and the labor market. As we discussed last chapter, the labor force consists of those employed and unemployed. People over the age

Exhibit 3-2

The Monthly Flows of Employment and Unemployment

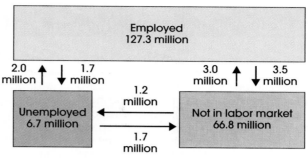

The U.S. labor market is in constant flux. The flows into and out of employment comprise about 4 percent of total employment. These figures are monthly averages from 1994 to 1998. Source: From Bleakley, Ferris, and Fuhrer. 1999. "New data on worker flows during business cycles." *New England Review*, July/August 1999:49–76.

Flows in and out of employment amount to about 4% of total employment.

of 16 and not in the labor force include those who have become too discouraged to look for work, full-time students, stay-at-home parents, some people with disabilities, retirees, people who are institutionalized, and people who choose not to work for pay. Some of these people and teenagers just turning 16 may decide to join the labor force. More than 15 percent of the unemployed—about 1 in 6—are new to the labor market (new entrants). The pool of potential workers includes both the unemployed and those not in the labor market.

Exhibit 3–2 shows the average monthly flows among the employed, unemployed, and those not in the labor force from 1994 through 1998. The monthly flows into employment comprise 4 percent of total employment. Three-fifths of this 4 percent are new entrants. The remaining new employees are those who had quit, had been laid off or fired from their previous jobs, or had been looking for work after having been out of the labor force.

The monthly flows out of employment also comprise about 4 percent of total employment. This is why the employment rate (employment-to-population ratio) stays roughly constant, or at least does not change wildly. People leave the employment pool because they quit jobs, or because their positions were eliminated. Job quitters in search of better possibilities account for about one-half of all those leaving the employment pool each month. Not all job losers become unemployed. Roughly two-thirds of those leaving a job exit the labor force altogether. The remaining job losers look for work and become part of the unemployed.

Vacancies. The picture Exhibit 3–2 creates is only half the story. The other half, its mirror image, is the picture of vacancies—posted jobs that cannot be or have not been filled. Vacancies arise for a variety of reasons. When employees leave their jobs voluntarily, vacancies open up. Newly established positions create vacancies as well. In the United States, the Bureau of Labor Statistics (BLS) reported that the number of jobs created between 1993 and 2000 exceeded the number eliminated by more than 10 million.

Although there are little data on how long it takes firms to fill a job opening, the BLS does collect data on how long people are unemployed. At the end of the 1990s and early 2000s there were so many vacancies in the U.S. economy that most people who became unemployed did not stay unemployed for long. The large flows in and out of employment help to keep the duration of unemployment low. In 2000, the BLS reported that the average duration of unemployment was less than

THE BRIEFING ROOM   Why Unemployment Has Been High in Europe

Over the past decade, unemployment has been high in Europe. Economists have several explanations why. One explanation is that European countries have extensive social safety nets for the unemployed that exceed those provided in the United States. Such programs reduce the incentive for the unemployed to find work. European countries also have stringent labor laws that limit the ability of firms to fire workers. While this may reduce the risk of becoming unemployed, it reduces firms' willingness to hire new workers. Once unemployed, it is hard to find a job. In Spain, for example, during the 1990s, about 50 percent of all unemployed remained unemployed for more than a year. This statistic compares to just over 10 percent in the United States.

Other labor laws set maximum work weeks, minimum overtime wages, and minimum vacation days. They impose taxes to pay for the countries' unemployment benefits, and limit the use of temporary workers. The list goes on. These laws increase the cost of doing business by directly increasing the cost of hiring and keeping employees. In effect, these laws reduce firms' willingness to hire new workers, and so there are few vacancies.

Another explanation for Europe's high unemployment is hysteresis. *Hysteresis* means that the behavior of economic variables today depends on history. High unemployment leads to higher unemployment, even if the cause of the previously high unemployment disappears. The explanation goes like this: High unemployment leads to a greater deterioration in skills necessary to be employed, a greater societal acceptance of being unemployed and collecting benefits, and the development of skills necessary to survive while unemployed.

Because of hysteresis, high unemployment can lower long-term growth. As the population loses its job skills and unemployment becomes more socially acceptable, the nation loses a larger and larger portion of its productive resources.

---

3 months, with 45 percent of the unemployed finding work within 5 weeks and 32 percent finding work within the fifth to fourteenth week of unemployment; 11 percent of the unemployed had not found work within 6 months. This is in contrast to European unemployment, wherein 60 percent of the unemployed have been unemployed 6 months or more. (See the accompanying Briefing Room, "Why Unemployment Has Been So High in Europe.")

Labor Market as Matchmaker. Why can't the unemployed find work immediately if there are always vacancies? Workers and firms must search for a suitable match. Businesses tell us that they can almost always find jobs for the "right people"—it is just not easy to find the right people. Our unemployed friends tell us that they can almost always get a job, but it is not the "right job." A well-functioning labor market directs the right people to the right jobs.

An analogy to dating may make the issue clearer. When you are searching for a date, you are looking for a good match. Some work out, some do not. The labor market works the same way. Employees and employers search for a good match. Just as it takes time to find a suitable spouse, it also takes time to find a suitable job—one that requires the right skills and pays the right salary. Likewise, it takes time to find an employee who has the right skills and is willing to work at the right pay.

Job searches and labor searches take time and money. Job searchers have to compose a résumé, look through the paper or the Internet to find job openings, and interview, most likely more than once for the same position. Firms have to advertise a position, review résumés, and interview potential hires. All of this takes time. Perhaps the job is far away from home, or does not pay quite enough. Maybe the worker wants a 30-hour-per-week schedule and the employer wants to hire someone for 40 hours. Because of job mismatch and job search time, there will always be some amount of unemployment, even when the economy is using its resources fully.

The Standard Supply and Demand Curves and the Dynamic Labor Market

To understand the dynamic nature of the labor market, you need to account for "matchmaking" considerations.

We will consider the dynamic nature of the labor market with a modification that Berkeley economist Bent Hansen worked out of the microeconomic supply-and-demand model you learned in your introductory economics class. In a labor market where the cost of looking for jobs and workers is zero and the match between vacancies and job seekers is instantaneous, the demand for labor is D and the supply of labor is S, shown in Exhibit 3–3(a). The static equilibrium (in which search costs are not considered) is point A, where the quantity of labor supplied equals the quantity of labor demanded; there is no unemployment.

As we know, however, unemployment and vacancies do exist; this can be explained by the costs and delays of the matchmaking process. To see how, we can make an adjustment to account for the labor market's dynamic aspects. Specifically, let S_M (the matched supply) be the number of workers who can actually find jobs at each wage, given the amount they are spending to search for jobs. At wage W_e, of the N_2 workers who are looking for jobs, only N_1 will find jobs. $N_2 - N_1$ will be unemployed. The ease of finding jobs depends on how many firms are looking for workers. Because at lower wages more firms are looking for workers, the lower the wage, the closer S_M is to S.

We can make the same adjustment to demand. Because of matchmaking costs and delays, D_M (the matched demand) shows the numbers of jobs filled at every wage, given the amount they are spending to search for jobs. At wage W_e, firms would like to hire N_2 workers, but they will fill only N_1 positions. $N_2 - N_1$ positions will go unfilled. Because more workers look for work as the wage rises, D_M gets closer to D as the wage rises.

The intersection of the S_M and D_M curves (point B) determines the equilibrium wage and employment level at which the market actually arrives. As you can see, at the equilibrium wage, W_e, the intersection of the two curves is at a lower level of employment, N_1, than we get from standard supply-and-demand curves. At wage W_e, firms are trying to hire N_2 workers but can only find N_1 suitable workers. Firms have vacancies, represented by $N_2 - N_1$. Likewise, at wage W_e, N_2 workers are

Exhibit 3-3

Supply and Demand for Labor

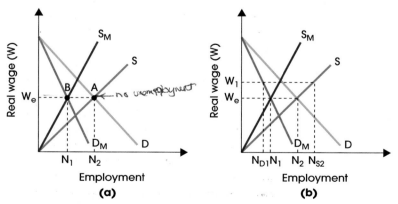

The standard demand-and-supply curves for labor do not account for matching problems in the labor market. *Panel a* takes into account search costs in the labor market by showing demand-and-supply curves that account for search costs. The equilibrium, point B, of demand and supply with search results in some unemployment ($N_2 - N_1$). *Panel b* takes into account the institutional and political pressures that lead to above-equilibrium wages and shows that an above-equilibrium wage of W_1 raises unemployment even further to $N_{S2} - N_{D1}$.

looking for work, but only N_1 workers are hired. Unemployment caused by the matchmaking process is represented by $N_2 - N_1$. An equilibrium exists, even though some workers and some firms remain disappointed.

The level of unemployment at the equilibrium wage is called **frictional unemployment**—the level of unemployment caused by mismatch and search in normal times when the wage is at the equilibrium level. Frictional unemployment in an economy results from the normal turnover in jobs and search by workers.

Frictional unemployment is not the only source of unemployment. Unemployment also arises from institutional and political pressures that raise wages above the equilibrium wage. Existing workers who have jobs, called insiders, often exert this pressure. To see why higher-than-equilibrium wages lead to unemployment, look at Exhibit 3–3(b), which is the same as Exhibit 3–3(a), except that the wage has been pushed above the equilibrium wage. Notice that because the prevailing wage, W_1, is above the equilibrium wage, W_e, the number of people looking for work increases from N_2 to N_{S2} while the number of workers firms want to hire falls from N_1 to N_{D1}. The pressure from insiders to raise wages has increased the number of unemployed. The unemployment caused by above-equilibrium wages is often called **insider–outsider unemployment.** Above-equilibrium wages help those who have jobs (insiders), but creates unemployment (outsiders).

This push for higher wages manifests itself in the market in many ways. Sometimes it occurs because of pressure by unions for higher wages; sometimes it occurs because of pressures from nonunion workers for higher wages; and then sometimes it works through government—a law setting a minimum wage that is higher than the equilibrium wage, for example.

Why do firms agree to pay higher-than-equilibrium wages? One reason is that workers are not identical. Some workers are more efficient than others and firms want to keep good workers. The "right" people are hard to find. By paying above-equilibrium wages, firms can be more selective about whom they hire. The high wage attracts a high number of applicants, reduces turnover of good workers (by offering workers wages that are higher than wages they would receive elsewhere), and maintains good employee relations (because workers know they are being well-paid). This above-equilibrium wage is sometimes called an **efficiency wage** because it can increase a firm's efficiency.

Whenever existing workers are paid above-equilibrium wages, firms can be reluctant to pay new workers the same wage they pay existing workers, even when the new workers are just as productive. This has led to a phenomenon in the United States called a dual wage structure. One way in which firms create a dual wage structure is to hire new workers as part-time workers, and not classify them as standard workers. Microsoft took this approach in the late 1990s and into 2000. The company filled more than one-third of its new positions from 1998 to 2000 with temporary workers. This led to a class-action lawsuit by temporary workers, who wanted the same stock options offered to regular employees. In response, Microsoft implemented a new policy in July 2000 that limited the length of temporary workers' contracts to 1 year and required a 100-day hiatus between assignments.

The Natural Rate of Unemployment

We add up frictional and insider–outsider unemployment to arrive at a level of unemployment that economies experience during normal times. This normal level

---

Unemployment at the equilibrium wage level is often called frictional unemployment.

Unemployment in excess of frictional unemployment is often called insider–outsider unemployment. It is caused by above-equilibrium wages.

Sometimes firms offer above-equilibrium wages to reduce turnover. Such above-equilibrium wages are called efficiency wages.

12

THE BRIEFING ROOM   Strategies to Lower European Unemployment

In an earlier Briefing Room feature, we discussed how European unemployment rates have been high in recent years. As you can imagine, policies to reduce these high rates have been an important topic of discussion among economists and European policy makers. Most of this discussion has been based on the economists' belief that the high unemployment stems from high natural rates of unemployment, and is not cyclical in nature. The natural rate of unemployment does not respond to demand-side policies, so most of their discussion has been about supply-side and structural policies. Some of the policies that have been recommended include the following:

- **Improve labor-force skills through education and training.** Higher skilled labor means more productive labor, which makes firms want to hire more workers, reducing unemployment. The problem with these policies is that education and training is often expensive, and the programs can quickly become self-serving for the educators, providing them with income but not providing workers with significant skills.

- **Reform (read: reduce) employment security laws.** It is very costly to fire workers in much of Europe. Firms must pay large separation payments. This makes firms worried about hiring in the first place. Therefore, paradoxically, these laws have the same effect as a tax on hiring. In the 1990s, many European countries relaxed their stringent labor laws, allowing firms more flexibility with regard to hiring, pay, and work-week hours.

- **Reduce regulation of work time and temporary jobs.** Firms will only hire workers if they think the workers' production will exceed their wages. Many European countries, however, have strong regulations that limit hours of work and prevent firms from hiring temporary and part-time workers. By reducing these regulations, firms are more able to shift production to meet the varying demands in the market.

- **Reform the level and duration of unemployment benefits.** Unemployment benefits pay people for not working, so the higher they are, the less likely the unemployed will want to work. By reducing unemployment benefits, you lower the reservation wage and increase the likelihood that workers will accept lower paying jobs.

There are, of course, many other similar types of policies, but these give you a sense of the kind of policies that governments are exploring to reduce their natural rate of unemployment.

It is possible for these policies to work. For example, Ireland's natural rate of unemployment fell by over 6 percentage points in the 1990s. During this time Ireland reduced unemployment benefits, reduced employment taxes, and increased efforts to train workers. It is one of the European Community's major success stories.

You can read more about these policy issues in *Implementing the OECD Jobs Strategy* (www.oecd.org).

---

of unemployment is what Alan Blinder was referring to when he said, at the Federal Reserve conference in Wyoming, ". . . central banks should seek to reduce the unemployment rate until it is just shy of the point where labor shortages begin to push up wages and the inflation rate accelerates." This rate is what we have been calling the *natural rate of unemployment* (the rate of unemployment that the economy can achieve, given current institutions).

What might change the natural rate? Generally accepted causes for the decline in the U.S. natural rate of unemployment in the past 20 years include demographic changes, changes in job-search costs, and structural changes in the economy, such as a change in union membership. (See the Briefing Room, "Strategies to Lower European Unemployment," for policies that government can implement to lower the natural rate.)

Lawrence Katz, a Harvard University economist, and Alan Krueger, a Princeton University economist, estimated that the aging of the Baby-Boom generation, an increase in the number of temporary employment agencies, increased incarceration rates, and the decline of union membership lowered the natural rate of unemployment by roughly 0.6 to 1.1 percentage points from the mid-1980s to the late 1990s.

The natural rate of unemployment is the rate that the economy can achieve, given current institutions.

Table 3-2

Causes of the Decline in the Natural Rate

Causes	Contribution (Percentage Point)
Aging of the Baby Boomers	0.40
Increasing number of temporary-help agencies	0.40
Increased incarceration rates	0.17
Decline in union membership	0.10
Total decline	*1.07*

Causes of the decline in the natural rate in the last 20 years include (1) the aging of Baby Boomers, (2) the increasing number of temporary-help agencies, (3) increased incarceration rates, and (4) the declining influence of unions.

Table 3–2 lists each factor, along with its estimated contribution to the decline in the natural rate.

Let us consider each factor. The aging of the Baby Boomers means fewer people are moving in the labor market so that the matched supply and demand curves are closer to the standard supply and demand curves. Young people are more likely to experience unemployment than are middle-aged and older people, who tend to settle into more permanent jobs. The aging of the Baby Boomers during the mid-1980s to late 1990s reduced the natural rate of unemployment by an estimated 0.4 percentage point.

Temporary-help agencies help reduce the cost of job matching so that firms can fill vacancies more quickly. The temporary-help industry grew tremendously during the 1990s. Katz and Krueger estimate that the temporary-help industry has reduced the natural rate of unemployment by up to 0.4 percentage point since the mid-1980s.

The third factor Katz and Krueger consider is the rise in the prison population over the past three decades. In 1970, two out of every 1,000 adults were in prison. In 1998, nine out of every 1,000 adults were in prison. Although prisoners are not counted as either employed or unemployed, prior to becoming incarcerated, many prisoners were unemployed. Katz and Krueger estimate that higher incarceration rates have reduced the natural rate of unemployment by an estimated 0.17 percentage point.

A final factor that has affected the natural rate of unemployment is union membership. The proportion of non-government workers who are members of labor unions has declined steadily from almost 25 percent in the mid-1970s to less than 10 percent today. Unions tend to raise wages for their members. As the proportion of unionized workers falls, therefore, the unemployment caused by above-equilibrium wages also falls. Katz and Krueger estimate that reduced union influence accounts for up to 0.1 percentage point of the decline in the natural rate of unemployment. All these factors reduce the unemployment rate by narrowing the gap between the matched and the standard supply and demand curves.

A factor they did not consider, but which is of increasing importance, is the effect of the Internet on the cost and duration of job searches. Consider the following example. An Internet service in New Hampshire, called Jobfind.com, posts want ads by employers and registers résumés from job seekers. Not only can want ads be updated daily, but the service will match résumés with jobs using keyword searches. Employers can screen job applicants on the Internet instead of in initial face-to-face interviews. This process reduces the cost of job and employee searches, allowing companies to consider a wider number of applicants. Such innovations increase the amount of information available and the speed and efficiency of job matches. These developments and government policies that reduce search costs will lower the natural rate of unemployment.

> Some economists believe that supply shocks (changes in the prices of significant inputs to production) affect the natural rate of unemployment.

Some economists believe that **supply shocks**—changes in the prices of imports or significant inputs to production or imported goods—also affected the natural rate of unemployment in the United States. The U.S. economy experienced several favorable price supply shocks in the late 1990s that put downward pressure on inflation. One favorable supply shock was the decline in the price of imports when the value of Asian currencies tumbled; another was the moderation in medical care inflation. According to a number of economists, these positive supply shocks allowed the U.S. unemployment rate to fall to 4 percent, well below the natural rate of 5.2 percent generally estimated at that time, without causing rising inflation. These economists argued that low unemployment put upward pressure on inflation, but the temporary favorable supply shocks offset that upward pressure and lowered inflation. This is the explanation that DRI and Wharton Econometrics, two U.S. forecasting firms, gave for why the unemployment rate fell below the natural rate without inflation rising in the late 1990s and into 2000.

> If supply shocks affect the natural rate, there is both a long-run and a short-run natural rate.

If supply shocks do change the natural rate of unemployment, then we need to distinguish between a long-run natural rate (the natural rate that excludes the effects of supply shocks) and a short-run natural rate (the natural rate that includes the effects of supply shocks). If supply shocks put upward pressure on prices, the short-run natural rate would be above the long-run natural rate. If, as was the case in the late 1990s, positive price supply shocks put downward pressure on prices, the short-run natural rate would be below the long-run natural rate. However, in 2000 those positive supply shocks ended. If this explanation is correct, we should expect increases in both inflation and unemployment between 2001 and 2003, unless, of course, something else changes.

Executive Summary

- Some unemployment is necessary in a dynamic economy. Flows in and out of employment comprise about 8 percent of total employment per month.

- Vacancies (unfilled jobs) are the flip side of unemployment. Unemployment and vacancies arise from job mismatch and above-equilibrium wages.

- Unemployment due to job mismatch is called *frictional unemployment*. Unemployment due to higher-than-equilibrium wages is called *insider-outsider* unemployment. The sum of the two equals the natural rate of unemployment.

- Aging Baby Boomers, growth in the temporary-help industry, increased prison population, reduced union membership, favorable supply shocks, and, possibly, lower search costs have contributed to the decline in the natural rate of unemployment since the mid-1980s.

Cyclical Unemployment and Cyclical Coordination Failures

The unemployment rate and the vacancy rate can vary around their own natural rates for reasons other than supply price shocks. Specifically, in recessions, unemployment

Exhibit 3-4

**The U.S.
Unemployment
Rate and Vacancy
Rate**

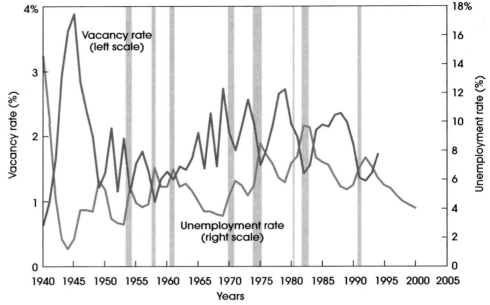

Vacancy and unemployment rates vary with the business cycle. The unemployment rate declines during expansions and rises during recessions. Vacancy rates move in the opposite direction. The *shaded bars* indicate recessions. Source: From the Bureau of Labor Statistics (stats.bls.gov) and Zagorsky, Jay L. 1998. "Job vacancies in the United States: 1923 to 1994." *Review of Economics and Statistics*, 1998:338–44.

Fluctuations around the natural rate of unemployment are caused by business cycles. Such unemployment is called *cyclical unemployment.*

Cyclical unemployment is caused by cyclical coordination failures involving dynamic feedbacks between decision makers.

rises; and, in expansions, unemployment falls. Exhibit 3–4 shows the unemployment rate through 2000 and the vacancy rate for the United States through 1994. The shaded regions indicate recessions. As you can see, the vacancy rate declines and the unemployment rate rises during recessions. The opposite occurs during expansions. Macroeconomic policy designed to limit fluctuations in output around its trend also tries to limit fluctuations in the unemployment rate above and below its natural rate. Unemployment that results when real output is below potential output is called **cyclical unemployment.** Cyclical unemployment exists because of cyclical coordination failures in the economy. **Cyclical coordination failures** are problems that develop in an economy because decisions by individuals feed back into the economy, augmenting the effect of the initial decision creating a mismatch between production and expenditures.

To understand cyclical coordination failures, think of a microphone and an amplifier. If the mike gets too close to the amplifier, the result is a chilling, high-pitched screech—sometimes a really loud screech. That screech is a result of dynamic feedbacks that occur between the mike and the amplifier when they are too close together. The resulting sound is not socially desirable. The socially desirable result is the simple amplification of the voice.

Cyclical coordination failures in the macroeconomy are caused by dynamic feedbacks. These coordination failures occur in the economy because of the interconnection of the components of the economy. When people change their spending, other people's income changes, which changes their spending, which . . . and so on. When these spending changes get too close together, and are not damped out by the law of large numbers, the result is a fluctuation in income and output, which no one wants, but it is, nonetheless, the result of their actions.

Exhibit 3-5

The Labor Market and the Business Cycle

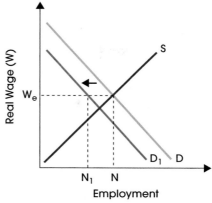

Economic recessions lead to a decline in the demand for labor. A fall in the wage may not eliminate the cyclical unemployment because the decline in wages, if widespread enough, will lead to a decline in income and a further drop in labor demand.

The cyclical coordination problem in the macroeconomy is made more difficult by the fact that businesses decide how much to produce based on how much they expect to sell. If confidence in future consumer demand falls, businesses cut production, and, as they do, the demand for labor falls. Exhibit 3–5 shows this decline as a shift to the left in the demand for labor from D to D_1. The number of workers hired falls from N to N_1. Because fewer people are working and the wage has not changed, total income and, therefore, total consumption expenditures, decline. Lower demand for consumer products and services causes firms to decrease production, and their demand for labor, even more. Firms' expectations become self-fulfilling. Unemployment is caused by the dynamic feedbacks when producers' and consumers' expectations are not coordinated.

In Exhibit 3–5, it looks as though a decrease in wages would eliminate the unemployment, but that assumes that demand for labor decreased in only one market. If demand declines for the economy as a whole, that analysis is problematic. The analysis of cyclical unemployment in the aggregate market (macroeconomic analysis) is more complicated than the analysis of an individual market (microeconomic analysis). If wages fall, workers' incomes fall, and this fall in income will decrease demand for workers even further, leading firms in many markets to produce less, not more. These issues involve complicated dynamics that will not be discussed in this chapter, but the observation that unemployment varies with the business cycle has led most policy-oriented macroeconomists to agree that cyclical unemployment is an important policy issue. (See the Q&A feature on why some economists believe cyclical unemployment does not exist.)

Costs of Cyclical Unemployment. Cyclical unemployment caused by cyclical coordination failures is not associated with significant increases in vacancies. A cut in production causes firms to terminate existing positions, resulting in workers losing jobs and firms canceling vacancies. Consequently, some macroeconomists view cyclical unemployment as a total loss to society. Not only are the unemployed unhappy, but so are firms. Firms would post vacancies if only they believed that the demand for their products would be there. If their argument is correct, the cost of cyclical unemployment is measured by the gap between actual output in the

The analysis of cyclical unemployment in the aggregate market is more complicated than the analysis of unemployment in an individual market.

QUESTION   Do all economists agree that some unemployment is cyclical?

ANSWER   No, a small group of economists, called real business cycle economists, argue that it does not exist, and a larger group of economists believe that the importance of cyclical unemployment is overstated.

Real business cycle economists argue that fluctuations in unemployment are a result of people's changing tastes and an economy's changing technology. This fits into their general belief that the economy is always producing at potential output. Therefore, fluctuations in output, and consequently unemployment, reflect changes in the amount an economy is capable of producing, or *real* phenomenon. Real business cycle economists would say that a 13 percent unemployment rate simply means that the economy is going through significant changes and that people want more leisure.

Other economists do not go this far, but they do argue that separating cyclical unemployment from other types is almost impossible; doing so serves little purpose

except to promote the desire of some macroeconomists to fight that unemployment with monetary and fiscal policy. For these economists, cyclical unemployment is not an objective measure, but the result of a judgment of what unemployment ought to be.

Policy macroeconomists, like ourselves, are sympathetic to the more moderate position, but argue that because policy requires normative judgments, one cannot escape the subjective element of measurement. The position—that cyclical unemployment cannot be measured—shows their general belief that monetary and fiscal policy should not be used to direct the economy. In policy, one cannot escape normative judgments; terminology and measurement inevitably have policy implications.

economy and potential output (what output would be when unemployment is at its natural rate and when there is no coordination failure) when output is below potential.

To figure out that loss of output, we need to know the relationship between unemployment and output. Exhibit 3–6 plots the annual percentage change in real output against the change in the unemployment rate from one year to the next for

---

Exhibit 3-6

Growth in GDP and Change in Unemployment

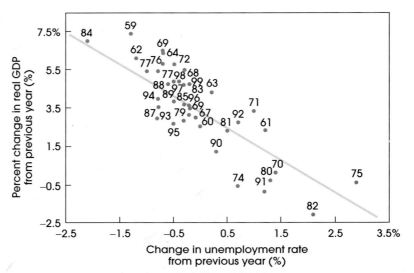

This exhibit depicts the observed relationship between the change in unemployment and growth in GDP, known as Okun's Rule of Thumb: A 1-percentage-point rise in unemployment is loosely associated with a 2-percentage-point reduction in the annual growth rate of real GDP.

the years between 1959 and 1999. Points in the upper left-hand corner represent years of rising output and falling unemployment. Points in the lower right-hand corner represent years of declining output and rising unemployment.

The *solid line* through the data points shows the approximate relationship between the unemployment rate and output. This relationship was first proposed as a rule of thumb by Arthur Okun in 1962, and it came to be known as Okun's Rule of Thumb. **Okun's Rule of Thumb** states that each percentage-point rise in unemployment is associated with a 2-percentage-point reduction in the annual growth rate of real gross domestic product (GDP). For example, if the unemployment rate rises from 5 percent to 6 percent, real GDP growth will typically slow by 2 percentage points.

Formally, this relationship can be stated as follows:

$$\%\Delta Q = 3.5 - (2 \times \Delta U) \qquad\qquad (3\text{-}1)$$

where $\%\Delta Q$ is the percent change in real GDP and ΔU is the change in the unemployment rate.

The 3.5 percent represents the annual growth rate of potential output. If the unemployment rate does not change, output will grow at its potential of 3.5 percent per year. If the unemployment rate increases by 1 percentage point, output will grow only 1.5 percent that year [3.5 − (2 × 1)]. If the unemployment rate increases by 2 percentage points, output will fall by 0.5 percent that year [3.5 − (2 × 2)].

Okun's Rule of Thumb states that a 1-percentage-point rise in the unemployment rate in today's greater than $10 trillion economy will reduce real GDP growth by about $200 billion, or about $2,000 per household that year. However, those losses are not shared equally among all households. New entrants to the job market and minorities tend to experience higher rates of unemployment on average. The higher rates of unemployment among new entrants and minorities means that they bear a disproportionately large share of the $200 billion in lost income.

Okun's Rule of Thumb is a rough-and-ready measure. It is not carved in stone. If the labor force participation rate increases, the unemployment rate can rise with no decline in the growth of real GDP. This occurred at times during the 1970s, as women entered the labor force in larger numbers. Similarly, employment can decline with no decline in the growth of real GDP if the employed become more productive. In the early 1990s, as large firms adjusted their production methods to increase productivity, unemployment sometimes rose even as output rose. Still, as a first approximation, Okun's Rule of Thumb gives policy makers a good starting point when estimating the cost of unemployment in terms of lost real GDP growth.

The Equity Costs of Unemployment. Even though unemployment, from a theoretical point of view, is not necessarily a sign of an ailing economy, society is always concerned with reducing unemployment. For individuals, the costs of being unemployed include lost income, a decline in skills if unemployment is prolonged, and a loss of self-worth. (Firms do not experience the same loss of self-worth when they have vacancies.) Individuals tend to define themselves by their jobs, and it can be psychologically devastating to lose their job. Jobs provide social standing; to lose a job is to lose social standing. Jobs also often provide a circle of friends, and to lose a job is often to lose friends, self-worth, and income. In short, the labor market is not

---

Okun's Rule of Thumb: Each percentage point rise in unemployment is associated with a 2-percentage-point reduction in annual growth rate of real GDP.

Okun's Rule of Thumb: $\%\Delta Q = 3.5 - 2 \times \Delta U$.

For individuals, unemployment can impose significant social and psychological costs.

Table 3-3

U.S. Unemployment by Age, Gender, and Race (%)

	1991	1992	1993	1994	1995	1996	1997	1998	1999	2000
All workers	6.8	7.5	6.9	6.1	5.6	5.4	4.9	4.5	4.2	4.0
All 16- to 19-year-olds	18.7	20.1	19.0	17.6	17.3	16.7	16.0	14.6	13.9	13.1
Males	7.2	7.9	7.2	6.2	5.6	5.4	4.9	4.4	4.1	3.9
Females	6.4	7.0	6.6	6.0	5.6	5.4	5.0	4.6	4.3	4.1
Blacks	12.5	14.2	13.0	11.5	10.4	10.5	10.0	8.9	8.0	7.6
Blacks (age 16–19)	36.1	39.7	38.8	35.2	35.7	33.6	32.4	27.6	27.9	24.7
Whites	6.1	6.6	6.1	5.3	4.9	4.7	4.2	3.9	3.7	3.5
Hispanics	10.0	11.6	10.8	9.9	9.3	8.9	7.7	7.2	6.4	5.7

Note: All workers include American Indians, Alaskan natives, and Asian and Pacific Islanders. The BLS does not report separate unemployment rates for these demographic groups.

Source: Table A–2 of the *Employment Situation*, published by the Bureau of Labor Statistics **(stats.bls.gov)**.

just another market. It is probably the one market that contributes the most to individuals' welfare, which is why it is the market on which economics focuses most.

In 2000, according to the BLS, even when unemployment was at an historic low of 4 percent, 5.7 million people said they were looking for work, but could not find it. Another 4.4 million people were not in the labor force, but said they wanted a job. That, by most people's standards, is a high cost. True, efficiency may require some unemployment, but the individuals who are experiencing the huge costs of unemployment share only a small fraction of society's gains in efficiency. A well-known joke illustrates the point: "A man comes home and tells his wife that he has good news and bad news. The good news is that he is on the forefront of the battle against inflation. The bad news is that he lost his job."

If unemployment were spread out equally among all major demographic groups, the equity costs would be far less, but it is not. Table 3–3 shows the wide variation in unemployment rates for various demographic groups. Economists break these numbers down so that policy makers can better understand the equity cost of unemployment.

Some groups experience higher rates of unemployment than do other groups.

As you can see in Table 3–3, unemployment rates among teen-agers are considerably higher than the overall unemployment rate in the economy. In 2000, the unemployment rate was 4.0 percent in the economy as a whole (and for individuals above the age of 20, it was about 3.4 percent), but teen-age unemployment was 13.1 percent. This difference has a number of explanations. Generally, teen-agers have more flexibility in whether to accept a job than do older people. (Teen-agers have parents who sometimes are willing to support them, and most teen-agers do not have a family they must support.) Teen-agers are trying out jobs, so, they naturally shift jobs a lot. Teen-agers are in and out of the job market, depending on their school status. Combined, these explanations support a much higher rate of unemployment for teen-agers than for other age groups.

The unemployment rate among Blacks and Hispanics as a whole has tended to be significantly higher than for Whites. Specifically, the unemployment rate for Blacks has generally been double that for Whites. Hispanics have fared a bit better. They have had slightly lower unemployment rates than have Blacks. Perhaps the most disturbing of the unemployment figures is among Black male teen-agers. During the 1990s, this group consistently experienced unemployment rates above 30 percent. Unemployment among Black female teen-agers, although lower than for Black male teen-agers, is also substantially higher than that of the White population as a whole.

What do these data tell us? They tell us that the aggregate unemployment rate hides the multidimensional nature of unemployment. Understanding unemployment means knowing the unemployment rates among the various groups in our society. Because unemployment hurts some demographic groups more than others, most economists believe that unemployment should be kept as low as possible, without generating accelerating or even increasing inflation. This historic tendency for inflation to rise as unemployment falls is called the Phillips curve.

THE PHILLIPS CURVE

The Phillips curve is a representation of the short-run inverse relationship between inflation and unemployment.

The **Phillips curve** is a representation of the short-run relationship between inflation and unemployment that has sometimes been observed in the economy. It is at the core of many working models of the economy that businesspeople and policy makers use.

The Phillips curve relationship tells policy makers the conditions for effective expansionary and contractionary policies. Exhibit 3–7 shows a hypothetical Phillips curve.

According to the Phillips curve, when inflation is high, unemployment tends to be low, and when inflation is low, unemployment tends to be high. That is, inflation and unemployment tend to be *inversely* related. First popularized in the 1950s by economist A. W. Phillips, the Phillips curve was thought by some economists to represent a stable set of choices between inflation and unemployment. Given the Phillips curve shown in Exhibit 3–7, if policy makers wanted to lower 7 percent inflation to 3 percent, for example, they would have to accept an unemployment rate of 8 percent instead of its current 4 percent. Points *A* and *B*, respectively, show these two choices.

This curve became popular because it captured a trade-off that had been observed at that time. It also provided a justification for government intervention

Exhibit 3–7

The Phillips Curve

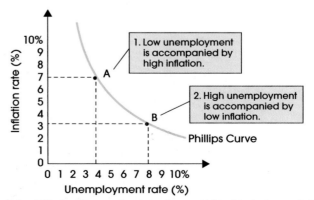

The Phillips curve is the historically perceived short-run relationship between inflation and unemployment. When inflation is high, unemployment tends to be low, and when inflation is low, unemployment tends to be high.

in the economy. If policy makers wanted lower unemployment, they would also have to accept higher inflation. All policy makers had to do to solve their dilemma of wanting both low unemployment and low inflation was to assign a cost and benefit to achieving each goal and choose the policy that resulted in the highest net benefit.

Of particular interest to policy makers were the Phillips curve's *position* and *slope*. The position of the Phillips curve showed attainable combinations of inflation and unemployment. Points to the left of the Phillips curve were unattainable. Monetary and fiscal policies could achieve only those combinations of inflation and unemployment along the Phillips curve. The slope of the Phillips curve determined the trade-off between inflation and unemployment, or the rate at which one goal must be given up to move toward achieving the other goal. If the Phillips curve were steep, a small decline in the unemployment rate would be achieved by accepting a relatively large rise in the inflation rate. If the Phillips curve were flat, a small decline in the unemployment rate would be accompanied by a smaller rise in the inflation rate. The Phillips curve appeared to be a promising policy-making guide to a trade-off between inflation and unemployment.

The Phillips Curve in the United States

Unfortunately for policy makers, the actual relationship between unemployment and inflation has not always conformed to the hypothetical Phillips curve shown in Exhibit 3–7. Exhibit 3–8 shows the relationship between inflation and unemployment for the United States between 1959 and 2000.

As you can see, no one trade-off is easily discernible over the entire period. When the Phillips curve gained acceptance as a policy guide, however, an inverse relationship between unemployment and inflation did exist, as shown by the downward-sloping dark red line connecting the years 1959 to 1969. When unemployment

Exhibit 3–8

Inflation and Unemployment, 1959 to 2000

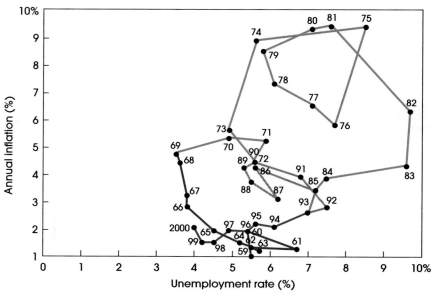

The Phillips curve, which shows the observed relationship between inflation and unemployment, has not remained stable over time. Source: From the Bureau of Labor Statistics (http://stats.bls.gov) and the Bureau of Economic Analysis (www.bea.doc.gov).

slowly fell from 5.5 percent in 1960 to 3.5 percent in 1969, annual inflation crept up from 1 percent to 4.7 percent.

Beginning in 1970 and until about 1984 the Phillips curve relationship broke down as the green line shows. During these years, both inflation and unemployment were high. The relationship reappeared briefly from 1985 to 1992, as shown by the gray line, but disappeared again from 1992 onward (shown in blue) as unemployment and inflation declined simultaneously. The point is that economists and policy makers must check whether observations about the relationship among variables carry over from one period into another.

The Short-Run and Long-Run Phillips Curves

The long-run Phillips curve is generally seen as vertical. In the long run, there is no trade-off between inflation and unemployment.

The substantial shifts in the Phillips curve have convinced most economists that a trade-off between inflation and unemployment that policy makers can use to make decisions does not exist in the long run. Today, the consensus view is that there are two types of Phillips curves: a long-run Phillips curve, represented by a vertical line positioned at the natural rate of unemployment, and a series of short-run Phillips curves that shift along the long-run curve. Exhibit 3–9 shows hypothetical examples of the long-run and short-run Phillips curves.

The vertical long-run Phillips curve shows economists' belief that the economy will always return to the natural rate of unemployment regardless of the inflation rate. Policy makers cannot lower the natural rate of unemployment in the long run by accepting a bit more inflation.

The short-run Phillips curve represents the short-run trade-off just discussed. It is, however, a difficult trade-off to use for policy purposes, because one never knows when that trade-off will change as the curve shifts to a new location. To compound the confusion, the natural rate itself changes, causing the long-run Phillips curve to shift as well. In the late 1990s and into 2001, the short-run Phillips curve had disappeared. Unemployment went below the commonly-accepted natural rate of 5.2 percent (which had been lowered in the late 1990s from 6.1 percent) while inflation fell. The lack of a rising inflation along with low unemployment has puzzled economists. Some economists say that the conditions are the result of structural changes in the economy, such as those that Katz and Krueger discuss.

Exhibit 3–9

The Long-Run and Short-Run Phillips Curves

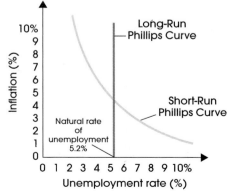

Most economists have given up the short-run Phillips curve as a guide for policy and focus instead on unemployment and inflation as separate problems. The long-run Phillips curve reflects this view. It is vertical at the natural rate of unemployment.

Even though the Phillips curve appears to shift and sometimes even disappear, for policy makers and businesspeople, the short-run–long-run Phillips curve relationship is still one of the most relied-on, short-term decision-making tools. The rules of thumb connecting inflation and the unemployment rate in models have been the following: *When the unemployment rate is below the natural rate, predict inflation to rise. When the unemployment rate is above its natural rate, predict inflation to fall.* For policy makers, this means the following: Enact contractionary policies when the unemployment rate is below its natural rate to avoid inflation, and enact expansionary policies when the unemployment rate is above its natural rate, unless you want to lower inflation. Alternatively, policy makers could implement policies that raise unemployment above its natural rate (create cyclical unemployment) to reduce inflation, as Paul Volcker, former chairman of the Federal Reserve Bank, did in the early 1980s. That is, policy makers can lower inflation, but at a cost of higher unemployment and lower output.

> When the unemployment rate is below its natural rate, inflation will rise. When the unemployment rate is above its natural rate, inflation will fall.

POLICY PERSPECTIVE: THE COST OF LOWERING INFLATION

Policy makers must understand trade-offs: "Achieving this goal will cost me so much in not attaining other goals." The Phillips curve represents an important (albeit ephemeral) trade-off. Another way to quantify the cost of policies that lower inflation is with a sacrifice ratio. The **sacrifice ratio** is the cumulative percent deviation of GDP from potential divided by the reduction in inflation achieved by that deviation. The concept is based on the Phillips curve and Okun's Rule of Thumb, which translates cyclical unemployment into lost real GDP.

> The sacrifice ratio is the cumulative percent deviation of GDP from potential divided by the reduction in inflation.

To see how the sacrifice ratio works, let's consider an example: the years 1980 to 1983. We selected this period because the Fed actively sought to reduce the inflation rate by slowing the economy. Annual CPI inflation was high in 1980 and the Fed decided it had to be reduced. It successfully used contractionary monetary policy to slow inflation down. The inflation rate fell from 12.5 percent in 1980 to 3.8 percent in 1983, a reduction of 8.7 percentage points. Inflation stayed low thereafter.

Table 3–4 shows how to calculate the sacrifice ratio. Column I shows the unemployment rate in each year. Column II shows the estimate of the natural rate of unemployment. Column III is the difference between the natural rate and the actual rate of unemployment (Column III − Column II). It is the cyclical unemployment created in each of the 4 years of disinflation.

Table 3-4

The Sacrifice Ratio for the United States, 1980 to 1983

	I Unemployment Rate −	II Natural Rate =	III Cyclical Unemployment	IV Loss of GDP	V Annual Inflation
1980	7.1%	6.0%	1.1%	2.2%	12.5%
1981	7.6	6.0	1.6	3.2	8.9
1982	9.7	6.0	3.7	7.4	3.8
1983	9.6	6.0	3.6	7.2	3.8
Sum			10.0	20.0	

Okun's Rule tells us that a 1-percentage-point rise in unemployment is associated with a 2-percentage-point reduction in the annual growth rate of real GDP. To calculate the sacrifice ratio, we restate Okun's Rule of Thumb in a slightly different way: Every percentage point of cyclical unemployment is associated with 2-percentage-point loss of a year's GDP from potential. If the unemployment rate in 1 year is at the natural rate, which was thought to be 6 percent in the early 1980s, there is no loss of real GDP from potential. Real GDP grows by 3.5 percent. If the unemployment rate is 7 percent one year, the loss of real GDP from potential that year is 2 percent. Instead of growing at a rate of 3.5 percent, real GDP grows by 1.5 percent.

We can use this to translate the cyclical unemployment in Table 3–4 into a loss of GDP for each year shown. We do that in Column IV. The cumulative loss of GDP is the sum of all the numbers in Column IV, or 20 percentage points. This is the numerator of the sacrifice ratio. The denominator of the sacrifice ratio is how much inflation fell. Column V shows inflation over this period. Notice that it fell from 12.5 percent to 3.8 percent, a reduction of 8.7 percentage points. To bring inflation down 8.7 percentage points, the economy lost accumulative 20 percent of real GDP. Therefore, the sacrifice ratio for the disinflation of the early 1980s was 2.3, (20/8.7). For each percentage point decline in inflation, 2.3 percent of real GDP was lost.

Is the 2.3 sacrifice ratio during the early 1980s high or low? Johns Hopkins University economist Laurence Ball studied 65 episodes of disinflation since 1960 for 19 countries. The average sacrifice ratio across all countries studied was about 1.4, lower than the sacrifice ratio in those countries during the early 1980s and lower than the 2.4 average for the United States since 1945. He also found that the short-run costs of disinflation vary significantly among countries.

Estimating sacrifice ratios gives policy makers quantitative information on which policy makers can base decisions about whether reducing inflation is worth the cost. Care must be taken, however: The relationship may be ephemeral, as was the Phillips curve. Since that study, inflation and unemployment in the United States have both fallen. Many factors, such as how quickly inflation is brought down, recent experience with inflation, and changing institutions, affect how costly disinflation will be. These issues are discussed in a later chapter.

The sacrifice ratio must be applied with care; the relationship may change.

There are two other reasons to apply the sacrifice ratio with care. The first is that the sacrifice ratio does not differentiate the degree of deviation of GDP from potential. GDP that is one percent below potential for three years is treated the same as being three percent below potential for one year. Some argue that this assumption is not true and that going cold turkey (a lot of unemployment in one year) is more effective at lowering inflation than a slow withdrawal (a little unemployment over a number of years). The evidence is mixed. The second is that policy makers have four goals: low unemployment, low inflation, smooth growth of output, and high growth. The sacrifice ratio does not take into account the effect of inflation on growth. If high inflation hurts long-term growth, accepting higher inflation to lower unemployment in the short run will jeopardize the high-growth goal, and the sacrifice ratio will overstate the costs of lowering inflation. This is because lower inflation will contribute to higher growth in later years, which will offset the previous loss of output that occurred when inflation declined. In the 1990s, economists, policy makers, and central bankers around the world deemphasized the low-unemployment goal and emphasized the low-inflation and high-growth goals. New Zealand, Canada, the United Kingdom, Sweden, Australia, Finland, Spain, Israel, and the European Union have, by official, written, mandate, made inflation the only target for their central banks.

Executive Summary

- Unemployment due to economic fluctuations is called *cyclical unemployment.*

- Okun's Rule of Thumb states that each percentage-point rise in unemployment is associated with 2-percentage-point reduction in the annual growth rate of real GDP. Formally, Okun's Rule of Thumb is $\%\Delta Q = 3.5 - (2 \times \Delta U)$.

- Unemployment is not distributed equally among all major demographic groups; unemployment has equity costs.

- The Phillips curve shows the inverse relationship between inflation and unemployment. This relationship has changed over time, leading economists to focus on a long-run Phillips curve that shows no relationship between inflation and unemployment.

CONCLUSION

Economics is about choice and the inevitable trade-offs among choices. Every policy has a cost, and the economic framework (there is no such thing as a free lunch) helps you find it. The macroeconomics that developed in the 1940s, 1950s, and 1960s was interpreted by policy makers as suggesting that, in macroeconomics, the cost element of policy was small, while the benefits were large. There were some free policy meals out there for the taking. All policy had to do was to increase aggregate expenditures, and unemployment could be costlessly reduced. The development of macroeconomics since that time has included reintroducing the costs of those policies, and putting the policy issues into better perspective.

Initially, through the Phillips curve, economists looked for the costs of expanding aggregate expenditures in terms of increased inflation. The short-run Phillips curve broke down in the late 1970s not because the costs had disappeared, but because the costs of policy had expanded—the free policy lunch was an illusion.

Most economists agree that our current view of macroeconomic policy, which emphasizes the costs as well as the benefits of expanding output, is more realistic. This does not mean, however, that there is no policy that is likely to improve the economy—once in a while policy makers can snitch a sandwich, and the goal of policy makers is to figure out when.

In future chapters, we will be looking more deeply into the relationships we have developed in this chapter. We will explore models that underlie the various views of the economy, and the institutional structure through which policies may operate, to give us a better sense of what policy can, and cannot, do.

Economists' current view of macroeconomics policy emphasizes the costs as well as the benefits of expanding output.

KEY POINTS

- The economy produces both unemployment and inflation. The U.S. government passed the Employment Act of 1946 and the Humphrey-Hawkins Act of 1978, which made both low inflation and low unemployment goals for both Congress and the Federal Reserve Bank.

- Inflation redistributes income from those who cannot or do not raise their prices to those who can and do raise their prices. This redistribution of income imposes costs on society.

- Inflation destroys the information contained in prices and makes predicting relative prices difficult, undermines institutions based on relatively fixed prices, reduces the usefulness of money and increases costs firms incur to change prices. All of these costs reduce long-run economic growth.

■ To the extent that inflation lowers long-term growth by diverting resources away from production and toward creating mechanisms to deal with inflation, it is sand to an economy. To the extent that inflation facilitates relative price changes, low rates of inflation are grease to an economy.

■ The flip side of unemployment is vacancies (unfilled jobs). In a dynamic economy, in which tastes and technology are constantly changing, some unemployment is necessary.

■ The labor market is a matchmaker. Employees and employers must search for a good match. Search costs lead to frictional unemployment.

■ The natural rate of unemployment is the result of search costs and the mismatch of skills, as well as an above-equilibrium wage. Policies that reduce search time or lower the wage toward the equilibrium wage will reduce the natural rate of unemployment.

■ Okun's Rule of Thumb states that each percentage-point rise in unemployment is associated with a 2-percentage-point reduction in the annual growth rate of real GDP. Formally, $\%\Delta Q = 3.5 - (2 \times \Delta U)$.

■ The short-run Phillips curve represents the perceived inverse relationship between inflation and unemployment. It suggests that lowering inflation comes at a cost of higher unemployment.

■ The short-run Phillips curve relationship is not stable and currently does not appear to exist.

■ The vertical long-run Phillips curve shows economists' belief that the economy will return to its natural rate of unemployment.

■ The sacrifice ratio is the cumulative percent deviation of GDP from potential divided by the decline in the inflation rate. The sacrifice ratio associated with the disinflation of the early 1980s is 2.3.

KEY TERMS

cyclical coordination failure 84
cyclical unemployment 84
efficiency wage 80
Federal Reserve Bank (the Fed) 68

frictional unemployment 80
insider–outsider unemployment 80
Okun's Rule of Thumb 87
Phillips curve 89

sacrifice ratio 92
supply shocks 83

QUESTIONS FOR THOUGHT AND REVIEW

1. Why do the goals of low inflation and low unemployment sometimes conflict?
2. Inflation makes society poorer because a dollar will not buy as much as it did before the inflation. Agree or disagree, and explain your answer.
3. Under what conditions does inflation redistribute income?
4. Describe the three categories of costs of inflation.
5. What do you think will happen to menu costs as more purchases are made over the Internet?
6. How can a small amount of inflation be beneficial to the economy?
7. How is the growth in flexible pay arrangements (stock options, bonuses tied to profits) likely to affect the amount of grease provided by inflation?
8. Why is some unemployment necessary?
9. Why don't the unemployed find work immediately if there are always job vacancies?

10. What are the three labor divisions for the working-age population? Characterize the flows between them.
11. Name three institutional pressures that lead to higher-than-equilibrium wages.
12. Describe four possible reasons why the natural rate of unemployment has fallen in the United States since the mid-1980s.
13. What would you predict would happen to the natural rate of unemployment if people become more willing to move large distances to take a job?
14. What are two policies that would reduce the natural rate of unemployment? (This requires reading "The Briefing Room feature, "Strategies to Lower European Unemployment.")
15. What causes cyclical unemployment?
16. According to Okun's Rule of Thumb, what is the cost of cyclical unemployment?

17. According to the Phillips curve, what is the cost of reducing the inflation rate?
18. Discuss the reliability of the Phillips curve as a forecasting tool. Do policy makers still rely on the Phillips curve? Why or why not?
19. What does the sacrifice ratio measure?
20. Would the costs of reducing inflation be the greatest for a steeper or flatter Phillips curve?

PROBLEMS AND EXERCISES

1. Explain the likely effect of each of the following events on the natural rate of unemployment:
   a. Women enter the workforce in greater numbers.
   b. The average age of the Baby Boomers rises to 45.
   c. The minimum wage falls 20 percent relative to the average wage rate.
   d. Union membership declines, resulting in fewer employees working under long-term contracts.
   e. A trade pact is signed that increases competition for domestic textiles, resulting in the loss of textile jobs, but increases vacancies in high-tech sectors.
   f. The economy enters a cyclical downturn.
   g. Congress passes a law imposing stiff penalties on firms who fire employees.
2. State Okun's Rule of Thumb. If output in an economy is $8 trillion and the unemployment rate falls from 6.0 percent to 5.5 percent, using Okun's Rule of Thumb, what would you predict to be the dollar change in real output?
3. How does the Phillips curve relate inflation to the difference between actual and potential output? (Use Okun's Rule of Thumb.)
4. Calculate the increase in real salary for each of the following inflation rates, assuming you negotiated a 3 percent pay increase:
   a. 1 percent.
   b. 3 percent.
   c. 5 percent.
5. Go to Jobfind.com on the Internet and answer the following questions:
   a. Select a job type, location, and position that interests you. How many jobs were posted? How many fit your skills?
   b. In what ways does this service reduce search costs for workers?
   c. In what ways does this service reduce search costs for employers?
6. Recalculate the sacrifice ratio from Table 3–4, assuming the natural rate is the following:
   a. 7 percent.
   b. 5 percent.

7. Show graphically, with the help of Exhibit 3–3, the effect of each of the following on the natural rate of unemployment:
   a. Union membership declines.
   b. The federal government raises the minimum wage.
   c. The Internet dramatically reduces the cost of searching for jobs and employees.
   d. The federal government reduces the number of months unemployment insurance is available to the unemployed.
8. Suppose the Phillips curve looks like the following (assume the natural rate of unemployment is 5 percent).

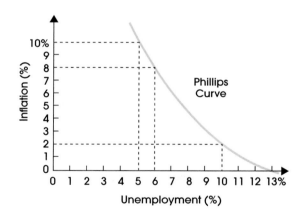

   a. Use Okun's Rule of Thumb to calculate the sacrifice ratio as the economy moves from 10 percent inflation to 8 percent inflation.
   b. Calculate the sacrifice ratio as the economy moves from 2 percent inflation to zero inflation.
9. Go to GPO Gate, which posts the 2000 *Economic Report of the President* (www.gpo.ucop.edu/catalog/erp00.html). Read the section, "What Has Held Inflation in Check?" in Chapter 2 to answer the following questions:
   a. How would you characterize the recent changes in inflation and the unemployment rate?

b. What is the Council of Economic Advisers' estimate of NAIRU (also the natural rate)? How does it compare with the unemployment rate in 2000?

c. What is likely to happen to inflation in the near future?

10. Find the most recent unemployment rates for the following groups from the Bureau of Labor Statistics' Home Page (stats.bls.gov):

a. Black; White

b. Married men, spouse present; women head of household

c. 16- to 19-year-olds; 20 and over

d. No high school diploma; high school diploma

e. Managerial workers; technical workers

f. What explanation can you give for the above differences you found in items (a) through (e)?

4

In the long run, we are simply in another short run.

—Joan Robinson

Understanding Policy for the Long Run and the Short Run

After reading this chapter you should be able to:

1. Draw the circular flow model and explain the economic flows among the various sectors of the economy

2. State the three assumptions of a basic production function

3. Define equilibrium for the economy, using aggregate demand and aggregate supply concepts

4. Define equilibrium for the economy, using investment and saving concepts

5. Describe the difference between long-run and short-run equilibria

6. Understand how fiscal policy affects the long-run and short-run equilibria differently

In 2000, U.S. consumer spending exceeded disposable income. The personal saving rate was −0.1 percent compared with an average of about 9 percent in past decades. Is this change in saving behavior helping or hurting the economy?

The saving rate has been a focus of economists for a number of years. For example, in the 1980s, policy makers were concerned with the low U.S. saving rate relative to Japan. Policy makers believed that the difference in saving rates, in part, explained why Japan's economy was booming, with average annual growth of 5 percent, while the United States' economy was growing only 2.5 percent per year. In the 1990s, however, Japan's boom fizzled, and the U.S. economy boomed, even though the Japanese personal saving rate remained significantly above the U.S. personal saving rate. Now policy makers argued that to get the Japanese economy growing again, Japanese consumers should stop saving so much and spend more.

Why, in one decade, was saving considered the cause of Japan's high growth and, in another, the reason for recession? And where does that leave our concern about the low personal saving rate in the United States? (See the Q&A feature about why the U.S. saving rate might not be as low as the official numbers suggest.) This chapter presents the framework that economists use to analyze the economy in both the long run and the short run and, in doing so, provides an answer to our questions.

THE CIRCULAR FLOW MODEL OF THE MACROECONOMY

We begin with an expanded circular flow model that gives a broad overview of the macroeconomy. The circular flow model shows how the sectors of the economy interact and provides us with a way to define equilibrium for the short run and the long run.

The circular flow model in Exhibit 4–1 is more complete than the one in Chapter 2; it shows all the key players in the economy—households, firms, the government, and foreigners—as well as the markets in which they interact. The three markets—factor, goods, and financial markets—are represented by the light green boxes. The **goods market** is where firms sell goods and services to households. The **factor market** is where households supply the factors of production in exchange for income. The **financial market** channels flows of saving back into the income stream.

The circular flow model also shows two types of flows: financial flows and real flows. The counterclockwise blue arrows between households and firms show real flows. Real flows include goods and services from firms to households and factors of production from households to firms. The clockwise red arrows between households and firms represent the financial flows that result from the real flows. Financial flows are flows of money. Connections between government and households and firms also include both real and financial flows.

This chapter deals with the size of the flows of goods and services. When the economy expands, the flows in the circular flow model increase because the amount of goods and services produced increases. Alternatively, when the economy goes into a recession or depression, the flows decline as the amount of goods and services produced falls. To understand what determines the flow of goods and services, we need to consider the function of each key player and how they interact.

Firms and Production

Firms purchase labor and capital from households in the factor market and transform those factors of production (inputs) into goods and services (output).

> The three central markets in an economy are the goods market, the factor market, and the financial market.

Exhibit 4-1

The Circular Flow Model

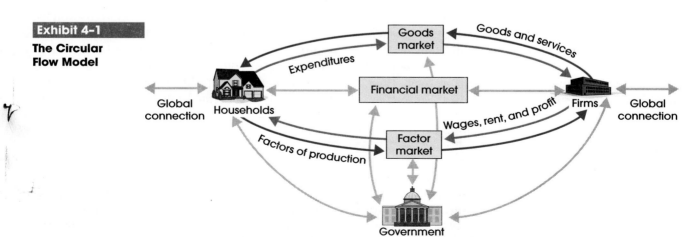

The circular flow model shows the flow of goods, services, and funds among households, firms, government, and foreigners. These key players interact in the factor market, goods market, and financial market. The financial market channels saving into investment.

QUESTION	Should we be concerned about the low U.S. personal saving rate?
ANSWER	Not necessarily. First, there are measurement problems and, second, we are more interested in private saving.

The personal saving rate has been falling steadily in the United States for about the past 20 years. Since 1995, the decline has been particularly steep and, in 2000, households spent more than their disposable income and dissaved 0.1 percent, as you can see in the following exhibit.

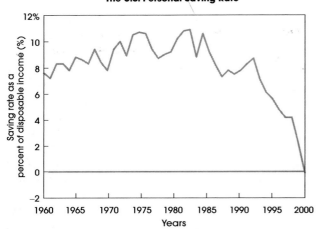

The U.S. Personal Saving Rate

This is not of particular concern because, as you will learn, our interest in the long run is with investment (expenditures on physical capital). Investment is determined by *total* saving in the economy, which includes saving by the private sector, government (surpluses), and foreign citizens (net capital inflows). Private saving is the combination of personal saving and retained earnings by firms. Retained earnings and saving by government and foreign citizens remained high during the 1990s, which meant that investment was high. High investment in the 1990s helped keep the U.S. economy booming.

Economists have even argued that the high retained earnings is what accounted for the decrease in the personal saving rate. High retained earnings led to higher stock prices and an increase in the wealth of private individuals who held stock. High retained earnings were one reason the stock market rose dramatically in the 1980s and 1990s. (The Dow Jones Industrial Average nearly tripled from 1980 to 1990 and nearly quadrupled from 1990 to 2000.)

A rise in the value of stocks increased the wealth of a majority of Americans either directly through their own stock holdings or indirectly through pensions. If government statistics had included the increase in wealth in its measure of personal income and saving, the personal saving rate would have been much higher. New York Fed economists Richard Peach and Charles Steindel, using a saving rate that counts stock market gains as saving and income, found that the U.S. saving rate declined very little in the 1990s.

Stock market gains aren't measured as income or saving in the national income and product accounts, but families often make consumption decisions based on changes in their wealth. Conventional wisdom is that Americans spend 2 percent to 4 percent of their increase in wealth each year. Instead of selling their stockholdings to spend, they spent more out of their monthly income, which lowered the measured personal saving rate. Low personal saving rates accompanied by stock market gains that are driven by high retained earnings reduce our concern about saving. However, when corporate profits fell and stock market prices fell at the end of 2000 and in early 2001, the personal saving rate became a much greater concern, and economists were carefully watching how these events influenced consumption and personal saving.

The production function is a simplified description of the relationship between inputs and outputs.

The transformation of the factors of production into output is called the production process. Economists generally use a very basic **production function—a** simplified description of the relationship between inputs and output in an economy—to refer to an aggregate of all production processes. The production function simplifies the millions of production processes in the economy—from steel making, to farming, to stock brokering—and combines them into a single production process. It also simplifies the factors of production. In reality, firms use many, many types of inputs (for example, labor with various skills, different types of machinery, developed and undeveloped land, and many kinds of raw materials), and technology is constantly changing. We combine these many inputs into only a few inputs to keep the analysis simple. Specifically, we discuss a production function that relates the level of output to two direct inputs—labor and capital.

> **Two inputs to production are capital and labor.**

The following is an example of a production function:

$$Y = F(K, L) \tag{4-1}$$
$$output = function\ of\ (capital,\ labor)$$

This equation tells us that firms use technology to transform labor and capital into output. **Labor** is the amount of labor used in production, often measured by labor hours. **Capital** is the physical goods used along with other raw materials in the production process—a computer, a desk, or a blast furnace. A law firm uses labor (the attorneys and staff) and capital (the building, desks, computers) to produce legal services (divorces, lawsuits, wills). A steel manufacturing plant combines labor (the steelworkers), capital (the blast furnace), and raw materials (iron ore, coke) to produce finished steel. What is important is that firms *transform* factors of production into goods and services. The firms do not take labor and capital (and raw materials) and sell those same inputs back to consumers. Rather, they change those inputs into a product or service. That's what the production function captures.

The production function can be thought of as a set of blueprints that tell how inputs are changed into outputs. These blueprints are always changing. When economists study the changing nature of the blueprints, they sometimes write the production function as Y = A · F(K,L). The "A" represents **technology**—the recipe for combining labor and capital to produce output, or the production process—and can change. As technology improves, we get more output with the same inputs. A law firm using computers and LEXIS/NEXIS technology can handle many more cases than one using typewriters and law books technology. Everyone agrees that technology is important. The problem is that measuring it, and determining its relation to output, is difficult—technology is often embodied in capital and labor. Technology often changes not just the recipe, but also capital and labor themselves, and is often directly unmeasurable. We can measure hours of work and number of machines, but when the labor and machinery embody technology, it is difficult to distinguish what part of the change in output is determined by labor and capital and what part is due to technology.

Assumptions About Production Processes

The production function for the economy is generally assumed to have the following attributes:

1. Output will increase as the quantity of inputs increases.
2. Output will increase by the same proportional increase in all inputs combined.
3. Output will increase by ever-smaller amounts as more of only one input is added, holding all other inputs and the production process constant.

The first attribute is rather obvious. Say you're a farmer and you've increased your acreage or hired more farmhands (inputs). With more of all inputs, you can produce more crops. The increase in output when one unit of input is added, holding all other inputs constant, is that input's **marginal product.**

The second attribute says that if you increase all inputs together by the same percentage, the amount produced also increases by that percentage. If this assumption holds true, a farmer who doubles his acreage and hires twice as many farm hands will double his crop. (This assumes that all land and labor are of equal quality.) If he tripled his acreage and farm hands, his crop would triple. Economists call this attribute **constant returns to scale**—the characteristic of the production function in which output rises by the same proportion as the increase in all inputs.

The final attribute says that output will rise by successively smaller amounts as more of one input is added, holding all other inputs constant. In the farming example, that means adding the first worker to an acre of land would increase crop production from zero to some level. Adding another farm worker would allow, say, better tilling or more seed sowing, but crop production would rise by less than the rise from the first worker because the first worker has to share the tools with the second worker and the acreage and number of seeds remains the same. Subsequent workers will have the same effect on output. Economists call this attribute **diminishing marginal product**—the decline in the amount that additional inputs contribute to output. A key to understanding diminishing marginal product is remembering that only one input is increasing—all other inputs are held constant.

Let's show you what we mean with a graph. Exhibit 4–2(a) shows an example of the relationship between labor and output in a production process. In this case, capital and technology are held constant. Only labor is allowed to vary. As you can see, output increases as labor is added. The slope of the production function shows the marginal product of labor. Notice that as labor is added, the addition to output gets smaller and smaller—diminishing marginal product. Output rises by 2 units when the fifth worker is added but by just over one unit when the sixth worker is added, because the other factors of production—tools, seeds, and land—must be shared among a greater number of workers. Diminishing marginal product is what makes the slope of the production function shown in Exhibit 4–2(a) get flatter as more labor is added. To make the math simple, economists assume that all production processes share these three attributes. This allows us to lump together all production processes into one production function.

So far, we've focused on the two inputs—labor and capital—holding technology constant. Let's now consider a change in technology. Technology increases production by altering the way a firm transforms capital and labor. Internet retailing, for example, increases retail transactions without building new retail outlets. The discovery of lasers dramatically increased the number of successful eye surgeries. Faster computers, which increase the speed of mathematical calculations, have increased production in a number of industries.

An increase in technology, represented by a larger numerical value for A, will lead to an increase in output (Y) for every combination of capital (K) and labor (L). Exhibit 4–2(b) shows the effect of a technological innovation on production. Initially with technology A_0, 4 units of labor and some fixed amount of capital, $\bar{K}$, produce 12 units of output. With technological innovation (represented by an increase from A_0 to A_1) the production function rotates upward so that, with the

---

Marginal product is the increase in output with the addition of one unit of input, holding all other inputs constant.

Returns to scale is a characteristic of production function that involves changing all inputs by the same proportion.

Diminishing marginal product: the decline in the amount that an additional input contributes to output, holding other inputs constant.

Exhibit 4-2

A Production Function

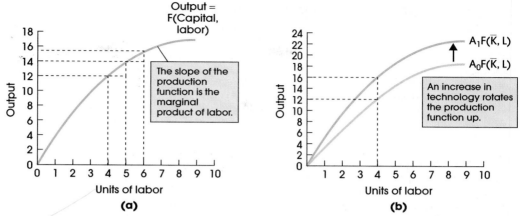

The production function in *panel a* shows how output changes as additional hours of labor are added while capital and technology are held constant. It exhibits diminishing marginal product. *Panel b* shows the effect of changes in technology on output. Initially with technology A_0 and capital $\overline{K}$, 4 units of labor produce 12 units of output. With the technological innovation, A_1, and keeping capital fixed at $\overline{K}$, the production function rotates up so that 4 units of labor produces 16 units of output.

same amount of capital, 4 units of labor can now produce 16 units of output. Before the innovation, 4 units of labor produced 12 units of output.

The difficulty of measuring technology caused economists, until recently, to assume that firms in the economy have no real control over either the level or the growth rate of technology. Using the terminology introduced in Chapter 1, we say that technology is **exogenous** (determined outside the model). This means that firms accept the available production technology. Although technology does advance over time, the assumption is that firms play no role in determining its path. This assumption simplifies our analysis of economic growth considerably. As we will see in Chapter 6, however, it does not fit the real world as well as we would like and, more recently, economists have been analyzing technology that is **endogenous** (determined within the model).

Exogenous means "determined outside the model."

Endogenous means "determined within the model."

Firms and the Factors of Production. When firms use capital, labor, and other factors of production, they must pay for them. The circular flow model shows that firms pay households income in exchange for both their labor and capital. Firms' payment for labor is called a wage. Firms' payment for capital is interest and profits, regardless of whether it pays out the profit as dividends or keeps it as retained earnings.

Retained earnings deserve some discussion. In their accounting procedures, economists assume that households own the firm and all its capital; firms are simply an intermediary between households as *producers* and households as *consumers*. Even though firms retain some earnings, households ultimately receive this profit, too, either because the value of firms' financial assets rises or because firms use the retained earnings to purchases additional capital. Increases in retained earnings and capital can push up the price of firms' stock, making households richer. Therefore, households, as owners of firms, benefit from profits either directly as dividend payments or indirectly as increases in the prices of stocks.

In 2000, investment (purchases of physical capital by firms, individuals, and government) was $2.2 trillion, which amounted to 22 percent of GDP. Fifty-seven

THE BRIEFING ROOM   Interest Rates Tend to Move Together

If you read the financial pages of any newspaper, you'll know that there are many interest rates in the economy, not just one. There's an interest rate for short-term bonds, long-term bonds, mortgages, and so on. Look in the newspaper or take a look at the Federal Reserve Bank's daily report on selected interest rates in its H.15 release. (You can find this H.15 release on the Internet at www.bog.frb.fed.us.)

The following exhibit shows nominal interest rates for corporate bonds, 30-year mortgages, and 3-month

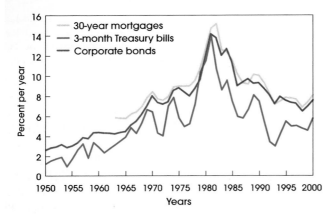

Treasury bills. As you can see, they differ, but they tend to move up and down together. The reason is substitution. If the interest rate on one bond differs from another, savers will tend to shift their funds to the bond with the higher interest rate. This pushes the interest rate on the bond with the higher rate down and the rate of the other bond up.

The differences in interest rates have to do primarily with risk. Risk depends on the bond's maturity (the time until the principal is repaid) and possibility of default. Because they have different maturities, a 30-year bond tends to have a higher interest rate than a 1-year note because the risk associated with price fluctuations is greater for bonds with a longer term to maturity: Changes in market interest rates change bond payments over a longer period of time for the bond and, therefore, have a greater impact on its price. Similarly, government bonds generally have a lower interest rate than corporate bonds with the same maturity. The government is more likely to repay its loans, so government bonds have less risk of default.

Changes in nominal interest rates are often the result of changes in expected inflation. Actual and expected inflation rose throughout the 1960s and 1970s, peaked in the early 1980s, and, except for small increases in the late 1980s, steadily declined through 2000.

Much of the investment in an economy is simply to cover depreciation.

percent of this investment, however, simply covered depreciation (the wearing out of capital during production). The remaining 43 percent was to add new capital to production—net investment. Personal saving was negative in 2000, drawing .1 percent away from net investment, corporate saving (retained earnings) financed 27 percent, and government and foreign saving financed the remaining 74 percent.

The Decision to Invest. Firms' decisions to invest depend on the opportunity cost of the investment. The decision is the same whether the firm uses retained earnings or borrows the funds to make the investment. A firm will invest if the earnings it expects to receive from using the capital exceed the interest it pays to finance the purchase (or the income it would earn from investing retained earnings elsewhere). The cost of an investment is the interest rate a firm pays to borrow the funds, or the interest rate it forgoes when investing those funds elsewhere.

The quantity of investment tends to vary inversely with the real interest rate.

Other things held constant, the interest rate (think opportunity cost of investment) and the quantity of investment demanded are inversely related. For example, suppose a firm is considering building a factory that will provide an 8 percent return on the firm's investment. If the interest rate is 14 percent, the project would not provide a sufficient return to pay the interest on the loan. Even if the firm could finance the investment without borrowing, it could do better lending that

Exhibit 4–3
Demand for Investment

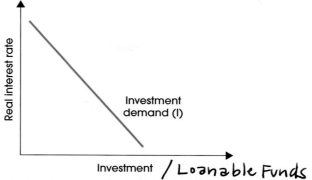

The demand for investment is inversely related to the real interest rate. When the real interest rate declines, the quantity of investment demanded rises.

money to another firm at 14 percent interest. Only when the interest rate falls below 8 percent will it make sense for the firm to build the factory.

As the interest rate falls, more and more investment projects become worthwhile. Let's take a closer look at the relationship between interest rates and investment. (When we use the term interest rate, we are referring to an average of all the many interest rates in the economy. We can do this because interest rates tend to move together. See The Briefing Room, "Interest Rates Tend to Move Together" for a further discussion.)

The interest rate relevant for investment decisions is the real interest rate, which, as you learned in Chapter 1, is the nominal interest rate less inflation. The reason investment decisions depend on the real interest rate is that inflation means that the price of goods is rising. A firm will expect the price of its goods, and therefore its revenue, to rise by the rate of inflation. The concept that is relevant to the firm's investment decision is the quantity of goods (a real value) it will have to produce to repay the loan. Other things equal a firm will be much more willing to borrow at 12 percent if the prices of its goods are rising by 10 percent per year than it would if the prices of its goods are rising by only 2 percent.

The quantity of investment demanded is inversely related to the real interest rate. Exhibit 4–3 shows this relationship. As interest rates rise, the quantity of investment demanded falls, which means that the demand for investment is a downward-sloping curve.

Households

Now let's consider the role of households in the circular flow of the economy. Households supply factors of production to firms and, in return, receive income. They use that income mainly to buy goods and services from firms. Consumption spending (C) is a flow from households to firms. The amount of income households have available to spend on consumption is called **disposable income** ($Y - T$)—income less government taxes plus government transfer payments (for example, welfare, food stamps, and unemployment compensation). Because transfer payments partially offset the effect of taxes on disposable income, we combine the two into one measure called taxes net of transfers (T)—taxes households pay less transfer payments they receive. (In this discussion, we assume transfers are zero and talk about taxes only.)

Executive Summary

- The circular flow model shows how households, firms, government, and foreigners interact in the economy. Although the financial flows are important, it is the change in the flows of goods and services that makes people better or worse off.

- Economists use the production function equation to express firms' production processes. On average, production processes exhibit three attributes:

  1. Output increases as the quantity of inputs increases.
  2. Output increases by the same proportional increase in all inputs combined.
  3. Output increases by ever-smaller amounts as more of only one input is added, holding all other inputs and the production process constant.

The last two attributes are called *constant returns to scale* and *diminishing marginal product*, respectively.

- Technological innovation allows firms to produce more output with the same quantities of inputs.

- Firms purchase capital from other firms by using funds borrowed from households or retained earnings. These expenditures, used to increase capital, are called *investment.*

- Firms invest less when the real interest rate rises and more when the real interest rate falls. That is, quantity of investment demanded is inversely related to the real interest rate.

Consumption tends to be related to disposable income. Therefore, it is often mathematically expressed by the following:

$$C = C_0 + mpc\,(Y - T) \tag{4-2}$$

Consumption function:
$C = C_0 + mpc\,(Y - T)$.

This equation says that households consume some amount (C_0) regardless of their income. In addition, households tend to increase consumption when their disposable income rises. The fraction of an increase in disposable income that households spend is the **marginal propensity to consume** (*mpc*). The *mpc* is a number between zero and one. For example, an *mpc* of .8 means that consumers spend 80 percent of any increase in their disposable income.

Disposable income that is not spent is saved. In terms of the *mpc*, the fraction of each additional dollar of disposable income saved is $1 - mpc$. If the *mpc* is .8, consumers save 20 cents of each dollar rise in disposable income. If the mpc falls to .7, the fraction of additional disposable income saved rises to .30. As disposable income rises, the level of both saving and consumption will rise. (Notice that we are particular in using the word *saving* instead of the word *savings*. The distinction between the two is explained in the Q&A feature.)

Saving by households (both personal saving and saving by households through their ownership of firms) is called **private saving** (S^p)—the difference between disposable income and consumption:

Private saving is the difference between disposable income and consumption.

$$S^p = (Y - T) - C \tag{4-3}$$
$$private\ saving = disposable\ income - consumption$$

Government

Government is another player in the circular flow of the economy. Government collects taxes from households, a portion of which it returns to households in the form of transfer payments. Government also purchases goods and services from firms and

QUESTION	What is the difference between *saving* and *savings*?
ANSWER	The amount of money you save from each paycheck is *saving* (without the "s") while accumulated saving is called *savings* (with the "s").

Saving (without the "s" at the end) is an economic flow concept (just like income, as you learned in Chapter 2), which means that it is measured over a period of time. For example, it makes no sense to say that you are saving $100 unless you specify when, or how frequently, you are saving it. Saying that you are saving $100 each month makes sense. The amount a person has saved (the accumulation of all past saving) is called *savings* (with the "s" at the end) and is an economic stock concept (just like wealth, as you learned in Appendix A of Chapter 2). Stock concepts are measured at a point in time. It does make sense to say that your savings is $100—if that's your total "in the bank" at a particular time.

What is the relationship between savings and saving? Saving each month will increase total accumulated savings. Mathematically, we can state this as ΔSavings =

saving. If you save $1,000 per month (a flow), your savings (a stock) will be $1,000 the first month, $2,000 the second month, and so on. Your savings increases by $1,000 each month.

For some people, the amount they save out of each paycheck today depends on how much savings they want for, say, retirement. If, for example, the price of people's stock holdings suddenly rises, they can reduce their monthly saving and still reach their desired level of savings. If you follow this approach, as the value of your savings rises for reasons other than your monthly contribution to savings, you will choose to reduce your monthly saving. This is exactly what happened in the United States in the late-1990s and early 2000s: As the value of the stock market rose (savings rose), the personal saving rate fell (monthly saving fell).

---

inputs from households. When the government spends more than it collects in taxes, it is running a budget deficit and must borrow the difference in the financial market.

When the government collects more taxes than it spends, it is running a budget surplus and it saves the difference. That saving is represented in the circular flow by the arrow from the government to the financial market. The difference between taxes and government spending is called **government saving** (S^g).

> **Government saving is the difference between taxes and government spending.**

$$S^g = T - G \qquad (4\text{-}4)$$
government saving = taxes − government spending

A budget deficit means negative government saving (also called *dissaving* or *borrowing*), and a budget surplus means positive government saving.

> **Fiscal policy involves varying government saving to offset fluctuations of private saving and thereby counteract fluctuations of output.**

A change in government spending or taxes implemented to affect output in the economy is called fiscal policy. Sometimes government uses fiscal policy to limit fluctuations in output. When the economy threatens to enter a recession, the government can use expansionary fiscal policy (increase spending and/or reduce taxes) to increase expenditures and output. Expansionary fiscal policy increases output by setting in motion a series of increases in total expenditures. Increases in government spending or reductions in taxes increase total expenditures, which lead to greater production and household income. Households spend some of this additional income, increasing total expenditures even more. An example of expansionary fiscal policy is President George W. Bush's bill in 2001 to cut taxes. One of the reasons he gave for cutting taxes was a need to counteract a slowing in the economy.

When output rises too quickly, leading to fears of inflation, the government can implement contractionary fiscal policy (reduce spending and/or increase taxes).

Exhibit 4-4

U.S. Budget Deficits During World War II

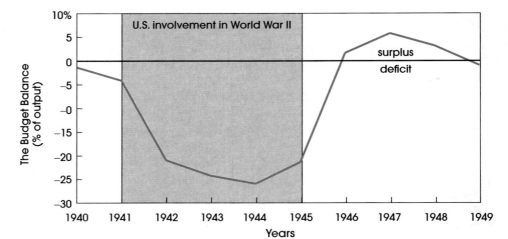

This exhibit shows how budget decisions are not just the result of fiscal policy. In this case, they were the result of entering World War II. Government expenditures rose considerably throughout U.S. participation in the war.

Contractionary fiscal policy has the opposite effect on the size of the circular flow. It reduces total expenditures, income, and output.

A classic example of an attempt at countercyclical fiscal policy is the Kennedy-Johnson tax cut in the early 1960s. When implemented in 1963 it reduced taxes as a percent of GDP by 1.8 percentage points. The tax cut increased the budget deficit and helped stimulate the economy. However, Congress and the President had started discussing a tax cut to stimulate the economy in 1961, when the U.S. economy was in the midst of a recession. By the time the tax cut was actually implemented in 1964, the economy had already almost fully recovered on its own, so the stimulation wasn't needed.

The Kennedy-Johnson tax cut illustrates a significant problem with countercyclical fiscal policy (policy designed to stabilize output in the economy)—it takes time for Congress and the President to formulate, debate, amend, and finally pass spending and tax legislation. Because the time between proposal and implementation is usually quite long, policy makers seldom use countercyclical fiscal policy.

Budget decisions generally are not made to achieve fiscal policy objectives. Instead, they are made for other reasons. For example, in the early to mid-1940s, the U.S. government increased expenditures to finance World War II. As Exhibit 4–4 shows, this led to large budget deficits. These deficits were the result of government's attempt to win the war, not to achieve fiscal policy objectives.

> Fiscal policy is not very useful, because budget decisions are generally not made to achieve fiscal policy objectives.

Global Connections

So far, we've discussed the circular flow model as if an economy did not interact with other economies in the world. From the discussion in Chapter 2, we know that the U.S. economy is very much connected with other economies through trade of goods and services as well as the flow of financial assets. The summary of a country's trade of goods and services with other countries is the **current account balance.** (Technically, the current account balance also includes the difference between income received by foreigners for their holdings of U.S. assets and income received by U.S. residents and firms for their holdings of foreign assets.) When the current account balance is positive (meaning exports exceed imports), we say that there is a current account surplus, and when the current account balance is negative (meaning imports exceed exports), we say there is a current account deficit. A country that runs a current account deficit is buying more goods and services than it is producing.

The current account balance gets most of the press coverage, but there is another global connection that is equally important. That connection is reflected in the capital account balance. When U.S. citizens purchase financial assets such as stocks and bonds from foreign firms, or real assets such as businesses or real estate, those purchases are considered a capital outflow. When foreigners purchase financial or real assets from U.S. firms or individuals, those purchases are considered a capital inflow. The difference between capital inflows and capital outflows is the **capital account balance.**

The capital account balance is the mirror image of the current account balance. To see why, think about what happens when the United States runs a current account deficit. That means that the dollars flowing abroad to purchase imports exceed the dollars flowing back for exports from the United States. Foreigners either keep the remaining U.S. dollars (which is a capital inflow to the United States) or use those dollars to purchase other U.S. assets, such as stocks or bonds (also a capital inflow to the United States). A current account deficit creates a capital account surplus of the same dollar amount. For example, if imports are $8 billion and exports are $6 billion, foreign purchases of U.S. assets must exceed U.S. purchases of foreign assets by $2 billion. The current account has a deficit of $2 billion, which is exactly offset by a capital account surplus of $2 billion. The U.S. is buying $2 billion more goods and services than it is producing, which is financed by net foreign inflows of $2 billion.

Another way to think about the capital account balance is that it represents foreign saving. The purchase of an asset is a form of saving. Therefore, a capital account surplus represents a net inflow of foreign saving, and a capital account deficit represents a net outflow of foreign saving. We, therefore, define **foreign saving** (S^f) as the flow of funds into an economy less the flow of funds out of an economy. Because the capital account balance and current account balance are mirror images of each other, foreign saving can be measured with either account:

> Foreign saving is the capital account balance. It also equals the negative of the current account balance.

$$S^f = capital\ account\ balance = (-)\ current\ account\ balance \qquad (4\text{-}5)$$

THE CIRCULAR FLOW, AS/AD MODEL AND EQUILIBRIUM IN THE ECONOMY

So far, using the circular flow model, we've broadly described what firms, households, and government do and how they interact with the international economy. Interactions among all these players take place in a market setting, which means that each is subject to market forces. For example, if households decide to save more, firms in the economy will be affected, because the supply of saving available for investment will have risen. If government decides to spend more, it will have to either increase taxes, leaving households with less disposable income, or increase its borrowing, reducing the supply of saving available to firms for investment. It is this interaction between the players in the economy that you need to picture when thinking of the paradox we posed at the beginning of the chapter: "Why was saving the cause of Japan's high growth in one decade and the reason for its slow growth in another decade?"

The interactions among players in the various markets are complicated. To simplify them, economists use a framework that combines the various forces into a model. If we can specify the equilibrium of that model, we know the direction the market forces are pushing the economy. The circular flow model gives us a basic framework for defining equilibrium in the economy.

Equilibrium in the circular flow model is usually incorporated into economic textbooks with the aggregate supply/aggregate demand (AS/AD) model—a formal representation of production and expenditures and how they are influenced by the price level. The aggregate supply (AS) curve represents the production side of the economy, where firms buy inputs from households and transform those inputs (through the production process) into output. The aggregate demand (AD) curve represents the expenditures side of the economy, where households, firms, government, and foreigners purchase goods and services from firms.

Because most of you may already be familiar with this model from your introductory economics class, the following presentation will be brief. We provide a more in-depth explanation of the model in a later chapter.

Aggregate demand is the sum of household consumption expenditures (C), firms' investment expenditures (I), government spending (G), and net exports ($X - M$). The aggregate demand (AD) curve shows an inverse relationship between the price level and quantity of real output demanded. As the price level falls, the quantity of real output demanded tends to rise. Aggregate demand is represented by a downward-sloping curve, as Exhibit 4–5(a) shows.

The position of the AD curve is determined by the levels of C, I, G, and $X - M$ for a given price level. If any of these components of aggregate demand rise without a change in the price level, the AD curve shifts right (for example, from AD_0 to AD_1 in *panel a* of Exhibit 4–5). If any of them fall, the AD curve shifts left (for example, from AD_1 to AD_0). Because monetary and fiscal policies affect the components of aggregate demand, they affect the position of the AD curve. Expansionary monetary and fiscal policies shift the AD curve to the right. Contractionary monetary and fiscal policies shift the AD curve to the left.

Aggregate supply is the output produced in the economy (Y) at various price levels. The aggregate supply (AS) curve shows how the price level and output respond to changes in aggregate demand. The shape of the AS curve distinguishes the long run from the short run. In the short run, the price level tends to be fixed and the short-run AS curve is represented by a horizontal curve at a fixed price level, as Exhibit 4–5(b) shows. This assumes that firms can increase production without increasing unit costs, and firms supply all that is demanded at the given price level. In the short run, output is determined by the components of aggregate demand. Increases in aggregate demand, therefore, lead to increases in output and no change in the price level.

In the long run, economists assume that firms produce at their sustainable capacity. Therefore, in the long run, aggregate supply is determined by potential output. Recall from Chapter 1 that potential output is the amount of goods and services an economy can sustainably produce with existing resources and technology. Because output is determined by available inputs and technology, changes in aggregate demand will lead only to price changes. This is shown graphically in Exhibit 4–5(b) by a vertical long-run AS curve at potential output. Increases in aggregate demand lead only to increases in the price level; decreases in aggregate demand lead only to decreases in the price level.

Aggregate demand: the sum of household consumption expenditures, firms' investment expenditures, government spending, and net exports at various price levels.

The AS curve shows how the price level and output respond to changes in aggregate demand.

The short-run AS curve is initially assumed to be horizontal. The long-run AS curve is assumed to be vertical at potential output.

Exhibit 4-5

The Aggregate Supply/Aggregate Demand Model

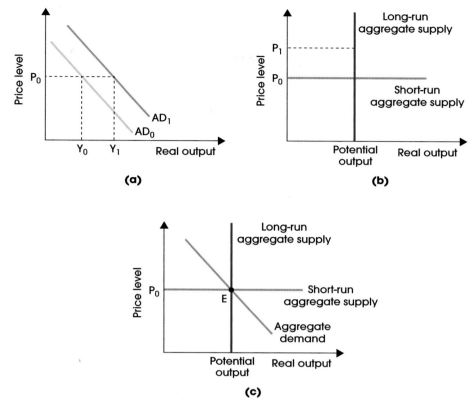

(a)

(b)

(c)

In the aggregate supply/aggregate demand model, the relationship between total expenditures and the price level is represented by a downward-sloping aggregate demand curve, as *panel a* shows. The relationship between total output and the price level is represented by two curves, as *panel b* shows. In the short run, the relationship is represented by a horizontal aggregate supply curve; in the long run, it is represented by a vertical aggregate supply curve. Equilibrium occurs where aggregate quantity demanded is equal to aggregate quantity supplied. Point *E* in *panel c* shows an economy in both short- and long-run equilibrium.

In equilibrium, aggregate quantity supplied equals aggregate quantity demanded. (Alternatively expressed, in equilibrium, the sum of all three forms of savings equal investment.)

Equilibrium occurs where the AS and AD curves intersect, as point *E* in Exhibit 4–5(c) shows, or when

$$aggregate\ quantity\ supplied = aggregate\ quantity\ demanded \qquad (4\text{-}6)$$
$$Y = C + I + G + (X - M).[1]$$

Another way to describe this same equilibrium is with saving and investment:

$$saving = investment \qquad (4\text{-}7)$$
$$S^p + S^g + S^f = I$$

To see how, in equilibrium, saving equals investment, first rewrite Equation 4-6 so that only investment (*I*) is on the right-hand side:

$$Y - C - G - (X - M) = I \qquad (4\text{-}8)$$

[1] *Y* denotes both income and aggregate supply, because aggregate supply creates an equal value of income.

Next, add and subtract taxes from the left-hand side (which we can do because $T - T$ is zero and you can add zero without changing the equation) and rearrange terms:

$$(Y - T - C) + (T - G) + (-)\, (X - M) = I \qquad (4\text{-}9)$$

$$\underbrace{(Y - T - C)}_{\substack{\text{private} \\ \text{saving}}} + \underbrace{(T - G)}_{\substack{\text{government} \\ \text{saving}}} + \underbrace{(-)\,(X - M)}_{\substack{\text{foreign} \\ \text{saving}}} = Investment$$

The first group of terms on the left-hand side, $(Y - T - C)$, is private saving (S^p). The second group is government saving (S^g). The last term is the capital account balance, or foreign saving, (S^f). That is, $S^p + S^g + S^f = I$, or saving = investment.

Let's go through a numerical example to see what these relationships are telling us. We begin by assuming that we are initially in equilibrium (saving equals investment). Now suppose that the government budget deficit rises by $200. This means that the government is borrowing an additional $200 from the financial market. If the economy is to remain in equilibrium (in which saving equals investment), either firms' investment will have to fall by $200 or some combination of private and foreign saving will have to rise by $200. The exact adjustment that takes place to keep the economy in equilibrium depends on many factors. An increase in government saving, conversely, will result in increased investment expenditures by firms, or decreased private and foreign saving.

Many adjustment combinations that maintain the savings–investment equality are possible. Exhibit 4–6 shows the relationship between investment expenditures, private and government saving (shown together as national saving) and foreign saving from 1980 to 2000. Notice that foreign saving makes up the difference between investment and national saving. This is just what we would expect from Equation 4-8.

Exhibit 4–6

National Saving, Domestic Investment, and Foreign Saving

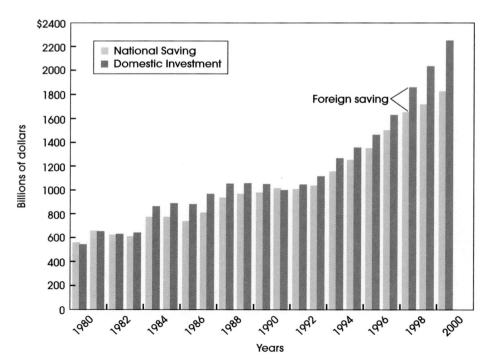

Domestic investment, national saving, and foreign saving are all related. For most years since 1980, the difference between domestic investment and the sum of government and private saving has been met by foreign saving. Source: *Economic Report of the President,* 2001, Table B–32.

Table 4-1

Saving and Investment in the United States

	National Saving					
I Year	**II** Private Saving +	**III** Government Saving +	**IV** Foreign Saving =	**V** Gross Domestic Investment –	**VI** Depreciation =	**VII** Net Investment
1994	$1199.3	–$43.4	$108.3	$1,264.2^a	$796.0	$468.2
2000	1297.1	528.0	427.9	2,253^a	1,257.1	995.9

SOURCE: Bureau of Economic Analysis **www.bea.doc.gov**

^{a}Investment figures exclude the statistical discrepancy of $58.5 billion in 1994 and –$83.7 billion in 2000.

In the late 1990s and 2000, government saving and foreign saving were important components of total saving and offset low personal saving.

Table 4–1 shows the detail for two of those years: 1994 and 2000. In 1994, federal, state, and local governments combined were running a $43.4 billion deficit, meaning that government was borrowing (dissaving) $43.4 billion. Private saving was $1,199.3 billion. The sum of the two, national saving, was $1,155.9 billion, which was lower than domestic investment, $1,264.2 billion, in 1994. The shortfall between national saving and investment, $108.3 billion was funded by foreign saving. Note that the current account balance was –$108.3 billion, and net capital inflow, or foreign saving, was $108.3 billion.

In 2000, U.S. government saving (federal, state, and local) was +$528 billion, meaning it was running a budget surplus. With an additional private saving of $1,297.1 billion, national saving totaled $1,825.1 billion. Investment was $2,253 billion. The difference between investment and national saving was $427.9 billion, the level of foreign saving. Saving and investment are kept equal through the interactions of foreigners, firms, households, and government in the market. This example shows how foreign saving financed much of the increase in U.S. purchases of capital from 1994 to 2000.

As we discussed above, much investment replaces capital that wears out in the process of production. The sixth column in Table 4–1 shows depreciation in each year, and the final column shows net investment (gross investment minus depreciation), which is the net addition to capital stock made in that year. Whereas gross domestic investment increased by $988.8 billion from 1994 to 2000, net domestic investment increased by a lesser $527.7 billion. It is net investment that drives economic growth.

Executive Summary

- Households earn income and pay taxes. The marginal propensity to consume (*mpc*) represents the fraction of an increase in disposable income that is spent. Disposable income less consumption is private saving (S^p).

- Government collects taxes and spends. Taxes, net of transfers, less government spending is government saving (S^g).

- Foreign saving (S^f) is flows of funds into an economy less flows of funds out of an economy. It is equal to the capital account balance, which is the mirror image of the current account balance.

- In equilibrium, aggregate quantity supplied equals aggregate quantity demanded. Two ways of saying this are:

  1. $Y = C + I + G + (X - M)$ (aggregate quantity supplied = aggregate quantity demanded)
  2. $S^p + S^g + S^f = I$ (saving = investment).

LONG-RUN VERSUS SHORT-RUN EQUILIBRIUM

The saving–investment (AS/AD equilibrium) holds for both the short run and the long run. However, the macroeconomy behaves differently in the two cases because the forces operating in the short run and long run differ. As a result, policies that can have a positive effect on the economy in the short run sometimes have a negative effect on the economy in the long run; the reverse can also be true. Understanding these divergent effects is key to answering the question posed at the beginning of the chapter about the effect of high Japanese saving on Japan's economy. Because policy will have different effects in the short and long run, it is important to understand the distinction between the two.

The key distinction between economists' long-run and short-run frameworks is the assumed wage and price responses to changes in demand. The short-run framework says that wages and prices tend to be institutionally fixed by custom, contract, and common business practice. When demand shifts, wages and prices, on average, tend not to move quickly to equilibrate demand and supply. Most goods markets in the United States are oligopolistic—comprised of a few major firms that set prices and make decisions based on each other's reactions. Oligopolistic firms tend not to adjust prices quickly when demand for their product changes. In labor markets, wages are generally set by firms or labor union negotiations. Because worker motivation is potentially tied to wages, firms tend to be hesitant to cut wages. The general assumption economists make is that wages are sticky in the short run. So, both wages and prices are assumed to be relatively stable in the short run.

> In the short-run framework, wages and prices are fixed. In the long-run framework, they are flexible.

In economists' long-run framework, wages and prices are assumed not to be constrained by institutions and instead move freely. This distinction between how prices and wages behave means that external changes in the economy, such as expansionary monetary and fiscal policy, result in different outcomes in the short run and the long run.

In the Short Run, Demand Rules

In the short run, production changes in response to changes in aggregate expenditures—the sum of consumption, investment, government spending, and net exports. Another way to think of this statement is that *in the short run, demand rules*—demand is the biggest factor in determining the level of equilibrium output. This is sometimes called **Hansen's Law**—in the short run, demand creates its own supply.

> In the short run, demand rules. (Hansen's Law)

Exhibit 4–7 shows the determination of equilibrium in the short run. Shifts in aggregate demand determine the level of output. If any one component of aggregate demand—say, government spending or investment expenditures—rises, then output also rises. If consumers become optimistic about their future income prospects and spend more, output will rise. Finally, if foreign economies expand, exports will rise, and output in the United States will rise. Through all this, aggregate quantity supplied (production) increases to accommodate increased aggregate demand. Exhibit 4–7 shows an increase in aggregate demand from AD_0 to AD_1 that is met with an increase in production from Y_0 to Y_1 with no change in the price level.

In the Long Run, Supply Rules

Now let's consider what happens in the long-run framework, in which prices move to bring about equilibrium. *In the long run, supply rules.* That means that, in the

Exhibit 4-7

**The AS/AD Model
in the Short Run**

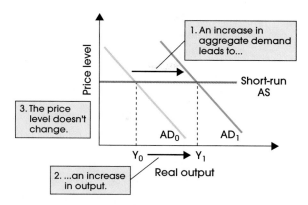

In the short run, firms change production to meet changes in aggregate expenditures at the given price level. Therefore, an increase in aggregate demand (from AD_0 to AD_1) would increase output from Y_0 to Y_1.

long run, the level of potential output is determined by the quantities of labor, capital, and technology operating through the production function. Only those factors that change labor, capital, and technology will affect potential output.

In the long run, we focus on potential output, which, by definition, is determined by the production function. Because potential output is not determined by either prices or aggregate demand, and, in the long run, firms produce at potential, supply is not affected by either prices or aggregate demand. This is sometimes called **Say's Law**—in the long run, supply creates its own demand. The argument is as follows: People work and produce goods because they want to purchase goods. So, the fact that people supply goods means there is a demand for an equal value of goods. That is, aggregate demand is determined by aggregate supply.

Exhibit 4–8 shows the determination of equilibrium in the long run. The supply of labor, quantity of capital, and state of technology determine potential output, and, in the long run, output equals that potential, independent of the quantity of output demanded. An increase in aggregate demand leads only to an increase in the price level because the economy cannot sustainably produce any more goods and services.

In the long run, supply rules. (Say's Law)

Exhibit 4-8

**The AS/AD Model
in the Long Run**

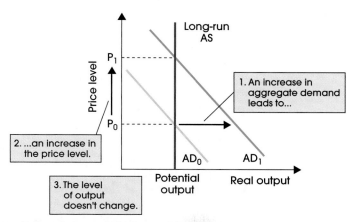

In the long run, changes in aggregate demand lead to changes in only the price level. For example, an increase in aggregate demand from AD_0 to AD_1 would lead to an increase in the price level from P_0 to P_1, with no change in real output.

As Exhibit 4–8 shows, an increase in aggregate demand from AD_0 to AD_1 leads to an increase in the price level from P_0 to P_1, with no change in real output.

Because total output is determined by potential output only, an increase in any component of aggregate demand must mean that some other component of aggregate demand must have fallen. For example, an increase in government expenditures must be offset by a decrease in expenditures by households, firms, or foreigners, or some combination thereof.

What does this say about policy options? Increasing demand will not help increase output in the long run. In the long-run, increased saving, because it leads to higher potential output, increases output—the opposite of what the short-run framework predicts. Only policies that increase capital, labor, or technology will increase output. In the long run, policies that increase saving—and, through saving, increase investment—increase income. An example of such a policy is the U.S. tax system, which provides incentives for long-term saving by allowing workers to subtract contributions to individual retirement accounts (IRAs) and 401(k)s from their taxable income.

The Equality of Saving and Investment

Let's now translate the propositions *in the short run, demand rules* and *in the long run, supply rules* into a saving–investment framework. The saving–investment framework helps us understand policy debates about the possible effect of increased government spending on the economy. It also explains the paradox about why saving can sometimes reduce output, and, at other times, increase output.

The equivalent to the long-run proposition that "Supply rules" is "Saving rules." In the long run, saving determines investment. The equivalent to the short-run proposition that "Demand rules" is "Investment rules." In the short run, investment determines saving. There's nothing magic about these relationships; they follow from the definitions of the long run and the short run.

Let's consider the short run first. When investment rises, output rises to meet the demand for new capital. As output rises, households' income rises. (Remember, households own all the factors of production.) Households spend a portion of that increase in income and save the rest. In the short run, an increase in investment expenditures leads to an increase in the level of saving.

A change in saving can affect the short-run equilibrium, but it does so through its effect on consumption. If households save a higher portion of their income, they are simultaneously choosing to spend a smaller portion. For government to save more, it must either reduce expenditures or raise taxes. Either way, total expenditures will fall. Finally, if foreign saving (represented by the capital account) rises, then net exports (represented by the current account) must fall, which also reduces total expenditures.

> In the short run, increased saving decreases output. In the long run, increased saving increases output.

Consumption, government expenditures, and net exports are all components of aggregate demand. In all three cases, the rise in saving—whether private, public, or foreign—is associated with a fall in some component of aggregate demand and a subsequent reduction in output. (Remember: In the short run, demand rules.) This is called the **paradox of thrift**—an increase in saving reduces output in the short run.

Now let's consider the relation between saving and investment in the long-run framework, where saving rules. In the long-run framework, changes in saving lead to equivalent changes in investment expenditures. If saving increases, there will be more saving available for firms to use for investment expenditures. More investment

THE BRIEFING ROOM   Blurring the Line Between Consumption and Investment

In the text our discussion of equilibrium is fairly tidy. For example, if consumers increase consumption, they decrease saving. The real world is not so neat and tidy. Not all consumption is the same. Some consumption (as measured by official government statistics) looks an awful lot like investment.

Take school, for instance. Is it a consumption good or an investment good? The national income accounts include most schooling as consumption, but it is also an *investment* in your future to the degree that it increases your skills, which enable you to produce (human capital). When activities are simultaneously investment and consumption, as is school, a society could have zero measured saving and still be growing significantly due to investment.

The line is also blurred for firms. Before 1998, the U.S. government did not count firms' expenditures on computer software as investment. Instead, it treated those expenditures the same as expenditures on paper clips. In 1998, the government changed its definition of investment to include computer software. That change substantially boosted the official estimates of investment.

The bottom line is that when economists evaluate the long-run impact of increases in consumption and investment, they must be aware of the definitional problems and do more than just look at the official numbers.

means more capital, and more capital, through the production function, means higher output. So, in the long run, higher saving leads to higher output.

Considering the different effects that changes in saving have on equilibrium output will cement in your mind the difference between the long run and the short run. In the short run, increases in saving lead to *decreases* in output, while, in the long run, increases in saving lead to *increases* in output. This means that policy makers with a short-term view tend to disregard the long-term effects of policies that reduce saving. Likewise, policy makers with a long-term view tend to disregard the effects of increased saving on output in the short run.

If you have a short-run view and want to increase output, promote policies targeted at expanding aggregate demand. Encourage consumption, increase government spending, and promote exports. If you have a long-run view and want to increase output, promote policies that contain supply incentives. Reduce personal income taxes to increase the benefits of working so that more people join the labor force. Discourage consumption (encourage saving) to make more funds available for investment. Encourage technological innovation. (See The Briefing Room, "Blurring the Line between Consumption and Investment," for an addendum to these policy precepts.)

Crowding Out

The debate about whether saving creates investment or investment creates saving plays an important role in the policy debates about the effects of government deficits on the economy. Economists emphasizing a long-run view (saving determines investment) argue that expansionary fiscal policy will not lead to higher output because the resulting budget deficits must be financed either by selling bonds or by replacing lost tax revenue. Specifically, government will have to borrow from the public an amount equal to the increase in government spending. Given a fixed saving pool, government borrowing will reduce the saving available for private investment. Therefore, the increase in government borrowing will decrease private investment spending.

Government spending tends to crowd out private spending.

The offset of private investment when government spending rises is called **crowding out.** In the long-run framework, crowding out is a necessary outcome because, in that framework, output is fixed at potential output. An increase in government expenditures must be accompanied by a decrease in private investment expenditures (otherwise, output would rise). This crowding out occurs tautologically (is true by definition), because output is fixed at potential output.

In the short-run framework, where investment determines saving, however, crowding out is not a tautological outcome. Saving and output are not assumed to be fixed by potential output; both are free to fluctuate. Given these assumptions, increased spending can expand output, which allows the level of saving to rise to meet the borrowing needs of the government. The saving available for investment does not necessarily fall. If the increased government spending leads to sufficiently higher output, and hence income, the level of saving can rise to finance the same amount of private investment as before. So, whereas in the long-run framework, crowding out is tautological, in the short-run framework, it is not. In the short run, there may be no crowding out.

Some discussions of crowding out are framed in terms of shares of output, where shares of output are calculated as government expenditures or private expenditures (the sum of consumption, investment, and net exports by businesses and households) as a percent of total output. This framework also makes crowding out tautological. An increase in the share of output going to government expenditures means that the shares of other expenditures must decrease. That's a tautology whether you're in the short run or the long run. For example, if the government share of output rises from 28 percent to 30 percent, the non-government share must fall from 72 percent to 70 percent. Because the total share must equal one, if the share of government spending rises, some combination of the other shares must fall.

Exhibit 4–9 shows that, in the U.S. economy, these shares have changed significantly over time. During U.S. involvement in World War II (1941–1945) and the Korean War (1950–1953), U.S. government spending rose as a share of output, while private spending fell. In the late 1960s, government spending gradually rose and hovered over 20 percent throughout the 1970s. In the 1990s, as Congress and

In the short-run framework, crowding out may occur. In the long-run framework, crowding out must occur.

If crowding out is discussed in terms of shares of output, government spending must crowd out private expenditures.

Exhibit 4–9

Share of Aggregate Spending in a Growing Economy

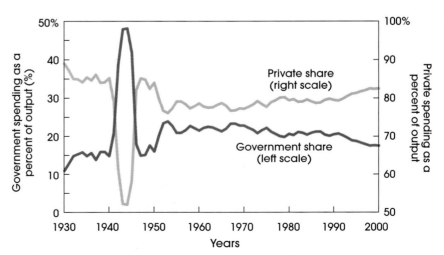

A rise in the share of one sector's spending must be offset by a combined decline in the shares of other sectors' spending. During World War II (1941-1945), U.S. government spending grew to nearly 50 percent of total output but returned to about 15 percent after the war. Private spending fell to close to 50 percent during United States' involvement in World War II. In the 1970s, government's share hovered around 20 percent of output, while, in the 1990s and in 2000, it fell to 17.5 percent.

the President worked to eliminate the budget deficit, the share of government spending fell and the share of private spending rose.

Crowding out in terms of relative shares of output is fundamentally different from crowding out in terms of absolute levels of spending. This difference has sometimes confused policy makers and economists. Crowding out in terms of relative shares, like the long-run crowding out when output is fixed by potential, is tautological. It follows, by definition, that total expenditures equal total output; an increase in one share will be offset by decreases in others, because the two lines in Exhibit 4–9 must sum to 100 percent.

The point to remember is that what happens to shares tells us little about what happens to absolute levels of spending. Say the government runs a deficit and spends more, increasing its share of total output. Will that increase reduce the level of spending by households, firms, or foreigners? The answer is unclear. Specifically, if output rises, the absolute level of investment or other private expenditures could increase, even as its share decreases. Whether this occurs depends on how much output increases.

One final point: Even if government spending reduces private investment, whether the result is desirable depends on the benefits of the government spending compared with the benefits of the private investment. The bottom line is that, when looking at the effects of crowding out, it is important to distinguish between the short run and the long run, and to distinguish between absolute levels of spending and relative shares of spending.

> Even if government spending reduces private investment, the results may or may not be desirable.

Executive Summary

- In the short run, changes in aggregate demand affect output; in the long run, they only affect the price level.

- In the long run, only changes in labor, capital, and technology affect the level of output.

- In the short run, an increase in saving causes output to fall. In the long run, an increase in saving causes output to rise.

- In the long-run, crowding out in terms of shares is tautological; it must occur. Crowding out in the short-run framework may or may not occur, depending on what happens to income.

POLICY PERSPECTIVE: CHOOSING BETWEEN THE SHORT-RUN AND LONG-RUN FRAMEWORKS

Whether to use a long-run or a short-run model largely depends on where the economy is thought to be relative to its long-run potential. If it is thought to be at potential, then the long-run framework is appropriate, because, by definition, the economy cannot sustain growth beyond potential. If it is thought to be below potential, then, according to the short-run framework, some force other than potential output is keeping the economy from expanding. Policy can be designed to expand output by countering that force.

Consider the late 1990s. The U.S. economy had been growing steadily from 1992 through 1998 without a recession. Beginning in late 1998 through early 2000, growth picked up significantly. It was not clear where the economy was relative to potential. Inflation was relatively low, suggesting that the short-run framework was appropriate for policy decisions. But if the economy were at or above potential, the long-run framework was appropriate and inflationary pressures could be expected to increase, unless aggregate demand fell. In 2001, it became clear that the economy was slowing, and policy makers became more concerned about recession than inflation. The short-run became the operative framework, and policy makers focused on how to stimulate output.

The policy problem is made all the more complicated by the possibility that the short run affects the long run. The conventional view (shared by one of your authors) is that the long run serves as an anchor for the short run, and the short run does not significantly influence the long run. Currently, the majority of economists probably agree with this position.

According to this view, in the short run, changes in aggregate demand can affect output either by pushing it above, or keeping it below, long-run potential. Output, however, always returns to its long-run potential, which is determined by supply factors, not demand factors. The short-run path of output over time is a deviation from that long-run path.

Path dependency means that what happens in one period affects what happens in later periods, so the economy can be analyzed only in an historical context.

An unconventional view (held by your other author) is that the long run is determined, in part (sometimes a significant part), by what happens in the short run through a process that is sometimes called **hysteresis**—the proposition that an economy's long-run equilibrium is path dependent. **Path dependency** means that what happens in one period affects what happens in later periods, so that the economy can be analyzed only within an historical context. In this view, when the economy expands in the short run, people create new opportunities for production and exchange. As markets grow and people learn to produce better through experience, potential output rises. The long run is not a fixed anchor, and trend growth is determined after the fact, not before.

Modeling such path dependency is extraordinarily complicated and seldom has definitive results. So, if it is true that the short run affects the long run, we cannot say much, formally, about the long run. Joan Robinson's quote at the beginning of this chapter, "In the long run, we are simply in another short run" (which was a modification of Keynes' famous quip, "In the long run, we're all dead"), captures this unconventional view. It was a view that was central to Keynesian thinking when Keynesian economics was in vogue. Which of these two views is right? The empirical evidence is vague, and arguments can be made for both sides.

Because most economists are conventional, in this text we present the conventional view, allowing our unconventional half a few comments here and there. But we will note that what's conventional, and what's unconventional, changes over time. What is considered an unconventional view now used to be the conventional view in the 1960s and 1970s.

Let's now return to the question with which we began the chapter: Why did economists believe high saving led Japan to high growth in one decade and low growth in another? The answer rests, in large part, on one's perspective. Taking a long-run perspective, a high saving rate will contribute to more capital and higher potential output. The Japanese have seen this happen. Their high saving rate over the past four decades helped them grow into one of the leading economies of the world.

Taking a short-run perspective, a high saving rate that's not accompanied by a high investment rate lowers expenditures, which lowers aggregate demand and output. Although the exact causes of Japan's economic slump in the late 1990s are complicated, almost everyone agrees that one of the problems was insufficient aggregate demand. Saving remained high, but investment was low. If the government had done more to boost aggregate demand, the economy would probably have expanded more than it did.

Japan took a two-pronged approach to solving its economic problems. It increased government spending and reduced interest rates to near zero to boost aggregate demand. It also reformed its financial sector, improving how it channels saving into investment. Whether these reforms were sufficient remains to be seen, but both are the type of policy proposals that one would expect from the analysis given in this chapter.

CONCLUSION

In this chapter, you learned how the sectors of the economy fit together in the circular flow model and about the general frameworks for thinking about the economy in the short run and the long run. In the short run, aggregate demand is key. In the long run, aggregate supply is key. You also learned that policy can have different, sometimes opposing, effects on the economy in the short run and the long run. Fiscal policy that stimulates the economy in the short run may lead to crowding out and lower output in the long run.

The long-run and short-run frameworks do not always lead to conflicting policy recommendations. Consider the U.S. economy at the end of the 1990s. Income growth was strong, unemployment was below what many economists thought was sustainable, and a surge in tax revenues had pushed the government budget into surplus for the first time in 30 years. Given these conditions, policy makers became concerned that the economy was overheating and inflation would soon increase. In such a situation, the appropriate short-run policy was to reduce aggregate demand by raising taxes or cutting government spending. This would have slowed the economy and lessened inflationary pressures. The appropriate long-run fiscal policy would have been to save the budget surplus, allowing more savings to flow into investment, thereby stimulating growth. So, both the short-run and the long-run frameworks called for increasing the budget surplus.

Is that what government did? The answer is no. Both parties bent over backward figuring out ways to spend the surplus—Republicans through tax cuts, and Democrats through new spending programs. So much for economists guiding policy.

> Policy makers do not always follow economists' advice, even when both the short-run and long-run models lead to the same policy recommendation.

KEY POINTS

- The circular flow model shows how firms, households, the government, and foreigners interact in the economy.
- Firms use labor, capital, and technology to produce goods and services.
- A basic production function is $Y = F(K, L)$. A production function that includes technology is sometimes written as $Y = A \cdot F(K, L)$.
- Production processes exhibit three attributes: (1) output increases as the quantity of inputs increases, (2) output increases by the same proportional

increase in all inputs combined, and (3) output increases by ever-smaller amounts as more of only one input is added—holding all other inputs and the production process constant.
- Households use income to pay taxes, consume, and save.
- Government saving is taxes net of transfers less government spending.
- The capital account balance represents foreign saving. It is the mirror image of the current account balance: $-(X - M)$.

- Equilibrium occurs when aggregate quantity supplied equals aggregate quantity demanded.
- An equivalent statement of equilibrium is that it occurs when saving equals investment.
- In the short run, prices do not move much. Instead, aggregate quantity supplied adjusts to meet aggregate quantity demanded.
- In the long run, prices are flexible, and movements in aggregate demand do not affect real output—only the price level.
- In the short run, an increase in saving causes output to fall. This is called the *paradox of thrift*.

- In the long run, an increase in saving causes output to rise.
- In the long-run framework, crowding out is tautological; it must occur. In the short-run framework, it may or may not occur, depending on what happens to income.
- Crowding out of expenditures, stated in terms of shares of output, is always tautological, because, by definition, total expenditures equal total output.

KEY TERMS

aggregate demand 110
aggregate supply 110
capital 101
capital account balance 109
constant returns to scale 102
crowding out 117
current account balance 108
diminishing marginal product 102
disposable income 105
endogenous 103

exogenous 103
factor market 99
financial market 99
foreign saving 109
goods market 99
government saving 107
Hansen's Law 114
hysteresis 120
labor 101
marginal product 102

marginal propensity to consume (mpc) 106
paradox of thrift 116
path dependency 120
private saving 106
production function 100
Say's Law 115
technology 101

QUESTIONS FOR THOUGHT AND REVIEW

1. Explain how a production function can have both diminishing marginal product and constant returns to scale.
2. Describe the production process for a job you have had (lawn mowing, babysitting, retail sales). Does your example fit the three attributes of the production function described in this chapter?
3. According to the circular flow model, who owns the factors of production? What does the owner receive in return for their use?
4. Describe an example of a recent technological innovation. How has this innovation led to more output?
5. Explain why the demand for investment is inversely related to the real interest rate.
6. What are the three things that households do with their income?
7. When the government spends more than it collects in taxes (runs a budget deficit), how does it pay for that spending?

8. When the government collects more tax revenue than it spends (runs a budget surplus), what happens to that extra revenue?
9. What is contractionary fiscal policy and when is it used? Describe the current economic situation. Does it call for expansionary or contractionary fiscal policy?
10. Explain why a current account deficit implies a net inflow of foreign saving, and why a current account surplus implies a net outflow of saving to foreign countries.
11. Suppose a group of Japanese citizens buys controlling interest in a U.S. corporation. From the perspective of the United States, is this transaction a capital inflow or outflow? How about from Japan's perspective?
12. What part of the economy does the aggregate supply curve describe? What part of the economy does the aggregate demand curve describe?
13. What assumption underlies the shapes of the short-run and long-run aggregate supply curves?

14. From a policy perspective, why is it important to distinguish between the long run and the short run?
15. Why according to the conventional view do changes in aggregate demand affect output in the short run but not in the long run?
16. How do changes in saving affect output in the short run? The long run?
17. What is *crowding out?*
18. What has happened to government's share of spending over the past 5 years? What does this mean about the private-sector spending share?
19. Does an increase in government spending necessarily crowd out private investment?

PROBLEMS AND EXERCISES

1. Suppose that households earn $1,000 in income, purchase $500 of consumption goods (half of which are imports), and pay $100 in taxes. Firms produce $450 worth of consumption goods ($250 is sold to domestic consumers and the remainder is exported). Government spending is $200. Calculate the amount available for firms to borrow for investment expenditures.
2. Now suppose that households earn $1,000 in income, purchase $500 of consumption goods, and pay $100 in taxes. Imports are $50 and investment expenditures are $400. Government spending is $50. How much are exports? What is the capital account balance?
3. Assume that private saving is held fixed. What would happen to investment expenditures in each of the following cases?
   a. The government budget balance falls and the current account balance rises.
   b. The government budget balance rises and the current account balance rises.
   c. The government budget balance rises and the current account balance falls.
   d. The government budget balance falls and the current account balance falls.
4. Suppose the economy is initially in equilibrium, with private saving of $20 billion, government saving of −$20 billion, and foreign saving of $10 billion. Assuming that investment expenditures remain unchanged, what possible adjustments could take place if the government suddenly started running a $5 billion budget surplus?
5. Look up the Congressional Budget Office's forecasts at www.cbo.gov (click on "Current Economic Projection" under Data Highlights). Calculate the real interest rate implied by their forecasts of short-term interest rates (3-month Treasury bill) and inflation (the CPI) for the next 5 years. Does the Congressional Budget Office expect real interest rates to rise or fall over the next 5 years? What do you expect to happen to investment expenditures?
6. Use the AS/AD model to illustrate what would happen to real output and the price level in the short and long run if the government used expansionary fiscal policy.

5

There has been a lot of progress during my lifetime, but I'm afraid it's leading in the wrong direction.

—*Ogden Nash*

The Neoclassical Growth Model

After reading this chapter you should be able to:

1. Briefly summarize the history of growth
2. List three types of policies economists suggest for promoting growth
3. Define steady-state equilibrium in the Solow growth model
4. Summarize the implications of the Solow growth model
5. Explain the effect of changes in saving rate, population growth, depreciation and technology in the Solow growth model
6. Describe the policy implications of the Solow growth model

Imagine two countries: Country A and Country B. On average, individuals in both countries earn $2,500 per year and their income has been growing by 1.5 percent per year. Each country has a choice:

1. Take a year off from work and have a year-long party. Resume work at the end of the year and continue to enjoy a 1.5 percent annual increase in income per person for years to come.
2. Spend that year investing in things that increase productivity, such as clearing land, building factories, and improving machinery, so that income per person can rise to 2.5 percent per year. In exchange, that country must give up the year-long party.

Annual growth of 1.5 percent seems reasonable, and the 1-percentage-point increase will add only $25 to income per person the first year. So the best choice is not obvious. Let's say that Country A chooses the party while Country B opts for the 2.5 percent growth. Now, let's turn the clock ahead 100 years. Country B's income per person is about $30,000, while Country A's is only $11,000. As you can see, a small difference in rates of growth over a long time period can make a big difference in a country's income.

The issue is not that hypothetical. For example, France and Argentina had roughly equal income per person in 1900, but over the next 100 years economic growth per person (percent change in real income per person) was about 2.2 percent per year in France and about 1.1 percent per year in

Argentina. Today, income per person in France is $24,000, compared with only $8,000 in Argentina. The point: What may appear to be small annual differences in growth rates compound and, over many years, lead to large differences in the levels of income per person. So, growth matters, and it matters in a big way.

Given the importance of growth, it isn't surprising that the questions, "What makes economies grow?" and "What policies will make our economies grow faster?" are central questions in economics.

A VERY BRIEF HISTORY OF GROWTH

Looking over millennia, output has increased over time. The growth rate of income increased in the early 1800s.

As you can tell from the discussion so far, some economies grow faster than others. But does economic growth vary over time? The answer is yes, definitely. Exhibit 5–1 shows how the world's income per person has changed over the past 2,000 years. Economic growth per person is the rate of change in income per person over time; the slope of the line in Exhibit 5–1 depicts average world economic growth per person. As you can see, for the first 1,500 years depicted, the world's economic growth was nearly stagnant. Starting around year 1500, at the same time market activity increased, economic growth rose to about 0.07 percent per year— too small to show in the graph.

At the beginning of the Industrial Revolution in the early 1800s, economic growth rose to about 0.2 percent per year and continued to accelerate to over 1.5 percent per year by the beginning of the twentieth century. In the 1950s, the modern era of economic growth per person began, with annual rates of 2.0 percent and above. Growth today remains high by historical standards, although it fluctuates over the decades and by geographic area.

Table 5–1 gives us a picture of the fluctuations of growth in various regions throughout the world over the past 180 years. As you can see, the modern era of North American growth (dominated by the United States) has been marked by three distinct periods of substantial growth. From about 1950 to 1973, output per person grew 2.5 percent a year, but rose only 1.5 percent per year from 1973 to 1995. Since then, our growth rate has increased to 3.2 percent.

Exhibit 5–1

Growth in World Economic Output Per Person over the Past 2,000 Years

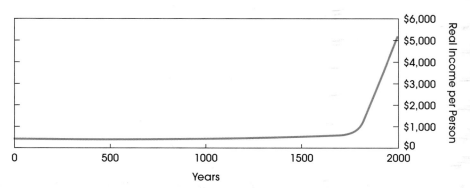

Real income per person before the early 1800s hardly changed at all. Beginning at about 1800, economic growth per person accelerated, rising by about 1.2 percent per year from 1820 to 2000. Today's economic growth rates are high by historical standards. Real income per person is measured in 1990 international dollars. Source: Based on Maddison, A. 1995. *Monitoring the World Economy.* Paris: OECD

Table 5-1

The Modern Era of Growth: 1820–2000

Average Growth Rates of Income per Person for Various Regions (1820 to the Present)				
	1820–1950	**1950–1973**	**1973–1995**	**1996–2000**
Western Europe	1.1%	3.9%	1.7%	2.0%
North America	1.6	2.5	1.5	3.2
Japan	0.8	8.0	2.5	0.1
Eastern Europe	1.1	3.8	−0.8	—
Latin America	1.0	2.5	0.6	—
China	−0.2	2.9	5.4	7.5
Other Asia	0.3	2.8	2.5	1.8
Africa	0.6	2.0	−0.3	—

Source: Maddison, Angus. "Poor Until 1820." *The Wall Street Journal* 1 January 1999, and author estimates.

Looking over decades, growth in output fluctuates and varies from area to area.

European economies grew even more quickly after World War II as they rebuilt factories and machinery that were lost during the war. That growth continued into the 1970s, but slowed in the 1980s and 1990s. Japan's growth rate has followed a similar trend.

From 1950 to 1995, the Asian Tigers—a group of Asian countries including Hong Kong (today part of China), South Korea, Taiwan, and Singapore—and most other Asian economies, including China, experienced tremendous growth. Their growth rates surpassed those of other developing, and even developed, countries. In the late 1990s, however, growth in many Asian Tiger economies slowed.

GROWTH, MARKETS, AND ECONOMICS

Today, economists generally suggest three types of policies for promoting growth:

Economists suggest three types of policies to promote growth: (1) maintain stable environments in which individuals have freedom to operate; (2) save and invest; and (3) educate the population.

1. *Maintain stable political, social, and market environments that give individuals freedom to operate.* Translated into policy, this means maintaining a strong system of private property rights and a well-established commercial code.
2. *Save and invest to build up the capital stock.* Translated into policy, this means creating a tax structure that encourages saving and investing.
3. *Educate the population.* Translated into policy, this means providing appropriate universal education and easy access to higher education.

Let's consider policy suggestion 1:

■ Maintain stable political, social, and market environments that give individuals freedom to operate.

The observation that growth increased enormously with the introduction and evolution of markets was evident to economists living during the Industrial Revolution. This observation became a central tenet of Adam Smith's *The Wealth of Nations*, the book that signifies the beginning of modern economics.

Smith's analysis of growth was vague, but it strongly emphasized individual freedom and markets as growth-promoting environments. Smith argued that markets allowed **specialization,** the concentration of individuals on the production of a good or on aspects of production, and **division of labor,** the splitting up of a task to allow specialization. He argued that markets create an economy in which individuals can specialize in certain tasks and still meet their needs for other goods. They use the income they earn producing some goods to buy other goods in the market. Because specialization and division of labor increase productivity (output per unit of input), markets lead to a higher standard of living for everyone.

How is productivity increased through specialization and division of labor? As people specialize, they become better at performing their tasks, exploiting their existing comparative advantage (ability to produce at a lower opportunity cost) and developing more advantages as they learn by doing. They develop new technologies, which allow them to produce the same amount with far fewer inputs.

Consider what life would be like without specialization and division of labor. You'd have to grow all your food, provide all your transportation, and build your living space. You'd need a lot of skills just to have the basics. Keeping up with your daily needs would be a challenge.

Now consider life with specialization. A dairy farm produces the milk you need. You don't have to know how it is produced, just where to buy it. You buy, rather than build, your car. It operates somehow; you're not quite sure how, and if it breaks down, you take it to a garage. Consider your education. Are you learning the skills that directly fulfill basic needs such as how to grow food or build a house? No, you are probably learning a set of skills that has little direct relevance to the production of most goods. But you'll most likely provide some good or service that will benefit the dairy farmer and auto mechanic and be able to do that at a lower opportunity cost than they could themselves. For most of the things you consume, you haven't the faintest idea of who makes them or how they are made, nor do you need to know.

As markets grow, more and more specialization is possible. For example, when Nike began making sneakers in the early 1960s, the market for specialty sneakers was concentrated in the United States. At that time, Nike made the shoes, marketed them, and sold them. Today, Nike shoes are sold all over the world, but Nike no longer makes shoes. It specializes in *coordinating* the process and contracts out all other aspects of its business, searching throughout the world for the least-cost producer for each element.

Because countries trade, the relevant market for many producers is the global market. The increasing globalization of the world economy is an example of the growth of markets. The gains from the division of labor and the advantages of specialization underlie economists' first policy suggestions for growth. It is why they generally favor free trade.

Western economies have markets, so in discussions of U.S. growth you'll hear much talk about free trade. Once a country has markets, the debate becomes whether the markets should be regulated and, if so, how much regulation is appropriate. Those debates, however, are about the operation of markets—not about whether markets should exist. So, the first policy suggestion is to give individuals freedom to operate within markets.

This policy suggestion is based on experience. Historically, economies that have stable governments and markets with little government interference grow quickly.

Markets allow for specialization and the division of labor. This specialization underlies productivity growth.

Let's consider a case study. In 1990, Poland took dramatic steps to move from a centrally planned economy to a market economy. (In a centrally planned economy, the government controls resource allocation, production levels, and prices.) Poland's government deregulated markets by allowing the market to determine prices, selling state-owned firms, cutting subsidies, and reducing import barriers. For the first 2 years, economic output declined, but in 1992, Poland's economy started growing. As more private firms emerged, an expanding private sector has led to growth in excess of 4 percent per year since 1992. The private sector now accounts for more than 60 percent of Poland's GDP, and that percentage is growing.

Let's now turn to policy suggestion 2:

■ Save and invest to build up the capital stock.

To give us insight into economists' thinking about growth, let's consider Adam Smith's vision of growth more carefully and how that vision has changed. Smith argued that because capital (the stock of physical goods used in the production process) allows people to specialize, the division of labor was closely tied to the use of capital. Labor increases as the population grows and more people join the labor force. Capital is different. Firms must produce it. Creating capital—investing—requires firms to divert some portion of current production away from consumption toward investment. Smith's analysis of growth has two aspects. The first concerns the gains to society that come from investment and increases in the capital stock. The second concerns the gains from specialization and division of labor. These two aspects of growth still apply and form the basis of economists' models of growth.

Depending on the rate of economic growth and the other policy considerations facing society, economists' interest in growth theory has waxed and waned. In the 1950s and 1960s, when U.S. policy makers were in a race to have U.S. growth outpace growth in the Soviet Union, interest in growth theory increased significantly. This interest led economists to develop formal models in which the principal engine of growth was its stock of capital: The more capital a country had, the faster the economy would grow.

The nature of U.S. production as it entered the twenty-first century was much different than production in the first part of the twentieth century. The modern picture of production changed from a giant steel mill with massive blast furnaces to a person sitting at a desk writing a computer program or tracking production. With this picture in mind, it becomes clear that knowledge, or knowledge embodied in capital, is what is very important to economic growth today. For example, advances in biochemistry and computing do not require enormous amounts of capital, but enormous amounts of knowledge. As this change in production occurred, economists' discussions and models of growth shifted from focusing on capital to focusing on human knowledge, technological change, and institutions. That shift has led to a stronger emphasis on policy suggestion 3:

■ Educate the population.

The more knowledge people have to apply to production, the faster the economy will grow. This has led to a focus away from physical capital toward **human capital**—the set of skills and the knowledge that enables individuals to produce.

Creating capital—investing—means devoting current production to building up capital stock for future production.

Modern industry focuses more on human capital than on physical capital.

More human capital leads to more productive research and development and greater technological advances. New technology also requires a more educated population.

We can see the importance of education in policy. In the United States, for example, President George W. Bush pledged to emphasize education during his administration. There are enormous debates about what leads to a better educated public, but educational standards and privatization of the supply of education through vouchers will likely be high on the policy agenda over the next few years. As with other factors contributing to economic growth, however, education alone is not enough. For example, the former Soviet Union had a well-developed educational system, but its growth fell behind that of the United States.

Executive Summary

- Small differences in growth rates generate large differences in income levels over long periods of time.

- After hardly changing at all for about 1,500 years, growth per person began to rise with the development of markets and accelerated with the beginning of the Industrial Revolution in 1800. Rates of growth in the modern era are high by historical standards.

- Perhaps one of the most important developments in the history of economic growth is the development of markets.

- Economists suggest three types of policies for promoting growth: (1) Maintain stable political, social, and market environments that give individuals freedom to operate; (2) save and invest to build up the capital stock; and (3) educate the population.

THE SOLOW GROWTH MODEL

We now turn to the neoclassical theory of growth, which is also called the Solow growth model. The **Solow growth model** (named for economist Robert Solow) is a model of growth that shows how technological innovation, saving, depreciation and population growth determine steady-state economic growth. This model provides the framework that economists use to discuss growth issues in general. Although its roots stem from aspects of classical economics of the eighteenth century, the Solow growth model was developed during the 1950s (which accounts for the "neo" [or new] part of the term *neoclassical*).

The Solow growth model is centered on the factors of production—or supply. Demand is given little emphasis. This focus is consistent with the proposition that, in the long-run, supply rules. Aggregate supply creates an equal amount of aggregate demand, so demand will always be sufficient to buy all the goods that are produced.

The Production Function

The Solow growth model begins with the production function:

$$Y = A \cdot F(K, L)$$

$$output = technology \cdot F\ (capital,\ labor).$$

(5-1)

Like the production function discussed in Chapter 4, this production function is assumed to have constant returns to scale and diminishing marginal product for both capital and labor.

Growth theory focuses on output per person, not total output, so we must convert the production function to a per-person production function. To avoid some technical difficulties, we assume that all people work, so labor and population are identical. (Although we know from our analysis of the labor market in Chapter 3 that this is not true, the results of the model will be unchanged as long as the labor force is a fairly constant fraction of the population.) This assumption, along with the assumption of constant returns to scale, allows us to divide output and all inputs by L:

$$Y/L = A \cdot F(K/L, 1) \qquad (5\text{-}2)$$

We simplify the notation further by using lowercase letters to represent quantities per person and by transforming the function into one where the "1" is embodied in the function:

$$y = A \cdot f(k) \qquad (5\text{-}3)$$

where y is output per person (Y/L), k is capital per person (K/Y), and A is measure of technology per person. The per-person production function tells us that *output per person is a function of capital per person*.

> The production function in the Solow growth model is a per-person production function.

Exhibit 5–2 shows a per-person production function. It has the same shape as the aggregate production function. The only difference is that capital per person (instead of capital) is on the horizontal axis and output per person (instead of total output) is on the vertical axis. The slope of the production function is the marginal product of capital. Aggregate output in an economy is the sum of each individual's output.

Given our assumptions, output per person rises if capital per person rises. For example, with k_0 capital per person, output per person is y_0. With one more unit of capital, $k_0 + 1$, output per person rises to y_1. Moving up along the production function represents an increase in output per person. Notice that as capital increases, output increases by successively smaller amounts. (The slope of the production function becomes flatter.) This is due to diminishing marginal product. Diminishing marginal product plays a central role in the Solow growth model. It gives the production function its shape and limits the effect that increasing capital has on the growth rate.

> Diminishing marginal product means that the per-person production function gets flatter as more capital is added to production.

Exhibit 5–2

A Production Function per Person

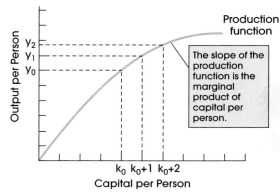

The production function per person shows how output per person changes as capital per person rises. The slope of the production function is the marginal product of capital. Because the marginal product of capital falls as capital per person rises, the slope of the production function also falls.

Forces That Increase Capital per Person: Saving and Investment

Holding technology constant, an increase in capital per person is the only direct determinant of a rise in output per person (growth). Therefore, if we can understand the forces that affect the level of capital in an economy, we can gain some insights into growth. We begin by considering the forces that increase capital: saving and investment. Investment refers to purchases of capital, which add to the stock of capital.

The level of investment depends on how much income people save. Hence, saving underlies increases in capital and growth. By assumption, all saving is translated into investment, so the two are identical. Saving and investment are assumed to be a constant fraction, v, of income. Thus,

> **Saving equals investment in the Solow growth model. Both are a constant fraction of income:** $I = S = vY$.

$$I = S = vY \tag{5-4}$$

As with the production function, we can translate this into a per-person relationship by dividing by L. Doing so gives us investment per person ($i = I/L$), which equals saving per person ($s = S/L$). Saving per person is a fraction, v, of income per person. So we have $i = s = vy$. For example, if the saving rate, v, is .04 and income per person is 200, saving per person, s, and investment per person, i, both equal 8. Because income per person is determined by capital per person, investment per person also depends on the existing stock of capital. Investment per person is related to the capital stock through the production function and the investment rate:

$$i = v[A \cdot f(k)] \tag{5-5}$$

Exhibit 5–3 shows the relationship between investment and capital per person. The production function tells us that the level of output for any level of capital per person, and v determines how much output is dedicated to investment. For example, with capital k_0, income per person is y_0. Of that income, vy_0 is investment. Because only a fraction of income is invested, the investment function always lies below the production function. The vertical distance between the production function and the investment function is the income per person less saving per person, or consumption per person.

Exhibit 5-3

Saving and Investment per Worker

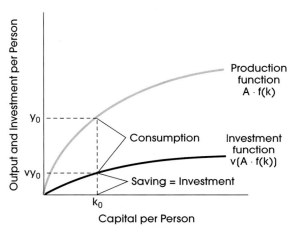

The difference between income and saving (also investment) at any level of capital is consumption per person. With capital k_0 and saving rate, v, income per person is y_0, investment per person is vy_0, and consumption per person is $y_0 - vy_0$.

Forces That Decrease Capital per Person: Population Growth and Depreciation

We now turn to two forces that decrease capital per person: depreciation and population growth. Let's start with depreciation (the wear and tear of capital). The rate at which capital depreciates is generally assumed to be a constant fraction, *d*, of existing capital. Depreciation reduces capital per person by the rate of depreciation times capital per person, or by *dk*. For example, if capital per person is currently 30 and capital depreciates at a rate of 10 percent, 3 units of capital per person will wear out during production, leaving 27 units of capital per person for the next period's production.

A second force that decreases capital per person is population growth. As population increases, capital per person declines, because existing capital is divided among a greater number of people. Population growth reduces capital per person by the rate of population growth times capital per person, or by *nk*. For example, if total capital is 6,000 and the initial population is 200, initial capital per person is 30. If the population grows at an annual rate of 2 percent, the population will grow by 4 to 204 in the next period, and capital per person will decrease to 6,000/204, or 29.4. Capital per person falls by 0.6. Population growth and depreciation, together, push down capital per person by *nk* + *dk*, or, alternatively expressed, by (*n* + *d*)*k*, each period.

> Population growth and depreciation both decrease the amount of investment that increases the capital stock.

Balanced Growth Investment

We have just described two sets of opposing forces that affect capital per person. Investment increases capital per person, while depreciation and population growth reduce capital per person. How these forces balance each other determines whether capital per person is rising or falling and, therefore, whether output per person is rising or falling.

The amount of investment that keeps capital per person constant is **balanced growth investment.** Mathematically, balanced growth investment is

> Balanced growth investment is the amount of investment that keeps capital per person constant. It is just enough to cover depreciation and population growth.

$$i = (n + d)k \qquad (5\text{-}6)$$

This equation tells us that to keep capital per person constant—simply keep up with population growth and replace worn-out capital—investment must equal the current capital per person times the rate of population growth, or *nk*, and the current rate of depreciation times the capital stock *dk*. Thus, for an economy to simply tread water and hold income per person constant, investment must offset the effects of depreciation and the population growth on capital per person. If there is no population growth and no depreciation of capital, balanced growth investment will be zero. No investment is needed to keep income per person constant.

In Exhibit 5–4, we show a **balanced growth investment line,** a line in the graph of the Solow growth model that tells us the amount of investment, *i*, needed to offset depreciation, *d*, and population growth, *n*. It is a straight line going through the origin, with a slope equal to the growth rate of the population plus the rate of depreciation, (*n* + *d*). (Slope measures the steepness of a curve. It tells how much the measure on the vertical axis rises for a 1-unit increase in the measure on the horizontal axis.) To illustrate the meaning of the balanced growth investment line, let's consider a numerical example. Assuming a depreciation rate of 0.02 and a population growth rate of 0.08, the slope of the balanced growth investment line is 0.1. Exhibit 5–4 shows this line. At point *A*, the capital stock per person is 2,000

> The balanced growth investment line is a straight line, with slope *n* + *d*.

Exhibit 5–4

Balanced Growth Investment Line

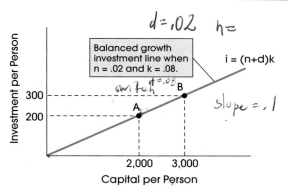

$d = .02 \quad h =$

The balanced growth investment line represents the rate at which the capital stock must increase to keep output per person constant. It is a straight line through the origin, with a slope equal to the growth of the population plus the rate of depreciation.

units (shown on the horizontal axis), and balanced growth investment is .1 × 2,000 = 200 units (shown on the vertical axis).

At higher levels of capital per person, depreciation is greater and more investment is needed for the growing population. Therefore, higher levels of capital require more investment to prevent capital per person from falling. Using the example in Exhibit 5–4, when capital per person rises to 3,000, balanced growth investment rises to 300.

To ensure that you are following this reasoning, answer the following question: What would the balanced growth investment line look like if there were no depreciation and no population growth. If you answered that it would be coincidental with the horizontal axis, you've got it.

Equilibrium in the Solow Growth Model

One of the surprising conclusions of the Solow growth model is that, given the assumptions, the economy will always be driven to an equilibrium in which the level of output per person does not change. This was quite different than predictions of earlier models. Earlier models indicated that growth was like a knife-edge—it either blew up or imploded unless the saving rate was just right. We show the conclusion of the Solow model in Exhibit 5–5, which combines both the investment function and the balanced growth investment line.

Exhibit 5–5

Steady-State Equilibrium

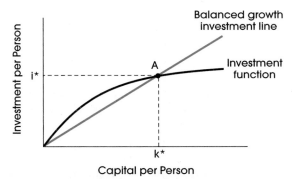

With the balanced growth investment line and the investment function, we can find the steady-state level of capital, which is where the two curves intersect. This is a steady state because at k^*, investment i^* adds just enough capital to offset the effects of depreciation and a rising population on the stock of capital per person.

The equilibrium in the Solow growth model occurs when output per person is constant. For this to happen, capital per person must remain constant. So, in equilibrium, investment per person must equal balanced growth investment. This occurs in Exhibit 5–5 at point A, where the investment function crosses the balanced growth investment line. At this point, capital per person is k^*; investment per person, i^*, is just sufficient to keep output per person constant. At k^*, income per person is neither rising nor falling.

This intersection of the balanced growth investment line and the investment function is called a **steady-state equilibrium**—a dynamic equilibrium in which central variables are not changing. In the Solow growth model, it means that capital and output per person are constant, even though the population is growing and capital is depreciating. At the steady-state equilibrium, investment adds just enough capital to replace depreciating capital and keep capital growing at the same rate that the population is growing. At the steady-state equilibrium, total output is growing along a balanced growth path. Along this balanced growth path, total output is rising at the rate the population is growing. Why is this a steady-state equilibrium? Because the forces affecting the amount of capital per person cancel each other out. Population growth and depreciation are offset by investment, and output per person remains unchanged. Capital per person doesn't change.

To confirm that k^* is a steady-state equilibrium, let's see what happens when the economy is off the balanced growth investment line at a point such as B in Exhibit 5–6. At point B, the investment function is above the balanced growth investment line. The economy is adding more capital than it needs to keep capital per person constant, so capital per person rises. As capital per person rises, the economy moves to the right along the investment function in the direction of the *arrows*. Output per person continues to rise, until investment is just enough to keep k constant. At point A, the economy is in a steady-state equilibrium.

Let's go through the process more carefully. Starting with k_0 capital in Exhibit 5–6, the economy produces y_0 output (income) per person. At this level of capital

> Steady-state equilibrium occurs where the investment function intersects the balance growth investment line. In the steady state, central variables do not change.

> If capital per person, k, differs from steady-state capital per person, k^*, output per person will rise (if $k < k^*$) or fall (if $k > k^*$).

Exhibit 5–6

Movement to Steady State

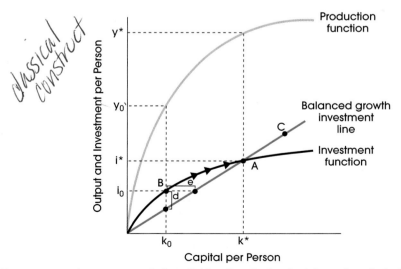

If an economy has an amount of capital less than its steady state, such as k_0 (point B), investment exceeds balanced growth investment (investment necessary to keep capital per person constant). That excess investment causes the capital stock per person (and output) to rise, (a movement to the right along the investment function). When the capital stock rises to k^* (point A), investment equals balanced growth investment, and there will be no more tendency for capital per person to change.

and income, the economy is at point B along the investment function. Investment per person is i_0, more than enough to keep capital per person constant. The "extra" investment is represented by the vertical length, d, below the investment function and above the balanced growth line. The excess investment contributes to a rise in capital per person, represented by horizontal length, e, and output per person increases. Because of diminishing marginal productivity, the successive increases in capital per person lead to smaller and smaller increases in y and, therefore, in i. Eventually, the economy reaches a steady state at which investment each period, i^*, is just enough to keep capital per person constant. The steady-state levels of capital and income are k^* and y^*, respectively. You can go through the same reasoning beginning at point C, showing that capital per person will be driven back to point A, at which capital per person and output per person remain constant.

Now that we've looked at steady-state equilibrium graphically, let's look at it using a numerical example. To simplify the presentation, we assume that depreciation is zero. Table 5–2 shows how an economy moves to a steady-state equilibrium. Column I shows the periods. Column II shows capital per person, which is

Table 5-2

A Numerical Example of Steady State

I Period	II k Capital	III $y = \sqrt{k}$ Output	IV $i = 0.4y$ Investment	V $nk = 0.1k$ Balanced Growth Investment	VI Change in k Excess Investment
1	9.000	3.000	1.200	0.900	0.300
2	9.300	3.050	1.220	0.930	0.290
3	9.590	3.097	1.239	0.959	0.280
4	9.870	3.142	1.257	0.987	0.270
5	10.139	3.184	1.274	1.014	0.260
10	11.342	3.342	1.347	1.134	0.213
20	13.110	3.621	1.448	1.311	0.137
21	13.247	3.640	1.456	1.325	0.131
100	15.950	3.994	1.597	1.595	0.003
101	15.952	3.994	1.598	1.595	0.002
199	16.000	4.000	1.600	1.600	0.000
200	16.000	4.000	1.600	1.600	0.000

Note: The numbers in this table are based on the following assumptions: $y = \sqrt{k}$, $n = 0.10$, $d = 0$. In period 0, $k = 9$ units and $v = 0.4$.

QUESTION   Is there a quick mathematical way to find the steady-state level of capital per person?

ANSWER   Yes.

We can also find the steady-state level of capital mathematically, using the equations for balanced growth investment $[i = (n + d)k]$ and the investment function ($i = vy$). Investment equals balanced growth investment when $vy = (n + d)k$. Using the same assumptions for the saving rate, population growth rate, and production as in Table 5–2, $v = 0.4$, $y = \sqrt{k}$, and $n = 0.1$ and $d = 0.0$. So, $0.4\sqrt{k} = 0.1k$. Solving this equation for k gives us k^*. To solve it, square both sides, giving $.16k = .01k^2$. Divide both sides by k, giving $.16 = .01k$ and finally divide both sides by .01 giving $k = 16$. the steady-state level of capital is 16 units per person.

the previous period's capital per person plus excess investment (columns II + VI). Output, shown in column III, is calculated using the production function $y = \sqrt{k}$.[1] Column IV shows investment per person at each period, which is the saving rate (0.4) times output per person. Column V shows balanced growth investment (how much the capital stock must rise to keep capital per person constant), which is population growth multiplied by capital.

The economy is not in a steady-state equilibrium in period 1. We know this because investment is greater than balanced growth investment (column IV > column V) and the capital stock is rising. Let's see how the economy moves toward its steady-state capital and output per person.

In period one, excess investment is .30 (column VI, row 1). This excess investment leads capital per person to rise from 9 to 9.3 (column II, row 2). Greater capital per person leads output to rise (to $\sqrt{9.3} = 3.05$ as column III, row 2 shows), which in turn leads to greater investment ($.4 \times 3.05 = 1.22$ as column IV, row 2 shows). But because there is more capital, balanced growth investment has also increased ($.1 \times 9.3 = .93$ as column V, row 2 shows). Subtracting balanced growth investment from investement ($1.22 - .93 = .29$ as column VI, row 2 shows), we see that excess investment has declined. This process will continue until actual investment equals balanced growth investment. At that point capital per person will not change and the economy will be in a steady-state equilibrium.

As you can see in Table 5–2, the rise in capital, and consequently output, gets smaller as the periods progress. For example, from period 4 to period 5, capital rises by 0.269 unit per person ($10.139 - 9.87$) and output rises by 0.042 unit per person ($3.184 - 3.142$). From period 20 to 21, the change is even smaller— capital per person rises by 0.137 unit ($13.247 - 13.11$) and output per person rises by only 0.019 unit ($3.640 - 3.621$). By the period 101, output is rising very slightly and investment exceeds balanced growth investment by a very small amount. By the period 200 the difference is totally imperceptible; investment is just enough to keep capital per person constant. The economy is in its steady-state equilibrium.

---

[1]This production function does not represent any particular real-world production process. We chose it because it is one of the easiest functions in a family of production functions that exhibit the four characteristics needed for a production function in the Solow growth model.

The numerical example of Table 5–2 illustrates two points. First, if an economy starts from a point off the balanced growth line, it will move toward that line. Second, as the economy approaches the balanced growth line, output grows at ever slower rates. Both of these conclusions follow from the assumption that the aggregate production function exhibits diminishing marginal product.

Executive Summary

- The Solow growth model shows how investment, through saving, affects growth and the level of income.

- The two elements of the Solow growth model are the investment function and the balanced growth investment line.

- The steady-state equilibrium in the Solow growth model is where investment per person, vy, equals balanced growth investment, $(n + d)k$. Graphically, the steady state is the point at which the investment function and balanced growth investment line intersect.

- In steady-state equilibrium, output grows at the same rate as the growth of the population.

IMPLICATIONS OF THE SOLOW GROWTH MODEL

Let's now step back and ask whether we have answered the original questions—what causes growth and what policies foster growth? So far, the basic Solow growth model tells us that, for a given saving rate, a given population growth and depreciation rate, and a given level of technology (recall that the model holds technology constant), the economy will eventually settle at a steady state, at which income grows at the growth rate of the population and income per person is constant.

This, however, is not what what we observe. For most economies, long-term growth in income exceeds the growth rate of the population. In other words, income per person rises over time. Our presentation of the Solow growth model is not yet complete because we haven't considered how changes in the saving rate, population growth rate, depreciation rate, or technology affect growth. The next step is to see whether changes in any of these four "givens"—the saving rate, the population growth rate, the depreciation rate, and technology—can account for economic growth. We consider changes in each of these givens in the following section.

An Increase in the Saving Rate

First, let's consider the effect of an increase in the saving rate, v, on an economy that starts with a steady-state level of capital and output per person—at k_0^* and y_0^* in Exhibit 5–7(a). A rise in the saving rate rotates the investment function up, raising investment at every level of capital per person. At the initial steady-state capital per person k_0^*, investment each period exceeds balanced growth investment and the amount of capital per person rises. As capital per person rises, output per person also rises until the economy reaches its higher steady-state equilibrium at k_1^* capital per person and y_1^* output per person. An increase in the saving rate increases output per person, but once the economy reaches its steady-state equilibrium, growth of output per person returns to zero.

Let's see how the economy moves from the original steady state at y_0^* to its new steady state at y_1^*. Exhibit 5–7(b) shows how output per person changes over time as a result of an increase in the saving rate. Time is on the horizontal axis and

Exhibit 5-7

Increase in the Saving Rate

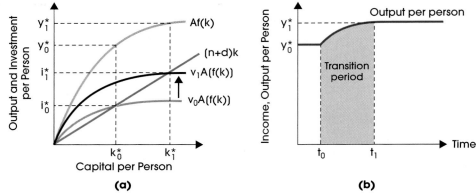

(a)   **(b)**

Panel a shows the effect of an increase in the saving rate on the steady state. An economy that was initially in a steady-state equilibrium now finds that its capital stock is rising, increasing output until a new steady state is reached, where, once again, the output rises only by the rate of growth of the population. *Panel b* shows how output per person rises as the economy moves from one steady state to another. In the transition period, output per person grows until it reaches its new higher steady state level of income. In the new steady state, income per person remains constant.

The transition period is the time during which an economy moves from one steady state to another steady state.

output per person is on the vertical axis. The time during which an economy moves from one steady state to another is called the **transition period.** Before time t_0, the saving rate is v_0 shown in Exhibit 5–7(a) in the lower investment function, and the economy is in a steady-state equilibrium—growing at the rate of the population, which keeps output per person at y_0^*. At t_0, the saving rate rises to v_1, shown in Exhibit 5–7(a) in the higher investment function. In the beginning of the transition period, output per person rises quickly, but as the economy approaches its steady state, growth of output per person slows and eventually returns to zero when output per person reaches a higher steady state at y_1^*. At time t_1, the transition period ends and the economy has reached its steady state.

The Solow model's conclusions about saving are the following:

Saving rate up → k^* up → i^* up → y^* up. In the steady state, growth rate doesn't change, and output per person remains constant.

■ A higher saving rate will lead to a higher level of capital per person and a higher income per person, but it will not lead to persistent growth per person. In the steady-state equilibrium, total income will grow at the rate the population is growing. Income per person does not grow in the steady state.

Although, in the transition period, total output grows faster than does the population, that growth is temporary. A higher saving rate does not lead to persistent economic growth. This follows from a production function with diminishing marginal product and constant returns to scale. In the long run, output and capital will grow at the rate of population growth. Economic growth per person will be zero. (If you're asking why economists don't advocate policies that would continually increase our saving rate to create economic growth per person, see the Q&A feature.)

These results have important implications for policy. To encourage more capital formation and a higher standard of living, policy makers have pushed for policies that increase saving rates. This is especially true in the United States, where private saving is comparatively low. U.S. policy makers have considered privatizing Social Security and expanding tax-free retirement and tax-free medical accounts. If the Solow model is a correct description of the economic growth process, these policies will increase the rate of economic growth for a period of time, leading to a higher

QUESTION   If increased saving increases output, shouldn't we try to save as much as possible?

ANSWER   Economists don't suggest saving all of our income, because then we wouldn't have any money left to buy goods and services.

Economists search for policies to maximize the welfare of the people in society. That welfare is generally assumed to depend on consumption. Saving is good because it is a means to higher future consumption, so economists advocate increasing our saving rate to increase output only if it also allows steady-state consumption to rise. In the Solow growth model, consumption per person is maximized where the vertical distance between the balanced growth investment line and the production function is maximized.

As drawn in the following exhibit, this occurs at k^*, where the slope of the balanced growth investment line equals the slope of the production function. To achieve this steady-state capital per person, an economy's saving rate must equal v^*, some positive fraction less than 1.

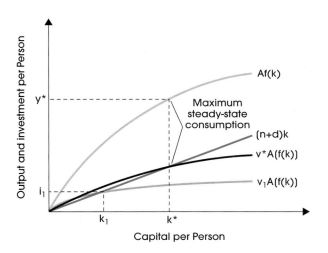

There is no reason why an economy's saving rate will be v^*. There are no forces in the model that will change an economy's saving rate to maximize consumption in the steady state. People in the economy must choose to save that fraction of their income.

Saving rates either above or below v^* will result in lower consumption per person in the steady state. Suppose an economy's saving rate is v_1, which is lower than v^*. Steady-state capital per person is k_1. Notice that, at this steady state, the slope of the production function is greater

than the slope of the balanced growth investment line. Remember, the slope of the production function is the marginal product of capital, and the slope of the balanced growth investment line is the sum of population growth and depreciation $(n + d)$.

Now suppose that people decide to raise their saving rate—just enough to increase capital per person by 1. Total output will increase by the marginal product of capital per person, but balanced growth investment will rise by the rate of population growth plus the rate of depreciation, $n + d$. Because the increase in output (the marginal product of capital per person) is greater than the rise in balanced growth investment $(n + d)$, steady-state consumption per person will rise. For any saving rate below v^*, an increase in the saving rate will lead to an increase in consumption in the steady state.

To make sure you are following this reasoning, think about what would happen if the economy started at v^* and decided to increase its saving rate. Moving to the right from v^*, you see that the slope of the production function is less than the slope of the balanced growth investment line. This means that the additional output produced with additional capital (the marginal product of capital per person) is less than what is required to cover depreciation and population growth in the steady state, so consumption falls. The level of saving (investment) that maximizes steady-state consumption is sometimes called the Golden Rule level of capital accumulation.

One of the implications of the Golden Rule is that if the government can get people to save the right amount, it could maximize steady-state consumption. Policy makers, however, face a dilemma if saving is below the Golden Rule. Future generations' consumption can be increased only if the current generation increases its saving rate and reduces its consumption during the transition period. When the saving rate rises, consumption dips below its current rate, but it rises thereafter and reaches a steady state that is higher than its current rate. The current generation would be willing to follow this path only if it follows the Golden Rule: Love thy neighbor as thyself. So, the current generation would need to care about future generations as much as it cares about itself.

Q
&
A

QUESTION   What is the difference between an increase in income per person and growth in economists' terminology?

ANSWER   In economists' terminology, *growth* refers to steady-state growth—a continual, not a temporary, increase in income per person.

Throughout this chapter, we refer to policies that affect growth and policies that affect the level of income per person. It is important, therefore, to understand the terminology economists use in distinguishing the two. In economists' terminology, a temporary increase in output per person is not called growth, but simply an increase in income.

To illustrate, let's revisit what the Solow growth model indicates will happen to income per person when the saving rate increases. The following exhibit shows that after the saving rate increases, income per person begins to rise until it reaches its new steady state at y_1^*. During the transition period (t_0 to t_1), income per person does grow, but this growth is temporary. Economists would say, therefore, that an increase in the saving rate, according to the Solow growth model, does not affect the growth rate of income per person in the steady state.

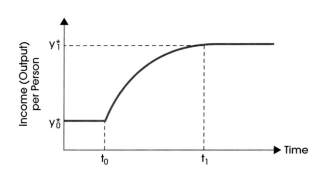

This temporary increase in income per person during the transition period is not steady-state growth. As economists use the term in growth models, *growth* means that income per person increases in steady-state equilibrium, which will last forever.

income per person. Once the economy reaches the new steady state, growth of total output will return to the rate of population growth, albeit at a higher output per person. That is, although in the steady state total output will grow, output per person will not. (The difference between higher economic growth per person and higher income per person is discussed further in the Q&A feature.)

A Change in Population Growth or the Rate of Depreciation

Next, let's consider whether an increase in population growth can lead to higher economic growth per person. A country can increase its population growth rate in a number of ways, such as raising tax deductions for dependents and allowing a higher rate of immigration. A higher population growth rate increases the amount of investment needed to keep capital per person constant. That is, for every k, balanced growth investment, $(n + d)k$, increases. Because $n + d$ is the slope of the balanced growth investment line, graphically this means that the balanced growth investment line rotates up. Exhibit 5–8 shows how the balanced growth investment line becomes steeper when the population growth rate rises from n_0 to n_1.

Assuming the economy begins with the steady-state equilibrium amount of capital, k_0^* (point A), when the population growth rate rises to n_1, the level of saving and investment that keeps capital per person at k_0^* rises to i_2, which is above the previous steady-state investment and saving levels, i_0^*. The capital stock is not increasing sufficiently to keep capital per person constant and capital is spread more thinly among a greater population. Capital per person falls, which leads to a decline in output per person. Output per person continues to fall until capital per

Exhibit 5-8

An Increase in Population Growth

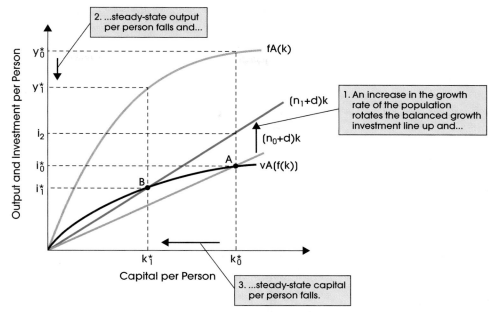

2. ...steady-state output per person falls and...

1. An increase in the growth rate of the population rotates the balanced growth investment line up and...

3. ...steady-state capital per person falls.

If an economy begins at steady-state level of capital per person, (point A), and the population growth rate rises to n_1, investment would have to rise to i_2, to keep capital per person at k_0^*. Equilibrium occurs at a lower level of investment i_1^*, capital k_1^*, and income per person y_1^* (point B).

person falls to its new steady state, k_1^* (point B). Steady-state output (income) per person, y_1^*, is also lower. The new steady-state equilibrium output per person remains constant at a lower income per person. Total output is growing at the new, higher population growth rate, n_1.

Population growth can explain sustained total output growth but not sustained output growth per person. The Solow growth model indicates that if population growth rises by 2 percentage points, total output growth will ultimately also rise by 2 percentage points, but output per person will fall. Population growth cannot explain sustained increases in economic growth per person because, in the steady state, output per person is constant. Conversely, a decline in the growth of the population will lower total output growth, raise output per person, but also not change economic growth per person. So, these are conclusions we draw from the effects of population growth:

> Population growth up → k^* down → i^* down → y^* down. In the steady state, growth rate increases; output per person remains constant.

- A rise in population growth leads to a permanently higher growth rate in total output, but lower output per person.
- A rise in population growth does not lead to a sustained increase in output per person.

Increases in depreciation affect growth the same way that an increase in the growth of the population does. The balanced growth investment line rotates up and to the left. At every level of capital per person, more of the investment must go to replacing worn out capital. Investment must increase to keep capital per person constant. Because less investment is available to increase the capital stock, greater depreciation leads to lower steady-state capital and output per person. Economic growth per person temporarily falls below the balanced growth line. Eventually, the economy reaches a new steady-state equilibrium at a lower level of capital and output per person. In the new steady-state equilibrium, output per person grows at the rate at which the population grows. Depreciation, like population growth, provides a reason why an economy needs investment to maintain income per person, but it does not explain economic growth per person. So, these are the conclusions we draw from the effects of depreciation:

- A rise in the rate of depreciation leads to lower output per person, but doesn't change the growth rate of total output or output per person.

A Change in Technological Progress

The last "given" we want to consider is a change in technology (A). How would a technological advance (an increase in A) affect growth? Consider today's personal computer, which makes it possible to complete a calculation in 2 minutes that had previously taken someone using a mainframe computer many weeks to complete. With the new computer, a person can do many more calculations during each hour of work than before. Such technological improvement increases output for every combination of capital and labor. That is, output per person will rise without any change in capital per person. Graphically, an increase in technology rotates the production function, and hence the investment function, up. At every level of capital per person, income is higher, which raises investment. Greater investment means capital per person, and therefore output per person, rises.

Exhibit 5–9 shows the effect of an increase in technology. At the original amount of capital per person, k_0^*, an increase in technology from A_0 to A_1 causes saving per person to exceed the amount necessary to keep capital per person constant. The amount of capital per person rises and output per person rises until

Exhibit 5–9

Technological Innovation

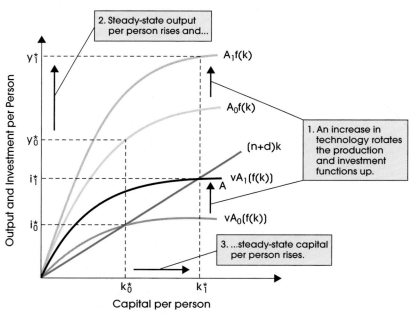

A technological innovation increases the amount of output (and income) that any combination of inputs can produce. The production function rotates up from $A_0(f(k))$ to $A_1(f(k))$. The investment function also rises $vA_0(f(k))$ to $vA_1(f(k))$. Capital per person continues to rise until the economy reaches a new steady-state level of income per person at y_1^*. At the new steady-state, investment, i_1^*, is just enough to keep capital and output per person constant.

investment returns to the balanced growth investment line at a higher level of capital per person, k_1^*, and a higher output per person, y_1^*. After the economy experiences a temporary growth spurt as it moves to the new higher steady-state growth path, it returns to its initial growth rate, with total output rising at the rate of population growth.

The technological innovation works essentially through two channels. First, technological innovation allows the same amount of capital per person to produce more output. Second, by stimulating saving, a technological innovation raises the amount of investment per person, increasing capital per person until the economy reaches a new, higher steady-state level of capital per person. A one-time increase in technology, however, will increase the growth rate of output per person only during a transition period. Because in the steady state output per person is constant, a technological innovation does not affect the steady-state growth rate of output per person. To affect the long-run economic growth rate per person, technological innovations must continue. Something similar to the one-time technological change described here must happen every year. We can summarize the conclusion of adding technology to the basic Solow growth model as follows:

Technological innovation up → k^* up → i^* up → y^* up; growth rate doesn't change; output per person remains constant.

- Technological innovation will raise output (and income) per person but will not lead to a permanently higher growth rate in output per person. In the steady state, total output will resume growing at the rate of population growth.

Conclusions About Saving, Population Growth, Depreciation, and Technological Innovation

We began this section wondering whether any of the exogenous variables (the givens) in the Solow growth model—saving rate, population growth rate, the depreciation rate, and level of technology—could answer this chapter's first policy question: What makes economies grow? We saw that an increase in the saving rate will increase income per person, and in the transition to a new steady state, income per person will grow. However, because of diminishing marginal productivity, economic growth per person will eventually slow and return to zero. Because only a steadily rising saving rate could explain persistent economic growth per person, and we do not observe steadily rising saving rates, increases in the saving rate cannot explain persistent economic growth per person.

An increase in population growth will lead to a higher level of total output, but lower output per person. Some studies do show that countries with high rates of population growth tend to have low incomes per person. A decrease in population growth will increase income per person, but the rise in economic growth per person is only temporary. In the steady state, economic growth per person will be zero. With population growth rates of 2 percent and less in most developed nations, a steadily falling population growth rate cannot explain sustained growth in income per person. Depreciation affects growth in a way that is similar to population growth. Changes in depreciation do not change steady-state output per person.

Although increases in saving and decreases in population growth do not lead to sustained economic growth per person, policies that promote saving and lower population growth are still popular policy choices for policy makers. Both lead to higher economic growth per person as the economy moves from one steady-state equilibrium to another. The transition period can last 20 to 30 years. So, even though, technically speaking, these policies do not affect growth in income per person in the steady state, a policy maker is typically concerned with more practical issues: What will raise economic growth per person while I'm in office, or over the next 5 to 10 years?

How about technology? A one-time increase in technology won't increase growth permanently. Technological advance must be continuous. Although this is a likely explanation for sustained economic growth per person, here is the rub: In the simple Solow growth model, technology is exogenous. So, the Solow growth model can explain economic growth per person by assuming steady growth in technology. Although the Solow model isolates technology as the cause of continuous economic growth per person, it does not explain why technology grows over time.

The basic Solow growth model has been modified and expanded in a number of ways so that it can answer such questions. For example, labor has been interpreted to embody technology and thereby incorporate technological increases. The Solow model also has been adjusted to incorporate increasing, rather than decreasing, returns to scale. Some of these adjustments are discussed in the next chapter.

Policies that promote saving and lower population growth lead to only temporary increases in growth. Despite this, they remain popular policies.

Executive Summary

- In the Solow model, an increase in the saving rate leads to an increase in the level of income per person, but it does not change the growth rate of income per person in the long run.

- An increase in population growth in the Solow model leads to lower income per person, but it does not change the growth rate of income per person in the long run.

- A rise in the rate of depreciation lowers output per person, but does not change the growth of output per person in the long run.

- In the Solow model, a technological advance increases income per person, but it does not lead to an increase in the growth rate of income per person in the steady-state equilibrium.

- Continual technological advances can lead to continuous growth of output per person.

POLICY PERSPECTIVE: INCENTIVES FOR SAVING AND INVESTMENT

How does the Solow growth model help us answer the policy question, presented at the beginning of the chapter "What policies will make our economies grow faster?" The Solow growth model, in some ways, underlies the long-run framework, in which saving is good for the economy in the long run.

The Solow growth model, however, adds a subtle qualification: There's a limit to higher growth rates that saving can achieve. An increase in saving, by increasing capital in the economy, temporarily pushes up the growth rate of output per person, but because of diminishing marginal productivity, the economy eventually slows and the steady-state growth of income per person falls to zero. Of course, an increase in the level of income per person is nothing to sneeze at, and policy makers have used the Solow model to justify policies to stimulate saving (see The Briefing Room, "Policies to Encourage Saving in Mexico"). Another point is that the transition from one steady state equilibrium to the next can take 20 to 30 years; the "temporary" boost in the growth in income per person can appear permanent.

Transition periods can last 20 or 30 years, which makes policies that temporarily increase growth, such as increased saving, popular, even though they do not increase steady-state growth.

Incentives for Saving

Consumption-based taxes are meant to stimulate saving.

One policy that many economists believe would stimulate saving is the replacement of the income tax with a **consumption-based tax**—a tax on spending. With

THE BRIEFING ROOM Policies to Encourage Saving: A Mexican Case Study

Because, in the transition period, greater saving leads to higher income per person and a higher growth rate of income per person, many governments have considered policies to encourage saving. Harvard economist Martin Feldstein looked at what the Mexican government could do to improve an economy in which average income per person is about one-fourth of the U.S. average. He recommended several changes to the existing tax laws, regulation of financial markets, and suggested a campaign to educate the public about saving. The following summarizes a few of his suggestions:

1. Change the laws to encourage people to buy life insurance. When you pay your insurance premium, the company invests part of your payment in stocks and bonds and other financial assets. Because of this, Feldstein points out that life insurance plans are a particularly good way for people to save. Feldstein recommends exempting much of the earnings of insurance companies from taxation or allowing individuals to deduct insurance premiums from taxable income to encourage more long-term saving through life insurance policies. Other countries have already adopted similar policies.

2. Change the restrictions on individual retirement accounts (IRAs). In Mexico, individuals must invest a substantial portion of their IRAs in government bonds, which earn a low rate of return. This restriction discourages saving. Removing this restriction could raise the return IRAs can earn and encourage more saving.

3. Remove restrictions on banks' ability to offer long-term savings accounts. In the United States, individuals can put their money into certificates of deposit (CDs), deposits that have early withdrawal penalties but pay interest rates higher than rates paid on savings accounts. In Mexico, banks do not offer CDs, because they are not allowed to penalize savers for early withdrawal. Removing this restriction would encourage banks to offer these long-term saving options.

4. Offer lottery bonds. Great Britain has successfully offered so-called lottery bonds. These are government bonds that pay slightly lower rates of return than non-lottery government bonds. Once a week, the government randomly draws bond serial numbers, and the winners receive substantial money prizes.

5. Reduce the high corporate and individual income tax rates. Feldstein argues that the tax on corporations and individuals in Mexico is so high that much of the economic activity takes place in the underground economy. If the government were to reduce the tax rates, tax revenues might actually rise, because businesses and individuals would have less incentive to limit reported income. Higher tax revenues would increase government saving, which would increase national saving.

6. Educate the public about existing tax incentives that encourage saving.

---

a consumption-based tax, total taxes paid depend on spending, not earnings. Say two individuals have incomes of $50,000 each. One spends $30,000, saving $20,000, while the other spends the entire $50,000. With an income-based tax, such as the one the United States has, they both pay the same amount of tax. In a consumption-based tax, the individual who saves pays a lower tax. By increasing the cost of consumer goods, a consumption-based tax provides an economic incentive to save.

In the late 1990s, the United States considered replacing all, or at least a portion, of its income-based tax with a consumption-based tax. A study by the Congressional Budget Office (CBO) estimated that switching to a consumption-based tax would raise the level of output per person between 1 percent and 10 percent. Consistent with the Solow growth model, however, tax reform was not expected to permanently raise the growth rate of income per person.

Although the United States does not have a broad-based consumption tax, it does have a variety of policies designed to provide incentives to save. For example, individual retirement accounts (IRAs) and individual medical accounts allow individuals to save a certain amount of their income tax-free. Another such policy is encouraging 401(k) plans, which reduce taxable income by the amount saved for retirement. In 2001 President George W. Bush signed a tax bill that expanded saving plans for retirement.

The connection between these targeted saving plans and their effect on saving and growth is subject to some debate. The problem is the degree to which such saving plans reshuffle existing wealth instead of creating new saving. For example, IRAs may not increase saving much; they may simply lead individuals to put the money they were already saving into a different form of saving. Some economists argue that such partial programs are simply giveaways to the rich, with little benefit to society in the way of increased saving.

Even the underlying theory behind pro-saving policies in general does not go unchallenged. There are two general arguments against them. The first argument involves equity issues. Because individuals with higher incomes generally save a greater percent of their income, these policies usually shift the tax burden from higher income individuals to lower income individuals. Politically, this makes this policy difficult to implement, and creates some opposition within the economics profession.

The second argument is theoretical. For saving to stimulate growth, it must be translated into investment. This does not always happen, and when it does not, additional saving can actually throw the economy into recession (the paradox of thrift). For a pro-saving policy to work, the institutional structure must be one in which there is sufficient demand for the goods produced.

Tax Incentives for Investment

Tax incentives for investment encourage investment. An example is an investment tax credit.

A second set of policies that many economists support at various times is **tax incentives for investment.** These are policies that lower the cost of investment, encouraging investment. For example, current U.S. tax laws allow small businesses to deduct up to $20,000 of expenditures on investment. These laws allow an immediate write-off—the equivalent to postponing taxation of income. Under normal rules, an investment must be depreciated over 3 to 25 years. With immediate write-offs, the business can deduct the cost of capital from taxable income the year that the capital is bought. If the tax rate is 25 percent, immediate write-offs can reduce taxes significantly in the initial year. In later years, the firm will have increased taxes, but by investing still more in the future years, it can postpone these taxes even further. In the 1980s, a variety of accelerated depreciation plans were introduced and expanded. Such policies that stimulate investment have been around for a long time. In the 1960s, the government introduced an **investment tax credit**—a government tax rebate to firms for their investment.

Because the Solow model emphasizes policies designed to stimulate saving and investment, it naturally deemphasizes other types of policies. It provides little guidance for policies to stimulate demand or to encourage technology. This points out why theories are so important even if one's focus is on policy: The theory sets the policy agenda and leads policy makers to look at the world in a certain way. In the next chapter, we explore some alternatives to the Solow growth model and see how these alternative theories change the focus of policy.

CONCLUSION

We began this chapter with a story and an observation. The story was about how, over long periods of time, small differences in growth rates can lead to large differences in income per person. The point of that story is that growth matters a lot. If a country can increase its average growth rate by even a fraction of a percent, income per person can rise substantially over a number of years. That is why economists spend a lot of time trying to figure out what determines growth and why policy makers are always seeking to increase growth.

Where are we today? Growth rates and levels of income per person differ greatly across countries around the world. To help explain these differences, we presented the Solow growth model, which focuses on the role of investment and saving in the growth process.

The Solow growth model helps us understand how saving and investment affect growth, but it doesn't explain all of the differences in growth across the world and it leaves us with few policy options for affecting long-term growth. We found that an increase in the saving rate, a decrease in the population growth rate, or a one-time increase in the state of technology will increase growth for a time, but, eventually, the economy will return to its steady-state growth path, where income per person is constant.

For many countries, the temporary increase in growth associated with increasing saving and investment carries large and long-lasting benefits. As a consequence, many policies have been formulated to encourage saving and investment. Only continual growth in technology, however, leads to continuous growth in income per person, and the Solow growth model leaves technology and technological change unexplained. So, as you will see in the next chapter, to fully explain differences in growth and provide useful advice to policy makers, it is necessary to go beyond the Solow growth model.

KEY POINTS

- Zero or very slow economic growth per person marked the first 1,500 years of the last two millennia. Since that time, economic growth per person has increased and is now about 1.5 percent per year.
- Small differences in the growth rates of two economies will lead to large differences in their levels of income over long periods of time.
- The most important development in the history of economic growth was the development of markets.
- The Solow growth model, a neoclassical model of growth, shows the relationship between the saving rate, capital per person, income per person, and the rate of economic growth per person.
- The steady-state equilibrium in the Solow growth model occurs where investment per person is equal to the balanced growth rate of capital.
- In the steady-state equilibrium in the Solow growth model, output and capital grow at the same rate as the population.

- An increase in the saving rate leads to an increase in income per person, but no long-term increase in the growth rate of income per person.
- An increase in the population growth rate leads to a decrease in income per person, but no long-term decrease in the growth rate of income per person.
- An increase in the rate of depreciation lowers output per person, but does not change steady-state output growth.
- An increase in technology leads to an increase in income per person, but no long-term increase in the growth rate of income per person.
- The policy focus of the Solow growth model is on saving, investment, and the supply side of the economy.
- The Solow growth model doesn't explain why output per person continually rises. It points to technology, which is outside the model, as the cause of economic growth per person. This pushes back the growth question.

KEY TERMS

balanced growth investment 132
balanced growth investment
  line 132
consumption-based tax 144

division of labor 127
human capital 128
investment tax credit 146
Solow growth model 129

specialization 127
steady-state equilibrium 134
tax incentives for investment 146
transition period 138

QUESTIONS FOR THOUGHT AND REVIEW

1. What factors account for the increase in growth starting around 1500 AD?
2. What are the three main policies that economists suggest for increasing growth? Give specific examples of each policy.
3. What do specialization and the division of labor have to do with economists' support of free trade?
4. What justification does the Solow growth model have for focusing on supply rather than demand?
5. What does the per-person production function tells us determines output per person?
6. What would be the shape of the production function if it exhibited constant marginal productivity? What if it exhibited increasing marginal productivity?
7. Describe how capital per-person is affected by changes in population growth, the rate of depreciation, and the saving rate.
8. What factors determine the amount of investment in the economy?
9. Describe in words what the balanced growth investment line represents.
10. Describe in words what a steady-state equilibrium is in the Solow growth model.
11. Suppose the economy's investment per person is above the balanced growth investment line. What will happen to bring this economy back to steady-state equilibrium?

12. Suppose the economy's investment per person is below the balanced growth investment line. What will happen to bring this economy back to steady-state equilibrium?
13. If the production function is $y = \sqrt{k}$ and the saving rate is v, what is the investment per-person function?
14. Assuming depreciation is d and the population is growing at a rate of n, what is the growth rate of total output in the steady state? What is the growth rate of per-person output in the steady state?
15. Does the basic Solow growth model explain the growth that we observe in the real world?
16. Use the Solow growth model to explain what will happen to growth of output per-person in the transition period and in the steady state in each of the following cases: (a) the saving rate decreases; (b) a virus wipes out the memories of one-third of the population; and (c) cloning increases population growth.
17. According to the basic Solow growth model, what is the source of continuous growth in output per person?
18. Why do policy makers focus on policies to encourage saving when the Solow growth model suggests that increased saving will not increase growth in the steady state?
19. Describe a policy the government can use to encourage saving. Describe a policy the government can use to encourage investment.

PROBLEMS AND EXERCISES

1. Consider two economies, A and B. Income per person is $30,000 in country A and $29,000 in country B. Income per person is growing at an annual rate of 2.5 percent in country A and at an annual rate of 3 percent in country B.
   a. Compare incomes per person between country A and B for the next 10 years.
   b. How many years does it take for country B to catch up with country A?

   c. At the end of 10 years, how much greater is income per person in country B compared with that in country A?
2. Demonstrate that the per-person production function $y = \sqrt{k}$ exhibits constant returns to scale and diminishing marginal product.
3. Suppose the production function is $y = \sqrt{k}$, the initial capital stock per person is 2, the depreciation rate is 10 percent, the population growth rate is 4 percent,

and the saving rate is 40 percent. What are output per person, capital per person, investment per person, and balanced growth investment per person in the first five periods of adjustment toward steady-state equilibrium?

4. Suppose the production function is $y = \sqrt{k}$, the initial capital stock per person is 2, the depreciation rate is 10 percent, the population growth rate is 4 percent, and the saving rate is 40 percent. What are capital per person, income per person, investment per person, and consumption per person in steady-state equilibrium?

5. Use the Solow growth model to graphically demonstrate what happens to output per person in the steady state when
   a. Population growth increases
   b. The saving rate declines

c. Technology increases
d. Capital depreciates more quickly

6. According to the Solow growth model, what happens to output per person during the transition period toward steady state when
   a. Population growth decreases
   b. The saving rate increases
   c. Technology decreases
   d. The depreciation rate falls

7. Go to the Web site datacentre.chass.utoronto.ca/pwt/index.html and look up the following data (called *topics*) on two countries of your choice: capital stock per worker (1985 International Prices) and real GDP per worker (1985 International Prices) from 1980 to 2000. Do the data match the prediction of the Solow growth model that output per worker is positively related to capital per worker?

6

If I have seen further, it is by
standing on the shoulders
of giants.

—*Sir Isaac Newton*

Beyond the Solow Growth Model

After reading this chapter you should be able to:

1. Give three reasons why it is important to go beyond the basic Solow growth model

2. Demonstrate how three modifications address the shortcomings of the basic Solow growth model

3. Distinguish between the Solow growth model and new growth theory

4. List four inputs to the production of technology

5. Explain how the ideas of Adam Smith and Joseph Schumpeter support the ideas in new growth theory

6. Discuss five growth policies recommended by new growth theory

Last chapter we introduced you to growth. We described the world's growth rates and presented a model to explain that growth—the basic Solow growth model. (In the remainder of this chapter when we say the "Solow growth model," we are referring to the *basic* Solow growth model presented in Chapter 5. We make this distinction to contrast it with the *extended* Solow growth model.) In this model, income per person depends on the saving rate, population growth, depreciation, and technology. Changes in any of these factors affect growth only during a transition period; in the steady state, there is no growth. A persistent increase in technology leads to permanent growth. However, the Solow growth model doesn't address how technological innovation occurs.

How well does the Solow growth model describe real-world growth? Economists have found that answering this question isn't easy. Comparing growth experiences over time and across countries means looking at many factors. As the Solow growth model suggests, factors that may appear to affect growth, such as changes in the saving rate or growth rate of the population, may be only moving an economy to a different equilibrium level of income per person, not to a different equilibrium growth rate. So, the problem becomes not only what factors to look at but also what time frame to consider.

We begin this chapter by looking at three reasons to go beyond the Solow growth model. We then introduce extensions of that model and new growth theory. You won't end up with definitive answers about what causes growth

The basic Solow growth model is not enough to explain persistent economic growth.

Economists cannot explain growth by the accumulation of capital alone.

(economists are still not quite sure), but you will learn two main points. First, the Solow model is not enough to explain persistent economic growth. Growth is the result of more than saving and investing; some countries have invested and have not grown. Economists cannot explain the totality of growth by the accumulation of capital. Second, policy makers must think more broadly about the policy options facing countries that wish to increase their growth rates. These policy options focus on developing environments that foster technological innovation rather than on only saving and investing.

THREE REASONS TO GO BEYOND THE SOLOW GROWTH MODEL

Many economists and policy makers look beyond the Solow growth model for three reasons:

1. The Solow growth model doesn't explain two important empirical observations: Growth rates have tended to accelerate over the past 180 years and poor countries aren't catching up to rich countries.
2. Sometimes, saving and investing—the policy prescription of the Solow model—do not lead to higher income per person.
3. Technological innovation accounts for much of the growth in developed economies, but the Solow growth model doesn't explain where that technological innovation comes from—or how to encourage it.

The Solow Growth Model Doesn't Fit the Facts

Predictions of the basic Solow growth model do not match two observations: Growth rates have accelerated, and incomes have not converged.

The predictions of a model should fit our observations of the real world. The Solow growth model predicted that (1) growth rates would decline over time as economies approached their steady states and (2) poor countries would grow faster than rich countries. In Chapter 5, however, you saw that world growth rates have not declined, but have accelerated from virtually zero up until the early 1800s when they accelerated to 1.5 percent and above. Table 6–1 shows that growth in the United States has been, for the most part, accelerating since 1800.

The second prediction of the basic Solow model that is not supported by the evidence is its **convergence hypothesis**—a prediction that, eventually, income per person of poor countries will catch up to that of rich countries. Convergence hasn't happened. Poor countries have tended to remain very poor, and rich countries have tended to remain very rich.

Table 6-1

Growth in the United States

Period	Annual Percent Change in Real GDP per Person
1800–1840	0.58
1840–1880	1.44
1880–1920	1.78
1920–1960	1.68
1960–2000	2.30

Source: *Historical Statistics of the United States: Colonial Times to 1970.* Washington, DC: The Government Printing Office, 1989, and the Bureau of Economic Statistics.

Comparison of Income per Person with the United States

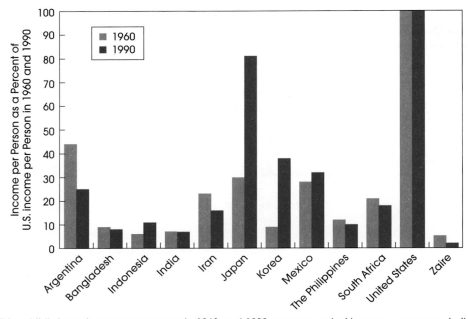

This exhibit shows income per person in 1960 and 1990 as a percent of income per person in the United States for 11 countries. If countries' incomes were converging, the blue bars would be higher than the red bars. Income per person is measured by nominal GDP per person. The most recent figures for Zaire are for 1989. Source: Temple, Jonathan. 1999. "The new growth evidence." *Journal of Economic Literature* 37(1):112–56.

We can look at the evidence in two ways. One way is to directly compare income levels over time. Exhibit 6–1 shows income per person for a group of countries as a percent of income per person in the United States in 1960 (the red bars) and 1990 (the blue bars). If countries' incomes were converging, all of the blue bars would be higher than all of the red bars. That is, the incomes per person of all countries would be converging to the level in the United States. Of the countries shown, Japan's income per person has progressed the furthest; income per person in Japan rose from 30 percent of U.S. income per person in 1960 to 80 percent in 1990. Other countries' progress is not as dramatic. In some countries, such as Argentina, relative incomes fell. Overall evidence shows that per-person incomes among countries have not tended to converge.

Another way to look at the evidence is to compare growth rates between poor and rich countries. If the income levels of poor countries are to catch up to those of rich countries, income per person in poor countries will have to grow faster than in rich countries. Before considering the evidence, let's see why the Solow growth model makes this prediction.

Suppose two countries, A and B, have the same saving rate, depreciation rate, population growth rate, and level of technology. The only difference is that country A's income per person is lower than country B's. According to the Solow growth model, country A is poor and country B is rich, because country A has less capital per person than country B, as Exhibit 6–2 shows. How about their growth rates? Because there is diminishing marginal product (the slope of the production function gets flatter), growth of income per person is greater in country A than in country B. So, according to the Solow model, *poor countries should grow faster than rich countries, all else held constant.*

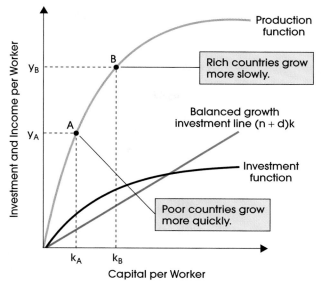

Country A is poorer than country B. Both countries are converging to the same steady-state level of income per person, but because of diminishing marginal productivity of capital, income per person is growing at a faster rate in country A than in country B, as the declining slope of the production function shows.

Now let's take a look at the evidence. If the basic Solow growth model is correct, the level and growth rate of income per person will be inversely correlated. Countries with low incomes should have high growth rates, and countries with high incomes should have low growth rates. Exhibit 6–3 is a scatterplot of growth rates and incomes per person for a number of countries. Each point represents one country's annual growth rate from 1960 to 1990 (measured on the vertical axis) and its level of income

Exhibit 6-3

Poor Countries Don't Grow Faster than Rich Countries

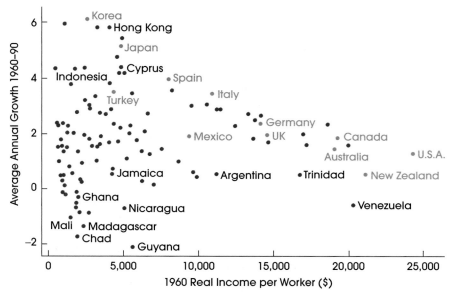

This scatterplot shows per capita growth rates from 1960 to 1990 and income levels in 1960 for a number of countries. The scatter of dots doesn't support the Solow model's conclusion that countries with high levels of income per capita grow more slowly than countries with low levels of income per capita. OECD countries are shown in green because they have similar economic attributes. Initial income levels and subsequent growth rates are inversely related for these countries. Source: Temple, Jonathan. 1999. "The new growth evidence." *Journal of Economic Literature* 37(1):112–56.

153

per person in 1960 (measured on the horizontal axis). If the scatterplot were to support the Solow growth model's prediction about income levels and growth rates, the points would be clustered from the upper left to the lower right of the graph. Interestingly, the United States had the highest income per person in 1960 and about average economic growth from 1960 to 1990. Many other developed countries, such as Canada, Australia, the United Kingdom, and Germany, are all clustered together. Chad had one of the lowest incomes per person in 1960 and nearly the lowest economic growth; it is clustered with a number of other low-income, slow-growth countries.

These two pieces of evidence tell us that, for the world as a whole, convergence hasn't happened. (While there is some tendency for upper-middle and high-income countries, to converge toward one another, that is not the case for poor countries. This raises the question: What is different about the poor countries that keeps them poor?) In general, poor countries are not growing faster than rich countries.

Saving and Investing Sometimes Don't Foster Growth

The second reason for going beyond the Solow growth model is that saving and investment don't always lead to growth. The Solow model focuses the analysis of growth on saving and investment and conveys the same message as the proverb of the grasshopper and the ant: The ant works all summer to store food for the winter, while the grasshopper squanders away his days basking in the sun. When winter comes, the ant has plenty to sustain himself, but the grasshopper has nothing. The Solow growth model suggests that poor countries—the grasshoppers—are poor because they have not sacrificed and saved as much as rich countries—the ants.

For poor countries, this model offers a straightforward (and morally appealing) recipe for success: Sacrifice, save, and invest, and your economy will prosper. But for many poor countries, this hasn't worked. For example, during its entire 80-year history, the Soviet Union saved and invested a tremendous amount in physical capital. When the Soviet Union broke apart in the late 1980s, most of the countries comprising the union had income levels comparable to those of *developing* countries. What went wrong? Why didn't saving and investing bring the Soviet Union to income levels comparable to the United States, Japan, or Western Europe? There are many other examples of countries around the world that have stagnated while investing heavily in physical capital. To be sure, some countries have saved, invested, and grown. But these varied experiences suggest that just saving and investing isn't enough. There must be something more.

Technology Is a Residual in the Solow Growth Model

The third reason for looking beyond the Solow growth model has to do with technology. When Solow developed his model of economic growth, he also developed a way to measure the contribution of factors of production to growth in total output, called growth accounting. An equation that shows the contribution of each factor of production to growth of total output is the **growth accounting formula.** It is derived from the Solow growth model. The growth accounting formula for the United States is

$$\%\Delta Y = \%\Delta A + 0.3\%\Delta K + 0.7\%\Delta L \qquad (6\text{-}1)$$

(Appendix A formally derives the growth accounting formula.) This formula divides the causes of growth of total output into three components: technological progress

---

The Solow growth model conveys the same message as the proverb of the grasshopper and the ant: Work hard, save, and invest.

For many countries, saving and investing alone has not worked.

The growth accounting formula: $\%\Delta Y = \%\Delta A + 0.3\%\Delta K + 0.7\%\Delta L$.

(which is assumed exogenous), growth of capital, and growth of labor. The growth rates of capital and labor are weighted by each factor's relative importance to production in the economy, which is determined by their relative income shares—the amount of income paid to each factor of production divided by total income. Capital is weighted by 0.3 because 30 percent of all income in the economy goes to the owners of capital. Labor is weighted by 0.7 because 70 percent of all income in the economy goes to labor. Despite the many changes in the U.S. economy since the end of World War II, these weights have basically remained unchanged.

Economists use this formula to indirectly measure technological progress. The growth rates of output ($\%\Delta Y$), capital ($\%\Delta K$), and labor ($\%\Delta L$) are all directly observable. The growth rate of output is real GDP growth. The growth rate of capital is investment minus depreciation, and the growth rate of labor is the growth of the labor force. Growth that is not explained by increases in capital or labor is assumed to be caused by the third factor—technology.

For example, suppose output, capital, and labor grow at annual rates of 3 percent, 4 percent, and 1 percent, respectively. Putting these percents into the growth accounting formula, we have $3 = \%\Delta A + 0.3(4) + 0.7(1)$, or $3 = \%\Delta A + 1.9$. The growth of capital and labor (appropriately weighted) accounts for 1.9 percentage points of the 3 percent real output growth. According to the model, the remainder of the growth must be due to a change in technology. Solving the growth accounting equation for the growth of technology, we get $\%\Delta A = 3 - 1.9 = 1.1$ percent.

This measure of technological progress in the Solow growth model is sometimes called the **Solow residual** because it measures the contribution of technological progress to growth after measurable factors are accounted for. It is what's left over—the residual. Some economists object to using this residual as a measure of technological progress, claiming that the residual shows our inability to correctly measure capital or labor or is due to other factors that may or may not be the result of technological progress.

Despite these objections, however, growth accounting is widely used to measure the contribution of the factors of production to growth. Most studies that use this equation find that the growth of technological progress accounts for a significant portion of growth in developed economies.

Exhibit 6–4 shows estimates of each factor's contribution to growth of total output for the United States since 1929. Capital accounts for 19 percent, labor accounts for 46 percent, and technology accounts for 35 percent of growth.

> Technology is a residual in the Solow growth model.

Exhibit 6–4

Contributions of Capital, Labor, and Technology to U.S. Growth

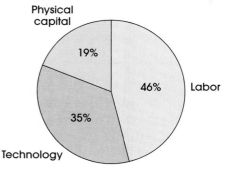

Increases in labor account for 46 percent of U.S. economic growth since 1929. Accumulation of capital accounts for 19 percent, and technological innovation accounts for the remaining 35 percent. Source: Edward F. Denison. 1985. *Trends in Economic Growth 1929–1982*. Washington, DC: The Brookings Institute, and author estimates.

Because technological progress accounts for over one-third of U.S. growth and because changes in labor and capital cannot explain fluctuations in growth rates, economists have pointed to changes in the rate of technological change to explain fluctuations in growth rates. In the mid-1970s, growth in most developed economies slowed, and that slowdown has been attributed to a slowdown in technological progress. It rose again in 1995 and that, too, was attributed to growth of technology. However, because economists don't have a good handle on how technology develops in the first place, it was difficult for them to explain why the rate fell so suddenly, or why it rose again. (See the Q&A feature on the labor productivity slowdown.)

Q & A	**QUESTION**	**Why did labor productivity slow in the mid-1970s and rise in the mid-1990s and 2000?**
	ANSWER	**Though economists have put forth several possible reasons, no one knows for sure.**

As we mentioned in Chapter 2, GDP per person in most industrialized economies began to grow more slowly during the mid-1970s and has increased recently. Labor productivity grew at an average rate of just over 1 percent per year from 1974 through 1995. From 1995 through 2000, labor productivity growth averaged nearly 2.0 percent per year. Although this rate was still not as high as the average productivity growth rate of 2.6 percent in the 1950s and 1960s, it is a substantial improvement over the average from 1974 to 1995.

Economists have provided several possible explanations for these changes. One "explanation" for the slowdown in the mid-1970s is that it didn't really occur: Economists just haven't measured productivity correctly. According to this argument, the increase in energy prices during the 1970s slowed measured productivity growth by increasing costs of total production, even though physical productivity did not change. Another explanation is that the ideas that generated the technology boom of the 1950s and 1960s dried up in the mid-1970s. Still another explanation is that low saving and investment rates in the United States during the 1960s reduced the growth of

capital per worker, which reduced the growth of output per worker—our measure of labor productivity. A final explanation is that an increase in government regulations increased the cost of production and slowed productivity. If a factory has to install a scrubber on its smoke stack, it will cost more to produce a given amount of output. That higher cost shows up as lower labor productivity.

Just as economists are unable to provide a complete explanation for the productivity slowdown in the 1970s, the recent upturn in productivity growth is also somewhat of a mystery. To explain it, some economists are simply reversing some of the above explanations. Others believe it is the result of the restructuring that occurred during the 1990–1991 recession, which caused firms to eliminate inefficiencies. Other economists attribute this upturn to a new technology shock—the widespread use of computers and the Internet. Still other economists claim that this is a temporary increase in productivity growth that will reverse, bringing the growth rate back to post-1973 rates. What do these continual debates tell us? One, the data aren't very good, and, two, the role of technology in growth is a very complicated subject.

Economists have used the growth accounting formula to analyze the causes of growth in other economies as well. A case of particular interest in the 1980s and early 1990s was the then fast-growing Asian economies called the Asian Tigers. Economist Paul Krugman estimated that nearly all of the growth in Asian Tiger economies was the result of increases in labor and capital. For example, in Singapore from 1966 to 1990, the labor force participation rate rose from 27 percent to 51 percent, and investment rose from 11 percent to 40 percent of total output. Krugman argued that technological progress in these economies was nearly nonexistent and, because of this, as diminishing marginal product set in, growth would eventually slow. Other economists, using different measures of capital and labor, disagreed. The World Bank, for instance, reported that technology accounted for one-third of Asia's growth since 1960. In the mid- to late 1990s, many Asian Tiger economies slowed, and some went into recession. Whether the slowdown means a slowing in long-term growth, however, is still debated today.

Executive Summary

- Three reasons to go beyond the basic Solow growth model: (1) It doesn't explain two important empirical observations: Growth rates have tended to accelerate over the past 180 years and poor countries aren't catching up to rich countries; (2) sometimes saving and investing do not lead to higher income per person; and (3) the source of technological progress, a large contributor to growth, remains unexplained.

- Estimates of the growth accounting formula suggest that technological progress accounts for a large portion of growth, but technology is not explained in the Solow growth model, leaving a large portion of growth unexplained.

MOVING BEYOND THE BASIC SOLOW GROWTH MODEL

Two approaches that go beyond the basic Solow growth model are (1) an expansion of the basic model; (2) new growth theory.

Economists have taken two approaches to improving our understanding of growth. The first approach is to expand the Solow growth model. The second approach is to develop a new framework, which economists call new growth theory. These approaches are not mutually exclusive; they simply emphasize different things. From a policy perspective, there is very little difference between these two approaches. Both emphasize policies that encourage technological innovation in addition to policies that emphasize capital formation.

Expanding the Solow Growth Model

Let's start by looking at how economists have expanded the Solow growth model. We made some pretty big assumptions in the Solow growth model that directly led to its predictions. For example, we assumed that countries are alike in every respect except their initial levels of capital per person. But what about differences in countries' topographies, geographic sizes, institutions, populations, cultures, and labor forces? All of these factors are likely to affect growth. So far in our analysis, we've assumed they are the same across all countries, but these factors differ considerably from country to country.

Conditional convergence predicts that incomes for countries with similar attributes will eventually become equal.

Conditional Convergence. One of the major predictions of the Solow growth model was convergence. The basic model predicted absolute convergence—income per person would equalize throughout the world. By changing the assumption that all countries' governments, institutions, and cultures are alike, absolute convergence is no longer predicted. However, what is called *conditional convergence* is still predicted. The **conditional convergence hypothesis** is the prediction that income per person for economies *with similar attributes* will eventually become equal. Looking back to Exhibit 6–3, you can see that the initial income levels and subsequent growth rates are inversely related for the OECD countries listed in green, which do have similar attributes.

What about countries with different attributes? Even though economies with different attributes are not expected to converge to the same level of income per person, the basic Solow growth model still predicts that their growth rates will converge to the rate of technological progress. There is some evidence to support this prediction. But the evidence is controversial, and the estimates of the rate at which economies converge are not precise. For example, a study by economists Robert Barro and Sali-i-Martin concluded that economies converge at a rate of 2 percent per year. However, when another economist, Jonathan Temple, reanalyzed the data, he found that the estimates of the rate of convergence range from 0 to 30 percent. With such large variance, it is difficult to attribute meaning to the average.

Explanations for Nonconvergence. Conditional convergence is a half-way point, and the empirical evidence is ambiguous. Some of the evidence suggests that there is no convergence at all—that the developed countries grow faster—creating an ever-increasing gap between rich and poor countries. Three possible explanations for how this could occur are (1) differences in the quality of labor force, (2) differences in institutions, and (3) increasing returns.

Differing Quality of Labor Among Countries. Workers differ among countries in terms of qualities such as education or health. For example, in the United States, one of the world's richest countries, 97 percent of adults are literate. In Haiti, one of the world's poorest countries, 45 percent of adults are literate. Similarly, countries with high rates of serious disease generally have less productive workforces than "healthier" countries. For example, economists John Gallup and Jeffrey Sachs found that high incidence of malaria reduced growth by 1.3 percentage points per year in afflicted countries.

> Differing quality of labor among countries can explain nonconvergence.

With such large differences in the quality of labor, using total employment or hours worked to represent the labor force in the Solow growth model might not meaningfully capture differences in the labor input; to do that, we must adjust the measure for quality differences. For example, say that two countries, A and B, have the same number of workers, but the quality of labor in developed country A is triple that of developing country B. Say also that developed country A has twice the capital of developing country B. Even though the developed country has twice the capital per person, it has less capital per person once adjusted for the improved quality of labor.

Let's consider the implications of this quality of labor argument for convergence with a numerical example. Suppose, as before, there are two countries—developed country A, which is growing faster than developing country B. Each has 100 workers, and country A has 600 units of capital, while country B has 300 units of capital. With only this information, the Solow growth model predicts the opposite of what we observe. It predicts that because developed country A has more capital per person, its income per person will grow at a slower rate than that of developing country B. This is because the diminishing marginal product of capital is much stronger in country A. It also predicts that, eventually, income per person would be the same in both countries.

If, however, we make an adjustment for the quality of workers, the Solow growth model's predictions change. If workers in developed country A are three times as productive as workers in developing country B, quality-adjusted labor is 300 in country A and 100 in country B. Taking into account differences in labor quality, developed country A has 2 units of capital per quality-adjusted worker compared with 3 units in developing country B. After making the adjustment for the quality of labor, capital per quality-adjusted person is *smaller* in the developed country and its marginal product of capital is *higher.* The Solow growth model would predict that the developed country would be growing more quickly. Not only that, but if the quality differences persist, it would predict that the developed country's steady-state income per person will be higher. An increase in the quality of labor is incorporated into the Solow growth model by rotating the production function up, which will lead to higher income in the steady state. Conditional convergence that adjusts for the quality of labor better matches our observations: Poor countries don't appear to be catching up.

As the above example shows, we can modify the Solow growth model to explain persistent differences in income per person. A country with 2 percent better quality workers than another country, perhaps resulting from a subsidy or tax incentive to attend college, will have a 2 percent higher income per person compared with the country with the lower quality of labor.

The problem comes in measuring the quality of labor. One way to integrate the quality of labor is to measure labor by human capital rather than by labor hours. Level of education is a measure of human capital. Years of education in advanced countries average 9.8 years, compared with 5.1 years in all developing countries. Economists have spent a great deal of effort estimating the effect of education on growth. Exhibit 6–5 shows one such well-known estimation by Robert Barro. He found a correlation between years of schooling for males and growth. Exhibit 6–5

Exhibit 6–5

Education and Growth

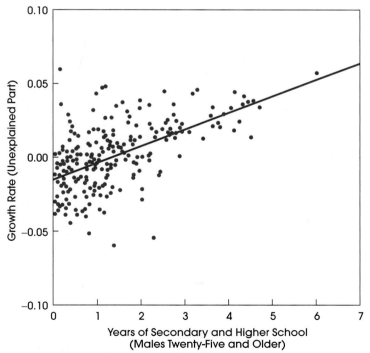

There is a clear, positive relationship between education and growth. Countries with a higher percentage of males attending secondary school or above have higher economic growth. Whether more education causes growth or growth causes more education is up for debate. Source: Robert Barro. 1997. *Determinants of Economic Growth.* Cambridge, MA: The MIT Press.

shows the relationship between schooling and economic growth for his sample of countries: A clear, positive relationship exists. Countries with a higher percentage of males attending secondary school or above also have higher economic growth than do countries with a less-educated population.

Economists are hesitant about these results for a number of reasons. First, Robert Barro didn't find the same correlation for female schooling, which is very puzzling: In many developing countries, women play central roles in the workforce, and, in other studies, female schooling has been shown to be important to growth. This suggests that Barro's measure of education might not be an accurate measure of human capital and that the correlation that he did find is spurious.

Second, even if the correlation is correct, it is an open question whether more schooling causes economic growth or whether economic growth leads to more schooling. (See the Q&A feature on correlation and causation.) Some economists argue that as countries grow, they can spend more money on education—that growth causes education. So, policies to promote education may not be the way to increase growth. They further argue that much of formal education serves to credentialize workers, determining who gets a limited number of jobs, but does not significantly improve the productivity of workers. They argue that the education that increases worker productivity in developing countries may be unrelated to the amount of formal education.

> Correlation does not necessarily imply causation.

Q & A	**QUESTION**	**What is the difference between correlation and causation, and is it important?**
	ANSWER	**Just because two variables are correlated doesn't mean one variable causes the other.**

The discussion of growth comes with a word of caution: *Correlation does not necessarily imply causation.* Suppose you are from a planet that is in desperate need of rain. You've been sent to earth to observe what causes rain and report back that your planet's problem is easy to solve. It seems that when earthlings carry large sticks attached to cloth or plastic, it usually rains sometime thereafter. When it rains, earthlings open their sticks to keep the rain coming. Your observation is based on correlation—you saw humans carrying umbrellas in the morning and rain in the afternoon—but, as we know, umbrellas do not cause rain. It is (the threat of) rain that makes people carry umbrellas.

The fact that growth is empirically related to increases in saving, investment, or what have you, does not necessarily mean that these inputs cause the growth. These inputs might just accompany the growth, which is caused by something that economists haven't yet discovered. Or, like the umbrella and rain example, causation may run contrary to what we know from other observations. As in the text example, instead of education causing growth, growth causes education. The moral: Although determining correlation is difficult, it is relatively easy compared to the problem of determining causation.

The education argument is another example of the problems that exist when one tries to draw inferences from available data, and why statistics and econometrics is such an important part of modern economics. In many cases, there simply are not enough data available to make definitive conclusions, and to draw even tentative conclusions at all requires sophisticated statistical techniques.

Differing Institutions. Another factor that the basic Solow growth model does not take into account, but which researchers have identified as influencing growth, is institutions. Institutions are the formal rules, customs, practices, and patterns of behavior that govern economic action. The Solow growth model assumes that all countries have the same institutions. If they do not, then this can be another reason why some countries grow faster than others—they have institutions that are better suited to growth.

Some economists have argued that institutions are so important that we should develop a whole new category of capital—social capital that captures institutions' role in the growth process. **Social capital** is institutions of a society, such as trust, customs, civic and government organizations, and laws, that positively affect growth. Social capital promotes growth by providing incentives to produce, invest in human capital and physical capital, and innovate. Trust, for example, can greatly affect the decision to produce. You would be less likely to start a restaurant if you couldn't trust your customers not to skip out on the bill. Likewise, you would be less likely to invest in capital if you thought that government might confiscate your earnings. The problem with social capital, however, is that it is difficult to measure, making it nearly impossible to quantitatively measure its effect on growth.

Stanford economist Robert Hall and National Bureau of Economic Research (NBER) economist Charles Jones created an index of social infrastructure that captures some elements of social capital. It includes measures of law and order and bureaucratic quality, which promote growth; corruption, risk of appropriation, and government repudiation of contracts, which halt growth. Using these measures they found a strong correlation between social capital and income levels. For example, Switzerland, Canada, and the United States, which have some of the highest incomes per person, had the highest indexes, while Zaire, Haiti, and Bangladesh, which are among the lowest income countries, had the lowest indexes. Of course, the correlation–causation caution must always be kept in mind.

Increasing Returns. A third adjustment that can be made to the basic Solow growth model is to allow for the possibility of increasing, rather than constant, returns to scale. A production function exhibits **increasing returns to scale** when an increase in all inputs leads to a proportionately greater increase in output, as Exhibit 6–6(a) shows. Exhibit 6–6(b) shows that a country with increasing-returns production

> Social capital is institutions of a society, such as trust, and laws that positively affect growth.

> Increasing returns to scale exist when an increase in all inputs leads to a proportionately greater increase in output.

Exhibit 6–6

Production Function with Increasing Returns

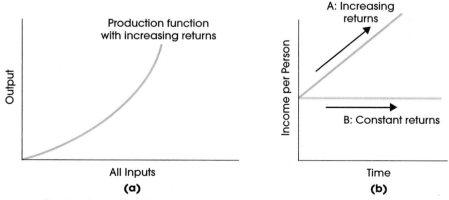

The production function in *panel a* exhibits increasing returns to scale. Output increases at an ever-increasing rate as all inputs increase. If an economy experiences increasing returns, it can follow growth path A in *panel b*, where per capita income is continually increasing. If it has constant returns, or if only some inputs are increased, so that diminishing marginal product offsets the increasing returns, the growth path could return to a path with zero growth per person, as shown by path B.

THE BRIEFING ROOM Virtuous Circles and Aggregate Demand

Once increasing returns are incorporated into the analysis of growth, a fixed, long-run rate of growth to which the economy always returns (as was assumed in the basic Solow growth model) seems far less likely. If increasing returns predominate in an economy, a key policy issue will then become the following: How do we get on the increasing-returns growth path? Expanding aggregate demand might be one way to do this.

The argument goes as follows: One determinant of investment in developing new technologies, and hence growth, is the expectation of demand. By increasing demand in the short run through expansionary monetary or fiscal policy, the government may (emphasize

may) push firms to spend more on producing new technologies and move the economy from a slow-growth path onto a virtuous circle. This virtuous circle will change the long-run growth path.

While increasing returns to scale opens up the possibility that, by increasing aggregate demand, the government can boost potential output, it does not suggest that increasing demand will be generally useful as a growth policy. Its usefulness is likely limited to specific circumstances, such as when the economy falls into an expectational conundrum. Ultimately, growth depends on supply and having a set of institutions that reward innovation and channel entrepreneurial energies in the right direction.

---

can have continual increases in income per person. This contrasts with constant returns, in which income per person doesn't change.

Increasing returns fundamentally changes the story that accompanies the growth process and removes any strong prediction of convergence. It creates the possibility of a **virtuous circle**, in which growth creates more growth. If increasing returns holds, then one of the reasons why countries grow is "because they grow." The country that grows first has a lead that will grow and grow, because a country's growth engenders more growth. (See The Briefing Room, "Virtuous Circles and Aggregate Demand" for a discussion of how virtuous circles provide a way for demand policies to affect long-run growth.)

Increasing returns creates the possibility of a virtuous circle.

We could assume that the production function in the Solow growth model exhibits increasing returns, but there is little motivation within the model for doing so. By focusing the analysis of growth on endogenous technological development, new growth theory provides that motivation.

Policy Implications of the Expanded Solow Growth Model. The basic Solow growth model focused policy on expanding capital; thus, it focused on policies that influence saving and investment. The expanded Solow growth model leads to a larger array of policy options. These policy options include expanding human capital through education, changing institutions to be more growth compatible, and creating incentives to move to industries that take advantage of increasing returns to scale. But the expanded Solow growth model does not give us significant direction as to which of these policies will work. That direction must come from one's broader understanding of growth and the growth process.

The expanded Solow growth model leads to a larger array of policy options, including expanding human capital, changing institutions, and directing production toward increasing-returns industries.

New Growth Theory

Some economists argue that expanding the Solow growth model is not enough, and that the broader understanding of growth will come through a broader understanding of technology. Their work goes under the name new growth theory. The focus of new growth theory is on endogenous technology, so whereas, in the Solow growth model, technology is a residual (outside of the production function), in new growth theory, technology is explained by the model. In fact, you can think of

New growth theory is a
theory that focuses on the
production of technology.
new growth theory as a theory of growth that focuses on the role of technology in growth. New growth theory focuses on the determinants of technology and, once that has been determined, integrates technology back into the economy's aggregate production function.

Nothing in new growth theory is necessarily incompatible with the Solow growth model; it simply brings the development of technology *into* the model. The focus on endogenous technology does, however, lead to a greater emphasis on increasing returns to scale and a de-emphasis of diminishing marginal products.

DETERMINANTS OF TECHNOLOGICAL INNOVATION

We now turn to the determinants of technological innovation, which is of primary interest to new growth theorists. In new growth theory, technology is not the product of a group of scientists who happen on discoveries. Instead, it is the result of a process that transforms inputs into technology. This can be described by the following production function for technology:

$$T = f(K, L, T, E) \tag{6-2}$$

Translated into words, the production function states that technology, an input in the production function for output, is itself a function of the capital (K) and labor (L) used to develop technology, the technology (T) used in that process, and the environment (E) in which that takes place.

Capital and Labor

The first two determinants—capital and labor—are familiar, but here they refer to the amount of capital and labor used in research and development. Because increases in technology are the natural outcome of research and development, the more a society invests in research and development, the higher will be its technological progress and growth. New growth theorists measure the amount countries spend on research and development, and argue that those countries that spend more on research and development will tend to grow faster than those that do not.

Technology

The third determinant, technology, refers to technology that is used in the development of new technologies. It is the methods and tools individuals use to come up with new ideas and new, more efficient ways of producing goods and services. If technology accelerates growth, then technology that is used to produce more technology is an accelerator of an accelerator. It increases the rate of growth of technology and, thereby, the rate of growth of the economy. This is the argument new growth theorists use to explain the increasing growth rates of developing economies over time.

Examples of technology that changed the process of developing technology are the transistor and the computer chip, which allowed researchers to study issues much more quickly and to solve mathematical problems that previously were beyond human calculation. These technologies have made it possible for people to develop more technologies. An example is the mapping of the human gene, which has led to new medicines and new techniques to diagnose disease. A complete mapping of the human gene was not possible without the use of computers. Therefore, the development of computers has led to technological progress (improved ability to diagnose and cure disease) in a totally different field.

More recently, easier access to ideas over the Internet has increased the speed at which information about innovations spreads. The Internet is an improvement in the technology of creating technology. The opening quotation by Sir Isaac Newton, "If I have seen further, it is by standing on the shoulders of giants," is Newton's recognition that his innovations were built on the innovations of those who preceded him. Technological innovation depends on past technology.

> General-purpose technologies are technologies that affect all aspects of production.

Technological developments can also be differentiated by how broadly they can be applied. **General-purpose technologies**—technologies that affect all aspects of production—have the strongest effects on growth. The development of the steam engine in the mid-1800s is an example of a general-purpose technology. Its development led to fundamental changes in all aspects of production and transportation, increasing productivity in a wide range of industries. In contrast, the spinning jenny, another innovation of that time, was not a general-purpose technology. It had a direct impact only in the textile industry.

In studying how general-purpose technologies have affected growth, researchers have found that, often, general-purpose technologies initially slow, rather than speed up, growth. The reason is that it is costly for people to integrate these new technologies into their production processes, and, initially, there are many failures. Adopting new technologies can be delayed even after efficient methods of production using these new technologies are developed. For example, at the time electricity was invented, manufacturers had just invested in production processes based on the steam engine. It was not cost effective to switch to electricity until their steam-based plants had depreciated sufficiently. As firms discover how to use these general-purpose technologies, they become much more efficient, and the technologies speed up growth significantly.

A more recent example of a general-purpose technology that initially did not speed up growth is the computer. In the first-half of the 1990s, firms were spending large amounts of money buying computers, with little increase in productivity. In the second-half of the 1990s, however, U.S. productivity growth picked up to over 4 percent per year.

> The S-curve phenomenon is the tendency for a new technology to initially slow down growth, and then significantly increase it.

The tendency for technological development to initially slow growth and then to speed it up has been called the S-curve phenomenon. Initially, you slide down the S (placed sideways), decreasing efficiency, and then you start climbing up the second part of the curve, increasing efficiency. Eventually, when the technology is fully integrated into production, it loses its effect, and growth must come from the development of a new technology.

The Diffusion of Technology, Convergence, and Increasing Returns

One of the interesting aspects of the development of technology is that it tends to be geographically concentrated. All places are not equally affected by technology. This creates a first-mover advantage, putting the area where it initially develops on an increasing-returns production function, and making that area or country grow while other countries find they are continually falling behind.

In explaining why this tends to be the case, new growth theorists have emphasized that there tends to be significant learning by doing in the technology development process. **Learning by doing** means the more one does something, the more productive one becomes. Learning by doing can work in a variety of ways. As you write more and more term papers, you internalize the process and, pretty soon, you can write a five-page, A paper in an hour. People who work with computers continually can deal with them far more efficiently than can those who do not.

Learning by doing means that the more one does something, the more productive one becomes.

Learning by doing gives a strong geographical component to technological development and leads to what are called *agglomeration effects.* **Agglomeration effects** occur when the concentration of firms producing similar goods in a geographic area increases productivity of all firms in the area. One cause of agglomeration effects is people working on new technologies getting together (agglomerate) and swapping ideas. As they do so, the cost of producing technological innovation falls. Instead of each person coming up with his own method of doing things, he can borrow ideas from others. New growth theorists argue that such interactions cause technological innovation to be geographically specific.

Agglomeration effects make growth happen in specific areas.

Workers in an industry learn the technological developments and then apply them to other industries in their geographic area. Examples are Silicon Valley in California or the Seattle area in Washington, which both have a concentration of high-tech firms. The growth that occurs in one sector leads to spin-offs in other sectors—spin-offs that initially take place in that same geographic area.

The slow geographic diffusion of some technology can lead to persistently different growth rates among areas. With agglomeration effects, once an area has begun producing new technologies, it can generate even more technological innovations and spin-offs, and keep on growing faster than other areas. This is one explanation economists give for why rich economies with access to advanced technologies, like the United States, continue to grow faster than poorer countries with less access to advanced technologies. Interestingly, the latest developments in communication and the Internet are making geography less important and, hence, may reduce agglomeration effects.

Economic Environment

A final determinant in the production function of technology—the economic environment—is crucial to technological innovation. Innovation is not just the result of purely scientific endeavors. Innovators and business people, motivated by profit, bring innovations to the marketplace in the form of new goods and services. New growth theory states that if a country wants to grow, it needs to create an environment in which entrepreneurs and innovators thrive and create new ideas. These institutions are similar to those discussed earlier—a stable government, protection of property rights, openness of trade, and enforcement of patent and copyright laws. Here, however, these institutions encourage not only production, but also innovation. Continual innovation will lead to positive and, possibly, ever-increasing growth rates.

Institutions That Promote Growth. The following example illustrates the importance of institutions to technological development. In one study, New York University economist William Baumol claims that the percentage of entrepreneurs in the general population is stable throughout time, even though the rate of technological progress is not. What does change are the institutions. In some time periods, the institutional settings, or "rules of the game," have encouraged economic growth. At other times, they have discouraged economic growth. For example, during the early Middle Ages, the social rule in England held that the eldest son inherited the property of the father and other sons entered either the clergy or the military. The eldest son had very little incentive to improve his crop yield because excess crops were handed over to the king. Enterprising younger sons made their mark by advancing in the military, where their efforts were most highly rewarded. The early Middle Ages marked a period of many military innovations but few innovations that were brought to market. Institutions at that time channeled innovative energy away from the production of goods and services for the masses and toward the military.

By the late Middle Ages, however, private property and the legal enforcement of private property rights became more widespread, providing an incentive to use resources productively. During this period, people developed ways to harness water power to produce goods for sale. The new rules generated tremendous growth as entrepreneurs directed their energy toward innovation for the marketplace.

Openness to Trade. Openness to trade is also an important aspect of institutions conducive to technological development. An economy that is open to trade will be able to import different products, and with those products will come different technologies. These technologies can themselves act as inputs for domestic innovation. Trade makes a variety of technologies and products available. Estimates of the effect of openness to trade suggest that moving from a closed economy (many barriers to trade) to an open economy (few or no barriers to trade) can add as much as 2.5 percentage points to annual growth.

Patents and Public Goods. An important consideration when trying to create an environment to foster technological development is the public-good aspect of technology. A **public good** is a good that, once created, can be used by everyone without diminishing the amount of the good available to others. National defense, for example, is a public good. The degree to which a technological development is a public good depends on whether it can be patented. A **patent** is legal protection that gives the holder the monopoly (sole ownership) rights to an idea or a product. If the technological innovation is an idea or a concept, rather than a good, then it is given a copyright, not a patent, but the legal protection is the same. Many aspects of a product can be copyrighted. For example, Corning has a copyright on the hue of "pink" it uses for its insulation. The U.S. Patent Office determines whether an innovation qualifies for a patent or copyright.

> A public good is a good that, once created, can be used by everyone without diminishing the amount available to others.

Nonpatented ideas are public goods; they are available to anyone at no cost. Once developed, they have the highest payoff in terms of growth, but, because they do not have a financial return to the originator, there is less incentive to create them. The decimal number system is an example of a nonpatented idea. Arabs developed a system of counting based on the decimal system in the 7th century; it was far more efficient than the Roman numeral system. (Have you ever tried multiplying CXVI times VI?) Had the Arabs copyrighted that idea (and had the copyright been enforceable), you would have to make a small payment to the holder of the copyright every time you multiplied using the Arabic numeral system.

> Patents both encourage and slow growth.

Even when ideas are patented, variations of them often are not, which means that other companies can produce those variations. To create such variations, most companies quickly buy other copyrighted and patented products and use reverse engineering—tearing products down to see precisely how they work. They then try to rebuild those products in a slightly different fashion, one that reproduces the result but doesn't violate the patent. Because innovations can be copied, other people can use them more cheaply than if they produced the innovations themselves. Microsoft did this when it developed its *Windows* technology. Apple had already developed a user-friendly computer desktop with a trashcan, folders, and files. Then, Microsoft came out with its *Windows* product and made just enough changes (such as replacing the waste basket with a recycling bin) to avoid violating Apple's copyright. Where reverse engineering is not possible, producers must buy the right to use the patented process or good, paying the creator for that right.

Because of their complexity and importance, regulations regarding patents and copyrights are growth policies that are much in debate. Should the government allow patents on various new technological developments? For example, consider Amazon.com's patent on the "one-click" online checkout model. Some policy makers believe that this practice is so basic, it should not be patentable. Other policy makers believe that not awarding patents in such cases reduces the incentives for companies to come up with innovations—it reduces technological progress.

Policy makers also debate whether pharmaceutical companies should be able to patent the drugs they sell. Some policy makers argue that because these drugs are so important to the public good, they should be affordable to everyone, especially the poor. Other policy makers argue that limiting the pharmaceutical companies' profits by eliminating or reducing patent production will limit their incentive to develop new drugs. The compromise that policy makers have worked out is that drugs are given a patent for a limited period, after which the drugs become "generically reproducible," and their price goes down considerably.

Monopolies do not end when a patent expires (typically, after 17 years in the United States). Companies spend large amounts of money to protect their brand names and to convince individuals that the "original" is preferable to the essentially identical generic. For example, Advil's patent has run out, but its manufacturer advertises heavily and many people buy Advil rather than an alternative ibuprofin generic brand.

If a technological development is patented, the public good element of that development is reduced, but the incentive for individuals to make the development is increased. In assigning copyrights, patents, and property rights, policy makers agree that societies must find a middle ground between giving individuals appropriate incentives to create new technologies (by giving them monopoly rights to those developments) and making that technology freely available to everyone, thereby spreading its benefits to a greater number of people. There is far less agreement on what the appropriate middle ground is.

In developing countries, the issue is even more complicated than how to adjust patent laws. Developing countries must decide whether to accept U.S. laws on patents or to develop laws of their own that allow much freer use of new technological developments. The United States naturally wants them to accept and enforce U.S. patents and copyrights and has made that acceptance a requirement for open trade relations. This puts great pressure on the other countries to comply in theory, but, in practice, to enforce the laws as weakly as possible. For example, the United States and China have an ongoing fight about the enforcement of U.S. copyrights on CDs and software. (You can buy a *Windows XP* CD in many of the open markets in China for under a dollar; that's below the license fee, so it is a good bet that they are "bootlegged"—produced out of copyright.) It isn't only CDs: We have received letters from people in China about how much they like using one of our books, which has never been sold in China by the publisher.

Executive Summary

- Economists have gone beyond the Solow growth model by (1) extending the basic model and (2) developing new growth theory.

- Economists have expanded the Solow growth model by accounting for differences in labor and institutions and by allowing for increasing returns to scale.

- When the basic model is extended, differences in quality of labor and institutions account for some of the differences in growth rates among countries.

- Increasing returns to scale leads to virtuous circles and persistent growth.

- New growth theory assumes that technological progress is the result of human effort that is guided by economic incentives.

- New growth theory focuses policy on investment in capital, labor, and institutions that lead to innovation.

- Patents provide firms with the incentive to develop new technologies.

- The public good aspect of technology is important for economic growth, because it allows the application of that technology to the production of goods and services and additional technologies to spread much more quickly.

IDENTIFYING THE CAUSES OF TECHNOLOGICAL DEVELOPMENT

Some economists argue that the growth process is too difficult to generalize into a model.

Economists who have studied technological innovation in depth have found the results of their study difficult to generalize. Each case seems to evolve in a different pattern. They have found that the way to get some general ideas of how growth occurs is to look at the history of growth through case studies. One person who has done so is Stanford economist Nathan Rosenberg, who writes:

> By "getting down into the trenches," examining the particular sequence of events and institutions within particular industries, one can extract insights into the process by which technological knowledge grows—knowledge of a kind that cannot be deduced from some merely theoretical framework. . . .
>
> Technological advance, almost by definition, is the result of costly experimentation and the assembly and manipulation of empirical data. While scientific theory sometimes guides the experimentation process, the precise design of an experiment and the mapping of its result into a new product or process are activities that cannot be deduced from theory. (*Exploring the Black Box: Technology, Economics, and History.* Cambridge: Oxford University Press, 1994:1–2.)

One conclusion from these case studies is that path dependency is central to the process of technological change and growth in economics. Path dependency means that decisions we make now affect what decisions we'll need to make later. In other words, we can understand the behavior of an economy only by understanding its history. History is fundamentally important.

A second conclusion is that we cannot model the decision process about technology by assuming that individuals have complete knowledge and full information about their economic environments. Rosenberg continues:

. . . historical analysis supports the view that technological change often takes place in quite information-poor and uncertain environments. This paucity of information on the part of decision-makers powerfully constrains their ability to assess the consequences of technical advance. However, neoclassical economic models of technological change *assume* very rich information environments, often only restricting the information available to the firm in one or at most two well-defined ways. Instead of proceeding from a natural starting point where firms possess little or no information and acquire information through experience and investment, most economic models of technological change assume that firms are aware of all the technological options available to them (leading to a well-defined production function). In addition, these models assume that firms possess complete information concerning the economic value of the technologies "induced" by expenditures on R&D. With these strong assumptions, it is simple to characterize the linear model of the science/technology/production interface, or to derive comparative statics using the neoclassical growth model. From this point of view, one aim of this book is to persuade the reader that simple linear analysis cannot satisfactorily explore the rich and interrelated terrains of technological change and economic growth. (p. 5)

Rosenberg's conclusion is that technological development is a complicated process that is difficult to capture in a model. By looking at case studies, we can begin to appreciate the enormous complexity of technological development and the varied factors that influence it.

NOT-SO-NEW GROWTH THEORY

New growth theory has developed over the past 25 years, but like most economic theories, the basic ideas and concepts of new growth theory aren't new. The concepts of new growth theory and economists' advice on how to get an economy to grow (create markets and give them freedom to operate, invest and save, educate society, and keep a stable government) are all ideas discussed by Adam Smith in the eighteenth century and economist Joseph Schumpeter in the early twentieth century.

Specialization and the Market

> Adam Smith emphasized the importance of specialization and the division of labor in the growth process with his famous pin factory example.

Consider Adam Smith's famous pin factory example of the advantage of specialization. At first, each worker makes an entire pin from start to finish. One worker has to learn all the necessary skills to finish the pin—cutting, sharpening, stamping, and soldering. However, if four workers together produced one pin—one worker cutting, one sharpening, one stamping, and another soldering—they could produce more pins in the same amount of time. As the workers learn their skills better, they produce even more pins.

The process of pin making that Smith describes was known before pin producers changed their production systems. The increases in output did not come from exogenous technological change. Instead, the gains came from discovering a better way of coordinating individuals' work so that they could specialize and spend less time switching tasks. The change in the method of making pins was motivated by the factory owner's desire to increase profits. That's endogenous technology.

The key to understanding growth, for Smith, was his discussion of trade, specialization, and the division of labor. Trade in markets was advantageous in large part because it expanded the market, allowing individuals and firms to further divide up work and specialize. Specialization encouraged learning by doing, setting up a positive feedback between trade and growth. Greater specialization increased output, which increased the market; increases in the market led to greater specialization, and the process began all over again. The incentive to organize production by specialization was to earn higher profits. These are all ideas that are consistent with new growth theory.

The Entrepreneur

Another early (twentieth-century) economist who approached growth theory from a "new" growth theory perspective was Joseph Schumpeter. Schumpeter was an original and broad-thinking economist, and one of the first modern economists to be concerned with growth. He emphasized the role of entrepreneurs (individuals who see opportunities to produce, coordinate, manage, and assume the risk of production) and their innovations. These entrepreneurs create major technological changes, which simultaneously drive the economy forward and modify the existing sociological structure.

Joseph Schumpeter emphasized the role of the entrepreneur in the growth process.

Economists have largely ignored the role of the entrepreneur in both micro- and macroeconomics. Instead, they merely assumed that supply and demand curves exist. However, ask yourself the following: Have you ever seen a "real" supply or demand curve? Or have you only seen what economists draw? Entrepreneurs must look at the world and create supply out of ideas and demand from a vision. Will the consumers want what is produced? Can the entrepreneur assemble the team that can produce the good at the estimated cost? Successful entrepreneurs earn profit; unsuccessful entrepreneurs' dreams are lost.

To think that the direction of our economy is determined by the dynamic vision of a few thousand entrepreneurs is a sobering thought for economic modelers, but it may hold a great deal of truth. Without these dynamic visionaries, no amount of macroeconomic policy will create a growing economy.

According to Schumpeter, the economy's growth depends on these entrepreneurs, and the industries they are in will be the leading industries, pulling the rest of the economy along with them. In the late 1700s, steam power and iron manufacturing were the driving forces. In the 1860s, railroads were the dynamic industry. Later, electronics, automobiles, and chemicals drove the U.S. economy. In the 1980s and 1990s, computers and biotechnology were the leading U.S. industries. Some economists claim that a new growth era has begun because of this recent wave of innovation. Exhibit 6–7 shows five waves of innovation.

Following Schumpeter's theory, entrepreneurs are a necessary ingredient of growth. However, entrepreneurs also need capital. Acquiring capital depends on the ability to get loans. Initially, individuals who apply innovations to production successfully make tremendous profits, and investors are willing to lend money to firms to buy capital. Imitators quickly follow, however, reducing profit levels, both because the imitators aren't able to apply the innovation as well as the original entrepreneurs and because the increase in the number of firms destroys the market power of individual firms. During these waves of innovation, the economic system grows. Finally, the innovation wave will run its course, and reduced profits will lead to tightened credit, forcing marginal firms out of business and the economy into a recession.

For Schumpeter, the process of capitalist economic growth is one of interdependent booms and busts. The innovative activities of entire groups of entrepreneurs

Exhibit 6-7

Waves of U.S. Innovation

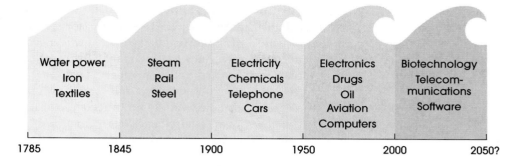

| Water power
Iron
Textiles | Steam
Rail
Steel | Electricity
Chemicals
Telephone
Cars | Electronics
Drugs
Oil
Aviation
Computers | Biotechnology
Telecom-
munications
Software |

1785   1845   1900   1950   2000   2050?

In the late 1700s, steam power and iron manufacturing were the driving forces. In the 1860s, railroads were the dynamic industry. Later, electronics, automobiles, and chemicals drove the U.S. economy. In the 1980s and 1990s, computers and biotechnology were the leading industries. Some economists claim that a new growth era has begun because of this recent wave of innovation.

create the growth, while the "busts," or depressions, weed out the inefficient and weak innovations, setting the stage for a new wave of growth. In Schumpeter's view, capitalism has a need for agony and ecstasy, and both combine to make for an ongoing system. Cycles are an inevitable and necessary part of the growth process.

According to Schumpeter, this freedom of entrepreneurial action gives capitalism its vitality, and this vitality makes capitalism superior to a communist or socialist organization of society. In capitalist or free-market societies, new ideas—mutations that can change not just the production of goods and services, but also the coordination of production and exchange—are continually arising, giving society an internal dynamic. In more regimented, socialistic societies, these ideas would not have the opportunity to flourish in the market.

Schumpeter admired and favored capitalism but did not think it would last. He saw the development of big business squeezing out the entrepreneur. Schumpeter argued that this growth of big business, combined with the destruction of the protective political state and the capitalist institutional structure, ultimately would end the growth, causing capitalist economies to stagnate after World War II. Clearly, Shumpeter was wrong. Capitalist countries have continued to grow, albeit more slowly than some may have hoped, and they have found a way to keep some capitalist spirit alive, even within large firms.

> Joseph Schumpeter wrongly predicted that capitalism would end because he believed big business would squeeze out the entrepreneur.

Executive Summary

- Growth experiences are difficult to capture in a model. Case studies illustrate how complex technological innovation really is.

- Smith focused on trade, specialization, and the division of labor in growth.

- Schumpter focused on the role of the entrepreneur in growth.

POLICY PERSPECTIVE: POLICIES TO AFFECT GROWTH

If technology is central to growth, in the way discussed above, countries will not necessarily converge to the same growth rates as the Solow growth model predicts. Instead, countries with high levels of capital and technology, an educated workforce, and institutions that foster innovation will continually grow faster than other countries. For the United States, the technology story is a comforting one. It suggests that the spin-offs from our current development will engender more growth and keep the United States growing at a faster rate than many other, less-developed countries.

Policy makers need only remember: "Them that has, get more; them that don't have, get less." So, try to get more, and soon. New growth theory says that, because South Korea is ahead of the Congo in technological development, it will continually have first shot at developing newer technologies and spinning off existing technologies to other industries. As it does, its growth rate will exceed the Congo's growth rate. South Korea will be in a virtuous circle and the Congo in a vicious circle; the Congo will not develop in the future because it isn't developing now.

The question for policy makers is, how can an economy avoid a vicious circle and get into a virtuous circle?

Reduce Protectionism

> Policies economists have recommended to encourage growth include the following: Reduce protectionism, establish private enterprise zones, lower tax rates, privatize, and create industrial policies.

New growth theory suggests that reducing barriers to trade can lead to increased growth. The United States reduced barriers to trade when it joined the North America Free Trade Association, and it continues to reduce barriers to trade through active membership in the World Trade Organization. Members of the World Trade Organization agree to hold down tariffs and restrict protectionism. The reasons such policies promote growth are that they increase competition and allow increases in specialization. For example, Bangladesh has specialized in producing clothing, and by increasing their clothing exports, they can buy far more goods than they could have produced domestically.

Politically, these "open economy" policies often come under fire because they displace workers and firms in the short run. However, economists focus on the long-run effects of free trade on growth, and through that growth, on long-run employment. Economists believe these long-run benefits generally trump the short-run costs. Economists Bradford DeLong and Lawrence Summers have found that countries that are relatively closed to foreign trade (because of high tariffs or restrictive quotas) grow, on average, 1.1 percent slower than countries that are open to foreign trade.

Establish Private Enterprise Zones

A politically popular pro-growth policy in the late 1990s was promoting private enterprise zones—geographic areas within which the public and the private sectors jointly work to improve employment opportunities in disadvantaged urban areas. The U.S. government gives businesses special tax benefits and other services if they relocate to these areas. The new businesses help the surrounding community by hiring local workers and encouraging related industries. The new businesses generate even more new businesses. New growth theory suggests that growth leads to growth. Private enterprise zones are the U.S. government's attempt to get that growth process started in a particular geographic area.

Lower Tax Rates

Some economists and policy makers advocate lowering tax rates to boost growth. Lowering tax rates can affect the economy two ways. First, lowering tax rates can increase aggregate demand, because people have more money to spend. The increased demand causes output to rise in the short run, and possibly the long run. Second, lowering tax rates can directly encourage suppliers to increase their production because profit per unit will rise. This second supply-side policy has been the focus of much debate in recent years. According to the supply-side view, by lowering tax rates, workers have a greater incentive to work, investors have a greater incentive to invest, and businesses have a greater incentive to produce. All of these incentives work toward increasing productivity and growth. There is significant debate over the size of the incentive effects from lower tax rates. Most economists believe that, in the short run, incentive effects are relatively weak, but, in the long run, they can be important.

Privatize

Privatization is government's sale of government-controlled activities to private, for-profit enterprises, or the transfer of current government activities to the private sector. The United States has considered proposals to privatize Social Security, education, the U.S. Postal Service, prisons, the police force, and roads. The general argument behind these proposals is that a private business can operate more efficiently than a government business, thereby lowering costs, even after making allowances for profit. Lower costs and higher productivity translate into more growth.

Have an Industrial Policy

Industrial policy is government policy of working directly with businesses, providing funds, research support, and encouragement to specific industries. Some policy makers take new growth theory's message—growth leads to more growth—to mean that the government should actively use industrial policies to promote certain industries in the hope that, as a result, there will be positive spill-over effects and increased technological growth.

Most economists agree that there are positive spill-over effects, but most economists also believe that industrial policy is often marked by major government failure; therefore, even though industrial policy may be worthwhile in theory, in practice, decisions are made for political, not economic, reasons, and often governments end up supporting the wrong technology. (See The Briefing Room, "Subsidizing Research and Development," for an example.)

The policy implication of new growth theory focuses on technological development, but the question of how best to encourage technological development is still open to debate. Table 6–2 summarizes several policies that economists and policy makers have suggested using to encourage growth and technology. Some of the

Table 6–2 Potential Growth Policies		
	• Create high capital investment to promote technological innovation. • Make education widely available. • Ensure political stability. • Establish well-defined property rights. • Promote aggregate demand policies to reduce economic uncertainty.	• Establish private enterprise zones. • Build industrial policies that promote technological innovation. • Lower tax rates. • Privatize government-owned businesses. • Increase openness to international trade by reducing trade restrictions.

THE BRIEFING ROOM   Subsidizing Research and Development

We have already seen how important new technology is to the growth process. It would seem natural that government would consider subsidizing the development of new technology, but this presents problems, because, if the idea is commercially viable, why wouldn't a private business develop it on its own? A project that requires government subsidization is questionable—perhaps it's too costly to ever be profitable.

Let's consider a famous case—the development of the supersonic passenger airplane. When Great Britain and France first proposed this idea, the U.S. aviation industry was the world leader. Supersonic technology promised to change the nature of flight; a trip from New York to Paris would take 3 hours instead of 6. The U.S. aviation industry felt it also needed to develop supersonic technology to maintain its leadership position.

However, these private U.S. companies felt that the risks of developing such a supersonic airplane were too great; the development costs were too high. They argued that they needed government to subsidize the effort. Britain and France were already collaborating on subsidizing and developing a supersonic transport—the *Concorde.* The debate was not simply between prosubsidization and antisubsidization forces. Many people also questioned the impact of supersonic flights on the environment and whether U.S. supersonic flights should be allowed at all.

After a year of debate, the U.S. government decided not to subsidize the project. The French and British introduced the *Concorde* in 1969 with great fanfare, but it was not a commercial success. The antisubsidization argument seemed to have been correct.

A few general points can be made from this case study. First, the political debate about subsidization will often center on reasons other than the financial viability of the proposal. In this case, it was primarily environmental concerns that scuttled the program in the United States. Had these concerns not existed, the subsidization arguments would likely have won. Second, governments make subsidization decisions within an international strategic context. What makes sense strategically can differ from what makes sense in a nonstrategic setting. The British and French governments subsidized the *Concorde* program, in part, because they felt that, through its defense contracting, the United States was already heavily subsidizing the U.S. aviation industry. European aviation needed subsidies to compete and to stay in business.

Their argument had validity. Many U.S. aviation firms had defense contracts that paid much of their overhead costs, implicitly subsidizing commercial airline development. In addition, the subsidized firm enjoys economies of scope (lower average costs of producing two related goods) and moves more quickly down the experience curve.

Should Britain and France have subsidized the *Concorde?* With hindsight, we can say, "Probably not." Without this hindsight, however, it is much harder to make the decision. For example, had our case study been of the French and British governments' decision to subsidize the *Airbus,* the subsidization option would have looked much better, because the *Airbus* has been a commercial success. As a result of subsidization, the *Airbus* has become a serious competitor to the U.S. company, Boeing.

---

policies are directly targeted at technology, while others are targeted at getting the growth process started with the idea that technological spill-overs will occur as a consequence.

CONCLUSION

Growth is likely to remain an area of primary concern for economists through the twenty-first century. The question that the policy science of macroeconomics asks is, "What policies should we adopt to achieve the level and type of growth we want?"

However, economists do not have a good handle on technological change nor on growth. We have models, but these models are based on highly restrictive assumptions that do not exactly fit the real world, and the conclusions we draw are based on those assumptions. This does not mean that the models are irrelevant. They help us understand the growth problem, but, as is the case with all economic

Growth models, like all models, must be used creatively and imaginatively— as a guide to common sense analysis—not mechanistically.

models, they should be used creatively and imaginatively—as a guide to common-sense analysis—not mechanistically.

The story of the ant and the grasshopper, which is also the story in the Solow growth model, is a good place to *start* thinking about differences in growth rates across countries. The Solow growth model highlights the role of saving and capital accumulation in the growth process. After comparing the Solow model's prediction with the data, however, we realize that there must be more to the story than just saving and capital investment. New growth theory states that economies that create environments that encourage technological advancement generate growth. Countries in which the environment is not conducive to technological innovation tend to fall behind and stagnate.

KEY POINTS

- Three reasons why it is important to go beyond the basic Solow growth model: (1) The Solow growth model doesn't explain why growth rates have tended to accelerate over the past 180 years and incomes of poor countries aren't catching up to those of rich countries. (2) Sometimes, saving and investing—the policy prescription of the Solow model—do not lead to higher growth. (3) Technological progress accounts for much of the growth in developed economies, but the Solow growth model doesn't explain where that technological progress comes from.

- Some economists have extended the basic Solow growth model to account for differences in quality of labor, institutions, and increasing returns.

- Increasing returns creates the possibility of a virtuous circle in which growth creates more growth.

- An alternative approach to the Solow growth model is to develop new growth theory, which makes technology a product of human effort and within the realm of policy makers.

- In new growth theory, technology is a function of capital, labor, technology, and the economic environment.

- Institutions that promote growth are openness to trade, patents, and public good aspects of technology.

- A policy issue regarding technology is whether to make a technological innovation a public good or a patented private good. Public goods have the highest return in terms of growth, but they also have the least incentive to be developed. Patented goods have the highest return for the developer but the least return in terms of growth.

- The Solow growth model states that economic growth policy should focus on boosting saving and investment. New growth theory states that economic growth policy should try to establish institutions that foster technological innovation. The two approaches are not incompatible.

- Adam Smith and Joseph Schumpeter took a "new" approach to economic growth even before new growth theory was formally developed. According to Smith, specialization and trade generate new opportunities for growth. According to Schumpeter, the individual entrepreneur plays an important role in the growth of an economy.

- New growth theory suggests that the following policies may increase growth: open the economy to trade, establish private enterprise zones, lower tax rates, privatize and adopt industrial policies that promote innovation.

KEY TERMS

agglomeration effects 165
conditional convergence
    hypothesis 157
convergence hypothesis 151
growth accounting formula 154
general-purpose technologies 164

increasing returns to scale 161
industrial policy 173
learning by doing 165
new growth theory 163
patent 166
privatization 173

public good 166
social capital 161
Solow residual 155
virtuous circle 162

QUESTIONS FOR THOUGHT AND REVIEW

1. What are the three reasons to go beyond the basic Solow growth model?
2. What is *convergence?* Demonstrate graphically how the basic Solow growth model predicts convergence.
3. How does the expanded Solow growth model explain differences in growth rates of output per person across countries?
4. According to the convergence hypothesis, which countries will grow faster—rich ones or poor ones? Is this what happens in the real world? Explain.
5. According to the growth accounting formula, what accounts for most of the growth in the United States? What accounts for the second largest portion of growth in the United States?
6. What is *conditional convergence?*
7. Describe three differences among countries that might explain the lack of convergence.
8. Does the positive correlation between education and growth mean that policy makers interested in getting their economies to grow faster should subsidize education? Explain.
9. What policies does the expanded Solow growth model suggest?
10. What is the difference between the expanded Solow growth model and new growth theory?
11. What is the role of general-purpose technologies in the development of technology growth? Give an example of a general-purpose technology.

12. What is *learning by doing,* and how does it lead to agglomeration effects?
13. Name three economic environmental factors that promote technological development.
14. How did institutions in the Middle Ages in England discourage innovation and growth?
15. How are ideas public goods? What can policy makers do to reduce the public-good aspect of ideas? Explain why this may be a desirable policy.
16. How does reverse engineering get around patent laws? What effect does this have on overall growth?
17. Why are case studies important to our understanding of technological development?
18. How are the ideas of Adam Smith related to new growth theory?
19. How are the ideas of Joseph Schumpeter related to new growth theory?
20. According to new growth theory, how can aggregate-demand management policies affect growth?
21. What is a *private enterprise zone?* According to new growth theory, how do private enterprise zones encourage growth?
22. How might privatization lead to higher growth?
23. What is *industrial policy?* How might it lead to higher growth?

PROBLEMS AND EXERCISES

1. Imagine that there are two countries—Richland and Poorland—with identical saving rates (30 percent) identical population growth rates (5 percent), and identical production functions ($y = \sqrt{k}$). For simplicity, assume there is no depreciation and no technological growth. The only difference between the two countries is their current levels of capital per person: Richland has capital per person equal to 25, while Poorland has capital per person equal to 16.
   a. Calculate the current level of income per person for both countries.
   b. Calculate the growth rate of income per person for both countries, starting at the current period and moving one period into the future.
   c. Plot income per person (on the vertical axis) and the growth rate of income per person (on the hori-

   zontal axis) for Richland and Poorland. Explain the pattern you observe.
2. Use the growth accounting formula to calculate the growth rate of technology, given a growth rate for labor of 1 percent, a growth rate for capital of 2 percent, and a growth rate for output of 3 percent.
3. According to the growth accounting formula, by how much will economic growth rise if the growth of the labor force increases by 1 percent? What if the growth of capital increases by 15 percent? Finally, what if the growth of technology increases by 3 percent?
4. Imagine two countries: Grad and Nograd. Grad has 1,000 pieces of capital and 25 highly educated and highly productive people. Nograd has 100 pieces of capital and 10 people who are uneducated and unskilled. Both have per-person production functions

of the form $y = \sqrt{k}$. Income growth per person in Grad is higher than income growth per person in Nograd.

a. Using the production-function provided, calculate capital per person and output per person in each country.

b. According to the basic Solow growth model, which country should be growing faster? Why?

c. Now assume that labor quality can be measured and the people of Grad are 20 times more productive than the people of Nograd. Calculate the quality-adjusted levels of capital per person and the marginal products of quality-adjusted capital per person for both countries. Do these new data match the prediction of the Solow growth model?

Deriving the Growth Accounting Formula

This appendix presents the derivation of the growth accounting formula presented in the chapter. The formula is derived from an aggregate production function with the three properties discussed in Chapters 4 and 5: output increases with increases in all inputs, constant returns to scale, and diminishing marginal product.

Economists often use a particular production function, called the *Cobb-Douglas production function*, to represent the aggregate production process:

$$Y = A \cdot K^a \cdot L^{(1-a)} \qquad (6A\text{-}1)$$

where a and $1 - a$ are the elasticities of output in relation to inputs; the values a and $1 - a$ can also be shown to equal the share of total income paid to capital and labor. For example, if a is 0.3, then 30 percent of the income in the economy is paid to capital and 70 percent is paid to labor.

To derive the growth accounting formula, we totally differentiate this production function to get

$$dY = (K^a \cdot L^{(1-a)}dA) \qquad (6A\text{-}2)$$
$$+ (aAK^{a-1} \cdot L^{(1-a)}dK)$$
$$+ [(1-a)AK^a \cdot L^{-a}dL]$$

Now we divide both sides by Y:

$$dY/Y = (K^a \cdot L^{(1-a)}dA)/Y \qquad (6A\text{-}3)$$
$$+ (aAK^{(a-1)} \cdot L^{(1-a)}dK)/Y$$
$$+ [(1-a)AK^a \cdot L^{-a}dL]/Y$$

Because $Y = AK^a \cdot L^{(1-a)}$, we can rewrite this as

$$dY/Y = (K^a \cdot L^{(1-a)}dA)/(AK^a \cdot L^{(1-a)}) \qquad (6A\text{-}4)$$
$$+ (aAK^{(a-1)} \cdot L^{(1-a)}dK)/(AK^a \cdot L^{(1-a)})$$
$$+ [(1-a)AK^a \cdot L^{-a}dL]/(AK^a \cdot L^{(1-a)})$$

which simplifies to

$$dY/Y = (dA)/A + (adK)/K + (1-a)(dL)/L \qquad (6A\text{-}5)$$

Because any term dX/X is roughly equal to the percentage change in X, we can write this even more simply as

$$\%\Delta Y = \%\Delta A + a\%\Delta K + (1-a)\%\Delta L \qquad (6A\text{-}6)$$

The general estimates of a is 0.3, making the growth accounting formula

$$\%\Delta Y = \Delta A + 0.3\%\Delta K + 0.7\%\Delta L \qquad (6A\text{-}7)$$

7

Inflation is always and everywhere a monetary phenomenon.

—*Milton Friedman*

Money, Inflation, and Exchange Rates in the Long Run

After reading this chapter you should be able to:

1. Define money and describe one way the Federal Reserve Bank affects the money supply

2. Write the equation of exchange

3. State the quantity theory of money and its theory of inflation

4. Demonstrate how market forces determine exchange rate values and how government can affect the value of its currency

5. Describe the balance of payments account and explain how it reflects the demand for and supply of currencies

6. Explain how an economy's inflation or exchange rate adjusts to private balance of payments surpluses, and deficits under fixed exchange rates

7. Use purchasing power parity theory to predict how inflation differentials lead to changes in nominal exchange rates

In early 2000, the Brazilian central bank sold $1 billion of Brazilian bonds to holders of U.S. dollars to increase its reserves of foreign currency. Brazil intended to use its foreign currency reserves to buy its own currency, called the *real* (pronounced "ree-ahl"), should its value begin to fall. Brazil wanted to defend its currency because, a year earlier, the real had depreciated more than 40 percent. Foreign investors had already lost billions of dollars during the collapse of Asian currencies in 1997 and the collapse of the Russian ruble in 1998. They didn't want to lose in Brazil, too, and they were threatening to pull their investment out of Brazil en masse.

Investors were particularly concerned because Brazil had introduced the real as a new currency just 5 years earlier as part of a plan to stop its economy's hyperinflation. Brazil's poor economic history in the 1990s, along with signs of accelerating inflation and rising fiscal problems, drove investors away, putting downward pressure on the Brazilian real. Even though, in early 2000, Brazil's economy began to recover and inflation fell to under 10 percent a year, Brazil still needed foreign exchange reserves to ward off future currency depreciations and to establish credibility that it would keep inflation low.

So far in our examination of the long run, we have focused exclusively on growth—the real economy, but as the case of Brazil illustrates, policy makers are also concerned about inflation and exchange rate fluctuations. What caused inflation in Brazil? Why was its exchange rate depreciating? What effect would these changes in inflation and the exchange rate have on the Brazilian economy? And, finally, can the Brazilian government offset any adverse effects of these changes? This chapter looks at such questions from a long-run perspective.

We begin this chapter by looking at domestic prices: What determines the average price level and the inflation rate within a country? We then look at international prices: What determines exchange rates? Finally, we look at how inflation and exchange rates are related and how policies to affect one often affect the other.

MONEY AND INFLATION

What causes inflation? The quotation at the beginning of this chapter gives some insight into that question: Countries with rapid growth in their money supply tend to have high inflation rates, while countries with lower rates of growth in their money supply tend to have low inflation rates. Of course, that answer leads to another question: Why does the money supply grow quickly in some countries and slowly in others? To answer this question, let's consider the nature of money.

What Is Money and Where Does It Come From?

Money is a financial asset that serves three functions. Money is

The three functions of money: a unit of account, a store of value, and a medium of exchange.

1. A unit of account
2. A store of value
3. A medium of exchange

A *unit of account* means that everything is priced in the units of money. In other words, when you buy a candy bar for $.50, a soda for $1, or a pair of shoes for $80, all of the prices are expressed in terms of dollars and cents. The dollar is the pricing standard for the United States. It is hard to imagine an alternative, but suppose that, instead of dollars, candy bars were the unit of account. The price of a soda would be listed as two candy bars and everything else in the store would be priced in terms of numbers of candy bars. (Your weekly paycheck would be stated in terms of the number of candy bars you earn in a week.)

The *store of value* function of money means that money holds its value over time (a good reason why candy bars are not used as money). Money is durable (doesn't melt in your pocket) and, one hopes, doesn't lose its value too quickly. Americans can cash their paychecks and carry dollars without fear that their dollars will become worthless. This is not the case with all currencies. In some developing economies with high inflation, currency loses its value quickly. People rush to spend their currency on goods and services, or to exchange it for another more stable currency, such as the U.S. dollar.

Money also functions as a *medium of exchange*. That is, it is universally accepted in transactions. It is possible that your roommate would accept two candy bars in exchange for a soda, but your college bursar would probably balk if you offered candy bars as payment for your tuition.

Throughout history, many commodities have served as money: gold, silver—even stones and cigarettes. Today, we think of money as a financial (rather than physical) asset: Currency and coins are the most obvious examples. Checking account balances also function as money. What about other financial assets, such as savings account balances or Treasury bills—are these assets money? The answer is yes and no. They are highly liquid. **Liquidity** is the ability to easily exchange one asset for another financial or real asset. Liquidity suggests saving account balances and Treasury bills should be included as money. You cannot, however, spend savings account balances directly. You must first transfer them into cash or your checking account. The same is true for Treasury bills. Whether Treasury bills and saving account balances should or should not be included as money is debatable.

The Federal Reserve Bank (the Fed), the agency responsible for measuring money in the United States, deals with the issue of what financial assets should be included in money by defining several measures that vary by degrees of liquidity. The most narrow and most liquid measure is M1 and includes only currency, coins, checking account balances, and travelers' checks. The broadest and least liquid measure is L, which includes M1, other forms of money, and short-term Treasury bills and savings bonds. Table 7–1 shows M1, L, and the measures of money that fall in between. (Throughout this chapter, we will keep things simple by assuming that money includes only those financial assets in M1—currency, coins, and checking account balances.)

Liquidity is the ability to change an asset into other things easily and without cost.

M1 is the narrowest and most liquid definition of *money*.

Table 7–1

Alternative Measures of Money

M1		
	• Currency	Coins and bills
	• Checkable deposits	Deposits in checking accounts
	• Travelers' checks	Checks issued by banks and accepted as cash
M2	• M1 plus	
	• Savings deposits	Deposits in accounts with no checking privileges
	• Small-time deposits	Deposits of less than $100,000 that have an explicit maturity and a penalty for early withdrawal
	• Money market mutual fund shares	Shares, held by individuals, of a fund that invests in short-term securities that come with check-writing privileges
M3	• M2 plus	
	• Large-time deposits	Deposits of greater than $100,000 that have an explicit maturity and a penalty for early withdrawal
	• Institutional money market fund shares	Shares, held by corporations, of a fund that invests in short-term securities that come with check-writing privileges
	• Repurchase Agreements (RPs)	Sales of securities with the agreement to repurchase
	• Eurodollars	Dollars or other currency deposited in banks outside the currency's country of origin
L	• M3 plus	
	• Highly liquid bonds	Short-term Treasury securities, commercial paper, savings bonds, and bankers' acceptances

The next question is, where does money come from? The U.S. Treasury prints the currency that circulates. But as Table 7–1 shows, money is more than just the currency in our pockets. What, then, determines the level of deposits, overnight repurchase agreements, and other categories that make up these broader measures of money? The answer is the financial system. It supplies the financial assets that people want.

The amount of financial assets that the financial system supplies is influenced by the Fed. The Fed influences the money supply primarily through open market operations. (Chapter 13 covers some other ways the Fed affects the money supply.) Open market operations are the Fed's purchase and sale of government securities (Treasury bills, notes, and bonds). When the Fed wishes to expand the money supply—follow expansionary monetary policy—it purchases U.S. government securities. It pays for the securities with its own IOUs, and it is these IOUs that serve as money. Look at a one-dollar bill. It is designated as a "Federal Reserve Note," has a picture of George Washington, and carries the motto "In God We Trust." Nowhere, however, is there an indication that it has value or that you can get anything for it. It is simply an IOU of the Fed.

When the Fed buys bonds, it pays for those bonds with its IOUs and thereby expands the money supply. When the Fed wishes to contract the money supply—implement a contractionary monetary policy—it sells part of its holdings of bonds, taking back its IOUs. So, the Federal Reserve Bank in the United States, or a country's central bank, creates money. (Changing the money supply leads to changes in interest rates, as discussed in the Q&A feature.)

> Open market operations are the purchase and sale of government securities by the Fed.

Q&A

QUESTION   I thought the Fed controlled the interest rate, not the money supply. Which does it control?

ANSWER   Since the early 1980s, the Fed has targeted interest rates. It targets them by changing the supply of money.

Our discussion centers on the Fed's control of the money supply, but newspaper reports of the Fed's actions generally focus on interest rates. That's because the Fed currently uses its control over the money supply to target interest rates. Here's how.

Banks in the United States are required to hold reserves at the Fed equal to a fraction of their deposits. Banks often find themselves with either too many or too few reserves. If they have too many reserves, they try to lend the excess reserves to other banks that have too few. These loans are usually for short periods of time (a day), and the interest rate that banks charge for these loans is called the federal (fed) funds rate. The Federal Reserve Bank does not set or mandate the fed funds rate. The term means that most of the borrowing in the federal funds market is to meet the required reserves of the Fed.

Although the Fed does not set the fed funds rate, it does have a great deal of influence over it in the short run. If the Fed uses open market operations to buy government bonds from the banking system, those purchases increase the amount of reserves in the system, because banks are exchanging government bonds for currency reserves. As reserves in the banking system increase, there is less need for banks to borrow from other banks to meet their reserve requirements. Lower demand for borrowing causes the fed funds rate to fall. If the Fed sells government bonds to the banking system, the total reserves decline and the fed funds rate rises.

U.S. monetary policy since the early 1980s has been aimed primarily at targeting the fed funds rate. When the Fed wants to raise the targeted rate, it decreases the money supply, reducing the amount of reserves in the banking system. When the Fed wants to lower the targeted rate, it increases the amount of reserves in the banking system.

The Quantity Theory of Money: The Equation of Exchange

Now that we've discussed the nature of money, let's see how money can be integrated into the long-run framework presented in the last two chapters. In the the long-run framework, growth models say that labor, capital, and technology determine real output, but they don't say anything about what determines the price level or inflation. Economists have a separate long-run model of inflation that focuses on money. So, in the long-run framework, there is a separation: Labor, capital, and technology determine real output, and money determines the price level—and, hence, nominal output (the value of all goods produced in an economy). The two analyses are independent of one another and are, therefore, divided. The separation of the real and nominal sectors in the long-run framework is called the **long-run dichotomy.**

The separation of the real and nominal sectors in the long-run framework is called the *long-run dichotomy.*

Economists' long-run theory of the money supply and demand is the quantity theory of money. In its simple form, the **quantity theory of money** states that the price level varies in direct proportion to the quantity of money. For example, if the money supply rises by 10 percent, the price level will also rise by 10 percent. The quantity theory of money is embodied in the **equation of exchange:**

The quantity theory of money states that the price level varies in direct proportion to the quantity of money.

$$MV = PY \qquad \textit{Classical construct} \qquad (7\text{-}1)$$

where M is the money supply, V is the velocity of money, P is the average price of goods and services sold in the economy, and Y is real income.

In the equation, P multiplied by Y is simply nominal income (nominal GDP)—the total dollar value of final goods and services purchased in the economy in a year. The **velocity of money** (V) tells us how many times each dollar is spent on average in a given year on final goods and services. To understand the velocity of money, it is important to realize that the total amount of money in the economy is considerably less than the total value of spending in the economy in a year, because money changes hands. For example, in 2000 the M1 money supply was approximately $1.1 trillion and nominal income was $9.96 trillion. This means that $1.1 trillion in money was used to pay for $9.96 trillion in final goods and services. Presumably, money was used each time something was purchased. Each dollar of M1 must have been used more than once. For example, say you buy a $4 hamburger at the student union. The student union uses that $4 to pay the supplier of beef, who uses some of it to buy gas for the delivery truck, and so on. The velocity of money tells us how many times, on average, money changes hands in a given year.

Executive Summary

- Money is any financial asset that serves as a unit of account, a store of value, and a medium of exchange.

- The Federal Reserve controls the money supply mainly through open market operations.

- The equation of exchange is written: $MV = PY$. It tells us that the money supply (M) times the number of times a dollar is spent on final goods and services in an economy in a year (V) equals nominal output (PY).

From the Equation of Exchange to the Quantity Theory

The quantity theory of money is a theory of the supply of and demand for money. When early classical economists first developed this equation in the 1600s, they assumed that the supply of money was determined exogenously. This assumption made institutional sense because, at that time, the supply of money equaled the value of gold held by a country (the gold standard). With the supply of money already given, economists needed only to analyze the demand for money to determine the "price" of money—the price at which quantity of money supplied equaled quantity of money demanded. (Think of the price of money as the amount of real goods you would have to give up to buy a unit of currency.) Then, because money serves as a unit of account, you could know the price level.

When using the equation of exchange to draw the connection between money and the price level, classical economists made three assumptions: The velocity of money (V) is constant, real output (Y) is determined independently of the money supply (M), and the direction of causation is from money to prices. Looking at the equation of exchange, $MV = PY$, you can see that if V is fixed and Y is independent of M, changes in M are identical to changes in P. Lastly, the direction of causation means that changes in money determine changes in the price level. Therefore, the quantity theory is

> To move from the equation of exchange to the quantity theory of money, make three assumptions: V is constant, Y is independent, and causation goes from left to right.

$$M\overline{V} \rightarrow P\overline{Y}$$

where the lines over V and Y mean that they are independent of changes in M. Let's now look more carefully at the assumptions.

First Assumption: The Velocity of Money Is Constant. Let's examine the assumption of constant velocity by considering how people determine how much money to hold. This decision depends on how much they spend and how easy or convenient it is to change other financial assets (such as mutual fund balances) into money. All else held constant, individuals would prefer to hold assets that pay interest such as bonds, until they need to make transactions. However, it is generally costly (in terms of time, inconvenience, and brokerage fees) to transform mutual fund shares into cash. Early classical economists argued that the convenience of transforming financial assets into spendable money depended on institutional features of the financial system. These features include how frequently people are paid (weekly, monthly) and the cost of converting money into financial assets and financial assets back into money (brokerage fees, banking convenience). Because these institutional factors do not change quickly over time, economists surmised that people's average cash holdings as a proportion of their income did not change quickly over time either. Average cash balances are M and nominal income is PY. So, early classical economists concluded that the ratio of money to income, M/PY, is fairly constant or changes slowly over time.

Because M/PY is constant, so too is velocity.[1] If the velocity of money is constant, the equation of exchange shows the relationship between the supply of money and nominal income. For example, if the supply of money is $800 billion and the velocity of money is 10, nominal income will be $8 trillion. If the supply of money rises to $900 billion, nominal income will rise to $9 trillion. In 2000, the velocity of money (M1 definition) in the United States was approximately 9.0, which means that a $1.1 trillion money supply supported a total nominal income of approximately $9.9 trillion.

---

[1]The equation of exchange tells us that if M/PY is constant, V is constant. To see how, divide both sides of the equation of exchange (MV = PY) by PY and by V. This gives us M/PY = 1/V. If M/PY is constant, V is constant.

Exhibit 7-1

The Velocity of Money in the United States

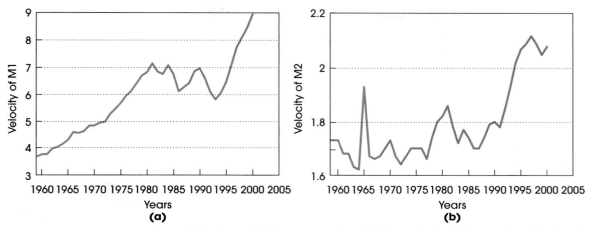

From 1959 to the mid-1970s, *panel a* shows that the velocity of M1 rose at a relatively constant rate in the United States. Since then, however, it has become difficult to predict. *Panel b* shows how the velocity of the broader measure of money, M2, is also not stable. Velocity is calculated by dividing *PY* (nominal income) by *M* (the money supply). Source: Board of Governors of the Federal Reserve System (www.federalreserve.gov).

Exhibit 7–1(a) graphs the velocity of money (M1) in the U.S. economy from 1959 to 2000. As you can see, it is not constant. Between 1959 and the mid-1970s, the velocity of money followed a fairly predictable trend. In about 1973, however, it rose unexpectedly, and, beginning in the early 1980s, it became quite unstable. As you can see in Exhibit 7–1(b), the velocity of M2 (a broader measure of money) is also not constant. So, while the quantity theory is neat and tidy, its assumption of a constant velocity of money does not fit reality. Nevertheless, economists use the quantity theory of money as a first step when thinking about money and prices in the long run.

Second Assumption: Real Output Is Determined by the Factors of Production. To draw the connection between money and the price level, economists make a second assumption. In the long run, real output (Y) is determined by the factors of production—the amounts of labor and capital and the state of technology in an economy. This means that real output is determined by factors outside the quantity theory of money; real output is exogenous. (You should be familiar with this second assumption after reading Chapters 5 and 6, so we won't go into it here.)

Third Assumption: Direction of Causation Goes from Money to Prices. The third assumption is the direction of causation. Classical economists argue that changes in the money supply cause changes in the price level. That is, the direction of causation goes from the money supply to the price level. Changes in the money supply are determined exogenously; they do not follow price level changes. (See The Briefing Room, "The Correlation Between Money Growth and Inflation," for an alternative view of the direction of causation.)

Conclusion: Inflation Is a Monetary Phenomenon. We can now put the three assumptions together and draw conclusions. Given our assumptions, nominal

---

THE BRIEFING ROOM   The Correlation Between Money Growth and Inflation

The long-run focus on money growth and inflation presented in this chapter is quite compatible with our conventional half's view of the economy; it is somewhat problematic for our unconventional half's view. The problems for our unconventional half are (1) the degree to which the facts support this relationship and (2) the assumption that money growth causes inflation. Let's briefly consider both problems.

While all economists agree that there is a connection between money growth and inflation for large changes in the money supply (say 30 percent or more), they would not agree that the connection exists for smaller changes. For example, in the United States over the past 10 years, there has been almost no connection between money growth and inflation, and predictions of inflation based on money growth have been wrong. So

our unconventional half would emphasize that the analysis is applicable only to large, not to small, changes in the money supply.

The second concern of our unconventional half is that the analysis takes an observed correlation between money growth and inflation and makes it into a causal relationship. Following economists Joan Robinson, Abba Lerner, and William Vickrey, our unconventional half sees the causal flow going from increased prices to money growth, rather than the other way around. When inflation rises, political pressures force governments and central banks to increase the money supply to avoid the recession that would result if they did not increase the money supply. The correlation between money growth and inflation is still there, but inflation is what is causing money growth; money growth is not causing inflation.

According to the quantity theory of money, inflation is always and everywhere a monetary phenomenon.

income (PY) is proportional to the supply of money (M). Therefore, a change in the money supply will result in a proportional change in nominal income. Real income (Y), however, is determined by the factors of production, so any remaining changes in nominal income must come entirely from a change in the price level (P). The quotation by Milton Friedman that opened this chapter, "Inflation is always and everywhere a monetary phenomenon" makes sense in light of this conclusion.

To see that the quantity theory of money is a theory of inflation (percent change in the price level), we have to rewrite the equation of exchange in terms of percent changes[2]:

$$\%\Delta M + \%\Delta V = \%\Delta P + \%\Delta Y \qquad (7\text{-}2)$$

According to our first key assumption, a constant or slowly changing velocity means that $\%\Delta V$ is fairly constant. With that assumption, the equation tells us that the growth rate of the money supply ($\%\Delta M$) will show up as some combination of inflation ($\%\Delta P$) and real output growth ($\%\Delta Y$). The second assumption, that real output is determined by factors other than the money supply, implies that the growth rate of the money supply will translate into inflation only. Three percent growth in the money supply will result in 3 percent inflation. Ten percent growth in the money supply will result in 10 percent inflation.

We can summarize the long-run model of inflation thus: Real output is determined by labor, capital, and the state of technology. The price level is determined by the quantity of money, and inflation results from a growing supply of money.

How Well Does the Quantity Theory of Money Work?

The prediction that the quantity theory of money makes—money growth determines inflation—is strong. It says, ultimately, that the policy makers at the Federal

---

[2]To get this formula, we use the rule that the percent change of a product of two factors equals the sum of the percent changes of each factor.

Exhibit 7–2
Inflation and
Money Growth

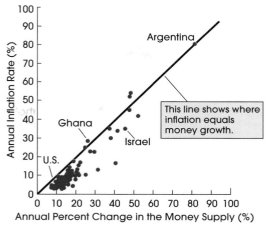

This exhibit shows the positive relationship between changes in the supply of money and inflation from 1960 to 1990 for 110 countries. Inflation is measured by the annual rise in consumer prices. Money growth is measured by annual rates of growth in M2. Source: McCandless, George, T., Jr. and Warren E. Weber. 1995. "Some monetary facts." *Quarterly Review*, Federal Reserve Bank of Minneapolis, 19(3):Summer.

Reserve (or the central bank in the country you are analyzing) are responsible for the inflation rate because they control the growth rate of the money supply. It is this theory that underlies the European Central Bank's singular policy goal of low inflation. This theory has also motivated some members of U.S. Congress to push for low inflation as the only policy goal of the Federal Reserve.

Let's see how well the prediction of the quantity theory matches the data. As you read at the beginning of the chapter, Brazil has had difficulty with inflation. In the 1980s, Brazil's most recent bout with hyperinflation was accompanied by high money growth. The dramatic decline in Brazil's inflation rate in the late 1990s was accompanied by slower money growth. The price level, on average, has risen over 40 percent per year in Brazil since 1900, and money supply growth has been similarly high over that same period. For countries, such as Brazil, with high rates of inflation, the connection between money growth and inflation is strong.

Exhibit 7–2 shows the relationship between money growth and inflation for 110 countries between 1960 and 1990. As you can see, there is a positive relationship between money growth and inflation, but it is not airtight, especially when inflation is low. The fact that the velocity of money can shift undermines the theory and suggests that, in practice, the quantity theory of money must be used with care.

For high inflations, money growth and price level growth are closely related; for low inflations, they are far less related.

Policy Implications of the Quantity Theory of Money

We can draw the following policy conclusion from the quantity theory of money: *To control the inflation rate, control the growth of the money supply*. Let's consider a real-world example of the problem caused by not containing growth of the money supply. During the early 1990s, Yugoslavia, experienced the second highest, and second longest, hyperinflation in world history. In January 1994, Yugoslavia's monthly inflation rate reached 313 million percent—that works out to an *hourly* inflation rate of 5.4 percent. A hamburger that cost 200 dinars (the Yugoslavian currency) for lunch cost 270 dinars for dinner!

Why did this happen? Excessive money growth. The government *ordered* the central bank to print money to pay for military operations, police forces, and other government needs. The central bank had to continuously pump more and more money into the economy. By 1994, the economy was in ruins and the dinar was worthless. At that point, the dinar ceased to be money; it was no longer a good store of value, nor was it used for transactions. Instead Yugoslavs, including the government, began to use German marks for domestic transactions.

This example illustrates two points. First, excessive money growth leads to excessive inflation—a prediction that follows directly from the quantity theory of money. Second, governments have priorities other than keeping inflation low. The central bank of Yugoslavia was directed by the Yugoslav government to increase the money supply at exorbitant rates because it had insufficient revenue to pay for the goods it wanted to buy. Governments that cannot raise revenue by taxing or issuing bonds can temporarily solve the problem by printing more money. They fully understand the inflationary consequences of increasing the money supply by so much, but, to keep the government from falling apart, they feel they have no other choice. So, in policy terms, we're left with the following: In the short run, with low inflation, the quantity theory of money is of questionable value because the velocity of money fluctuates. Therefore, the value of the theory lies in the long run for high inflations. However, high inflation caused by increases in the money supply is usually the result of political problems. Solving the inflation problem often means solving those political problems before stopping the growth of money.

The Inflation Tax. When the government pays for goods by printing money, it does not violate the "no free lunch principle" you learned about in your principles course. Somebody must pay for those goods. Let's see how they pay. The quantity theory of money states that an increasing money supply will increase the price level, which means that the value of money is continually shrinking. As the value of money falls, people who hold cash become poorer. That's how people end up paying. Let's consider this more carefully.

The printing of money reduces the value of cash because inflation reduces the number of goods and services that each dollar can buy. Economists call this an **inflation tax.** No one receives an actual tax bill, but the holders of cash do "pay" by having to use more dollars to buy the same number of goods and services than before the inflation. Whenever the government prints money, it "earns" a profit, called seingiorage. **Seigniorage** is the difference between the cost of printing the money (almost zero) and the value of that money. Seigniorage is a source of revenue for government and is one way government can pay for expenditures.

Most changes in the money supply are not caused by printing money, but instead by open market operations. However, the seigniorage principle works with open market operations, too. Suppose the Treasury (the agency that manages financing needs of government purchases) sells a bond to purchase a military airplane from a defense contractor. If the Fed purchases that bond, it is creating money by giving the government money in return for the bond. The defense contractor who sells the plane to the government uses the money to pay its workers and parts suppliers. According to the quantity theory of money, as that extra money is spent in the economy, the average price level rises. Holders of cash will find that their money is worth a little less than before the government bought its own bond.

Central Bank Independence. The United States pays for most of its spending through taxation and relies very little on seigniorage from inflation. The U.S. has a

Often, when governments increase the money supply enormously, it is because of deep political and fiscal problems, which lead them to believe that they have no other acceptable option.

The inflation tax is the seigniorage that government receives for money growth as the result of inflation.

well-developed set of institutions with which to collect revenue from other sources (income taxes, sales taxes, property taxes). The inflation tax is usually a tax of last resort. Developing and transitional economies that lack those institutions often resort to the inflation tax. Harvard economist Robert S. Kravchuk tells an example of the Ukraine: In 1991, the Ukraine gained independence from Russia, and the economy fell into recession. Tax revenue declined, and government expenditures rose as the government attempted to support failing state enterprises. Faced with the possibility of a complete collapse, the government printed more karbovanets (Ukraine's currency) to pay for the persistent budget deficits. The ensuing hyperinflation in 1992 and 1993 resulted in an inflation tax of over 100 percent of total output paid for by the holders of karbovanets.

The inflation tax is not especially relevant for the United States. Even if the U.S. government needed the income from the inflation tax, the Federal Reserve would probably be slow to comply, because the Federal Reserve is largely insulated from political pressures. Members of the Board of Governors, the Fed's governing body, serve 14-year terms and are appointed, not elected. Without changing the Fed's charter, Congress and the President cannot order the Fed to print more money. The Fed must report its actions to Congress twice a year, but aside from amending the Federal Reserve Act (the act that established the Fed in 1913), the Congress and the President have little say about how the Fed conducts monetary policy.

> Central bank independence allows it to make politically unpopular decisions in the short run to prevent inflation in the long run.

The Fed's independence allows it to make politically unpopular decisions, such as using contractionary monetary policy to keep inflation from rising in the long run, even though there may be no apparent inflation. Contractionary monetary policy means lower output growth and higher unemployment in the short run. The unemployment it creates lessens the chances that politicians will be re-elected. The Fed's independence provides political cover for contractionary monetary policy and is one reason why the United States has been able to keep inflation relatively low.

Over the past 20 years, economists and policy makers have become aware of the importance of central bank independence in controlling inflation. Several countries, including New Zealand, Canada, Sweden, and the United Kingdom, have made their central banks more independent and, as they have done so, have lowered their inflation rates.

THE LONG-RUN DICHOTOMY

The proposition underlying the quantity theory of money (in the long-run, the price level, and the price level only, is determined by the quantity of money) is the long-run dichotomy mentioned earlier. This dichotomy states that, in the long run, the real sector, where real output is determined, and the nominal sector, where the price level is determined, can be analyzed separately. Prices relevant in the real sector are relative prices, not absolute prices. A relative price change occurs when the price of one good changes compared with the prices of other goods. An absolute price change is when all prices (and wages, because wages are also a price) change.

Economists argue that, in the long run, relative price changes can be analyzed separately from absolute price changes. That's because relative price changes affect demand-and-supply decisions, while absolute price changes do not. Suppose a frost in Florida reduces the orange harvest, causing the price of orange juice to rise relative to the price of apple juice. Economic theory tells us that the quantity of orange

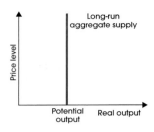

The long-run dichotomy is simply another way of stating that, in the long run, the AS curve is vertical.

juice demanded will fall, while the demand for apple juice will rise. Alternatively, if the absolute price level rises (the price of both orange juice, apple juice, and all other goods, including wages, all rise by the same percent), the quantity of oranges demanded will not change. Although all prices have risen (nominal quantities have risen), each item costs the same relative to all other items, and demand-and-supply decisions do not change (real quantities have not changed).

The basis of the long-run dichotomy is that changes in the money supply lead to changes in absolute, not relative, prices in the long run. Because absolute price changes do not affect demand-and-supply decisions, they do not affect how much real output is produced or the composition of that output. Therefore, in the long run, changes in the money supply cause changes in absolute prices only, not changes in real output. The long-run dichotomy is simply another way of stating that, in the long run, the aggregate supply curve is vertical, as you saw in Chapter 4.

Executive Summary

- Three assumptions turn the equation of exchange into the quantity theory of money: (1) the velocity of money is constant, (2) real output is determined independently of the money supply, and (3) changes in the money supply cause changes in the price level.

- According to the quantity theory of money, money growth causes inflation.

- Data show that, over long spans of time, money growth is positively correlated with inflation.

- Seigniorage is the revenue the government receives from the inflation tax.

- Central bank independence is important for avoiding excessive use of the inflation tax.

- The long-run dichotomy states that an economy's price level is independent of the quantity of real output that the economy produces.

EXCHANGE RATES AND INFLATION

So far, the discussion has concentrated on inflation in the context of the domestic economy. To fully understand the effects of inflation and the policy dilemmas it poses, we need to consider it in an international setting. A change in the price level for a country will affect its economic relationships with other countries. For example, say that Mexico's price level goes up 14 percent and the United States' price level remains constant. The immediate effect, if we assume no other changes occur, is that the price of Mexican goods will become more expensive (in terms of pesos) in both countries, leading people to buy more U.S. goods and fewer Mexican goods. For both countries, the effects of these changes will often be undesirable. Most likely, however, other changes will occur. Adjustments will take place in either the exchange rate (the price at which one currency is exchanged for another currency), the price level in Mexico, or the price level in the United States.

Countries are faced with such dilemmas every day, which means that the international dimension of inflation and money is a central policy issue. The main policy point is that the price level and the exchange rate of a country are related: Whenever the price level changes in one country, the price of that country's goods relative to other countries also changes, unless the country's exchange rate changes

Exhibit 7-3

**An Exchange
Rate Table**

EXCHANGE RATES
(Wednesday, May 9, 2001)

The New York foreign exchange mid-range rates below apply to trading among banks in amounts of $1 million and more, as quoted at 4 P.M. Eastern time by Reuters and other sources. Retail transactions provide fewer units of foreign currency per dollar.

| I | U.S. $ EQUIV. | | CURRENCY PER U.S. $ | |
| | II | III | IV | V |
COUNTRY	Wed	Tue	Wed	Tue
Argentina (Peso)	1.0003	1.0003	0.9997	0.9997
Australia (Dollar)	0.5247	0.5158	1.9057	1.9389
Belgium (Franc)	0.0219	0.0219	45.5895	45.6540
Brazil (Real)	0.4421	0.4456	2.2620	2.2440
Britain (Pound)	1.4207	1.4251	0.7039	0.7017
Canada (Dollar)	0.6500	0.6483	1.5385	1.5425
Chile (Peso)	0.001660	0.001661	602.4500	602.1500
China (Renminbi)	0.1208	0.1208	8.2775	8.2785
Colombia (Peso)	0.0004242	0.0004235	2357.5000	2361.5000
.				
.				
.				
Mexico (Peso)	0.1086	0.1086	9.2090	9.2050
Netherland (Guilder)	0.4015	0.4010	2.4905	2.4940
New Zealand (Dollar)	0.4282	0.4192	2.3354	2.3855
Norway (Krone)	0.1098	0.1099	9.1035	9.0977
Switzerland (Franc)	0.5742	0.5734	1.7417	1.7439
Taiwan (Dollar)	0.03043	0.03043	32.8600	32.8600
Thailand (Baht)	0.02195	0.02192	45.5550	45.6250
Turkey (Lira)	0.00000086	0.00000087	116500.0000	114500.0000
United Arab (Dirham)	0.2723	0.2723	3.6730	3.6730
Urugay (New Peso)	0.07657	0.07667	13.0600	13.0430
Euro	0.8849	0.8836	1.1301	1.1317

This exchange rate table from *The Wall Street Journal* illustrates the price of foreign currencies in terms of the U.S. dollar. Columns II and III report how many dollars could have been purchased with one unit of each foreign currency on Tuesday, May 8, 2001, and on Wednesday, May 9, 2001. Columns IV and V report how much foreign currency was needed to purchase one dollar on Tuesday, May 8, 2001, and on Wednesday, May 9, 2001.

too. To make this relationship clear, you need some background information on exchange rates.

When a person from one country wants to buy goods from someone in another country, the buyer must pay for those goods with currency from the seller's country. For example, to import goods or to purchase assets from Mexico, an American must first exchange dollars for pesos. So, when people from different countries trade goods, they are simultaneously creating a need to trade currencies. When buying goods from a foreign country, you need to know that country's exchange rate. You can find exchange rates in a table, such as the one in Exhibit 7–3, from *The Wall Street Journal*. The exchange rates in Exhibit 7–3 show the amounts of various currencies it takes to buy one U.S. dollar. For example, looking at column IV you'll see that on Wednesday, May 9, 2001, 9.2 pesos bought one U.S. dollar. The peso-per-dollar exchange rate was 9.2.

Exchange Rate Determination

The key to understanding how the "price" of currencies, or the exchange rate, is determined is to realize that both market forces and government forces are at work. The market forces work just like the demand and supply for any good. If the quantity of a currency supplied exceeds the quantity demanded, that currency's price (in terms of the other currency) will fall. For example, if the supply of dollars exceeds the demand for dollars the euro price of dollars might fall from 1.12 to 1.00. If the quantity of a currency supplied is less than the quantity demanded, that currency's price will rise.

Exhibit 7–4(a) shows the demand and supply of dollars in terms of Mexican pesos. To make the analysis simple, we assume that only Mexico and the United States exchange currencies. Because there are two units of account (dollars and pesos), we must specify the price—either pesos per dollar or dollars per peso. The convention is to state the exchange rate in terms of how much of the foreign currency it will cost to buy one unit of the domestic currency. Following this convention, the exchange rate in Exhibit 7–4 is the number of pesos it takes to buy one dollar. At the equilibrium exchange rate, for example, one would receive 9 pesos for every dollar. (The price axis, therefore, is labeled "price of dollars in pesos"). Now let's consider the forces underlying the supply and demand curves. First, take the demand for dollars by Mexicans. Mexicans need dollars for two reasons:

> The demand for foreign currency is derived from domestic demand for foreign goods and assets.

1. To pay for imported goods and services from the United States
2. To buy assets in the United States

Exhibit 7–4

Flexible and Fixed Exchange Rates

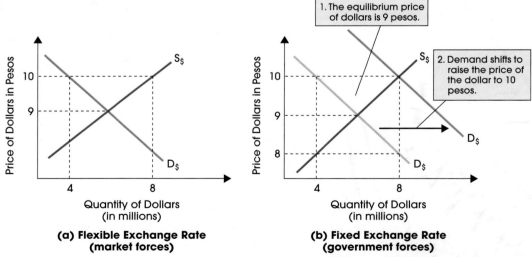

In *panel a*, the exchange rate is determined by the supply and demand for dollars; it is a flexible exchange rate. *Panel b* shows how a government must buy or sell its currency to keep its value at a legally set price that is different from the market-determined price. If the United States wanted to fix the value of the dollar at 10 pesos per dollar, it would have to buy the excess supply of dollars ($4 million) using foreign reserves of pesos. Alternatively, if the United States wanted to fix the value of the dollar at 8 pesos per dollar, where excess demand is $4 million, it would have to sell 4 million dollars in exchange for pesos.

In other words, the demand for dollars by Mexicans is derived from their demand for U.S. exports and assets. Assuming all works well, as the relative price of the dollar rises from 9 to 10 pesos per dollar, for example, Mexicans will have to give up one more peso for every dollar, raising the peso-cost of U.S. goods and assets. Consequently, Mexicans will demand fewer U.S. goods and assets and, accordingly, fewer dollars. This results in the negatively sloped demand curve for dollars shown by $D_\$$ in Exhibit 7–4(a).

The supply of foreign currency is derived from foreign demand for domestic goods and assets.

The supply of dollars is derived from Americans' demand for Mexican goods and assets. As the price of dollars in terms of pesos rises (pesos buy fewer dollars) from 9 to 10 pesos per dollar, the price of pesos in terms of dollars falls. Americans can get one more peso for every dollar, reducing the dollar price of Mexican goods. In this case, Americans will buy more Mexican goods (law of demand). Assuming they need to buy more pesos to do so, Americans will supply more dollars to the market. This means that the supply of dollars is a positively sloped supply curve, like $S_\$$ in Exhibit 7–4(a).

The intersection of supply and demand, in this case at a price of 9 pesos for one dollar, is the market equilibrium exchange rate. At this rate, the quantity of dollars supplied and demanded are equal.

Government Intervention in the Exchange Market. Governments can directly affect the foreign exchange market in two ways. The first way is by choosing whether their currency is convertible. A **convertible currency** is a currency that people can freely exchange for another currency. The United States has a convertible currency. Americans can buy pesos, euros, yen, or any other convertible currency without any government restrictions. Some countries, however, do not allow people to freely buy and sell their currencies. Those countries' currencies are **nonconvertible currencies.**

Convertibility is the degree to which a currency can be exchanged for another currency without restriction.

Nonconvertibility can have many dimensions. For example, a currency might be convertible on the current account (you can sell a currency to buy foreign goods), but nonconvertible on the private capital account (you cannot sell a currency to invest—buy financial assets—in another country). Most developing countries have, to some degree, nonconvertible currencies in regard to their capital account. Most developed countries, however, have fully convertible currencies. Where currencies are in some way nonconvertible, black or grey markets in the currency usually emerge. Two exchange rates develop: the legal rate and the black market rate.

Governments can influence the value of their currency by buying and selling their currency; when they do so at a given exchange rate, we say there is a fixed exchange rate.

A second way governments directly affect the foreign exchange market is by buying and selling currencies to affect the value of its currency. If the government buys and sells its own currency only to keep the exchange rate at a predetermined level, it has a fixed exchange rate. A country that lets the market completely determine the value of its currency has a flexible exchange rate. When a country has a flexible exchange rate, the government does not intervene—buy or sell currencies—to affect the exchange rate. Between these two extremes is a partially flexible exchange rate wherein government enters the foreign exchange market to buy or sell currencies to keep the exchange rate within a predetermined range.

The effect of government intervention is graphically demonstrated in Exhibit 7–4(b). The market value of the dollar is 9 pesos per dollar. If the United States wants to raise the exchange rate value of the dollar to 10 pesos per dollar, it will have to buy $4 million dollars with its holdings of pesos. In this case, the government is buying up the excess supply of its currency so that the exchange rate does not fall, as it would naturally tend to do due to market forces. (This is why Brazil sought the foreign currency reserves in exchange for the $1 billion of Brazilian bonds it sold in early 2000.) If the United States ran out of pesos, it would have to make the dollar nonconvertible, or it would have to give up the fixed exchange rate, allowing the value of the dollar to fall to its market equilibrium, 9 pesos per dollar. If the United States wanted to lower the value of the dollar to 8 pesos per dollar, it would have to sell $4 million dollars (buy pesos) to eliminate excess demand. If it stopped selling dollars, the value of the dollar would rise to its market equilibrium, 9 pesos per dollar.

Changes in Exchange Rate Values. The changing value of a currency has its own terminology, which depends on whether a country has a flexible exchange rate or a fixed exchange rate. In the case of a flexible exchange rate, if the value of a currency goes down relative to another currency (one gets fewer foreign currency units for each domestic currency unit), we say that the domestic currency **depreciates.** For example, when the euro was first introduced January 1999, one euro was worth $1.16. By December 2000, one euro was worth only $0.89. The euro depreciated against the dollar almost steadily from January through December 2000.

> When a flexible and partially flexible exchange rate changes, it either appreciates or depreciates; when a country allows its fixed exchange rate to change, it either devalues or revalues its currency.

If the price of the domestic currency rises (one gets more foreign currency units for each domestic currency unit), the domestic currency **appreciates.** The Japanese yen appreciated against the dollar for most of the early 1990s. In January 1990, 100 yen exchanged for $0.69 and in June 2001, 100 yen exchanged for $0.80.

When talking about fixed exchange rates a different terminology is used. If a country has a fixed exchange rate and the government allows its currency to depreciate, the country **devalues** its currency. If the government allows its currency to appreciate, the country **revalues** its currency.

Exhibit 7–5 shows the value of the dollar from 1973 to 2000, stated as an index of a composite of currencies. The index is a weighted average of the foreign exchange value of the dollar against the currencies of a group of ten U.S. trading partners weighted by the volume of trade with each country. The index is set to 100 in 1973. An index less than 100 means that, on average, one dollar buys fewer foreign currency units than it did in 1973, while an index greater than 100 means that, on

Exhibit 7–5

The Value of the Dollar

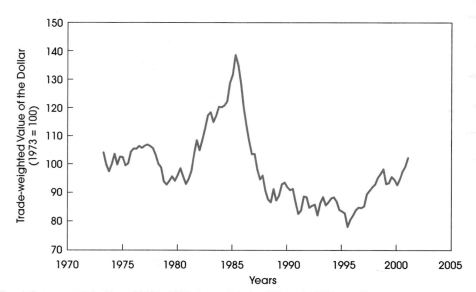

The dollar appreciated from 1973 to 1985, depreciated until the mid-1990s, and has been on an upward trend since. Source: Board of Governors of the Federal Reserve System (www.federalreserve.gov).

average, one dollar buys more foreign currency units than it did in 1973. We start the graph in 1973 because prior to 1973, the United States had a fixed exchange rate and the value of the dollar was constant. In 1973, the United States adopted a partially flexible exchange rate policy. The value of the dollar appreciated from 1973 to 1985, depreciated from 1985 to the mid 1990s, and has appreciated steadily since.

Now that we have covered the basic mechanics of exchange rate determination, we will dig a little deeper to understand the sources of demand and supply for a currency. This requires a further development of the balance of payments account, which were initially discussed in Chapter 4.

The Balance of Payments Account

The supply and demand for currencies is derived from the demand for goods and assets among countries. The United States, through the U.S. Department of Commerce, records the transactions of goods and assets between the United States and the rest of the world in the **balance of payments account.** Behind each purchase or sale of a good or asset that is recorded in the balance of payments account, there is also a purchase or sale of foreign currency. The balance of payments account tells us whether there is a net inflow or outflow of currency from a country. Changes in a country's balance of payments change the supply and demand for currencies, which, as we'll see, affects a country's exchange rate.

The balance of payments account is comprised of the current account, the private capital account, and the official reserves transactions account (Table 7–2). We will explain each account in turn.

> The balance of payments account is comprised of the current account, the private capital account, and the official reserves transactions account.

Table 7–2		
The Balance of Payments Account, 2000		**Billions of Dollars**
Current Account		
1. Exports		1,070
2. Imports		1,438
3. Trade balance (1) − (2)		−368
4. Net investment income		−14
5. Official transfers		−53
6. Current account balance (3) + (4) + (5)		−435
Private Capital Account		
7. Foreign purchases of U.S. assets (capital inflow)		952
8. U.S. purchases of foreign assets (capital outflow)		553
9. Capital account balance (7) − (8)		399
Official Reserve Transactions Account		
10. Official transactions		−1
11. Statistical discrepancy		37
12. Private balance of payments (6) + (9) + (11)		1
13. Balance of payments (12) + (10)		0

Even though the official reserve transactions account is essentially zero, the private capital account and the current account do not sum close to zero because the data for each account come from different sources, which often results in a statistical discrepancy. In 2000, there was a statistical discrepancy of $37 billion (line 11). Source: Bureau of Economic Analysis **(www.bea.doc.gov).**

The Current Account. The **current account** is a record of the flow of currencies that results from the trade of goods and services to and from the rest of the world, the flow of short-term investment, and flow of foreign aid. It is composed of three main categories: trade, net investment income, and official transfers. The trade balance, shown in line 3 of Table 7–2, is the difference between exports, which results in an inflow of dollars, and imports, which results in an outflow of dollars. In 2000, the U.S. trade balance was −$368 billion. Net investment income, shown in line 4 of Table 7–2, is income that U.S. residents and firms receive from their holdings of foreign assets less income foreigners receive from their holdings of U.S. assets. In 2000, net investment income was −$14 billion, a net outflow of income. Official transfers, shown by line 5, are payments of foreign aid. As has been true for most years, the United States provides foreign aid to other countries, which represents an outflow of currency. The sum of the trade balance (line 3), net investment income (line 4), and official transfers (line 5) equals the current account balance (line 6). The current account balance was −$435 billion in 2000, meaning items in this account resulted in a net *outflow* of U.S. dollars.

> The current account records the flow of currencies resulting primarily from the trade of goods and services to and from the rest of the world.

The Private Capital Account. The **private capital account** is a summary of flows of currencies among countries, resulting from the purchase and sale of assets between a country and the rest of the world. When a foreign company invests in the United States (the Japanese firm Toyota builds a plant in the United States), that investment will show up on the private capital account as a capital inflow. Foreign purchases of U.S. assets equaled $952 billion in 2000 (line 7 in Table 7–2). Foreign purchases of U.S. assets are offset by U.S. purchases of foreign assets. For example, a purchase of a foreign bond by a U.S. citizen, is recorded as a capital outflow on the U.S. private capital account. U.S. purchases of foreign assets equaled $553 billion in 2000 (line 8). The difference between the two, called the *capital account balance* (line 9), was $399 billion in 2000, meaning the value of U.S. assets purchased by foreigners exceeded the value of foreign assets purchased by U.S. citizens. The capital account shows a net *inflow* of dollars.

> The private capital account records the flow of currencies resulting from the purchase and sale of assets between a country and the rest of the world.

In recent years, technological developments have integrated world financial markets, allowing people to buy and sell foreign assets much more easily. As a result, the private capital account has gained importance in international economic issues. Individuals and companies have large financial assets that they are willing to move to another country if they see the opportunity to earn a higher rate of return. Interest rates play an important role in determining expected returns. When interest rates rise in one country relative to another, money flows into the country with the higher interest rate and out of the country with the lower interest rate.

Official Reserve Transactions Account. The final component of the balance of payments account is the **official reserve transactions account.** This account is a record of government purchases and sales of currencies. Official reserve transactions for the United States in 2000 are listed in line 10 of Table 7–2. Notice that official reserve transactions are $1 billion. This is extremely small relative to the flows in the other accounts, which tells us that, for 2000, for the year as a whole, the United States did not significantly buy or sell dollars to affect the dollar's value.

> The official reserve transactions account is a record of government purchases and sales of currencies.

The **private balance of payments** (line 12) is the sum of the current account and the capital account balances. When the exchange rate is determined by market forces alone (the government does not buy or sell currency to affect the value of its

> The private balance of payments is the sum of the current account and the capital account.

| Q & A | QUESTION | Which is preferable, a balance of trade surplus or deficit? |
| | **ANSWER** | It depends. |

Newspaper accounts often portray a balance of trade deficit as bad and a surplus as good. Such an unqualified view is wrong. The correct view is that it depends on the specifics.

A balance of trade deficit means that the nation is consuming more goods and services than it is producing. Because more consumption is preferred to less, one could say that a trade deficit is preferred to a surplus. But this statement is not entirely right either. The trade deficit must be financed by selling financial assets such as stocks and bonds as well as real assets, such as real estate and firms.

As foreigners acquire more and more U.S. assets, more and more income must be paid to foreigners. How these payments will affect future consumption depends on what expenditures were financed by the capital inflows. If they were used for investment expenditures that expanded the productive capacity of domestically owned businesses, borrowing could raise future consumption—as long as the resulting income was more than enough to cover payments to foreigners. If the borrowing is used to finance only consumption, eventually the country will have to forgo consumption to repay the debt. Without having much more information about the specific circumstances, you cannot say which is preferable, just as you cannot say whether it is better to borrow or to lend.

currency), the private balance of payments equals zero. This should be no surprise. What this says is that the inflow of dollars must equal the outflow of dollars (quantity supplied must equal quantity demanded).

Relationships in the Balance of Payments Account. Because the balance of payments account measures flows of currencies between a country and the rest of the world, it also measures the supply of and demand for a country's currency. If a country's currency is convertible (as are most of the major currencies of the industrial countries), the quantity of a currency supplied equals the quantity demanded, because, by definition, *convertibility* means anyone who wants to buy or sell a currency can do so.

For a convertible currency, the sum of the current account, the private capital account, and the official reserve transactions accounts, collectively known as the *balance of payments* (line 13), must equal zero. This doesn't mean that the *private* quantity supplied always equals the *private* quantity demanded. If private balance of payments (line 12) don't sum to zero, government must be buying or selling currency.[3] A private balance of payments deficit (net outflow of currency) must be offset by government purchases of its domestic currency, and a private balance of payments surplus (net inflow of currency) must be offset by government purchases of foreign currency.

As long as governments are willing and able to make up the difference between private demand and supply for a currency, a country's private balance of payments deficit or surplus can continue indefinitely. If the government isn't willing to continue buying and selling currency on the foreign exchange market, the government

> For a convertible currency, the balance of payments—the sum of the current account, the private capital account, and the official reserve transactions account—must be zero.

[3]They may not sum to zero because the data for the current and capital accounts come from different sources, which often results in a statistical discrepancy. In 2000, there was a statistical discrepancy of $37 billion (line 11 in Table 7–2).

will have to adopt a flexible exchange rate. Because government purchases of currencies offset any private balance of payments deficit or surplus, when we speak of a private balance of payments deficit or surplus, we mean that the central banks had to step in and make up the difference between the private supply and demand for the currency.

The example of Brazil with which we opened the chapter shows how this works. In 2000, Brazil bought its own currency to eliminate the excess supply of reals and maintain the value of its currency. The Brazilian official transactions account had a positive entry in 2000. (The Q&A feature discusses whether a country would prefer a balance of trade surplus or deficit.)

When the official reserve transactions account is zero, the private capital account is the mirror image of the current account; if one account is in surplus, the other account must be in deficit. In Table 7–2, the official reserve transactions account is essentially zero, so the current account deficit (outflow) is covered by the capital account surplus (inflow).

Executive Summary

- The nominal exchange rate is the value of one currency stated in terms of another currency.

- If a currency is convertible, the government places no restrictions on its purchase or sale. If a currency is nonconvertible the government restricts its purchase and sale and black market exchanges usually develop.

- Flexible exchange rates are determined by the interaction of supply and demand in the market. Demand for foreign currency is derived from domestic demand for foreign goods and assets.

- Supply of foreign currency is derived from foreign demand for domestic goods and assets.

- Fixed and partially flexible exchange rates require the government to buy and sell foreign currency to maintain a certain exchange rate.

- The balance of payments accounts record the flow of goods and services, income payments, and assets in and out of a country. It is divided into the current account, the capital account, and the official reserve transactions account.

- A country with a flexible currency has a private balance of payments of zero.

Balance of Payments Forces: Price Levels and Exchange Rates

Now let's return to our example of the United States and Mexico and consider what happens when the price level in one country rises faster than the price level in another country. In this example, the price level in Mexico rose by 14 percent and the price level in the United States remained constant. What happens next depends on whether the country has a fixed or a flexible exchange rate.

Let's assume both exchange rates are flexible. The 14 percent rise in Mexico's price level means that the demand for pesos will fall and the demand for dollars will rise, causing the peso to depreciate. The demand and supply for the two currencies will continue to change until the peso has depreciated against the dollar by the difference in the rates of inflation. When the peso depreciates by 14 percent against the dollar, Mexicans will get 14 percent fewer dollars for their pesos. But, assuming Mexican wages rise with the price level, Mexicans can buy the same amount of goods and services as before.

Similarly, for Americans, the price of Mexican goods has risen 14 percent in terms of pesos, but pesos cost 14 percent less, so Americans can also buy the same amount of Mexican goods and services as before. Under these circumstances, the

When inflation differs among countries with flexible exchange rates, we would expect the value of the country's currency with the greater inflation to fall relative other currencies.

amount of exports and imports for each country will remain unchanged. The changing exchange rates bring us right back to the same balance of payments equilibrium with which we started.

Next, let's consider what happens when exchange rates are fixed. As prices in Mexico rise, the supply of pesos rises and the demand for pesos falls. If the United States and Mexico started with a zero balance of payments prior to the price-level increase, the Mexican balance of payments would move into deficit and the U.S. balance of payments would move into surplus. Exhibit 7–6 shows the situation facing Mexico and the United States. The demand-and-supply curves represent those that exist after the rise in the price level. One peso can be exchanged for 10 cents (as Exhibit 7–6[a] shows), or, alternatively, one dollar can be exchanged for 10 pesos (as Exhibit 7–6[b] shows). Each country's demand–supply imbalance will have to be offset through buying and selling of official reserves; either Mexico or the United States would both buy pesos with dollars. These actions can temporarily hold the dollar–peso exchange rate fixed, but this works only if the United States is willing to sell dollars to buy pesos or Mexico has large reserves of dollars with which to buy pesos.

It was just this situation—a rising price level—that prompted Brazil to sell the $1 billion worth of Brazilian bonds in the example given at the beginning of this chapter. Brazil was acquiring foreign reserves in the event that its currency began to depreciate again, and it wanted to maintain the value of its currency.

To see what will eventually happen once these reserves run out, let's consider an example using the gold standard, which was the system used 250 years ago. The gold standard is an international institutional arrangement whereby a country is bound to provide a specified amount of gold in exchange for one unit of its currency. Under the gold standard the value of each country's currency is related to a specific amount of gold. The amount of money in a country was determined by the amount of gold it had. If the standard for the British pound were £1 for 1 ounce of gold, people could go to the British central bank and get 1 ounce of gold in exchange for each British pound. Under the gold standard, a country with a balance of payments deficit (the quantity of its own currency supplied is greater than the quantity demanded) had to pay off that deficit with its gold. It had to ship gold to the country with the surplus.

> When inflation differs among countries with fixed exchange rates, the country with the higher inflation rate will tend to lose official reserves.

> When a country runs out of reserves, it must devalue its currency.

Exhibit 7–6

The Balance of Payments Under a Fixed Exchange Rate

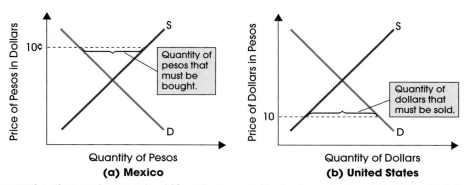

In *panel a*, at an exchange rate of 10 cents per peso Mexico has a balance of payments deficit, meaning the quantity of pesos supplied exceeds the quantity demanded. To maintain this fixed exchange rate, Mexico would have to buy pesos with reserves of dollars. This would decrease the money supply in Mexico. In *panel b*, at an exchange rate of 10 pesos per dollar, the United States has a balance of payments surplus. To maintain this fixed exchange rate, the United States must buy pesos and sell dollars. This increases the United States' money supply.

In our example, if Mexico were under a gold standard and it ran a deficit, it would lose gold to the United States. With less gold, Mexico's money supply would decrease. The United States would gain gold, and its money supply would increase. The money supply change would cause the price level to change (assuming the quantity theory of money held true). The price level would fall in the country with a balance of payments deficit (Mexico) and rise in the country with a balance of payments surplus (United States).

How much would the price levels rise and fall? They would rise and fall by the amount necessary to bring both countries back to a zero balance of payments. If the price level in the United States rose 7 percent and the price level in Mexico fell 7 percent, the relative prices faced by people in both countries would be what they were before. If each country began with a zero balance of payments, both countries would return to a zero balance of payments. Therefore, the result of a rise in the Mexican price level with fixed exchange rates is that the price levels in Mexico and the United States would adjust to bring the prices back to where they started.

Real Exchange Rates

The real exchange rate is the nominal exchange rate adjusted for price level differences among countries.

Economists have developed a terminology to describe prices of a composite of goods in one country relative to other countries that takes into account both exchange rates and differing rates of inflation between countries. Economists call the exchange rate adjusted for price-level differences among countries the **real exchange rate.** When price levels in both countries change by the same proportion, a change in the **nominal exchange rate**—the price at which one currency is exchanged for another currency—is also the change in the real exchange rate. (The nominal exchange rate is the exchange rate we're talking about so far. This exchange rate is often referred to as the *nominal exchange rate* to distinguish it from the real exchange rate.) If, however, the price level rises more quickly in one country compared with another, the change in the nominal exchange rate between two countries will differ from the change in the real exchange rate.

Let's consider a couple of examples. Say the price level rises 5 percent in the United States and 0 percent in the European Union, and that the dollar–euro nominal exchange rate remains constant. This means that U.S. goods become more expensive for Europeans—the real euro–dollar exchange rate has fallen 5 percent. A euro will buy 5 percent fewer U.S. goods than before.

To see how to calculate the real exchange, consider the following example. Suppose that the price of a dollar in terms of euros is 1.5, which means that 1.5 euros buys one dollar, or, equivalently, 67 cents buys 1 euro. In this case we would say the euro-to-dollar exchange rate is 1.5. This nominal exchange rate alone does not tell us whether goods and services are more or less expensive in Europe compared with the United States. To answer this question, we have to know the prices of goods in both countries. Say that a movie ticket costs $7 in the United States and 10.50 euros in the European Union. Because each dollar buys 1.5 euros, the prices of movies in both locations are identical: $7 can buy a movie in both the United States and the European Union (7 × 1.5 = 10.5 euros). Extending this example to a composite of all goods, the real exchange rate gives us a measure of the amount of goods your money will buy in another country.

The real exchange rate of a domestic currency (price of domestic currency in terms of foreign currency) can be expressed as follows:

$$E_R = E \times \left(\frac{P_{domestic}}{P_{foreign}} \right) \qquad (7\text{-}3)$$

If we are talking about the United States E is the nominal exchange rate of the dollar (the price of the dollar in foreign currencies), E_R is the real exchange rate of the dollar (the real price of dollars in foreign currencies), $P_{domestic}$ is the U.S. price level, and $P_{foreign}$ is the foreign price level. If the prices of composite goods are identical in both countries, the real exchange rate equals the nominal exchange rate. If the movie ticket had referred to a price of a composite of goods, we would have the following:

$$E_R = 1.5 \times (7/10.5) = 1$$

On average goods, adjusted for price levels, cost the same in both countries.

Determining real exchange rates is very difficult, as you will see in the next section's discussion of purchasing-power parity. Generally, the discussion is of changes in, not the level of real exchange rates. Converting Equation 7–3 to percent changes we have the following:

> Changes in the real exchange rate equals changes in the nominal exchange rate plus domestic inflation minus foreign inflation.

$$\%\Delta E_R = \%\Delta E + \%\Delta P_{domestic} - \%\Delta P_{foreign} \qquad (7\text{-}4)$$

where $\%\Delta E_R$ is the percent change in the real exchange rate of the domestic currency (price of domestic currency in foreign currencies), $\%\Delta E$ is the percent change in the nominal exchange rate (price of domestic currency in foreign currencies) $\%\Delta P_{domestic}$ is the inflation rate in the domestic country, and $\%\Delta P_{foreign}$ is the inflation rate in the foreign country.

Let's consider the example of Mexico discussed above (here Mexico is the domestic country). The price level in Mexico rose by 14 percent and the peso depreciated by 14 percent against the dollar (one received 14 percent more pesos for every dollar). Putting these values into the equation ($\%\Delta E_R = -14\% + 14\% - 0\% = 0$), we find that the nominal exchange rate of the peso (price of pesos in dollars) adjusted so that the real exchange rate did not change at all.

As a second example, let's consider a change from the U.S. perspective (where the U.S. is the domestic country). Let's say the price level in Mexico rises by 14 percent while the price level in the United States rises by 5 percent. Let's also say that the nominal exchange rate of dollar (price of dollars in terms of pesos) rises by 3 percent. Given these assumptions the change in the real exchange rate of the dollar (real price of the dollar in pesos) equals:

% change in real exchange rate of the dollar = 3% + 5% − 14% = −6%

In words this equation states that the change in the real exchange rate of the dollar equals the change in the nominal dollar exchange rate (+3 percent) plus the change in the price level in the United States (+5 percent) minus the change in the price level in Mexico (+14 percent). The real exchange rate of the dollar has fallen by 6 percent. (Alternatively, the real exchange rate of the peso has risen by 6 percent.) The combination of effects is the equivalent to a rise in the nominal exchange rate of the Mexican peso (price of pesos in terms of dollars) of 6 percent with constant price levels.

Purchasing-Power Parity

The prices and exchange rates illustrated in the real exchange rate formula raise the question about what is the *correct* real exchange rate, if there is one. One way economists estimate the real exchange rate is with purchasing-power parity. **Purchasing-power parity** theory states that the amount of tradable goods and services a currency can buy (its purchasing power) should be the same in all countries. This theory is based on one of the central laws of economics—the **law of one price,** which states that, in competitive markets, the same good (accounting for transportation and other relevant costs) cannot sell for two different prices. Applied internationally, the law of one price becomes purchasing-power parity. Specifically, purchasing-power parity states that exchange rates and/or prices will adjust so that tradable goods sell for the same price. In terms of real exchange rates, purchasing-power parity states that the real exchange rate for countries in which goods are tradable will be one. Thus:

$$E_R = 1 = E \times \left(\frac{P_{domestic}}{P_{foreign}} \right) \qquad (7\text{-}5)$$

or

$$P_{foreign} = E \times P_{domestic}$$

For example, if the price level of tradable goods were twice as high in the United States as in New Zealand (both of whose currencies are called dollars) the New Zealand dollar would cost two U.S. dollars.

The adjective "tradable" is important because the law of one price is based on competition and there will be competition only when goods are traded. Building rents will not necessarily equalize; prices of VCRs will have a much stronger tendency to equalize.

Both the law of one price and purchasing-power parity are based on the assumptions that economies are highly competitive and that markets will quickly move prices of tradable goods in response to profit opportunities. Suppose, for example, that you go to a farmers' market and different farmers are selling identical apples at different prices. The economics you learned in your principles course suggests that the invisible hand will quickly move the prices of the apples to a single price as the high-price farmers lower their prices to attract customers or the low-price farmers raise their price in response to the high level of demand for their apples. This is an example of the law of one price.

Extending this concept to the international setting, the law of one price states that identical apples should sell for identical prices in all countries. For example, if apples are selling for more in Thailand than they are in the United States, some entrepreneur will see an opportunity to earn a profit by buying up the apples in the United States and selling them in Thailand. Other entrepreneurs will do the same. As the demand for apples in the United States rises, the price of the apples will rise. As the supply of apples rises in Thailand, their price will fall. This will continue until apples cost the same in both countries.

What does it mean for prices to be identical between Thailand and the United States? If you buy an apple in the United States for $0.10, that same $0.10 will buy you enough bahts (Thailand's currency) to purchase one apple in Thailand.

THE BRIEFING ROOM   Purchasing-Power Parity and the Price of Big Macs

According to purchasing-power parity, identical tradable goods in two countries should cost the same after taking into account exchange rates, transportation costs, tariffs, and taxes. *The Economist* magazine periodically publishes the prices of McDonald's Big Mac hamburgers from different countries around the world. To the degree that hamburgers are identical goods, we can use their prices to evaluate how closely purchasing-power parity works in the real world.

The following table shows the prices of Big Macs in various countries, stated in their native currencies. Column IV shows the exchange rate for each country.

I	II	III	IV	V
		Price of Big Mac in Local Currency	Exchange Rate[a]	Price of Big Mac ($)
Country	Currency			
The Philippines	Peso	59.00	50.30	1.17
China	Yuan	9.90	8.28	1.20
Russia	Ruble	35.00	28.90	1.21
Poland	Zloty	5.90	4.03	1.46
Brazil	Real	3.60	2.19	1.64
Taiwan	Dollar	70.00	32.90	2.13
Mexico	Peso	21.90	9.29	2.36
United States	**Dollar**	**2.54**	**1.00**	**2.54**
United Kingdom	Pound	4.08	1.43	2.85
Denmark	Kroner	24.75	8.46	2.93
Switzerland	Franc	6.30	1.73	3.65

[a]Market exchange rate (April 17, 2001). Source: *The Economist*, April 19th, 2001, "Big Mac Currencies."

Column V converts the price of Big Macs from domestic currency to dollars, using market exchange rates. For example, in China, a Big Mac costs 9.90 yuan. To buy a Big Mac in China, we would have to convert dollars to yuan. One dollar buys 8.28 yuan, and we need 9.90 yuan to buy the Big Mac. Therefore, we need to exchange $1.20 (9.90/8.28) to purchase a Big Mac in China. If purchasing-power parity had held, the Big Mac would have cost $2.54 (or 21.03 yuan), the same as in the United States. Because the Big Mac costs less in China than in the United States, purchasing-power parity states that too many yuan are exchanged for each dollar at the current exchange rate—the yuan is undervalued compared with the U.S. dollar. The exchange rates for those countries where the Big Mac costs less than $2.54 are *under*valued. The exchange rates for those countries where the Big Mac costs more than $2.54 are *over*valued.

The Big Mac Index is fun, but in actuality, the Big Mac is not a good reference product for the law of one price. One reason is that *The Economist* does not take into account transportation costs, tariffs, and taxes when reporting prices. A second reason is that the tradable components of the Big Mac (special sauce, lettuce, cheese, pickles, onions, etc.) are only a portion of the total cost of a Big Mac. Buildings and domestic labor, also inputs to the production of Big Macs, are not tradable goods and therefore their prices do not face the same pressure to equalize.

Of course, the differences between this example and the farmers' market example are the following: The distances between markets are large, and the countries may have different taxes and tariffs. For this reason, we have to assume that the price you pay for an apple in Thailand includes the transportation costs and any tariffs or taxes. (See The Briefing Room, "Purchasing-Power Parity and the Price of Big Macs.")

There is another question we must consider in purchasing-power parity: What goods and assets are being bought and sold? Remember, the balance of payments consists of both a capital account and a current account, so the relevant price level includes both goods and assets. Measured price indexes include only goods and services. If demand for a country's assets were high, so the prices of their assets are higher than other countries' assets, and the real exchange rate is one, we would expect that country's prices of goods and services to be lower to offset the difference in the price of assets.

If purchasing-power parity holds, changes in nominal exchange rates will be determined by differences in inflation rates. You can see this by looking back

When applying purchasing-power parity, one must remember that the relevant price level includes the prices of both a country's goods and its assets.

Exhibit 7-7

The Nominal Exchange Rate and Inflation

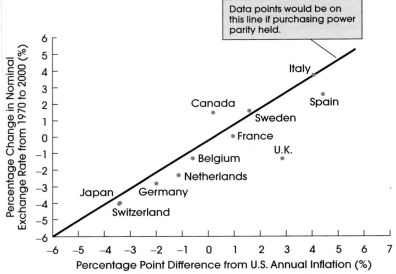

This exhibit plots inflation differentials between the United States and 11 other countries against the percent change in each country's exchange rate from 1970 to 2000. Because the data points cluster along a straight line, this exhibit supports the proposition that changes in the nominal exchange rate are determined, in part, by relative inflation rates between foreign and domestic economies. The inflation differential is the average inflation rate less U.S. average inflation from 1970 to 2000 in each country. Source: *International Financial Statistics* (www.imf.org).

at Equation 7–4. If the real exchange rate does not change, we can rewrite it thus:

$$\%\Delta E = \%\Delta P_{foreign} - \%\Delta P_{domestic} \qquad (7\text{-}6)$$

The nominal exchange rate, stated in foreign currency per unit of domestic currency, will rise when foreign inflation is greater than domestic inflation and will fall if it is less than U.S. inflation. Exhibit 7–7 plots countries' inflation rates less the U.S. inflation rate against the change in their exchange rates (foreign currency per U.S. dollar). If purchasing-power parity theory held, the nominal exchange rate would fall along the *solid line*. Although the predicted relationship doesn't hold perfectly in the real world, this graph does show that inflation is an important force in moving the nominal exchange rate. Countries with relatively high rates of inflation (such as Italy) have depreciating currencies. Countries with relatively low rates of inflation (such as Switzerland) have appreciating currencies.

POLICY PERSPECTIVE: EXPORTING INFLATION

Purchasing-power parity brings together the inflation analysis and exchange-rate analysis. It suggests that long-run movements in exchange rates are determined to a significant degree by differences in inflation rates among countries and that the long-run equilibrium must be the same whether countries have fixed or flexible exchange rates. If they have fixed exchange rates, the price levels in the countries adjust. If they have flexible exchange rates, the nominal exchange rates adjust. In both cases, the real exchange rate will not change and will be determined by real forces such as labor, capital, and technological progress. So, in the long run, the equilibrium real exchange rate will be the same whether there are fixed or flexible exchange rates.

From a policy perspective, it is important to focus on the adjustment path of exchange rates and inflation as the economy moves to the long-run equilibrium. The adjustment paths under flexible and fixed exchange rates can be quite different and require different types of policy responses. When exchange rates are flexible, inflation differentials will lead to changes in the nominal exchange rate only, and the country does not need to buy or sell its currency, or have other adjustment policies.

> With flexible exchange rates, inflation in one country does not tend to cause inflation in another country; with fixed exchange rates, inflation in one country often leads to inflationary pressure in other countries.

When exchange rates are fixed and countries remain committed to fixed exchange rates, higher inflation in one country can turn into higher inflation in other countries. Such an adjustment process took place in the 1960s when the United States and most other industrialized countries were operating with a fixed exchange-rate system. Under that exchange-rate system (called the *Bretton Woods system of fixed exchange rates*), the United States tied the dollar to the price of gold ($35 per ounce) and other countries tied their currencies to the dollar.

Throughout the 1960s, the growth of the money supply in the United States exceeded that of most other countries. Consistent with the quantity theory, this growth of the U.S. money supply was accompanied by an increase in inflation in the United States relative to inflation abroad. To keep the dollar from depreciating, other countries began buying up the excess supply of dollars, thereby increasing the supplies of their own currencies. They could have turned their dollars in to the United States, demanding gold in return, but most did not because they knew that the United States did not have enough gold reserves to cover them. They knew that if they did turn them in, the system of fixed exchange rates would break down. So, under these arrangements, the other countries were forced to increase their money supplies and inflate their price levels to match U.S. inflation. The United States, in essence, exported inflation. France, in particular, was not happy with this situation. In 1971, France decided to turn its dollars in to the United States for gold, and this forced the world economy off the Bretton Woods fixed exchange rate system.

Since that time, the world has had a continually changing international exchange-rate regime. There is no universal fixed exchange-rate system, but countries can tie their currency to other currencies. When they do so they create the possibility of financial crisis. Consider the Asian financial crisis of the late 1990s. A number of Asian countries had tied their currencies to the dollar, but their inflation rate was higher than the U.S. inflation rate. Because they, not the United States or other countries, were maintaining the fixed exchange rate, the other world economies did not increase their money supplies when they ran balance of payments surpluses with these countries. Instead, Asian countries, alone, had to buy their own currencies to hold up their exchange rates. When their reserves of foreign currencies ran out, a crisis erupted and the Asian countries had to undertake a number of adjustments, which we will consider in later chapters on short-run international issues. This crisis spread to Brazil and helped create the situation discussed in the introduction to this chapter. Investors were selling Brazilian assets, which put downward pressure on the real. Brazil responded initially by spending its foreign reserves to support its currency, but it finally let the market largely determine the value of the real.

Table 7-3
Summary of the Long-Run Models

	Key Assumptions	Key Predictions	Key Policy Implications
Solow Growth Model Long-run, steady-state model that focuses on the role of saving and investment in the growth process	• Supply is determined by the factors of production. • Supply creates its own demand. • Technology is exogenous to the model. • Diminishing marginal product • Constant returns to scale	• The economy will grow at the rate the population grows. • Per capita growth will be zero. • Growth rates among countries will converge.	• Government can increase growth in the intermediate run by implementing policies to increase saving and investment. Nothing can be done to affect per capita growth in the long run—the economy always returns to its steady-state growth path.
New Growth Theory Long-run model that focuses on technological advance and trade in the growth process	• Supply creates its own demand. • Technology is affected by policy. • Increasing returns to scale	• Policies can increase per capita growth. • Growth engenders more growth. • Growth rates will accelerate over time. • Rich countries' and poor countries' incomes may not converge.	• Government can increase growth by (1) implementing policies that encourage technological development, (2) reducing protectionism, (3) lowering tax rates, (4) privatizing activities, (5) industrial policy.
Quantity Theory Long-run model of inflation. Real output is determined by aggregate supply, and the price level is determined by aggregate demand—or the quantity of money.	• Based on the equation of exchange: $MV = PY$ • Real output is determined by the factors of production. • Velocity of money is constant. • Direction of causation goes from money to prices.	• Inflation will rise by the same percentage as the rise in the money supply.	• To control inflation, control the growth of the money supply. • Central banks should be independent of politics.
Purchasing-Power Parity Long-run model of exchange rates	• The law of one price holds for internationally traded goods.	• The real exchange rate equals 1. • In the long run, nominal exchange rates are determined by inflation differentials.	• In the long run, the government can control the nominal exchange rate by controlling only the inflation rate.

Executive Summary

- Through its effect on the balance of payments, inflation differentials put pressure on the nominal exchange rates to change.

- The currency of the country with the higher inflation will tend to depreciate and vice versa.

- Under fixed exchange rates, a balance of payments deficit will lead to a decline in the domestic money supply, and a fall in the price level.

- Under flexible exchange rates, a balance of payments deficit will lead to a depreciation of a country's currency.

- The real exchange rate of a domestic currency is the nominal exchange rate of the domestic currency adjusted for differences in price levels.

$$E_R = E \times \left(\frac{P_{domestic}}{P_{foreign}} \right).$$

- Changes in the real exchange rate follow the formula: $\%\Delta E_R = \%\Delta E + \%\Delta P_{domestic} - \%\Delta P_{foreign}$.

- Purchasing-power parity predicts that the real exchange rate will tend towards 1. That is, the price of goods and services among countries, adjusted for the exchange rate, will be the same in all countries.

CONCLUSION

The four long-run models are the Solow growth model, new growth theory, the quantity theory, and purchasing-power parity.

This chapter concludes our discussion of the long run. At this point, it's a good idea to pause and summarize what you have learned before starting on the short run. Table 7–3 provides a summary of the long-run models, as well as their key assumptions, predictions, and policy implications. These four models give you a fairly complete picture of economists' vision of the long run.

Real output is determined by capital, labor, and technology. The inflation rate is determined by the growth rate of money, and nominal exchange rates are determined by inflation differentials. These long-run forces tell us where the economy is eventually headed. However, economies often deviate from their long-run paths for long periods of time. Policy makers don't want to hear, "Eventually, this will happen." They want to know what will happen now. They want to know what will happen in the short run. In the next four chapters, we will discuss the short run.

KEY POINTS

- Money is a financial asset that serves as a store of value, a unit of account, and a medium of exchange.
- The Federal Reserve Bank controls the money supply mainly through open market purchases and sales of government securities.
- The equation of exchange is $MV = PY$.
- The long-run dichotomy asserts that the level of real output supplied in the economy is independent of the level of prices.
- The equation of exchange, combined with the assumption of a constant velocity and the long-run dichotomy, becomes the quantity theory of money, which predicts that the price level is proportional to the money supply—or money growth causes inflation.
- The quantity theory of money says that to control inflation, control the growth of the money supply. The problem with this policy prescription is that there is usually another problem—government may have to print money just to keep from falling apart.
- The profit government earns from printing money is called seignorage. Seignorage is one way government pays for its expenses.
- The nominal exchange rate is the price of one currency in terms of another. For example, a euro–dollar exchange rate of 1.15 means that it takes 1.15 euros to buy one dollar.

- Flexible exchange rates are determined by the interaction of supply and demand in the market while fixed and partially flexible exchange rates require the government to buy and sell foreign currency to maintain a certain exchange rate.

- The balance of payments records the transactions of goods and assets between a country and the rest of the world. It is composed of the current account, the capital account, and the official reserve transactions account.

- The balance of payments account reflects the demand for and supply of a currency. A country with a flexible currency always has a private balance of payments of zero.

- Under flexible exchange rates, an increase in a country's inflation rate relative to inflation elsewhere will cause that country's currency to depreciate.

- A country with a fixed exchange rate and a balance of payments deficit must reduce its money supply, which causes prices to fall in the long run. A country with a flexible exchange rate and a balance of payments deficit will experience a depreciation of its currency.

- The real exchange rate is the nominal exchange rate adjusted for differences in price levels.

$$E_R = E \times \left(\frac{P_{domestic}}{P_{foreign}} \right).$$

- Changes in the real exchange rate follow the formula: $\%\Delta E_R = \%\Delta E + \%\Delta P_{domestic} - \%\Delta P_{foreign}$.

- The real exchange rate adjusts the nominal exchange rate for differences in price levels among countries.

- Purchasing-power parity states that two identical goods in two different countries should have the same price after accounting for the exchange rate.

KEY TERMS

appreciate 194
balance of payments account 195
convertible currency 193
current account 196
depreciate 194
devalue 194
equation of exchange 183
inflation tax 188

law of one price 202
liquidity 181
long-run dichotomy 183
money 180
nominal exchange rate 200
nonconvertible currency 193
official reserve transactions
    account 196

private balance of payments 196
private capital account 196
purchasing-power parity 202
quantity theory of money 183
real exchange rate 200
revalue 194
seigniorage 188
velocity of money 183

QUESTIONS FOR THOUGHT AND REVIEW

1. What is money?
2. Why does the Federal Reserve collect and publish data on several different measures of money?
3. Are grocery store coupons considered to be money?
4. How does the Federal Reserve increase and decrease the money supply through an open market operation?
5. What is the long-run dichotomy?
6. What is the quantity theory of money?
7. State the equation of exchange and explain what the velocity of money means.
8. What three assumptions are needed to transform the equation of exchange into the quantity theory of money? Do those assumptions hold in the real world? Is the quantity theory an accurate description of the relationship between money growth and inflation in the long run?

9. According to the quantity theory of money, what will happen to the price level if the money supply increases by 10 percent? What will happen to real output?
10. What are the policy implications of the quantity theory of money?
11. What is the inflation tax? Why do some countries rely heavily on it, while others do not?
12. What is an exchange rate?
13. What is the difference between a convertible currency and a nonconvertible currency? Give an example of a restriction on the convertibility of currency. Why do some countries have nonconvertible currencies?
14. What is the difference between a currency that has appreciated and a currency that has been revalued?
15. What would the United States' capital account balance be if there were a $60 billion current account surplus and flexible exchange rates?

16. If an economy with a fixed exchange rate has a balance of payments deficit, is the exchange rate above or below the equilibrium exchange rate? Describe what is happening to the official reserve transactions account.
17. When is the private balance of payments account not in balance?
18. What distinguishes the private balance of payments from the balance of payments?
19. Can the balance of payments indicate whether a country has a fixed, flexible, or partially flexible exchange rate?
20. What is the difference between the real exchange rate and the nominal exchange rate?
21. What is purchasing-power parity? How is it related to the law of one price?
22. According to the purchasing-power parity hypothesis, what causes the nominal exchange rate to change over the long run?
23. What adjustments will take place if the price level in the United States rises relative to the foreign price level, assuming that the real exchange rate remains unchanged and government maintains a fixed nominal exchange rate.

PROBLEMS AND EXERCISES

1. Go to the Board of Governor's home page and look up the minutes from the most recent Federal Open Market Committee meeting (www.federalreserve.gov/fomc). What open market operation was required to meet the Fed's policy objectives that were determined at that meeting?
2. Look up the data on the M1 money supply and nominal GDP from the latest *Economic Report of the President* (w3.access.gpo.gov/eop). Click in the option to download the current statistical tables.
   a. What is the velocity of money for the past 5 years? What do these numbers mean?
   b. Has velocity remained constant over the past 5 years?
3. Go to www.NewsEngin.com/neFreeTools.nsf and choose "all items" and "U.S. City Average" to get to the cost of living calculator.
   a. What was the value of $1,000 today in the year you were born? Using this answer, what is the cumulative amount of inflation from the year you were born to the present time?
   b. What was the buying power of $2 in 1933 (the trough of the Great Depression)? Using your answer, determine the cumulative amount of inflation from 1933 to the present.
   c. According to the quantity theory of money, what accounts for the inflation you found in your answers to items a and b?
4. Look up today's peso–dollar and yen–dollar exchange rates at the following Web site: www.x-rates.com.
   a. Has the peso appreciated or depreciated against the dollar over the past 120 days?
   b. Has the yen appreciated or depreciated against the dollar over the past 120 days?
   c. What are the dollar–peso and dollar–yen exchange rates?
5. On which account (the current or capital) will the following transactions be recorded?
   a. A resident of China buys a share of stock in U.S. corporation.
   b. A resident of China buys a refrigerator made in the United States.
   c. A group of Chinese residents buys controlling interest in a U.S. baseball team.
6. What will happen to the nominal exchange rate if the price level in the United States rises relative to the foreign price level, assuming that the real exchange rate remains unchanged?
7. If the price of a single scoop of Ben and Jerry's ice cream is $1.50 in the United States and $2.00 in Canadian dollars, and purchasing-power parity holds, what would be the Canadian dollar–U.S. dollar exchange rate?
8. If the price of a single scoop of Ben and Jerry's ice cream is $1.50 in the United States, the Canadian dollar–U.S. dollar exchange rate is 1.11, and purchasing-power parity holds, what would be the price of a scoop of Ben and Jerry's ice cream in Canadian dollars?
9. Calculate the change in the real exchange rate of the dollar in each of the following cases:
   a. the value of the dollar rises 10 percent, U.S. inflation is 5 percent, foreign inflation is 7 percent.
   b. the value of the dollar rises 5 percent, U.S. inflation is 8 percent, foreign inflation is 8 percent.
   c. the value of the dollar falls 7 percent, U.S. inflation is 3 percent, foreign inflation is 6 percent.

8

In the long run, we are all dead.

—J. M. Keynes

The Determination of Output in the Short Run

After reading this chapter you should be able to:

1. List the assumptions and implications of the short-run macroeconomic model

2. Use the multiplier model to determine equilibrium in the goods market

3. Explain how changes in autonomous expenditures and fiscal policy affect output in the multiplier model

4. Discuss how equilibrium is determined in the money market

5. Explain how monetary policy affects the money market equilibrium

6. Discuss how monetary and fiscal policy affect the economy in the short run

CNN once reported that the size of Alan Greenspan's briefcase is an indicator of the direction of monetary policy. If the briefcase looks heavy, said CNN, the chairman of the Fed is carrying lots of documentation to convince other members of the Federal Open Market Committee (FOMC), the U.S. committee that directs monetary policy, that monetary policy needs to change. If the briefcase looks light, then monetary policy is likely to remain unchanged.

The previous chapters developed the long-run model of the economy, which we use to explain the economy's growth path. According to that model, changes in the money supply—monetary policy—have no effect on real output; they only affect the price level. Concern with the weight of Alan Greenspan's briefcase, however, comes primarily from an interest in what would happen to real output, not prices. If monetary policy does not affect real output, why are policy makers and businesspeople interested in what the chairman of the Fed is thinking? The reason is that, in the short run, monetary policy *does* affect real output. Any hint about the direction of monetary policy is also a hint about the direction of real output.

This chapter begins to explore economists' short-run model, which economists use to explain business cycles—the fluctuations of real output over time. This model is adapted from a model proposed by J. M. Keynes in the mid-1930s. Keynes argued that the long-run model did not match the real-world economy. The long-run model assumed that the economy would always return relatively quickly to its long-run growth path. In the 1930s, that assumption definitely did not fit reality well.

Economists' short-run
model is adapted from
a model proposed by
J. M. Keynes in the 1930s.

In the 1930s, the economy was well below its potential: Real output fell 30 percent between 1929 and 1933, and unemployment rose to 25 percent. Keynes and other economists at the time recognized that the economy wasn't behaving as the long-run model predicted. They developed a new, short-run model to understand why. Their model shifts the focus away from aggregate supply (the focus of long-run models in Chapters 5 through 7) to aggregate demand, which can be affected by both monetary and fiscal policy. They argued that insufficient aggregate demand caused the Great Depression. Their explanation was that aggregate demand had fallen, creating a glut of goods, which led firms to cut production and lay off workers. This reduced aggregate demand even more. They agreed that unless something pulled aggregate demand back up, output would remain below potential. In the short-run model, output can deviate from potential, possibly for substantial periods of time. Policy makers use the short-run model today when they think about business cycles and policies to deal with them.

THE IS/LM MODEL

The short-run model focuses
on aggregate demand;
the long-run model focuses
on aggregate supply.

To explain the role of aggregate demand in the economy in the short run, we start by assuming that the price level is fixed. This is consistent with how we distinguished the short run from the long run in Chapter 4. In the short run, the price level is completely fixed; in the long run, it is completely flexible. (In Chapter 11, we adjust the model to allow the price level to change in the short run.) What a fixed price level means graphically is that the aggregate supply curve is horizontal, as Exhibit 8–1 shows. With this aggregate supply curve, changes in aggregate demand cause changes in output, not prices. You will recall from Chapter 4 that this is Hansen's law (in the short run, whatever is demanded is supplied). Firms increase or decrease production to meet expenditures at the current price level. If aggregate demand is high (AD_1), output will be high (Y_1). If aggregate demand is low (AD_0), output will be low (Y_0). Aggregate expenditures (the quantity of aggregate demand at a given

In the simplest short-run
model, the price level is
assumed to be fixed.

Exhibit 8–1

Aggregate Supply When Prices Are Fixed

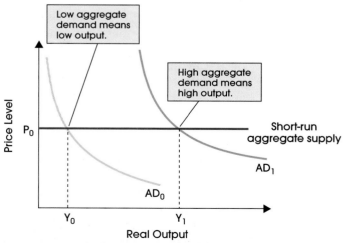

With completely fixed prices, the aggregate supply curve is horizontal. Aggregate demand determines real output. If aggregate demand is high (AD_1), real output is high (Y_1). If aggregate demand is low (AD_0), real output is low (Y_0).

THE BRIEFING ROOM   A Pragmatic View of Fixed and Flexible Price Models

Advocates of both the long-run and short-run models know that their assumptions about prices don't always match reality. The long-run model assumes prices are completely flexible, while the short-run model assumes prices are fixed. Each model includes these extreme assumptions to make the models easier. Advocates of the long-run model know that, in the short run, prices tend to be fixed, but they argue that this is temporary and that long-run forces will eventually control what happens to prices.

Advocates of the short-run model know that the price level is not always fixed but argue that fixed-price models serve as a useful approximation to the real-world economy. Furthermore, they argue that the level of potential output is ambiguous, and that the best policy is to push the economy beyond its potential by expanding aggregate demand and creating a "high-pressure" economy. Firms will be induced to develop new technology, which will lead to increasing returns and increased productivity, which will hold prices down, even as the labor market tightens and wages rise.

From the 1940s until the 1970s, the short-run view was the conventional view. In the 1970s, inflation rose, even though the economy was far below what had been thought to be potential output. It was no longer reasonable to assume, even approximately, that prices were fixed. The long run became the focus of attention. In the 1990s, there was another change in the economy. In particular, the U.S. economy continued to grow, squeezing unemployment to record lows, but inflation didn't rise. Newspapers frequently reported of a "new economy" in which technological innovation had worked to keep productivity apace with increasing demand. With this new development, the short-run model once again became the relevant tool to analyze the economy because the price level was relatively stable and output seemed able to meet demand, even when unemployment was low. As you can see, throughout the past 70 years, the relevance of the short-run assumption of fixed prices for analyzing short-run movements in the economy has fallen in and out of favor. We suspect it will continue to do so in the future.

The AD curve looks simple, but it is not. It is fundamentally different from the demand curve of a single good.

Underlying the AD curve is a complicated analysis, which is embodied in the multiplier model, the money demand and supply model, and the IS/LM model.

price level) determine real output. (See The Briefing Room, "A Pragmatic View of Fixed and Flexible Price Models," for more discussion.)

The aggregate demand curve looks simple, but it is not. You might at first be tempted to think about the aggregate demand curve as just another demand curve—a curve showing that as price rises, quantity demanded falls and vice versa. But aggregate demand is fundamentally different from the demand for a single good. That's because the aggregate demand curve relates the price level of all goods (not just a single good) to the quantity of all goods in an economy. You can see this in Exhibit 8–1: The price level is on the vertical axis and real output is on the horizontal axis. The shape of the aggregate demand curve, therefore, is not the result of substitution among goods. The aggregate demand curve is an equilibrium curve. It shows the combinations of price and income levels at which both the goods and the money markets are in equilibrium. If the economy is not in equilibrium, forces will push it toward equilibrium; the model can guide our forecasts of the economy.

Underlying the aggregate demand curve is the **IS/LM model,** which looks at the combinations of equilibria in the goods market and the money market and considers how they interact. The IS/LM model is the main focus of this chapter. We begin our discussion of the goods market by deriving the **multiplier model**—a model of the economy that shows how changes in expenditures have a multiplied effect on aggregate output. The multiplier model combined with an investment model leads directly to the IS curve, which shows equilibrium in the goods market. In the second half of the chapter, we look at a model of the demand and supply of money that leads to the LM curve, which shows equilibrium in the money market. Exhibit 8–2 shows these components of the model. Behind the aggregate demand curve are the IS and LM curves. The AD curve is based on those other models. By combining the IS and LM curves, we can describe the aggregate demand side of the economy.

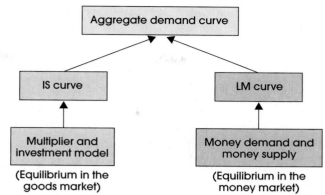

Exhibit 8-2
The Models Behind Aggregate Demand

Behind the aggregate demand curve are the IS and LM curves. The IS curve is based on the multiplier model, and the LM curve is based on a model of money demand and supply. By combining the IS and LM curves, we can describe the aggregate demand side of the economy.

THE MULTIPLIER MODEL

The multiplier model is a model of the goods market—the market where goods and services are bought and sold. Total expenditures on goods and services are called **aggregate expenditures (AE)**—the sum of consumption expenditures by households (C), investment expenditures by firms (I), government expenditures (G), and net exports ($X - M$):

$AE = C + I + G + (X - M)$.

$$AE = C + I + G + (X - M). \tag{8-1}$$

These are the same expenditure categories you read about in Chapters 2 and 4. In this chapter, we develop each of these categories further by distinguishing between two types of expenditures: expenditures that vary with the level of income in the economy, known as **induced expenditures,** and expenditures that are independent of the level of income in the economy, known as **autonomous expenditures.**

Induced expenditures vary with the level of income; autonomous expenditures are independent of the level of income.

Let's begin with consumption by households. As you learned in Chapter 4, household consumption varies with the level of income in the economy. The marginal propensity to consume (mpc) measures the change in consumption for each additional dollar of disposable income (income less taxes). For example, if the mpc is .8 and disposable income rises by $100, consumption expenditures will rise by $80. The $80 increase is induced consumption.

In addition, people consume a minimum level regardless of income. For example, a person might spend $4,000 a year regardless of the level of income. That $4,000 is autonomous consumption. If income is zero, the $4,000 would come out of savings. Just because autonomous consumption is independent of income doesn't mean it cannot change. Autonomous consumption could rise if consumers become more optimistic about the future (maybe you expect to get a big raise in the next year or the value of your stock portfolio rises).

The consumption function states that consumption is a linear function of disposable income: $C = C_0 + mpc(Y - T)$.

Total consumption expenditures are the sum of autonomous consumption (C_0) and induced consumption ($mpc(Y - T)$). The **consumption function,** a mathematical expression of the relationship between consumption and income, is written as

$$C = C_0 + mpc(Y - T) \qquad (8\text{-}2)$$

where Y is income, T is taxes and $Y - T$ is disposable income. Some taxes, such as property taxes, don't depend on income, while others, such as income taxes, are a fraction of income. Total taxes, therefore are the sum of taxes that are paid regardless of income, T_0, and taxes that depends on income, tY:

$$T = T_0 + tY \qquad (8\text{-}3)$$

where t is the tax rate.

The remainder of the components of aggregate expenditures are investment, government expenditures, and net exports. The general assumptions about each are

$$I = I_0$$
$$G = G_0$$
$$X = X_0$$
$$M = M_0 + mY$$

where X_0 is autonomous exports, M_0 is autonomous imports, and m is the marginal propensity to import. Investment, government expenditures, and exports are fixed to keep the model simple, and imports depend partly on income.

We initially assume that t and m are zero so that taxes and imports do not change with income. The assumption allows us to show the intuition of the multiplier more easily. (We will relax this simplifying assumption later.) Combining the expenditures of households, firms, and the government, we have aggregate expenditures:

$$AE = \underset{\substack{Consumption \\ function}}{C_0 + mpc(Y - T_0)} + \underset{\substack{Autonomous \\ investment}}{I_0} + \underset{\substack{Autonomous \\ government \\ spending}}{G_0} + \underset{\substack{Autonomous \\ net\ exports}}{(X_0 - M_0).} \qquad (8\text{-}4)$$

Exhibit 8–3 shows the aggregate expenditures (AE) curve. Given our initial assumptions that the only component of aggregate expenditures that varies with income is induced consumption, the slope of the aggregate expenditures curve is the marginal propensity to consume. The y-intercept of the aggregate expenditures curve (where aggregate income is zero) is the sum of autonomous expenditures.

Equilibrium in the Multiplier Model

Equilibrium in the multiplier model, Y_e, is where aggregate expenditures equal aggregate output (or, equivalently, aggregate income). In equilibrium, whatever is demanded is supplied, so all we need to do is figure out where total expenditures equal income.

We do this in equation 8–5, setting aggregate expenditures equal to income

$$Y_e = C_0 + mpc(Y_e - T) + I_0 + G_0 + X_0 - M_0 \qquad (8\text{-}5)$$

Equilibrium in the multiplier model occurs where aggregate expenditures equal aggregate production; this is true only on the 45-degree line.

Exhibit 8-3

Aggregate Expenditures Curve

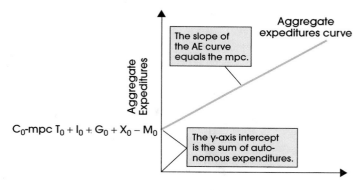

The aggregate expenditures curve shows the level of expenditures for each level of income. At zero income, expenditures equal $C_0 - mpcT_0 + I_0 + G_0 + X_0 - M_0$. The slope of the aggregate expenditure curve is the marginal propensity to consume.

Algebraically manipulating this equation (moving all the Y's to one side and factoring out a Y; in Appendix A we show those manipulations for a more general multiplier model) we get the **multiplier equation**—an equation that tells us that equilibrium income equals the multiplier times autonomous expenditures:

$$Y_e = \frac{1}{1 - mpc}[C_0 - mpcT_0 + I_0 + G_0 + (X_0 - M_0)] \qquad (8\text{-}6)$$

The equation can be divided into two components. The first component $(1/1 - mpc)$ is called the **multiplier**—the change in output that results from a one-dollar change in autonomous expenditures; the second component is the sum of all autonomous expenditures.

> The multiplier is the change in output that results from a one-dollar change in autonomous aggregate expenditures.

The equation tells us that to determine equilibrium income you multiply autonomous expenditures by the multiplier. For example if the sum of autonomous expenditures is $3,000 and the multiplier is 5, equilibrium income will be $15,000.

> The simple multiplier equals $1/(1 - mpc)$.

The multiplier is calculated by dividing 1 by $1 - mpc$. (This is the multiplier because our initial assumptions only allowed consumption to vary with income. Later we will show the multiplier when taxes and imports are allowed to vary with income.)

The following table presents the multipliers associated with a number of marginal propensities to consume.

> As the *mpc* increases, the multiplier becomes larger.

$$Multiplier = \frac{1}{(1 - mpc)}$$

Multiplier	mpc
2.0	0.5
2.5	0.6
3.3	0.67
4.0	0.75
5.0	0.8
10.0	0.9
100.0	0.99

Notice that, as the marginal propensity to consume gets closer to 1, the multiplier gets larger and larger. A small change in autonomous expenditures will have a large effect on total income or output.

The *mpc* in the United States is close to .8, which, if the multiplier were $1/(1-mpc)$, should result in a multiplier of 5. Most forecasting models that professional and government economists use, however, have multipliers closer to 2. A reason for the difference is the simplifying assumptions we made ($t = 0$ and $m = 0$) to let us focus on the intuition of the multiplier. To get a more realistic multiplier, let's eliminate those simplifying assumptions. As you will see, the effect of changes in income on expenditures is partly offset by these two other factors: (1) tax payments and (2) purchases of imports increase with income, *reducing* the multiplier.

Let's see what happens to the multiplier when we take into account the tax rate and marginal propensity to import. Suppose your income rises by $1. You will pay a fraction (t) of that income in taxes to the government, reducing your disposable income by t. So, spending rises by only $mpc(1 - t)$. You also spend a portion of your increase in income on imports (m). Spending on imported goods is subtracted from aggregate expenditures because we are interested in how an increase in income generates additional spending on *domestic* goods.

> The marginal propensity to expend includes taxes on income and induced expenditures on imports in the multiplier; the $mpe = mpc(1 - t) - m$.

To include the effect of these factors in the multiplier, we replace the *mpc* with a broader term, the **marginal propensity to expend (mpe)**—the fraction of an increase in income that is spent when taxes on income and induced expenditures on imports are taken into account. Therefore, the more general multiplier equation is

$$Y_e = \frac{1}{1 - mpe} \times (autonomous\ expenditures) \tag{8-7}$$

The marginal propensity to expend is:

$$mpe = mpc(1 - t) - m,$$
$$or\ equivalently$$
$$mpe = mpc - mpc \times t - m \tag{8-8}$$

The more-inclusive *mpe* replaces the *mpc* in the formula for the multiplier to give us

> The more general multiplier equals $\frac{1}{(1 - mpe)} = \frac{1}{1 - mpc(1 - t) + m}$

$$Multiplier = \frac{1}{(1 - mpe)} = \frac{1}{[1 - mpc(1 - t) + m]} \tag{8-9}$$

With an *mpc* of 0.8, t of 0.25, and m of 0.1, the *mpe* is 0.5 and the multiplier becomes $1/0.5 = 2$, which is much closer to the observed multiplier in the United States. (Appendix A derives the complete multiplier model.)

We can also see the determination of equilibrium income graphically. Exhibit 8–4 shows the 45-degree line in black together with the aggregate expenditures curve in blue. It has aggregate expenditures on the vertical axis and aggregate output on the horizontal axis. Therefore, the 45-degree line shows where aggregate expenditures equal aggregate output. All points along the 45-degree line are possible points of equilibrium. Because the 45-degree line shows all points of equilibrium, and the aggregate expenditures curve tells us aggregate expenditures at every level of income, equilibrium must be where the two curves intersect. Equilibrium will be at point A in Exhibit 8–4, where output, Y_0, equals expenditures, AE_0. At point A, households earn

Exhibit 8-4

Aggregate Expenditures and Equilibrium

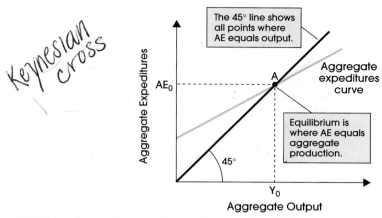

Keynesian cross

The 45° line shows all points where AE equals output.

Aggregate expenditures curve

AE_0 ⸱⸱⸱⸱⸱⸱⸱⸱⸱ A

Aggregate Expenditures

Equilibrium is where AE equals aggregate production.

45°

Y_0

Aggregate Output

Equilibrium income is where aggregate expenditures just equal aggregate output. This is at point *A*, where the 45-degree line (all points where aggregate expenditures equal aggregate output) and the *AE* curve intersect.

income, Y_0, which determines their consumption. The sum of those expenditures plus expenditures by the government, firms and foreigners equal aggregate output, Y_0.

An Example of Equilibrium

A numerical example of equilibrium will help to illustrate the determination of equilibrium. Assume autonomous consumption (C_0) is $100, investment ($I_0$) is $200, government spending (G_0) is $50, taxes ($T_0$) are $0, and net exports ($X_0 - M_0$) are $0, and the marginal propensity to consume (mpc) is .9. We can solve for equilibrium income using the multiplier equation by multiplying autonomous expenditures times the multiplier. Autonomous expenditures equal $350 (100 + 200 + 50), and the multiplier equals 10 (1/[1 − .9]), so equilibrium income is $3,500 (10 × 350).

An alternative method is to graph the aggregate expenditures function:

$$AE = 350 + .9Y$$

↳ mpc

We can see this graphically in Exhibit 8–5, which is a graph of the AE curve (AE = 350 + .9Y) with the 45-degree line. The slope (the *mpc*) is .9 and the vertical axis intercept (the sum of autonomous expenditures) is $350. The AE curve intersects the 45-degree line at an income level of $3,500 so $3,500 is our equilibrium income.

Adjustment Forces toward Equilibrium

To give you an intuitive sense of why $3,500 is equilibrium income let's consider what would happen at different levels of income. Say that income is $2,000. Given our aggregate expenditures curve (AE = 350 + .9Y), when income is $2,000, aggregate expenditures equal 350 + .9(2,000) = $2,150. Because aggregate expenditures exceed output, firms find that inventory is running down and they increase production, moving the economy along the expenditures function toward point A.

As firms increase production, they pay more income, which causes aggregate expenditures to rise even further. For example, suppose that firms increase production by $150, the production shortfall when income was $2,000. As production (and hence income) rises to $2,150, aggregate expenditures rise to $2,285

Exhibit 8-5

**Illustration of
Equilibrium in the
Goods Market**

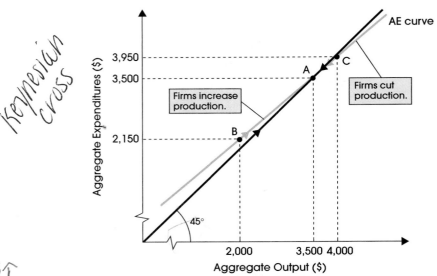

Keynesian cross

I ↓ R T M↓T

Equilibrium is where the 45-degree line and the aggregate expenditures curve intersect. Equilibrium in the example shown in this exhibit occurs at point A, where aggregate output and aggregate expenditures are $3,500.

$(350 + .9 \times 2,150)$. Firms find their inventories are still depleted, but now by $135 $(2,285 - 2,150)$. The process is repeated: Firms increase output and expenditures rise. This process continues until output reaches $3,500. At income of $3,500, aggregate expenditures also equal $3,500 so there is no further reason for firms to change output; the economy is in equilibrium.

Let's next look at what happens if income is higher than equilibrium income. Specifically let's say income is $4,000. At an income of $4,000, expenditures are $3,950 (point C). Firms find they have unsold goods and unplanned inventory accumulation. They cut production, which reduces income and expenditures, and the economy works its way back to point A. (See The Briefing Room, "Just-in-Time Inventory Management," for a discussion of how technological advances in inventory management may be affecting the adjustment process and the business cycle.)

The role of the 45-degree line should now become clear. At levels of output (or income) where the expenditures line is above the 45-degree line, expenditures exceed output (aggregate quantity demanded exceeds aggregate quantity supplied), inventories are depleted, and firms respond by increasing production. At levels of output where the expenditure line is below the 45-degree line, expenditures are less than output (aggregate quantity supplied exceeds aggregate quantity demanded), inventories accumulate, and firms respond by reducing production. At the level of output where the 45-degree line crosses the aggregate expenditure curve, the goods market is in equilibrium.

The Multiplier Effect When Autonomous Expenditures Change

The use of the multiplier model is generally concerned with determining what the effect of a change in autonomous expenditures will be. We can determine this relationship by modifying equation 8-7 slightly to tell us how changes in autonomous expenditures will affect income. Doing so gives us $\Delta Y = $ multiplier $\times \Delta$autonomous expenditures. More specifically we have:

Exhibit 8-6

A Change in Autonomous Expenditures

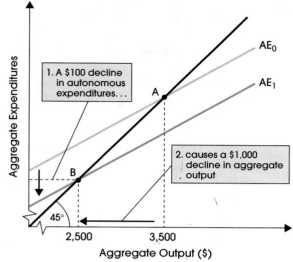

This exhibit demonstrates the multiplier. Equilibrium is initially at point *A*, where output is $3,500. A decrease in autonomous investment expenditures of $100 causes output to fall by $1,000 (a multiplier of 10) to $2,500, point *B*.

$$\Delta Y = \left(\frac{1}{(1 - mpe)} \right) [\Delta C_0 - \Delta mpc T_0 + \Delta I_0 + \Delta G_0 - \Delta(X_0 - M_0)] \qquad (8\text{-}10)$$

In words this equation tells us that the change in equilibrium income resulting from a change in autonomous expenditures will be equal to the multiplier times the change in autonomous expenditures.

Let's now consider an example of a decline in autonomous investment of 100. Income will decline by the multiplier $\times$ 100. In Exhibit 8–6 we show this graphically. There we see that the $100 decline in investment causes the aggregate expenditures curve to shift down by $100: from AE_0 to AE. With an mpc of .9 this leads to a $1,000 decline in equilibrium income—$[1(1 - mpc)]\Delta I$. The multiplier will be different for different marginal propensities to consume.

The Multiplier Process

Table 8–1 shows a numerical example of the multiplier process when the marginal propensity to consume is .9 and firms reduce autonomous investment expenditures

Table 8-1

Numerical Example of the Multiplier Process

	Change in Expenditures	Cumulative Change	Change in Output and Income	Cumulative Change
Step 1	−$100	−$100	−$100	−$100
Step 2	−90	−190	−90	−190
Step 3	−81	−271	−81	−271
.				
.				
.				
Equilibrium	$0	−$1,000	$0	−$1,000

THE BRIEFING ROOM *Just-in-Time Inventory Management*

Some economists suggest that new inventory systems have helped reduce fluctuations in output in the United States. The following exhibit shows how low inventory levels have become as a percent of sales.

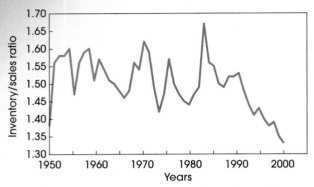

Source: The Department of Commerce (www.doc.gov).

The inventory–sales ratio shows the value of the goods companies have in stock relative to the value of the goods they sell. From the 1960s to the early 1980s, the inventory–sales ratio fluctuated between 1.42 percent and 1.60 percent. In the 1980s, when firms started using just-in-time inventory systems, that ratio began to drop. In 2000, the ratio was about 1.3 percent.

What is just-in-time inventory? The next time you buy something at a store, notice that the clerk punches in numbers or scans the coded label. That information feeds into the store's information system and guides purchasing managers in their ordering decisions. The purchasing managers know the sales of each product immediately and can replenish inventory quickly. This faster flow of information has allowed firms to hold smaller inventory—to have it shipped so it gets there "just in time."

Some economists believe this change has dampened, or even eliminated, business cycles. If firms hold large inventories and demand for their products falls, they will have to cut way back on production, possibly laying off workers until the excess inventories are sold. If firms hold small inventories when demand for their product falls, they may have to reduce production by only a small amount, laying off fewer workers for a shorter period of time.

Economists Margaret M. McConnell and Gabriel Parez Quiro argue that computer technology has allowed businesses to track both production and sales closely, so they can adjust production more quickly than ever to changes in expenditures and avert an inventory build-up. This better information allows businesses to adjust production immediately when demand changes, eliminating the jumps in inventory and production that lead to business cycles. Time will tell whether just-in-time inventory management will result in fewer, and less severe, business cycle fluctuations in the future.

---

by $100. At first, total output and income declines by $100 (step 1). Because income falls by $100, however, expenditures fall again by $90 (.9 × 100). Output, in turn, falls by another $90, for a total cumulative decline (so far) of $190 (step 2).

The process continues another round. Because income has declined $90, people reduce their expenditures again, this time by $81 (.9 × $90). Total output has now fallen $271 (step 3).

The process continues and each time income falls by smaller and smaller amounts, until expenditures equal production. Because expenditures in the economy vary with the level of income, any change in income caused by a change in autonomous expenditures will lead to further changes in aggregate expenditures and income. That's the multiplier at work. At the end of the multiplier process, the cumulative decrease in output is $1,000—10 times the initial decline in investment expenditures.

As you can see, the multiplier process amplifies changes in autonomous expenditures into fluctuations in output, or business cycles. An increase in autonomous expenditures will push economic output up, and a decrease will push economic output down. That's what happened in 1990. The U.S. economy had been slowing. As oil prices rose in mid-1990, consumer confidence fell and consumers cut back their expenditures. The multiplier amplified the initial decline and the economy went into recession. Policy makers are interested in minimizing these fluctuations because of (1) the inflation that can result when output exceeds potential output and (2) the unemployment that occurs when output is below potential output.

Fiscal Policy and the Multiplier

The multiplier model offers a way for policy makers to offset business cycle fluctuations caused by unwanted shifts in autonomous expenditures: Increase or decrease autonomous government expenditures, and the multiplier will augment the effect of that change on output. If a small decrease in autonomous expenditures causes output to fall by a multiple of that decrease, then government can use fiscal policy (increase government expenditures or decrease taxes) to bring output back to its original level, smoothing out what otherwise would be a business cycle. In terms of our example so far, an increase in government spending equal to the initial decline in autonomous expenditures can bring the economy back to its initial equilibrium output. The decline in autonomous expenditures is offset by an increase in government spending so that the two expenditure changes cancel each other out.

So, if government can respond to changes in autonomous expenditures by changing its expenditures in the opposite direction, then, in the multiplier model, government can completely eliminate business cycles. The effectiveness of this approach depends on the assumptions of the multiplier model. Specifically, the model assumes that government can recognize when autonomous expenditures shift and can change its expenditures fast enough to offset them. These assumptions are rarely met. In fact, since 1940, Congress has not been able to pass legislation to counter any of the recessions until after the economy already began to recover on its own. This makes fiscal policy a far less effective tool than it appears to be in the model.

> When government changes spending, output will change by $\dfrac{1}{(1 - mpe)}$ times that amount.

The multiplier tells us that when government changes spending by a certain amount, output will change by $1/(1 - mpe)$ times that amount. When government raises or lowers taxes instead of changing spending, the effect on output needs to be slightly modified. Taxes affect expenditures only indirectly through their effect on disposable income. When taxes are decreased, people have more disposable income to spend and consumption expenditures rise, but not by the full amount of the tax cut. People will consume a fraction and save a fraction of the increase in their disposable income. Expenditures will rise initially by the mpc times the change in taxes. Because the initial effect of taxes is through disposable income, the net effect reduces the multiplier to $-mpc/(1 - mpe)$, where the negative sign means that an increase in taxes reduces aggregate expenditures.

> When government changes taxes, output will change by $\dfrac{-mpc}{(1 - mpe)}$ times that amount.

Let's briefly go through an example. Say output is $4,000 and desired output is $4,080, the mpe is .5 and the mpc is .9. The government wants to use fiscal policy to increase output by $80. How much should it change spending, or taxes? To answer this we first calculate the multiplier, $1/(1 - .5) = 2$, and the tax multiplier, $-.9/(1 - .5) = 1.8$. To increase output by 80 we need to increase government spending by 80/2, or $40. Alternatively we could cut taxes by 80/1.8 or $44.44.

Executive Summary

- The short-run macroeconomic model assumes that prices are fixed. Changes in aggregate demand cause changes in output, not changes in prices.

- Equilibrium in the multiplier model is where aggregate expenditures equal aggregate output. It equals the multiplier × autonomous expenditures.

- Changes in autonomous expenditures have a multiplied effect on equilibrium output. The multiplier is
$$\frac{1}{(1 - mpe)} = \frac{1}{(1 - mpc(1 - t) + m)}.$$

- When the tax rate, t, and the marginal propensity to import, m, are assumed to be zero, the multiplier equals $\dfrac{1}{(1 - mpc)}$

THE IS CURVE

The IS curve shows all combinations of real interest rates and income levels where expenditures equal production. (The goods market is in equilibrium.)

The multiplier model shows how equilibrium is determined in the goods market and how changes in autonomous expenditures affect that equilibrium. In the next section, we use the multiplier model as a building block for the IS curve, the part of the IS/LM model that examines the goods market. The **IS curve** shows all combinations of real interest rates and incomes where expenditures equal production, or where the goods market is in equilibrium. (See the Q&A feature for an explanation of the significance of the letters *IS*.) In the multiplier model, we assumed that investment expenditures are autonomous. As you saw in Chapter 4, however, firms take into account the cost of borrowing when making investment decisions. The reason is that, for any investment decision, the firm's primary interest is how much profit the firm will earn from the investment expenditure. It weighs the cost and the benefit of the investment. The cost of the investment is directly related to the real interest rate (the nominal interest rate adjusted for inflation).

For example, if a firm wants to build a new factory, it can borrow the funds from a bank or issue a bond. In both cases, it must pay back the loan with interest. If the firm uses retained earnings to fund the investment, it will forgo interest payments it could have earned had it loaned the retained earnings to others. As the real interest rate rises, the cost of the investment will rise and firms will borrow less and lower their investment expenditures. The opposite is true as the real interest rate falls. We can show this by changing our investment function to

$$I = I_0 - I(r). \qquad (8\text{-}11)$$

The first term, I_0, is investment that is independent of the interest rate. The second term, $I(r)$, captures the inverse relationship between investment and the real interest rate. In our aggregate expenditures diagram, a change in the real interest rate shifts the expenditures line (AE) up or down.

Let's consider an example. Suppose the total output is $1,000, the real interest rate is 6 percent, and the multiplier is 2. This equilibrium is represented by point A in Exhibit 8–7(a). Further, assume that, for every percentage point decline in the real interest rate, investment expenditures rise by $100. What will happen if the

---

Q&A

QUESTION   What do the letters *IS* stand for in IS/LM?

ANSWER   They stand for the equality of *investment* and *saving* in equilibrium.

You may be wondering why the IS curve is called the IS curve. Here's why: Remember, from Chapter 4, that equilibrium in the macroeconomy can be described in two ways: Aggregate supply equals aggregate demand, or investment equals saving. The IS curve describes points of equilibrium in the goods market. Therefore, all along the IS curve investment equals savings, hence the name IS.

interest rate falls to 4 percent? Investment will rise by $200, which, as Exhibit 8–7(a) shows, shifts the expenditures curve up by $200. Equilibrium output rises from $1,000 to $1,400 (point *A* to point *B*)—the multiplier times the initial rise in investment.

Exhibit 8–7(b) shows the two levels of equilibrium income associated with the two real interest rates from the aggregate expenditures diagram shown in Exhibit 8–7(a). As the real interest rate falls from 6 percent to 4 percent, equilibrium income rises from $1,000 to $1,400. These are two points on the IS curve.

Exhibit 8-7

Derivation of the IS Curve

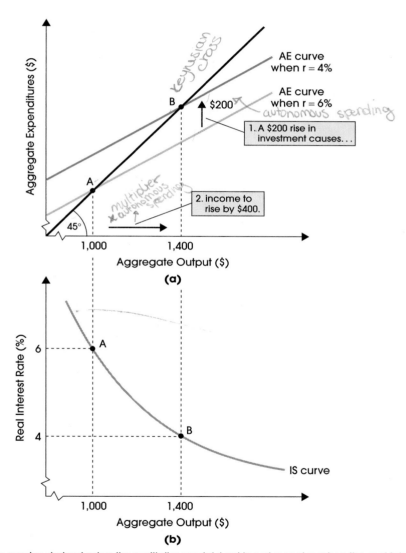

The IS curve can be derived using the multiplier model. Looking at *panel a,* when the real interest rate declines from 6 percent to 4 percent, investment expenditures rise by $200, shifting the expenditures function up and raising equilibrium income from $1,000 to $1,400. Equilibrium income rises by $400—the increase in investment times the multiplier. Looking at *panel b,* the IS curve shows combinations of interest rates and incomes at which the goods market is in equilibrium. Transferring the interest rate and income combinations, points *A* and *B,* from *panel a* to *panel b* gives two points along an IS curve.

The IS curve slopes downward to the right.

The IS curve slopes downward to the right because a decline in the real interest rate causes investment expenditures to rise, which, through the multiplier process, leads to a greater rise in income. The IS curve shows that, for the goods market to remain in equilibrium, a decline in the interest rate must be accompanied by an increase in income.

The Shape of the IS Curve

The IS curve adds an interest rate component to the multiplier model and shows the general inverse relationship between the real interest rate and aggregate expenditures: As the real interest rate falls, aggregate expenditures rise. To forecast the economy and to make policy recommendations, policy makers want to know more than just the direction of change—they want to know *by how much* expenditures will change with a given change in the real interest rate. The shape of the IS curve—whether it is steep or flat—reflects the sensitivity of investment to changes in the real interest rate and the size of the multiplier.

The shape of the IS curve reflects the sensitivity of investment to changes in the real interest rate and the size of the multiplier.

Two things happen when the interest rate changes. First, a change in the interest rate causes investment expenditures to change, shifting the aggregate expenditures curve. Second, the change in aggregate expenditures caused by the change in investment expenditures leads to further changes in aggregate expenditures through the multiplier process. If both of these effects are large (investment is very sensitive to real interest rate changes and the multiplier is large), changes in real interest rates will be associated with large changes in equilibrium income, and the IS curve will be flat. If both effects are small (investment is insensitive to real interest rate changes and the multiplier is small), expenditures will not change by much when interest rates change, and the IS curve will be steep.

Exhibit 8–8 shows the case in which investment expenditures are not very responsive to changes in the interest rate and the multiplier is small. As the real interest rate falls from r_0 to r_1 in Exhibit 8–8(a), the aggregate expenditures line shifts upward by a small amount (ΔI). A small multiplier means that the aggregate expenditure line is relatively flat, so the change in investment leads to a small change in equilibrium income and to a relatively steep IS curve, as Exhibit 8–8(b) shows. If, however, investment changes by a lot when the real interest rate changes and the multiplier is large, the IS curve will be relatively flat (the opposite of what is shown in Exhibit 8–8(b)).

It is possible that the two forces will not reinforce each other. The multiplier may be large and investment may be unresponsive to real interest rate changes, or vice versa. In these cases, the relative sizes of the real interest sensitivity and multiplier effects will determine whether the IS curve is steep or flat.

Shifts in the IS Curve

Changes in autonomous expenditures and taxes (such as fiscal policy) will shift the IS curve.

Changes in autonomous expenditures and taxes will shift the IS curve. For example, an increase in autonomous investment expenditures will shift the aggregate expenditures curve up. Through the multiplier process, this leads to a greater increase in equilibrium income. Because equilibrium income has risen for every interest rate, while equilibrium income has increased, the increase in investment expenditures shifts the IS curve out to the right.

Exhibit 8-8

The Slope of
the IS Curve

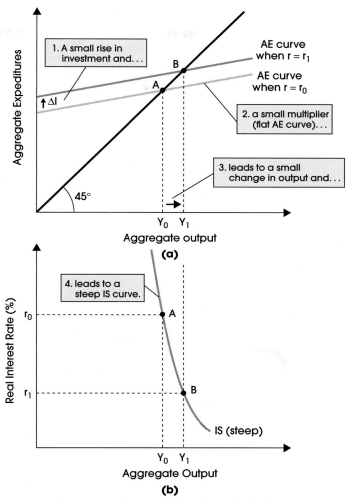

When investment expenditures are not responsive to changes in the interest rate and the multiplier is small, the IS curve is steep. *Panel a* shows a flat *AE* curve because the multiplier is small. When the interest rate rises, the *AE* curve shifts up. Equilibrium income rises from point *A* to point *B*. The same two points are shown in *panel b*, with their associated interest rates. Because equilibrium income doesn't rise by much, the IS curve is steep.

Alternatively, if businesses expect sales to slow in the future and consequently reduce investment without a change in the real interest rate, equilibrium income will be lower at each interest rate, and the IS curve will shift in to the left. Changes in autonomous consumption, autonomous net exports, autonomous taxes, and autonomous government spending also shift the IS curve. How much the IS curve shifts depends on the multiplier. Specifically, the IS curve shifts to the right or left by the multiplier times the change in autonomous expenditures.

Consider government spending. Suppose the economy is at point *A* in Exhibit 8–9 and government believes that output, $3,000, is undesirably low. If the multiplier is 3, government can increase its spending by $1,000 and, through the

Exhibit 8-9

**Shifting the
IS Curve**

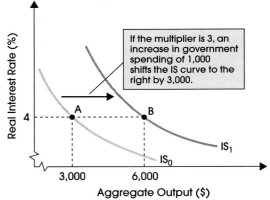

The IS curve shifts when autonomous expenditures change or when taxes change. The IS curve shifts by the multiplier times the change in autonomous expenditures. In this exhibit, government expenditures rise by $1,000 and the multiplier is 3. The IS curve shifts to the right by $3,000 (3 × $1,000).

multiplier process, increase income to $6,000 (point B). Because the real interest rate remains at 4 percent, investment expenditures do not change and the IS curve shifts to the right by $3,000 (the multiplier times the change in government expenditures), from IS_0 to IS_1.

Executive Summary

- The IS curve shows how in the goods market equilibrium output varies inversely with the real interest rate.

- The shape of the IS curve depends on the responsiveness of investment to changes in the real interest rate and the size of the multiplier.

- If investment is unresponsive to changes in the real interest rate and the multiplier is small, the IS curve is steep and vice versa.

- Changes in autonomous expenditures shift the IS curve to the right and to the left by the multiplier times the change in autonomous expenditures.

- Fiscal policy shifts the IS curve to the right and to the left.

THE LM CURVE

The IS curve shows us the combination of real interest rates and levels of output or income at which the goods market is in equilibrium. But where does the interest rate come from? What determines whether it is high or low? In the short-run model, the answer is: The interest rate is determined by the supply and demand for money in the **money market**—a financial market in which highly liquid assets (money) are traded. Equilibrium in the money market is described by the LM curve. The **LM curve** shows all combinations of income levels and interest rates at which the money market is in equilibrium. (If you're curious about what the letters *LM* represent, see the Q&A feature.)

The Demand for Money

Money can include many different liquid assets. In this chapter, as in the last chapter, we will use M1 as our measure of money. M1 includes currency and checking

Q & A	QUESTION	What do the letters *LM* stand for?
	ANSWER	They stand for the terms *liquidity* and *money*.

The *L* comes from the fact that money demand is often represented by *L* for *liquidity*, because money is a highly liquid asset. The *M* represents money supply, so *LM* represents the points where *L* equals *M*—or money demand equals money supply.

account balances as well as travelers' checks. We are not including other financial assets—savings account balances, stocks, bonds, and gold—as money. (Remember, the division between what is and is not money is somewhat arbitrary.) The general equation for the demand for money is

$$M^D = M^D(Y, i) \tag{8-12}$$

where M^D represents the demand for money, Y is income, and i is the nominal interest rate. Notice that while investment decisions depend on the real interest rate, money demand depends on the nominal interest rate. (Appendix B presents an explicit function of the demand for money.) Let's consider how both income and the nominal interest rate affect the demand for money.

Income and the Demand for Money. People hold money mainly to buy goods and services. Holding money makes buying easy. You can't exchange a stock or bond for a candy bar and soda at a convenience store. Therefore, in deciding how much money people want to carry, the first thing they think about is how much they want to spend. Spending—and the demand for money—rises when income rises, and it falls when income falls. So, the demand for money and spending are positively related to income.

> The demand for money varies positively with income and the quantity of money demanded varies negatively with interest rates.

Interest Rates and the Demand for Money. Like every activity, there is an opportunity cost to holding money. (See the Briefing Room, "What Happens to Money Demand When Money Pays Interest.") The opportunity cost of holding money is the chance to earn interest. Money generally pays no, or very little, interest. So, when deciding how much money to carry, you balance that cost (you forgo interest) against the benefit (transactions are easy). Suppose that, on being paid, you convert your entire paycheck to bonds. You'll earn interest on your entire paycheck, but when you need to buy something, you'll have to call your broker to sell some bonds. This is both inconvenient and costly. Most likely, you keep a portion of your paycheck as money and buy financial assets—savings account, mutual fund, stocks, bonds—with the remainder. For convenience, we will call all of these other financial assets *bonds*.

As the interest rate rises, you will want to hold less money and more bonds—you are willing to pay the broker's fees and suffer the inconvenience because you earn a higher return. All else held constant, the higher the interest rate, the less money you will hold. The lower the interest rate, the more money you will hold. Therefore, the demand for money is inversely related to the interest rate.

(

THE BRIEFING ROOM   What Happens to Money Demand When Money Pays Interest?

In the early 1980s, banks and saving and loan institutions began offering checking accounts that paid interest. Before that time, saving accounts paid interest and checking accounts did not. The demand for M1 (currency plus checking account balances) rose as people shifted their funds from saving accounts to (more liquid) checking accounts.

If money pays interest, then why would they bother buying bonds when the interest rate rises? The answer is that the interest rate paid on money is lower than the interest rate on bonds, and generally does not move one-for-one with other interest rates in the economy. For example, when interest rates on bonds rise, checking account interest rates generally stay the same or rise by less. This means that the opportunity cost of holding the checking account balance rises with the increase in the spread between the interest rate paid on bonds and on checking account balances. So interest rates still affect money demand, but to determine the true opportunity cost we have to look at interest rate spreads—the difference between interest rates on financial assets and the interest rate on checking account balances—that difference tells us the effect that a change in interest rates will have on the quantity of money demanded.

The choice between bonds and money is affected by the nominal interest rate that bonds are paying, because the nominal interest rate is the opportunity cost of holding money. At this point in our discussion of the short-run model, we are assuming that the price level is fixed so that inflation is zero. Therefore, the nominal interest rate is equal to the real interest rate, allowing us to write money demand as $M^D = M^D(Y, r)$. Keep in mind, however, that, in general, money demand depends on the nominal interest rate, while investment expenditures depend on the real interest rate.

Exhibit 8–10(a) shows the inverse relationship between money demand and the interest rate. As the interest rate falls, the quantity of money demanded rises. For example, if the interest rate falls from r_0 to r_1, the quantity of money demanded rises from M_0 to M_1. All other factors that affect the demand for money (income, for example) shift the demand for money. A rise in income from Y_0 to Y_1, for example, will shift the money demand curve to the right, as Exhibit 8–10(b) shows. The demand for money rises at every interest rate. Money demand will also shift to the left when income falls.

Autonomous Influences on Money Demand. Income and the interest rate are the two main factors influencing the demand for money, but there are other influences as well. We call these other influences autonomous factors. An example of an autonomous influence on money demand is an innovation in the financial services industry that reduces the cost of converting less liquid financial assets into money. This innovation reduces the demand for money because people would prefer to earn interest. For example, before the invention of the automatic teller machine (ATM), you had no choice but to go to the bank to transfer funds from your saving account (not part of M1) to your checking account (part of M1). You had to physically go to the bank, stand in line, and present your request to the teller, who made the transfer. With ATMs and Internet banking, you can now transfer the funds yourself at any time of the day or night. Because the cost of transferring funds from one account to another (shoe-leather cost) has dropped, the demand for money has dropped as well. The lower demand for money can be represented graphically as a shift in the demand for money in to the left.

The demand for money will shift because of autonomous influences, such as changes in expectations or innovations in financial markets.

Exhibit 8-10

Interest Rates, Income, and the Demand for Money

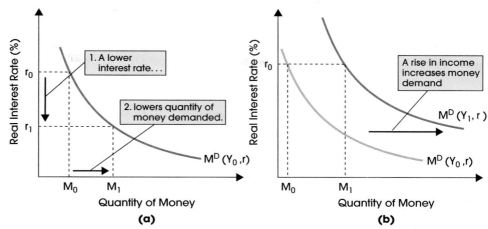

Panel a shows the inverse relationship between the quantity of money demanded and the interest rate. If the interest rate falls from r_0 to r_1, the quantity of money demanded rises from M_0 to M_1. The demand for money rises as income rises. Panel b shows that a rise in income increases the quantity of money demanded at every interest rate. A rise in income from Y_0 to Y_1, for example, will shift the money demand curve to the right. At interest rate r_0, the demand for money rises from M_0 to M_1. Changes in income shift the demand for money.

Another autonomous factor influencing money demand is *expected* interest rates. One reason you might hold money is to buy bonds. If you think bonds' interest rates will rise in the future, you will hold onto your money and buy bonds later. There are two reasons to wait. The first reason is that you would rather earn a higher interest rate. The second reason is subtle: If you were to buy a bond now and the interest rate rose, the price of the bond you bought would fall. (A review of the relationship between the price of bonds and the interest rate appears in the accompanying Q&A feature).

The price of the bond may fall so much that the decline in its value is not covered by the bond's interest payments. Holding the bond may result in a negative return. In such cases, money, even though it pays little or no interest, can be an attractive part of your portfolio. Holding money allows you to avoid a loss. Therefore, if people expect interest rates to rise, the demand for money will rise. When interest rates are expected to fall, however, the price of bonds can be expected to rise and the demand for money will fall. People will want to hold bonds so that they can benefit from the rise in the price of the bond.

At "normal" rates of interest, beliefs about the direction of interest rates will generally differ sufficiently, so that expected interest rates are not a factor in the demand for money. Economists don't have a precise definition for a normal interest rate, but most people have a sense of when the interest rate is unusually high or unusually low. As interest rates fall from what is considered a normal level, a majority of people may begin to believe interest rates will rise. Because they expect interest rates to rise, the demand for money will rise. However, if a majority of people believe that interest rates will continue to fall, the demand for money will fall.

The Supply of Money

The supply of money is assumed to be fixed in the simplest model.

We now turn to the supply of money. To keep the analysis simple, we assume that the supply of money is fixed by the Federal Reserve Bank. A fixed money supply,

QUESTION   What is the relationship between changes in interest rates and bond prices?

ANSWER   As the interest rate in the economy rises, bond prices fall.

To understand the relationship between changes in interest rates and money demand, it is important to understand the relationship between changes in interest rates and the price of bonds. As the interest rate in the economy falls, bond prices rise; as the interest rate rises, bond prices fall. To see how this happens, consider this example. Suppose you buy a $1,000 two-year bond with a fixed annual coupon rate of 10 percent. (To keep it simple, we assume no compounding.) After the first year, you will receive a $100 interest payment and, after the second year, you will receive another $100 interest payment plus the principal of $1,000.

Now suppose that after holding the bond for a year (and collecting the first $100 interest payment), you decide to sell it. This is not uncommon; there is an active secondary market for bonds. How much can you sell your bond for? At the time you bought it, the market interest rate for such bonds was the same as its coupon rate, 10 percent, but suppose now that the market interest rate is 12 percent. This means that newly issued bonds will have a 12 percent coupon rate. Someone can buy a $1,000 bond that will pay them $120 at the end of the first year. If someone buys your bond for $1,000, this person would still only get $100 interest payments, because the coupon rate doesn't change. To entice someone to buy your bond with a coupon rate that is lower than market interest rates you will, therefore, have to lower its price. (You cannot change the interest payment.) You would lower the price so that the interest payment of $100 was 12 percent of whatever the buyer paid for your bond. The price that someone would pay can be figured by solving the following equation for the new price of the bond, P_B, which matures in one year.

$$P_B = \frac{amount\ to\ be\ paid\ in\ one\ year}{1 + interest\ rate\ in\ the\ economy} = \frac{1,100}{1.12}$$

$$P_B = \$982.14$$

You can see that the price of the bond went down when the interest rate went up. To make sure that you've got this concept, try figuring out the price of the bond if the market interest rate after one year falls to 8 percent. You should see that the price of the bond rises.

graphically, is a vertical line, as Exhibit 8–11 shows. Notice that the money supply is the same, $\overline{M}^s$, regardless of the interest rate.

The Determination of the Interest Rate

The equilibrium interest rate is the interest rate at which the quantity of money demanded equals the quantity of money supplied. In Exhibit 8–11, equilibrium is where the demand-and-supply curves intersect, point A, at an interest rate of r_0. At interest rates above r_0, such as r_2, the quantity of money supplied, $\overline{M}^s$, is greater than the quantity of money demanded, M_2. People would prefer to hold more bonds and less money, so, as a result, people buy bonds. As the demand for bonds rises, the price of bonds also rises, leading to a decline in the interest rate. People continue to demand more bonds until the interest rate falls to r_0.

At interest rates below r_0, such as r_1, the quantity of money demanded, M_1, exceeds the quantity of money supplied, $\overline{M}^s$. At such low interest rates, people are holding more bonds than they would like and begin to sell their bonds. As the supply of bonds rises, their price falls and the interest rate rises. This continues until the interest rate rises to r_0, at which point, the quantity of money supplied equals the quantity of money demanded.

Exhibit 8-11

The Determination of the Equilibrium Interest Rate in the Money Market

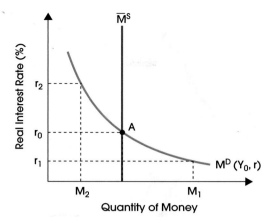

The equilibrium interest rate in the money market is determined by the intersection of the supply and demand for money. In this exhibit, the equilibrium is at point A, where the interest rate is r_0.

The Derivation of the LM Curve

The LM curve shows all combinations of income levels and interest rates at which the money market is in equilibrium.

With an understanding of the money market, we're now ready to derive the second part of the IS/LM model—the LM curve. As stated earlier, the LM curve shows all combinations of income levels and interest rates at which the money market is in equilibrium. It summarizes the effects of shifting income on the equilibrium interest rate. As discussed, income is an important determinant of the demand for money. An increase in income increases the demand for money, which increases the equilibrium interest rate. Exhibit 8–12(a) shows this. The economy begins at point A, where the interest rate is 4 percent and aggregate income (and output) is $2,000. When income rises to $4,000, demand for money shifts out to the right. At a 4 percent interest rate, people want to hold more money than is available. The interest rate rises to 6 percent, decreasing the quantity of money demanded, enough so that the money market is at equilibrium (point B).

Exhibit 8-12

Derivation of the LM Curve

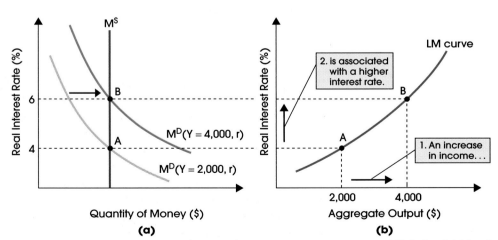

In *panel a,* when income rises from $2,000 to $4,000, the demand for money shifts to the right, leading to an increase in the real interest rate from 4 to 6 percent (points A to B). These are two combinations of income levels and interest rates at which the money market is in equilibrium, which means that they are two points on the LM curve in *panel b.* The LM curve shows all combinations of interest rates and income levels at which the money market is in equilibrium.

Transferring the combinations of equilibrium income levels and interest rates from Exhibit 8–12(a) to 8–12(b) gives us two points on the LM curve—points *A* and *B*. The first combination (income of $2,000 and interest rate of 4 percent) and the second combination (income of $4,000 and interest rate of 6 percent) are two combinations of interest rates and income levels where the money market is in equilibrium. Showing *all* possible combinations of income and interest rates at which the money market is in equilibrium gives us the entire LM curve. As you can see by the positive slope of the LM curve, equilibrium interest rates and income levels are *directly* related. As income rises, people demand more money. Because the money supply is fixed, the interest rate must rise to reduce the quantity of money demanded. An increase in income is associated with an increase in the interest rate.

> The LM curve slopes upward.

The Shape of the LM Curve

We know the LM curve slopes upward, but how steep or flat is it? The slope of the LM curve depends on two factors:

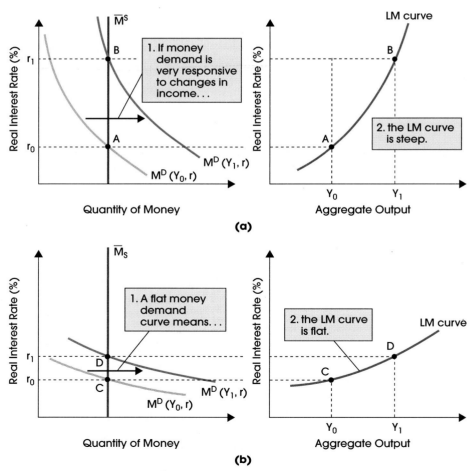

The slope of the LM curve depends on the responsiveness of money demand to changes in income and the interest sensitivity of the quantity of money demanded. *Panel a* shows how the LM curve is steep when money demand is responsive to changes in income. *Panel b* shows that the LM curve is flat when money demand is not very responsive to changes in the interest rate.

1. The responsiveness of money demand to changes in income
2. The interest sensitivity of the quantity of money demanded

Let's consider these effects one at a time. Exhibit 8–13(a) shows how the slope of the LM curve depends on the responsiveness of money demand to changes in income. If the demand for money is very responsive to changes in income, when income rises from Y_0 to Y_1, the demand for money shifts by a large amount, requiring a large increase in the interest rate to keep the money market in equilibrium (from point A to point B) and a steep LM curve. If, however, the demand for money is not responsive to changes in income, the demand for money shifts by a smaller amount, resulting in a smaller increase in the interest rate and a flatter LM curve.

Exhibit 8–13(b) shows how the slope of the LM curve also depends on the interest sensitivity of the quantity of money demanded (the slope of the demand for money). When a small change in the interest rate leads to a large change in the quantity of money demanded, an increase in income will lead to a relatively small increase in the interest rate (from point C to point D), and the LM curve is relatively flat. In this case, when income changes, the interest rate doesn't need to change by much to restore equilibrium in the money market. When the quantity of money demanded is hardly sensitive to changes in interest rates, the interest rate rises by a lot in response to the change in income, and the LM curve is relatively steep. In summary, the LM curve is steeper the more sensitive money demand is to changes in income, and the less sensitive the quantity of money demanded is to changes in interest rates.

> The shape of the LM curve depends on the responsiveness of money demand to changes in income and the interest sensitivity of the quantity of money demanded.

Shifts in the LM Curve

> When factors other than income shift the demand for money, the LM curve shifts.

The position of the LM curve depends on the supply of money and factors other than income that affect the demand for money. Let's begin by looking at two factors that affect the demand for money:

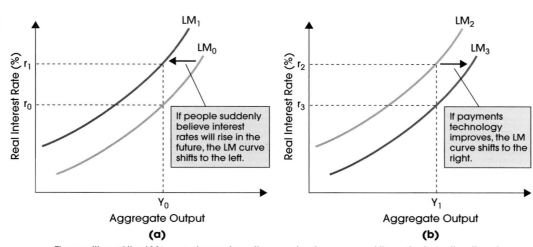

Exhibit 8-14

Shifts in the LM Curve

(a)
Aggregate Output

If people suddenly believe interest rates will rise in the future, the LM curve shifts to the left.

(b)
Aggregate Output

If payments technology improves, the LM curve shifts to the right.

The position of the LM curve depends on the supply of money and those factors other than income that affect the demand for money. In *panel a*, the LM curve shifts in to the left because people are choosing to hold more money in anticipation of rising interest rates. In *panel b*, the LM curve shifts out to the right because payments technology has reduced the demand for money.

1. People suddenly expect interest rates to rise in the future.
2. Payments technology improves, and more people use computers for financial transactions.

In the first case, the demand for money rises as people hold more of their income as money in anticipation of purchasing bonds with higher interest rates. The rise in money demand increases the equilibrium interest rate at every level of income, shifting the LM curve to the left, as Exhibit 8–14(a) shows. For example, at income Y_0, the interest rate is initially r_0. With expectations of higher interest rates, the interest rate that is consistent with equilibrium in the money market rises for every level of income. At income Y_0, the equilibrium interest rate is r_1.

In the second case, the demand for money falls because the cost of changing bonds to money falls. You simply click a button on your computer rather than calling your bond trader, filling out forms, and waiting for the payment to arrive by "snail-mail." The reduction in money demand lowers the interest rate at every level of income, shifting the LM curve out to the right, as Exhibit 8–14(b) shows. At income Y_1, the interest rate that is consistent with equilibrium in the money market falls to r_3.

Monetary Policy and the LM Curve

A primary reason we are interested in the LM curve is that, through monetary policy (the deliberate control of the money supply to affect the economy), the Fed can control the position of the LM curve and, hence, equilibrium income. If the Fed increases the money supply, the supply curve for money shifts to the right, for example from $\overline{M}_0^s$ to $\overline{M}_1^s$, as Exhibit 8–15(a) shows. Because income doesn't change, people find they are holding more money than they want (the quantity of money supplied exceeds quantity demanded) and they purchase bonds, which reduces the interest rate. This process continues until the interest rate falls. At income Y_0, interest rates fall from r_0 to r_1 (point A to point B).

Exhibit 8-15

Monetary Policy and the LM Curve

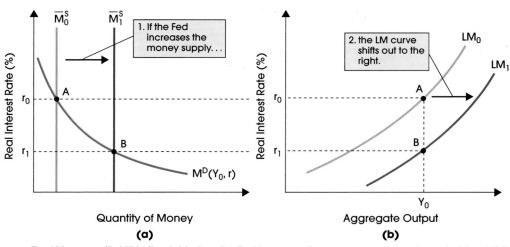

The LM curve will shift to the right when the Fed increases the money supply, as shown in this exhibit. If the money supply increases from $\overline{M}_0^s$ to $\overline{M}_1^s$ when income is Y_0, the interest rate falls from r_0 to r_1 to keep the money market in equilibrium. The LM curve will shift to the left when the Fed decreases the money supply.

Expansionary monetary policy shifts the LM curve out; contractionary monetary policy shifts the LM curve in.

Graphing the new LM curve after the increase in the money supply, we see that an increase in the money supply shifts the LM curve out to the right from LM_0 to LM_1 as in Exhibit 8–15(b). Initially, the interest rate associated with Y_0 is r_0 (point A). After the increase in the money supply, the interest rate associated with Y_0 is r_1 (point B). A decrease in the money supply shifts the LM curve in to the left.

Exhibit 8–15(b) shows that the Fed's ability to move the LM curve depends on its ability to affect the interest rate. As discussed in Chapter 7, the Fed most directly controls the short-term nominal interest rate, called the *fed funds rate*. The **fed funds rate** is the interest rate that banks charge each other for overnight loans (federal funds). The Fed buys and sells bonds daily to keep the federal funds rate close to a particular target. To implement expansionary monetary policy, it buys bonds. Because banks have more cash, the demand for fed funds falls and the federal funds rate falls. To implement contractionary monetary policy, the Fed sells bonds. Banks have less cash, raising the demand for fed funds and the fed funds rate rises. The Fed has significant control over this short-term interest rate. In the IS/LM model, we assume that this change in the short-term nominal interest rate affects the real interest rate of securities with longer maturities that affect investment decisions.

Throughout the rest of this chapter, we assume that all interest rates in the economy move with the fed funds rate, and, therefore, the Fed has precise control over them all. In the next chapter, we discuss some limitations of this assumption and how expectations can play a large role in the effectiveness of monetary policy.

SHORT-RUN EQUILIBRIUM

Now that we have demonstrated equilibrium in both the goods market and the money market, we are ready to put them together and find the level of income and real interest rate for which both markets are simultaneously in equilibrium. It is this equilibrium combination of interest rates and income levels that economists, using the IS/LM model, forecast for the economy. Exhibit 8–16 puts both curves together.

Remember that, all along the LM curve, the money market is in equilibrium. All along the IS curve, the goods market is in equilibrium. The only point at

Exhibit 8-16

Equilibrium in the IS/LM Model

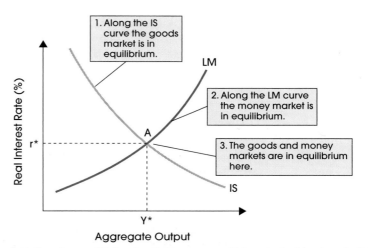

The IS/LM model tells us the equilibrium level of income and interest rate. It is where both the money market and the goods market are in equilibrium (point A) or where the IS and LM curves intersect.

Full equilibrium in the IS/LM
model occurs when the
IS curve intersects the LM
curve.

which both markets are in equilibrium at the same time is where the two curves intersect. In Exhibit 8–16, this occurs at point A, where the real interest rate is r^* and income is Y^*. By definition, at any point other than A, at least one market will be in disequilibrium and forces will be pushing the economy toward the equilibrium.

The equilibrium described by the IS/LM model is a short-run equilibrium. For given levels of autonomous expenditures and taxes and a given money supply, the economy will tend to move toward point A. In the long-run model, the equilibrium level of output is the potential output in the economy, determined by the factors of supply. In the short run, the economy may not be at potential output; equilibrium output may be higher or lower than its potential.

To know whether output at point A in Exhibit 8–16 is above or below potential, we need to estimate what output would be if all factors of production were fully utilized. If income at point A were below potential, policy makers would be concerned, because unemployment would be above the natural rate, factories would be idle, and raw materials would be underutilized.

POLICY PERSPECTIVE: OFFSETTING SHOCKS WITH MONETARY AND FISCAL POLICY

Now that you know how to find equilibrium in the goods market, the money market, and the economy as a whole, it is time to remember why you are learning this framework. You are trying to explain business-cycle fluctuations—short-term deviations from the potential growth path of the economy.

How does the IS/LM model explain these fluctuations? Imagine that the economy is initially operating at potential income Y_0 in Exhibit 8–17(a). Something happens to move the economy away from that equilibrium—perhaps firms and households reduce their autonomous expenditures. A reduction in expenditures is shown as a leftward shift in the IS curve in the direction of *arrow A,* which causes the level of income to fall to Y_1—a recession.

Most economists view the economy as being continuously hit with these shocks—or unanticipated changes in the IS and LM curves. When negative shocks occur, unemployment rises and aggregate income falls. Positive shocks may cause the economy to move above its potential, which causes inflationary pressures to rise. In any case, deviations from potential output are undesirable. Since the end of World War II, the focus of much of monetary and fiscal policy in the United States has been on offsetting or reducing the effects of these shocks.

In theory, fiscal and monetary policy can offset undesirable economic shocks. According to the IS/LM model, expansionary fiscal policy or expansionary monetary policy can offset a recession caused by a negative spending shock. As Exhibit 8–17(a) shows, expansionary fiscal policy shifts the IS curve in the direction of *arrow B* and the economy returns to its original position, with the real interest rate and level of income the same as before. Exhibit 8–17(b) shows what happens to output and the real interest rate when the Fed uses expansionary monetary policy to offset the shock. An increase in the money supply shifts the LM curve to the right, from LM_0 to LM_1 in the direction of *arrow C.* Output returns to its original level at Y_0, but the interest rate falls to r_2, lower than it previously was.

Exhibit 8-17

**Offsetting a
Negative IS Shock**

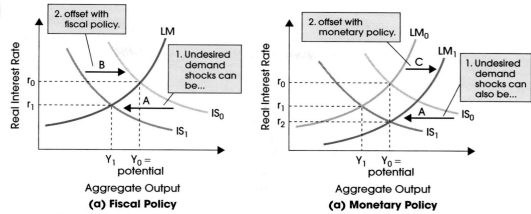

(a) Fiscal Policy   **(a) Monetary Policy**

Panel a shows how increases in government spending or reductions in taxes can offset a reduction in autonomous private spending and bring the economy back to potential. *Panel b* shows how expansionary monetary policy also can offset the shock.

Policymakers could, in principle, use either fiscal or monetary policy to offset these undesirable shocks in expenditures. Using fiscal and monetary policy to offset cyclical shocks to the economy is called **aggregate demand management.** Policy makers are managing, or attempting to control, the level of aggregate demand to move the economy to potential output.

Shocks to the economy can originate in the money market as well. If the introduction of Internet transactions (e-money) reduces the demand for money sufficiently (shifting the LM curve to the right) to push aggregate output above potential, policy makers can use either contractionary fiscal or monetary policy to reduce inflationary pressures.

The IS/LM model makes policy look much more mechanical and definitive than it actually is. These mechanics are a necessary first step in analyzing the effects of policy on the economy in the short run, but it is important to remember they are only a first step. The real world is much more complicated than the model, and all of our simplifying assumptions must eventually be considered when applying the model. Still, the IS/LM model is helpful in providing some structure to a complicated set of interrelationships.

To see the problems with fine-tuning the economy, consider the opening story of this chapter. At the time that CNN reported the story about Alan Greenspan's briefcase, most economists and policy makers believed the U.S. economy was operating well above potential output and inflationary pressures were building. The question at the time was whether Mr. Greenspan and other Fed policy makers should use contractionary monetary policy to try to cool the economy and bring it back down to potential. Greenspan and the FOMC did use contractionary policy throughout most of 1999 and early 2000, but the inflation they worried about never materialized and the economy continued to grow. In early 2000, the economy slowed enough to replace inflationary worries with worries of recession, and people still watched Greenspan's briefcase for clues to future monetary policy actions.

Aggregate demand management is when policy makers use fiscal policy (shifts the IS curve) and monetary policy (shifts the LM curve) to offset cyclical shocks to the economy.

In the IS/LM model, fine-tuning with monetary and fiscal policy is easy; in reality, it is very hard.

Executive Summary

- The quantity of money demanded is inversely related to the interest rate. When the interest rate rises, the quantity of money demanded falls. When the interest rate falls, the quantity of money demanded rises.

- Changes in income change the demand for money. When income rises, the demand for money rises; when income falls, the demand for money falls.

- In our IS/LM model we assume that the supply of money is fixed by the Federal Reserve Bank.

- The LM curve shows the combinations of income levels and interest rates at which the money market is in equilibrium.

- When the Fed increases the money supply the LM curve shifts out to the right.

- Factors other than income, such as expectations about the interest rate and changes in payment technology, that affect the demand for money shift the LM curve.

- The slope of the LM curve depends on the responsiveness of money demand to changes in income and the sensitivity of the quantity of money demanded to changes in interest rates.

- The goods and money markets are in equilibrium simultaneously where the IS and LM curves intersect.

- In the IS/LM model contractionary fiscal policy leads to lower interest rates and lower output. Contractionary monetary policy leads to higher interest rates and lower output.

CONCLUSION

This chapter has been largely technical, setting out the mechanics of the IS and LM curves. The technical derivation of the IS and LM curves is sufficiently difficult that we felt it best to stick with the basics here, and save the debates and interpretations for later. However, we want to emphasize one point before this chapter ends: Managing aggregate demand to offset business cycles is not simply a matter of applying the mechanics illustrated in this chapter. In the real world, policy makers face numerous challenges. Often, the outcomes of their policies are not what they intended. In the next chapter, we will try to give you a feel for some of the challenges in using IS/LM analysis to guide policy in the real world.

KEY POINTS

- In the short-run macroeconomic model, aggregate demand determines the level of real output, and prices are assumed to be completely fixed.
- Goods market equilibrium occurs at the point where total expenditures equal total output.
- Changes in autonomous expenditures have a multiplied effect on equilibrium output. The multiplier is

$$\frac{1}{1 - mpe} = \frac{1}{1 - mpc(1 - t) + m}$$

- The IS curve represents the combinations of interest rates and levels of aggregate output that are consistent with equilibrium in the goods market. Along the IS curve interest rates are inversely related to output, and vice versa.

- Increases in autonomous expenditures and decreases in taxes cause the IS curve to shift out to the right, and decreases in autonomous expenditures and increases in taxes cause the IS curve to shift in to the left. The shift equals the change in autonomous expenditures times the multiplier.
- The shape of the IS curve reflects the sensitivity of investment to changes in the real interest rate, and the size of the multiplier.
- The demand for money is a function of the interest rate, the level of income, and the expected interest rate.
- The intersection of money demand and money supply determines the interest rate.

■ The LM curve represents the combinations of interest rates and levels of aggregate output (or income) that are consistent with equilibrium in the money market. Along the LM curve interest rates are directly related with output.

■ The shape of the LM curve depends on the responsiveness of money demand to changes in income and the interest sensitivity of the quantity of money demanded.

■ Increases in the money supply shift the LM curve out to the right, given a fixed demand curve for money. Decreases in the money supply shift the LM curve in to the left, given a fixed demand curve for money.

■ Equilibrium in the economy as a whole (both the goods market and the money market) is represented by the intersection of the IS and LM curves. Fiscal policy affects the position of the IS curve, and monetary policy affects the position of the LM curve.

■ Expansionary fiscal policy shifts the IS curve to the right. Expansionary monetary policy shifts the LM curve to the right.

KEY TERMS

aggregate demand management 237
aggregate expenditures 213
autonomous expenditures 213
consumption function 213
fed funds rate 235

induced expenditures 213
IS curve 222
IS/LM model 212
LM curve 226
marginal propensity to expend 216

money market 226
multiplier 215
multiplier equation 215
multiplier model 212

QUESTIONS FOR THOUGHT AND REVIEW

1. What assumption about prices in the short run allows us to focus exclusively on aggregate demand as the determinant of equilibrium output? What does this assumption imply about the shape of the short-run aggregate supply curve?

2. In what way is the aggregate demand curve different from the individual or market demand curves you learned about in microeconomics?

3. What is the difference between an autonomous expenditure and an induced expenditure?

4. What three components of aggregate expenditures depend on the level of aggregate income? Describe these relationships.

5. What is equilibrium income if the mpe is .8 and autonomous expenditures are $900?

6. What adjustments take place when aggregate expenditures exceed aggregate output? Will the economy eventually reach equilibrium? Why or why not?

7. Why do changes in autonomous expenditures and taxes have a multiplied effect on aggregate output?

8. What is the difference between the marginal propensity to consume and the marginal propensity to expend?

9. How does fiscal policy affect aggregate expenditures?

10. Define the *IS curve*. Why does it slope downward?

11. How does a change in autonomous expenditures affect the position of the IS curve? How does fiscal policy affect the position of the IS curve?

12. How do the size of the multiplier and the interest sensitivity of investment demand influence the slope of the IS curve?

13. List three factors that affect the demand for money and describe the relationship between each of the factors and the demand for money.

14. Explain how a change in the money supply leads to a change in the interest rate.

15. Define the *LM curve* and explain why it slopes upward.

16. Name two factors that shift the LM curve. Describe the direction of the shift caused by changes in each of these factors.

17. Describe how the responsiveness of money demand to changes in income and the interest sensitivity of money demand influence the slope of the LM curve.

18. Over what interest rate does the Fed have the greatest control?

19. Define *aggregate demand management*.

PROBLEMS AND EXERCISES

1. Suppose that the aggregate consumption function is $C = 100 + .8(Y - T)$; taxes are $T = 10 + .05Y$; imports are $M = 5 + .10Y$; investment is 400, government expenditures are 200, and exports are 100.
   a. What is equilibrium income, consumption, taxes, and net exports?
   b. Illustrate equilibrium using the aggregate expenditures/45-degree line diagram.
   c. If government spending rises to 250, what happens to equilibrium levels of income, consumption, taxes, and net exports? Demonstrate your answer graphically.
   d. What is the size of the multiplier in this economy?

2. Derive two points on the IS curve graphically.
   a. Graphically show what happens to the IS curve when government expenditures increase.
   b. How is the size of the shift in the IS related to the amount by which government expenditures increased?
   c. Using a separate graph, demonstrate what happens when government decreases taxes.

3. The text explains how the introduction of Internet technology lowered the demand for money.
   a. How would the demand for money be affected if banks start charging fees for withdrawing funds from e-accounts?
   b. Illustrate the impact of this change on interest rates by using the demand-and-supply curves for money.

4. Derive two points on the LM curve graphically.
   a. Demonstrate what happens to the LM curve when expected interest rates rise.
   b. On a separate diagram, show what happens when there is an increase in the money supply.

5. Suppose the economy is initially in equilibrium. Use separate IS and LM diagrams to show the impact of each of the following on equilibrium income and interest rates:
   a. Autonomous consumption expenditures fall.
   b. Monetary policy is used to offset the effects of the decline in consumption expenditures.
   c. Fiscal policy is used to offset the effects of the decline in consumption expenditures.

6. Suppose the economy is initially in equilibrium. Use separate IS and LM diagrams to show what would happen to equilibrium income and the interest rate for each of the following:
   a. Payments technology change so that it is less costly to transfer wealth from interest-bearing financial assets to money.
   b. Monetary policy offsets the effects of the change in payments technology.
   c. Fiscal policy offsets the effects of the change in payments technology on income.

The Algebra of the Multiplier Model

In the text, we presented a numerical example of the multiplier model. Here we present the more general algebraic form of that model. The subscripted zero denotes autonomous components of spending and taxes; Y denotes real income. The components of aggregate expenditures are the following:

Consumption

$$C = C_0 + mpc(Y - T) \qquad (8A\text{-}1)$$

where mpc is the marginal propensity to consume.

Taxes

$$T = T_0 + tY \qquad (8A\text{-}2)$$

where t is the tax rate.

Investment

$$I = I_0 \qquad (8A\text{-}3)$$

Government Spending

$$G = G_0 \qquad (8A\text{-}4)$$

Exports

$$X = X_0 \qquad (8A\text{-}5)$$

Imports

$$M = M_0 + mY \qquad (8A\text{-}6)$$

where m is the marginal propensity to import.

Aggregate expenditures (AE) equal the sum of the expenditure components:

$$AE = C + I + G + X - M \qquad (8A\text{-}7)$$

Substituting Equations (8A-1) through (8A-6) into (8A-7), we have

$$AE = C_0 + mpc(Y - T_0 - tY) \\ + I_0 + G_0 + X_0 - M_0 - mY \qquad (8A\text{-}8)$$

Equilibrium in the multiplier model occurs where aggregate expenditures equal aggregate output:

$$AE = Y$$

Replacing AE with the right-hand side of (8A-8) gives us

$$C_0 + mpc(Y - T_0 - tY) + I_0 + G_0 + X_0 - M_0 - mY = Y$$

Isolating the terms with Y in them on the left:

$$Y[1 - mpc(1 - t) + m] = \\ C_0 + I_0 + G_0 + X_0 - mpcT_0 - M_0$$

Finally, solving for Y:

$$Y = \left(\frac{1}{1 - mpc(1 - t) + m} \right) \\ \times (C_0 + I_0 + G_0 + X_0 - mpcT_0 - M_0) \qquad (8A\text{-}9)$$

You should recognize the term $[1/(1 - mpc(1 - t) + m] = 1/(1 - mpe)$ as the multiplier. Equation (8A-9) can be used to show how a change in any one of the expenditure components will affect aggregate output: A one-unit change in autonomous consumption, investment, government expenditures, and net exports will cause output to change by $[1/(1 - mpc(1 - t) + m]$. A one-unit change in autonomous taxes will cause output to change by $-mpc[1/(1 - mpc(1 - t) + m)]$.

The Algebraic Determination of the IS Curve and the LM Curve

THE IS CURVE

Algebraically, we can derive the IS curve by modifying the investment demand in Appendix A to include the real interest rate. Equation (8A-3) becomes

$$I = I_0 - dr \qquad \text{(8B-1)}$$

where d is a positive constant that measures the interest rate sensitivity of investment and r is the real interest rate.

With the new investment demand equation, aggregate expenditures become

$$AE = C_0 + mpc(Y - T_0 - tY) \qquad \text{(8B-2)}$$
$$+ I_0 - dr + G_0 + X_0 - M_0 - mY$$

Equilibrium in the goods market is the point at which aggregate expenditures equal aggregate output:

$$AE = Y$$

Substituting equation (8B-2) into the equilibrium equation gives us

$$C_0 + mpc(Y - T_0 - tY) + I_0 - \qquad \text{(8B-3)}$$
$$dr + G_0 + X_0 - M_0 - mY = Y$$

Isolating the terms with Y on the left gives us

$$Y[1 - mpc(1 - t) + m] = \qquad \text{(8B-4)}$$
$$C_0 + I_0 - dr + G_0 + X_0 - mpcT_0 - M_0$$

Dividing each side by $[1 - mpc(1 - t) + m]$ gives us equilibrium income:

$$Y = \left(\frac{1}{1 - mpc(1 - t) + m} \right) \qquad \text{(8B-5)}$$
$$\times (C_0 + I_0 - dr + G_0 + X_0 - mpcT_0 - M_0)$$

Equation (8B-5) is the IS curve. It shows the inverse relationship between the interest rate r and aggregate output Y. The equation shows the negative relationship with the negative sign in front of the term dr.

THE LM CURVE

Algebraically, we can state the demand for money as the following equation. (For simplicity, we assume that all relationships can be described by linear functions and the function is separable.)

$$M^D = j_0 + kY - hr \qquad \text{(8B-6)}$$

where M^D is demand for money, j_0 is a constant to be determined empirically, k is a positive constant measuring the sensitivity of money demand to changes in income, and h is a positive constant measuring the sensitivity of the demand for money to changes in the interest rate.[1]

The money supply is assumed to be determined exogenously:

$$M^S = \overline{M}^S \qquad \text{(8B-7)}$$

To find equilibrium in the money market, we equate money demand and money supply:

$$M^S = M^D$$

By substitution,

$$\overline{M}^S = j_0 + kY - hr \qquad \text{(8B-8)}$$

Adding hr to both sides and dividing by k yields

$$Y = (\overline{M}^S + hr - j_0)/k \qquad \text{(8B-9)}$$

or

$$Y = \overline{M}^S/k + hr/k - j_0/k \qquad \text{(8B-10)}$$

---

[1]Although money demand depends on the nominal interest rate, we use the real interest rate here because the price level is assumed to be fixed, in which case, the nominal interest rate equals the real interest rate.

This is a positively sloped linear function relating equilibrium income and interest rates, given the money supply and the constants h and k. Notice that the first term, $\overline{M}^s/k$, is one version of the simple quantity theory where k is the inverse of velocity. The second term makes velocity no longer constant; rather, it varies with interest rates. Graphing this equation—as done in Exhibit 8–12(b)—gives us the LM curve.

The elder grasps the LM with his left hand and the IS with his right and, holding the totem out in front of himself with elbows slightly bent, proceeds in a straight line. . . . The grads of the village skip gaily around him at first, falling silent as the trek grows longer and more wearisome, . . . At long last the totem vibrates, then oscillates more and more; finally, it points, quivering, straight down. The elder waits for the grads to gather round and then pronounces, with great solemnity, "Behold, the Truth and Power of the Model."

—Axel Leijonhufvud

Policy Analysis with the IS/LM Model

After reading this chapter you should be able to:

1. Explain how crowding out limits the effect of fiscal policy on output and how a liquidity trap limits the effect of monetary policy on output

2. Describe policies that a government must undertake to achieve various interest rate and output targets

3. Use the IS/LM model to describe three policy actions in U.S. history

4. State four interpretation problems with monetary policy and two interpretation problems with fiscal policy

5. List three implementation problems of monetary and fiscal policy

6. Explain why policy makers use policy rules to deal with interpretation and implementation problems of policy

In early 2000, the U.S. economy was in its longest expansion on record. This expansion was driven partly by rising autonomous consumption and investment from the booming stock market. Policy makers at the Federal Reserve feared that inflation would soon rise, so they worked to slow the economy by using contractionary monetary policy. By the end of 2000 and into 2001, the Fed's concern about inflation turned into a fear of recession, so the Fed switched to expansionary monetary policy.

The mechanics of the IS/LM model that you learned last chapter will help you to understand the theory underlying these actions. The initial expansion was caused by an increase in autonomous expenditures, which shifted the IS curve to the right, causing output to rise. Contractionary monetary policy shifted the LM curve to the left, raising real interest rates and offsetting the increase in output. Then, autonomous expenditures decreased and the Fed countered with expansionary monetary policy.

More generally, if the IS/LM model accurately reflects the economy, business cycles should not be a problem. In the IS/LM model, countering those cycles is easy—identify a shift in IS or LM and counter that shift with an offsetting shift with fiscal or monetary policy. Unfortunately, in the real world, using policy to counter short-term business-cycle fluctuations is far from easy. The mechanics you learned in Chapter 8 are an important first step, but, as you will see, figuring out what shocks are hitting the economy and then pulling the levers of policy is a complicated process with many problems.

This chapter introduces you to some of the problems of using the IS/LM model in the real world. At the end of the chapter, we revisit the Fed's actions in the late 1990s and early 2000 to see how these real-world problems affected its monetary policymaking.

A CLOSER LOOK AT FISCAL AND MONETARY POLICY

Expansionary fiscal policy shifts the IS curve out to the right; contractionary fiscal policy shifts it in to the left. Similarly, expansionary monetary policy shifts the LM curve out to the right; contractionary monetary policy shifts the LM curve in to the left. Let's consider how this happens. In doing so, we will see how the goods market and the money market interact, and how the effectiveness of fiscal and monetary policy depends on the shapes of the IS and LM curves.

Fiscal Policy

> When government uses fiscal policy, the IS curve shifts by the change in autonomous expenditures times the multiplier.

Let's begin by looking at fiscal policy. Suppose that the economy is initially at income of $6,000, shown in Exhibit 9–1(a). The government decides to increase expenditures by $500, and the marginal propensity to expend is .5, so the multiplier is 2 [1/(1 − .5)]. As you learned in Chapter 8, the IS curve will shift to the right by $1,000 (= 2 × 500). Notice, however, that income will rise by less than $1,000 (to $6,600) at the intersection of the new IS curve and the original LM curve.

Why doesn't output rise by the full multiplier times the rise in government expenditures? The reason is that as output, and, therefore, income, starts to rise, the demand for money rises as well. As long as the Fed holds the money supply fixed, people must sell bonds to increase their holdings of money. An increase in the supply of bonds leads to a decline in their price and a rise in the interest rate. Exhibit 9–1(a) shows the interest rate rising from 4 percent to 5 percent. The higher interest rate causes investment expenditures to decline, partly offsetting the

Exhibit 9-1

Crowding Out

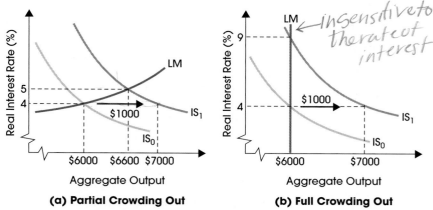

(a) Partial Crowding Out   **(b) Full Crowding Out**

Expansionary fiscal policy shifts the IS curve out to the right. In *panel a*, income does not rise by the full multiplier effect because the interest rate rises from 4 percent to 5 percent. The higher interest rate causes investment to fall, which partly offsets the effect of the expansionary fiscal policy. When this occurs, fiscal policy is said to "crowd out" private investment. *Panel b* shows how expansionary fiscal policy can be completely offset by a decline in investment.

rise in income caused by the increase in government expenditures. Remember, a decline in investment expenditures that is the result of a rise in the interest rate is represented by a movement up to the left along the IS curve.

This example illustrates crowding out—the decline in investment expenditures caused by a rise in interest rates when government expenditures rise. The increase in government spending crowds out private investment expenditures so that income rises to only $6,600. An increase in government spending has a direct, desirable effect—it increases income or output. It also has an indirect, undesirable effect—it increases interest rates, which decreases private investment expenditures.

The degree of crowding out depends on the shapes of the LM and IS curves. The steeper the LM curve and the flatter the IS curve, the greater the degree of crowding out. Let's consider how this works with the LM curve. When the LM curve is horizontal, the interest rate does not change when the IS curve shifts to the right. Increases in government spending do not crowd out investment expenditures, and output rises by the full multiplier times the rise in government spending. In the example in Exhibit 9–1(a), if there were no crowding out, output would rise by $1,000 (2 times $500).

The LM curve also can be vertical, as Exhibit 9–1(b) shows. In this case, changes in government expenditures have no effect on output. The $500 increase in government spending shifts the IS curve to the right by $1,000, but, as aggregate expenditures rise, the interest rate rises to 9 percent. Investment expenditures fall, completely offsetting the increase in government expenditures. Output remains at $6,000. Complete crowding out will occur if the quantity of money demanded is totally insensitive to changes in the interest rate (a vertical LM curve). The interest rate will keep rising until the initial rise in government expenditures is offset with a similar decline in investment expenditures. With complete crowding out, fiscal policy affects only interest rates, not output.

Monetary Policy

Now let's take a closer look at monetary policy in the IS/LM model. When the Federal Reserve expands the money supply, the LM curve shifts to the right, as Exhibit 9–2(a) shows. The Fed expands the money supply by purchasing government bonds on the open market. As the Fed buys bonds, their price rises and the interest rate falls. As the interest rate falls, investment expenditures rise and, as investment expenditures rise, the level of income in the economy rises. In Exhibit 9–2(a), expansionary monetary policy shifts the LM curve from LM_0 to LM_1. This causes the interest rate to fall from r_0 to r_1 and equilibrium output to rise from Y_0 to Y_1. Expansionary monetary policy lowers interest rates and raises equilibrium output in the short run.

As with fiscal policy, the effectiveness of monetary policy on changing output depends on the shapes of the IS and LM curves. A steep IS curve means that investment expenditures are not sensitive to changes in the interest rate. Monetary policy works by changing interest rates, which affect investment. The less sensitive investment expenditures are to changes in the interest rate (steeper IS curve), the less effective monetary policy will be. When the IS curve is vertical (investment demand is not affected by the interest rate at all), monetary policy will not change output at all. A flat IS curve (investment demand is very sensitive to changes in the interest rate) means monetary policy will be very effective at changing output.

Some of the effect of fiscal policy on income is offset by the decline in investment (crowding out) caused by the rise in the interest rate.

The degree of crowding out depends on the shape of the IS and LM curves; the steeper the LM curve and the flatter the IS curve, the greater the degree of crowding out.

Complete crowding out occurs if the LM curve is vertical.

Monetary policy shifts the LM curve.

The effectiveness of monetary policy on changing income depends on the shapes of the IS and LM curves. The flatter the IS curve the more effective monetary policy is in changing income.

Exhibit 9-2

A Closer Look at Monetary Policy in the IS/LM Model

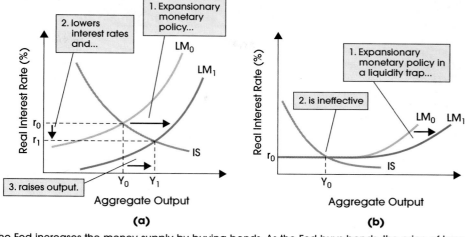

The Fed increases the money supply by buying bonds. As the Fed buys bonds, the price of bonds rises and the interest rate falls, shifting the LM curve out to the right in *panel a*. As the interest rate falls, investment expenditures increase and output rises. *Panel b* shows a liquidity trap. At very low interest rates, expansionary monetary policy may not be able to push interest rates down any lower. Investment may not be stimulated and monetary policy will have no effect on output.

> When the LM curve is horizontal, the economy is in a liquidity trap, and monetary policy (which shifts the LM curve to the right and left) has no effect on interest rates or income.

Monetary policy also has no effect on output when the LM curve is horizontal, as Exhibit 9–2(b) shows. The LM curve is horizontal when the quantity of money demanded is extremely sensitive (in fact, infinitely sensitive) to changes in the interest rate. This special case is called the **liquidity trap**—a situation in which monetary policy does not affect the interest rate or investment. Liquidity traps are most likely to occur at unusually low interest rates, when interest rates can only rise. In Exhibit 9–2(b), for example, expansionary monetary policy shifts the LM curve from LM_0 to LM_1, but because the LM curve is flat in the range where the economy is (around Y_0), expansionary monetary policy is completely ineffective. The interest rate remains at r_0 and output remains at Y_0.

Some economists believe that the United States faced a liquidity trap in the 1930s and Japan faced a liquidity trap in the late 1990s. The evidence in both cases, however, is not conclusive, because IS and LM curves cannot be observed directly in the real world. What sometimes looks like a failure of interest rates to respond to monetary policy also can be a failure of monetary policy to expand the money supply enough. For example, some economists argue that the Fed in the 1930s and the Bank of Japan in the 1990s did not expand the money supply sufficiently to expand the economy. (For details, see The Briefing Room, "Was Japan in a Liquidity Trap in the late 1990s?".)

Achieving Short-Run Policy Goals with Monetary and Fiscal Policy

Understanding the mechanics of IS/LM means understanding how the effectiveness of monetary and fiscal policy depends on the interest rate sensitivity of money demand and investment demand. By now, you should associate effective fiscal policy with a flat LM curve, and effective monetary policy with a flat IS curve. So, why don't policy makers simply determine the shapes of the curves and base policy on those shapes? They would if they could, but, often, they cannot. The interest rate sensitivities of investment and money demand are difficult to observe, and those interest rate sensitivities can change unpredictably over time. Nonetheless, the

When interest rates become so low that the central bank cannot push them any lower, the possibility of a liquidity trap exists. In March 1999, the interest rate on overnight loans in Japan (equivalent to the fed funds rate in the United States) fell to 0.01 percent (a hundredth of one percent!) per year. That meant that a bank could borrow $1 million overnight and pay only 27 cents in interest. Some analysts thought that the low interest rate on overnight loans was a clear indication that Japan was in a liquidity trap (a horizontal LM curve) and that the Japanese central bank's monetary policy was ineffective. Others argued that expanding the money supply wouldn't help because Japanese firms did not want to borrow and invest in new plants and equipment, even at low interest rates. According to this argument, the problem was that the IS curve was vertical, not that the LM curve was horizontal. To support their argument, they pointed out that expanding the money supply significantly would have created inflation, which would make the real interest rate negative, and thereby increase investment if investment were responsive to real interest rate changes. Empirically, because the Central Bank of Japan did not try to aggressively expand the money supply, it is difficult to determine which of these was the case.

IS/LM analysis provides an initial framework through which we can understand monetary and fiscal policy.

Table 9–1 summarizes the policy directives inherent in the IS/LM framework. It tells what happens to output and interest rates when government implements monetary or fiscal policy. Table 9–2 gives examples of actions that government takes to implement each type of policy. If the government uses expansionary fiscal policy to increase output, the interest rate will rise. This is the situation shown in Exhibit 9–1(a). If government uses expansionary monetary policy to increase output, the interest rate will fall. This is the situation shown in Exhibit 9–2(a). Which policy the country uses will most likely depend on practical considerations—which policy is easiest to implement.

If a country finds that its output is far above potential, it can either reduce the supply of money and accept a higher interest rate or reduce government expenditures and lower interest rates. We show both scenarios in Exhibit 9–3. If the Fed uses contractionary monetary policy, it sells bonds on the open market, which lowers the price of bonds and raises interest rates. Investment

The combination of monetary and fiscal policy determines what will happen to interest rates and aggregate output in the IS-LM model.

Table 9–1

Short-Run Outcomes of Policies Choices

Output Goal	Interest Rate Goal	Policies
Increase	Increase	• Expansionary fiscal policy
Increase	Decrease	• Expansionary monetary policy
Increase	No change	• Expansionary fiscal and monetary policy
Decrease	Decrease	• Contractionary fiscal policy
Decrease	Increase	• Contractionary monetary policy
Decrease	No change	• Contractionary fiscal and monetary policy
No change	Increase	• Expansionary fiscal policy and contractionary monetary policy
No change	Decrease	• Contractionary fiscal policy and expansionary monetary policy

Table 9-2

Examples of Monetary and Fiscal Policies

Type of Policy	Action Taken
Expansionary fiscal policy	• Increase expenditures (financed by the Treasury selling bonds).
Expansionary monetary policy	• The Fed buys bonds.
Contractionary fiscal policy	• Raise taxes (the Treasury retires debt).
Contractionary monetary policy	• The Fed sells bonds.

expenditures fall, which lowers output. Exhibit 9–3(a) shows this by a leftward shift in the LM curve from LM_0 to LM_1. Income falls from Y_0 to Y_1, and interest rates rise to r_1.

If the government uses contractionary fiscal policy to lower output, it must accept lower interest rates. We show this in Exhibit 9–3(b). Contractionary fiscal policy shifts the IS curve from IS_0 to IS_1, output falls from Y_0 to Y_1, and the interest rate falls to r_2. If a country does not care what happens to interest rates, it can use either monetary policy or fiscal policy alone to achieve its output goals.

If a government has both an interest rate goal and an output goal, its policy choices are limited. If it wants to increase output and lower interest rates, it will have to use expansionary monetary policy. If it wants to decrease output and lower interest rates, it will have to use contractionary fiscal policy.

By using both expansionary monetary and fiscal policies, the government can expand output without changing interest rates.

When a government wants to change only interest rates or only output, keeping the other constant, monetary policy and fiscal policy must work together, because, when used alone, monetary and fiscal policy generally change both output and interest rates. For example, suppose the economy is initially at point A in

Exhibit 9-3

Policy when the Economy Is Above Potential

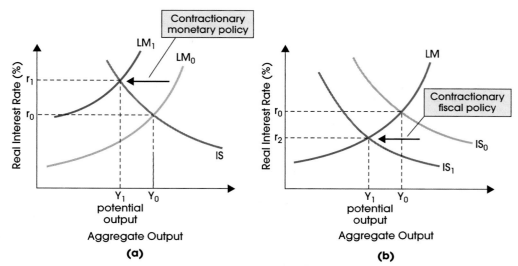

Contractionary monetary and fiscal policies reduce output when the economy is above potential. Contractionary monetary policy *(panel a)* will also raise the real interest rate, while contractionary fiscal policy *(panel b)* will lower the real interest rate.

Exhibit 9-4

Interactions Between Monetary and Fiscal Policy

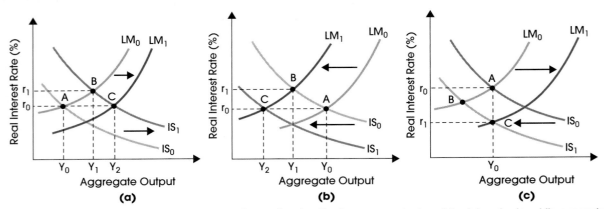

In *panel a*, expansionary fiscal policy increases output and the interest rate, while expansionary monetary policy pushes the interest rate down and increases output even further. In *panel b*, contractionary monetary policy is accompanied by contractionary fiscal policy. This combination keeps interest rates constant and reduces output by a lot (from Y_0 to Y_2). In *panel c*, expansionary monetary policy is accompanied by contractionary fiscal policy. This combination keeps output constant and reduces interest rates (from r_0 to r_1).

Exhibit 9–4(a), and the government wants to increase output but keep interest rates constant. To do so, it must use a combination of expansionary monetary and fiscal policy. In Exhibit 9–4(a), expansionary fiscal policy shifts the IS curve out from IS_0 to IS_1. Output will rise to Y_1, and interest rates will rise to r_1 (point B). To offset the rise in interest rates, the government must use expansionary monetary policy to neutralize the effect that expansionary fiscal policy has on interest rates. Expansionary monetary policy shifts the LM curve from LM_0 to LM_1, output rises even further to Y_2, and interest rates return to r_0 (point C).

The monetary policy shown in Exhibit 9–4(a) is accommodative monetary policy. **Accommodative monetary policy** prevents a rise in interest rates that would otherwise occur when a government increases its deficit. Such policy makes sense when the economy is far below its potential and there is little possibility of inflation. In the late 1990s, Japan implemented both expansionary monetary and expansionary fiscal policy to get the economy out of a decade-long slump, but there was debate about whether it was too little or too late.

Consider another example. Suppose a government wants to lower output with contractionary monetary policy without raising interest rates. It would have to use a combination of contractionary monetary policy and contractionary fiscal policy. In Exhibit 9–4(b), contractionary monetary policy shifts the LM curve from LM_0 to LM_1, and output falls from Y_0 to Y_1, while the interest rate rises from r_0 to r_1 (point B). So, to keep the interest rates at r_0, the government will have to reduce spending or increase taxes to shift the IS curve from IS_0 to IS_1. Output will fall even further, and the interest rate will return to its original position (point C).

To make sure you understand how combinations of monetary and fiscal policy affect the economy, suppose the government wanted to lower interest rates but keep output unchanged. What policies would you suggest it use? If you advised

To lower the interest rate with no effect on income, use contractionary fiscal policy and expansionary monetary policy.

using a combination of expansionary monetary and contractionary fiscal policies, you've got it. Look at Exhibit 9–4(c). Contractionary fiscal policy shifts the IS curve from IS_0 to IS_1, and expansionary monetary policy shifts the LM curve from LM_0 to LM_1. Output remains unchanged at Y_0, and the interest rate falls to r_1. Exhibit 9–4(c) demonstrates offsetting policy, in which monetary and fiscal policies move in opposite directions to change the interest rate but keep output unchanged.

Government uses offsetting policies to affect interest rates without changing output. Offsetting policies make sense when the economy is close to or at its potential level of output. In the United States, the Federal Reserve promised offsetting policy—expansionary monetary policy—if Congress reduced the deficit in the mid-1990s. Throughout the mid- to late 1990s, Congress reduced the deficit. Output increased, not decreased, in part because the Fed offset the effects of contractionary fiscal policy with expansionary monetary policy.

Executive Summary

- Increases in government spending have an expansionary effect of increasing output, but tend to increase interest rates, which leads to lower investment spending. This offsetting of private investment by government spending is called crowding out.

- Complete crowding out occurs when interest rates rise sufficiently so that investment expenditures decline by the same amount as the increase in government spending. In this case, fiscal policy is ineffective in changing output.

- If the quantity of money demanded is very sensitive to changes in the interest rate, the LM curve may be horizontal and the economy may be in a liquidity trap. In this case, monetary policy is ineffective in changing output.

- Governments can simultaneously use monetary and fiscal policies to attain both an output goal and an interest rate goal. Accommodative monetary policy prevents a rise in the interest rate that otherwise would occur when government increases spending or decreases taxes. Offsetting policies are monetary and fiscal policies that work together to change interest rates, keeping output unchanged.

REAL-WORLD MONETARY AND FISCAL POLICY

Now that we've been through the basics of IS/LM, let's use it to interpret some historical events. Let's begin with the Great Depression. From 1929 to 1933, U.S. output fell 30 percent and unemployment rose to 25 percent. The economy was far below potential. Franklin D. Roosevelt's New Deal increased government spending, reducing the budget balance somewhat from a surplus in 1929 to a deficit in the mid-1930s. Once the United States entered World War II in 1941, however, government expenditures rose enormously and the government deficit rose from 3 percent of GDP in 1940 to nearly 30 percent in 1943. (For comparison, in the early 1990s, policy makers were concerned about a U.S. deficit of less than 5 percent of GDP.)

Exhibit 9–5(a) shows the effect of increasing government expenditures. A shift in the IS curve from IS_0 to IS_1 increased output from Y_0 to Y_1, far above potential. Because the Fed agreed to hold interest rates constant to help government finance the war, the Fed was forced to supplement expansionary fiscal policy with expansionary monetary policy. This is shown by a shift in the LM curve from LM_0 to LM_1, keeping interest rates at r_0 and increasing output further to Y_2. Interest rates did

Exhibit 9-5

Real-World Policy and the IS/LM Model

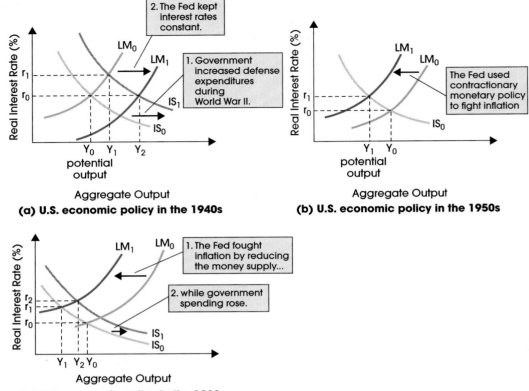

2. The Fed kept interest rates constant.

1. Government increased defense expenditures during World War II.

(a) U.S. economic policy in the 1940s

The Fed used contractionary monetary policy to fight inflation

(b) U.S. economic policy in the 1950s

1. The Fed fought inflation by reducing the money supply...

2. while government spending rose.

(c) U.S. economic policy in the 1980s

This exhibit shows three examples of real-world U.S. policy explained with the IS/LM model. *Panel a* shows expansionary fiscal policy during World War II in the 1940s accommodated by expansionary monetary policy. *Panel b* shows contractionary monetary policy of the 1950s. *Panel c* shows the mix of contractionary monetary policy and expansionary fiscal policy during the Reagan era of the 1980s.

remain low. In fact, some short-term interest rates remained under 1 percent throughout World War II.

Now let's consider another scenario. In the mid-1950s, the U.S. economy was expanding, and annual inflation rose to about 3 percent. To fight inflation, the Fed tightened the money supply, as shown in Exhibit 9–5(b). The LM curve shifts from LM_0 to LM_1. Short-term interest rates rose from 1.6 percent in 1954 to 3.9 percent in 1957. Business investment dropped 16 percent, and consumer expenditures on durable goods fell as the economy moved up along the IS curve. Real output fell, and the economy entered a recession in August 1957.

The 1980s provide a similar story of contractionary monetary policy, but this time, monetary and fiscal policy worked in opposing directions. In the early 1980s, Paul Volcker was the chairman of the Federal Reserve Bank. At that time, inflation was approaching 12 percent—very high by U.S. standards. The Fed thought that maintaining stable prices outweighed keeping the economy at potential output, so it dramatically reduced the growth rate of the money supply to bring the inflation rate down. Exhibit 9–5(c) shows the situation. Contractionary monetary policy shifted the LM curve from LM_0 to LM_1, reducing output from Y_0 to Y_1 and raising interest rates from r_0 to r_1.

At the same time, Ronald Reagan took office in January 1981 with two goals: to reduce taxes and to increase military defense spending. The mix resulted in an expansionary fiscal policy, shifting the IS curve from IS_0 to IS_1, which increased interest rates further from r_1 to r_2, but offset some of the effect of contractionary monetary policy on output, pulling the economy from Y_1 to Y_2. The economy was in a recession, but the recession was probably smaller than it would have been had expansionary fiscal policy not partially offset the contractionary monetary policy.

PROBLEMS USING IS/LM TO ANALYZE POLICY IN THE REAL WORLD

The analysis of the economy using the IS/LM model presented here is very neat, but it is also mechanical. It states that when the government sees a recession, it simply increases government spending, reduces taxes, or increases the money supply. If the government sees the economy overheating, it does the opposite. It is a bit like driving a car with monetary and fiscal policies as the steering wheel. It sounds too easy to be true, and it is. In the real world, politics, lags, and uncertainties make aggregate demand management policies difficult to implement with precision. Real-world policymaking is more like riding a bull than driving a car.

Two types of problems emerge as we move from the IS/LM model to talking about real-world policy: interpretation problems and implementation problems. Interpretation problems center on knowing how to interpret real-world events within the IS/LM framework. Implementation problems are those involved with undertaking the policy. Let's examine interpretation problems first.

Real-world policymaking is more like riding a bull than driving a car.

When we apply the IS/LM model to the real world, we run into interpretation problems and implementation problems.

Interpretation Problems

Models inevitably make implicit and explicit assumptions that don't quite fit the real world. To interpret real-world events with a model, one must adjust the model to fit the real world. Doing so always involves problems, and we call the problems that arise interpretation problems.

The Interest Rate Problem. The first problem we have when using the IS/LM model to analyze real-world monetary policy is how to interpret the interest rate. The IS/LM model tells us that when the Fed tightens monetary policy, the interest rate will rise. In the real world, this presents two problems. The first problem is that when there is inflation, real interest rates and nominal interest rates will differ. To apply the model, one must decide which is relevant.

The second problem is that there are many interest rates in the economy. Section C of *The Wall Street Journal,* for example, lists interest rates for Treasury bills, certificates of deposit, corporate bonds, and fed funds, to name just a few. The Fed has direct influence over only the fed funds rate—the interest rate that banks charge each other for overnight loans. The interest rate problem is that the fed funds rate isn't the interest rate that households and firms care about when they are

Deciding which interest rate is the relevant one is an important interpretation problem.

deciding how much to borrow. So, if the Fed is to have any influence on the economy, it has to be able to affect—if not directly control—the interest rates that are relevant for borrowing decisions made by households and firms, as well as the fed funds rate. This is much harder for the Fed to do.

Why Interest Rates Differ. Interest rates differ from one another for a number of reasons. We will focus on two:

1. Interest rates differ according to the likelihood that the borrower will repay the loan.
2. Interest rates differ by their term to maturity.

One reason why interest rates differ is **default risk**—the possibility that the borrower will not pay back, or will default on, the loan. Lenders charge a higher interest rate to those borrowers who have a greater chance of default. The extra amount of interest that is added to compensate the lender for lending to a risky borrower is called a risk premium. The United States government has never defaulted on a loan and the probability that it will do so in the future is extremely low. Thus, the interest rates on Treasury bills and bonds do not include a significant risk premium, and their interest rates are often cited as examples of risk-free interest rates. Other interest rates are higher because they include risk premiums. An example is the interest rate on corporate bonds, which tend to be higher than the interest rates on U.S. government bonds.

A second reason why interest rates on bonds might differ is the risk of interest rate fluctuations. These interest rate fluctuations change the price of long-term bonds more than short-term bonds. Because long-term bond prices fluctuate more than short-term bond prices, they are riskier. To compensate for this risk, long-term bonds tend to have higher interest rates than short-term bonds. For example, the interest rate on the 3-month Treasury bill is usually different from the interest rate on the 30-year Treasury bond, even though the default risks are the same.

The Yield Curve. While as a general proposition long-term bonds have higher interest rates than short-term bonds, this is not always the case. The relationship between the interest rates on long- and short-term bonds can be seen in the **yield curve**—a curve that shows the relationship between bonds' maturities and interest rates. Exhibit 9–6(a) shows a typical upward-sloping yield curve. The horizontal axis shows the term of the bond, and the vertical axis shows the interest rate. Notice that the yield curve is upward sloping. For example, the yield (or interest rate) on the 30-year bond is 5.6 percent, while the yield on the 3-month T-bill is 4.0 percent.

The yield curve can take many shapes, depending on inflation expectations. An increase in expected future inflation will tend to steepen the yield curve, and a decrease in expected inflation in the future will tend to flatten the yield curve. If inflation is expected to fall, the yield curve can become inverted; short-term securities will have higher interest rates than will long-term securities. Exhibit 9–6(b) shows an inverted yield curve. Alternatively, if the inflation rate is expected to rise in the future the upward slope of the yield curve will increase.

By focusing on one interest rate, the IS/LM model misses the fact that policy will not always have the same effect on the interest rates of different securities. The IS/LM model assumes that policy affects all interest rates similarly—that the slope

> The yield curve shows the relationship between bonds' maturities and interest rates.

Exhibit 9–6

Yield Curves

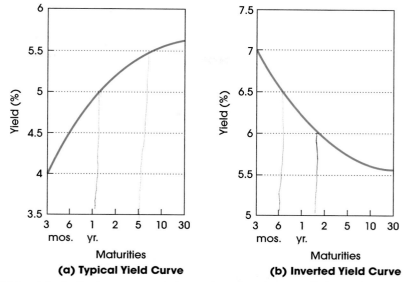

(a) Typical Yield Curve   (b) Inverted Yield Curve

The yield curve typically slopes upward—longer term bonds generally have higher yields than shorter term bills. However, occasionally, the yield curve inverts *(panel b)*, meaning that shorter term bills have higher yields than longer term bonds.

If monetary policy affects expectations of inflation, the long-run interest rate can respond differently than the short-run interest rate to monetary policy.

of the yield curve doesn't change. Given that assumption, when the Fed pushes up the fed funds rate, it also pushes up long-term interest rates. Often, that assumption doesn't hold. Say, for example, that the Fed runs contractionary monetary policy. In the IS/LM model, this will push up interest rates and slow the economy. The only interest rate it will definitely push up, however, is the short-term (fed funds) interest rate. If that contractionary monetary policy signals to investors that inflation will fall in the future, it could *push down* long-term interest rates, which are the ones that affect long-term investment decisions. In that case, the contractionary monetary policy could have expansionary effects.

Anticipation of Policy Problems. A second interpretation problem of the IS/LM model is that it does not take into account the effect of people's expectations of policy actions. For example, say that investors expect the Fed to increase the money supply some time in the next two months. Based on that expectation, investors will most likely expect interest rates to fall once the money supply is increased. An investor planning to buy a bond in the next month or two would rather buy it sooner while the price is low instead of waiting until later when the price will be higher (lower interest rates). So, the expectation of future monetary policy causes the demand for bonds to increase immediately. The increased demand for bonds causes the price of bonds to rise and the interest rate to fall *before* the policy action is taken. The interest rate can move just on the *anticipation* of Fed policy.

To make matters more confusing, expectations of future policy actions rarely (if ever) match Fed action. Say that the Fed increases the money supply by less than expected. People who purchased bonds in expectation of Fed action sell the bonds once their value doesn't rise as much as they thought. This will push the price of bonds down and the interest rate up. What we observe is that the interest rate *rises* after the Fed increases the money supply—the opposite of what the IS/LM model predicts.

Monetary Tools and Credit Condition Problems. A third interpretation problem of the IS/LM model comes from the economy's institutional structure. The IS/LM model assumes that investment depends on interest rates only, and it implicitly assumes that interest rates are the driving force in determining investment. In the real world, investment determination depends on other factors as well. One factor is credit conditions—the willingness of banks to lend, independent of the interest rate. Low interest rates do not necessarily mean that banks want to (or will) lend more money.

When making lending decisions, banks are primarily interested in the risk-adjusted spread—the difference between the rates at which they lend money and the rates at which they "borrow" money—adjusted for risk. That spread may not change with a change in interest rates, and may change even when interest rates remain constant. Moreover, banks sometimes vary their lending standards without varying the interest rate (see the Q&A feature on why banks sometimes change their lending standards instead of changing the interest rate). Banks want to lend to individuals who have alternative sources of funds and are most likely to repay loans. If banks increase the amount of collateral they require for lending, look more closely at business plans, value assets lower than they would have otherwise, or become more concerned about individuals' likelihood of repayment, they will decrease loans, even if the interest rate remains constant.

> Banks are interested in the risk-adjusted spread between their borrowing cost and their lending rate.

Changes in credit conditions can either augment or offset the effect of monetary policy. Either case makes the net effect of monetary policy unpredictable. It's like having brakes that sometimes grab—when they do, they can throw the economy into a spin. For example, in 1988, the Fed tightened monetary policy slightly and expected a modest slowing of economic output. At the same time, however, Federal Reserve Bank regulators began scrutinizing bank balance sheets more carefully in an attempt to avert the problems that had led to the savings-and-loan bailout earlier in the decade. As a result of increased scrutiny, banks raised their lending standards. The combination of these policies slowed the economy more than desired and, beginning in late 1989, the Fed reversed its policy and reduced the fed funds rate to get the economy going again.

The Fed continued to reduce rates into 1990, but the reduction in rates did not stimulate the economy much; the tight credit conditions overwhelmed the effects of expansionary monetary policy. Some businesses and households in the economy could not get loans at any interest rate. So, here we have a case in which banks did not increase lending, even to what would have been reasonable ventures. Contrary to what the IS/LM model would predict, even though interest rates were falling, bank lending was declining. The economy fell into recession.

The Interest Rate Target Problem. A fourth interpretation problem associated with monetary policy in the IS/LM model concerns the way monetary policy is implemented. In recent years, the Fed, and most other central banks around the world, target an interest rate rather than the money supply. The IS/LM model presented so far incorporates monetary policy with a change in the money supply. A change in the money supply shifts the LM curve and causes interest rates to move along the IS curve. Currently, when policy makers talk about changing monetary policy in the real world, they talk about changing interest rates—not the money supply. The policy emphasis is on interest rates—not on monetary aggregates.

> Currently, monetary policy generally targets an interest rate rather than the money supply.

If we think of monetary policy as choosing an interest rate rather than changing the money supply, we need to incorporate the monetary policy rule into the LM

QUESTION   Why don't banks raise interest rates instead of tightening lending standards when the Fed contracts the money supply?

ANSWER   Raising interest rates may attract high-risk borrowers.

If banks are nervous about loan repayment when the Fed contracts the money supply, why don't they just raise the interest rate they charge on loans enough to compensate them for increased risk and let the demanders of those loans decide on how much money they want to borrow at that new higher rate? The reason banks don't do this has to do with a phenomenon called adverse selection.

To explain adverse selection, let's begin by reviewing the role that banks play in the economy. Banks do more than simply take the money you deposit in your account and loan it to the next person who walks through the door; they screen and evaluate borrowers. In fact, banks specialize in evaluating the information necessary to decide who gets a loan and who does not. Is the loan going to be used to buy lottery tickets, a car, or a great investment project? Does the borrower have a steady income? Has the borrower paid back loans in the past? These are all questions (except about the lottery tickets) the banks generally ask a borrower before deciding whether to make a loan.

Adverse selection occurs when poor-quality products are overrepresented in markets, because buyers and sellers cannot directly observe the quality of the product. Take the used-car market, for example. You cannot tell whether a used car is a "lemon" just by looking at it, but used cars are more likely to be lemons than are new cars because people tend to want to get rid of lemons. So, a greater proportion of used cars being offered for sale are lemons than are new cars.

What does this have to do with banking? When banks issue loans, they are not 100 percent sure of the borrower's ability to pay back the loan. They can require all sorts of information from borrowers, but the future remains unknown. There is no guarantee that the borrower will repay the loan. There are always risks associated with lending. Sometimes, even when banks have screened applicants very carefully, borrowers still default on their loans.

Now think about the pool of borrowers that remain when the bank raises its interest rate. The people who apply for loans at higher interest rates are more likely to be high-risk borrowers (people who are accustomed to paying a risk premium). These are people who are less likely to pay back their loans and perhaps couldn't get a loan at a lower rate because they are high-risk borrowers. Higher rates of interest not only increase the risk of default because interest payments are higher, but also discourage those with good credit from taking out loans.

In other words, at the higher interest rate, the market will adversely select the high-risk borrowers. More "lemons" will apply for loans. And more loans will go sour. Banks, therefore, may want to keep interest rates at a moderate level and tighten the requirements for getting a loan (higher income, larger down payment). Adverse selection is one reason why the rise in the interest rate potentially understates the effect of contractionary monetary policy. Banks may raise rates slightly but reduce the number of loans they make, to avoid the adverse selection problem.

An effective LM curve is the LM curve that exists when the money supply is determined by a monetary policy rule.

curve. That is, the money supply is determined by the interest rate rule within the model. This changes our derivation of the LM curve, which was based on the assumption that the money supply was fixed. Instead of an upward-sloping LM curve, we now have a flat curve, which might be called an effective LM curve. The effective LM curve does not have a fixed money supply underlying it. Instead it has a money supply that follows a prespecified policy rule. Therefore, an **effective LM curve** is the LM curve that exists when the money supply is determined by a monetary policy rule. The difference between the two LM curves is the following: Any change in the money supply shifts the standard LM curve; only those changes in the money supply that deviate from the policy rule shift the effective LM curve. (Technically, the effective LM curve is a locus of points on a shifting LM curve.)

Exhibit 9–7

**An Effective
LM Curve That
Is Horizontal**

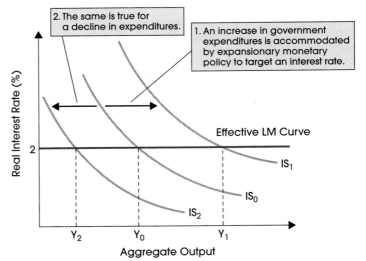

This exhibit demonstrates a Fed policy rule of targeting the interest rate. To keep the interest rate at its target, the Fed offsets the effect of any shifts in the IS curve on the interest rate with accommodating monetary policy. The Fed essentially maintains an effective LM curve that is horizontal at the targeted interest rate.

When the Fed targets an interest rate, the effective LM curve is horizontal at the chosen interest rate. For example, suppose the Fed has chosen a real fed funds rate of 2 percent for its target, as Exhibit 9–7 shows. At that 2 percent interest rate, the Fed will offset the effect of any shifts in the IS curve on the interest rate by using accommodative monetary policy. If output is at Y_0 and autonomous expenditures increase, pushing the IS curve right and increasing money demand, the Fed will increase the supply of money to keep the interest rate at 2 percent, and output will rise to Y_1. If autonomous expenditures fall, pushing the IS curve left and decreasing the demand for money, the Fed will decrease the money supply so that the interest rate remains at 2 percent, and output will fall to Y_2. By accommodating shifts in the IS curve, the Fed is essentially maintaining an effective LM curve that is horizontal at the targeted interest rate.

When the effective LM curve is horizontal, contractionary and expansionary monetary policies are represented as shifts up or down in the targeted interest rate. For example, to implement contractionary monetary policy, the Fed will raise the fed funds target, pushing the effective LM curve upward. To run expansionary monetary policy, the Fed will decrease the fed funds rate target, pushing the effective LM curve downward.

The Budget Problem: Cyclical and Structural Budgets. The problems associated with interpreting the IS/LM model for the real world are not limited only to monetary policy and interest rates. There are also interpretation problems with fiscal policy. To talk about shifting the IS curve with fiscal policy, we have to talk about the surplus or deficit of the federal government budget. If the government is running a deficit, fiscal policy is expansionary; if it is running a surplus, fiscal policy is contractionary. The reality is not that clear-cut, creating a number of problems when we try to relate the IS curve to discussions of policy in the real world.

The first problem is that the deficits and surpluses not only influence the economy, but also are determined by the state of the economy. As the economy expands,

Fiscal policy is usually discussed in terms of the budget deficit or surplus, but there are many different types of budgets.

Deficits and surpluses not only influence the economy, but also are determined *by* the economy.

Exhibit 9-8

Structural and Cyclical Deficits and Surpluses

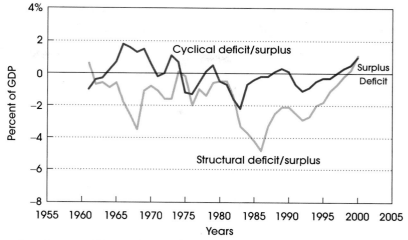

Deficits and surpluses are determined by both policy and the state of the economy. The portion due to the state of the economy is known as the cyclical deficit or surplus. The structural deficit or surplus is the budget balance that would exist if the economy were at potential. Source: The Congressional Budget Office (www.cbo.gov).

income rises and tax revenues rise, causing the budget deficit to decrease (or the surplus to increase) automatically. So, to determine whether fiscal policy is expansionary or contractionary, we must have a measure that removes the automatic changes in spending and taxes.

To separate the effects of these automatic changes on the budget balance from the effect of policy on the budget balance, economists have developed two terms— the *structural budget surplus or deficit* and the *cyclical budget surplus or deficit.* The **structural budget surplus or deficit** is the fiscal budget balance that would exist when the economy is at potential output. The **cyclical budget surplus or deficit** is that portion of the fiscal budget balance that exists because output is above or below potential output. When the economy is operating below potential, the cyclical deficit balance pulls the entire budget toward deficit. When the economy is operating above potential, the cyclical budget surplus pulls the entire budget toward surplus. The actual budget balance is the sum of the structural balance and the cyclical balance.

The U.S. structural and cyclical budget surpluses and deficits as a percent of GDP are shown in Exhibit 9–8. During the recessions of 1974, 1981, and 1991, the cyclical budget balance was in deficit. There has been a cyclical budget surplus since 1996, but there had been a structural deficit from 1962 until 1998; in 1999 the structural budget deficit turned to a surplus.

The difference between the actual budget balance (the difference between tax revenue and expenditure) and the structural deficit widened during the late 1990s as the economy grew beyond economists' estimates of potential output. For example, in 1998, the actual budget surplus was $69 billion. Because the economy was thought to be operating above potential, tax revenues were higher and expenditures were lower by a combined $87 billion than what they would have been if the economy had been at its potential output. That means that the economy was running an $18 billion structural deficit (69 − 87 = −18). The cyclical surplus was the $87 billion caused by the economy being above potential. Adding the cyclical surplus (87) to the structural deficit (−18) gives us the actual $69 billion surplus.

To make sure you understand, let's consider another numerical example. Suppose that the actual deficit is $50 billion, and that the deficit falls by $20 billion for every percentage point increase in output. Also, suppose that output is 2 percentage points below potential. At potential output, revenue would be $40 billion higher, so the structural deficit of the economy is $10 billion (50 − 40) and the cyclical portion of the deficit is $40 billion. Adding the structural component of 10 and the cyclical component of 40, we get the actual deficit of $50 billion.

Movements in the structural budget balance, not the actual budget balance, are what are represented by shifts in the IS curve. Structural budget changes show policy changes, while cyclical budget changes reflect economic conditions and are incorporated in the shape of the IS curve. An increase in the structural budget balance shifts the IS curve in to the left. A decrease in the structural budget balance shifts the IS curve out to the right.

The Budget Problem: Accounting Methods. A second problem with interpreting surpluses and deficits as a measure of fiscal policy is that surpluses and deficits depend on the accounting methods used to determine the U.S. government budget, and the chosen method may not capture the effect fiscal policy is having on the economy. To understand this, it is important to know a little about the accounting that goes into calculating the budget balance. The budget balance shows the difference between tax revenue and government expenditures. In accounting terms, the U.S. reports its budget in large part as a **cash-flow budget**—a budget based on an accounting system in which revenues and expenses are counted only when cash is received and spent.

Problems with the Cash-Flow Budget. A cash-flow budget can be misleading at times. To see why, let's consider a hypothetical example. Suppose you earn $24,000 and spend $21,600. Suppose also that you promised your boss you'd work during the next year an extra 5 hours a week for nothing, helping him build a house. (That's the only way he would give you the job.) Using a cash-flow accounting system, you have a surplus of $2,400 this year, because you do not include the future obligation to work. Cash-flow accounting, however, does not accurately capture your financial situation. Assuming you value your time at $15 per hour, you have an additional obligation of $3,750 for the extra 5 hours per week (assuming you work 50 weeks a year), so, from an economist's point of view, you have a deficit of $1,350.

We point out this issue because, each year, the government incurs significant future obligations, but those obligations are not considered part of the budget. For example, in the late 1990s, the U.S. budget was in surplus, in large part because current Social Security taxes were significantly above current Social Security expenditures. The excess was placed in a Social Security trust fund, but nonetheless boosted the budget balance (the taxes are part of total government revenue). At this same time, obligations for Social Security and Medicare, which represent future obligations to the recipients of those retirement benefits, grew. In other words, the government was already obligated to pay out much of the current revenue as future retirement benefits.

A budget that includes the expected value of future expenditures and revenues is called an **obligation budget.** If future obligations exceed future trust fund accumulations, the obligation budget balance is lower than the cash-flow budget balance. If, alternatively, future trust fund accumulations exceed future obligations, the obligation budget is higher than the cash-flow budget.

Whether the obligations budget or the cash-flow budget is more appropriate for considering the fiscal impact of the deficit depends on whether people base their spending on their cash income (in which case, the cash flow budget is appropriate) or on their lifetime income (in which case, the obligations budget is more appropriate).

Ricardian Equivalence. Some economists argue that the trust fund and the obligations that it represents in large part offset each other and should be totally removed from the budget calculation when using the "budget balance" figure. In fact, they argue that deficits don't change total spending at all. This argument is called the Ricardian equivalence theory, named for David Ricardo, an early nineteenth-century British economist. In its strictest interpretation, **Ricardian equivalence** states that financing government spending by borrowing has the same impact on consumption and aggregate output as does financing spending by increasing taxes.

> Ricardian equivalence states that, because individuals fully anticipate future tax payments, financing government spending by borrowing has the same impact on consumption and aggregate output as does financing spending by increasing taxes.

Underlying Ricardian equivalence is the assumption that people make their consumption decisions based on lifetime income. If the government decides to cut taxes and doesn't change spending, the cash-flow budget balance would fall and the government would have to borrow to make up for the shortfall in revenue. Ricardian equivalence states that the effect of a decrease in government taxes on disposable income today will be offset by an equal rise in future taxes, so that their lifetime income will not change. People will save the increase in disposable income resulting from the decrease in taxes today to pay for taxes later—taxes that will repay the larger government debt. Whether the government changes the budget balance by increasing or decreasing taxes, Ricardian equivalence states the effect will always be offset by consumers who expect a reduction or increase in their future taxes, and hence their disposable income.

Suppose, for example, that Congress decides to cut taxes while holding spending constant. To the keep spending constant with less tax revenue, the government must incur more debt. According to the standard IS/LM model, a cut in taxes will cause consumption expenditures and output to increase in the short run. According to the Ricardian equivalence proposition, the tax cut will not cause consumption or output to rise, because people will save the tax cut to pay for future tax obligations that result from the increase in the debt.

Only a small number of economists believe that Ricardian equivalence holds perfectly and that changes in the budget balance caused by changes in taxes have no effect on consumption or output. Most economists find it hard to believe that people perceive the exact future tax obligation of current government debt. But most economists also believe that Ricardian equivalence does play some role in people's decisionmaking.

In the IS/LM model, if Ricardian equivalence is true, changes in taxes will not shift the IS curve. If it is not true, changes in taxes will shift the IS curve, and if it is partly true, then changes in taxes will shift the IS curve but by less than the multiplier suggests. The bottom line is that Ricardian equivalence makes the effect of tax changes (fiscal policy) on the IS curve and on the economy uncertain because it is nearly impossible to measure how people change their views of future tax obligations in response to changes in current taxes.

Using IS/LM in the Real World: Summarizing the Interpretation Problem. As you can see, using the IS/LM to analyze the real world has its problems. Monetary policy affects not just one interest rate; it affects many interest rates. Monetary policy is often implemented in terms of policy rules, which contradicts the assumption that the money supply is exogenous. The IS/LM model also does not take into account the fact that monetary policy affects bank lending in the economy independent of the interest rate.

There are also problems interpreting fiscal policy. First, economists generally use the budget balance as a guide to the direction of fiscal policy. Which budget balance to use is unclear. The budget balance is the result of accounting rules that might not show the effect of the budget on the economy. Economists disagree about which accounting rules best show the effect of the budget on the economy. Second, the budget balance not only affects the economy, but also is affected *by* the economy. We separate the budget balance in two—a cyclical component and a structural component—and use the structural component as a measure of the direction of fiscal policy.

Executive Summary

- Monetary policy is difficult to measure for three reasons: (1) The interest rate in the IS/LM model does not capture the effect of monetary policy on all the interest rates in the economy, (2) expectations of future policy actions affect interest rates and (3) changes in an economy's credit conditions can affect the level of investment expenditures independent of the interest rate.

- Most central banks, including the Federal Reserve, target an interest rate which means the effective LM curve is horizontal at the targeted interest rate.

- Measuring fiscal policy using the reported budget balance is problematic for three reasons: (1) The budget balance is affected not only by policy, but also by the state of the economy; (2) the budget balance measure depends on the accounting method used and it is unclear what that method is; (3) financing government spending by borrowing may have the same impact on consumption and output as does financing spending with taxes.

Implementation Problems of Monetary and Fiscal Policy

Even if policy makers can solve the interpretation problems of the IS/LM model, there remain severe problems with implementing policies recommended by the model. Implementing fiscal and monetary policies is not as easy as shifting the IS or LM curves. It is often difficult to know where the economy is relative to potential output, because potential output is difficult to measure and because data on the current state of the economy are imprecise and available only after a time lag. Put simply: It is difficult to implement policy quickly—it takes time to formulate and enact the policy. We now briefly discuss these uncertainties and lags.

Uncertainty About Potential Output. One macroeconomic policy goal is smooth growth of output. In other words, keep output as close to potential output as possible. In reality, economists and policy makers are never quite sure where potential output is and whether the economy is above or below it. For example, during the last half of the 1990s and into 2000, the economy expanded rapidly. Most economists and policy makers believed that the economy had expanded well beyond potential output. However, the usual warning sign of an economy above potential—increasing inflation—failed to appear, so they kept raising their estimates.

Such uncertainty makes it difficult to implement policies in the real world. It also increases the possibility that policy makers will make costly mistakes by using contractionary policy when the economy is below potential, creating too much

Because there is enormous uncertainty about where potential income is, the appropriate monetary and fiscal policy is often unclear.

unemployment, or using expansionary policy when the economy is above potential, creating too much inflation.

Information Lag. The IS/LM model assumes that Congress, the President, and the Federal Reserve see what is happening in the economy and instantly alter their policies to fix any problem. In the real world, it takes time to recognize what is happening. There is an **information lag**—a delay between a change in the economy and knowledge of that change in the economy.

The government tries to collect as much timely and accurate economic information as it can, but such information is difficult to collect and disseminate quickly. The Department of Commerce reports quarterly GDP a full month after the quarter has ended, and it then revises its report several times as more information about the economy becomes available.

Implementing monetary and fiscal policies requires knowing where the economy is relative to potential output and knowing what policy to use. The Fed collects anecdotal evidence on the state of the economy every six weeks, and other reports come out monthly, but those numbers must be pieced together into a "big picture." In 1990, for example, it wasn't clear that the economy was in a recession until it was almost out of it. Some political analysts believe that policy makers didn't act quickly enough, and that failure to act cost then President Bush (father of George W. Bush) his re-election.

> Data become available only with a lag, and, thus, we often don't know precisely what is currently going on in the economy.

Policy Implementation Lag. The IS/LM model assumes that policy takes effect immediately. The reality is quite different. Once information about the economy becomes available, the policy has to be formulated and implemented. In the case of fiscal policy, there is a large **implementation lag**—a delay between the time policy makers recognize the need for a policy action and when they can institute that policy. Congress and the President need to formulate legislation, debate it, amend it, and pass it. This process can take months or even years. In the meantime, the economy may have changed completely.

The Kennedy-Johnson tax cut of 1963 is a classic example. In April 1960, the economy entered a recession. In January 1961, President Kennedy took office. He proposed cutting taxes to stimulate aggregate demand to bring the economy out of the recession. After working its way through Congress, legislation that called for an $11.5 billion tax cut was finally passed three years later, in 1963. (That $11.5 billion is equivalent to roughly $150 billion in today's dollars, or 2 percent of GDP.) The tax cut stimulated consumer spending and aggregate output, just as our IS/LM model predicts, but it was too much too late. By 1963, the economy had come out of the recession on its own and was believed by almost all economists to be at or above the potential level of output. The tax cut served only to exacerbate inflationary pressures. This experience points out a major problem with using fiscal policy to stabilize the economy. By the time an economic problem is identified, policy is formulated, and legislation is passed, the economy is likely to have changed.

> Fiscal policy has a long implementation lag.

Monetary policy makers also face information lags as well as uncertainties about the effect of their policies and the level of potential output. However, monetary policy can be implemented quicker than fiscal policy. The Federal Open Market Committee (FOMC), the policymaking body of the Fed, meets every 6 weeks to decide on monetary policy. The FOMC's policy decisions are implemented immediately by the Federal Reserve Bank of New York. Moreover, the chairman of the Board

> Monetary policy has a shorter implementation lag and is the primary policy government uses to influence the economy.

of Governors can consult with the other members of the board between regularly scheduled meetings to make changes in policy if needed. That's what happened in early 2001. The Fed cut interest rates weeks before its next meeting in response to data indicating a slowing economy. Because of the shorter implementation lag and the fact that fiscal policy has focused mainly on deficit reduction since the late 1980s, monetary policy has taken over as the main policy tool for offsetting shocks to the U.S. economy.

How Policy Makers Deal with the Interpretation and Implementation Problems

Interpretation and implementation problems make it difficult for policy makers to precisely forecast the effect of their policies on the economy. To cope with this, policy makers do not try to "fine-tune" the economy by responding to every small change in output. Instead, they try to steer the economy in a generally desirable direction. Discretionary fiscal policy is reserved for major recessions or superheated booms.

Even though the United States seldom uses discretionary fiscal policy, fiscal policy still influences the economy through what are called *automatic stabilizers*. **Automatic stabilizers** are programs that are built into the budget that change expenditures or revenue countercyclically without new legislative action. Table 9–3 lists examples of U.S. government programs that are automatic stabilizers. They are responsible for much of the cyclical portion of the deficit.

Let's consider how two automatic stabilizers—unemployment insurance and income taxes—work. When the economy falls into a recession, government spending on unemployment insurance increases, which provides income for unemployed individuals and keeps them spending. Alternatively, when the economy expands, income tax revenues increase, which gives individuals less money than they otherwise would have and slows the expansion. Neither of these programs requires discretionary action by government. They operate automatically.

The fact that discretionary fiscal policy has been used in U.S. history, and continues to be used in countries with prolonged recessions, keeps alive the *expectation* that government would use fiscal policy in an emergency. This expectation can help stabilize the economy. For example, if firms think the government will step in to

> Automatic stabilizers are programs that are built into the budget that change expenditures or revenue countercyclically without new legislative action.

Table 9–3

Examples of Automatic Stabilizers

Unemployment insurance	When output falls and more people become unemployed, transfer payments to individuals, and, therefore, government expenditures, automatically rise.
Temporary Assistance for Needy Families (TANF), food stamps, and Medicaid	When income falls, more people become eligible for these welfare payments. Transfer payments to individuals, and, therefore, government expenditures, automatically rise.
Progressive income tax system	When income rises, more income is taxed at higher marginal tax rates. The opposite occurs when income falls. This dampens fluctuations in consumption.

increase demand, they will not cut production when demand falls because they will expect demand to rebound. In that case, the expectation of the policy has done the work, and the policy is not needed.

Monetary policy has fewer implementation problems than does fiscal policy, but it has them nonetheless. A key problem is the effect of monetary policy on expected inflation. Here's the problem: If expansionary monetary policy causes expectations of inflation to rise, monetary policy will have less impact on real output. Part of the effect of monetary policy will be to increase the price level. So, the Fed and other central banks work hard to convince individuals that monetary policy will not be inflationary. One way they do this is by setting monetary policy according to rules (predetermined responses), rather than by discretion (responses based on judgment) or the current situation.

Central banks can have monetary rules that are explicitly stated or rules that are implicit in their actions. The European Central Bank has an explicit rule in its charter that it will fight inflation and only inflation, although it doesn't specify how it will fight it. Over the past decade, central banks around the world (including the Fed) moved closer to establishing explicit rules by stating their policy goals and their strategies to achieve those goals. For example, the Reserve Bank of New Zealand, by law, must attempt to keep CPI inflation between 0 and 2 percent a year. The Reserve Bank has discretion over how to achieve that goal, but it must explain its strategies to the government when the CPI rises above that range. Establishing rules helps central banks manage the impact of expectations on the effectiveness of monetary policy.

The U.S. Fed does not have an explicit rule committing it to fighting only inflation, but Fed officials state publicly that the Fed's main objective is to fight inflation. They seem to be following an implicit rule that the Fed will change monetary policy inversely with inflation. (When inflation rises, it will contract the money supply and vice versa.) Most economists and businesspeople, therefore, believe that the Fed will increase its interest rate target when inflation rises, and the greater the inflation, the higher it will raise its interest rate target. If the policy rule convinces people that the central bank will not allow inflation to rise, expectations of inflation will not change. (We will discuss monetary policy rules further in Chapter 13.)

THE POWER OF IS/LM

The preceding discussion should have convinced you that just because you understand IS/LM analysis, you do not necessarily understand the workings of short-run policy. Don't, however, let that discourage you about the model's usefulness. There's a positive side: If you have followed IS/LM analysis, you have made a major step toward understanding the macroeconomy. For example, consider what two Nobel Prize winners, James Tobin and Robert Solow, have to say about the IS/LM model.

James Tobin has said, "I do not think the apparatus (IS/LM) is discredited. I still believe that carefully used and taught, it is a powerful instrument for understanding our economies and the impacts of policies upon them." Robert Solow concurs and argues that IS/LM is useful in "training our intuition, to give us a handle on the facts." Solow argues that the IS/LM model has survived because it has proven to be a marvelously simple and useful way to organize and process some of the main macroeconomic facts.

We agree with both Solow and Tobin, which is why IS/LM has been given a central role in this book: Used imaginatively, by individuals who recognize it for what it is—a first step—the IS/LM model is an enormously powerful tool for understanding short-run movements in the economy. On the other hand, we also agree with the critics—if IS/LM is used mechanically, as a model of what actually happens in the world, it can be more harmful than helpful.

The analogy of learning to play the piano may make the argument clearer. You don't play Beethoven's *Moonlight Sonata* when beginning piano; you first learn scales—and you play *Chopsticks* again and again. When you have fully mastered one skill, you move up, and you keep moving up. It's the same thing when learning economics. As an exercise, IS/LM analysis is superb, as long as you remember that it is *Chopsticks,* not *Moonlight Sonata.*

In the final analysis, the economy is far more complicated than any two-dimensional graph. But you have to start somewhere, and IS/LM is a good place to start. If you understand the analytics of IS/LM—what gives the curves the shapes they have, and what shifts the curves—then you have the thought process for analyzing the short-run economy. It is this thought process, not the knowledge of the IS/LM model's conclusions, that is economic thinking.

Despite its problems, the IS/LM model is useful; it provides the framework within which economists and policy makers view policy.

Executive Summary

- Three implementation problems of monetary and fiscal policies are (1) uncertainty about potential output, (2) delayed and incomplete information about the state of the economy, and (3) the time it takes legislators to enact laws.
- Fiscal policy has a large implementation lag. Monetary policy has a short implementation lag.
- Automatic stablizers change government expenditures and taxes without new legislative action.
- Policy rules that affect expectations can stabilize an economy without any action.
- The IS/LM model is a first step in understanding short-run movements in economic output.

POLICY PERSPECTIVE: UNCERTAINTY AND POLICY IN THE 1990S

Let's return to our discussion of U.S. monetary policy in the late 1990s and early 2000s and see what the IS/LM model tells us, now that we've presented the limitations of applying the model to the real world. In the mid-1990s, the U.S. economy experienced increased growth and falling interest rates. Fiscal policy looked contractionary, but that contractionary effect was offset by a significant increase in investment and consumer spending, which was caused by the rise in the stock market. Monetary policy makers faced a dilemma. Should the Fed follow expansionary policy to offset the effects of contractionary fiscal policy, or should it use contractionary policy to slow the economy? The debate centered around potential output. How close was the economy to its potential?

Here's what people knew. In 1996, the economy grew by 3.6 percent, rising at an annual rate of 4.6 percent during the final quarter of 1996. Indications were that it was continuing to grow at this fast pace going into 1997. The Dow Jones Industrial Average was over 6,000 at the end of 1996, having doubled in 4 years. Because the Fed thought the economy was above potential and because it thought that inflationary pressures were building, in March 1997, it tightened monetary policy, raising the fed funds rate by one-quarter percentage point. Despite this rise, the economy kept growing at a fast pace throughout 1997. Moreover, contrary to economists' predictions, the inflation rate fell.

As the Fed waited for inflation to arrive, other problems arose. The financial crisis that began in Asia in late 1997 appeared to be spreading to Latin America and Russia. In late summer of 1998, Russia was forced to devalue the ruble, and prices on the U.S. stock market fell. These events caused a financial investment firm, Long-Term Capital Management, to lose $120 billion during the second half of 1998. This huge financial loss threatened to send prices in the fragile world financial market into a tailspin. In response, the Fed switched its policy focus from inflation fighting to fighting a possible recession. Specifically, the Fed arranged a private bailout of Long-Term Capital Management and reduced the fed funds rate by one-half percentage point in October 1998. Why did it do this? The Fed feared that the domestic and foreign financial turmoil would lead to a contraction of bank lending, further slowing the economy.

By the summer of 1999, fears of a global depression had disappeared, and some of the economies hardest hit by the financial crisis of 1997 began to show signs of recovery. The U.S. economy continued to grow—by over 4 percent during the first quarter of 1999. Again fearing inflation, the Fed raised the fed funds rate one-quarter percentage point, tightening monetary policy in the summer of 1999. It continued to raise interest rates through 2000. Despite these increases, the economic expansion continued, but inflation remained low. More and more economists came to believe that the old speed limits of economic growth no longer applied.

This story illustrates the uncertainty surrounding policy. Uncertainty about potential output, uncertainty about the effect of the global economic slowdown on the U.S. economy, and uncertainty about the effect of its own monetary polices caused the Fed to reverse policies twice in the course of 3 years.

Monetary policy at the end of the 1990s and early 2000s was judged a success. The economy grew rapidly, with low inflation. But the truth be told, it is impossible to tell whether that growth was due to good luck or to good policy.

CONCLUSION

> The IS/LM model is useful as long as it is used with care—as an interpretative, not a mechanical, model.

In Chapter 8, you learned the mechanics of the IS/LM model. In this chapter, you learned about the difficulties of applying the IS/LM model in the real world. The bottom line is this: For many macroeconomic discussions, the IS/LM model is extremely useful for understanding the basics of what is happening in the economy in the short run. But it is only useful if it is used with care—as an interpretative, not a mechanical, model.

Often, the predictions of the mechanical IS/LM model do not fit the real world, but with an understanding of the interpretation and implementation problems, the IS/LM model still provides an excellent framework for understanding policy. The next chapter adds a complication to the IS/LM model—the foreign sector of the economy. In Chapter 10, you will see how the IS/LM model helps organize our thinking about international issues.

- The effectiveness of monetary and fiscal policy depends on the slopes of the IS and LM curves.
- When investment demand is very sensitive to the interest rate or when money demand is not sensitive to the interest rate, there is perfect crowding out, and fiscal policy is ineffective.
- When investment demand is not sensitive to the interest rate or money demand is very sensitive to the interest rate (the liquidity trap case), monetary policy is ineffective.
- Policy makers can achieve various interest rate and income goals by using fiscal and monetary policies.
- Policy makers used expansionary monetary and fiscal policy to increase output and keep interest rates low during the 1940s. Policy makers used contractionary monetary policy to lower inflation during the 1950s. Policy makers used expansionary fiscal policy and contractionary monetary policy during the early 1980s.
- Four interpretation problems with monetary policy are (1) there are many interest rates in the economy, (2) people's expectations of policies affect interest rates, (3) credit conditions also affect expenditures, and (4) the central bank targets interest rates making the effective LM curve horizontal.
- The Fed directly affects short-term interest rates. Investment decisions depend on long-term rates. The yield curve describes the relationship between short-term and long-term interest rates. The rates of short and long-term securities differ from each other because of risk and expected inflation.
- The Fed affects output not only through the effects of interest rates on borrowing decisions, but also by affecting credit conditions in the economy. Looking only at changes in interest rates may understate the effect of Fed policy on investment.
- An increase in the government budget deficit may be due to factors other than a change in policy. It could be due to a change in the economy or a change in accounting procedures.
- Because government reports the budget on a cash-flow basis, it misses future obligations that may impact current consumer expenditures.
- An obligations budget includes future spending government has promised. Ricardian equivalence supports a focus on the obligations budget as an accurate picture of fiscal policy.
- In the real world, information lags, implementation lags, and uncertainty about potential output make implementing aggregate demand management policies difficult.
- Automatic stabilizers help counteract business cycles without new legislative action.
- It is important to consider anticipations of policy when using the IS/LM model to analyze real-world policy changes. In the 1990s, central banks established policy rules, such as stating numerical inflation targets, to help manage the effect of expectations on policy.

accommodative monetary policy 250
automatic stabilizers 264
cash-flow budget 260
cyclical budget surplus or deficit 259

default risk 254
effective LM curve 257
implementation lag 263
information lag 263
liquidity trap 247

obligation budget 260
Ricardian equivalence 261
structural budget surplus or deficit 259
yield curve 254

1. In the IS/LM model, why wouldn't an increase in autonomous expenditures cause output to rise by the full multiplier times the change in expenditures?
2. Under what conditions will fiscal policy have no effect on output in the IS/LM model?
3. What is a liquidity trap? Under what conditions will one exist?
4. Why does an increase in the money supply reduce interest rates, and an increase in government spending increase interest rates?

5. Policy makers want to increase equilibrium output without increasing interest rates. What policy or combination of policies would you recommend?

6. Policy makers want to lower interest rates but keep equilibrium output the same. What policy or combination of policies would you recommend?

7. What monetary policy would the Fed use to accommodate an increase in government spending? Describe a real-world example of when the Fed used this type of policy.

8. What monetary policy would the Fed use to offset the effect of an increase in government spending on output? Describe a real-world example of when the Fed used this type of policy.

9. What are the two reasons why interest rates on bonds of different maturities usually differ?

10. What is the yield curve? Name one reason why the yield curve could be inverted.

11. Why is the Fed concerned about how its policies affect the yield curve?

12. How can an increase in the money supply lead to an increase in interest rates and still be consistent with the predictions of the IS/LM model?

13. Why might contractionary monetary policy reduce investment spending by more than would be suggested by the resulting rise in interest rates?

14. What is the effective LM curve, and under what assumptions about the conduct of monetary policy is it the relevant curve to use in the IS/LM model?

What is the shape of the effective LM curve when there is an interest rate target?

15. Why does the government's budget balance automatically change with the level of economic activity?

16. In what way might the reported budget deficit or surplus be a misleading guide to whether fiscal policy is expansionary or contractionary?

17. What is the difference between the structural deficit and cyclical deficit?

18. What is the difference between a cash flow budget and an obligation budget? What kind of budget is the U.S. government budget?

19. Why does Ricardian equivalence imply that a tax cut will not affect the economy?

20. What are the three main implementation problems associated with using fiscal and monetary policy to manage aggregate demand?

21. How does uncertainty about potential output affect the ability of policy makers to implement policy?

22. How do automatic stabilizers help to overcome the implementation lag associated with fiscal policy?

23. Which has a longer implementation lag, monetary or fiscal policy? Why?

24. Defend the following: The IS/LM model is a useful tool for analyzing the real world despite the problems associated with interpreting and implementing its policy recommendations.

25. How did uncertainty about potential output affect Fed policy in the last half of the 1990s?

PROBLEMS AND EXERCISES

1. Congratulations! You have just been appointed head of the Council of Economic Advisers in Funlandia. Demonstrate, graphically, the policy or policies you would recommend to your president in each of the following situations.
   a. The economy is below potential and interest rates are high. The president would like to bring the economy back to potential and lower interest rates.
   b. The economy is above potential, but interest rates are just right. The president would like to bring the economy back to potential but keep interest rates the same.
   c. The economy is at potential, but interest rates are high. The president would like to keep the economy at potential but lower the interest rate.
   d. Now that you have shown the president how she can manage aggregate demand on paper by shifting the IS and LM curves, explain to her why conducting policy in the real world is not so easy.

2. Suppose the economy is currently below potential output. What type of policy would you recommend to bring it back to potential output in each of the following cases? Demonstrate your answers graphically.
   a. The demand for money is completely insensitive to interest rate changes (does not respond at all to changes in the interest rate).
   b. The demand for money is infinitely responsive (extremely responsive) to changes in the interest rate.

3. Suppose it is an election year and the President and Congress have just passed a big spending bill to boost the economy and increase their chances of re-election.
   a. What policy action would the Fed take to offset the effect of this policy on output? Demonstrate your answer graphically.
   b. Now suppose the country goes to war and government spending rises even more. What policy action

would the Fed take to accommodate this fiscal policy? Demonstrate your answer graphically.

4. Suppose the budget surplus rises by $10 billion for every percentage-point rise in output. Calculate the structural and cyclical budget surplus or deficit in each of the following situations.

a. The economy is currently 2 percentage points above potential and the budget deficit is $20 billion.

b. The economy is currently 4 percentage points below potential and the budget deficit is $30 billion.

c. The economy is at potential output, with a $10 billion surplus.

5. In November 1999, the European Central Bank (ECB) contracted the money supply to raise interest rates. Short-term interest rates rose in reaction to this policy action, but long-term interest rates fell. Draw the yield curve before and after the ECB's policy change and explain why long-term and short-term interest rates reacted differently to the decrease in the money supply.

6. Use the IS/LM model to demonstrate what happens when taxes are cut in each of the following situations:

a. The Ricardian equivalence does not hold.

b. The Ricardian equivalence holds.

7. Use the IS/LM diagram to describe U.S. fiscal and monetary policies during the 1990s.

The Complete Algebraic Fixed-Price Model

In Appendix B of Chapter 8 we presented the algebra of the IS and LM curves. In this appendix we put those two curves together to determine the equilibrium values of real income and the real interest rate algebraically.

From Chapter 8, Appendix B, the equation for the IS curve is

$$Y = \left(\frac{1}{1 - mpc(1 - t) + m}\right)$$
$$(C_0 + I_0 - dr + G_0 - mpcT_0 + X_0 - M_0) \quad (9A\text{-}1)$$

and the equation for the LM curve is

$$Y = M_0^s/k + hr/k - j_0/k \quad (9A\text{-}2)$$

Our goal is to solve equations (9-A1) and (9-A2) for the equilibrium values of real income, Y, and the real interest rate, r, given all the components that make up the IS and LM curves. The algebra gets pretty complicated, so before we solve these equations, we will group some of the terms together. First, let's define an autonomous spending variable, A_0, to equal all autonomous spending:

$$A_0 = C_0 + I_0 + G_0 - mpcT_0 + X_0 - M_0$$

When any component of autonomous spending rises (or autonomous taxes fall), A_0 rises. When any component of autonomous spending falls (or autonomous taxes rise), A_0 falls.

Next, we define a multiplier z:

$$z = \frac{1}{1 - mpc(1 - t) + m}$$

Using these simpler terms, we can rewrite equation (9A-1) as

$$Y = zA_0 - dzr \quad (9A\text{-}3)$$

Solving Equation 9A-3 for r gives us

$$r = A_0/d - Y/dz \quad (9A\text{-}4)$$

Now we substitute this formula for r from the IS equation into Equation 9A-2, the equation for LM:

$$Y = M_0^s/k + (h/k)(A_0/d - Y/dz) - j_0/k$$

To solve for Y, we first bring all the terms with Y to the left side:

$$Y(1 + h/kdz) = M_0^s/k - j_0/k + hA_0/kd$$

and solve for Y:

$$Y = [dz/(kdz + h)](M_0^s - j_0) + zhA_0/(kdz + h) \quad (9A\text{-}5)$$

Notice that d, k, and h and the multiplier (z) are all positive. This shows that an increase in the money supply, M_0^s, will lead to higher output; an increase in autonomous money demand, j_0, will lead to a lower output; and an increase in autonomous spending, A_0, will lead to a rise in output.

To find the equilibrium interest rate, we substitute Equation 9A-5 into Equation 9A-4:

$$r = A_0/d - [1/(kdz + h)](M_0^s - j_0) - hA_0/d(kdz + h)$$

Simplifying further, we get

$$r = -[1/(kdz + h)](M_0^s - j_0) + [kz/(kdz + h)]A_0 \quad (9A\text{-}6)$$

From this equation, we can see that an increase in the money supply, M_0^s, causes the interest rate to fall. An increase in autonomous money demand (j_0) causes the interest rate to rise, and an increase in autonomous spending (A_0) causes the interest rate to rise.

Because the algebra becomes complicated so quickly, you can see why economics professors generally focus either on general functional forms or on geometry in the pedagogical models they present to students.

10

The only thing that has driven more men crazy than love is the currency question.

—Benjamin Disraeli

We don't study macroeconomic policy from an international perspective, because there is no world government to implement policies.

Short-run Fluctuations in an Open Economy

After reading this chapter you should be able to:

1. Explain why the interest rate must rise when income rises to keep the balance of payments in equilibrium

2. Demonstrate, using the IS/LM/BP model, the effects of monetary and fiscal policy when exchange rates are flexible

3. Demonstrate, using the IS/LM/BP model, the effects of monetary and fiscal policy when exchange rates are fixed

4. List four policies other than monetary and fiscal policies that affect the balance of payments

5. Describe the effectiveness of monetary and fiscal policy for small, internationally open economies, using the Mundell-Fleming model

6. List the advantages and disadvantages of a common currency

During the 1990s, Mexico and several Asian economies suffered severe recessions, partly because they pursued policies to keep their exchange rates fixed. Why did they pursue those policies? What did they hope to achieve by fixing their exchange rates? Why was the sudden devaluation of those exchange rates associated with recession in those countries?

So far in our analysis of the short run, we have focused on what happens in an individual economy without considering how that economy interacts with foreign economies. But that analysis is incomplete. You cannot really understand domestic macroeconomics without understanding international economics.

In a sense, the correct way to study macroeconomics is from the perspective of the world economy, because only the world economy includes all interactions of economic variables and, hence, is fully "macroeconomic." We don't study macroeconomics from this perspective because there is no world government to undertake world economic policy. Instead, we focus on open-economy macroeconomics. An open economy is an economy that trades goods, services, real assets, and financial assets with other countries. The degree of openness—the number of barriers to trade—varies from country to country. No country is totally open (no trade barriers), and no country is totally closed (boundaries stop all flows of factors of production and products). Western economies are quite open, while many developing countries are closed to varying degrees, although international pressures for trade liberalization (the removal of barriers to trade) continue to increase their openness.

Let's start our analysis of the open economy by looking at how international factors change the IS/LM model presented in the last two chapters. In a closed economy, expansionary fiscal policy shifts the IS curve out to the right, increasing interest rates and income. This was the end of the story. However, in an open economy, monetary and fiscal policy have international repercussions: domestic policy actions affect a country's balance of payments, balance of trade, and capital flows.

For example, higher interest rates caused by expansionary fiscal policy increases the flow of capital into a country, and the higher income leads people to import more goods and services. Depending on the relative strengths of these effects, the exchange rate either rises or falls. A change in the exchange rate, in turn, affects imports and exports. To have a full analysis of the open economy, we need to take these various international effects into account.

To apply the IS/LM analysis to an open economy, we need to combine it with the analysis of the balance of payments (the balance between the flow of goods and assets going out of a country and coming into a country) introduced in Chapter 7. We first review the balance of payments, the capital account balance, the current account balance, and the official reserve transactions account. Then we develop the BP curve—a curve that integrates international factors into the IS/LM model. With the BP curve, we can talk about the importance of international issues to macroeconomic policy. To keep the analysis simple, as in the previous two chapters, we continue to assume the price level is fixed.

THE OPEN-ECONOMY SHORT-RUN MACROECONOMIC MODEL

In Chapter 7, you learned that the private balance of payments (the current account balance plus the private capital account balance) is in equilibrium when it equals zero. For the private balance of payments to be in equilibrium, either both the current account balance (the difference between exports and imports) and the private capital account balance (the difference between private capital inflows and outflows) must be zero, or each must offset the other so that, combined, they balance to zero. If the current account is in deficit, the private capital account must have a surplus equal to the size of the current account deficit and vice versa.

> When the exchange rate is flexible, if the current account is in deficit, the private capital account must have a surplus.

When the current account and private capital account balances do not sum to zero, the private balance of payments is not in equilibrium. And when the private balance of payments is not in equilibrium, the private quantity of currency demanded does not equal the private quantity supplied. A private balance of payments that is in deficit means that the private quantity of currency supplied exceeds the private quantity of currency demanded. If the country has a flexible exchange rate, the currency will depreciate until the demand–supply equilibrium (or, equivalently, the private balance of payments equilibrium) is restored. Alternatively, a private balance of payments surplus means that the private quantity of currency demanded exceeds the private quantity of currency supplied. If the country has a flexible exchange rate, the currency will appreciate until the private balance of payments equilibrium is restored.

If a country wants to maintain a fixed exchange rate and the private balance of payments is not in equilibrium, the government will have to intervene in the foreign exchange market. If the private balance of payments is in deficit, a country will have to buy up the excess supply of its currency. If the private balance of payments is in surplus, it will have to sell its own currency to eliminate the excess demand for its currency. These transactions are recorded on the official reserve transactions account. Whether a country has a flexible or fixed exchange rate, its balance of payments, including both the private account and official reserve transactions account, must always be zero. The balance of payments and exchange rates are an additional consideration for government when deciding its policies.

THE BP CURVE

The BP curve is a combination of interest rates and income levels at which the private balance of payments is in equilibrium.

Economists integrate international factors into the IS/LM model using the **balance of payments (BP) curve**—a curve that represents combinations of interest rates and income levels at a given exchange rate at which the private balance of payments is in equilibrium. We start by assuming that the official reserve transactions account is zero, so the BP curve is determined solely by the private balance of payments account. We can, therefore, derive the BP curve by considering how the current account and the private capital account change with various interest rates and income levels. Let's start with the current account.

Because the largest component of the current account is net exports (exports minus imports), the current account balance tends to move primarily with net exports. So, we focus on how net exports change as a country's domestic income changes. Exports have little relation to domestic income; they depend mainly on foreign economic conditions. When foreign income rises, foreigners buy more of a country's exports; when it falls, they buy less. So, in relation to domestic income, exports are exogenous (determined outside the model).

Imports are directly related to domestic income. When domestic income rises, consumers buy more domestic and imported goods and services. Because exports are exogenous and imports vary directly with income, net exports vary inversely with income. We illustrate this relationship in Exhibit 10–1(a). We've chosen an arbitrary level of income, Y_0 (point A), at which the current account balance is zero (imports equal exports). As income rises to Y_1 (point B), imports rise, and because exports do not change, the current account balance turns into a deficit. If income falls from Y_0 to Y_2 (point C), imports fall and the current account balance turns into a surplus.

The other component of the private balance of payments is the private capital account. The private capital account balance is the difference between the outflow and inflow of financial capital. All else held constant, financial capital will flow into countries that offer investments with the highest rate of return. (A lot of factors other than the interest rate also affect capital flows. The two most important are default–risk and movements in expected exchange rates. We hold both of these constant for now.) If a foreign investor can earn 8 percent on a 30-year U.S. government bond and 6 percent on a 30-year European Union (EU) bond, the foreign investor would buy the U.S. bond. More generally, if interest rates in the United States rise above interest rates in other countries, more capital will flow into the United States than out, pushing the capital account balance into surplus. If interest

Exhibit 10-1

Deriving the BP Curve

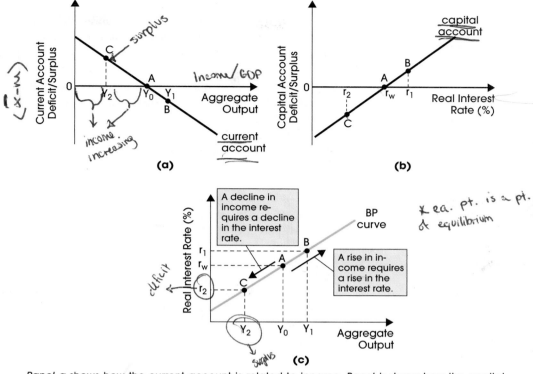

Panel a shows how the current account is related to income. Panel b shows how the capital account is related to real interest rates. Panel c puts panels a and b together to show combinations of interest rates and income levels where the sum of the current and capital accounts is zero.

rates in the United States fall below interest rates in other countries, more capital will flow out of the United States than in, pushing the capital account into deficit. We illustrate this relationship in Exhibit 10–1(b). The interest rate, r_w, represents the world interest rate—an average of interest rates outside of the United States. At point A, the interest rate in the United States equals the world interest rate (r_w) and the capital account is in balance. As the interest rate rises to r_1 (point B), the capital account balance moves into surplus (more capital is flowing in than out), and as the interest rate falls to r_2 (point C), the capital account falls into deficit (more capital is leaving the country than entering).

Points Along the BP Curve

Because the balance of payments is the combination of the current and capital accounts, we can derive a BP curve by putting the two curves in Exhibits 10–1(a and b) together. Remember, all along the BP curve, the private balance of payments is zero. We know from Exhibits 10–1(a) and 10–1(b) that the current account is zero at income Y_0 and that the private capital account is zero at interest rate r_w. This gives us point A on the BP curve in Exhibit 10–1(c). What if income increases to Y_1 (point B in Exhibit 10–1[a])? If income increases, the current account will be in deficit. To keep the balance of payments in equilibrium, the interest rate must rise enough to bring the capital account into surplus to exactly offset the current account deficit. That is, to maintain a private balance of payments equilibrium when income rises, interest rates must rise to r_1 (point B in Exhibit 10–1[b]). This is a second point on the BP curve—point B in Exhibit 10–1(c).

If income falls to Y_2 (point C in Exhibit 10–1[a]), the current account will move into surplus and the interest rate must fall to r_2 (point C in Exhibit 10–1[b]) to bring the capital account into deficit to offset the current account surplus. Because interest rates must rise when income rises to keep the balance of payments in equilibrium, the BP curve is upward sloping, as Exhibit 10–1(c) shows. A rise in income requires a rise in the interest rate. A decline in income requires a decline in interest rates.

A numerical example will help you understand the BP curve. Exhibits 10–2(a) and 10–2(b) show the current account and capital account balances, respectively, from Exhibit 10–1, but this time with numbers. At point C in Exhibits 10–2(a) and 10–2(b), the current account and the capital account are zero at income 300 and interest rate 10 percent, respectively. Point C (income = 300 and interest rate = 10 percent) in Exhibit 10–2(c), is one point on the BP curve. From Exhibit 10–2(a), we see that if the income level rises to 400 (point D), the current account deficit is 20. From Exhibit 10–2(b), we can see that the interest rate must rise to 12 percent to create an offsetting capital account surplus of 20 (point D). Thus, at income level 400 and interest rate 12 percent, the balance of payments will also be in equilibrium. This is shown as point D in Exhibit 10–2(c).

> The BP curve is upward sloping, like the LM curve.

Exhibit 10–2

Numerical Example of Deriving the BP Curve

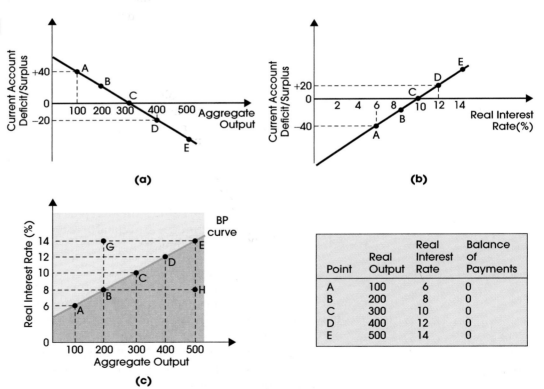

Point	Real Output	Real Interest Rate	Balance of Payments
A	100	6	0
B	200	8	0
C	300	10	0
D	400	12	0
E	500	14	0

Points A through E in *panel c* show the combinations of interest rates and income levels where the balance of payments is in equilibrium (zero). These combinations are also listed in the table. Points off the BP curve in *panel c* represent points of disequilibrium. To the left of the BP curve—the *yellow shaded area*—there is a balance of payments surplus. To the right of the BP curve—the *tan shaded area*—there is a balance of payments deficit.

The table accompanying Exhibit 10–2 provides a number of interest rate and income combinations from Exhibits 10–2(a) and 10–2(b), where the current and capital accounts offset each other. We use these combinations to complete the BP curve, as shown in Exhibit 10–2(c). Notice in the table that for a country to maintain a balance of payments equilibrium, higher levels of interest rates have to accompany higher levels of incomes.

Points off the BP Curve

Let's also look at combinations of interest rates and income levels off the BP curve and determine whether the balance of payments is in surplus or deficit. At any point to the left of the BP curve (the *yellow shaded region*), the balance of payments is in surplus; at any point to the right (the *tan shaded region*), it is in deficit. At point *G* in Exhibit 10–2(c), the balance of payments is in surplus because, given income level 200, the interest rate is higher than the interest rate that is consistent with a balance of payments equilibrium (8 percent). Capital flows into the country more than offset the current account deficit. So, the quantity of the country's currency demanded exceeds quantity supplied. For the balance of payments to be in equilibrium, the interest rate would have to fall, reducing capital inflows, the country's income would have to rise, increasing imports, or some combination of the two would have to occur. By similar reasoning, you should be able to demonstrate that, at point *H,* the balance of payments is in deficit and the quantity of the country's currency supplied exceeds quantity demanded.

The Slope of the BP Curve

The BP curve shows that, to maintain a balance of payments equilibrium, interest rates must rise as income rises. Policy makers are interested in more than just the general relationship, however. They also want to know *by how much* interest rates must rise when income rises. In other words, policy makers are interested in the *slope* of the BP curve. If the BP curve is steep, to maintain a balance of payments equilibrium, the interest rate must rise by a large amount for a given increase in income. If the BP curve is flat, to maintain balance of payments equilibrium, the interest rate must rise by a small amount for a given increase in income.

Two factors determine the slope of the BP curve:

1. The responsiveness of capital flows to differences between the domestic and world interest rate
2. The responsiveness of imports to income

As capital flows become more responsive to differences between domestic and world interest rates, the BP curve becomes flatter. For example, if a slight increase in the domestic interest rate above the world interest rate brings in a flood of foreign capital, the BP curve will be very flat. A slight increase in interest rates is sufficient to bring in enough foreign capital to offset a decrease in the current account caused by an increase in income. As you will find later in the chapter, small economies in which capital is allowed to flow freely have horizontal BP curves.

As imports become more responsive to changes in income (the marginal propensity to import increases), the BP curve becomes steeper. A given rise in income will cause a relatively greater decline in the current account and require a

---

Margin notes:

To the left of the BP curve, the balance of payments is in surplus; to the right, it is in deficit.

The slope of the BP curve is determined by the responsiveness of capital flows to interest rates and the responsiveness of imports to income.

The more responsive capital flows are to interest rates, and the less responsive imports are to income, the flatter the BP curve.

relatively greater rise in the capital account. As imports become more responsive to changes in income, the interest rate will have to rise by more to attract greater inflows of capital to restore balance of payments equilibrium.

Policies That Shift the BP Curve

Four policies that shift the BP curve are exchange rate policies, import controls, export drives, and capital controls.

Exchange Rates Policies. Policy makers can influence the BP curve's position with a number of policies. The most common is exchange rate policies. Until now, we have assumed that the official reserve transactions account is zero and the exchange rate does not change. These two assumptions might be inconsistent with one another. If the exchange rate is flexible, a change in the exchange rate will cause the BP curve to shift until the economy is in a balance of payments equilibrium. Alternatively, if the exchange rate is fixed, the government will have to buy and sell its currency in the foreign exchange market to bring the balance of payments into equilibrium at the fixed exchange rate; the official reserve transactions account will not be zero. More generally, by buying or selling currency in the foreign exchange market, a central bank can influence the price of its currency relative to other currencies around the world. Movements in the exchange rate affect the balance of payments equilibrium and are represented by shifts in the BP curve.

Suppose, for example, that a central bank wants to stimulate exports by depreciating its currency. To depreciate its currency, it sells domestic currency in exchange for foreign currency. With a lower exchange rate, the price of imports rises and the price of exports falls. The current account balance rises, pushing the balance of payments into surplus. The balance of payments equilibrium can be restored with a decline in the capital account balance, a decline in the current account balance, or a combination of the two. This means the combination of income and interest rates that will keep the balance of payments in equilibrium will shift to the right.

Exhibit 10–3 shows an example of the effect of a currency depreciation. Initially, at point A on BP_0, the balance of payments is in equilibrium. The depreciation increases exports and decreases imports, pushing the balance of payments into surplus. If the balance of payments is to remain in equilibrium, either income must rise or the interest rate must fall to bring the balance of payments back to equilibrium. One possibility is that only the interest rate changes. In this case, income doesn't change and the interest rate falls to reduce the capital account balance enough to offset the rise in the current account surplus caused by the depreciation. The economy moves to point B on BP_1. The interest rate associated with balance of payments equilibrium is lower for every level of income. In other words, the BP curve shifts down.

We can also see this as a shift of the BP curve to the right. Suppose income changes to bring the balance of payments into equilibrium. Because the interest rate doesn't change, income rises sufficiently to increase imports and decrease the current account balance to restore a balance of payments equilibrium. The economy moves to point C on BP_1. The new BP curve, BP_1, represents all combinations of income and interest rates at which the balance of payments is in equilibrium at the lower exchange rate. (Sometimes, depreciating one's currency has the opposite effect—it worsens the current account. See the Q&A feature on the J-curve on page 280 that

Exhibit 10-3

The Effect of a Depreciation of a Currency

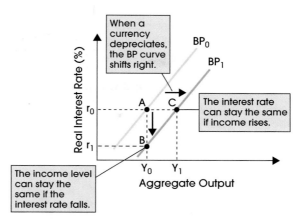

When a currency depreciates, the BP curve shifts right.

The interest rate can stay the same if income rises.

The income level can stay the same if the interest rate falls.

Starting from point *A*, a currency depreciation will cause the BP curve to shift down and to the right. Points *C* and *B* represent possible interest rate and income combinations at which the balance of payments is in equilibrium. At point *C*, the interest rate remains the same, requiring a rise in income. At point *B*, income remains the same so that the interest rate must fall.

explains how a currency depreciation can initially worsen a country's trade deficit and thereby possibly worsen the balance of payments deficit.) If the central bank had, instead, appreciated its currency, the BP curve could have shifted up (or to the left).

This discussion shows you why exchange rate policy is a key policy for government. Lowering the exchange rate shifts the BP curve out; increasing the exchange rate shifts the BP curve in. When exchange rates are flexible, the BP curve shifts in the same way on its own, leaving the government to focus on domestic policy.

Import Controls and Export Drives. Policies that control imports also affect the balance of payments. Import controls are policies that forbid or discourage the importing of goods, pushing the current account toward surplus. Because import controls will reduce a current account deficit (or expand a current account surplus), points that had represented a balance of payments equilibrium now are points of surplus. Keeping interest rates constant, income will have to rise to bring the current account back to its original position, where the balance of payments was in equilibrium. Import controls shift the BP curve to the right.

Examples of import controls include tariffs, quotas, and voluntary restraint agreements. **Tariffs** are taxes on imports. They are the common trade restriction. **Quotas** place quantitative limits on what a country can import, and a **voluntary restraint agreement** is an informal agreement between two countries, in which one country limits its exports to the other. They work much the same as quotas. In the early 1980s, for example, Japan voluntarily agreed to limit the number of automobiles exported to the United States. The World Trade Organization now strongly discourages such voluntary agreements.

A second policy that shifts the BP curve to the right is an export drive. An **export drive** is a policy that promotes a country's exports, using a combination of subsidies and international appeals to buy its exports. The European Union, for example, pays firms to export a number of agricultural goods. In fact, about 45 percent of the E.U. government budget is devoted to the agricultural sector. Because subsidies lower the cost of production, they allow firms to better compete with the prices of international competitors. By making their exports more price competitive, the European Union has been able to increase its world market share of a number of

A fall in the exchange rate shifts the BP curve out to the right; a rise in the exchange rate shifts the BP curve in to the left.

Any policy that reduces imports or increases exports shifts the BP curve out to the right.

QUESTION Is it possible that a currency depreciation leads to a decrease in the current account and thereby in the balance of payments? If so, why?

ANSWER Yes. Initially, a depreciation of a country's currency can worsen the trade deficit because it takes time for people to adjust their buying patterns. After a time, the trade deficit, however, will improve. This is known as the *J curve effect.*

Although the open-economy macroeconomic model predicts that when a country's currency depreciates, the BP curve shifts to the right, economists have found that, empirically, this doesn't always happen right away. In fact, when a currency depreciates, the current account (or the trade deficit) initially worsens, pulling the BP curve to the left, not to the right.

Why does a depreciation initially worsen the trade deficit? The reason is that the value of a country's imports and exports is determined by both price and quantity. When a country's currency depreciates, the price of imports rises and the price of exports falls. Often countries are slow to cut back on imports; they continue to import the same quantities for a while at the higher prices, and then gradually cut down. The opposite happens with exports. Other countries also are slow to increase their quantity of imports, even though prices have declined. What this means is that in the short run, the price effect outweighs the quantity effect, and the trade deficit worsens. As the quantity effect picks up and dominates, the trade balance improves. For example, suppose a family has planned a vacation to Europe and the exchange rate changes, making the trip more expensive. They will probably still go, worsening the trade deficit. They may plan a domestic vacation next time, though, improving the trade deficit.

Consider a numerical example. The European Union sells Volkswagens for 21,600 euros and the United States sells computers for $1,800. With those prices and a euro–dollar exchange rate of 1.2 euros per dollar, the United States buys 100 VWs from the European Union at dollar cost of $18,000 each, and the European Union buys 999 computers from the United States for a euro cost of 2,160 euros each. So, U.S. imports are $1,800,000 ($18,000 × 100) and exports are $1,798,200 ($1,800 × 999). The United States has a trade deficit of $1,800. Now suppose the dollar depreciates to 1.05/1 (euros for dollars), lowering the euro price of computers to 1,890 euros ($1,800 × 1.05) and raising the dollar price of VWs to $20,571 (21,600/1.05). Initially, this price change will have little effect on quantities. Suppose the quantity of VWs bought decreases to 99, while the quantity of computers bought rises to 1,000. Now calculate the balance of payments to the United States. Exports will be $1,800,000 ($1,800 × 1,000) and imports will be $2,036,529 ($20,571 × 99). The U.S. trade deficit rose to $236,529. Assuming no change in the capital account, the U.S. balance of payments did not improve with depreciation of the U.S. currency. It actually worsened.

The reason depreciation can hurt the balance of payments in the short run lies in the numbers chosen in our example—different numbers would have given "better" results. The example, however, is not totally arbitrary. In fact, it is typical of the short-run experience of many countries with balance of payments deficits.*

In the long run, the numbers tend to change as the volume effects increase and the long-run demand curves for both exports and imports respond more to changes in the exchange rate. This tendency of the balance of payments to worsen initially following a depreciation of a currency and then improve after a period of time has been called the *J curve,* because the pattern of a worsening deficit changing to a surplus looks like the letter J on a graph. A hypothetical J curve is shown in the following exhibit. At time T_1, the currency depreciates, causing the trade balance to fall. Over time—in this case, at time T_2—the trade balance improves.

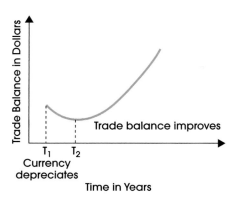

Obviously there are limits. A continual fall of the price of dollars would make United States assets such a bargain that those in the European Union would be flocking to the United States to buy up everything. In technical terms, we would say that the market is locally, not globally, unstable.

Q & A

QUESTION What does sterilization in open-economy macroeconomics mean?

ANSWER It means that a government offsets the effect that a shifting BP curve has on its IS and LM curves.

To keep the analysis of the open economy manageable, we have assumed that movements along, and shifts in, the BP curve do not affect the IS or LM curves. In actuality, this is not true—international policies *do* affect these curves. For example, when capital controls are implemented, shifting the BP curve, the LM curve also will shift.

Actually, assuming that these effects don't exist for monetary policy is not so far off the mark. This is the way the United States conducts monetary policy. The central bank counteracts the effect of international capital flows on the domestic money supply with a process called sterilization—offsetting international monetary flows with domestic monetary actions. The central bank increases or decreases the money supply by just enough to offset the outflow or inflow of international funds to neutralize the effect of a purchase or sale of currency on the domestic

money supply. So, when the Fed buys a foreign currency, it usually simultaneously sells an equal amount of bonds to keep the money supply constant. The assumption we use in this section of the chapter is that any international effects on the LM curve are sterilized.

Changes in exchange rates, and policies to affect the position of the BP curve, also affect net exports and the IS curve. For example, a currency depreciation that increases exports, decreases imports, and shifts the BP curve to the right will also shift the IS curve to the right. Although, in reality, the effect of exchange rate policies on the IS curve is seldom sterilized, to keep the analysis simple, we assume that it is. This allows us to concentrate on shifts in the BP curve. (We remove this assumption when we discuss a small open economy because, in small open economies, it is impossible to sterilize these effects.)

---

agricultural goods. By increasing exports, points on the BP curve that had represented balance of payments equilibria are now points of surplus. Keeping interest rates constant, income will have to rise to increase imports and bring the balance of payments back to equilibrium. That is, export drives shift the BP curve to the right.

Capital outflow controls shift the BP curve out to the right.

Capital Outflow Controls. Capital outflow controls are policies that limit the amount of capital that can leave the country, directly reducing any private capital account deficit. Essentially, the government tells individuals they must save domestically even if they could get a higher return elsewhere. Controls of this kind are generally hard to enforce. Moreover, they tend to induce retaliatory controls by other countries.

Small, developing countries, however, are unlikely to face retaliation, and many limit the outflow of capital. For example, Jamaica, a small, developing country, does not allow its citizens to own foreign capital. Capital outflow controls create a non-convertibility on the private capital account, and a majority of developing economies use this policy. These controls are meant to reduce the demand for foreign currency and keep the domestic currency from depreciating. Controls on the outflow of capital that do not also affect capital inflows will move the capital account toward surplus and shift the BP curve to the right. Capital outflow controls, however, will also reduce capital inflows. Foreign investors are less likely to invest in countries if they cannot take the profits of their investment back home or cannot divest themselves easily.

Interaction of a Shifting BP Curve with the IS and LM Curves

As is usually the case, foreign factors interact enormously with domestic factors. Specifically, policies that shift the BP curve will also affect the IS and LM curves.

For example, when a country sells its own currency and buys foreign currency, its currency depreciates and the BP curve shifts to the right. In doing so, the central bank increases its money supply, shifting the LM curve to the right. A currency depreciation also leads to higher net exports, shifting the IS curve out to the right. To keep our analysis as manageable as possible, at this point we will ignore the effect that changes in the exchange rate have on the LM curve. Technically, we are assuming that effects of changes in the value of the exchange rate on the IS and LM curves are sterilized—that the government also implements policies that offset the effects on the IS and LM curves. (The Q&A feature discusses sterilization further.)

> Sterilization is government's use of monetary or fiscal policy to offset the effects of changes in the value of a currency on the IS or LM curves.

Executive Summary

- **Policies designed to achieve domestic goals will also affect a country's international goals.**

- **Increases in domestic income will push the current account toward deficit, meaning the quantity of currency supplied exceeds the quantity demanded, and there will be pressure for the value of the currency to fall.**

- **Increases in domestic interest rates will push the capital account toward surplus, meaning the quantity of currency demanded exceeds the quantity supplied, and there will be pressure for the value of the currency to rise.**

- **The BP curve represents combinations of interest rates and income levels at which the economy maintains a balance of payments equilibrium.**

- **For points to the left of the BP curve, the balance of payments is in surplus. For points to the right of the BP curve, the balance of payments is in deficit.**

- **A fall in the value of a country's currency shifts the BP curve to the right. A rise in the value of a country's currency shifts the BP curve to the left.**

- **Import controls, export drives, and capital controls are designed to shift the BP curve to the right.**

POLICY ANALYSIS WITH THE IS/LM MODEL AND THE BP CURVE

> Internal balance occurs when the government achieves its goals for interest rates and output.

> External balance occurs when the government achieves its goals for its trade balance, balance of payments, and its exchange rate.

The BP curve adds a new level of analysis to the IS/LM model. Generally, policy makers discuss open-economy policy issues in reference to internal balance and external balance. When the government achieves its goals for interest rates and output, the economy is said to be in **internal balance.** When the government achieves its goals for its trade balance (if it has a flexible exchange rate), or for its balance of payments (if it has a fixed exchange rate), together with its goal for its exchange rate, the economy is said to be in **external balance.** A country that meets all of these goals simultaneously is in internal and external balance. So, the policy game is to shift the IS, LM, and BP curves to achieve the desired internal and external balances simultaneously. Let's go through a few examples so you can be sure that you understand how the IS, LM, and BP curves interact.

Monetary and Fiscal Policy in the Open Economy

Let's start with Exhibit 10–4(a), which shows the IS, LM, and BP curves together. Notice that both the BP and the LM curves are upward sloping. As the curves are drawn, the LM curve is flatter than the BP curve. However, this need not be the case—the BP curve could be flatter than the LM curve. The relative slopes of the BP and LM curves depend on factors such as how sensitive the quantity of money demanded is to the interest rate and how sensitive imports are to changes in income, to name just two. (A good review of both curves is to specify the conditions under

Exhibit 10-4

**Fiscal and
Monetary Policy
with the BP Curve**

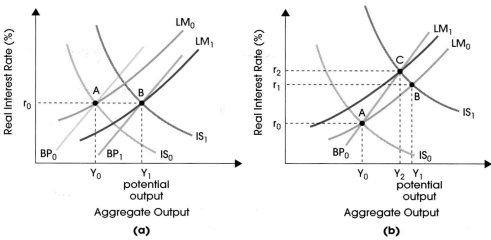

Panel a shows how a country that wants to increase output but maintain an interest rate must accept a decline in the value of its currency when exchange rates are flexible. *Panel b* shows a country that wants to increase output with expansionary fiscal policy but also maintain a fixed exchange rate. If it doesn't have enough reserves to keep the exchange rate fixed, it must contract the money supply to raise interest rates sufficiently to increase the capital account balance and reduce income. The reduction in income increases the current account balance to maintain external equilibrium.

which the BP curve would be flatter than the LM curve.) Internal balance occurs where the IS and LM curves intersect at the desired interest rate and income level. External balance occurs at the desired balance of payments, which, for ease of exposition, we assume also means that the official reserve transactions account is zero.

Say that the economy is at point *A* in Exhibit 10–4(a). The government is satisfied with its interest rate (r_0), but output (Y_0) is below potential. The desired internal balance is for output to be at potential. To increase output but keep the interest rate at r_0, the government uses a combination of expansionary monetary and fiscal policy, which shifts the IS and LM curves out to IS_1 and LM_1. Interest rates remain at r_0, and income rises to Y_1 (point *B*). If the exchange rate is flexible, the increase in the money supply will cause the currency to depreciate, increasing exports to match the increased imports. The BP curve shifts out to BP_1 to meet the new internal equilibrium, and the economy is in both internal and external balance (point *B*).

Consider the same scenario, but, this time, the exchange rate is fixed. In this case, the exchange rate doesn't depreciate automatically when the IS and LM curves shift. External balance remains along the original BP curve, even after the economy has moved to point *B* in Exhibit 10–4(a). The economy now has a current account deficit (imports increase and exports remain constant). The balance of payments is in deficit, so the quantity of currency supplied exceeds the quantity demanded, creating pressure for the currency to depreciate. To maintain its fixed exchange rate, the government will have to buy the excess supply of its currency, using its reserves of foreign currency.

If the deficit continues for a long enough time period, eventually the country will run out of foreign reserves. It will either have to devalue its currency, which would cause the BP curve to shift out to the right through point *B*, or compromise on its domestic goals and reduce income back to Y_0 with contractionary monetary and fiscal policy. A country can increase income and maintain its interest rate target only if it has enough foreign reserves to offset its private balance of payments deficit.

With a flexible exchange rate system, the BP curve shifts to the internal equilibrium.

In the IS/LM/BP model, the government can achieve both internal and external balance by using various combinations of monetary and fiscal policy, as long as it doesn't care about the structure of the balance of payments between the capital account and the current account.

A country cannot run a balance of payments deficit forever; at some point, it will run out of foreign reserves.

Exhibit 10–4(b) shows a third example of an economy that has moved away from its external balance. Suppose the country has a fixed exchange rate but no foreign reserves. It wants to increase income, but it has no particular interest rate target. In this case, the government can use expansionary fiscal policy to increase output. Expansionary fiscal policy is illustrated as a shift in the IS curve from IS_0 to IS_1. Income rises to Y_1 and the interest rate rises to r_1 (point B). At point B, however, the balance of payments is in deficit. To restore private balance of payments equilibrium, the central bank can use contractionary monetary policy to increase interest rates enough to bring in capital flows to offset the increase in imports. By running contractionary monetary policy that shifts the LM curve from LM_0 to LM_1, it achieves the desired domestic goal of increasing output and maintains its balance of payments equilibrium. Note, however, that to maintain a balance of payments equilibrium, it has to accept a rise in interest rates.

These examples show that a country with flexible exchange rates doesn't need to consider the problem of achieving external balance directly. With flexible exchange rates, the balance of payments is always in equilibrium—the exchange rate adjusts so that the quantity of currency demanded equals the quantity supplied (the private balance of payments is zero). A country with flexible exchange rates can pursue its internal goals and let the exchange rate adjust to maintain external balance.

A country with fixed exchange rates, however, will have more difficulty achieving external and internal balance simultaneously. The limitation that the need to balance international payments (given fixed exchange rates) places on a country's fiscal policy and monetary policy is called the **balance of payments constraint.**

A country that wants to increase output but maintain a fixed exchange rate must spend its foreign currency reserves or contract the money supply and accept a higher interest rate. Both policies have risks. If a country uses its foreign currency reserves to maintain a fixed exchange rate, it risks exhausting its reserves, requiring the central bank to abandon its fixed exchange rate, risking a rapid depreciation. This is what happened in Mexico in the early 1990s and in several Asian countries in the late 1990s. Unfortunately, a rapid depreciation of currency is often associated with other problems—primarily, increasing inflation.

A country can maintain its fixed exchange rate by adjusting its internal policies to achieve the desired external balance. For example, a country can contract its money supply to maintain a fixed exchange rate. This can discourage domestic investment and throw the economy into a recession. In the late 1990s, Brazil's central bank raised its interest rates to nearly 30 percent to keep its currency from depreciating, and the result was a recession.

In summary, the balance of payments constraint places limits on a country's ability to expand output with fiscal or monetary policy while trying to maintain a fixed exchange rate. To get around these limits, countries sometimes use policies to increase exports, limit imports, or bring in new capital flows.

Countries with a fixed exchange rate have a balance of payments constraint that places a limit on their monetary and fiscal policies.

Policies That Directly Affect the Balance of Payments Constraint

In addition to using fiscal and monetary policies to achieve external and internal balance, governments can use exchange rate policies, import controls, export drives, and capital controls to directly affect their balance of payments and achieve external and internal balance. To achieve internal balance, suppose the government uses a combination of expansionary monetary and fiscal policy to increase output while keeping the interest rate unchanged (the same as in Exhibit 10-4(a) except

Exchange rate policies, import controls, export drives, and capital controls can all be used to adjust the BP curve.

with a fixed exchange rate). In Exhibit 10–5, these policies shift the IS and LM curves out to IS_1 and LM_1. Internal balance moves from point A to point B—interest rates remain at r_0 and income rises to Y_1. External balance, however, remains at point A, where there is a balance of payments deficit. If the government wants to maintain a fixed exchange rate, it will have to use its foreign currency reserves to buy the resulting surplus currency. Eventually, the government will run out of foreign currency reserves. An alternative to buying up the excess supply of currency is for the government to impose import controls, tariffs, or quotas, or launch export drives to shift the BP curve out to BP_1. By pursuing policies that increase exports and decrease imports, the country can bring the balance of payments back to equilibrium and achieve both internal and external balance at point B without devaluing its currency.

Instituting policies to affect the balance of payments curve, however, could create problems of their own. Import restrictions reduce the incentive for domestic firms to remain competitive. Two reasons why Japanese cars were outselling American cars when the Japanese agreed to voluntary restraints on exports in the early 1980s were that the cars were both better and, at the prevailing exchange rates, cheaper than American models. If the U.S. automobile industry was to compete with foreign producers, it would have to cut wages and increase productivity. The Japanese competition gave the U.S. auto industry the "kick in the pants" it needed to make the difficult adjustment. (The kick-in-the-pants argument is the standard one against all barriers to trade. The rebuttal is that not every kick in the pants stimulates an industry. Some merely hurt or, even worse, destroy it.) However, the agreement with Japan did not insulate U.S. automakers from Japanese competition. Japan stuck to the limits but changed the mix of cars it exported—from mostly low-price models to expensive cars—to maintain high profits. Not only did this policy fail to eliminate the U.S. balance of payments deficit, it also increased Japanese automakers' presence in the U.S. auto market.

External balance becomes an issue only if a country has a fixed or a partially flexible exchange rate. If a country is willing to have a flexible exchange rate (accept the exchange rate determined by the market), the country will always be in

> Policies that affect the balance of payments curve often create problems of their own.

Exhibit 10–5

Achieving External Balance

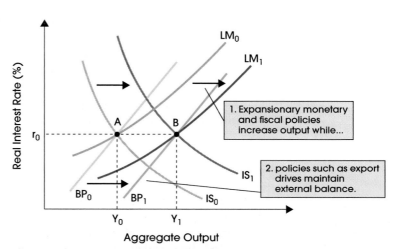

If a country follows policies that take it off its balance of payments curve, it can institute policies that directly affect the balance of payments constraint, such as imposing import controls or launching export drives to increase the balance of payments constraint.

THE BRIEFING ROOM   The Importance of Expectations and the South Korean Won

The balance of payments constraint states that unless a country is sitting on a hoard of foreign money, gold, or other financial assets other countries will accept, a private balance of payments deficit cannot continue indefinitely.

The possibility of the government giving up its fixed exchange rate policy can become a self-fulfilling expectation. Say, for example, that foreign investors think a country is about to run out of foreign reserves and allow the value of its currency to fall. To avoid losses from such a fall, the investors will sell their holdings of that country's assets, creating pressure for the currency to depreciate, even if there had been none before. This means that the expectation of a falling currency requires government to spend even greater foreign reserves to maintain a fixed exchange rate. As investors are increasingly able to transfer large quantities of currency from country to country (called hot money), few countries have sufficient reserves to withstand a speculative run on their currency (massive sale of currency) in the face of expectations of a fall in its price. Eventually, the country would

have to abandon the fixed exchange rate and either devalue its currency or adopt a flexible exchange rate policy.

This is a large part of what happened in South Korea in December 1997. The South Korean government was working hard to keep the financial crisis in Thailand from spreading to its own economy. To give investors confidence that its currency would not fall, the Korean government reported that it had $30 billion in foreign currency reserves. When it later confessed to having just $10 billion, investors lost confidence in the won (South Korea's currency). They quickly sold their holdings of South Korean won-denominated assets, which put pressure on the price of the won to fall. The South Korean government was unable to offset the dramatic increase in the supply of its currency. The won depreciated by 30 percent in just a few days. This example shows the risk that countries with a fixed exchange rate face: Once they run out of foreign currency reserves, the price of their currency can fall rapidly.

Most countries are willing to let their currencies fluctuate within a range, and will intervene when the exchange rate is outside that range.

external balance. Most countries, however, are not willing to allow the market to fully determine the value of its currency, but are willing to let their exchange rate fluctuate within a range. When the exchange rate fluctuates outside the desired range, even countries that generally have a flexible exchange rate (such as the United States) will often intervene in the foreign exchange market. A country, however, has limited ability to offset exchange rate fluctuations.

The United States ran up against the balance of payments constraint in the 1970s. Throughout the 1960s, the United States had a fixed exchange rate and a balance of payments deficit. Bound by the Bretton Woods system of fixed exchange rates, foreign central banks had to buy up the surplus of dollars, paying for them with their own currencies. As they did so, they accumulated more and more dollars and were forced to increase their domestic money supplies to pay for the dollars. The increased money supplies led to inflation and, eventually, these countries said, "No more." Something had to give. The "something" was the Bretton Woods system of fixed exchange rates among countries. Ironically, the U.S. trade deficit worsened in the 1980s, as the world developed an enormous demand for U.S. dollars and dollar-denominated assets.

From the 1940s to the 1970s, the international economy operated under the Bretton-Woods system of fixed exchange rates.

Part of the reason for the increased demand for dollar denominated assets was that expansionary fiscal policy in the early 1980s had caused interest rates in the United States to rise (think of a rightward shift in the IS curve). The increase in U.S. interest rates attracted foreign investors and the dollar appreciated. As the dollar appreciated, exports fell and imports rose, causing the trade balance to worsen. Although the United States made several attempts to bring the value of the dollar down by intervening in the foreign exchange market, these interventions had limited success. In a market in which about $3 trillion is traded daily, with limited foreign reserves, governments can affect the value of currencies mainly by affecting expectations. (See The Briefing Room, "The Importance of Expectations and the

South Korean Won," for an example of the importance of expectations in foreign currency markets.) The primary feasible way for the United States to reduce foreign demand for dollars was to reduce deficit spending (reduce expansionary fiscal policy). Deficit reduction became an important issue in the 1980s, in part because policy makers recognized it as a way to reduce the trade deficit.

POLICY IN A SMALL OPEN ECONOMY: THE MUNDELL-FLEMING MODEL

So far, we have presented the BP curve as an upward-sloping curve—increases in domestic output must be accompanied by increases in the domestic interest rate to maintain private balance of payments equilibrium. The increased interest rate attracts foreign capital to offset the decrease in the capital account balance caused by the rise in output.

By assuming the BP curve is upward sloping, we are implicitly assuming that real interest rates can differ among countries. That is, capital does not flow from country to country to eliminate all real interest rate differentials. This assumption is reasonable for large economies such as the United States. For small economies that are internationally integrated, this assumption is not as reasonable. For example, before becoming a member of the European Union, Belgium couldn't maintain a domestic interest rate that was different from Germany's. When it tried to raise its interest rate above that of Germany's to slow its economy, capital flowed from Germany to Belgium, which pushed the interest rate in Belgium back to the German interest rate.

> In a small open economy with perfect capital mobility, the BP curve is horizontal. Such countries must take the interest rate as given.

In small, internationally integrated economies, it is more reasonable to assume **perfect capital mobility**—investors can buy and sell all the assets they want across countries with no additional cost and risk. With perfectly mobile capital, real interest rates are the same across all countries, because any interest rate differential is eliminated by the flow of capital. Capital will flow to any economy with higher interest rates, lowering its interest rate until the differential no longer exists. This means that the BP curve is horizontal, as in Exhibit 10–6. That is, the capital flows

Exhibit 10-6

Mundell-Fleming Model

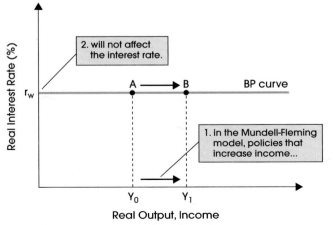

For small, internationally integrated economies with perfect capital mobility, the BP curve is horizontal at the world interest rate, because the slightest force that moves the domestic interest rate away from the world rate results in a flood of capital outflows or inflows that keeps the domestic interest rate at the world rate.

The IS/LM/BP model in
which the BP curve is flat is
called the *Mundell-Fleming
model.*

will totally overwhelm any change in current account flows. Economists call this model the **Mundell-Fleming model**—a model of an open economy in which capital is perfectly mobile.[1] The assumption of a horizontal BP curve is also known as the *small country assumption.* The flows of capital in small-economy countries are sufficiently large, compared with the size of the economy, to warrant the assumption that capital is perfectly mobile.

To see why perfect capital mobility means that the BP curve is horizontal, suppose an economy starts in a balance of payments equilibrium, in which the domestic interest rate equals the world interest rate, r_w, and income is Y_0—point A in Exhibit 10–6. If income rises to Y_1, the current account balance will fall as more goods are imported. To maintain balance of payments equilibrium, the decline in the current account balance must be offset by an increase in the capital account balance. When the BP curve is upward sloping, the only way to generate that increase in the capital account is to have the interest rate rise above the world interest rate, to attract capital inflows. When capital is perfectly mobile, however, capital flows are assumed to be so responsive to interest rate differentials that the slightest force that increases the domestic interest rates would result in a flood of capital that keeps the interest rate at the world interest rate. As the economy moves from point A to point B along the horizontal BP curve in Exhibit 10–6, the current account balance falls and the capital account balance rises, but the interest rate remains at the world interest rate.

The key difference between the upward-sloping BP curve and the horizontal BP curve is the assumption about capital flows. The upward-sloping BP curve represents a balance between changes in trade flows (the current account) and capital flows (the capital account). Neither flow plays a dominant role in the adjustment toward equilibrium. As the current account balance falls, the interest rate rises, pushing the capital account balance up enough to offset the decline in the current account balance. Because of the balancing of these two flows, it is possible for an economy to maintain an interest rate that is different from the world interest rate. The ability to do this greatly expands a country's policy options.

With a horizontal BP curve, capital flows dominate trade flows, so much so that a country cannot choose to have an interest rate that is different from the world interest rate. This is very constraining for policy (as you will see in the next section). Massive changes in capital flows will prevent a country from achieving external balance at an interest rate that is different from the world interest rate.

Policy in the Mundell-Fleming Model with Fixed Exchange Rates

Let's see how perfect capital mobility changes the effects of expansionary fiscal policy on output when the exchange rate is fixed. Suppose we're looking at Iceland. The economy begins at point A in Exhibit 10–7(a). The IS curve shifts right from IS_0 to IS_1 when the government increases spending or decreases taxes. Income and the interest rate begin to rise, which brings in significant amounts of foreign capital. To buy Icelandic capital, foreigners have to exchange their currency for kronur (Iceland's currency). The increased demand for kronur causes the kronur to appreciate. To keep its exchange rate fixed, the central bank in Iceland must buy foreign

In the Mundell-Fleming
model, fiscal policy must be
accompanied by accom-
modative monetary policy.

[1]Robert Mundell and J. Marcus Fleming, famous international economists, developed this model in the 1960s. Robert Mundell won the Nobel prize in economics in 1999 for his work on exchange rates and open-economy macroeconomics.

Exhibit 10-7

Policy in an Open Economy with Perfectly Mobile Capital and Fixed Exchange Rates

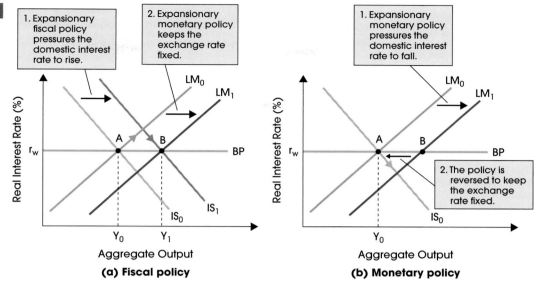

In *panel a,* expansionary fiscal policy shifts the IS curve to the right. As forces begin to push interest rates up, capital flows into the country, creating a balance of payments surplus. To keep the balance of payments in equilibrium and the value of the kronur fixed, the central bank of Iceland must increase the supply of kronur, shifting the LM curve to the right. In *panel b,* expansionary monetary policy pushes interest rates and the value of the kronur down. To maintain the fixed exchange rate, either the central bank of Iceland must reverse its expansionary monetary policy or the government must implement expansionary fiscal policy, which shifts the IS curve to the right.

currency to eliminate excess demand at the set rate. Because the central bank is supplying more kronur, the money supply in Iceland increases. Exhibit 10–7(a) shows the increase in the money supply with a shift of the LM curve from LM_0 to LM_1. Ultimately, equilibrium income rises to Y_1 and the domestic interest rate remains at r_w, the world interest rate (point *B*).

The preceding discussion points out a difference between open-economy analysis with a horizontal BP curve and the analysis with an upward-sloping BP curve. In the upward-sloping case, we assumed, for simplicity's sake, that exchange rate intervention did not affect the LM curve. (The central bank sterilized the changes in the money supply.) With a horizontal BP curve, capital flows are so large that it is impossible for the central bank to sterilize exchange rate interventions; it cannot have an independent monetary policy.

Next, let's consider how monetary policy works with fixed exchange rates and perfectly mobile capital. Income in Iceland again begins at Y_0, and interest rates equal the world interest rate, r_w—point *A* in Exhibit 10–7(b). Suppose the central bank in Iceland decides to increase the money supply. This puts pressure on the domestic interest rate to fall and the kronur to depreciate. To keep the exchange rate fixed, policy makers have two choices. Their first is to use expansionary fiscal policy to push the IS curve to the right, so the interest rate doesn't fall. The second is to reverse the monetary policy action and move the LM curve back to its original position (point *A*).

These two examples illustrate how monetary and fiscal policies are connected in a small open economy with a horizontal BP curve. Neither policy can be used successfully without the other. When fiscal policy is used, monetary policy has to step in to maintain the fixed exchange rate. When a central bank uses monetary policy, fiscal

When the BP curve is horizontal, capital flows are so large, it is impossible for the central bank to sterilize exchange rate interventions.

In the Mundell-Fleming model with fixed exchange rates, monetary and fiscal policy must be coordinated.

policy has to step in to maintain the fixed exchange rate. If policy makers want to simultaneously maintain a fixed exchange rate and move the economy to a different level of income, both monetary and fiscal policy must be used in a coordinated fashion.

Policy in the Mundell-Fleming Model with Flexible Exchange Rates

Let's now consider how monetary and fiscal policy work in the case of flexible exchange rates and perfect capital mobility. Again, suppose we are talking about Iceland. Iceland's economy starts at point A in Exhibit 10–8(a). Policy makers wish to increase income to Y_1, (point B). By using expansionary fiscal policy (cutting taxes or increasing spending), the IS curve shifts out to the right to IS_1. As the domestic interest rate begins to rise, capital flows into Iceland, the demand for kronur rises, and the kronur appreciates. With flexible exchange rates, the government allows the kronur to appreciate, and it continues to do so as long as fiscal policy is pushing the interest rate above the world interest rate. However, the kronur will not appreciate forever. (That would mean there is no equilibrium in this economy.) The kronur's appreciation causes imports to rise and exports to fall. Net exports decline, pushing the IS curve back to IS_0. Once the economy returns to point A, the kronur stops appreciating, because the interest rate has fallen back to the world interest rate. Fiscal policy has no effect on output in this case because net exports fall to exactly offset the effect of the expansionary policy. The expansionary effect of fiscal policy is exported to other economies. So, a small open economy with flexible exchange rates cannot use fiscal policy to increase output.

In our analysis of the large open economy with an *upward*-sloping BP curve, we assumed that the effect of changes in net exports on the IS curve is sterilized by offsetting fiscal policies, and we focused on how the BP curve shifted in response to

> In the Mundell-Fleming model with flexible exchange rates, fiscal policy will be ineffective, because changes in net exports will offset fiscal policy.

Exhibit 10-8

Policy in an Open Economy with Perfectly Mobile Capital and Flexible Exchange Rates

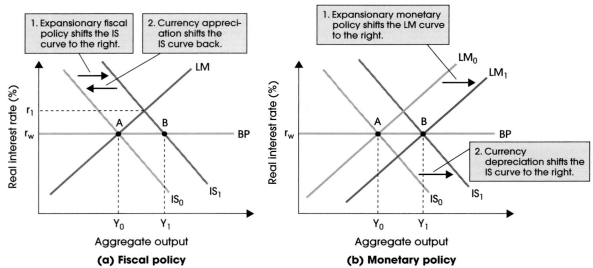

(a) Fiscal policy

(b) Monetary policy

At point A, the economy is equilibrium. *Panel a* shows how expansionary fiscal policy will increase domestic interest rates and cause large capital inflows. Increased demand for the domestic currency to purchase capital will drive the exchange rate up until imports fall enough to push the IS curve back to its original location. In *panel b*, expansionary monetary policy shifts the LM curve to the right. As the interest rate begins to fall, the domestic currency depreciates and the capital account falls. As the currency depreciates, net exports rise, pushing the IS curve to the right.

those changes. (If net exports fall, the government increases spending or reduces taxes, and if net exports rise, it lowers spending or increases taxes.) In the small open-economy with a *horizontal* BP curve, we cannot ignore the effect of changes in net exports on the IS curve, because the government cannot (practically speaking) offset these movements. For example, in Exhibit 10–8(a), to offset the effect of declining net exports, Iceland would have to continue pushing the IS curve to the right, with ever-expanding fiscal policy. The budget deficit would balloon to astronomical levels, and, eventually, Iceland would be unable to finance additional expenditures. The IS curve would shift back as net exports declined.

In the Mundell-Fleming model with flexible exchange rates, a combination of monetary and fiscal policy can be used to achieve any desired income level.

As you can see, a small open economy with flexible exchange rates lacks the ability to undertake independent fiscal policy. However, as with the case of fixed exchange rates, it can use coordinated monetary and fiscal policy to move along the horizontal BP curve—it just cannot be above or below the horizontal BP curve. In the case of expansionary fiscal policy, the central bank can expand the money supply, shifting the LM curve to the right, until the interest rate falls back down to the world interest rate at point *B* in Exhibit 10–8(a).

In the Mundell-Fleming model with flexible exchange rates, expansionary monetary policy forces net exports to change to validate the expansionary monetary policy.

Finally, let's consider using monetary policy to expand output. Exhibit 10–8(b) shows what happens when the central bank increases the money supply to expand the economy and increase output. The economy begins at point *A*. As the LM curve shifts from LM_0 to LM_1, the interest rate begins to fall, which precipitates capital outflows as Icelandic investors seek the higher rates of return in foreign countries. To invest in foreign countries, these investors must exchange their kronur for foreign currencies. The demand for kronur falls and its value depreciates, which causes exports to rise, imports to fall, and the current account balance to rise. Once again, we cannot ignore the effect of changes in net exports on the IS curve. Net exports will continue to rise (shifting the IS curve to the right) until the interest rate equals the world interest rate (r_w) and income rises to Y_1 (point *B*). Table 10–1 summarizes the effectiveness of monetary and fiscal policy in the Mundell-Fleming Model.

Monetary Policy and Inflation in the Open Economy

From this analysis, it appears that a small open economy with perfect capital mobility can increase output to any level it desires. The policies it uses to do so, however, are limited. If the country has flexible exchange rates, it must use expansionary

Table 10-1

Policy Effectiveness in the Mundell-Fleming Model

	Fixed Exchange Rate	Flexible Exchange Rate
Monetary policy	Ineffective in changing income by itself; offset by capital inflows or outflows. Effective when coordinated with fiscal policy	Effective in changing income; causes net exports to change to validate monetary policy
Fiscal policy	Effective in changing income because it forces an accommodative monetary policy	Ineffective in changing income by itself; net exports will change to offset it. Effective when coordinated with accommodative monetary policy

monetary policy to increase output. If the country wants to maintain a fixed exchange rate, it must use both expansionary fiscal policy and expansionary monetary policy. Regardless of whether a country has flexible or fixed exchange rates, the constraint of world interest rates requires that it increase the money supply to increase output.

These policies, however, generally cannot be used in the real world, because the assumption of a fixed price level (which we have maintained throughout Chapters 8, 9, and 10) is unlikely to hold true in the small, open-economy model. From the quantity theory of money, we know that generally higher growth in the money supply will lead to higher domestic inflation. The threat of inflation places an additional constraint on policy makers in the open economy, and considerably reduces their policy options.

Trade Policies

In our discussion of the large open economy with an upward-sloping BP curve, we considered policies that shift the BP curve, such as exchange rate intervention, capital controls, import quotas, and exports drives. None of the policies works independently in a small open economy with a horizontal BP curve because it is not possible to shift the BP curve—it is a horizontal line fixed at the world interest rate. Consider a country that tries to boost net exports by using a combination of import quotas and export drives. As net exports rise, the IS curve would shift to the right, pressuring the interest rate to rise above the world interest rate. As capital flowed into the country, the increased demand for the domestic currency would cause the currency to appreciate. The appreciating currency would cause net exports to decline, pushing the IS curve back to its original position—completely undoing the effect of the import quotas and export drives. The country would have to use expansionary monetary policy in conjunction with the import quotas and export drives if it wanted to boost net exports.

Executive Summary

- An economy is in internal balance when the government achieves its domestic goals. An economy is in external balance when the government achieves its trade and exchange rate goals.

- A large country with imperfectly mobile capital (upward-sloping BP curve) and flexible exchange rates *can* pursue domestic policy goals without regard for whether the balance of payments is in equilibrium. The exchange rate will adjust to bring the balance of payments into equilibrium.

- A large country with imperfectly mobile capital (upward-sloping BP curve) and fixed exchange rates *cannot* pursue domestic policy goals without regard for whether the balance of payments is in equilibrium. If the policies create a balance of payments deficit, the country will have to buy up the excess supply of its currency, using its foreign reserves. It will eventually run out of reserves.

- Countries can use capital outflow controls, import controls, tariffs, quotas, or voluntary export restraints to shift the BP curve and achieve external balance.

- The Mundell-Fleming model of the open economy assumes that capital is perfectly mobile. This model is useful for the analysis of small open economies. In this model, the BP curve is horizontal. Countries cannot pursue policies to change their interest rates, because capital flows are so large, they push the interest rate back to the world interest rate.

- A small open economy with perfect capital mobility must use monetary policy and fiscal policy combined. Neither works independently.

INTERNATIONAL POLICY COORDINATION

Apart from the case of voluntary restraint agreements, we have assumed so far that countries do not coordinate policies with other countries. In some sense, this is true: Countries ultimately conduct policy independently. Because policies in one country affect other countries' economies, however, many countries work to form a coordinated world policy. A variety of international organizations exist that coordinate policies and provide aid to countries to pursue macroeconomic goals.

International Organizations

Numerous international organizations attempt to coordinate policies of their member countries.

We divide international organizations into three groups: organizations that coordinate international financial flows, organizations that coordinate international trade flows, and regional and special-issue organizations. Table 10–2 shows some important organizations in each of these groups.

Table 10–2
International Organizations

INTERNATIONAL FINANCE ORGANIZATIONS

International Monetary Fund (IMF) (www.imf.org): Helps coordinate international financial flows

World Bank (www.worldbank.org): Helps developing countries obtain low-interest loans

INTERNATIONAL TRADE ORGANIZATIONS

World Trade Organization (WTO) (www.wto.org): Works toward free trade in goods and services and mediates trade disputes among member countries

REGIONAL AND SPECIAL-ISSUE ORGANIZATIONS

Group of 7: A group of seven countries (Britain, Canada, France, Germany, Italy, Japan, and the United States) that promotes trade negotiations and coordinates economic policies among its members

Organization of Petroleum Exporting Countries (OPEC) (www.opec.org): A group of 13 major oil exporting countries in the Middle East, Far East, Africa, and South America, established to create greater cooperation and coordination among member countries, to help prevent the price of oil from falling too low

Organization for Economic Cooperation and Development (OECD) (www.oecd.org): A group of countries from Europe and North America, plus Japan, Australia, New Zealand, Mexico, the Czech Republic, Hungary, Poland, and South Korea, that promote economic cooperation among its members

North American Free Trade Agreement (NAFTA): Established to eliminate trade barriers among Mexico, the United States, and Canada

European Union (www.europa.org): Seeks to integrate member countries by eliminating trade barriers and establishing a common currency among member countries: Belgium, Germany, France, Italy, Luxembourg, the Netherlands, Denmark, Ireland, the United Kingdom, Greece, Spain, Portugal, Austria, Finland, and Sweden

International organizations attempt to coordinate policies among countries; they encourage countries to undertake policies that benefit the world, even if those policies only slightly benefit them, and attempt to prevent one country from undertaking policies that benefit it but hurt other countries. An example of the type of financial intervention in which these countries engage is a series of agreements to support or change the value of major currencies. In 1985, the G-5 (G-7 less Canada and Italy) signed the Plaza Accord to lower the value of the U.S. dollar. Combined, they sold $10.2 billion (of dollars) in 2 months, and the value of the dollar fell, although some observers argued that it was falling anyway. In 1987, the G-6 (G-7 less Italy) signed the Louvre Accord to keep the value of the dollar from declining below 1.8 marks to the dollar. In 2000, the G-5 countries agreed to purchase $3 billion to $5 billion (of euros) to stop a nearly 2-year decline in the euro's value.

These agreements work primarily through expectations. The reason is that even a coordinated intervention is generally too small (less than 1 percent of the total volume of currency transactions) to make a significant difference in exchange rates. The coordinated action by government tells currency dealers that they will work toward a change. Currency dealers react by either buying or selling that currency, which magnifies the initial effect of the government intervention.

An example of the importance of policy coordination is the breakdown of the Bretton Woods system of fixed exchange rates. Recall that in the early 1970s the United States was running expansionary monetary policy and a somewhat expansionary fiscal policy, maintaining relatively low rates of interest. Exhibit 10–9 shows this with a shift in the LM curve from LM_0 to LM_1 and a shift in the IS curve from IS_0 to IS_1. The mix of policies moved the economy from point A to point B, caused a balance of payments deficit, and put pressure on the dollar to depreciate. To maintain a fixed exchange rate with the dollar, other countries had to buy the excess supply of dollars by printing more of their currencies—increasing their money supplies. This significantly expanded foreign countries' money supplies and led to higher inflation. Foreign countries claimed that the United States was "exporting inflation." In response, they pressured the United States to use contractionary aggregate demand policy to bring the

Exhibit 10-9

International Policy Coordination

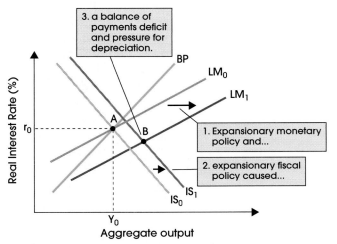

In the early 1970s, the United States was running expansionary monetary policy and slightly expansionary fiscal policy. This caused a balance of payments deficit and put pressure on the dollar to depreciate. Because exchange rates were fixed at that time, foreign countries were forced to increase their money supplies to buy up excess dollars.

balance of payments back into equilibrium at the fixed exchange rate. The United States argued that these countries should use more expansionary monetary and fiscal policy. The examples presented in this section illustrate how economies are linked. The Briefing Room, "The Locomotive Theory," discusses these links further.

A Common Currency for Europe

A common currency sets policy coordination into an institutional structure, putting independent monetary policy into a straight-jacket.

The European Union is comprised of the 15 countries shown in Exhibit 10–10. Between January 1999 and January 2002, eleven of these countries adopted a common currency—the euro. Like a fixed exchange rate, a common currency will constrain individual countries from pursuing independent monetary policies. However, a common currency is a more significant commitment than a fixed exchange rate. No longer can these E.U. countries achieve their domestic goals by depreciating their currencies. A common currency institutionalizes policy coordination—putting independent

Exhibit 10–10

The European Union

The European Union comprises 15 countries (labeled): Austria, Belgium, Denmark, Finland, France, Germany, Greece, Ireland, the United Kingdom, Italy, Luxembourg, the Netherlands, Portugal, Spain, and Sweden. Eleven of these countries have agreed to share a common currency, the euro. (See www.europa.eu.int)

THE BRIEFING ROOM   The Locomotive Theory

The locomotive theory states that one country takes the lead in expanding the world economy, pulling the other countries along, whether they like it or not. The United States, for example, used the locomotive theory to argue that Germany and Japan should expand their economies in the late 1970s. Had they done so, U.S. exports would have increased and the United States would not have had to use as strong a stimulative monetary and fiscal policy as it did. More generally, the locomotive theory supports the argument that countries must coordinate their macroeconomic policies so that each country does its fair share of the pulling and is not pulled where it does not want to go. The locomotive theory sounds great, but it is difficult to implement. Japan rejected the U.S. proposal.

Where the policy is in the interest of both countries, it can work. In the early 1980s, there was again pressure on Japan to stimulate its economy as a means of pulling the world economy out of its slump. Because Japan was running a trade surplus of $18 billion with the United States and had an inflation rate of under 5 per-

cent, Japanese policy makers felt that such an expansionary policy was both feasible and advantageous. Expanding Japan's economy helped stimulate the sluggish U.S. economy, improve the U.S. balance of payments, and reduce the political pressure other countries were exerting on Japan to cut exports. Japan followed the same policy in the early 1990s, when the world economy once again fell into recession. Again, the U.S. economy expanded.

A country need not be pulled; it can always offset the upward and downward effect of net exports on aggregate demand with domestic monetary and fiscal policy. However, when the country's economy is small, such offsetting monetary and fiscal policy is almost impossible. Even if such policies are not impossible, international effects can make domestic monetary and fiscal policy hostage to the actions of foreign countries. Small economies often feel as if they are at the end of a whip. There is a saying in many developing countries that expresses this sentiment: "When the United States coughs, developing countries get pneumonia."

---

monetary policy in a straightjacket. These countries will no longer be able to expand their money supplies independently because they will no longer have their own currency. A common currency is like having one LM curve for the entire region. Individual countries no longer have their own LM curves. The difference between a fixed exchange rate and a common currency is a bit like the difference between living together and getting married in a country that does not allow divorce. Once a group of countries adopts a common currency, there is no going back.

The advantages of a common currency are:

Advantages of a common currency include reduction in exchange rate risk, reduction in transaction costs, and economies of scale.

1. *Reduction in exchange rate risk.* Having one currency eliminates exchange rate risk, leading to more stability in the capital markets.
2. *Reduction in transactions costs.* Once countries agree to a single currency, there is no exchange of currencies among members, which means a reduction in the cost of exchanging one currency for another. Just as Americans can use dollars for transaction purposes in all 50 states, E.U. businesses and travelers are able to do the same with the euro in E.U. countries.
3. *Economies of scale.* Some economists expect the euro to rival the U.S. dollar as a reserve currency for governments. This means that the European Union gets interest-free loans (as countries hold euros as reserves). In addition, if international contracts are written in euros rather than in dollars, transaction costs for E.U. companies decline.

Individual E.U. countries face two major disadvantages from the adoption of a common currency:

Disadvantages of a common currency include loss of independent monetary policy and loss of nationalism.

1. *Loss of independent monetary policy.* Individual E.U. countries can no longer use expansionary monetary policy to stimulate their economies or depreciate their

THE BRIEFING ROOM   The Dollarization of Ecuador

Maintaining confidence in a national currency is especially difficult for governments that have had a history of trouble with inflation and sudden currency devaluations. Ecuador illustrates this point. During much of the late 1990s in Ecuador, prices rose by over 30 percent per year and Ecuador was forced to devalue its currency both rapidly and in large increments. Each time Ecuador devalued the sucre (Ecuador's currency), foreign investors lost money. As a result, it became increasingly difficult for Ecuador to attract foreign capital. The Ecuadorian economy contracted.

To bring back foreign capital, Ecuador needed to eliminate exchange rate risk and restore the confidence of foreign investors. So, in September 2000, Ecuador adopted the U.S. dollar as its official currency. Adopting another country's currency is an extreme form of a fixed exchange rate. By adopting the dollar, Ecuador is unable to devalue its currency and unable to expand the money supply and create inflation. Ecuador no longer controls its currency; the U.S. Fed does. Ecuador's hope is that this extreme measure will add stability to the economy and also signal to foreign investors that it is serious about maintaining a stable currency. Ecuador, however, also recognizes that the dollar has the same disadvantages of a common currency, and that by adopting the dollar it loses its ability to run an independent monetary policy.

---

currency. For example, say France was in a recession while the other E.U. economies were booming. If France had its own currency, and did not feel obliged to maintain a fixed exchange rate, it could run expansionary monetary policy to offset the recession. With a common currency, the monetary policy is the same in all E.U. countries; there is only one money supply and one central bank.

2. *Loss of nationalism.* The loss of control over one's currency reduces the fiscal policy options of a country. The ability of a country's central bank to print money and buy bonds means that the government can never go bankrupt as long as the central bank bails it out. Lower risk of default makes a country's bonds more attractive to investors. With a common currency, that is not the case: government doesn't have a central bank to bail it out. This may make it harder and more expensive (by increasing the default risk premium) for countries to run expansionary fiscal policy financed by the sale of bonds. Critics of the common currency argue that losing a national currency is like losing national identity or heritage. For example, the British pound sterling has been a symbol of Britain, much as the British monarchy has, and despite the problems of both these symbols, the British are reluctant to part with either.

The Maastricht Treaty set up the rules for a common currency in Europe.

Weighing the Advantages and Disadvantages of a Common Currency. The E.U. senators felt that the advantages outweighed the disadvantages, and, in an agreement reached in 1991, known as the **Maastricht Treaty,** they specified a set of conditions that countries would have to meet to be part of the monetary union. The treaty set stringent rules regarding a country's inflation rate, exchange rate stability, and debt and deficit as percentages of GDP—all indicators of economic stability. Each country that wished to join the European Union also had to hold a referendum (a vote by all citizens) to see whether its citizens ratified its E.U. membership. In January 1999, eleven members of the European Union began recording transactions and keeping accounts in both the euro and their own currencies. In January 2001, the euro replaced these members' national currencies. Britain was not planning to adopt the euro in 2001, and Denmark's citizens voted not to adopt the euro as their currency in 2000. (See The Briefing Room, "The Dollarization of Ecuador," for a unilateral move to adopt another country's currency.)

Technical Requirements of Optimal Currency Areas. The adoption of the euro by the European Union raises broader questions: What is an optimal currency area? Should the entire world use a single currency? Or should there be many different currencies? For example, is Europe an **optimal currency area**—a group of countries suitable for adopting a common currency without significantly jeopardizing domestic policy goals? Is the United States an optimal currency area, or would the United States be better off with two currencies—say, one for east of the Mississippi and one for west of the Mississippi?

As economists have explored the issue of optimal currency areas, they have found that it is not so much geographical size, but the type of production and nature of economic events that take place within the area that are significant. Criteria for an optimal currency area include significant labor mobility, wage rate flexibility, a broad range of industries, and diverse demand shocks.

How do European Union countries fit these criteria? Countries of the European Union appear to have a reasonably broad range of industries to merit a common currency. Similarly, the shocks they experience are somewhat diverse. In this regard, the European Union is comparable to the United States, making it a good candidate for a common currency. However, labor mobility in the European Union is highly restricted compared with that in the United States, and wage rates are not very flexible, making the European Union a poor candidate on these grounds. So, on technical grounds, the evidence for a successful optimal currency area in the European Union is mixed.

> Optimal currency areas require significant labor mobility, wage-rate flexibility, a broad range of industries in the entire area, and diverse demand shocks.

Political Requirements of Optimal Currency Areas. Another requirement for an optimal currency area is political cohesiveness. Political cohesiveness would allow income to flow from one area to another to achieve what independent monetary policy would achieve when a recession hits one area but not another. For instance, if France experienced a recession, income transfers such as unemployment insurance and welfare payments could flow to it from the countries experiencing booms. Some of the equalizing effects from these transfers would have been achieved with independent monetary policies.

Such political cohesiveness is limited in the European Union. In fact, the lack of a central government and a common fiscal policy, such as exist in the United States, is probably the European Union's biggest shortcoming in its move to a common currency. Their leaders know this, but they hope that the move to a single currency will lead to greater political and fiscal integration. However, many economists fear that the European Union is putting the cart before the horse, and could lead to serious problems.

> Political cohesiveness is the biggest problem facing the European Union in its attempt to establish a common currency.

Executive Summary

- Countries recognize that the economies of the world are interconnected and have developed international organizations to coordinate policies among countries.

- In adopting a common currency, the members of the European Union will benefit from reduced exchange rate risk, reduced transactions costs, and economies of scale, as well as greater political integration.

- The costs of a common currency are loss of independent monetary policy and loss of nationalism.

- Members of the European Union hope the benefits of a common currency will outweigh the costs.

- Criteria for an optimal currency area include significant labor mobility, wage rate flexibility, a broad range of industries, and diverse demand shocks.

POLICY PERSPECTIVE: CURRENCY CRISES IN EMERGING ECONOMIES

The experience of Mexico and several Asian economies during the 1990s illustrates the problems that can arise as countries deal with international issues. Mexico had a growing current account deficit financed by large foreign capital inflows. In addition, Mexico was partially fixing the peso to the dollar. (It allowed the exchange rate to change by a preset amount each year.)

The reliance on foreign capital inflows to finance a growing trade deficit is fine as long as the foreign capital keeps flowing into the economy, but it can cause problems when it stops. For example, in early 1994, political instability in Mexico led to a sharp reduction in foreign capital inflows, causing the exchange rate to fall faster than the depreciation planned by the Mexican government.

For most of 1994, the Mexican government stuck to its plan of gradual depreciation by buying up pesos with its reserve of U.S. dollars. In late 1994, however, it became clear that the Mexican government would soon run out of U.S. dollars and would eventually have to abandon its gradual depreciation. Currency traders detected this and sold pesos, forcing the government to abandon its plan immediately. (Traders make money by anticipating movements in exchange rates—buy low, sell high—so there will be pressure for anything that can be expected to happen to happen immediately.) The peso's value started to plummet. The peso's rapid depreciation led to further panic among foreign investors, who pulled out more of their capital. To steady its currency, the Mexican government was forced to run contractionary monetary and fiscal policies in a way that raised interest rates. (The Mexican economy is small, but not that small, so the BP curve was not flat.) This increased capital inflows and decreased demand for the more expensive imports, halting the depreciation of the peso, but also threw the Mexican economy into a recession.

Mexico was left with a sagging economy and a large amount of international debt that was now more expensive to repay because its currency was worth less than before. The U.S. Treasury, along with the International Monetary Fund (IMF), arranged for $40 billion in loans to help Mexico repay its foreign debts. These loans helped restore investor confidence and, in 1996, foreign capital began flowing back into Mexico and its economy started expanding again.

Just as Mexico was recovering from its currency crisis, another currency crisis was brewing across the Pacific Ocean. In late summer 1997, Thailand had a rising trade deficit and a falling exchange rate. To slow the decline of the value of the Thai baht, the Thai government had to buy bahts with dollars on the foreign exchange market. In August 1997, Thailand announced it would soon run out of foreign currency reserves. Investors began pulling their money out of Thailand and several other Southeast Asian economies in anticipation of currency devaluation. The reduction in capital inflows to Indonesia, the Philippines, Malaysia, and Singapore forced those countries to devalue their currencies as well. To help them pay back their foreign debt, the U.S. Treasury and the IMF arranged loans for these countries.

The common thread in these two cases is that large capital inflows suddenly stopped and reversed themselves at a time when the government was trying to maintain an orderly exchange market by having fixed exchange rates.

If relatively fixed exchange rates are part of the problem, why did these governments have them? The fixed exchange rates help them attract foreign investors. Suppose you are a U.S. company wishing to build a factory in Mexico. Your factory will earn profits in pesos and you will then exchange those profits for dollars. A

Despite their problems, countries tend to use partially fixed exchange rates, although less so than in the past.

fixed nominal exchange rate between pesos and dollars is attractive to you because it eliminates one type of uncertainty—you will still face uncertainty about how much profit you will earn, but at least you will be certain about how much that profit, once earned, will be worth in terms of dollars. So, a fixed nominal exchange rate, backed by a government that can credibly defend that exchange rate, is thought to encourage foreign investment, which emerging economies need.

Given the problems that sudden changes in capital flows can cause for countries, the disadvantage of fixed exchange rates appears to outweigh its advantage for many countries. As of late 1999, Mexico, Thailand, Indonesia, the Philippines, Malaysia, and Singapore had abandoned fixed exchange rates and were leaning much more toward flexible exchange rates. Most of these countries were doing well in 2000. However, as the world economy resumed its expansion, it was unclear how much of that success was due to their foreign exchange policies.

CONCLUSION

A country cannot consider its domestic goals without considering its international implications. The IS/LM/BP framework allows one to do so, and makes difficult issues understandable. As we hope has been apparent from this chapter, the issues in open-economy macroeconomics are extraordinarily interesting and every bit as complicated and politically charged as are issues in domestic macroeconomics. Whatever the correct solutions to open-economy macroeconomic problems, we can expect these problems to become increasingly important for the United States.

With international transportation and communication becoming faster and easier, economies are increasingly becoming integrated. More and more of macroeconomics will be open-economy macroeconomics, even for large countries like the United States.

KEY POINTS

- Policies designed to achieve domestic goals will also affect a country's international goals.
- When income rises, the current account will move toward deficit. To maintain a balance of payments equilibrium, interest rates need to rise to increase the flow of capital into the country and bring the capital account toward surplus. The BP curve summarizes this relationship.
- The balance of payments (BP) curve shows the combination of interest rates and levels of income for which balance of payments is in equilibrium. Its position depends on variables other than interest rates and income such as exchange rates and tariffs.
- The more responsive capital flows are to interest rates, the flatter the BP curve. The more responsive imports are to income, the steeper the BP curve.
- A fall in the exchange rate shifts the BP curve to the right; a rise in the exchange rate shifts the BP curve to the left. Any policy that increases net exports shifts the BP curve to the right; any policy that decreases net exports shifts the BP curve to the left.
- When an economy is to the left of the BP curve, the balance of payments is in surplus and there is pressure for the currency to appreciate. If exchange rates are flexible, the BP curve will shift to the left.
- When an economy is to the right of the BP curve, the balance of payments is in deficit and there is pressure for the currency to depreciate. If exchange rates are flexible, the BP curve will shift to the right.
- The BP curve affects the power of monetary and fiscal policy. In large open economies, if exchange rates are flexible, policy makers don't have to worry about maintaining a balance of payments equilibrium. The value of the country's currency will be in equilibrium.

- A large open economy with a fixed exchange rate can increase income and maintain its interest rate target only if it has sufficient foreign reserves to offset its private balance of payments deficit.
- Countries with fixed exchange rates have a balance of payments constraint that places a limit on the effectiveness of fiscal policy.
- A country can use capital outflow controls, import controls, and exchange rate policies to achieve simultaneous external and internal balance. Or, it can change its internal balance to achieve external balance.
- Under perfect capital mobility, the BP curve is horizontal at the world interest rate.
- In the Mundell-Flemming model with fixed exchange rates, monetary and fiscal policy must be coordinated.
- In the Mundell-Flemming model with flexible exchange rates, fiscal policy will be ineffective because changes in net exports will offset fiscal policy. But a combination of monetary and fiscal policy can be used to achieve any desired income level.
- A small open economy with perfect capital mobility cannot use monetary policy or fiscal policy independently.
- The members of the European Union have adopted a common currency—the euro—in hopes of increasing trade and capital flows among countries, as well as encouraging greater political integration. The largest risk of adopting a common currency is that individual countries will lose their ability to conduct independent monetary policy.
- Optimal currency areas require similar industries in all countries, significant labor mobility, broad range of industries in the entire area, and diverse demand shocks.

KEY TERMS

balance of payments constraint 284
balance of payments curve 274
capital outflow controls 281
export drive 279
external balance 282

internal balance 282
Maastricht Treaty 297
Mundell-Fleming model 288
optimal currency area 298
perfect capital mobility 287

quotas 279
tariffs 279
voluntary restraint agreement 279

QUESTIONS FOR THOUGHT AND REVIEW

1. Why is it important to study open-economy macroeconomics?
2. What does it mean for a country to have a private balance of payments equilibrium?
3. Why does a country with a flexible exchange rate always move toward a private balance of payments of zero?
4. Why does the BP curve slope upward?
5. What factors determine the slope of the BP curve? Explain how the slope of the BP curve varies with each factor.
6. Describe one exchange rate policy and explain how it shifts the BP curve.
7. What is an import control and how does it affect the BP curve?
8. What is a capital outflow control and how does it affect the BP curve?
9. What is the difference between internal and external balance?
10. How does the balance of payments constraint affect a country's choice of macroeconomic policies?
11. What type of policies other than monetary or fiscal policy can a government use to achieve external balance? Give an example of such a policy.
12. What does *perfect capital mobility* mean, and what does it imply about the shape of the BP curve?
13. What is the Mundell-Fleming model? Under what circumstances is it the appropriate model?
14. What does it mean for the central bank to sterilize exchange rate interventions? Why is it impossible for a small open economy to sterilize its exchange rate interventions?
15. Why is fiscal policy, used alone, ineffective in a small open economy with flexible exchange rates?
16. Why is monetary policy, used alone, ineffective in a small open economy with fixed exchange rates?
17. Why don't trade policies work in small open economies?

18. How did the United States export inflation during the Bretton Woods era of fixed exchange rates? Why did it do so?

19. What are the advantages and disadvantages of a common currency?

20. What are the technical and political requirements of an optimal currency area? Does the European Union satisfy these requirements?

21. What events led up to the currency crises in Mexico and Asia during the 1990s? What could these countries have done differently to prevent these crises?

PROBLEMS AND EXERCISES

1. Suppose a country has a balance of payments deficit.
   a. Is there an excess supply of its currency or an excess demand for its currency?
   b. Assuming the country has a flexible exchange rate, will its currency depreciate or appreciate to bring the balance of payments back to equilibrium?

2. Consider a large open economy with a flexible exchange rate. The economy is currently well below potential at the intersection of the IS/LM and BP curves, but the government is satisfied with the interest rate.
   a. What combination of fiscal and monetary policies could it use to move output to potential but keep interest rates unchanged? Demonstrate your answer with the IS/LM/BP model.
   b. What are the adjustments that would take place to restore balance of payments equilibrium?

3. Consider a large open economy with a fixed exchange rate. The economy is currently well below potential at the intersection of the IS/LM and BP curves. The government wishes to use fiscal policy only to move output to potential, and it has sufficient foreign reserves.
   a. Illustrate the impact of using fiscal policy to move the economy to potential, using the IS/LM/BP diagram. Is the private balance of payments in deficit or surplus at the new level of output and interest rate? What actions will the government have to take to maintain a fixed exchange rate? What hap-

pens if the government does not have sufficient foreign reserves?
   b. Use the IS/LM/BP diagram to illustrate the combination of fiscal and monetary policies necessary to move the economy toward potential and, at the same time, maintain a private balance of payments equilibrium.
   c. Consider the situation in item (b), but this time, assume that the government does *not* want to use monetary policy to bring about a private balance of payments equilibrium. What other policies could it use to maintain a private balance of payments equilibrium following the expansion of fiscal policy? Illustrate your answer, using the IS/LM/BP diagram.

4. Demonstrate the effect of expansionary fiscal policy in the Mundell-Fleming model, when
   a. Exchange rates are flexible
   b. Exchange rates are fixed

5. Demonstrate the effect of expansionary monetary policy, using the Mundell-Fleming model, when
   a. Exchange rates are flexible
   b. Exchange rates are fixed

6. Go to the International Monetary Fund's web-page (www.imf.org). Under the heading "What's New?", the IMF lists its recent policy actions. Describe a recent policy action taken by the IMF. What was the justification for this action?

7. Demonstrate what happened during the 1994 Mexican currency crisis, using the IS/LM/BP diagram.

11

Models should be as simple

as possible, but not more so.

—Albert Einstein

Aggregate Supply and Aggregate Demand

After reading this chapter you should be able to:

1. State the determinants of the slope of the AD curve and describe what factors shift the curve

2. State the determinants of the slope of the AS curve and describe what factors shift the curve

3. Demonstrate how prices and output adjust to economic shocks in the short run and the long run

4. Show how the AS/AD model modifies the impact of policy in the IS/LM model

5. Explain how policy makers can respond to aggregate shocks to the economy and why economists debate how policy makers should respond

6. Describe how expectations affect policy in the AS/AD model

7. Use the AS/AD model to describe what happened to the U.S. economy in the late 1990s

In IS/LM analysis, the price level is assumed to be fixed.

The last three chapters introduced you to the IS/LM model. You should now be able to discuss monetary and fiscal policy using the IS/LM model in both a domestic and an international context.

A central assumption of the IS/LM model in those chapters is that the price level is fixed; that is, there is no inflation. In reality, however, inflation is an important concern to policy makers. The importance of inflation to policy makers is evident in the U.S. Fed's actions in the late 1990s and early 2000. Even though annual inflation in the United States was at a 30-year low of about 2 percent, in 1999 the Fed implemented contractionary monetary policy to slow the economy because it feared that the growing economy would ultimately lead to accelerating inflation. This fear stemmed from policy makers' estimates that the economy had expanded beyond potential output. Based on past experience, when the economy exceeded potential output, inflation rose. Policy makers were anticipating a similar result, and implemented contractionary monetary policy in late 1999 and into 2000.

To understand these events and policies, we need to introduce the price level into the short-run model. The model economists use to show the relationship between real output and the price level is the aggregate supply/aggregate demand (AS/AD) model, first introduced in Chapter 4. The AS/AD model is a formal representation of production and expenditures and how they are influenced by the price level. Policy makers and economists use the AS/AD model to analyze short-run movements in the price level and aggregate output. We begin by introducing the aggregate demand curve.

AGGREGATE DEMAND

The AD curve shows combinations of price levels and income levels at which both the goods market and the money market are in equilibrium.

The **aggregate demand (AD) curve** shows the combinations of price levels and income levels at which both the goods market and the money market are in equilibrium. It really isn't an aggregate demand curve at all—it's a goods market/money market equilibrium curve.[1] The AD curve is a downward-sloping equilibrium curve that has the aggregate price level on the vertical axis and aggregate output on the horizontal axis.

The Slope of the AD Curve

As discussed in Chapter 8, the aggregate demand curve is not the same as a demand curve in microeconomics. In microeconomics, the price of a single good is on the vertical axis and the quantity of a single good is on the horizontal axis. A demand curve for a single good is downward sloping because, as a good's price rises, people buy less of it, substituting other goods for it. Because the AD curve is for the entire economy (all goods), substitution cannot be the reason why it is sloped downward. There are no other goods that can be substituted. Instead, the foundation of the AD curve lies in the IS/LM model you learned in Chapters 8 and 9. To derive an AD curve, we have to consider how a change in the price level, everything else held constant, will affect equilibrium expenditures and output. We will concentrate on two effects: the interest rate effect and the international effect.[2]

Interest rate effect: P up → Real M down → r up → Investment down → Quantity of AD down.

The Interest Rate Effect. The **interest rate effect** states that, as the price level rises, the real money supply decreases, causing interest rates to rise, causing investment expenditures, and therefore, the quantity of aggregate demand to fall. To understand the interest rate effect, it is important to differentiate between nominal money supply, the actual quantity of money in the economy, and **real money supply,** the quantity of money divided by the price level. The real money supply is a measure of the purchasing power of money—the amount of goods and services that money can buy.

For example, if you have $10 and candy bars cost $1, you can buy 10 candy bars. If the price of candy bars doubles to $2, that same $10 can purchase only five candy bars. When the price level doubles, the purchasing power of $10 falls to $5.

---

[1]We attempted to call it by a better name, but, after a spirited fight, we have succumbed and now use the standard AD terminology. As long as you remember that this curve is derived from the IS/LM model, is an equilibrium curve, and has no relationship to the demand curve you learned about in principles of microeconomics, it doesn't matter what it is called. Other economists have attempted to solve the problem by developing an alternative AS/AD model with inflation on the vertical axis. See Appendix A for an introduction to the alternative approach.

[2]Economists have offered other explanations of the relationship between the price level and aggregate quantity demanded, but the interest rate effect and the international effect are two of the most important, and to keep the analysis manageable, we will only discuss them.

Likewise, if the nominal money supply is $1 trillion and the price level doubles, the amount of goods and services that people can buy with that $1 trillion—the real money supply—falls to half.

So, when the price level rises, the real money supply falls, even though the nominal money supply does not. Because people find that their cash holdings are not sufficient for the goods and services they wish to purchase, they sell bonds to make up for the decline of the real money supply. As they sell bonds, the supply of bonds increases, bond prices fall, and interest rates rise. As interest rates rise, investment expenditures fall, which reduces total expenditures. So, a rise in the price level, through its effect on interest rates, leads to a decline in expenditures. This explanation of the effect of a rise in the price level on expenditures would be equivalent to a shift in to the left of the LM curve.

International effect: *P* up → Net exports down → Quantity of AD down.

The International Effect. The **international effect** states that if nominal exchange rates are fixed, as the price level rises, net exports, and therefore the quantity of aggregate demand, will fall. An increase in the price level will cause exports to become more expensive for foreign buyers and imports to become less relatively expensive for domestic buyers. As a result, people in a country purchase more imported goods and fewer domestic goods, and foreign consumers buy fewer goods from that country. Net exports, which are a component of aggregate demand, fall. This shifts the IS curve in to the left.

If the exchange rate is flexible, the exchange rate may adjust to offset the change in the price level. If a change in the exchange rate completely offsets the change in the price level, the IS curve does not shift at all. (This is the case when purchasing-power parity holds perfectly.) If it only partly offsets the change in the price level, the IS curve shifts by a smaller amount than when the exchange rate is fixed.

Both the interest rate and international effects are shown in Exhibit 11–1. A rise in the price level, through the interest rate effect, shifts the LM curve to the left, from LM_0 to LM_1, leading to a decline in real output, Y_0 to Y_1, as the economy moves from point A to point B. In addition, the rise in the price level, through the

Exhibit 11-1

Interest Rate and International Effects

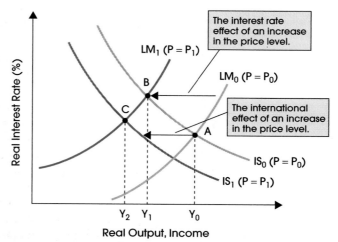

A rise in the price level reduces the real money supply and shifts the LM curve to the left, from LM_0 to LM_1. This is the interest rate effect. A rise in the price level also reduces net exports and shifts the IS curve to the left, from IS_0 to IS_1. This is the international effect. Output falls from Y_0 to Y_2 when the price level rises from P_0 to P_1.

international effect, shifts the IS curve from IS_0 to IS_1, further reducing income from Y_1 to Y_2, as the economy moves from point B to point C. Including both the interest rate and the international effects means that when the price level rises from P_0 to P_1, output falls from Y_0 to Y_2 (point C in Exhibit 11–1).

Deriving the AD Curve from the IS/LM Model

Because the AD curve represents the combinations of price levels and output levels at which the goods market and money market are in equilibrium, we already have derived two points on the AD curve. We can see this in Exhibit 11–2, which shows the IS/LM model in the top panel and the AD curve in the bottom panel. Notice that in the lower exhibit, the price level is on the vertical axis and real output is on the horizontal axis. At the initial price level, P_0, the goods and money markets are in equilibrium when income is Y_0—point A in Exhibit 11–2(a). This is also one combination of price and income on the AD curve—point A in Exhibit 11–2(b).

When the price level rises from P_0 to P_1, the LM and IS curves shift in to the left, giving us a new equilibrium output level, Y_1—point B in Exhibit 11–2(a). The LM curve shifts to the left because of the interest rate effect, while

Exhibit 11–2

From IS/LM to AD

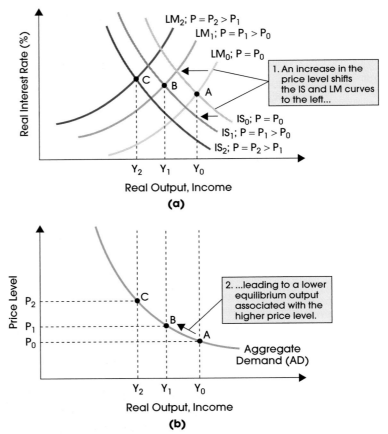

Because the AD curve is a combination of price and income levels where the goods and money markets are in equilibrium, we can use the IS/LM model to derive an AD curve. An increase in the price level from P_0 to P_2 in *panel a* shifts the LM and IS curves to the left and reduces income from Y_0 to Y_2. Points A, B, and C are three price and income combinations along the AD curve, shown in *panel b*.

the IS curve shifts to the left because of the international effect. (We're assuming that the exchange rate is not perfectly flexible and does not rise to offset the decline in the price level.) Combining the new price level, P_1, with the new equilibrium real output level, Y_1, gives us a second point on the AD curve—point B in Exhibit 11–2(b).

Let's now derive a third point. Say that the price level rises to P_2. Using the same reasoning as before, this will shift the LM and IS curves further to the left—to LM_2 and IS_2—causing equilibrium output to fall to Y_2 (point C) in Exhibit 11–2(a). Combining this lower equilibrium real output Y_2 with the higher price level P_2, we get a third point on the AD curve—point C in Exhibit 11–2(b). Continuing this exercise for all possible price levels, we derive the entire AD curve—all price and income combinations at which the goods market and the money market are in equilibrium. As you can see, it is a downward-sloping curve. As the price level rises, aggregate expenditures decline.

One aspect of the AD curve that interests policy makers is how much aggregate expenditures change when the price level changes, in other words, the slope of the AD curve. If expenditures change by only a little for a given change in the price level, the AD curve is steep. If expenditures change by a lot for a given change in the price level, the AD curve is flat.

The slope of the AD curve depends on the strength of the interest rate and international effects (how far the IS and LM curves shift) as well as the factors that determine the slopes of the IS and LM curves. (The flatter the IS and LM curves, the flatter the AD curve.) The larger the interest rate and international effects, the flatter the AD curve. The smaller the interest rate and international effects, the steeper the AD curve. For example, if the economy has flexible exchange rates and purchasing-power parity holds so that the real exchange rate tends to remain constant when the price level changes, the international effect is eliminated and aggregate expenditures become less responsive to changes in the price level (the AD curve becomes steeper).

One more thing to note about the slope: A larger marginal propensity to consume means that the quantity of aggregate demand changes much more when the price level changes. In technical terms, the greater the size of the multiplier, the flatter the AD curve. We know this because the slope of the IS curve depends on the size of the multiplier. As the multiplier gets larger, the IS curve becomes flatter, and so the quantity of aggregate demand also becomes more responsive to changes in the price level.

Factors That Shift the AD Curve

The AD curve shows the relationship between the price level and aggregate expenditures. Anything that causes aggregate expenditures to change (holding the price level constant) will shift the AD curve. From the IS/LM model, we know that any factor that shifts the IS or LM curves will change expenditures at every price level. The same factors that shift the IS and LM curves will also shift the AD curve.

For example, an increase in the money supply shifts the LM curve to the right, increasing equilibrium income at price level P_0. This effect is shown in Exhibit 11–3(a). The economy begins at point A. Expansionary monetary policy shifts the LM curve from LM_0 to LM_1, and output rises to Y_1 when the price level is P_0. Exhibit 11–3(b) shows the effect on the AD curve. Point A on AD_0 in Exhibit 11–3(b) corresponds to point A in Exhibit 11–3(a). Expansionary monetary policy

The AD curve is derived from determining various equilibria of IS and LM curves at various price levels.

The slope of the AD curve depends on the slopes and shifts of the IS and LM curves.

Shifts in autonomous expenditures will shift the AD curve.

Expansionary monetary and fiscal policy shift the AD curve to the right; contractionary policy shifts the AD curve to the left.

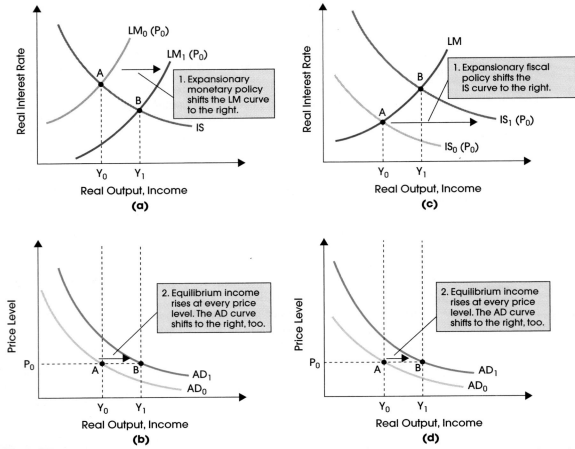

Exhibit 11-3

Factors that Shift the AD Curve

Anything that causes aggregate expenditures to change (holding the price level constant) shifts the AD curve. *Panels a* and *b* show how an increase in the money supply shifts the AD curve to the right. *Panels c* and *d* show how an increase in government spending or a reduction in taxes shifts the AD curve to the right.

increases equilibrium income at price level P_0 to Y_1, which means that the new AD curve must go through point *B* in Exhibit 11–3(b). The increase in expenditures from expansionary monetary policy shifts the AD curve out to the right, as Exhibit 11–3(b) shows. Other factors that shift the LM curve, such as a decrease in autonomous demand for money, also shift the AD curve out.

Exhibit 11–3(c, d) show the effect of expansionary fiscal policy. Exhibit 11–3(c) shows how expansionary fiscal policy shifts the IS curve from IS_0 to IS_1. Aggregate expenditures rise to Y_1 at price level P_0, which means that the AD curve shifts from AD_0 to AD_1 in Exhibit 11–3(d). Increases in any autonomous component of aggregate expenditures also shift the AD curve out to the right.

Anything that causes aggregate expenditures to change (holding the price level constant) whether through the IS or LM curve, shifts the AD curve. Shift factors include fiscal policy, monetary policy, changes in autonomous expenditures, and changes in autonomous money demand. While the AD curve shows aggregate expenditures at each price level, without aggregate supply, we don't know the equilibrium level of output and the equilibrium price level.

Executive Summary

- The AD curve shows combinations of price levels and income levels at which both the goods market and money markets are in equilibrium.

- The AD curve slopes downward because (1) a rise in price level increases real interest rates, which lowers investment expenditures and output (the interest rate effect); and (2) a rise in the price level lowers net exports and output (the international effect).

- The flatter the IS and LM curves and the larger the interest rate and international effects, the flatter the AD curve.

- Fiscal policy, monetary policy, changes in autonomous expenditures, and changes in autonomous money demand shift the AD curve.

AGGREGATE SUPPLY IN THE SHORT RUN

The AS curve shows how the price level responds to changes in aggregate demand.

The **aggregate supply (AS) curve** is a curve that shows how the price level responds to changes in aggregate demand. Just as the AD curve is not like a demand curve for a single good, the AS curve is not like the supply curve for a single good that you studied in your microeconomics course. The AS curve is based on pricing institutions of an economy and shows how the price level typically responds to changes in aggregate demand.[3]

The Slope of the AS Curve

In Chapters 8 through 10, we implicitly assumed that the AS curve was horizontal—that the price level did not change as aggregate demand changed. (This assumption allows individual prices to change, as long as some go up and some go down to even out the overall price level.) The horizontal short-run AS curve fits reality reasonably well in many cases: For example, through much of the 1990s, the price level did not change by much as output rose. In other cases, however, the horizontal short-run AS curve doesn't fit well with reality. In this chapter, we expand the analysis and consider an upward-sloping AS curve in which the price level rises as output rises, and vice versa.

In this book, we concentrate on changes in the prices of factors of production as the explanation for the slope of the AS curve.

Although economists have a number of explanations for the slope of the AS curve, to keep the analysis simple, we concentrate on the prices of factors of production (input prices) as the sole cause. This makes some sense, because changes in input prices tend to be a predictor of changes in the price level. Theoretically, economists focus on input prices by assuming that firms set their prices using a **cost-plus-markup rule.** Cost-plus markup is a pricing system in which a firm sets prices above input costs high enough to result in a desirable profit margin while keeping its products competitive. An example of a cost-plus-markup rule is to set price 50 percent above input costs. Using this rule, if a CD costs $6 to produce, the firm will sell it for $9. If firms use a cost-plus-markup rule, fluctuations in prices mirror fluctuations in costs.

If firms use a cost-plus-markup rule, fluctuations in prices mirror fluctuations in costs.

Cost-plus-markup pricing rules are used in most macroeconomic forecasting models. These models predict future price-level changes by looking at changes in

---

[3]In microeconomics, a firm or industry supply curve is based on the firm's marginal cost of production. It tells us the quantity that a competitive firm will supply given a price. In the specification of the AS curve presented in this chapter, firms are considered price makers. They determine price subject to demand and competitive conditions. Because firms are price makers, the AS curve is not directly related to the marginal cost of production.

Exhibit 11-4

**The AS Curve—Its
Slope and Shifts**

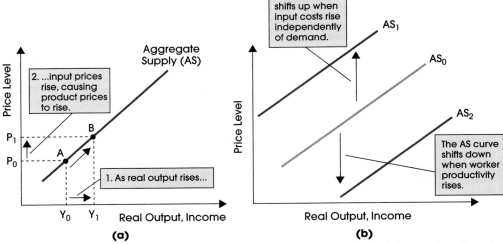

The short-run AS curve is upward sloping, as *panel a* shows. As real output rises, so does the price level. *Panel b* shows a shifting AS curve. Aggregate supply will shift when input prices change independently of demand or when worker productivity changes.

the prices of inputs such as labor, capital, and raw materials. If wages rise, while productivity remains constant, economists predict that firms will increase prices to maintain a constant markup over labor and other costs. Models emphasize labor costs because, for most firms, labor is the greatest input cost.

In the mark-up pricing model when input prices are fixed, regardless of demand (by either formal or informal long-term contracts), the AS curve will be horizontal. Put another way, if input costs aren't changing, the price level will remain constant. Input costs, however, could change. When the demand for goods and services increases, firms increase their demand for inputs such as labor. When all firms demand more inputs, and the market supply of the factors of production is upward sloping, firms' costs will rise. Firms will respond by raising their product prices, resulting in an upward-sloping AS curve, as Exhibit 11–4(a) shows. As aggregate output increases (the economy moves from point A to B), the price level increases.

> When input prices remain fixed, output prices tend to remain constant.

We could say much more about the theoretical reason for upward-sloping AS curves, but we won't. We will stop here because our interest is policy, and the relationship we emphasize—the connection between input prices and output prices—is the relationship that is important in applied policy models.

Factors That Shift the AS Curve

Let's now consider factors that shift the AS curve. In a cost-plus-markup model, anything that reduces the costs of production independent of demand will shift the AS curve down, and anything that increases the costs of production independent of demand will shift the AS curve up.

> If workers expect increases in inflation, they raise their nominal wage and the AS curve shifts up.

One factor that will shift the AS curve is inflationary expectations by workers. Because a higher price level reduces the purchasing power of workers' wages, if workers expect the price level in the economy to rise in the future, they will negotiate for higher wages to compensate them for that higher cost of living. That is, they will negotiate for higher **nominal wages** (the wage they receive) to keep their **real wages** (the nominal wage adjusted for inflation) constant. Because, at a higher price level, workers require a higher nominal wage for every quantity of labor supplied, the labor supply curve shifts up. Firms will have to increase worker pay, the costs of production will rise, and the AS curve will shift up. Exhibit 11–4(b) shows the effect of this shift in the supply of labor on the AS curve as a shift from AS_0 to AS_1. If workers expect increases in inflation, the AS curve shifts up.

> Increases in labor productivity shift the AS curve down.

Wages aren't the only factor that affect the costs of production. Changes in productivity also affect the costs of production independent of demand. For example, if labor productivity rises, firms will be able to produce more with the same number of workers, reducing the cost of production. Increases in productivity, therefore, shift the AS curve down, as Exhibit 11–4(b) demonstrates, from AS_0 to AS_2.

Although the focus has been on labor, the same reasoning for the relationship between the price level and output can be applied to any factor of production. Adverse supply shocks—sudden increases in the price of important inputs to production caused by such things as natural disasters, oil supply disruptions, and large agricultural losses—will shift the AS curve up, and sudden decreases will shift it down. Many economists believe that the dramatic increases in the world price of oil in the 1970s increased firms' cost of production and shifted the AS curve up. They believe this was the cause of the higher price level and lower real output at that time. The opposite happened in the mid-1990s when oil prices declined. In this instance, the AS curve shifted down, reducing the price level and increasing real output.

In summary, anything that increases the price of inputs, independent of demand, will shift the AS curve up, and anything that decreases the price of inputs, independent of demand, will shift the AS curve down.

SHORT-RUN EQUILIBRIUM IN THE AS/AD MODEL

Now that we've introduced both the AS and AD curves, we're ready to consider equilibrium. In Exhibit 11–5(a), we combine the AS curve with the AD curve. Short-run equilibrium in the AS/AD model occurs where the AS and AD curves intersect—where aggregate quantity of real output supplied equals aggregate quantity of real output demanded. Point A in Exhibit 11–5(a) is an example of equilibrium. When aggregate demand is AD_0, at real output levels above Y_0, inventories are building up and firms cut production. At real output levels below Y_0, aggregate expenditures exceed aggregate production, inventories are being depleted, and firms respond by increasing production. When an economy is in equilibrium, aggregate expenditures equal aggregate production.

> Short-run equilibrium in the AS/AD model occurs where the AS curve intersects the AD curve.

Now let's consider when an economy moves away from its equilibrium because of a shift in either the aggregate demand curve or the aggregate supply curve. These shifts might be due to monetary or fiscal policy (for aggregate demand) or a supply shock (for aggregate supply). Consider an economy that is in equilibrium at point A in Exhibit 11–5(a). Expansionary monetary policy shifts the AD curve to the right, from AD_0 to AD_1. (Remember: The entire IS/LM analysis lies behind the AD curve, so the multiplier and interest rates are all coming into play in any shift of the AD curve.) At the original price level (P_0), aggregate expenditures (Y_2) exceed aggregate production (Y_0) and inventories are running down. As firms increase production to meet the increase in expenditures, the demand for labor increases and

> When the AS curve slopes up, part of the effect of an increase in AD on real output is offset by the rise in the price level.

Exhibit 11-5

Short-Run Equilibrium

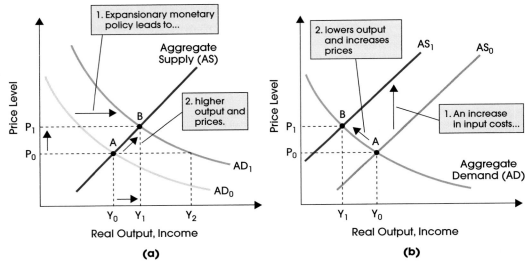

Short-run equilibrium occurs where the AD curve intersects the short-run AS curve. *Panel a* shows how increases in aggregate demand lead to both a higher price level and higher real output. *Panel b* shows how increases in input prices that shift the AS curve up lead to a higher price level but lower real output.

wages rise because of the upward-sloping supply curve for labor. The rise in the price level, through the interest rate effect and the international effect, reduces the aggregate quantity demanded. The economy moves from point A to point B.

If the price level had remained constant, as we assume it did in the IS/LM model, output would have increased to Y_2. With flexible prices, real output increases to only Y_1. This is an important conclusion of the short-run AS/AD model: *The effect of any increase in aggregate demand on real output is partially offset by a higher price level.*

As another example, suppose a significant portion of a country's capital is damaged by an earthquake. This reduces the availability of factors of production, increases production costs, and shifts the AS curve up from AS_0 to AS_1 (see Exhibit 11–5[b]) as firms raise their prices to maintain their profit margin. The increase in the price level reduces the aggregate quantity demanded and the economy moves from point A to point B. In the short-run AS/AD model, *significant increases in factor prices raise the price level and reduce real output.*

LONG-RUN EQUILIBRIUM IN THE AS/AD MODEL

So far, we've discussed short-run equilibrium in the AS/AD model. We know from Chapters 5 through 7, however, that the economy behaves differently in the long run. In the long run, potential output rules. We now expand the AS/AD model and consider long-run equilibrium.

Long-run equilibrium occurs where the aggregate quantity of real output demanded equals potential output. We know from Chapter 4 that potential output is the amount of output an economy can produce when capital and labor are fully utilized. Potential output does not depend on the price level and is, therefore, represented graphically by a vertical line when the price level is on the vertical axis and real output is on the horizontal axis. The vertical line in Exhibit 11–6(a) is an

Exhibit 11–6

Long-Run Equilibrium

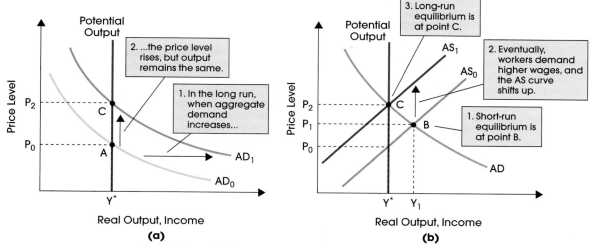

Panel a shows that long-run equilibrium real output is determined entirely by potential output. In the long run, changes in aggregate demand do not affect real output, only the price level. In the short run equilibrium output need not equal potential. When output is above potential, input prices will begin to rise and the AS curve will shift up, as *panel b* shows. This adjustment continues until the economy is at both short- and long-run equilibrium at potential output at point *C*.

example of the relationship between potential output and the price level. Graphically, long-run equilibrium is where the AD curve intersects the potential output line, such as at points *A* and *C* in Exhibit 11–6(a).

Because potential output is independent of the price level in the long run, changes in aggregate demand will not affect real output. In the long run, changes in aggregate demand will only change the price level. For example, if aggregate demand rises from AD_0 to AD_1 (Exhibit 11–6[a]), real output remains at Y^* and the price level rises to P_2. This is the long-run dichotomy, which states that the real sector (where real output is determined) and the nominal sector (where the price level is determined) can be analyzed separately. This dichotomy underlies the policy conclusion that changes in aggregate demand can affect real output only in the short run. In the long run, aggregate demand affects only the price level. In the AS/AD model, therefore, potential output provides a long-run anchor for real output.

This is not to say that the potential output never changes. The location of the line representing potential output on the real output axis depends on the amount of labor, capital and technology available to an economy. Growth in any of these factors shifts the potential output line out to the right, but, usually, in policy discussions of short-run issues such as stabilization, potential output is taken as given.

Adjustment from Short-Run to Long-Run Equilibrium

Long-run equilibrium occurs where the AD curve intersects potential output; thus, potential output provides a long-run anchor for real output.

The economy is in both long-run equilibrium and short-run equilibrium when the AS and AD curves intersect at potential output. If for some reason the short-run equilibrium differs from the long-run equilibrium, the economy will be pulled toward the long-run equilibrium through an adjustment that involves changing input prices. Let's examine how this happens.

We begin by considering a short-run equilibrium in which real output is greater than potential output. In Exhibit 11–6(b), long-run equilibrium is at point C. Short-run equilibrium is initially at point B—where the short-run AS curve, AS_0, intersects the AD curve. At this short-run equilibrium, real output, Y_1, exceeds potential output. The economy can temporarily operate above potential because, in the short run, workers will work overtime, factories and machinery can be pushed harder, and firms can process raw materials more quickly. Unless potential output rises (from an advance in technology or a rise in the labor force participation rate, for example), the short-run equilibrium at Y_1 will be temporary.

One reason the short-run equilibrium is temporary is that, at the short-run equilibrium, the workers' perception of the price level does not match the true price level. This explanation for a short-run equilibrium that differs from the long-run equilibrium is called the **worker-misperception model**—a model of aggregate supply in which worker's perception of the price level is constant along an upward sloping AS curve. Changes in worker's perceptions of the price level, by shifting the supply of labor, shift the AS curve. As they change their beliefs, the equilibrium changes. Let's consider this more carefully. By definition, at each point on the short-run AS curve, AS_0, workers believe that the price level is P_0—the price level at which the AS curve intersects potential output. The only place where their perceptions are correct is where real output equals potential output, which is why potential output is the only long-run equilibrium. In the long-run equilibrium, workers' perceptions must match reality.

At short-run equilibrium B, however, their perceptions are not correct. The price level is actually P_1. Firms are getting existing workers to work overtime by offering them a higher nominal wage, but because the price level has also risen, their real wage has not risen. Eventually, workers realize that the price level has risen and demand higher nominal wages. Their demand for higher wages is represented by a shift up in the supply curve for labor—the nominal wage rises at every quantity of labor supplied. The short-run AS curve shifts up in Exhibit 11–6(b). The labor supply and AS curves continue to shift up until the short-run AS curve is AS_1 and the price level in the economy matches workers' expectations. At that point, the economy is at point C. Real output returns to potential output, Y^*, and the price level rises to P_2, which equals the price level perceived by workers. The economy is in both a short- and long-run equilibrium. As you can see the driving force in the adjustment from the short-run to the long run is workers' perceptions of the price level. In short-run equilibrium, perceptions can differ from actual values because we assume that in the short-run workers focus on nominal wages. In the long run they cannot differ; in the long run, workers focus on real wages to determine quantity of labor supplied. In the long run, the short-run AS curve must intersect the AD and potential output curves at the same location.

Let's now consider an opposite scenario, in which the short-run equilibrium is below the long-run equilibrium, as Exhibit 11–7(a) shows. The initial short-run equilibrium is at point A, where real output is lower than the long-run equilibrium real output. When output is below potential, the labor adjustment process works in reverse. The short-run AS curve, AS_0, is based on worker misperception that the price level is P_0 when it is actually P_1. At real output Y_1, there is an excess supply of workers (the unemployment rate is higher than the natural rate of unemployment). As workers realize that the price level is lower than they previously thought (their real wage is higher than they previously thought), firms can negotiate with workers to accept lower nominal wages. This shifts the supply curve for labor down and, as

The price level that workers expect is the same along each AS curve. It is the price level at which the AS curve intersects the potential output line.

The economy adjusts from long-run to short-run equilibrium because wages change as workers realize that their real wage is not what they thought it was.

Exhibit 11-7

Alternative Adjustments to Long-Run Equilibrium

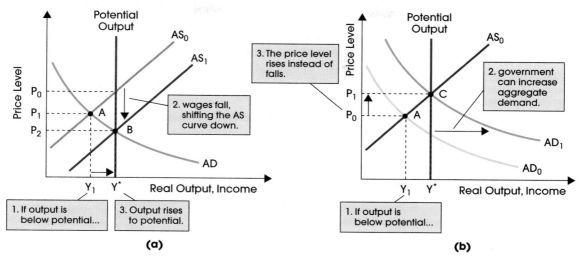

Panel a demonstrates the adjustment of an economy's short-run equilibrium to the long-run equilibrium. When output is below potential, input prices will begin to fall and the AS curve will shift down. This will continue until the economy is at both short- and long-run equilibrium at potential output at point B. Panel b shows the most likely adjustment of an economy that is below potential. Government will likely increase aggregate demand to avoid a decline in the price level. In the long-run the economy returns to potential output at point C.

it does so, shifts the short-run AS curve down. This shifting down continues until the economy returns to potential output, Y^*, at an even lower price level, P_2. At point B, the economy is in both a short- and long-run equilibrium. The supply of labor consistent with AS_1 is based on correct perceptions of the price level.

The implications of the analysis can be made clearer by defining an *effective aggregate supply curve* as the aggregate supply curve at which workers' perception of the price level equals the actual price level. (The effective aggregate supply curve is a locus of points at which a shifting aggregate supply curve intersects the potential output curve.) By definition, the effective aggregate supply curve is a vertical line that is coincident with the potential output curve because the only place where the perceived price level equals the actual price level is where the AS curve intersects the potential output curve.

Importance of Government Intervention to Adjustment

The adjustments from short-run to long-run equilibrium described above are theoretically plausible. In fact, for the case of increases in the price level, the adjustments tend to match the process that policy makers generally believe to be true. However, they don't match the adjustment process described when the economy is below potential (see Exhibit 11–7[a]). In this case, economists adjust the typical adjustment story about movement to equilibrium, because government policy (or expectations of government policy) becomes part of the adjustment process.

Most governments, when faced with an economy that is significantly below potential, try to boost aggregate demand rather than let the price level fall, so the adjustment process that works through a falling price level seldom occurs. Instead

When short-run equilibrium is below potential output, the adjustment process seldom occurs through a fall in the price level; government generally intervenes and shifts the AD curve back out to potential output.

of allowing the price level to fall, the government increases aggregate expenditures with either expansionary monetary or fiscal policy, which brings the economy back to potential output. Exhibit 11–7(b) shows this scenario. As before, the economy begins at point A. To keep the price-level adjustment from occurring, the government implements expansionary monetary or fiscal policy, shifting the AD curve to the right. The price level rises to that level expected by workers, and real output increases to potential. The economy ends up at point C, which is both a short- and long-run equilibrium.

Importance of Expectations to the Time of Adjustment

We should point out that the time periods of the short run and long run have no predetermined length or duration. Instead, they are determined by the ability of firms, consumers, and workers to recognize changes in the price level and incorporate those changes in their decisions. For example, if workers immediately take into account the effect of changing price levels on their real wages, the economy will always be in the long–run equilibrium at potential output. Economists who emphasize rational expectations (discussed later in the chapter) believe that if future economic events, such as changes in aggregate demand, are anticipated, the economy will always be in long-run equilibrium, because firms, workers, and consumers will have incorporated changes in the price level into their decisions as the changes occur.

Executive Summary

- The short-run AS curve is upward sloping because firms set prices based on costs. As aggregate demand increases, demand for inputs increase and their prices rise.

- The AS curve shifts up and down when input prices change independently of demand, worker expectations about the price level changes, or worker productivity changes.

- Short-run equilibrium occurs where the AD and AS curves intersect. Long-run equilibrium occurs where the AD curve intersects the potential output line.

- If the economy is above potential, input prices will rise and the AS curve will shift up until the economy returns to potential in the long run.

- If the economy is below potential, either input prices will fall and the AS curve will shift down until the economy returns to potential in the long run, or government will expand aggregate demand, shifting the AD curve out, allowing the economy to arrive at potential output and a higher price level.

WHY WOULD EQUILIBRIUM OUTPUT EVER DEVIATE FROM POTENTIAL?

To keep our analysis simple, we have focused on one reason why the short-run equilibrium could be different from the long-run equilibrium. That reason is the worker-misperception model. Economists have offered some other reasons, and it may be helpful to survey these to put the short-run argument into perspective.

All of these explanations are interesting, and we could spend an entire chapter on each, but we won't. As long as you know that the short-run equilibrium can differ from the long-run equilibrium, and when they do differ, an adjustment process toward long-run equilibrium is set in motion, you'll be in good shape to consider policy issues.

The Imperfect Information Model

Output can deviate from potential because of worker misperception, imperfect information, and implicit contracts.

The **imperfect information model** is a model of aggregate supply that bases the upward slope of the AS curve on firms' and workers' lack of information about absolute and relative prices. It is a generalization of the worker-misperception model. This explanation also relies on the distinction between real and nominal. In this model, however, workers aren't the only ones who are fooled into thinking the price they receive has risen when it actually hasn't. In the imperfect information model, firms can be fooled in the short run as well.

Firms see the nominal price of their products rise and perceive it as a relative price increase and, therefore, increase the quantity supplied. They don't realize that other prices in the economy have also risen. Short-run output can exceed long-run output. The implications of this imperfect information model for the long run are identical to the worker misperception model. Once firms realize that their relative prices haven't changed, they will cut production and the economy will return to its natural rate of unemployment and its potential level of output.

The Sticky Wage and Price Model

The **sticky wage and price model** is a model of aggregate supply that assumes that firms have implicit or explicit contractual relations with their customers not to raise their prices, even if demand increases. So, it is not the fact that firms and individuals are fooled that leads them to not increase their prices and wages in response to an increase in aggregate demand; it is that they have a contractual agreement not to do so. For example, many unions and firms sign 3-year contracts that set wages for the contract period.

Firms generally do not have explicit contracts with customers, but, in these models, firms have implicit contracts in which they have agreed not to raise their price. Raising their price during a shortage would be seen as taking advantage of customers and may lead the consumer to buy from another firm. For example, right before a hurricane, a flashlight's value increases 10-fold, but firms (those that intend to stay in the market) sell them at the normal price, because not doing so would violate their implicit contract with their customers. Implicit contracts say that, in the short run, such firm–customer relationships are widespread. Firms meet the increases in demand for their product by increasing output. A sufficient number of firms, however, raise both price and production so that overall both output and the price level rise. The implicit contracts established, however, are temporary; in the long run, all prices will gravitate to equilibrium, and the economy will return to its natural rate of unemployment and its potential level of income.

THE AS/AD AND THE IS/LM MODELS

The AS/AD model is an expansion of the IS/LM model in two ways. First, it allows for a changing price level and second it integrates the long run back into the IS/LM model. Let's consider the relationship between the two models by considering them together in Exhibit 11–8. We start at an initial equilibrium (point A) and assume government wants to expand output. In the IS/LM model, this would call for either

Exhibit 11-8

Relationship Between IS/LM and AS/AD

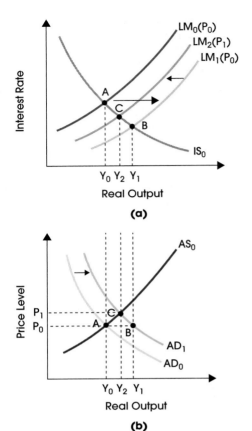

Because the aggregate supply curve is upward sloping, the effect of expansionary monetary policy on real output is partially offset by a rising price level. *Panel b* shows expansionary monetary policy leads the price level to rise. *Panel a* shows how the rise in the price level shifts the LM curve back slightly to the left.

expansionary monetary or fiscal policy. Say that the government runs expansionary monetary policy; the LM curve shifts out to LM_1 and equilibrium output rises from Y_0 to Y_1. The new equilibrium is at point B. In the AS/AD model, this expansionary monetary policy causes the AD curve to shift out to AD_1. To determine the amount by which the AD curve shifts, extend a vertical line from the new IS/LM equilibrium (point B) to the AS/AD graph at the initial price level, P_0.

If the AS curve were perfectly elastic (the implicit assumption in the IS/LM model), point B would be the new equilibrium in both models. But with an upward sloping AS curve, it is not. The price level will rise from P_0 to P_1. Compared to the IS/LM equilibrium (point B), the AS/AD equilibrium (point C) is at a higher price level, P_1, and a lower level of output, Y_2. The reason for this is that the simple IS/LM equilibrium (point B) is not the final equilibrium. The higher price level has to be brought back into the IS/LM model. The higher price level reduces net exports (the international effect) and reduces the real money supply (the interest rate effect).

To keep the analysis simple, let's assume that only the interest rate effect is operative. In that case, the higher price level causes the real money supply to decline, shifting the LM curve to the left to LM_2. Where will the new equilibrium be? It must be at Y_2, the same level of output as is determined in the AS/AD model.

As you can see, the upward sloping AS curve reduces the quantitative effectiveness of aggregate demand policy on real output and changes some of the effect into a rise in the price level. The more inelastic the AS curve, the more aggregate demand policy impacts the price level, instead of real output. In the long run, the AS/AD model tells us that the only achievable real output level is potential output. The effective AS curve is vertical, and output will always return to potential. The LM curve will shift back to its initial position and monetary policy will be ineffective. Therefore, in the long run, the AS/AD model undermines the effectiveness of both monetary and fiscal policy if they are targeted to achieve a level of real output other than potential output.

AGGREGATE DEMAND MANAGEMENT IN THE AS/AD MODEL

As you can see the AS/AD policy model incorporates the IS/LM model, but is more general because it incorporates the effects of a changing price level. Because it is more general, it allows a neater exposition of policy. Let's now return to a discussion of policy in the AS/AD model.

Offsetting Aggregate Demand Shocks

The policy response to a demand shock is clear in the AS/AD model: Offset negative demand shocks that push the economy below potential with expansionary fiscal or monetary policy. Offset positive demand shocks that push the economy above potential with contractionary monetary or fiscal policy. In either case, government can bring real output and the price level to their original levels, which is assumed to be the levels desired by policy makers. A policy problem only arises if for some reason the government is aiming at a real output equilibrium that is not consistent with potential output. In the long run, any such policy will fail.

Offsetting Aggregate Supply Shocks

Offsetting AS shocks through monetary and fiscal policy is more difficult than offsetting AD shocks.

An aggregate supply shock is harder to handle through aggregate demand management policies. If the AS curve shifts up as the result of a supply shock, such as an increase in the price of oil, prices rise and output falls. This type of shock, called an adverse aggregate supply shock, causes **stagflation**—a simultaneous decrease in output and increase in inflation.

To counter the decline in output in a stagflation, policy makers could use expansionary monetary or fiscal policy. To counter the rise in prices, policy makers could use contractionary monetary or fiscal policy. Unfortunately, policy makers cannot use both expansionary and contractionary policy at the same time. An adverse aggregate supply shock creates a policy dilemma. Policy makers must choose between boosting output and suffering higher inflation, or dampening inflation and suffering lower output. In the 1970s, policy makers in the United States chose to offset the decline in output and, as a consequence, the expansionary monetary policy raised inflation.

Uncertainty and Policy

In reality, offsetting shocks is much harder than it is in the model.

Although aggregate demand management is straightforward in the model, it is far from straightforward in reality. Policy makers face many obstacles in trying to implement these policies in the real world. All of the obstacles discussed in Chapter 8 in the context of the IS/LM model apply here. Policy makers face both recognition and implementation lags. They also face uncertainty about the effect of their policy and about the level of potential output. The AS/AD model adds yet another dimension of uncertainty to the policy discussion: How will the effect of policy be split between real output and inflation?

Exhibit 11-9

Adjustment After an Adverse Supply Shock

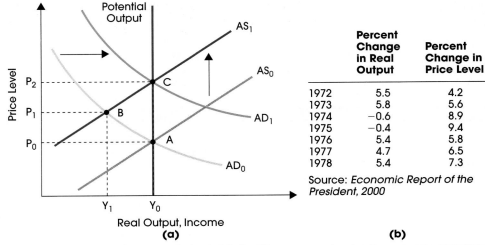

	Percent Change in Real Output	Percent Change in Price Level
1972	5.5	4.2
1973	5.8	5.6
1974	−0.6	8.9
1975	−0.4	9.4
1976	5.4	5.8
1977	4.7	6.5
1978	5.4	7.3

Source: *Economic Report of the President, 2000*

(a)　　　　　　　　　　　　　　　**(b)**

Panel a shows how an adverse supply shock shifts the AS curve up and pushes the economy away from its initial long-run equilibrium at point *A*. If the government wants to limit the effect of the shock on output, it will run expansionary policy and shift the AD curve out to the right. If government does nothing, the AS curve eventually will shift back to its original position, the price level will fall, and output will return to potential at point *A*. *Panel b* shows stagflation during the mid 1970s—output declined and inflation rose.

A Supply-Shock Case Study

Let's consider an adverse supply-shock episode more carefully. From 1974 to 1975, the Organization of Petroleum Exporting Countries (OPEC) cut production, which quadrupled the price of oil. Because oil is an important input to the production of many goods, the increase in its price caused the AS curve to shift upward, as Exhibit 11–9(a) shows. The AS/AD model predicts that the shift would cause real output to decrease, pushing output from Y_0 to Y_1 and prices up from P_0 to P_1. (Short-run equilibrium moved from point *A* to point *B*.) Looking at the data for the United States in Exhibit 11–9(b), we can see that this is exactly what happened. The U.S. economy went into a recession in November 1973 that lasted until March 1975 (16 months). During that time, inflation rose from 4.2 percent a year to over 9 percent a year.

The AS/AD model shows that this adverse supply shock can be countered if the government runs expansionary fiscal or monetary policy, shifting the AD curve from AD_0 to AD_1. In this case, the economy would end up at a new equilibrium, point *C*, but this would push the price level up further, and may cause workers to expect inflation to rise. Workers would push for even higher wages, which would lead to another upward shift in the AS curve. If government chooses not to use expansionary policy, the excess supply of workers would lower wages and the AS curve would eventually shift back to its original position. This path to equilibrium would mean a downward shift in the AS curve, from AS_1 to AS_0.

Here is what happened in response to the oil price shocks of the 1970s: Initially, the Fed accommodated the price rise somewhat with expansionary monetary policy. Inflation began to increase, but a recession was not avoided. Through the late 1970s, the Fed maintained expansionary monetary policy and inflation rose. In 1979, the Fed changed its focus from recession to inflation and implemented contractionary monetary policy, shifting the AD curve back substantially. The U.S. economy fell into a severe 6-month recession in early 1980 and again into a 16-month recession

THE BRIEFING ROOM Potential Output and Inflation in the FAIRmodel

Most government and professional forecasters use large-scale econometric models to forecast the macroeconomy. A large-scale econometric model is a set of interrelated equations that describe aggregate relationships in an economy. These equations are roughly based on the AS/AD framework that you are learning in this chapter. The model's specification of potential output and the output gap are central to these models' predictions for macroeconomic variables such as unemployment, output, and inflation. If actual output rises above potential output, the models predict that inflation will rise; if output dips below potential, the models predict that inflation will fall.

An example of a real-world econometric model that forecasts the economy is the FAIRmodel, constructed by Professor Ray Fair of Yale University. In his model, the equation showing how inflation responds to aggregate demand is

$$Inflation = 0.0039 \times GDPGAP + other\ terms,$$

where GDPGAP is the percent difference between actual GDP and potential GDP. This equation states that when actual GDP is 1 percent above potential GDP, inflation rises by 0.39 percentage points. If actual GDP is 1 percent below potential, this equation predicts that the inflation rate will fall by 0.39 percentage points.

Policy makers at the President's Council of Economic Advisers, the U.S. Federal Reserve Bank, and other government agencies either forecast the economy with their own large-scale econometric models or purchase forecasts from private forecasting firms. The same is true for private firms, such as investment companies, banks, and just about any firm whose business decisions require as accurate a forecast as one can get.

Source: FAIRmodel (fairmodel.econ.yale.edu).

in mid-1981. Inflation began to fall, and, in late 1982, the economy began expanding. By the late 1980s, annual inflation fell to about 4 percent and unemployment fell to about 5.5 percent.

Economists and policy makers typically debate what is the best response to an adverse supply shock. Should policy makers use aggregate demand policies or leave the economy alone? Generally, policy makers take a combination of the two approaches. Much of the choice depends on estimates of how long it will take the economy to move on its own, and what the sacrifice ratio, the ratio of the total output lost during a disinflation to the percentage-point decline in the rate of inflation, will be. (See Chapter 3 for a further discussion.) In general, when faced with an adverse supply shock, government increases aggregate demand, but not enough to prevent some increase in unemployment.

The Real Business-Cycle Perspective on Policy

Real business-cycle economists emphasize technology shocks as the cause of fluctuations in the economy; they advise a laissez-faire policy.

The analysis of business cycles and stabilization policy, using the AS/AD model, is the standard approach most policy makers take. Some economists, however, called **real business-cycle economists,** emphasize technology shocks as the source of output fluctuations in the economy. They argue that many fluctuations in the economy stem from changes in "real phenomenon"—the amount of goods and services an economy is capable of producing. They argue that many of the fluctuations are not deviations of output from potential, but fluctuations of potential output. (Some real business-cycle economists argue that the best estimate of potential output is current output.) They further argue that the goal of macroeconomic policy should not be to smooth out fluctuations. Real business-cycle economists say that, because it is hard to tell whether a change in output is caused by a change in potential output or a shift in the short-run demand or supply curve, the best economic policy is laissez faire (that is, not to intervene).

INFLATION, POTENTIAL OUTPUT, AND THE OUTPUT GAP

Real-life policy discussions of macroeconomic policy generally focus on the output gap.

Real-life policy discussions about adjustment from the short-run equilibrium to the long-run equilibrium usually focus on the **output gap**—the difference between actual output (measured by real GDP) and potential output (measured by potential GDP). Actual output is the short-run equilibrium output; potential output is the long-run equilibrium output.

Exhibit 11–10 shows the historical U.S. data on the output gap and its relationship to inflation. A positive output gap (a gap above zero) means that actual output is above potential output; a negative output gap (a gap below zero) means that actual output is below potential output. In general, when the output gap is positive, the inflation rate tends to rise. You can see that this happened from the mid-1960s to about 1970, and again in the late 1970s and early 1980s, as well as in the early 1990s. When the output gap was negative, the inflation rate tended to fall. In the late 1990s, however, the economy operated above what economists believed to be potential output, and inflation remained low. (See The Briefing Room, "Potential Output and Inflation in the FAIRModel," for an example of a forecasting model that uses the output gap to predict the behavior of the economy.)

Unfortunately, potential output is hard to measure. Estimates of it are based on historical evidence on output growth and unemployment rates at which inflation has started to increase. (See the Q&A feature for an explanation of three methods of estimating potential output.) In recent years, these estimates have not been especially good, as the economy has exceeded estimated potential output without generating significantly increasing inflation.

In recent years, economists have not done well in predicting potential output.

For example, in the late 1990s, the U.S. economy was thought to be above potential output: Short-run equilibrium was at a higher output than long-run equilibrium. Economists predicted significant rises in the price level, but that didn't happen. Instead, the price level remained relatively constant, and income remained high.

Exhibit 11-10

Inflation and the Output Gap

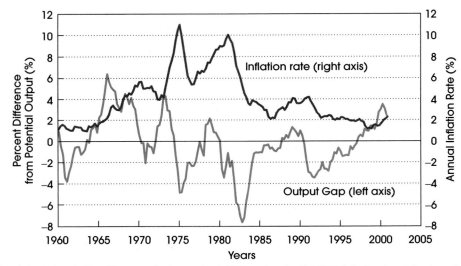

The output gap is the difference between real GDP and potential GDP. Inflation tends to rise when actual output is above potential output, and fall when actual output is below potential output. This relationship broke down in the 1990s. Source: The Bureau of Economic Analysis (www.bea.doc.gov) and Congressional Budget Office (www.cbo.gov).

Q & A

QUESTION   How do economists estimate potential output?

ANSWER   They use statistical and econometric techniques that use data from the recent past.

The recommended policy action for an economy above potential output is the opposite of the recommended policy action for an economy below potential output. So, the usefulness of the short-run model for analyzing policy depends on policy makers' ability to estimate potential output.

Economists use three methods to estimate potential output. The first method is purely statistical. It entails estimating trend growth in actual GDP and adjusting previous estimates of potential GDP for that trend.

A second method for estimating potential output focuses on the amount of labor, capital, and technology available to the economy. Economists combine their estimates of available labor, capital, and technology with an estimated aggregate production function to arrive at an estimate of potential output. The red line in the accompanying exhibit shows an estimate of potential output using this method, along with actual output in blue. According to this estimate, at the end of 2000, in the United States, actual output ($9.39 trillion) was roughly 2.4 percent above potential output ($9.17 trillion).

A third method is to focus primarily on the unemployment rate and the trend growth rate of GDP. Economists estimate the natural rate of unemployment as the rate of unemployment that exists at the trend growth rate of GDP. Potential output is output that exists when the unemployment rate is equal to the natural rate.

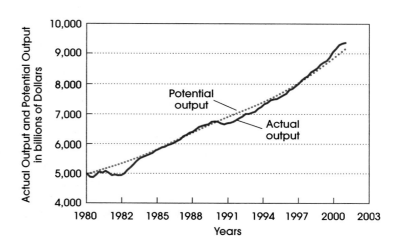

Source: Author estimates and the Bureau of Economic Analysis.

A simple explanation for why inflation did not rise is that potential output rose significantly (the AS curve shifted to the right), which would mean that the output gap wasn't positive in the late 1990s. The problem with this explanation is that few economists predicted that potential output would rise so dramatically, and, if policy makers are to base policy decisions on potential output, they must be able to anticipate changes in potential output before they happen.

The policy debate now is whether the experience in the second part of the 1990s and at the turn of the twenty-first century was a one-time occurrence due to special factors or whether the economy entered a new paradigm, in which previous methods of calculating potential output were no longer relevant. Among journalists, the "new paradigm" view is popular, but professional and government macroeconomists point to "special factors" as an explanation for what occurred in the late 1990s. Most economists still base their forecasts of inflation on how close the economy is to potential output, although they have raised their estimates of potential output.

Despite economists' difficulty in predicting potential output accurately, potential output is still central to macroeconomic policy models and to the AS curve, so you should understand the concept of the output gap, but you should also know to apply it with caution.

THE IMPORTANCE OF EXPECTATIONS

> Expectations are central to macroeconomic policy; they determine whether a policy's short-run or long-run effects will dominate.

The AS/AD model provides a framework for policy discussions that allows us to integrate the price level and expectations of inflation into our policy story. Let's consider the policy story the AS/AD model tells. In the short run, demand shocks can affect real output because either people make mistakes predicting future price level and inflation or people's reactions to changes in aggregate demand are constrained by institutions. In the long run, however, people correct their mistakes and are no longer constrained; the economy will always gravitate to its potential output.

Let's see how this process works. Suppose people did not expect the changes brought about by a negative demand shock. In the short run, there would be more unemployed resources—labor and other inputs—than usual. Once people adjust their expectations downward and have the opportunity to renegotiate contracts, wages and other input prices will eventually fall. While input prices are adjusting downward, the economy is operating below its potential, with unemployment above the natural rate because of the negative demand shock. The more the shock is a surprise, the more difficult it will be for people to adjust their expectations and their wage contracts, and the longer the unemployment will persist.

More generally, when a change in aggregate demand is not anticipated, prices and wages do not adjust immediately, and output falls below or rises above potential. When a change in aggregate demand is anticipated, prices and wages adjust fully, with little or no change in output. Using the same reasoning, in the AS/AD model, people's expectations play a central role in the effect of a policy on the economy. These expectations determine whether the policy's short-run or long-run effects will dominate. The expectation of a policy will have the same result as the policy itself.

Let's consider how expectations of policy affect our model. Suppose the economy is initially at potential output and price level P_0 (point A), as Exhibit 11–11 shows, and the government announces that it plans to cut taxes. Most likely, it will

Exhibit 11-11

Expectations and the AS Curve

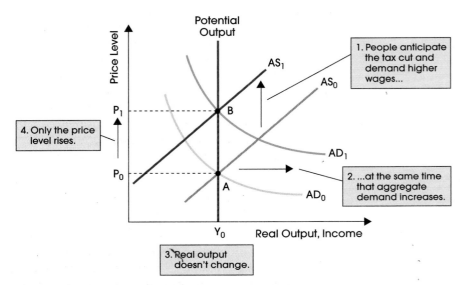

If people (firms and workers) expect a demand increase that leads to a higher price level, they will adjust their prices and the AS curve will shift up at the same time that the AD curve shifts. The expansionary policy will not increase output at all. It will increase only the price level.

take months before Congress passes the tax legislation and the President signs the bill as law, so the policy will not be implemented for a long time. However, because the tax cut was announced, some people will anticipate the tax cut and some firms will increase production in expectation of higher sales. Some people might even increase their spending before the tax cut goes into effect. Thus, the expectation of the policy shifts the AD curve out, which means that the policy will begin to work even before it is implemented. (The corollary to this insight is that when the expected policy is actually implemented, it will be less effective than it otherwise would have been.)

The expectations argument can be carried even further. Because we assume that the economy starts at potential output, people will expect the tax cut to lead to a rise in the price level. Workers will recognize this and ask for higher wages, shifting the AS curve up. If the model is correct, the tax cut is correctly anticipated, and there are no institutional restrictions on changing prices, the tax cut will move the economy from point *A* to point *B* with little or no increase in output, and with an increase in prices.

Reasonable Expectations

Because expectations play a key role in policy effectiveness, economists have spent a lot of time considering how people form them. Most economists agree that the majority of people form **reasonable expectations**—expectations based on relevant information, as processed by "reasonable" people. That's the easy part. The hard part is determining what set of expectations are reasonable and how those expectations are formed. Most research suggests that people form expectations with a combination of extrapolations from the past and predictions of the future, based on expert's views, which, in turn, are based on theory.

What does it mean to use relevant information when predicting inflation? Suppose you live in an economy where prices constantly rise over time. You would make an effort to keep your wages growing at the rate of inflation by asking for a raise each year to cover the expected inflation over the coming year. Over time, you would figure out what data are relevant for future inflation. Perhaps you'd keep a record of your expenses and figure out how much they would rise each year. Perhaps you'd look up the Consumer Price Index in the newspaper, or pay attention to forecasts published in the financial press. Over time, you'd use what works and discard what does not.

To the extent possible, you would also try to avoid making systematic mistakes. This means that if you underpredict inflation for a few years in a row, you learn and try to eliminate this underprediction in the future. This does not mean that you will not make mistakes—you may zig when the economy zags—but you will not make the same mistake over and over again.

Rational Expectations

Our description of how people form expectations is reasonable and widely accepted. It says that people are purposeful in their efforts to predict inflation. This assumption is consistent with most economists' view that people act purposefully when making any choice, whether it is which soft drink to buy or what expectations to have. For modeling purposes, some economists, however, prefer a stronger assumption, called *rational expectations*. Rational expectations are a subset of reasonable expectations.

Reasonable expectations are expectations based on all relevant information but involving some uncertainty as to what model of the economy is the correct one.

THE BRIEFING ROOM   An Unconventional View of Expectations and the AS/AD Story

Most economists and policy makers use the AS/AD model with either reasonable or rational expectations to analyze short-term movements in the economy. Our conventional half believes that the assumptions underlying the AS/AD model are reasonable, and that the AS/AD model should be the primary model we teach. Our unconventional half questions some of the assumptions underlying the AS/AD model.

Our unconventional half believes that aggregate demand policy can matter not only in the short run, but also in the long run. Unanticipated changes in aggregate demand can affect the short run (that's the conventional story), but they can also affect the long run by altering individuals' and firms' behavior. According to the unconventional view, potential output is much more ambiguous than the standard model suggests. In this view, the long-run potential output of an economy is not a fixed point. Within a fairly wide range, there are many levels of potential output at which the economy can be in equilibrium. Potential output depends on aggregate demand.

For example, if aggregate demand expands the economy beyond its previous potential, firms will develop new ways to produce with less labor and other inputs, thereby increasing productivity. These technological changes can offset the inflationary pressure and increase potential output. Thus, technological change can be brought about by high aggregate demand. Pushing the economy beyond potential output in the short run can actually increase potential output.

From this unconventional perspective, because potential output is so ambiguous, policy should focus on the short run, not on the long run, and it should try to keep output as high as possible. Policy makers should look for inflationary pressures, but they should not try to curtail expansions simply because the economy is operating at output levels above what was previously thought of as "potential." The economy is a bit like the runner training for a race. By pushing the runner (the economy) beyond his previous potential, you increase that potential.

Rational expectations are expectations that are based on the predictions of an underlying economic model. The economists' model is what distinguishes rational from reasonable expectations. If, for example, an economist's model predicts that a change in Fed policy will lower the inflation rate, people will use that model to predict a drop in the inflation rate. As a requirement in modeling, when assuming there is a single model that correctly describes an economy, assuming rational expectations make a lot of sense. It simply means that people will eventually figure out the model and base their expectation on that model. If there is a correct and knowable model, it would be irrational to do otherwise. Rational expectations are simply expectations consistent with the model. For policy purposes, the assumption is less useful. The problem is that we don't know whether our model is right. (Judging from past experience, it often is not.)

> Rational expectations are expectations based on the underlying model of the economy.

Policy and Expectations

The difference between reasonable expectations and rational expectations is a matter of degree. How reasonable is it for economists to expect that their model captures what is happening in the economy and that people use that model? The more stable the economy and the more consistently policy impacts the economy, the more reasonable expectations become rational expectations. If a model works, people will come to believe it and base their expectations on it. People figure out how the economy works, and they incorporate any systematic change in policy into their expectations.

The less stable the economy and the less consistent policy's impact on the economy, the less likely reasonable expectations will be rational. People will have a difficult time trying to figure out how the economy works. (In fact, they may never figure it out.) Rational expectations assumes a much higher degree of economic understanding on the part of economists and on the part of the average person than does reasonable expectations.

The distinction between rational and reasonable expectations is important in determining how one views the effect of policy on the economy. According to rational expectations, any expected systematic change in aggregate demand policy has no impact on real output; it affects only the price level. This follows because, in economists' long-run model of the economy, aggregate demand policy cannot affect real output. According to reasonable expectations, the model can always be changing; economists, and other people, are never sure what the correct model is. In such a world, systematic policy may have an impact on the economy. Of course, with the economy constantly changing, the policy may not have the desired effect. (The Briefing Room, "An Unconventional View of Expectations and the AS/AD Story," discusses one way that short-run policy may affect long-run equilibrium.)

THE AS/AD MODEL IN AN INFLATIONARY ENVIRONMENT

According to the AS/AD model, a decrease in aggregate demand will cause output and, eventually, the price level to fall, as input prices fall and the economy returns to potential output. As mentioned previously, before input prices begin to fall, government (usually) steps in and uses expansionary fiscal or monetary policy to expand the economy. People come to expect these policies, and an inflationary bias becomes built into the economy—the price level goes up much more often than it goes down. This story is consistent with the empirical evidence: Since the end of World War II, the U.S. economy has always had some inflation.

In an inflationary environment, decreases in aggregate demand do not lead to declines in the price level but to disinflation—declines in the percent change in the price level, or inflation. For example, in the early 1980s, contractionary monetary policy caused aggregate demand to fall, pushing the economy into recession. The inflation rate fell from 9.2 percent in 1980 to 3.7 percent in 1985. Similarly, in the early 1990s,

In an inflationary environment, decreases in aggregate demand lead to disinflation, not deflation.

Exhibit 11-12

Inflation in the AS/AD Model

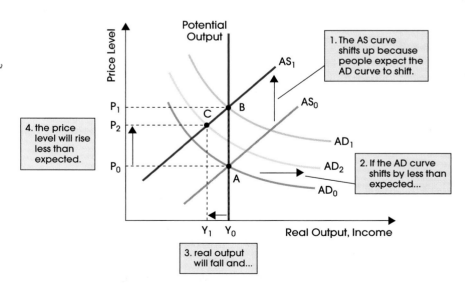

If aggregate demand does not rise by as much as expected, output can decline with the price level still rising, as this exhibit shows. Aggregate demand is expected to rise to AD_1. In anticipation of that, people change their prices and the AS curve shifts to AS_1. If aggregate demand increases to only AD_2, the economy will end up at point C, where output has fallen and the price level is higher than at point A.

contractionary monetary policy caused aggregate demand to fall, pushing the economy into recession. The inflation rate fell from 3.9 percent in 1990 to 2.2 percent in 1993.

We can interpret the AS/AD model in the context of some underlying expected rate of inflation. Suppose, for example, that people have come to expect prices to rise at about 3 percent per year on average. Those expectations will become built into input prices and the overall price level. Suppose the economy starts off at point A in Exhibit 11–12, with inflation expected to increase by 3 percent because aggregate demand is expected to shift to AD_1. If the inflation is completely anticipated, then the AD and AS curves will slide up the potential output line to point B, keeping output unchanged and causing prices to rise by the expected full 3 percent.

If, instead, aggregate demand rises by less than expected (to AD_2), the price level will rise by less than expected and output will decline. The economy will move to point C in the short run. Similarly, if aggregate demand rises by more than expected, the economy will go beyond potential and prices will rise by more than expected.

In summary, we can use the aggregate demand and supply analysis to explain movements in the economy with persistent inflation if we assume that people make decisions based on the expectation of an always-expanding aggregate demand. A decline in aggregate demand relative to expectations will therefore mean that prices rise by less than expected rather than actually falling.

Executive Summary

- Three explanations why short-run equilibrium deviates from long-run equilibrium are (1) the worker misperception model, (2) the imperfect information model, and (3) the sticky wage and price model.

- The AS/AD model reduces the quantitative effects of monetary and fiscal policy on real output compared to the IS/LM model.

- The less elastic the AS curve, the greater the effect of monetary and fiscal policy on the price level rather than on real output.

- The policy response to a change in aggregate demand is more straightforward than to a change in aggregate supply. An adverse aggregate supply shock both lowers output and raises the price level. Policy makers must choose between output and inflation.

- The more a movement in aggregate demand is expected, the larger the price response and the smaller the real output response in the short run.

- Following a shock to aggregate demand or aggregate supply, input prices adjust, which shifts the AS curve until the economy returns to potential output.

- When a change in aggregate demand is fully expected, prices and wages will adjust fully with little or no change in output.

- The AS/AD model can explain changes in inflation if we assume that people make decisions based on expectations of inflation.

POLICY PERSPECTIVE: U.S. POTENTIAL OUTPUT IN THE LATE 1990s

To get a better feel for the AS/AD model, let's apply it to the situation in the beginning of this chapter: the U.S. economy in the late 1990s. In the late 1990s, real output in the United States appeared to be well beyond what most economist thought was potential output. According to the *Congressional Budget Office's* measure of potential output, real GDP was almost 3 percent above potential output. In previous decades, when output rose that far above potential, the inflation rate increased, but in the late 1990s, the inflation rate did not increase; it fell.

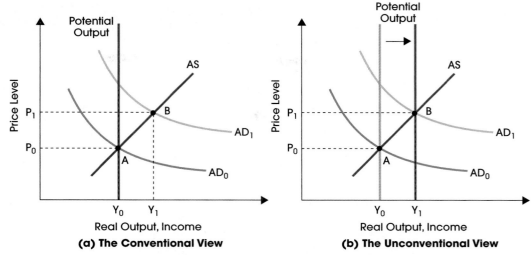

Exhibit 11-13

The U.S. Economy at the End of the 1990s

(a) The Conventional View

(b) The Unconventional View

The conventional view of the late 1990s U.S. economy is that consumption and investment expenditures were pushing the AD curve to the right, so that the economy exceeded potential, as *panel a* shows, creating inflationary pressure. The unconventional view is that increases in aggregate demand pulled potential output to the right, so that the economy remained in both short- and long-run equilibrium, as *panel b* shows.

> Reality and the model can usually be made consistent by explanations based on changes in assumptions and unexpected occurrences.

The conventional view, shown in Exhibit 11–13(a), was that the economy was being pushed beyond potential output by high consumption and investment demand, aided by not-too-contractionary monetary policy. Of course, a problem for proponents of this view was that inflation had fallen instead of risen, but they explained that special factors kept inflation from rising. Medical care inflation was unusually low, and commodity prices, import prices, and computer prices were falling. These special factors contributed to a drop in the inflation rate despite the increased demand pressures. According to this view, inflationary pressures were building. It was believed that when the factors that were keeping prices low disappeared, the Fed would need to implement contractionary monetary policy to bring output down to potential.

One unconventional view, shown in Exhibit 11–13(b), held that the increase in aggregate demand pushed potential output up along with it. The higher demand led firms to invest in research and development, which increased technology and shifted potential output out. This started a virtuous circle of growth in which more demand led to increased productivity, which led to less inflationary pressure. Measures of potential output based on past economic performance were too low. According to this view, inflationary pressure was not building during this period and the Fed's best policy option was to leave monetary policy alone, or maybe even expand monetary policy. (See the Briefing Room, "The Politics of Potential Output," for information about the politics of potential output.)

Another unconventional view was the real business-cycle view. Economists who held this view also believe that the best explanation for the 1990s was that potential output shifted to the right, but not because aggregate demand increased. They attributed the increase in potential output to a positive technological shock that had nothing to do with government's aggregate demand policy. Their policy prescription was laissez-faire.

THE BRIEFING ROOM   The Politics of Potential Output

In 1995, potential output went from being an obscure concept discussed only in economics textbooks to one making U.S. headline news. Congress and the President were formulating a bill that would balance the federal government's budget by 2002. The negotiations reached a stalemate in December 1995 because Congress and the President had slightly different estimates of what potential output would be in 2002. The President's estimate came from the Office of Management and Budget (OMB), while Congress' estimate came from the Congressional Budget Office (CBO).

The slight difference in estimated potential output made a big difference in estimated revenues in 2002. Congress had a smaller estimated potential output: It believed that GDP would be smaller, and income tax revenue would be smaller in 2002 than the President's estimate. This meant that spending would have to be cut by more than the President's economist at OMB had estimated. The then-Speaker of the House, Newt Gingrich, told the press that Congress' number was more accurate than the President's because it was calculated by the nonpartisan CBO. (In reality, both OMB's and CBO's numbers were plausible, given the amount of uncertainty surrounding the estimate of potential output.) Congress and the President did reach a compromise but not until the federal government shut down for an entire month because Congress refused to sign spending bills until an agreement was reached to balance the budget in 2002.

After 3 years of very robust economic growth, the budget deficit turned into a surplus in 1998—four years ahead of schedule. Moreover, CBO projected surpluses at least through 2010. These projections were based on their estimates of potential output in the economy. At that point, Newt Gingrich complained about CBO's estimates of potential output, saying they were too low. At the time, Congress was trying to pass a tax-cut bill, and the larger the projected level of potential output in the future, the more tax revenue the government would have and the more it could give back in the form of a tax cut. The moral of the story is that economists will offer a number of estimates of potential output and politicians will choose the estimate that best suits their desired policy.

Economists have offered a number of explanations for why potential output has risen. Edmund Phelps, an economist who popularized the concept of the natural rate of unemployment, has suggested that the stock market plays a role. As stock prices rise, firms invest in more capital, which boosts labor productivity and leads to greater potential output.

Other economists have suggested that international issues play a role. If workers are worried about international competition, they may not push for significantly higher wages when unemployment remains low. Still other economists have suggested that a connection between aggregate demand and potential output exists. They argue that when demand is high, firms develop new technology, potential output shifts out, and no price increase is necessary. If this is true, potential output can be dragged out by increases in demand, and the independence between potential output and demand is broken.

Whatever the reason, throughout the late 1990s, economists kept increasing their estimates of the economy's potential output, as the economy exceeded their previous estimates without generating the predicted inflation.

The debate over whether the Fed ought to have contracted the money supply in the late 1990s was complicated by the large increase in stock market prices. Many economists felt that stock prices were overvalued—a symptom of unsustainable expectations of future growth, what some people have termed irrational exuberance. At some point, economists argued that the expectations bubble would burst, and the virtuous circle of increasing growth would implode.

Through 1999, the Fed waffled between the various views. It raised interest rates twice in an attempt to restrain potential inflation, but it did so hesitantly. Moreover, a number of times when it could have raised interest rates, it did not. After raising interest rates six times by mid-2000, the Fed seemed to shift views. It began leaning toward the unconventional views and raised its estimate of potential output growth substantially. Because the Fed raised the rate at which it believed the economy could grow without increasing inflationary pressures,

Table 11-1

Summary of the Short-Run Models

Model and Brief Summary	Key Assumptions	Key Predictions	Key Policy Implications
IS/LM A short-run model of real output. Real output is determined by the level of expenditures (aggregate demand). The two components are the IS curve (goods market equilibrium) and the LM curve (money market equilibrium).	• The price level is fixed. • Equilibrium in the goods market is determined by aggregate expenditures. • Equilibrium in the money market is determined by the demand and supply of money.	• Fiscal policy and monetary policy can directly affect real output. • Expansionary fiscal policy leads to higher interest rates and higher real output. • Expansionary monetary policy leads to lower interest rates and higher real output. • Crowding out can limit the effectiveness of fiscal policy. • A liquidity trap can limit the effectiveness of monetary policy.	• Government can smooth business cycles by using monetary and fiscal policy.
IS/LM/BP (Large Country) A short-run model of real output that includes the international sector. The upward-sloping BP curve shows where the balance of payments is zero.	• The price level is fixed. • Forces constantly push the economy toward IS/LM equilibrium and balance of payments equilibrium.	• If a country has flexible exchange rates, the exchange rate adjusts to domestic IS/LM equilibrium. • A country with fixed exchange rates may have difficulty achieving its domestic goals.	• If exchange rates are flexible, government need not worry about maintaining balance of payments equilibrium. It can focus on domestic goals. • Government can adjust exchange rates, import controls, export drives, and capital controls to achieve domestic goals.
Mundell-Fleming model An IS/LM/BP model for a small open economy. The BP curve is horizontal at the world interest rate.	• The price level is fixed. • Capital will flow in and out of a country to keep domestic interest rates at the world interest rate.	• If exchange rates are fixed, expansionary fiscal policy must be accompanied by expansionary monetary policy. • If exchange rates are fixed, expansionary monetary policy must be accompanied by expansionary fiscal policy. • If exchange rates are flexible, expansionary fiscal policy can affect the economy only if monetary policy is also expansionary.	• Government must accept the world interest rate. • To increase output, an economy should run expansionary fiscal and monetary policies.
AS/AD model A model that integrates the long run and the short run. The AD curve is downward sloping. The AS model determines how changes in aggregate expenditures are split between changes in output and the price level.	• Prices are flexible. • A fall in the price level leads to higher aggregate demand because of the international and interest rate effects. • The more people expect a change in aggregate demand, the less that change will affect real output.	• Increases in aggregate demand lead to increases in real output. • Adverse aggregate supply shocks lead to lower output and higher prices. • Changes in aggregate demand that are perfectly anticipated have a smaller impact on real output and a larger impact on the price level compared to when the changes are anticipated.	• When the economy is below potential output, it should run expansionary monetary or fiscal policy to increase real output. • When the economy is above potential output, it should run contractionary monetary or fiscal policy to reduce real output and avoid inflation. • When the economy is at potential output, policy should be neutral.

Most real-world policy choices are a compromise among competing views.

no contractionary policy was necessary. In 2001, when the economy's growth seemed to slow, entering into what some economists call a growth recession (a significant slowdown in economic growth but with growth still positive), the Fed implemented expansionary monetary policy. However, the Fed kept a close eye on inflation and stood ready to shift back to the conventional view if inflation picked up. Like most real-world policy choices, the Fed's choice was a compromise among competing views.

CONCLUSION

In this chapter, we showed how the changes in the price level affect the analysis of short-run movements in the economy. Most of the basic lessons from the earlier chapters on fixed-price models (Chapters 8 through 10) still held—an increase in aggregate demand causes output to rise, and a decrease causes output to fall. In this chapter, however, we saw that, along with changes in output come changes in the price level.

The addition of the possibility of the price level changing makes the discussion of policy a bit more complicated. When policy makers use aggregate demand policies to stimulate the economy, they want to know how much of the bad (higher inflation) they will have to accept to get the good (higher output). When policy makers use aggregate demand policies to dampen inflation, they want to know how much of the bad (reduced output) they will have to accept with the good (lower inflation).

Although this chapter does not give you definitive answers to these questions (economists don't have any), it does present the framework within which the questions are examined. The mix of good and bad outcomes from aggregate demand management policy depends on how close the economy is to potential output, how quickly expectations adjust, the state of input prices, and the AS curve. With this information, economists attempt to design policy. (Table 11–1 summarizes the short-run models covered in Chapters 8 through 11.)

KEY POINTS

- The aggregate demand (AD) curve is a downward-sloping curve that shows the combinations of price levels and income levels at which both the goods market and the money market are in equilibrium. The AD curve can be derived from the IS/LM model.
- The AD curve slopes downward because of the interest rate effect and the international effect. Fiscal policy, monetary policy changes in autonomous expenditures, and changes in autonomous demand for money shift the AD curve.
- The aggregate supply (AS) curve shows how the price level responds to changes in aggregate demand.
- In the short run, the AS curve shifts when the price of inputs to production change independently of demand, when worker productivity changes, or when the expected price level changes.
- All along the AS curve, the expected price level is constant; it is that price where the AS curve intersects potential output.

- Potential output is a central element in policy makers' models of the economy. It determines where the economy is headed in the long run.
- Short-run equilibrium occurs where the AS and AD curves intersect. This is also a long-run equilibrium if they intersect at potential output.
- Economists have three explanations why the economy may not always be in long-run equilibrium: the worker misperception model, the imperfect information model, and the sticky wage and price model.
- The AS/AD framework guides policy makers' response to shocks to an economy. An aggregate demand shock can be countered by a change in fiscal or monetary policy that shifts the AD curve in the opposite direction.
- Offsetting an adverse aggregate supply shock is more difficult. Government must choose among

fighting inflation, fighting recession, and doing nothing.
- Real business-cycle economists believe that business cycles result from changes in potential output and that government should not offset these changes.
- The AS/AD model brings the price level into the analysis and reduces the quantitative effects of monetary and fiscal policy on real output compared to the IS/LM model.
- The less elastic the AS curve, the greater the effect of monetary and fiscal policy on the price level rather than on real output.
- Reasonable expectations assume that people use relevant information and avoid systematic mistakes when forming expectations. Rational expectations go further, by assuming that people use economists' models of the economy when forming expectations.

KEY TERMS

aggregate demand curve 304
aggregate supply curve 309
cost-plus-markup rule 309
imperfect information model 317
interest rate effect 304
international effect 305

output gap 322
nominal wages 311
rational expectations 326
real business-cycle economists 321
real money supply 304
real wages 311

reasonable expectations 325
stagflation 319
sticky wage and price model 317
worker misperception model 314

QUESTIONS FOR THOUGHT AND REVIEW

1. List and explain two reasons why the AD curve slopes downward.
2. Define the *real money supply,* and explain why it is important in understanding the shape of the AD curve.
3. Under what circumstances will the international effect be inoperative?
4. List the factors that shift the AD curve, and explain how each of them shifts the curve.
5. What is the short-run AS curve? What are on the axes?
6. What is a cost-plus-markup rule? How is it related to the short-run AS curve?

7. List the factors that shift the AS curve, and describe how each of them shifts the curve.
8. What happens to output and the price level in the short run when aggregate demand rises?
9. What happens to output and the price level in the short run when there is a significant rise in the price of inputs?
10. Explain how the economy adjusts back to long-run equilibrium following an increase in aggregate demand.
11. Explain how the economy adjusts back to long-run equilibrium following a significant increase in input prices.

12. How do changes in the expected price level affect the AS/AD model?

13. How do expectations affect the length of time it takes to adjust from a short-run equilibrium to a long-run equilibrium?

14. How does government intervention affect the way that the economy adjusts to long-run equilibrium from a short-run equilibrium that is below potential?

15. Describe the three main theoretical reasons why equilibrium output may differ from potential output.

16. How does the upward slope of the AS curve modify the policy results of the IS/LM model?

17. What type of policy would the government use to offset a negative aggregate demand shock if it wanted output and the price level to return to their original levels?

18. What type of policy would the government use to offset the effect of a negative aggregate supply shock (a large increase in the price of oil) if it wanted to keep *output* where it had been prior to the shock? What is the undesirable side effect of this policy?

19. What type of policy would the government use to offset the effect of a negative aggregate supply shock (a large increase in the price of oil) if it wanted to keep the *price level* where it had been prior to the shock? What is the undesirable side effect of this policy?

20. What is stagflation? How should policy makers react to it? How did they react to it during the 1970s?

21. What is the real business-cycle view of economic fluctuations, and what does it imply about the role of aggregate demand management policies?

22. What is the output gap, and how is it related to inflation?

23. Explain why correctly anticipated aggregate demand management policies may have no impact on real output.

24. What is the difference between reasonable expectations and rational expectations?

25. Explain how the effectiveness of aggregate demand management policy depends on whether people form their expectations reasonably or rationally.

26. How can the aggregate demand and supply model be adapted to explain economies in which the price level is always rising (economies with persistent inflation)?

27. What are the two views of where the U.S. economy was relative to potential output at the end of the 1990s? What is the appropriate policy reaction to each view?

PROBLEMS AND EXERCISES

1. Show the effect of each of the following on the economy in the short run, using the AS/AD model. Assume that the economy begins at both the short-run and the long-run equilibrium.
   a. The price of oil rises dramatically.
   b. A technology boom increases productivity dramatically.
   c. The dollar depreciates significantly relative to the currencies of our trading partners.
   d. Congress and the President cut taxes.
   e. The Fed increases the money supply.

2. Answer problem 1 (a–e) again, but this time, show the adjustment in the long run, using the AS/AD model.

3. Demonstrate graphically how the AS/AD model modifies the results of the IS/LM model assuming the interest rate effect is inoperative, but the international effect is operative. (Make sure to go through each step of the analysis relating the shifts in the AS/AD model with the IS/LM model.)

4. Answer problem #3 again, but this time showing only the long-run effects.

5. Use the AS/AD model to show the short-run impact of a decrease in autonomous consumption expenditures. On the same diagram, show the effect of government policy used to prevent the price level from falling.

6. Use the AS/AD model to show how the government would offset the effects of a decrease in autonomous investment expenditures on real output and the price level, using aggregate demand management policy.

7. Use the AS/AD model to show how the government would offset the effects of an increase in the price of oil on the price level, using aggregate demand management policy.

8. Use the AS/AD model to show how the government would offset the effects of an increase in the price of oil on real output, using aggregate demand management policy.

9. Use the AS/AD model to show the impact of a systematic increase in the money supply in each of following cases:
   a. The increase in the money supply is unexpected.
   b. The increase in the money supply is completely anticipated and people can change their wages and prices.

10. Use the AS/AD model to illustrate the two views of the U.S. economy at the end of the 1990s. (Use a separate diagram to illustrate each view.)

An Alternative AS/AD Model

The aggregate supply/aggregate demand model presented in the text has been subjected to much debate. The complaints include the fact that (1) the curves are not supply-and-demand curves in the microeconomic sense, and hence can be misleading to students; and (2) the model's underlying dynamics do not adequately capture how the economy arrives at equilibrium.[1]

Economists have suggested numerous alternative models, but variations of the one we presented in the text still dominate. Because our book focuses on conventional models for policy, and doesn't dwell on theoretical issues, we showed you the standard AS/AD model with a minimum of theoretical discussion. We did not discuss alternative constructions, such as the Post Keynesian AS/AD model (a model constructed by Paul Davidson, a leading Post Keynesian economist) or any other variations of the AS/AD model, because these alternative constructions are not widely used.

Recently, however, an influential group of macroeconomists (John Taylor, David Romer, and Ben Bernanke) have been advocating, and using, an alternative AS/AD model that develops the AS and AD curves in a model with inflation and real output on the axes.[2]

Although the AS and AD curves in this model look the same as those in the text, they are different: This model has *inflation not the price level* on the vertical axis. Economists who support this alternative AS/AD model argue that this model is more in line with real-world pol-icy discussions, because policy makers think in terms of an inflation–real output trade-off. Although this is an advantage, the disadvantage is that the microfoundations of this model are complicated and obscure, which makes it difficult for students to learn and apply. Because instructors weigh both teachability and applicability, the jury is out as to whether this new model will replace the standard model. However, because you may see this alternative construction in other courses, we briefly present it in this appendix.

First, we develop the foundations of the two curves. Then, we discuss equilibrium of the model. Finally, we apply the model to policy issues.

THE AGGREGATE DEMAND CURVE

With inflation on the vertical axis, the reasons presented in the chapter for why the AD curve is downward sloping are no longer applicable. Those reasons related the quantity of aggregate demand to the price level, not to inflation—the rate of change in the price level. Hence, we must look for an alternative reason to justify a downward-sloping AD curve. We do this by making monetary policy endogenous, the same way we did in Chapter 9 when discussing the horizontal LM curve. (Recall from Chapter 1 that *endogenous* means "determined within the model.") This AD curve is based on a Fed policy reaction function in which the Fed changes the money supply and the interest rates automatically in response to changes in inflation. The AD curve, therefore, embodies a Fed policy rule. If the Fed does not follow the policy rule, the model breaks down.

The way in which these alternative models endogenize monetary policy is with the Taylor rule, which we introduce in Chapter 13. The Taylor rule is an equation

---

[1]See David Colander, "The stories we tell: A reconsideration of AS/AD analysis," *Journal of Economic Perspectives,* 1995;9(3):169–88, for a discussion of these and other complaints.

[2]See David Romer, "Keynesian macroeconomics without the LM curve," *Journal of Economic Perspectives,* 2000;14(2):149–69, and John B. Taylor, "Teaching modern macroeconomics at the principles level," *American Economic Review,* 2000;(May):90–94.

Exhibit 11–A1
The Alternative AS/AD Model

This model has inflation, not the price level, on the vertical axis. The AD curve slopes down because the model assumes that the Fed will target a lower interest rate when inflation is lower. Lower interest rates lead to higher investment expenditures and higher real output. The AS curve is horizontal because people do not change their expectations of inflation quickly. Potential output is independent of inflation. Short-run equilibrium is at point A, where AS and AD intersect.

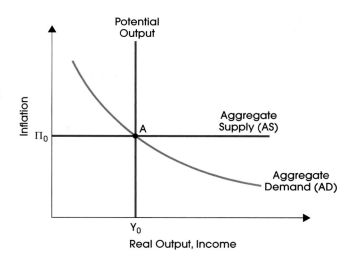

that describes how the Fed sets the fed funds interest rate target based on inflation and output growth. According to the Taylor rule, when the inflation rate rises above the Fed's target rate (2 percent to 3 percent, for example) or output rises above potential, the Fed will raise the fed funds rate target enough to raise the real interest rate. The higher real interest rate causes investment expenditures and, therefore, aggregate expenditures to fall. This monetary policy rule produces the downward-sloping aggregate demand curve shown in Exhibit 11–A1, because the Fed will react to the higher inflation rate (denoted by Π) by setting a higher real interest rate, which will lower the quantity of aggregate demand.

Shifts in the AD curve are caused by changes in fiscal policy or in the monetary policy rule. Expansionary fiscal policy shifts the AD curve to the right, while contractionary fiscal policy shifts the AD curve to the left. Monetary policy will also shift the AD curve, but in a way that is slightly different from that of the standard AS/AD model. *The AD curve will shift only if the Fed changes its policy rule.* For example, if the Fed decides to target a higher real interest rate for each level of inflation, the AD curve will shift in to the left. If the Fed decides to target a lower real interest rate for each level of inflation, the AD curve will shift out to the right.

THE AGGREGATE SUPPLY CURVE

The AS curve in this model is generally presented as a horizontal line in the short run and by potential output (a vertical line) in the long run, as Exhibit 11–A1 shows. The short-run AS curve is horizontal because of inflation inertia caused by slowly moving expectations of infla-

tion. The justification of the long-run vertical potential output curve is similar to reasons we gave in the text for the fixed potential output line: Real output does not depend on inflation or the price level in the long run.

EQUILIBRIUM

Short-run equilibrium occurs where the AD curve intersects the short-run AS curve. Long-run equilibrium occurs where the AD curve intersects potential output. Point A in Exhibit 11–A1 shows an economy in both long- and short-run equilibrium.

As is the case with the standard model, the time period that distinguishes the short run from the long run is ambiguous. What distinguishes the two is how quickly expectations adjust to changes in the inflation rate. If short-run equilibrium and long-run equilibrium differ, as expectations of inflation change (and prices become more flexible), the AS curve shifts to meet the long-run equilibrium.

Exhibit 11–A2 shows two examples of an economy that adjusts from a short-run to a long-run equilibrium. Exhibit 11–A2(a) shows an economy in short-run equilibrium below potential output at point A. The excess productive capacity and increased unemployment lead people to lower their expected inflation, which shifts the AS curve down until the economy reaches potential output at point B and expected inflation equals actual inflation. Exhibit 11–A2(b) shows an economy in short-run equilibrium *above* potential at point C. Unemployment is pushed below the natural rate, and firms exceed their sustainable productive capacity, leading people to increase their expected inflation, which shifts

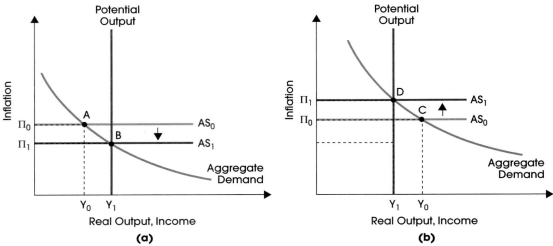

Exhibit 11–A2
Adjustment to Long-Run Equilibrium

Panel a shows an economy that begins at a short-run equilibrium below potential output. Because the unemployment rate is below the natural rate of unemployment and firms have excess capacity, people lower their expectations of inflation. This shifts the AS curve down, from AS_0 to AS_1, until the economy reaches potential output and a lower rate of inflation at point B. *Panel b* shows the opposite scenario.

the AS curve up until the economy reaches potential output at *D*.

POLICY ANALYSIS

Let's now consider three policies to show how this model works. In Exhibit 11–A3(a), we consider expansionary monetary policy (changing the policy rule) in a situation in which the economy was initially in both long- and short-run equilibrium.

We begin with AD_0 and AS_0, with an equilibrium at point *A* in Exhibit 11–A3(a) and consider a change in the Fed's policy rule that reflects *expansionary monetary policy*. Specifically, the Fed sets a lower real interest rate target for every inflation rate. Expansionary monetary policy shifts the AD curve out to AD_1, which, in the short run, increases real output without increasing inflation. As expectations of inflation rise, however, the short-run AS curve shifts up. It continues to shift up until it reaches AS_1 and the economy returns to potential output.

Exhibit 11–A3(b) shows the effect of contractionary fiscal policy. The economy begins at point *A* with AD_0 and AS_0. Some combination of tax increases and government spending cuts will cause the AD curve to shift in to the left, from AD_0 to AD_1. Aggregate quantity demanded is lower at each real interest rate targeted by the Fed for

each inflation rate because aggregate spending has fallen at every rate of inflation. The economy will initially move to short-run equilibrium at point *B*. As inflationary expectations adjust downward, the AS curve will shift downward to AS_1 and the economy will return to potential output at point *C*.

Finally, Exhibit 11–A3(c) shows the effect of an adverse supply shock such as a sudden increase in the price of oil. The economy begins at point *A* with AD_0 and AS_0. An increase in the price of oil shifts the AS curve upward to AS_1 and the economy moves to short-run equilibrium at point *B*. At point *B,* however, unemployment is below the natural rate and there is excess capacity in the economy. People expect wages and prices to decline, offsetting the rise in the price of oil, and, therefore, adjust their expectations of inflation down, shifting the AS curve back down to AS_0, where the economy returns to potential output at point *A*.

CONCLUSION

The presentation in this appendix has been brief, but it should be sufficient to give you a sense of this alternative AS/AD model. Notice that the general policy result is the same with this model as it is with the standard model, and that many of the adjustment stories are similar. The difference is that the net effect of aggregate

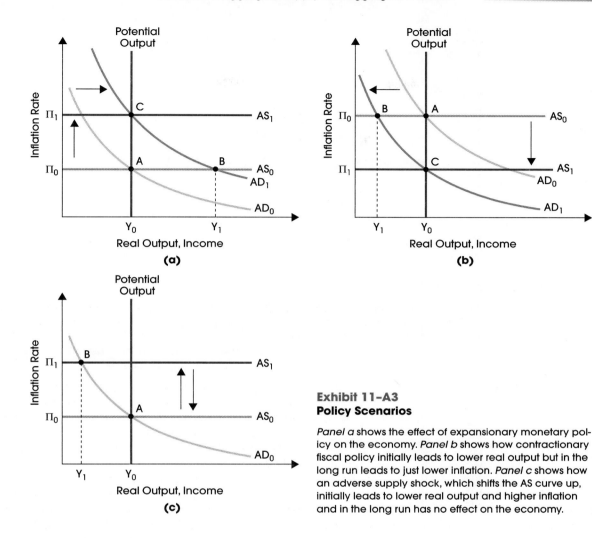

Exhibit 11-A3
Policy Scenarios

Panel a shows the effect of expansionary monetary policy on the economy. *Panel b* shows how contractionary fiscal policy initially leads to lower real output but in the long run leads to just lower inflation. *Panel c* shows how an adverse supply shock, which shifts the AS curve up, initially leads to lower real output and higher inflation and in the long run has no effect on the economy.

demand policies is on inflation, not on the price level. In the short run, aggregate demand policy affects real output, but, in the long run, the effect is on inflation. As you can see, the models basically come to the same results in terms of policy. Unless you are going further in your study of economics, in which case, you need to delve into the foundations of policy more carefully, you can use either model.

12

In the long run we're all
dead is one of the dumber
things that Keynes said.

—Robert Lucas

Microfoundations of
Consumption and Investment

After reading this chapter you should be able to:

1. Explain why microfoundations are important for understanding macroeconomic policy

2. Calculate the present value of a future sum of money

3. Discuss the permanent income and life-cycle hypotheses and describe their implications for macroeconomic policy

4. Use the concept of the marginal efficiency of investment to describe the relationship between interest rates and investment expenditures

5. Describe the difference between debt and equity financing

6. Explain the factors that determine the price of bonds and the price of stocks

7. Discuss why we should view policy as a process

Short-run macroeconomic models that policy makers use (and those presented in this book) focus on empirical regularities. The following are two examples of such regularities:

1. Consumption generally changes by a fraction of the change in income.
2. Investment tends to vary inversely with the interest rate.

Economists look for empirical regularities, incorporate them in their models, and then use those models to predict what will happen in the economy. The consumption function, for example, is based on the empirical regularities about consumption and forms the basis of the IS/LM and AS/AD models. Implicit in the predictions of the models and the policies they support is the assumption that those regularities will continue. Empirical regularities are what guide policy decisions.

Because empirical regularities can change suddenly, they do not always provide a sound basis for policy. When empirical regularities change, the impact of policy can change. Therefore, economists supplement their use of empirical regularities with deductive reasoning. They study macroeconomic issues, using models that predict what will happen based on general principles about individual choices, not empirical regularities.

An example of a breakdown of an empirical regularity occurred in the late 1960s. At the time, many U.S. policy makers believed that there was a long-run trade-off between inflation and unemployment. (You should recognize this trade-off as the Phillips curve, presented in Chapter 3.) That presumed trade-off was based on models that focused on the empirical regularity of rigid nominal wages. According to these models, increases in aggregate demand cause the price level to rise and lead firms to increase employment and output with little effect on wages. This model worked well for a while, but in the late 1960s and early 1970s, it performed poorly. Expansionary fiscal and monetary policy of the 1960s produced a lot more inflation, without the reduction in unemployment the model predicted.

Economists Milton Friedman and Ned Phelps had warned policy makers that their model was wrong. They based their warning on a deductive model, which states that when the price level rises, nominal wages will rise, but because people care about real, not nominal, wages, employment and production will not rise. Their deductive model predicted that, as the demand for workers rises, wages also start to rise, and that the short-run trade off between inflation and unemployment will break down. In the early 1970s, after Friedman and Phelps' prediction came true, macroeconomists started paying a lot more attention to deductive models to understand the macroeconomy.

MICROFOUNDATIONS

Microfoundations approaches macroeconomic relationships from a study of the decisions of individuals.

Logical deductive models are in the realm of microeconomics. Instead of being built on empirical regularities, as they are in macroeconomics, microeconomic models are built on first principles—logical deductive reasoning. Macroeconomics builds down, while microeconomics builds up. Microeconomics starts by analyzing the decisions of rational individuals and expands to an understanding of the aggregate economy. Developing macroeconomic relationships from an analysis of individual decisions is the study of **microfoundations.** Microfoundations plays a role in a number of aspects of macroeconomics. In this chapter, we focus on the microfoundations of consumption and investment decisions. We do so because changes in output are often the result of changes in these two components of aggregate expenditures.

The Role of Microfoundations of Consumption and Investment

Microeconomics is about choices and opportunity cost. It explores how rational individuals allocate their scarce resources. (See the The Briefing Room, "Rational Versus Purposeful Behavior," for a discussion of the rationality assumption.) Microfoundations of macroeconomics is the study of choices that are relevant to macroeconomic issues and the implications of those choices for macroeconomic policy.

Microfoundations sheds some light on how the structure of the economy might change in response to policy.

One important macroeconomic policy issue is fluctuations of output over time: Why do these fluctuations exist, and should government use monetary and fiscal policy to try to offset them? Studying the microfoundations of consumption and investment decisions sheds some light on the nature of these fluctuations and how they might change in response to policy.

THE BRIEFING ROOM   Rational Versus Purposeful Behavior

All economists believe that individuals are purposeful—people have reasons for what they do—and that price incentives play a role in decisions. Economists disagree about the best way to analyze these decisions. The standard microfoundations approach is to assume that individuals are perfectly rational both today and over time. Economists argue that even though this approach exaggerates the rationality that individuals exhibit, the assumption provides a base model from which we can understand the role that microfoundations play.

Some economists (real business-cycle advocates) even argue that anything other than models built up from microfoundations that assume full rationality is "voodoo economics" with no scientific merit. Some macroeconomic textbooks focus entirely on such choices, which essentially makes macroeconomics a sub-branch of microeconomics that focuses on choices over time. (Appendix A describes the beginning of such an approach; it presents a formal analysis of choices over time.)

Other economists argue that the macroeconomy is too complicated to even bother with microfoundations—that we can only usefully look at purposeful behavior within a small set of choices and over short periods of time. People's minds are not up to making choices over large sets and over long periods of time. These economists argue that macroeconomics built on fully rational microfoundations is the celestial mechanics of a nonexistent world.

Most economists are somewhere in between the two positions. They use standard, empirically determined relationships (such as the consumption function) as the foundation of their macroeconomics and supplement it with an analysis of microfoundations where it makes sense to do so. Of course, where microfoundations makes sense is subject to debate. Economists studying the psychological foundations of economics run experiments to determine how people actually behave, to find out if they can get a better understanding of purposeful behavior.

For example, if the economy is in a recession, the government might cut taxes to boost aggregate demand. The model you learned in Chapters 8 through 11 shows that a reduction in taxes will lead to an increase in output. Looking at the microfoundations of consumption and investment, however, we will see that how the tax cut affects output depends on people's perceptions of the tax cut. Based on microfoundations a permanent tax cut should affect aggregate demand more than a temporary tax cut. Looking at the microfoundations of consumption and investment provides us with additional considerations regarding policy.

Choices that are especially important to macroeconomic policy issues are choices over time, or what are called **intertemporal choices.** By adding an intertemporal dimension to the analysis, microfoundations enriches the macroeconomic model and challenges or modifies some of the policy conclusions. Intertemporal choices depend heavily on the concept of **present value**—the current value of a future flow of income. So, let's now turn to a consideration of present value.

> Present value is the current value of a future flow of income.

Present Value

Most people know that, say, $100 now will not have the same buying power as $100 will 10 years from now. Nonetheless, often people add up income streams over time as if it were. For example, you will often see a newspaper headline that announces that a baseball player has received a contract for, say, $30 million. If you read the article closely, you will generally see that most of that $30 million is paid in the future. The present value of the contract is far less than $30 million. For example, if the interest rate is 10 percent and the contract calls for $30 million to be paid as one lump sum 20 years from the date the contract is signed, the actual contract is worth (that is, its present value is) "only" $4.5 million. If the interest rate is 15 percent, the contract's value falls to less than $2 million. These values represent the amount of money you would have to save now at the stated interest rate in order to have that much in the future. (If you invest $2 million at 15 percent, you will have almost $33 million in 20 years.)

Present Value and Interest Rates. To understand how to calculate present value, consider the relationship between the interest rate and the value of a sum of money 1 year from now. Suppose your grandmother promises to give you $10,000 when you graduate from college a year from now. What is that $10,000 a year from now worth today? One way to think about this is to ask yourself how much money you would have to put in the bank today at the current interest rate (r), so that 1 year from now you would receive $10,000 in principal and interest. That amount is the present value, written as PV_1, where the subscript 1 indicates that the money is to be paid 1 year from now. To calculate PV_1, we solve the following equation:

$$PV_1 \, (1 + r) = \$10,000$$

or

$$PV_1 = \frac{\$10,000}{(1 + r)}$$

At a 10 percent interest rate, for example, PV_1 = $9,090.91. If you were to put $9,090.91 in an account that pays 10 percent interest annually, you would receive $909.09 in interest in 1 year. Adding that to the principal of $9,090.91 gives you $10,000.

At a 12 percent interest rate, PV_1 = $8,928.57, and at a 20 percent interest rate, PV_1 = $8,333.33. As you can see, as the interest rate rises, the present value of the future sum falls. The present value of a future sum of money varies inversely with the interest rate.

In general, the present value of a future sum of money X to be received 1 year from now is

$PV_1 = X/(1 + r)$.

$$PV_1 = \frac{X}{(1 + r)} \tag{12-1}$$

where r is the interest rate and X is the amount of money to be paid in 1 year.

Present Value over Multiple Years. Let's consider a few basic extensions. Suppose your grandmother says that she will give you $10,000 when you graduate 2 years from today. What is the present value of that sum of money if the interest rate is 5 percent?

When you want to calculate the present value of money paid more than 1 year into the future, you have to take into account the fact that interest is paid on the principal and any accrued interest. This is called compounding. Remember, the present value of $10,000 received 2 years from today would be that amount of money you would have to put into the bank now to receive $10,000 in principal and interest 2 years from now. If you put PV_2 into the bank, after 1 year you would have $PV_2(1 + r)$. If you keep that amount in the bank for another year, you will have $PV_2(1 + r)(1 + r)$, which must just equal $10,000:

$$PV_2(1 + r)(1 + r) = \$10,000$$

Solving for PV_2, we get

$$PV_2 = \frac{10,000}{(1 + r)^2}$$

If the interest rate is .05, $PV_2 = \$9,070.30$. You can see from this example that the present value of some amount of money paid 2 years from today is less than the present value of that same amount of money paid 1 year from today. In general, for a given interest rate, the further into the future a payment is made, the smaller is its present value. The formula for the present value of any sum X, n years from today, is

$$PV_n = \frac{X}{(1 + r)^n} \tag{12-2}$$

Exhibit 12–1 shows how the present value of $10,000 declines as the payment date is pushed further into the future. If the interest rate is .05, the present value of $10,000 is $7,835.26 in 5 years, $3,768.90 in 20 years, and $76.04 in 100 years.

We can also use the concept of present value to calculate the value today of a future *flow* of payments over time. Suppose that you are going to get $10,000 not only next year, but every year for 5 years. The present value of that stream of annual payments can be calculated by simply adding together the present values of the five payments of $10,000:

$PV_{1-n} = X_1/(1 + r)$
$+ X_2/(1 + r)^2 + \ldots$
$+ X_n/(1 + r)^n$.

$$\$PV_{1-5} = PV_1 + PV_2 + PV_3 + PV_4 + PV_5$$

$$\$PV_{1-5} = \frac{\$10,000}{(1 + r)} + \frac{\$10,000}{(1 + r)^2} + \frac{\$10,000}{(1 + r)^3} + \frac{\$10,000}{(1 + r)^4} + \frac{\$10,000}{(1 + r)^5}$$

Exhibit 12-1

The Present Value of $10,000 at 5 Percent Interest

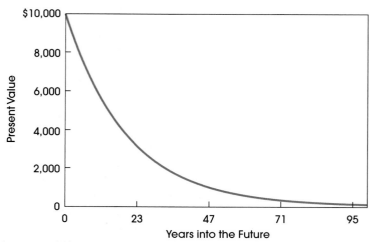

This exhibit shows the value today of $10,000 paid 0 to 100 years from today. The longer until the sum is paid, the lower its value.

If the interest rate is .05, $\$PV_{1-5} = \$43,294.77$; if the interest rate is .08, $\$PV_{1-5} = \$39,927.10$. It's a pretty messy calculation. Economists generally use financial software to calculate the present value of annual flows of income. The general relationship between present value and interest rates carries over to annuities. Present value varies inversely with the interest rate. This fact is important in macroeconomics. For example, when interest rates rise, the prices of bonds with fixed interest payments fall because the present value of the bond's future payments falls. Present value is also the reason why, when interest rates fall, the prices of bonds rise.

When interest rates rise, bond prices fall.

Executive Summary

- Microeconomic foundations of macroeconomics looks at how rational individuals and firms make consumption and investment choices over time.

- Choices over time begin with calculating the present value of future sums of money.

- The present value of an amount of money to be received in the future is the value of that money today.

- The present value of a future sum of money varies inversely with the interest rate: $PV_1 = \dfrac{X}{(1 + r)}$

- The present value of a given sum of money declines the further into the future that money is received.

CONSUMPTION

We now turn to a consideration of how present value helps us to understand individuals' consumption decisions. Think of the marginal propensity to consume (*mpc*), a key variable in the aggregate consumption function. The marginal propensity to consume is also an important determinant of the size of the multiplier and, consequently, in determining how changes in autonomous spending will affect output. Because of the importance of the consumption function to short-run macroeconomic models, economists have devoted significant time to measuring both the consumption function and the size of the marginal propensity to consume. Present value lets us approach the consumption decision from a microeconomic perspective.

First, a little background information. John Maynard Keynes first introduced the consumption function in his book, *The General Theory of Employment, Interest and Money* (usually referred to as *The General Theory*), published in 1936. He postulated that consumption depended on disposable income (Y^d) and "other factors," which he called *autonomous consumption,* represented by C_0:

$$C = C_0 + mpcY^d$$

This is the consumption function that forms the basis of the aggregate expenditures curve. Keynes did not have any formal empirical evidence that consumption actually conformed to this equation. In 1936, data analysis was labor intensive (computers had not been invented) and much data just weren't available. What led Keynes to this relationship were common sense and an understanding of people's decisions. Later economists collected data to measure this relationship and check its validity, which meant estimating both autonomous consumption (C_0) and the marginal propensity to consume (*mpc*). To estimate the consumption function (find values for C_0 and mpc), economists refined statistical techniques (especially regression analysis) to find the "best fitting" relationship for observed data.[1]

As economists gathered data and began estimating the consumption function during the 1940s and 1950s, they discovered that different sets of data generated very different estimates. For example, looking at long-term averages (10 years, for example) of consumption and disposable income, economists found that the mpc was close to .9 and that autonomous consumption, C_0, was zero:

$$C^{LR} = .9Y^d$$

where C^{LR} is the long-run consumption function. In the long run, autonomous consumption is zero, and for every dollar increase in disposable income, consumption rose by 90 cents. However, when these economists looked at short-term averages (annually, for example) of consumption and disposable income, they found a smaller mpc (about .75) and positive autonomous consumption (C_0). Using annual data from 1929 through 1941, economists estimated the short-run consumption function:

$$C^{SR} = 26.5 + .75Y^d$$

where C^{SR} is the short-run consumption function. This estimate means that, in the short run, consumption in the economy is $26.5 billion plus 75 percent of disposable income. Consumption rises by 75 cents for every dollar increase in disposable income. Somehow, individuals spent a smaller portion of income in the short run than in the long run.

A useful way of seeing the difference between the long-run and short-run consumption functions is to consider the **average propensity to consume (apc),** which is consumption divided by disposable income:

$$apc = \frac{C}{Y^d} \tag{12-3}$$

The apc tells us the fraction of total income that is consumed. In the long run, apc is constant and equal to the mpc:

$$apc^{LR} = \frac{C^{LR}}{Y^d} = \frac{.9Y^d}{Y^d} = .9$$

In the short run, apc varies inversely with income:

$$apc^{SR} = \frac{C^{SR}}{Y^d} = \frac{26.5}{Y^d} + .75$$

When economists first looked at the relationship between these two consumption functions, some thought it suggested that the economy was in for future

> The long-term marginal propensity to consume is bigger than the short-term marginal propensity to consume.

---

[1]A typical method to find a "best fit" is *ordinary least squares,* which identifies the line that minimizes the sum of the squared vertical distances from the actual data points and the line. Ordinary least squares is covered in statistics and econometrics courses.

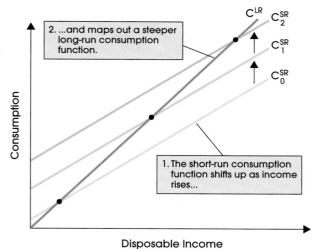

Exhibit 12-2

Relationship Between the Short- and Long-Run Consumption Functions

The short-run consumption functions C_0^{SR} through C_2^{SR} are flatter than the long-run consumption function, C^{LR}. The marginal propensities to consume are greater in the long run. The short-run consumption functions also intersect the y-axis at a value greater than zero. That is, in the short run, autonomous consumption is positive; in the long run, it is zero. Over time, the short-run consumption function shifts upward to trace out the long-run consumption function.

trouble. If the correct consumption function is the short-run consumption function, then, as income rises over time, the *apc* will fall. If consumption were to fall as a proportion of disposable income, assuming investment did not grow, aggregate demand might not be sufficient to keep the economy growing. Economists called this condition **secular stagnation**—the tendency of economic growth to slow over time. (Policy makers were very worried about secular stagnation in the 1940s and 1950s, because the Great Depression was still very much in everyone's mind. Would the economy sink back into depression?)

During the 1940s and 1950s, economists reconciled the two conflicting estimates for the consumption function. Basing their analysis on microeconomic reasoning, they reasoned that there are two separate, but compatible, consumption functions—a short-run consumption function that describes how income and consumption are related over short periods of time, and a long-run consumption function that describes how income and consumption are related over longer periods of time. As income rises and people incorporate those increases into their consumption decisions, the short-run consumption function shifts up along the long-run consumption function, as Exhibit 12–2 shows. So, over long periods of time, secular stagnation would not be a problem, because the *apc* along the long-run consumption function does not fall with income.

The two most prominent microfoundations theories that seek to explain the relationship between these two consumption functions are the permanent income hypothesis and the life-cycle hypothesis. Both theories start with the premise that people simultaneously choose how much to consume now and how much to consume in the future. To make these decisions, they look at how much income they earn now and how much they expect to earn in the future, as well as how much savings they have accumulated. This is an important difference from the original formulation of the consumption function, which assumed that people based their consumption only on current disposable income.

The Permanent Income Hypothesis

The **permanent income hypothesis,** first suggested by Milton Friedman in 1957, states that people base their consumption decisions on the present value of their expected future income. To illustrate what this means, suppose you are given a lump-sum payment of $60,000 to spend over the next 2 years. You could spend $5,000 the first year and $55,000 the second; $60,000 the first year and nothing the second; or any other combination that adds to $60,000. Friedman suggested that most people prefer to keep consumption as evenly divided between the 2 years as possible. In this example, he would assume that you would spend $30,000 each year.

According to this hypothesis, during years in which income is temporarily high, people will save most of the temporary portion in case income temporarily dips in the future. During years in which income is temporarily low, people borrow (or use savings) to maintain their level of spending. Consider a recent college graduate, Sandy, who just started her first job. The job pays well enough for Sandy to afford a modest apartment and a car. She uses her credit cards to furnish the apartment and buy a new wardrobe. (Blue jeans and sneakers from her college days will no longer do.) She accumulates a lot of debt. By going into debt, she is choosing to consume part of her future income today. She anticipates that her income will rise, allowing her to pay her credit card loans and still maintain her desired level of consumption in the future. Down the road, she may even start to save for retirement (although this is a very distant event in her mind). In making these choices, Sandy is deciding how much she wants to consume now and how much she wants to consume in the future.

If Sandy knew exactly what her income was going to be each year for her entire working life, she could calculate the present value of that income. Friedman called the annual average of the present value of future income permanent income. If Sandy plans to work for 20 years, earning Y_0 in the current year, Y_1 in next year, and so on, we can use the present value formula to write her permanent income as

$$Y^P = \left[Y_0 + \frac{Y_1}{(1 + r)} + \frac{Y_2}{(1 + r)^2} + \ldots + \frac{Y_{19}}{(1 + r)^{19}} \right] / 20$$

The reason we divide by 20 is to get the present value of the average amount of income that will be available for consumption in each of Sandy's 20 working years. So, how does this present value calculation reconcile the two consumption function estimates? Friedman argued that, in the short run, most changes in income are transitory or temporary. Over longer periods of time, these transitory movements average to zero. Empirical studies that used annual data, therefore, picked up mostly transitory movements in income and consumption. These studies found a relatively low *mpc* because people were saving much of the temporarily high income to augment consumption when income would be temporarily low. Empirical studies that used 10-year averages (long-run data) picked up mostly permanent movements in income and consumption.

Another way to see the different responses in consumption is to think about how you would react to an increase in your income in a given year. Suppose that one year, your income rises from $70,000 to $80,000. Initially, you might expect that most of the increase is temporary, so you increase consumption by only a small amount, say $6,000, saving the rest in case your income falls in the future. With this information, we can calculate our short-run *mpc* to be .6. However, if your income remains at $80,000 for a few years, you will change your calculation for your permanent income and increase your yearly consumption by, say, $9,000, so your long-run *mpc* would be .9.

The Life-Cycle Hypothesis

At the same time that Friedman was working on the permanent income hypothesis, economist Franco Modigliani was formulating a theory to explain the differences in the short-run and long-run consumption functions, which he called the *life-cycle hypothesis*. The **life-cycle hypothesis** is a theory of consumption that states that people try to even out their consumption expenditures over their lifetimes. Modigliani's theory reconciles the conflicting consumption functions in much the same way that Friedman's hypothesis did. Like Friedman, Modigliani argued that people base their consumption decisions on the present value of their lifetime incomes, but Modigliani also tried to explain how saving changes over one's lifetime.

> According to the life-cycle hypothesis, people try to smooth out their consumption over their lifetimes.

Modigliani suggested that consumption, income, and saving vary over a person's working life according to the diagram in Exhibit 12–3. As you can see, consumption stays the same each year. During their working years, people's income exceeds consumption, and people save and accumulate assets. At retirement, people begin to

Exhibit 12-3

Life-Cycle Hypothesis

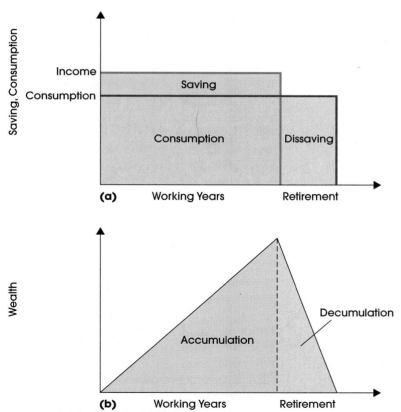

Panel a shows disposable income, consumption, and saving during a typical person's working years, and consumption and dissaving during retirement. During a person's working years, income exceeds consumption and he accumulates savings. During retirement, he draws down his savings; that is, he dissaves. *Panel b* shows how wealth rises during a person's working years and falls during his retirement. At death, wealth is completely exhausted.

dissave, drawing down their accumulated assets. At the exact moment of death, one's assets have been completely depleted. This is actually a simplified version of the story we told about Sandy. In reality, most people (like Sandy) dissave at the beginning of their careers, as they establish their households. In their middle years, they accumulate savings, and during their retirement, they dissave.

Modigliani was one of the first to point out the importance of assets for consumption decisions, which was an important discovery, because it states that the value of assets such as stock holdings or houses can influence consumption expenditures. Following the formulation of Modigliani's theory, economists began including a measure of accumulated wealth in empirical formulations of the consumption function. They found that the *mpc* out of accumulated wealth was roughly .03 to .06. This means people spend 3 to 6 cents of every $1 increase in wealth.

How Well Does the Life-Cycle Hypothesis Theory Fit the Facts?

Modigliani formulated the life-cycle hypothesis to reconcile the differences between the long-run and short-run consumption functions. However, his hypothesis makes additional predictions that don't seem to match the real world. Two predictions that have been extensively researched are that the elderly dissave and that people smooth their consumption.

> The elderly dissave less than predicted by the life-cycle hypothesis.

Dissaving Among the Elderly. According to the life-cycle hypothesis (see Exhibit 12–3), the elderly dissave during retirement. Although retired elderly do dissave on average, they do not dissave as much as the life-cycle theory predicts. This presents a puzzle: If people save during their working years to smooth their consumption, why aren't they dissaving as much as the theory predicts during retirement?

Economists have proposed two different explanations. The first is that people's lifespans are uncertain; therefore, they may be hesitant to dissave too quickly and risk running out of savings before the end of their lives. Although there is some truth to this explanation, it does not completely explain the lack of dissaving among the elderly; people can purchase annuities that guarantee an income for life when they retire. In addition, uncertain medical expenses are covered by government and private insurance plans. A second reason why the elderly do not dissave as quickly as the life-cycle hypothesis predicts is that they may want to leave an inheritance to their children. Students we talk with generally hope that this is the correct explanation.

Consumption Smoothing and Transitory Income Changes. Another observation inconsistent with predictions of the life-cycle hypothesis is that people do not tend to smooth their consumption as much as the model predicts. According to the life-cycle hypothesis, the *mpc* out of transitory income is expected to be only 5 percent to 10 percent as large as the *mpc* out of permanent income. The data show the *mpc* out of transitory income to be about 30 percent as large as the *mpc* out of permanent income. In other words, people are not smoothing consumption as much as expected.

To understand this puzzle, we need to look more closely at one of the key assumptions of the life-cycle (and permanent income) hypothesis—the assumption that people base current consumption on the present value of expected future income. How do people form expectations of future income? Early studies of these hypotheses suggested that people base their estimates of future income on past income, using simple rules of thumb such as the average income over the past several years. Modern economists have expanded on this, suggesting that people form expectations about future income using rational expectations. Recall from Chapter 11 that *rational expectations* means that they use all available information, avoid making systematic mistakes, and know the economic model that is generating their lifetime incomes.

If people form their expectations rationally, they make their current consumption decisions based on all that they know about their future income. Anticipated changes in income, then, would not change consumption when they occur; they would change consumption when they become known. Only unexpected changes in income would affect consumption decisions as people update their expectations of their permanent income. Because people are rational, the only changes in income that are unexpected are random.

If this explanation were true, all observed changes in consumption would be random changes. They aren't. Expected increases in income tend to lead to increases in consumption. So, people either do not form rational expectations about future income or are unable to borrow against future income to finance their present consumption. Let's take a closer look at these possible explanations.

It is possible that the life-cycle theory failed because people really aren't rational when they form their expectations about future income. Perhaps people are more myopic, less forward-looking, than the life-cycle model assumes. The life-cycle model doesn't assume that people know exactly what their income will be throughout their lifetimes, but it does assume that people have a forecast or general assessment in the back of their minds when they are deciding how much to consume. Perhaps even this idea is going too far. Many people simply might not know how to predict future income or might not have much faith in any such predictions. For these people, it is easier to let their consumption follow their current incomes; consumption smoothing is too difficult, so consumption rises and falls with income.

The second possible explanation is that people may be liquidity constrained. Even if people could perfectly anticipate their lifetime earnings, it is unlikely that they could borrow enough from future income to completely smooth their consumption over their lifetimes. People facing a liquidity constraint would have to put off desired purchases until their income actually rises, even if that rise is fully anticipated.

Consider your own lifetime income. As a college graduate, you will likely get a well-paying job and have a fair amount of economic security. You will probably earn enough to afford a house, a car, and a nice vacation every year. However, if you tried to walk into a bank today and explain that you deserve a loan so you could buy all of those things now, the loan officer would show you the door. You are liquidity constrained—you are not able to borrow against your lifetime income. Imagine Bill Gates, after dropping out of Harvard, walking into a bank and telling them he planned to become the wealthiest person in the world in a few years and he would like a $10 million loan against that future income. The world is too uncertain for banks to take such a risk. So, even Bill Gates, in his early years, was likely liquidity constrained.

The fact that the elderly do not dissave as much as expected or that people tend to smooth their consumption less than expected is not consistent with the life-cycle hypothesis. That is not to say that the life-cycle hypothesis is totally invalid. Rather, it is to say that the basic hypothesis needs to be modified or extended to include the possibilities that people are myopic or liquidity constrained, or that the elderly save in order to leave inheritances.

What the Permanent Income and Life-Cycle Hypotheses Mean for Policy

The permanent income and life-cycle hypotheses contain two macroeconomic policy lessons. The first lesson is that permanent policies will have more impact on the economy than will temporary policies. The second lesson is that monetary policy can affect consumption through its effect on people's wealth.

Permanent Versus Temporary Policies. Let's begin with the difference between temporary and permanent macroeconomic policies. If people think a policy, such as a tax cut, is permanent and will affect their permanent or lifetime income, that policy will have a larger impact on consumption and, therefore, on the economy than if they think the policy is temporary. According to the permanent income and life-cycle hypotheses, if a person believes a tax cut is temporary, she will spend only a portion of her additional disposable income this year, saving the rest to increase consumption in future years. So, consumption will rise by a little each year in response to the temporary tax cut. If, instead, she thinks the tax cut is permanent, she will spend all of the increase in disposable income this year because she knows she will have the same increase in disposable income to spend in the next year and all future years. She doesn't need to save part of the increase in income for future consumption. So, consumption will respond more to the permanent tax cut than to the temporary tax cut.

Permanent policies will have more impact than will temporary policies.

U.S. policy makers have attempted several times to manage aggregate demand through temporary changes in taxes. During the Lyndon Johnson Administration in 1968, Congress enacted a temporary tax increase to slow the economy. Government implemented the tax because the economy was expanding well above potential due to increased spending on defense and social programs. The effect of the policy was minimal; people hardly changed their spending.

Under President Gerald Ford, Congress enacted a temporary tax cut to bring the economy out of the 1974–1975 recession. As the life-cycle and permanent income hypotheses predict, most of the tax cut was saved and the policy was ineffective. Several economists criticized President Jimmy Carter's proposal for a temporary tax cut in 1977 on the grounds that it would increase the budget deficit without producing the desired stimulating effect. They based their criticism on the life-cycle and permanent income hypotheses.

Policy makers seem to have learned that the impact of temporary spending and tax policies on output is often small. But the political effect of these policies can be large, which means that politicians will most likely continue to use them. In 1992, for example, President George H. Bush proposed reducing the amount of income taxes withheld from paychecks during each tax year in an effort to stimulate spending. This was not a reduction in taxes, only a reduction in withholding. The same amount of taxes would be due on April 15 each year. It was clear to most economists and policy makers that the economic impact would be small, but the political impact (the President could say that he had taken action to stimulate the economy!) was large, and political impact often drives real-world policy.

The Wealth Effect and Monetary Policy. The second microfoundations lesson for macroeconomic policy is that monetary policy can influence the economy through not just income, but also asset prices and wealth. According to the life-cycle hypothesis, changes in accumulated wealth will affect consumption. Economists have estimated that the *mpc* out of wealth is 3 to 6 cents of every dollar increase in wealth. If monetary policy can also affect wealth, it can affect not only investment expenditures, but also consumption expenditures. For example, contractionary monetary policy, by raising interest rates and lowering investor confidence, could lead to lower stock market prices. By reducing income, it could also lower housing prices. Stocks and housing values are two important sources of wealth. Contractionary monetary policy that reduced wealth would, according to the life-cycle hypothesis, lead to lower consumption. This adds another channel by which the Fed affects the economy. The effect that the changing value of wealth has on the economy is known as the **wealth effect.**

> Monetary policy can affect consumption through its effect on people's wealth.

This wealth effect was particularly important during the late 1990s and into 2000 when rising stock prices generated a tremendous increase in stock market wealth. Although the *mpc* out of wealth is small, the rise in wealth during this period was so large that consumption expenditures rose significantly. Consumption remained high, offsetting the contractionary fiscal policy, and kept the economic expansion going. Economists estimated that the wealth effect contributed roughly 1.5 percentage points to annual growth during 1999 and early 2000. By raising interest rates in 1999, the Fed slowed investment and reduced the growth of the stock market, which slowed consumption. By the end of 2000, stock prices had dipped and the growth of consumption expenditures had slowed considerably, although in 2001, stock prices rose somewhat.

Executive Summary

- The short-run and long-run consumption functions differ: The short-run consumption function has a positive autonomous component, C_0, and a lower *mpc* than the long-run consumption function. The long-run consumption function has no autonomous component, C_0.

- The permanent income and life-cycle hypotheses assume that people try to smooth their consumption over their lifetimes by saving transitory increases in income and dissaving to maintain consumption during transitory decreases in income.

- According to the permanent income and life-cycle hypotheses, the short-run consumption function has a lower *mpc* and a positive autonomous component, because most short-term movements in income are dominated by transitory changes.

- The elderly do not dissave as much as the life-cycle hypothesis predicts, perhaps because they are uncertain about the timing of their deaths or they wish to bequeath money to their children.

- People tend not to smooth consumption as much as the life-cycle and permanent income hypotheses predict, either because people are myopic (are unable to forecast future income) or because they are liquidity constrained (are unable to borrow against future income).

- Fiscal policy actions, such as tax cuts, that people perceive to be temporary will have a smaller impact on the economy than will fiscal policy actions that people perceive as permanent.

- The life-cycle hypothesis suggests that monetary policy can affect consumption through its effect on stock market wealth.

INVESTMENT

We now look at how economists use microfoundations to improve their understanding of investment. In the earlier discussion of investment, we assumed that investment expenditures are inversely related to interest rates, meaning that, as interest rates go up, investment goes down, and as interest rates go down, investment goes up. That explanation was sufficient for laying out the short-run model, but it leaves open the important microeconomic questions of how firms decide on investment expenditures and the exact role of the interest rate in that decision. To answer these questions, we look at the microfoundations of investment expenditures.

Let's consider the decision a firm faces if it has to borrow to invest. In any investment project, the primary concern is, or should be, the bottom line: How much profit will the firm earn on that investment? The answer depends on two things: receipts from selling the output of the investment project (the quantity of output it will produce times the selling price) and the cost of producing that output. If "correctly measured" receipts are greater than "correctly measured" costs, the investment is worthwhile.

What makes the analysis of investment difficult is that receipts from an investment project do not come in immediately. Instead, they come in over a period of time. For example, a $100 investment in a machine might result in revenue of $40 per year for 3 years. The firm must decide whether it is worthwhile to buy the machine. One approach to answering this question is to compare the marginal efficiency of investment (the benefit) with the interest rate (the cost).

The Marginal Efficiency of Investment

The investment decision can be analyzed in a number of ways, all of which are versions of the present value analysis. We will concentrate on the marginal efficiency

The *mei* is the rate of return that makes the present value of a project's cash flow equal to its initial cost.

of investment approach. The **marginal efficiency of investment (mei)** is the rate of return that makes the present value of a project's cash flow equal to its initial cost. If the *mei* is higher than the relevant interest cost of the funds for the firm, the firm should invest. For example, the firm should invest if the interest rate is 14 percent and the *mei* is 20 percent.

In our example, the initial investment is $100 and the cash flow resulting from that investment is $40 in each of 3 years. To determine the return on the investment we ask, "What interest rate would make the present value of the future cash flow equal to the cost of the initial investment?" We can use the present value formula to answer that question:

$$100 = \frac{40}{(1 + mei)} + \frac{40}{(1 + mei)^2} + \frac{40}{(1 + mei)^3}$$

The $100 is the present value of $40 for 3 years. Instead of calculating the present value, given an interest rate *r*, we are calculating the rate of return (*mei*) that equates the present value of the flow of earnings to the current cost of the investment. Solving for the *mei*, we have[2]

$$mei = 9.5 \ percent$$

To see the logic of this calculation, consider a $100 investment that has its return of $120 in 1 year rather than $40 per year for 3 years. Because the entire return is in one period, the equivalent formula is

$$100 = \frac{120}{(1 + mei)}$$

In this case,

$$mei = 1.2 - 1 = 0.2, \ or \ 20 \ percent$$

Shortening the payback period by 2 years has caused the *mei* to rise from 9.5 to 20 percent. If the payback period were 2 years, the *mei* would have been

$$100 = \frac{60}{(1 + mei)} + \frac{60}{(1 + mei)^2}$$

$$mei = 0.131, \ or \ 13.1 \ percent.$$

Let's consider another example. Suppose Bighats.com is an Internet retailer of hats for big heads. A new college graduate started this business out of his parents' basement. Now that sales have taken off, he needs more space to hold inventory and is

---

[2]Most financial calculators can make this calculation automatically. This calculation is also called the *internal rate of return*. To calculate the internal rate of return on a financial calculator, you have to supply the initial cost of the project, the revenue stream, and the number of years that the project will generate revenue. If you don't have a calculator, you can solve the equation, but that's a real pain. We don't suggest it.

considering buying a small warehouse. He must choose whether to borrow money to finance this investment expenditure or continue to stick it out in his parents' basement. That choice depends on whether his expected sales will cover the purchase price of the building plus the interest payment on the loan and still earn a decent profit. Suppose the warehouse will cost $40,000 and will increase revenue by $10,000 for 10 years. The *mei* for this project would be

$$\$40{,}000 = \frac{\$10{,}000}{(1 + mei)} + \frac{10{,}000}{(1 + mei)^2} + \dots + \frac{10{,}000}{(1 + mei)^{10}}$$

In this case, *mei* = 0.214, or 21.4 percent, so assuming he can borrow money at less than 21.4 percent, it is a good investment.

Summarizing, to decide whether an investment project makes sense, compare the *mei* with the rate of interest (*r*). The decision rule is

> If *mei* > *r*, undertake the investment project.
> If *mei* < *r*, do not undertake the investment project.

If *mei* > *r*, undertake the investment project; if *mei* < *r*, don't invest in the project.

A firm will normally have a variety of investment projects from which to choose and will rank those projects according to their marginal efficiencies of investment. A fall in the interest rate (with no change in expected returns) will make projects that were unattractive at a higher interest rate now worth undertaking. For example, if the interest rate decreases from 6 percent to 3 percent, all investments with an *mei* between 6 percent and 3 percent now become worthwhile.

Adjusting for Risk

If determining whether to invest were as easy as described above, firms would have little trouble determining which projects to undertake: They would undertake those projects with the highest *mei*. Unfortunately, it is not that easy. Generally, firms do not know the returns of an investment project. At best, they have some idea of the probabilities of various returns. For example, who could have imagined that Pokemon would be a tremendous success? Some lucky or bright entrepreneur must have correctly predicted that such characters would have wide appeal. Put simply, businesses must make decisions based on their expectations about the returns of a project.

The economic approach of estimating returns on a risky project is to estimate the probabilities of a project's success and to determine the project's expected value (*EV*). The decision maker then compares *expected* returns based on expected values. Say, for example, that a Furby project has a 1 percent chance of making $1 million and a 99 percent chance of making nothing, while a project to produce some other toy has a 100 percent chance of making $10,000. The expected value of each project is the product of the probability of a particular return and the amount of the return.

Multiply expected returns by the probability of those returns occurring to adjust for risk.

> *Expected value of Furby* = 0.01($1,000,000) + 0.99(0) = $10,000
> *Expected value of alternative toy* = (1.0)$10,000

The projects' expected values are equal. A firm that doesn't care about the risk associated with either choice would be indifferent between these two choices because they have the same expected value. Suppose, however, the firm is risk-averse, meaning that it tries to avoid risk because it does not have the financial resources to survive if the investment project yields a zero return. To account for risk aversion, we subtract a risk premium from the expected value of the risky alternative. The greater the risk, the greater the risk premium. So, in the preceding example, a risk-averse firm might value the first alternative less than the second alternative, even though the expected values are identical. Risk preferences vary among firms and can be important in determining a firm's choice of investment projects.

We could say more about how firms move from rough ideas about a project (subjective probabilities) to the *mei*. An entire course, corporate finance, is devoted to these issues, but for now, we will assume that firms can determine a project's *mei*.

Executive Summary

- The marginal efficiency of investment (*mei*) is the rate of return that would make a project's cash flow equal to its initial cost.

- Firms use these decision rules when deciding whether to invest in a project: If *mei* > *r*, invest in the project; if *mei* < *r*, do not invest in the project.

- To adjust for risk, multiply the expected return by the probability that the return will be forthcoming.

- Firms base their investment decisions on expected future profits, which are inherently uncertain.

Choosing a Method of Financing Investment Expenditures

So far, we have evaluated the investment decision, assuming firms borrow the funds from a bank to make the investment. But firms need not always borrow. Besides borrowing from a bank, firms can borrow by selling bonds, issuing stock, or use retained earnings. Investment decisions entail choosing among methods of financing.

To understand how firms select their method of financing, let's introduce some finance terms. When a firm borrows money from a bank or issues bonds, it is undertaking or using **debt financing.** When a firm issues stock, it is using **equity financing.** These two methods of financing differ in repayment, control, and liability.

Debt financing requires the firm to pay interest to the lender (either the bank or the bond holder), which is usually at a fixed interest rate and for a fixed term. Equity financing doesn't require periodic payments. Instead, the firm is obligated to share its profits, some of which may be periodically paid out as dividends.

It may seem that equity financing is the best option because it does not require fixed payments. What the firm gives up, however, is part ownership and control. Stockholders generally have the right to participate in the election of the board of directors and vote on important firm decisions. Although small investors rarely exert much influence, large investors, such as insurance companies or stock mutual funds, can greatly influence business decisions by the firms in which they own stock. In contrast, a bondholder has no voice in the operation of the firm. Control over business decisions is a primary factor when a firm chooses between debt financing and equity financing.

Another difference between debt financing and equity financing is that if a firm goes bankrupt, it must pay its bondholders and banks first when it liquidates its assets. Only remaining assets are distributed to shareholders.

Firms also must consider external constraints to its financing decisions. Which will give the firm the greatest access to funds—bonds or stocks? To

To finance projects, firms must choose between debt financing and equity financing.

understand this issue, we have to look more closely at the determination of bond and stock prices.

Bond Prices and Interest Rates

Above, we stated that a bond can be valued with the present value formula and that its price varies inversely with the interest rate. Let's now look more closely at that relationship. The first thing to note is that a bond is a promise to pay some specified amount at some future date. To keep things simple, suppose a firm issues a bond that promises to pay the holder $100 in 1 year. What is the most you would be willing to pay for that bond? Letting the price of the bond be represented by P_B, you should answer, the present value of the future payment ($100):

$$P_B = \frac{\$100}{(1 + r)}$$

(If this wasn't your answer, you may want to review the previous section on present value.) If the interest rate in the economy is 5 percent, $P_B = \$95.24$, and if the interest rate in the economy is 7 percent, $P_B = \$93.46$.

The same basic principle can be applied to calculate the price of bonds with longer maturities and those that pay periodic interest. For example, suppose a firm issues a 2-year, $100 bond that pays 10 percent interest each year. At the end of the first year, the bondholder will receive a $10 interest payment, and at the end of the second year, she will receive another $10 interest payment plus the principal of $100. The calculation for the price of the bond in this example will be

$$P_B = \frac{\$10}{(1 + r)} + \frac{\$110}{(1 + r)^2}$$

Interest Rate on Similar Bonds. The interest rate that is relevant to this calculation, r, is the interest rate paid on similar bonds (bonds issued by firms with a similar credit rating). If the interest rate of similar bonds is the same (10 percent), the price of this bond will be its face value ($100). If the interest rate on similar bonds is higher, say 12 percent, the amount people would be willing to pay would be lower than the face value of the bond. In this case, $P_B = \$96.62$. The bond will sell for less than its face value to compensate the holder for the fact that the interest payment is lower than on similar bonds. If, alternatively, the interest rate on other bonds is lower than the interest rate on this bond, say, 8 percent, people would be willing to pay more than its face value. They'd be willing to pay $103.57. The firm selling the bond can earn a premium on the bond (of $3.57) because the bond promises to pay the bond holder a higher interest than could be earned elsewhere on similar bonds.

Term to Maturity and Risk of Default. In our discussion of bonds and interest rates, we have assumed that people decide how much to pay for a bond based solely on the interest rate (r) that investors use to calculate the present value. In reality, bondholders consider two other factors: the term of the bond and the risk that the firm will default on its promise (not pay interest or the principal).

In Chapter 9, we discussed how the term to maturity affects a bond's interest rate and introduced the yield curve (a curve that shows the relationship between

The longer the maturity of a bond, the more its price will vary with interest rate changes.

Bonds have varying degrees of default risks and are classified by ratings.

bonds' maturities and interest rates). The yield curve is usually upward sloping because longer-term bonds include a premium for greater risk. Even bonds with the same term to maturity, however, may pay different interest, because firms do not have the same probabilities of paying the interest and repaying the principal. A firm with a high probability of default will have to pay a premium to compensate investors for the higher risk.

It is difficult for an investor to gather all of the information necessary to calculate a firm's probability of default. Fortunately, several companies specialize in providing such information. The largest and most well known is Moody's Investors Service. (You can search for sample bond ratings at www.moodys.com.) Moody's rates bonds according to their risk of default, giving a rating of Aaa to the highest quality (lowest probability of default) and a rating of Baa to the medium-quality bonds. Bonds receiving a rating of C have the highest default risk.

Exhibit 12–4 shows interest rates of Moody's Aaa and Baa bonds. Notice that the interest rates tend to move together over time, but that interest rates on Baa-rated bonds are persistently higher than those on Aaa-rated bonds, reflecting the premium for risk.

So, in sum, bond prices vary inversely with interest rates, and the interest rate on bonds varies directly with the term to maturity and risk of default of bonds. If the risk of default rises, so will the interest rate that bondholders require. Understanding the relationship between interest rates and the investment decision more carefully, we can see how monetary policy can affect investment decisions. Contractionary monetary policy that raises market interest rates reduces the price bondholders are willing to pay for corporate bonds. This, in turn, raises the cost of borrowing to firms and reduces the number of investment projects that firms will undertake, reinforcing the conclusion from earlier chapters that contractionary monetary policy will reduce investment expenditures. Likewise, expansionary monetary policy, by lowering the cost of borrowing, will increase investment expenditures. Therefore, we see that the general relationships that we used in our macroeconomic model have microeconomic foundations.

Exhibit 12-4

Bond Yields

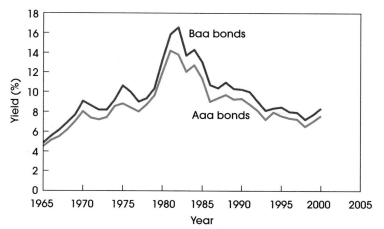

The yields on Baa-rated bonds and Aaa-rated bonds tend to move together. Baa-rated bonds are sold at a higher yield to compensate bondholders for the greater risk of default, compared with Aaa-rated bonds.

Q
&
A

QUESTION   Can the present value formula explain why Internet stock prices rose so high?

ANSWER   Yes, if profits are expected to grow, the valuation of a stock can become extraordinarily high.

The annuity formula assumes a constant annual payment. If profits are expected to rise, the valuation goes up. The closer the expected growth rate of profit is to the rate of interest rate, the more valuable is the stock. To see this, let's say that the profits are expected to grow at the rate of interest. The present value becomes:

$$PV = \frac{X(1 + g)}{(1 + r)} + \frac{X(1 + g)^2}{(1 + r)^2} + \ldots + \frac{X(1 + g)^n}{(1 + r)^n}.$$

In this case, the growth rate (g) and the discount (r) factors cancel out making the present value the infinite sum of the current profit. That sum is infinite, which means that whatever you pay for the stock, it's a good buy. In reality, profits cannot grow indefinitely, and the growth rate of profit must at some point fall. When people suddenly come to believe that the growth rate of profits will fall, the value of the stock will fall suddenly, as happened with the price of Internet stocks in late 2000 and early 2001.

Stock Prices

Stock prices reflect the present value of the future stream of profits per share.

We have discovered what determines the price of a bond. What about the price of a share of stock? The standard view of stock prices is that they reflect the present value of the future stream of profits per share that a firm is expected to earn over its lifetime, adjusted for the riskiness of that return. Putting aside risk for a moment, suppose that a firm is expected to earn $10 profit per share into the indefinite future and that the current interest rate is r. The stock price, P_S, will be

$$P_S = \$10 + \frac{\$10}{(1 + r)} + \frac{\$10}{(1 + r)^2} + \frac{\$10}{(1 + r)^3} \ldots$$

If we assume that the firm will earn $10 per share forever, the price of a share of stock will be[3]

$$P_S = \frac{\$10}{r}$$

At a 5 percent interest rate ($r = .05$), $P_S = \$200$, and at a 7 percent interest rate, $P_S = \$142.86$. Changes in the price of a share of stock, therefore, will arise from changes in the expected profits per share of the firm and changes in the interest rate. The annuity formula can also be used to approximate the value of long-term bonds. After 30 years, the contribution of future payments is relatively small, so as an approximation of the price of a long-term bond, one can also use this formula (especially when the interest rate in the economy is relatively high). Therefore, when the current interest rate is 12 percent, a 30-year $1,000 bond with a 10 percent coupon rate will cost approximately $833 (100/.12).

The preceding calculation of stock and long-term bond prices ignores the role of risk. In the real world, however, risk is an important determinant of stock prices

---

[3]The present value of an infinite stream of $10 payments is: $P_S = \$10 + \$10/(1 + r) + \$10/(1 + r)^2 + \$10/(1 + r)^3 + \$10/(1 + r)^4 \ldots$ If we factor out the $10, this can be rewritten as $P_S = \$10[1 + 1/(1 + r) + 1/(1 + r)^2 + 1/(1 + r)^3 + 1/(1 + r)^4 \ldots]$. The term inside the brackets is called a *geometric series*. This geometric series sums to $1/r$. Thus, the present value of this infinite stream is simply $10/r$.

QUESTION	What is an example of a risk rating for stocks?
ANSWER	Betas are a typical risk rating for stocks.

The financial press often talks about the riskiness of a stock in relation to its *beta*. A stock's beta measures the relationship between the rate of return on a particular stock and the rate of return on the stock market as a whole. Suppose, for example, that a company has a stock with a beta of 1. This means that the rate of return on that stock tends to move one-for-one with the rate of return on the stock market as a whole. If the stock market rises by 3 percent, the price of the stock with a beta of 1 will tend to rise by 3 percent as well. Likewise, if the stock market falls by 3 percent, the price of a stock with a beta of 1 will tend to fall by 3 percent. If a particular stock has a beta greater than 1, its return tends to move up and down by more than the stock market. For example, a beta of 1.5 means that if the stock market rises by 3 percent, that stock price will tend to rise by 4.5 percent. This might sound pretty good, but when the market falls by 3 percent, that stock price will tend to fall by 4.5 percent. Stocks with betas of less than 1 have returns that generally vary by less than the market. Notice that we have used terms like *tends to* and *generally* when describing the relationship between a stock's return and the market's return. The reason we've used these terms is that betas describe a statistical relationship. They measure what happens, on average, when the market rises or falls by a certain percent.

We can classify a stock's riskiness based on its beta. If a stock has a beta less than 1, it is considered less risky than the stock market. If a stock has a beta greater than 1, it is more risky than the stock market, and if a stock has a beta equal to 1, it is as risky as the stock market. The following table shows betas for a few selected companies in mid-2000. (These betas will change over time.)

Betas for Selected Companies

Company	Beta
General Mills	0.65
Tootsie Roll Industries	0.70
Humana	1.10
Coca-Cola	1.10
Payne Webber	1.90
Lehman Brothers	1.90

Note that a stock's beta measures only the systematic risk of stock—the risk that is tied to the stock market as a whole. There is also firm-specific risk that is not captured by the beta. Investors avoid this firm-specific risk by diversifying their portfolios—not keeping all their eggs in one basket.

(just as risk is an important determinant of bond yields). One of the measures of *risk* is how variable the stock price is expected to be relative to the overall stock market.[4] A share of stock whose price is expected to vary more than the average of all stock prices will have a higher return (it will appreciate in value more than average) than a share of stock whose price is expected to vary about as much as the average of all stocks in the stock market.

Expected Profits. According to one explanation of the determination of stock prices, stock prices are based on investors' expectations about the expected profit stream and risk of a firm. An entire industry is devoted to gathering information about companies and assessing their future profitability and risk. Investment firms such as Merrill Lynch, Lehman Brothers, and Dean Witter specialize in gathering such information. (See the Q&A feature on betas, one measure of risk of a firm's stock price.)

---

[4]This is sometimes called *systematic* risk because it describes the systematic movement of a share of stock relative to the entire stock market.

First, investors assess the profitability of a company, then they look at the price of its stock. If the share price seems low, given expected profits and expected risk, they will buy. If it seems high, given expected profits and expected risk, they will sell or not buy. In the process of buying and selling, the price will tend to move toward the market's expected present value of future profits per share adjusted for risk.

According to this view of stock price determination, the large increase in stock prices during the late 1990s and early 2000s is the result of increased expected profits. Investors believed that firms in the United States, particularly technology firms, e-commerce firms, and dot-com firms, would earn enormous profits in the future. As long as nothing happened to change those beliefs, stock prices would remain high.

Speculative Bubbles. There is an explanation for stock prices, however, that does not rely solely on expected future profits. Some economists and policy makers believe that asset markets are subject to **speculative bubbles**—inflated asset prices that are not based on expected future profits.

A price bubble occurs when investors buy stocks solely on the belief that they can sell them for a higher price in the future—independent of the present value of the expected profits per share of the firm. As long as investors speculate that someone will buy the stock at a higher price, they will keep bidding the price higher and higher. The reason this situation is called a *bubble*, of course, is that bubbles sometimes burst. When stock market bubbles burst, prices of most stocks plummet.

At the time that stock prices are rising, it is impossible to tell whether they are rising because of a speculative bubble, rising expected future profits, or some combination of both. The reason is that expected future profit is a nebulous concept. Despite the mountains of objective analysis that go into assessing the profitability of firms, in the end, the ultimate assessment is subjective. (See the Briefing Room, "Using the Price–Earnings Ratio to Assess Stock Values," to learn about the price–earnings ratio, one of the common objective measures of stock valuations.)

Now that you have seen explanations of how stock and bond prices are determined, let's return to the question of which method of finance—stocks or bonds—gives a firm greater access to funds. The answer depends on what is happening to interest rates and stock prices. If interest rates are low and stock prices are low relative to the firm's expected future profits, the firm would be better off issuing bonds, because issuing bonds will cost less. If interest rates are high and stock prices are high, the firm would be better off issuing stock, because the cost of issuing stocks will be less than the cost of issuing bonds.

Tobin's-*q* Theory of Investment

Nobel-prize-winning economist James Tobin developed a microeconomic theory that incorporates stock prices into the firm's investment decision. Tobin postulated that the firm's own stock prices influence the firm's decision to invest. Recall that the owner of a share of stock in a corporation is really part owner of the corporation and all of its assets. You can, therefore, think of the shareholders as owning the machinery and equipment on the factory floor as well as the factory itself. Putting aside the possibility of speculative bubbles for a moment, the price that someone is willing to pay for a share of stock reflects the company's expected future profits or, alternatively, how much profit the company's current capital is expected to generate now and in the future.

Expected profits are very uncertain, so the price of a stock can change suddenly.

A speculative bubble occurs when investors buy stocks solely on the belief that they can sell them at a higher price in the future.

THE BRIEFING ROOM   **Using the Price–Earnings Ratio to Assess Stock Values**

Stock investors sometimes look at the price-earnings (PE) ratio when assessing whether a stock is "correctly" priced. The PE ratio is the price of a share of stock divided by the earnings per share of the firm. For example, if a share of IBM costs $80 and IBM's profit per share is $8, then its PE ratio is 10 (= 80/8).

Investors use PE ratios to assess whether a stock (or a group of stocks) is undervalued or overvalued. A low PE ratio means that the stock's price is low compared with the current earnings of the firm. As long as investors think that the firm's earnings will remain high, this low PE ratio could signal that the stock's price is too low. A high PE ratio means that the stock's price is high compared with the firm's current earnings. As long as investors think that the firm's earnings will remain low, this PE ratio could signal that the stock's price is too high.

We have avoided giving you a magic PE ratio to look for when evaluating whether a stock is over- or underpriced. That's because there isn't one. We can assess only whether a particular PE ratio is high or low relative to other stocks or relative to some other time period.

Another reason that the PE ratio is difficult to interpret is that it compares the current price with the current earnings of the firm. Our analysis in the text suggests that the price of a share of stock is related to *expected future* earnings—not necessarily to current earnings. PE ratio analysis implicitly assumes that current earnings are correlated with future earnings—when current earnings are high, future

earnings will be high, and when current earnings are low, future earnings will be low.

PE ratios are useful only if current earnings are related to future earnings. That may not be the case during periods of rapid technological innovation. The following exhibit shows the PE ratio for the Standard & Poors 500 stock index from 1881 to 2000. The average PE ratio from 1871 to 2000 was 15.8. The average PE ratio from 1997 through the end of 1999 was 40. The late 1990s was a period of rapid technological innovation in computing and telecommunications. During that period, PE ratios rose to historic highs (in fact because many of these companies had no current earnings, the PE ratios were uncalculable), only to crash in 2001.

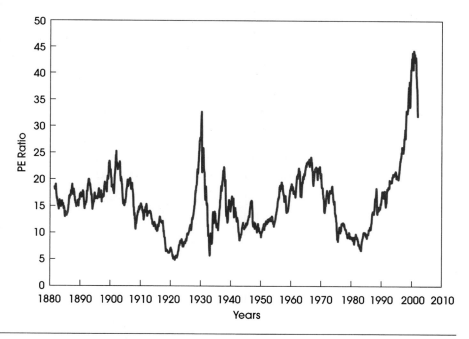

Tobin suggested that firms base their investment decision on the value of their outstanding stock relative to the replacement cost of their capital. The total value of outstanding stock reflects how much the market values the current capital. The ratio of the market value of current capital to the cost of replacing that capital is called **Tobin's-q:**

$$Tobin\text{'s-}q = \frac{market\ value\ of\ current\ capital}{cost\ of\ replacement\ capital} \tag{12-4}$$

The numerator is the market's expectation of future profits generated by the firm's present capital. The denominator is the cost of replacing that capital. If q is greater

Tobin's-*q* theory of investment states that investment depends on whether the market value of current capital divided by the cost of replacement capital is greater or less than 1.

than 1, the stock market valuation of the firm's existing capital in terms of its potential to earn profit exceeds the cost of that capital and it is worthwhile for the firm to add more capital. If *q* is less than 1, the market valuation of capital is less than its replacement cost and the firm should not invest in new capital.

Suppose, for example, a firm is thinking about investing in a new factory that will cost $20 million. If investing in the new factory raises the market value of the firm's outstanding stock by more than $20 million (*q* is greater than 1), the firm should invest in the factory because stock market investors believe it will earn the company more in future profits than it will cost. If investing in the new factory raises the market value of the firm's outstanding stock by less than $20 million (*q* is less than 1), the firm should not invest in the new factory. The empirical evidence on Tobin's-*q* is mixed. Investment expenditures and stock market prices are positively related, indicating that firms take the value of their outstanding stock into account when making investment decisions. However, the empirical evidence is not strong enough to accept the theory totally.

In Chapter 8, you learned how monetary policy affects investment expenditures in the IS/LM model. A reduction in the money supply causes the interest rate to rise and investment expenditures to fall. Tobin's-*q* theory suggests another channel, through which monetary policy affects investment expenditures. A reduction in the money supply raises the interest rate. Holding the return on stocks constant, an increase in the interest rate will cause investors to switch from holding stocks to holding bonds, wherein they will get a relatively higher rate of return. The decline in the demand for stocks will cause stock prices to fall and, according to Tobin's-*q* theory, investment will fall as well.

Summing Up: Policy Implications of the Microfoundations of Investment

The microfoundations of investment provide a firmer underpinning for the standard relationships assumed in macro between interest rates and other variables in the economy. They also point to policies other than monetary policy that will affect investment decisions. Tax credits, for example, will raise future expected profits. Policy makers, therefore, can use tax credits to stimulate investment.

Another policy implication is that monetary policy has an additional channel through which to affect investment—namely, the stock market. If a tightening of monetary policy leads to higher interest rates, investors will shift away from stocks and start buying bonds. Stock prices will fall and, according to Tobin's-*q* theory, so will investment expenditures.

POLICY PERSPECTIVE: THE IMPORTANCE OF EXPECTATIONS

A common theme in our discussion of the microfoundations of consumption and investment is that individuals consider the future when making choices. Intertemporal choices tell us that policy is best seen as a process, not as an event.

Consider, for example, the lesson about permanent and temporary tax cuts. Microfoundations tell us that people and firms make intertemporal choices based on the present value of future income and profits. A $100 permanent reduction in taxes will increase the present value of future income and profits by more than will a $100 temporary tax cut. A permanent tax cut will have a larger positive impact on both consumption and investment, because it will affect the whole stream of future income and profits.

In the context of modern macroeconomics, it does not make sense to talk about the effects of an increase in the money supply, a tax cut, or an increase in government spending as isolated events. Instead, we must consider policy in terms of a whole series of present and future changes. People draw conclusions about the permanence of a policy based on past government behavior, called a policy regime. A **policy regime** is a rule that people believe is guiding policy.

For example, during the 1960s and early 1970s, the U.S. government increased spending on the Vietnam War and on social programs. When individuals and firms looked to the future and tried to form expectations about what the government might do with taxes and spending, they formed those expectations in the context of the fiscal policy regime at the time—expansionary fiscal policy. During the 1980s and early 1990s, U.S. fiscal policy sought to reduce the government budget deficit. Policy during that period was also interpreted within the context of that policy regime.

Another implication of intertemporal macroeconomic theory is that **credibility**— the degree to which people believe that an economic policy will be implemented—is an important determinant of the policy's effectiveness. Throughout the 1990s, for example, Congress and the President talked about establishing a credible deficit reduction plan. They knew that if people believed that the deficit was going to fall, long-term interest rates would fall, which would make it easier to reduce the deficit (because interest payments would be lower). Similarly, the Fed continually tries to maintain its credibility as an inflation fighter in order to keep inflationary expectations from rising. That's because it is more difficult to reduce inflation when people expect inflation. Finally, if Congress can convince the American public that a tax cut is permanent, there will be a larger stimulative impact on output than if people think a tax cut is temporary.

> A policy regime is the underlying rule that people believe the government is following in its policy.

> Credibility is an important determinant of a policy's effectiveness.

Executive Summary

- Firms finance investments by using retained earnings, selling bonds (debt), or selling shares of stock (equity).

- Firms consider the fact that holders of debt (bonds) have first claim on a firm's assets, while holders of equity participate in electing the board of directors and voting on key decisions of the firm in the decision about what method of financing to use.

- The price of a bond equals the present value of the flow of payments less a premium for risk.

- The price of a share of stock equals the present value of the stream of profits per share less a premium for risk.

- Stock prices can rise for no other reason than investors believe the price of the stock is going up.

- Such speculative bubbles are subject to bursting and rapidly falling stock prices.

- Tobin's $q = \dfrac{\text{market value of current capital}}{\text{cost of replacement capital}}$

- When Tobin's-q is greater than 1, firms invest. When Tobin's-q is less than 1, firms do not invest.

- Permanent changes in investment tax laws will have a larger impact on investment expenditures than will temporary changes.

- An alternative channel by which monetary policy affects investment is through Tobin's-q.

- Intertemporal choice implies that policy is best thought of as a process—an effective policy regime.

- The effectiveness of a policy depends on its credibility.

CONCLUSION

Economists no longer analyze government policy actions as isolated events—a one-time change in taxes or government spending. Instead, they analyze government policy actions as a whole sequence of events—changes in government spending and taxes stretching out into the foreseeable future. This means that the effect of a particular policy will depend critically on its perceived effect on future policy actions. Of course, our earlier discussions took this into account, but by considering microfoundations, these issues become clearer. Whether microfoundations is the future of macroeconomics is unclear, but all economists agree that microfoundations adds insight to both models and policy.

KEY POINTS

- Microeconomic foundations have refined and augmented the policy advice that macroeconomists give.
- In general, present value is today's value of some future amount of money. $PV_{1-n} = \dfrac{X_1}{(1+r)^1} + \dfrac{X_2}{(1+r)^2} + \cdots + \dfrac{X_n}{(1+r)^n}$
- The higher the interest rate, the lower the present value of a future sum of money.
- The greater number of years until a sum is paid, the lower its present value.
- The short-run consumption function has a lower *mpc* than the long-run consumption function. It also has an autonomous component and the long-run consumption function does not.
- The permanent income and life-cycle hypotheses assume that people try to smooth their consumption over their lifetimes.
- According to the permanent income and life-cycle hypotheses, a temporary tax cut has a smaller impact on consumption expenditures than does a permanent tax cut.

- The marginal efficiency of investment (*mei*) is the rate of return that makes a project's cash flow equal to its initial cost.
- If *mei* > *r*, a firm should undertake the investment project. If *mei* < *r*, it should not.
- *Debt financing* means borrowing or issuing bonds. *Equity financing* means selling shares of stock.
- The price of a bond depends on the interest rate, the term to maturity, and the default risk of the bond.
- The price of a share of stock depends on the interest rate, expected future profits of the company, and the riskiness of the stock.
- The main differences between debt financing and equity financing are the terms of repayment, control, and liability.
- Tobin's-$q = \dfrac{\text{market value of current capital}}{\text{cost of replacement capital}}$
- According to Tobin's-*q* theory, when *q* > 1, firms will invest, and when *q* < 1, they will not invest. Tobin's q gives monetary policy another channel to affect investment.
- *Intertemporal choice* implies that policy is a process and that a policy's effectiveness depends on its credibility.

KEY TERMS

QUESTIONS FOR THOUGHT AND REVIEW

1. What are microeconomic foundations and why are they important to macroeconomic policy?
2. What are intertemporal choices? Give an example of an intertemporal choice.
3. What is present value and how does it affect intertemporal choices?
4. Describe how the present value of a future sum of money varies with the interest rate.
5. Describe how the present value of a future sum of money varies with the payment date.
6. Describe the differences between the short-run and long-run consumption functions. How are the differences relevant for macroeconomic policy?
7. How does the permanent income hypothesis reconcile the differences between the short-run and long-run consumption functions?
8. How does the life-cycle hypothesis reconcile the differences between the short-run and long-run consumption functions?
9. Describe the pattern of lifetime consumption that the life-cycle hypothesis predicts.
10. What are the possible explanations for why elderly people do not dissave as quickly as the life-cycle hypothesis predicts?
11. Why is consumption more volatile than the life-cycle hypothesis predicts?
12. What is the policy implication of the permanent income and life-cycle hypotheses?
13. What is the marginal efficiency of investment and how does it relate to the present value formula?
14. Explain how a firm would use the concept of marginal efficiency of investment to determine whether to invest in a particular project.
15. What factors does a firm consider when deciding between debt financing and equity financing?
16. Use the concept of present value to explain why the price of a bond is inversely related to the interest rate.
17. Demonstrate how the price of a share of stock is determined using the present value concept.
18. What is a speculative bubble? What is the potential role for policy when there is a speculative bubble in the stock market?
19. What is Tobin's-q theory of investment?
20. What are the policy implications of the microeconomic foundations of investment?
21. How does intertemporal choice change our view of policy?
22. Why is credibility an important determinant of the effectiveness of policy?

PROBLEMS AND EXERCISES

1. Your great uncle just died and left you $1 million, but there is a catch—you can't collect it until you are 40 years old. What is that $1 million worth to you today if the interest rate is 5 percent? 7 percent? 12 percent? (Assume you are currently 20 years old.) (This question requires a calculator.)
2. (This question requires a financial calculator.) Assume your tuition is $25,000 per year for 4 years. Your college offers two different tuition-payment plans. One plan allows you to pay $25,000 each year. The other plan allows you to make one payment of $93,000 at the start of your freshman year. Which plan would you take at each of the following interest rates (assuming tuition payments are due at the beginning of each year):
   a. 3 percent
   b. 8 percent
   c. At what interest rate would you be indifferent between the two plans?
3. Redraw the top half of Exhibit 12–3 to show Sandy's consumption and income pattern.
4. Redraw Exhibit 12–3 (both graphs), assuming people wish to leave a bequest to their children.
5. (A calculator would be a help in answering this question.) Bighats.com wants to purchase a hat-packing machine that costs $40,000. This machine is expected to bring in revenue of $46,000 four years from now and then break.
   a. Calculate the marginal efficiency of investment for this project.
   b. Would the firm invest in this project if the interest rate were 3 percent?
   c. What if the interest rate were 7.5 percent?
6. Assume you have a $100 bond, with a 10 percent coupon rate, that has 1 year left until maturity. Calculate the amount for which you could sell this bond at each of the following interest rates:
   a. 7 percent
   b. 10 percent
   c. 12 percent

7. Suppose you are considering an investment project that has a 5 percent probability of generating $100,000 profit and a 95 percent chance of generating a $20,000 profit. What is the expected value of that investment project?

8. Calculate the price of a share of stock for a firm that is expected to earn $20 per share forever for each of the following interest rates:

a. 3 percent

b. 8 percent

c. 12 percent

Two-Period Model of Life-Cycle Consumption

In the chapter, we gave an example of Sandy's intertemporal choices. In this appendix, we look at these choices more formally.

Recall that Sandy is a recent college graduate who just started her first job. She needs a lot of things—a car, an apartment, business clothes, food, and so forth. Although her salary can cover some of the cost, she can't pay for it all. She must decide how many of her current needs to fill—how much should she borrow? She's also starting to think about her needs during retirement—how much should she save for the future?

In choosing how many goods and services to buy this year, Sandy must think about not only her current disposable income, but also any income she plans to earn in the future, any past saving or accumulated wealth, and the rate of return on that wealth. Let's say Sandy plans to work for 45 years and be retired for

20 years. If we try to think about how much Sandy will decide to consume in each of these 65 years of life, it will be overwhelmingly (and unnecessarily) complicated. So, we will simplify the problem for Sandy by dividing her life into two time periods. In the first period of her life she works, earning an annual income of $90,000. In the second period of her life she retires, receiving annual Social Security benefits of $12,000. She came into the first period of her life with a stock mutual fund valued at $50,000, which represents her accumulated wealth.

Our first task is to determine Sandy's lifetime consumption possibilities. One option is for Sandy to spend her income and her accumulated savings during the first period of her life and her Social Security benefits in the second period of her life. Point A in Exhibit 12–A1 shows this possibility. Consumption expenditures are $140,000

Exhibit 12–A1
Lifetime Consumption Possibilities

The line in the graph shows all of the consumption possibilities that Sandy faces. The extremes are point B, where Sandy consumes all income in the second period, and point C, where she consumes all income in the first period. The line connecting the two points shows all other possible combinations.

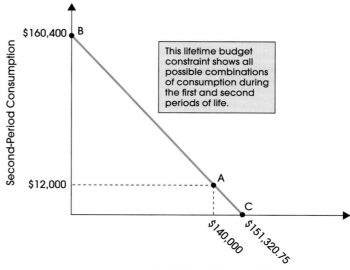

($50,000 + $90,000) in the first period of her life and $12,000 in the second period of her life.

A second possibility is for Sandy to consume nothing during the first period of her life, saving all of her income to augment consumption expenditures during the second period of her life. If Sandy puts her first period income into her stock mutual fund and that fund earns a rate of return r, her consumption will be 0 in the first period. The second period consumption equals:

$$(90,000 + 50,000)(1 + r) + (12,000)$$

For example, if the stock mutual fund earns a 6 percent return, Sandy's second period consumption will be $160,400. For a 6 percent return, this consumption combination is shown as point B in Exhibit 12–A1.

A third possibility is for Sandy to consume nothing during the second period of her life and to borrow against future earnings (her Social Security benefits) so she can spend more than her current income and wealth during the first period of her life.

What is the maximum that Sandy can borrow? Here is where our concept of present value comes in. Sandy can borrow the present value of her future income, or $12,000/(1 + r)$. For example, if the interest rate is .06, PV_1 = 12,000/1.06 = 11,320.75. If Sandy borrows $11,320.75 at .06, she will pay back the principle ($11,320.75) plus the interest ($679.25), which just equals $12,000.

If Sandy borrows against her future income at 6 percent and then adds these borrowed funds to her first-period income and accumulated wealth, her lifetime consumption will be $151,320.75 (50,000 + 90,000 + 12,000/1.06 + 0). This combination of first- and second-period consumptions is illustrated as point C in Exhibit 12–A1.

THE INTERTEMPORAL BUDGET LINE

The three scenarios we have illustrated represent only a small subset of all of the possible combinations of first- and second-period consumption that Sandy can consume. By varying the amount she borrows or saves, Sandy can consume anywhere along the line shown in Exhibit 12–A1. This line is called the *lifetime budget constraint* because it incorporates Sandy's lifetime earnings and shows the possible combinations that she can consume, given those lifetime earnings.

Sandy can divide her consumption expenditures any way she'd like as long as it is on or inside her lifetime budget constraint. If we assume that Sandy does not want to leave a bequest (she wants to spend her last dime

just before she draws her last breath) and that more consumption gives her more happiness, she will always operate on her lifetime budget constraint rather than inside it.

THE INTERTEMPORAL INDIFFERENCE CURVES

Our next task is to determine which combination of consumption expenditures Sandy will actually choose. To figure that out, we need to characterize Sandy's preferences—the combination that will make Sandy the happiest.

It is not possible to actually measure how happy Sandy will be for a particular combination, but we *can* compare that particular combination with other combinations of first- and second-period consumption and ask which combination would likely make Sandy happier, or whether she would be indifferent between the two combinations.

To illustrate, suppose we arbitrarily choose the combination $C1_0$, $C2_0$ to start, which is point w in Exhibit 12–A2. If we compare that combination with point z, where Sandy has the same first-period consumption ($C1_0$) but lower second-period consumption ($C2_1$), it is clear that Sandy would be happier with point w. Now think about how we can make Sandy just as happy as she was at her initial point but with the lower second-period consumption $C2_1$. To make up for the lower second-period consumption, we would have to give her more first-period consumption, possibly moving her to point y at $C1_1$, $C2_1$. The difference between w and y is that Sandy has traded lower second-period consumption to have higher first-period consumption, but both points give her the same level of happiness. In other words, Sandy is indifferent between points w and y.

We can present Sandy with a variety of trade-offs of first- and second-period consumption and trace out the points that give her the same level of happiness as w and y. These points will form a curve called an indifference curve—combinations of first- and second-period consumption that give Sandy the same level of happiness. Exhibit 12–A2 shows the indifference curve, labeled I_1, going through points w and y.

We can repeat this exercise by starting at a different consumption combination other than $C1_0$, $C2_0$ at point w. Suppose we start at point q, which makes Sandy less happy than she is at any of the points on I_1. If we trace out all the points Sandy is indifferent to, starting at point q, we will form another indifference curve, I_2. In principle, there are an infinite number of these indifference curves, stacked one next to the other. As we move up and to the right, we reach higher indifference curves and higher levels of happiness.

Before we use these curves to figure out the combination of first- and second-period consumption that Sandy will actually choose, it is important to understand the reason why indifference curves are shaped the way we have drawn them—why they are downward sloping and why they are bowed in toward the origin of the graph. It should be clear why they are downward sloping—as Sandy gives up some first-period consumption, she needs

more second-period consumption to stay at the same level of happiness.

The bowed-inward shape, however, implies that for each additional dollar of first-period consumption Sandy gives up, she needs more and more second-period consumption to keep her at the same level of happiness. Let's assume Sandy starts with $40,000 worth of consumption in both periods of her life, point A in Exhibit 12–A3. If we take away $5,000 in second-period consumption, we must give Sandy $7,000 in first-period consumption to stay on the same indifference curve (point B). Now, if we

Exhibit 12–A2
Lifetime Consumption Possibilities

Sandy is indifferent between points *w* and *y* on indifference curve I_1. She prefers all points along I_1 to all points along I_2.

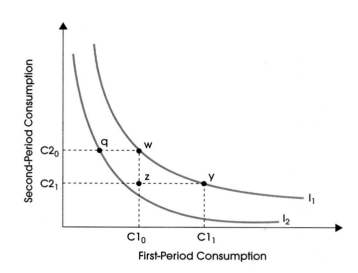

Exhibit 12–A3
Shape of the Indifference Curve

Indifference curves are generally bowed in toward the origin because people will be equally happy with less consumption during one period only if they are given more and more consumption in the other.

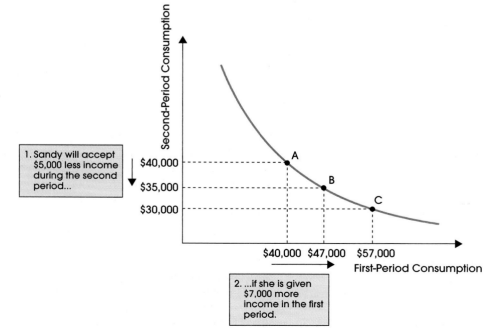

1. Sandy will accept $5,000 less income during the second period...

2. ...if she is given $7,000 more income in the first period.

take away an additional $5,000 in second-period consumption, we must give her back even more first-period consumption, $10,000, to stay at the same level of happiness (point C). If we keep taking away $5,000 in second-period consumption, we will have to give her greater and greater amounts of first-period consumption to keep her on the same indifference curve.

This example illustrates what it means for Sandy's indifference curves to be bowed inward, but what is the economic intuition here? The bowed-inward shape reflects the property of consumption in the permanent income and life-cycle hypotheses—people like to smooth their consumption as much as possible over their lifetimes. For example, the smaller second-period consumption is, compared with first-period consumption, the bigger the premium or extra first-period consumption Sandy requires to keep her at the same level of happiness.

INTERTEMPORAL EQUILIBRIUM

Now it's time to put together Sandy's indifference curves and her lifetime budget constraint to determine the combination of consumption expenditures that she can afford and that will make her the happiest. Exhibit 12–A4 shows the highest indifference curve Sandy can achieve while still meeting her intertemporal budget constraint.

Sandy will try to get to the highest indifference curve, but she cannot exceed her lifetime budget constraint. This means that she will choose the point on indifference curve I_1 that is tangent to her lifetime budget constraint (touches at one point). Any movement from this point to the right or to the left will leave Sandy on a lower indifference curve, and she will be less happy.

Given the way we've drawn the curves, the tangency is at point A, where Sandy's consumption combination is $77,864.08 the first period and $77,864.08 the second. At point A, Sandy is consuming less than her first-period income and more than her second-period income. In other words, she is saving $12,135.92 ($90,000 − $77,864.08) during her first period of life and drawing down her savings during her second period of life. To calculate Sandy's second period consumption we add her first period saving to her first period wealth, multiply by an assumed 6 percent rate of return and then add that product to her second period income:

$$C_2 = (\$12,135.92 + \$50,000) \times 1.06 + \$12,000 = \$77,864.08.$$

We have intentionally drawn Sandy's indifference curve to make her consumption equal in both periods. This is consistent with reality. Most people earn more during the first period of their lives (their working years) and because most people wish to smooth their consumption over their lifetimes, they save to supplement their earnings when they are retired. This illustrates the pattern of consumption proposed in Modigliani's life-cycle theory of consumption.

TEMPORARY AND PERMANENT CHANGES IN INCOME

Now that we have set up how Sandy makes her intertemporal consumption choice, let's see how she will change that choice when her income changes. There are two different types of income changes we want to consider: a temporary change and a permanent change. We begin with a temporary change. Suppose Sandy gets a

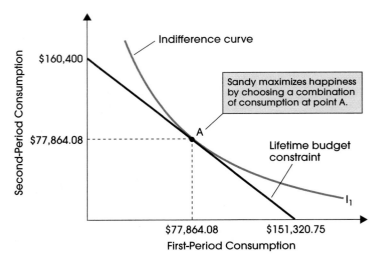

Exhibit 12–A4
Optimal Consumption Choice

Sandy chooses to consume $77,864.08 in both periods of her life. This combination places her at the highest indifference curve, I_1, that is tangent to her lifetime budget constraint (touches it at only one point).

bonus at work, which raises her wage by $2,000 in the first period of her life, leaving her second-period earnings unchanged at $12,000. The effect of this change is illustrated in Exhibit 12–A5.

Sandy's lifetime budget constraint shifts out and becomes slightly less steep because her first period income rises but not her second. She chooses a new lifetime consumption combination $78,893.21 in the first period and $78,893.21 in the second period (point B). The temporary increase in income led to an increase in Sandy's first-period and second-period consumption. Sandy used part of the $2,000 ($1,029.13) to increase

consumption in the first period of her life, and she saved the remainder ($970.87) to add to her second-period consumption. This is another illustration of the consumption smoothing principle. Sandy consumes part of her bonus and saves part to supplement her second-period consumption. Notice that Sandy's marginal propensity to consume (mpc) out of this temporary increase in income is .51 (1029.13/2000).

Now let's consider a permanent change in income. By *permanent change,* we mean that Sandy's first-period and second-period earnings both rise by $2,000. The effect of this change is illustrated in Exhibit 12–A6.

Exhibit 12–A5
Temporary Increase in Income

Sandy's budget constraint shifts out when her first-period income rises. She saves part of the increase to smooth lifetime consumption.

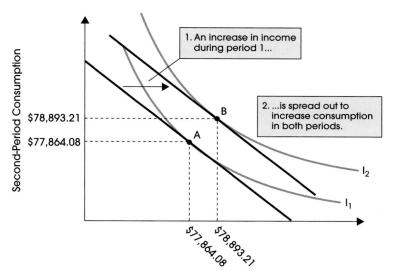

Exhibit 12–A6
Permanent Increase in Income

Sandy's budget constraint shifts out when her lifetime income rises. Her consumption increases by the rise in income, or $2,000, in both periods—from point A to point B.

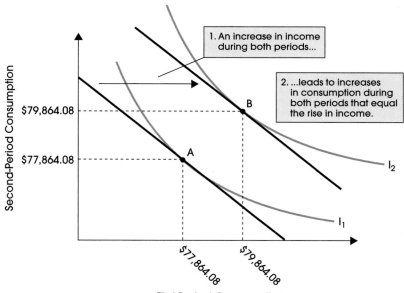

Again, Sandy's lifetime budget constraint increases (shifts out) but it shifts out further and the slope changes by less. Faced with this budget line she chooses a new consumption combination: $79,864.08 in the first period and $79,864.08 in the second period. This time, consumption in both periods increases by the full amount of the increase in income. Sandy doesn't need to spread the increase in income across the two periods, because the increase is permanent. There is no reason for Sandy to increase her saving during the first period of her life, because she knows that the income increase will remain through the second period of her life. In a sense, consumption is automatically smoothed by the permanent nature of the income change. Notice that Sandy's marginal propensity to consume (mpc) out of this permanent change in income is 1 (2000/2000). This model illustrates the empirical observation that we pointed out at the beginning of the chapter: the short-run *mpc* is smaller than the long-run *mpc*.

13

The Nuts and Bolts of Monetary Policy

A squirrel in the forest had a particular taste for fish. He finally went to the wise old owl for some guidance and counsel. After listening to his story, the owl advised the squirrel that the way for him to satisfy that desire was to become a kingfisher. So the squirrel happily went away, ran up a tree over a brook, and imagined himself a kingfisher so he could catch some fish.

Of course, imagination was not enough. The squirrel discovered he was still a squirrel. After sitting in the tree for a while, he returned to the owl in a state of some agitation and railed, "You told me the way to satisfy my desire to get some fish was to become a kingfisher, but you haven't told me how to do that. I am still a squirrel." The owl replied, "Look, you came to me with a problem. I gave you some sound policy advice. The rest is operational detail."

—Paul Volcker

After reading this chapter you should be able to:

1. Describe the structure and targets of the Federal Reserve Bank

2. List three tools of monetary policy and explain how they affect the money supply

3. Explain how banks create money

4. Name two operating targets and two intermediate targets the Fed uses to achieve its ultimate targets

5. Describe the operational conduct of the Fed

6. Summarize the debate about rules versus discretion

7. Use the Taylor rule to measure the direction of monetary policy

As you enter the lobby of the Federal Reserve Bank of San Francisco, you will see an electronic video game. The object of the game is to hit a moving target with a dart from a moving arm. With both the arm and the target moving, most visitors miss the target.

The game is there to demonstrate the difficulties of implementing monetary policy. Monetary policy "shoots from a moving arm," as you will see when we consider the operational details of monetary policy. Ultimately, policy actions of the Federal Reserve System (the Fed) influence output and inflation, but the influence is not direct, and many other factors also affect output and inflation.

The Fed has targets given to it by law. Its official targets are *to promote maximum employment, stable prices, and moderate long-term interest rates.* What each target means is ambiguous, however, and the conventional interpretations change over time. Consider the Fed's problem in the late 1990s when unemployment had fallen below what most economists had previously considered the natural rate. Some economists argued that the unemployment target had moved; others argued that inflation was just around the corner. By early 2000, inflation still had not risen. Even so, the Fed began to implement slightly contractionary monetary policy. The policy perspective at the end of this chapter discusses how the Fed justified its actions.

In reality, the Fed's problem is even more complicated than the video game suggests. A more telling game would be one modeled after a Rube Goldberg

**A Rube Goldberg
Pencil Sharpener**

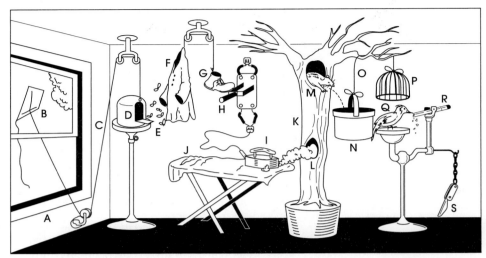

Directions: Open window *(A)* and fly kite *(B)*. String *(C)* lifts small door *(D)* allowing moths *(E)* to escape and eat red flannel shirt *(F)*. As weight of shirt becomes less, shoe *(G)* steps on switch *(H)*, which heats electric iron *(I)* and burns hole in pants *(J)*. Smoke *(K)* enters hole in tree *(L)*, smoking out opossum *(M)*, which jumps into basket *(N)*, pulling rope *(O)* and lifting cage *(P)*, allowing woodpecker *(Q)* to chew wood from pencil *(R)*, exposing lead. Emergency knife *(S)* is always handy in case opossum or the woodpecker gets sick and can't work. **Source:** www.rube-goldberg.com

> The Fed's official targets are to promote maximum employment, stable prices, and moderate long-term interest rates.

cartoon. If you hit the first moving target, it releases a second dart when hit. That second dart is supposed to hit a second moving target, which, in turn, releases a third dart aimed at yet another moving target. Given the complicated path that monetary policy follows, it should not be surprising that the Fed often misses its ultimate targets. Some economists pose this question: Would the Fed be better off not even trying to play the game?

This chapter explores how monetary policy works by considering the nuts and bolts of the U.S. monetary and financial system. We first consider some of the institutional features of the Federal Reserve Bank, the U.S. central bank. Then we take a broader look at the nature of financial assets and liabilities and the role of money in the U.S. financial system. Next, we look at the operational details of monetary policy, giving you a feel for what playing the monetary policy game is like. Finally, we consider some recent issues in monetary policy in light of earlier chapters.

THE FEDERAL RESERVE BANK

Monetary policy is the set of policies a country's central bank undertakes to influence the money supply and interest rates, and, thereby, to influence the level of economic activity and amount of inflation in the country. The central bank in the United States (the agency responsible for monetary policy) is called the Federal Reserve (the Fed). In addition to conducting monetary policy, the Fed has oversight control of the financial system in the United States. (See The Briefing Room, "The Fed's Role of Maintaining Financial Stability," on page 378 for a discussion of this broader role.) Because the Fed is the central player in monetary policy, let us briefly consider its organizational structure.

The Fed is the U.S. central bank; it is composed of 12 regional banks and has seven Governors, appointed for 14-year terms.

Technically, the Fed is not just one bank; it is a system of banks, called the Federal Reserve System. It is composed of 12 regional Federal Reserve Banks, the Board of Governors of the Federal Reserve, the Federal Open Market Committee, and about 4,000 member banks. The seven-member Board of Governors oversees the entire system. The President of the United States appoints each governor for a term of 14 years, although most governors choose not to complete their terms. The President also designates one of the governors to be the chairperson of the Fed (in 2001, this was Alan Greenspan) for a 4-year term. A chairperson can serve multiple terms, and this chairperson is sometimes referred to as the second most powerful person in Washington, D.C. (the most powerful being the President of the United States).

The Federal Reserve System has 12 districts, which are shown in Exhibit 13–1. Each district has one main regional Federal Reserve Bank, which operates under the general supervision of the Board of Governors. However, since 1935, the districts, except for the Federal Reserve Bank of New York, have had little direct power over the banking system. District banks and their branch banks gather information about business and banking conditions in their geographic regions, and the presidents of the regional Feds report that information to the Board of Governors in Washington, D.C.

The FOMC is the key committee that decides monetary policy.

The **Federal Open Market Committee (FOMC)** is a group of officials within the Federal Reserve System who make the key decisions that affect the money supply and interest rates (monetary policy). Preparation for these meetings consumes much of the staff's time at the Board of Governors. The press carefully follows its meetings, and you will likely read about monetary policy in the newspapers the day after FOMC meetings.

Voting members of the FOMC include the seven appointed members of the Board of Governors, the president of the New York Fed, and a rotating group of four other district bank presidents. All presidents of the district Federal Reserve Banks attend the FOMC meetings, but only five get to vote at any one meeting.

Exhibit 13–1

The Federal Reserve System

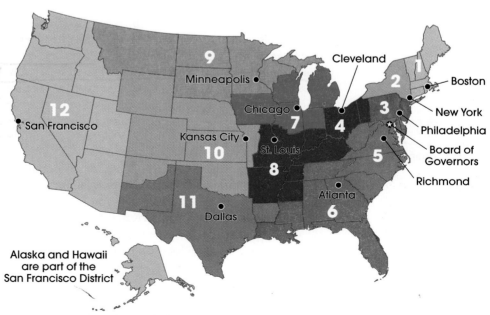

The Federal Reserve has 12 districts. Each district, which has a main regional Federal Reserve Bank located in the city labeled in this exhibit, covers banking operations in several states. Source: www.federalreserve.gov/otherfrb.htm

THE BRIEFING ROOM　　The Fed Role of Maintaining Financial Stability

This chapter focuses on monetary policy because most of the day-to-day debate about the Fed concerns monetary policy. However, the Fed has a broader responsibility that goes beyond monetary policy—to maintain the financial stability of the United States. The Fed is entrusted with this responsibility because it, and it alone, has the right to issue money. That sole right gives the Fed enormous power and responsibilities.

To see what this role means, imagine that there is a sudden monetary crisis and a run on banks. In a run on a bank, large numbers of people lose faith in the banking system and "run" to the bank to withdraw their money. In our system of fractional reserves, banks do not have sufficient money on hand to cover all demand deposits, and the bank would have to close. In this case, assuming the bank is ultimately solvent, it can borrow as many Federal Reserve Notes from the Fed as it needs to meet the demand for currency by its customers. As soon as people realize they can easily exchange their demand deposits for cash, they will not want to, and the run on the bank will end. The Fed's role as a lender of last resort gives it an important role in maintaining overall financial stability. When a crisis occurs, the Fed can lend funds to troubled banks.

The stock market crash of October 1987 is a similar crisis that was limited by the Fed action. The value of stock portfolios fell 23 percent and many brokers tried to get loans to tide them over. It looked as if the stock market would crash even further. The Fed lent large amounts of funds to banks and encouraged them to make loans to brokers, which they did, avoiding a meltdown in the stock market. This "maintaining financial stability" could also be expressed as preventing the "institutional coordination effect" from becoming operative. It was the Fed's failure to prevent such an effect in 1933 that many economists believe led to the Great Depression.

A more recent example occurred in August 1998. The unexpected devaluation of the Russian ruble sent shock waves through the financial sector, and one financial firm in particular, Long-Term Capital Management, suffered large losses (52 percent for the year). The Fed thought that if Long-Term Capital Management went out of business there would be widespread panic in the financial markets. The Fed, therefore, arranged meetings between Long-Term Capital Management and several banks and brokerage houses in order to work out a way to save the firm. The private companies did find a solution, but the point of this story is that the Fed played a role in facilitating the meetings because of its interest in maintaining financial market stability.

Because the president of the Federal Reserve Bank of New York is a continuing voting member of the FOMC, the New York Fed has more power than other district banks. The New York Fed also operates the open market desk and the foreign exchange desk. The open market desk buys and sells government securities for the Fed, the primary way the Fed affects the money supply. The foreign exchange desk buys and sells foreign currencies to implement the Fed's exchange rate policy.

The Fed is technically owned by its member commercial banks, but all of its earnings (except for 6 percent annual dividend payments to its member banks) go to the federal government. The federal government is liable for the debts of the Federal Reserve banks.[1]

The Fed is a bankers' bank. Private individuals cannot deposit money with the Fed, nor can they borrow from it; only banks can. The Fed, and only the Fed, can issue notes and create currency. If you look at a dollar bill, you will see that it is a Federal Reserve Note. Currency is merely an obligation or IOU of the Fed, "backed" by the federal government. That means that the Fed agrees to give you a dollar bill in exchange for a dollar bill. Nothing else.[2]

> The Fed is technically owned by its member commercial banks, but most of its earnings go to the government.

---

[1] The Fed earns revenue from interest on the assets it owns (primarily government bonds). After paying expenses and dividends, it returns its "profits" to the Federal government.

[2] The term *backed* may be a bit misleading, because the backing of the dollar is only a moral obligation; the government is required only to give you another dollar bill to replace your current one.

One final point: While the Fed does not depend on Congress for its financing and, therefore, is not responsible to Congress, the Humphrey Hawkins Act requires the Fed to report to Congress twice a year regarding its activities. Because Congress could pass a law that takes away the Fed's independence (over the years, a number of bills have unsuccessfully attempted to do so), the Fed tries not to alienate Congress. Its independence is not total.

Executive Summary

- The Fed's official goals are to promote (1) maximum employment, (2) stable prices, and (3) moderate long-term interest rates.

- The Federal Reserve Bank is the semi-autonomous U.S. government agency in charge of monetary

policy in the United States. There are 12 regional Federal Reserve Banks.

- The FOMC makes the decisions that affect the money supply and interest rates (monetary policy) in the economy.

MONETARY POLICY

Fed policy shifts the LM and the AD curves.

Let's now turn to monetary policy. By doing so, you will have a much better understanding of what we mean when we say that the Fed shifts the LM and the AD curves out (expansionary monetary policy) or the LM and AD curves in (contractionary monetary policy). With this understanding, you will be in a much better position to apply macroeconomic models to the real world.

First, we discuss the tools that the Fed uses to conduct monetary policy—what the Fed can do and what effects those actions have on interest rates, inflation, and output. (Appendix A presents a brief history of monetary policy actions.) Then, we look at the operational conduct of monetary policy, showing you a Fed directive and explaining how the Fed implements that directive. We then step back and show how real-world monetary policy fits the description of the video game at the beginning of this chapter. Finally, we talk about recent monetary policy issues.

The Tools of Monetary Policy

The three tools of monetary policy are changing the reserve requirement, changing the discount rate, and open-market operations.

The Fed can create and destroy money, so it can control, or at least influence, the money supply and interest rate, and through those measures, affect other economic variables. The Fed has three tools with which to influence the money supply: changing the reserve requirement, changing the discount rate, and buying and selling bonds (open-market operations). Exhibit 13–2 shows how two of these tools—the discount rate and open market operations—affect the banking system. We will discuss the specific workings of these tools when we discuss the operational conduct of monetary policy.

The fraction of bank deposits that the Fed requires banks to hold as reserves is the reserve requirement.

Changing the Reserve Requirement. The Fed requires banks to hold a fraction of their deposits as reserves. **Reserves** are cash in banks' vaults or bank deposits at the Fed. The fraction of bank deposits that the Fed orders banks to hold as reserves is the **reserve requirement.** For example, if you deposit $100 in a checking account at your bank and the reserve requirement is 10 percent, the bank must hold $10 of the deposit as cash in its vault or as deposits at the Fed. Because the reserve

Exhibit 13-2

The Fed's Tools

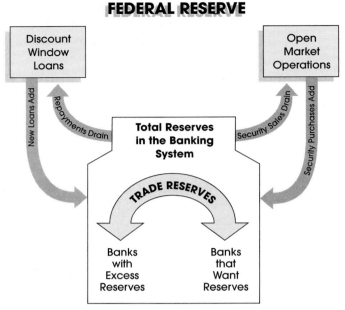

This flow diagram illustrates how two of the Fed's tools—discount window lending and open-market operations—affect the amount of reserves in the banking system. By changing the amount of reserves, the Fed can affect the money supply. Source: Federal Reserve System.

> The monetary base is currency in circulation and the reserves in the banking system.

requirement determines how much of a bank's deposits the bank can lend, it establishes the relationship between reserves and the money supply. Reserve requirements are set by the Board of Governors and, therefore, are another monetary policy tool. The total reserves in the banking system and currency in circulation is known as the **monetary base.**

Reserves pay no interest, so banks hold as few reserves as possible. The required reserve ratio that the Fed sets is generally higher than necessary for normal business operations, and banks generally reach the minimum reserve requirement before they are short of cash. Today, reserve requirements are set only on transactions deposits such as demand deposits, NOW accounts, and ATS (automatic transfer from savings) accounts. Reserve requirements are 3 percent of transaction accounts between $5 million and $44 million, and 10 percent above $44 million. (You can find the current reserve requirements in Table 1.15 of the current *Federal Reserve Bulletin*.) Although the Board of Governors can change the reserve requirement, it rarely does so. The reserve requirement was last changed in April 1992.

> The discount rate is the interest rate that the Fed charges banks to borrow reserves.

Changing the Discount Rate. A second tool available to the Fed to influence the money supply is changing the discount rate. The **discount rate** is the interest rate the Fed charges banks that borrow reserves from the Fed. Because the loans are Fed IOUs, and because Fed IOUs held by banks are reserves, this borrowing increases reserves. Banks borrow from the Fed through what is called the discount window. They generally do so when their reserves are insufficient to meet the minimum amount required by law. Raising the discount rate discourages borrowing and decreases the money supply. Decreasing the discount rate encourages borrowing and increases the money supply.

As banks increase their borrowing from the Fed, they acquire more reserves, allowing them to increase their lending, which expands the total money supply. In theory, this means that, by changing the discount rate, the Fed can influence the money supply. In practice, however, banks are hesitant to borrow from the Fed unless they absolutely have to. The Fed frowns on banks that borrow from it and might tell its bank examiners to audit these banks more carefully than usual to see why they need to borrow. Banks are also fearful that word will get out to the public that they have borrowed too often at the discount window and may be experiencing difficulty. Instead, banks borrow reserves from other banks in the federal funds market at a market interest rate called the fed funds rate.

At one time, the Fed used the discount rate as a barometer to signal its intentions. It raised the discount rate to indicate its desire to contract the money supply, and lowered the rate to indicate its desire to expand the money supply. Banks responded to these signals and changed their lending practices accordingly, affecting the total money supply. This custom has broken down because certain aggressive banks borrowed all they could from the Fed whenever it was profitable for them to do so. In response, the Fed now adjusts the discount rate to stay close to the fed funds rate, although there is still debate over how free banks are to use the discount window to meet normal funding needs. Table 13–1 lists the discount rate and fed funds rate since 1990.

Open-Market Operations. The tool that the Fed uses most often to affect the money supply is open-market operations. **Open-market operations** are the Fed's buying and selling of government securities. To see how this tool affects the money supply, suppose the Fed sells bonds to the public. The public pays for these bonds with checks drawn on commercial bank accounts, and made out to the Fed. The Fed presents these checks to the commercial banks, which give the Fed money out of its reserves. A bank draft paid on an account reduces bank reserves by the amount of the draft, in this case, the amount of the bond sold to the public. If the bank does not have more reserves than the Fed requires, the decline in reserves sets in motion a multiplied contraction in the money supply.

> *the interest rate that banks charge each other for overnight loans*

The discount rate is usually kept slightly below the federal funds rate.

Open-market operations are the main way the Fed affects the money supply.

Table 13-1

The Discount Rate and Federal Funds Rate

	Fed Funds Rate	Discount Rate
1990	8.10	6.98
1991	5.69	5.45
1992	3.52	3.25
1993	3.02	3.00
1994	4.21	3.60
1995	5.83	5.21
1996	5.30	5.02
1997	5.46	5.00
1998	5.35	4.92
1999	4.97	4.62
2000	6.24	5.73

Rates are annualized using a 360-day year or bank interest.

Source: The Federal Reserve System (**www.federalreserve.gov**).

When the Fed sells bonds, the money supply decreases; when it buys bonds, the money supply increases.

Alternatively, if the Fed wants to increase the money supply, it buys bonds, paying for them with checks drawn on the Fed's accounts. These Fed checks are IOUs of the Fed and, just like currency, increase bank reserves, even though they are merely accounting entries. The ease of open-market operations makes it the most commonly used tool in controlling the money supply.[3] To execute open-market operations, the Fed maintains a portfolio of government securities.

The Money Multipliers and Fractional Reserve Banking

The three policy tools of the Fed are related to the money supply through the money multiplier and the monetary base. Open-market operations and discount window lending affect the monetary base (reserves plus currency in circulation), while changing the reserve requirement affects the money multiplier. The relationship between the money supply, the money multiplier, and the monetary base is as follows:

$$money\ supply = money\ multiplier \times monetary\ base. \qquad (13\text{-}1)$$

This equation states that the money supply is some multiple of the monetary base. The money multiplier is the result of a **fractional reserve banking** system, in which banks hold only a fraction of their deposits in reserve and lend the remaining fraction. (See The Briefing Room, "Matching Asset and Liability Maturities," for a discussion of bank's lending practices. Appendix B gives a more detailed presentation of fractional reserve banking using balance sheets.)

The money multiplier increases the effect of changes in the monetary base on the money supply.

The **money multiplier** tells us the relationship between the monetary base and the money supply. A money multiplier of 5 means that the money supply is five times the monetary base. Each dollar of the monetary base generates multiple dollars in the money supply because that monetary base serves as reserves for all bank deposits. Banks can lend the remaining bank deposits, which are either held by the public as cash or deposited at banks. In either case, these loaned funds are included in all the standard measures of the money supply.

Whenever banks make loans, they create money in the same way the Fed creates money when it issues its IOUs. The money multiplier simply tells us the amount of money that banks are capable of creating for a given monetary base and reserve requirement. Let's see how the money-creation process works.

Say the Fed conducts an open-market operation: It buys a $100 bond from an individual and gives that individual $100 in currency. With that open-market operation, the Fed has created $100. The individual then deposits the $100 at a bank. He now has $100 in his checking account, which is considered money. So, he still has $100 in money. The bank, however, now has $100 more in reserves, and because the United States has a fractional reserve system, the bank can loan out some portion of the increase in reserves. That loan is new money. If the bank keeps 10 percent of deposits as reserves, when it lends $90 of its new deposits, the bank increases the money supply by $90.

These actions are only the first step in the money-creation process. The new $90 in money works its way back to the bank as $90 in new deposits, which supports

---

[3]For the conduct of open-market operations in government debt, the amount of government debt must be sufficient to support a continual market in that debt. Someone must almost always be buying or selling. For many developing countries, the market in government debt is too "thin," and, thus, this is not the main tool of monetary policy.

THE BRIEFING ROOM   Matching Assets and Liability Maturities

Banks operate by taking in deposits and making loans. In doing so, they serve as intermediaries between lenders and borrowers. The deposits they take in are their liabilities, and the loans they make are their assets. Their income consists of the difference between what they pay for deposits and what they earn on loans. The lenders to banks are people who hold checking accounts at the bank; these accounts pay either low or no interest rates. These checking accounts are payable on demand, which is why they are called demand deposit accounts. Twenty or 30 years ago, most of a bank's liabilities were payable on demand, while many of its assets were long-term and could not be collected early. Banks were borrowing "short" and lending "long," leaving them in a vulnerable position if all the banks' "short" lenders demanded their cash. This problem can create periodic runs on banks, when many depositors withdraw their money at the same time, leaving banks unable to pay others who wish to withdraw their money.

The changing institutional structure of banking has reduced the difference in time to maturity between liabilities and assets. New financial instruments have developed that allow banks to sell loans they have already made and to take in deposits with relatively long maturities. Today, banks practice simultaneous asset management and liability management. They carefully try to match the maturity of their assets (loans) with the maturities of the liabilities (deposits). As this happens, new financial institutions and new financial assets are continually being created.

additional loans that increase the money supply even further. In each round, the amount of additional money created becomes smaller and smaller until banks are fully loaned out, at which point the money-creation process ends. In our example, if banks hold 10 percent of their deposits as reserves, the $100 increase in the monetary base supports a $1,000 increase in the money supply.

The reason a fractional reserve banking system works is due to the law of large numbers, which states that a large number of repeated actions will converge to the average of all actions. Even though the balance in any particular checking account can be withdrawn at will, on average, total deposits in the bank change very little. Net deposits and net withdrawals on any particular day generally offset each other, and banks can pay withdrawals with new deposits. To handle normal operations, banks need only hold reserves for a small portion of their deposits. As mentioned, the reserve requirement generally exceeds the amount of reserves banks would otherwise choose to carry.

If the reserve requirement is the fraction r, each time the bank makes a loan, it must keep r of that loan on reserve. Continuing our example, when the individual deposited the $100 he received from selling the bond, reserves rose by $100. The bank was then able to make new loans (create money) in the amount of $(1 - r) \times 100$. When the loans are spent, the money makes its way back to the bank as deposits so that an additional $[(1 - r)(1 - r)] \times 100 = (1 - r)^2 \times 100$ is created, and so on. Extending this, we have the mathematical series,

$$[(1 - r) + (1 - r)^2 + (1 - r)^3 + \ldots] \times 100$$

The simply money multiplier is 1/r.

which can be simplified to $(1/r) \times (100)$.[4] So, the **simple money multiplier** is

$$1/r \qquad\qquad (13\text{-}2)$$

---

[4]This simplification is based on the fact that a series $1 + x + x^2 + x^3 + \ldots$ where $0 < x < 1$ sums to $1/(1 - x)$. Substituting $1 - r$ for x in the equation gives us $1/[1 - (1 - r)]$, or $1/r$.

This is the money multiplier when no one holds currency and banks hold no more reserves than the Fed requires.

The similarity between the money multiplier and the expenditures multiplier (discussed in an earlier chapter) sometimes leads to confusion. Money is a stock; income is a flow. The amount of money in the economy is *not* directly related to the income in the economy (although it is indirectly related through the quantity theory). Although the reasoning behind the two multipliers is similar, the multipliers describe totally different processes. The money multiplier magnifies a one-time change in the money supply that results from the Fed's actions. The expenditures multiplier affects the income flow in the economy and must be supported by a continuous stream of spending or saving.

Complications in the Money-Creation Process. The previously described money-creation process depends on some simplifying assumptions. They include:

1. There is one bank.
2. There are no excess reserves.
3. Individuals hold no cash.

In practice, none of these assumptions holds true, so the money-creation process and the real-world money multiplier are more complicated than we have described.

The One-Bank Assumption. When there are many banks, no individual bank can rely on loans returning to its vaults as deposits. The money returns to the banking system, not to a particular bank. We assume that there is only one bank so we can talk about the banking system as a whole, rather than focusing on the interaction among banks.

The No-Excess-Reserves Assumption. The assumption that the bank can loan out additional funds if it wants to makes it seem that the reserve requirement determines the size of the multiplier. Those reserve requirements merely set a lower limit on what a bank must hold in reserve; banks are free to hold more. Reserves that banks hold above what the Fed requires are called **excess reserves.** Excess reserves reduce the money multiplier. The percentage of deposits that banks hold in excess reserves, *e,* must be added to the reserve requirement, making the money multiplier with excess reserves

$$\frac{1}{(r + e)} \tag{13-3}$$

The Individuals-Hold-No-Cash Assumption. Generally, people keep a fraction of their money as cash, depositing the remainder. The fact that people hold cash decreases the size of the new deposits that are created from any initial inflow of money into the economy. For example, if the reserve requirement is 10 percent and individuals hold some fraction of their deposits as cash, an even greater fraction of new loans will be lost from each round of the money-creation process. Increases in publicly held currency reduce the size of the multiplier.

QUESTION Where does the formula for the complex money multiplier come from?

ANSWER We'll show you here.

First, let's isolate the multiplier by rewriting Equation 13-1 so that the multiplier is on the left-hand side:

$$multiplier = \frac{money\ supply}{monetary\ base}$$

The money supply equals demand deposits plus currency in circulation, and the monetary base is currency in circulation plus total reserves. Thus, let's rewrite the equation for the multiplier as

$$multiplier = \frac{demand\ deposits + currency}{currency + total\ reserves}$$

Further, because total reserves equals required reserves plus excess reserves,

$$multiplier = \frac{demand\ deposits + currency}{currency + required\ reserves + excess\ reserves}$$

Dividing the numerator and denominator by demand deposits,

$$mutiplier = \frac{\left(\dfrac{demand\ deposits}{demand\ deposits} + \dfrac{currency}{demand\ deposits}\right)}{\left(\dfrac{currency}{demand\ deposits} + \dfrac{required\ reserves}{demand\ deposits} + \dfrac{excess\ reserves}{demand\ deposits}\right)}$$

Letting c be the currency–deposit ratio, r be the required reserve ratio, and e be the excess reserve ratio, we can rewrite this equation as

$$multiplier = \frac{1 + c}{r + c + e}$$

The complex money multiplier is $(1 + c)/(r + c + e)$.

The Complex Money Multiplier. The formula for the money multiplier that takes excess reserves and publicly held currency into account, or the **complex money multiplier,** is

$$\frac{(1 + c)}{(r + c + e)} \tag{13-4}$$

where r is the required reserve–deposit ratio, c is the currency–deposit ratio, and e is the excess reserve–deposit ratio. (See the Q&A feature for a derivation of the equation for the complex money multiplier.) To see how this works, suppose that the Fed purchases a $100 bond as before, that the reserve requirement is 10 percent, the currency–deposit ratio is 25 percent, and the excess reserve–deposit ratio is zero. The individual who sold the $100 bond keeps 25 percent of his deposits as currency, so he deposits $80 in the bank and holds $20 as currency. You can confirm that the currency–deposit ratio is 25 percent by dividing currency holdings ($20) by deposits ($80).[5] The monetary base and the initial money supply increase by $100. Banks loan out 90 percent of the $80 (or $72), and of that amount, 80 percent (or $57.60), returns to the bank. At this stage, the money supply has increased by $172 (an increase in bank deposits of $137.60, or $80 + $57.60, and an increase in currency in circulation of $34.40, or $20 + $14.40). Carrying this process through to the end, we arrive at an increase in the money supply of $357 and a money multiplier of 3.57.

---

[5] Because the currency-to-deposit ratio is 25 percent, the ratio of currency to money you receive is 20 percent. The ratio of currency to total money held is $c/(1 + c) = .25/(1 + .25) = .2$, or 20 percent.

Examples of the Money-Creation Process. Now that you have learned about the money multiplier, let's reconsider the tools of monetary policy in relation to Equation 13-1. Open-market operations and changing the discount rate affect the money supply by changing reserves, a component of the monetary base. Open-market operations directly change the amount of reserves in the banking system. Changing the discount rate makes it either more or less costly for banks to borrow from the Fed, thereby indirectly influencing the amount of reserves. Changes in the monetary base are then augmented, through the money multiplier, into larger changes in the money supply. Finally, changing the reserve requirement affects the size of the money multiplier, and thereby, affects the money supply that a given monetary base can support.

Let's consider some examples. We begin with a change in the reserve requirement. Say the currency–deposit ratio is .4 (which is approximately its true value) and the reserve requirement is increased from 10 percent to 20 percent. Using the complex money multiplier $(1 + c)/(r + c + e)$, you can calculate the multiplier before and after the increase in the reserve requirement. With a 10 percent reserve requirement, the money multiplier is 2.8 $[(1 + .4)/(.1 + .4 + 0)]$. With a 20 percent reserve requirement, the money multiplier is 2.33 $[(1 + .4)/(.2 + .4 + 0)]$. The money supply decreases by about 20 percent. Because manipulating the reserve requirement has such a big effect on the money supply, any changes the Fed makes to it are generally very small, and, as mentioned earlier, this tool is seldom used.

Next let's say that the Fed conducts contractionary open-market operations by selling bonds. Suppose the required reserve ratio is 10 percent, the currency–deposit ratio is .4, banks hold no excess reserves, and the Fed sells $1,000 in bonds. In this case, the money supply will decline by the change in the monetary base (−$1,000) times the multiplier, 2.8 $[(1 + .4)/(.1 + .4)] \times$ ($1,000), or $2,800. Because open-market operations are easily executed, they are the Fed's most often used monetary policy tool.

Finally, suppose the Fed decreases the discount rate by .5 percentage points, which increases reserves by $200. Assume also that the reserve requirement is .1, the currency–deposit ratio is .3, and the excess reserve–deposit ratio is .1. To find the increase in the money supply, multiply the increase in the monetary base, $200, by the money multiplier, 2.6 $[(1 + .3)/(.1 + .3 + .1)]$. The money supply increases by $520. Although, at one time, discount lending was the Fed's primary monetary policy tool, today the Fed generally changes the discount rate when it changes the federal funds rate it targets.

Monetary Policy Tools and Interest Rates. Throughout this book we have emphasized the Fed's practice of targeting the interest rate, so why focus so much on how the three tools affect the money supply? We emphasize the money supply because, for a long time, monetary policy focused on the money supply and economists fell into the habit of discussing monetary policy in this regard. Because the money supply and short-term interest rates are closely related, this does not present a problem. Recall from Chapters 8 and 9 that when the Fed increases the money supply, the LM curve shifts to the right, lowering the interest rate; and when the Fed reduces the money supply, the LM curve shifts to the left, raising the interest rate. So, each of the three tools can be translated as affecting the interest rate as well. Actions that reduce the money supply (open-market sales of bonds, increases in the discount rate, and increases in the reserve requirement) will increase the interest rate. Actions that increase the money supply (open-market purchases of bonds,

Monetary policy can be viewed as affecting either the money supply or the interest rate.

decreases in the discount rate, and decreases in the reserve requirement) will decrease the interest rate.

Executive Summary

- The Fed's three tools for influencing the money supply are open-market operations, changing the discount rate, and changing reserve requirements.

- Banks play a role in the money-supply process by creating demand deposits.

- The simple money multiplier is $1/r$. The complex money multiplier, when individuals hold currency and banks hold excess reserves, is $(1 + c)/(r + c + e)$.

- Open-market sales decrease the monetary base and decrease the money supply by the money multiplier times the decrease in the monetary base. Open-market purchases increase the monetary base and increase the money supply by the money multiplier times the increase in the monetary base.

- Reductions in the discount rate encourage borrowing of reserves by banks and also increase the monetary base. Through the money multiplier, the money supply increases by a multiple of the increased discount window borrowing. The opposite occurs when the Fed increases the discount rate.

- Reductions in the reserve requirement increase the money multiplier and increase the money supply. Increases in the reserve requirement decrease the money multiplier and decrease the money supply.

THE OPERATIONAL CONDUCT OF MONETARY POLICY

A good way to learn how monetary policy works in practice is to look at how the Fed conducts its normal operations and see how that relates to our previous discussion. The FOMC is the central decision-making body of the Fed, so let's consider the operation of monetary policy in reference to one of the eight annual meetings at which the FOMC decides the direction of monetary policy.

Three Colored Books

In preparation for this meeting, the staffs of the various regional Feds and of the Board of Governors, whose job it is to follow the economy and the financial sector, prepare briefings for the various members of the FOMC. Much of this information is contained in three books.

The Beige Book—information about regional business conditions.

- *The Beige Book*   This book, prepared by the 12 regional Fed staffs, reports the economic conditions in the various regions based on data collected in each region and conversations that staff members have with local businesses. (Different sources sometimes contradict each other—businesses can think the economy is doing lousy, but the data don't support that conclusion. When that happens, Fed economists analyze the sources even more carefully to discover the source of the discrepancy.)

The Green Book—presents a 2-year economic outlook.

- *The Green Book*   The staff of the Board of Governors prepares a summary of the 2-year economic outlook for the FOMC meeting. Together with the *The Beige Book, The Green Book* provides the general background information for monetary policy decisions.

The Blue Book—presents recent economic developments and the three policy options.

- *The Blue Book*   This book, prepared by the Board of Governors staff, surveys the recent and projected developments related to money, bank reserves, and interest rates and presents three monetary policy options. While the other two books provide general background information, *The Blue Book* provides specific background information.

FOMC members receive these books in advance of their meeting. The FOMC meeting, regularly scheduled eight times a year, is attended by all the regional Fed bank presidents, together with selected staff, but only the governors and five bank presidents vote. At the beginning of the meeting, members discuss past economic events and the effectiveness of monetary policy since the last meeting. They then consider the three monetary policy scenarios presented in *The Blue Book*. Usually, these three options seek to continue the current monetary policy stance, contract monetary policy slightly or expand monetary policy slightly.

FOMC Directives

At the end of the meeting, members of the FOMC vote to execute open-market operations in accordance with a specific directive. This directive becomes the guiding directive of monetary policy until the next FOMC meeting. You can find the directive in FOMC minutes. The following is one from the June 2000 meeting:

> At the conclusion of this discussion, the Committee voted to authorize and direct the Federal Reserve Bank of New York, until it was instructed otherwise, to execute transactions in the System Account in accordance with the following domestic policy directive:
>
> > The Federal Open Market Committee seeks monetary and financial conditions that will foster price stability and promote sustainable growth in output. To further its long-run objectives, the Committee in the immediate future seeks conditions in reserve markets consistent with maintaining the federal funds rate at an average of around 6½ percent.
>
> The vote also encompassed approval of the sentence below for inclusion in the press statement to be released shortly after the meeting:
>
> > Against the background of its long-run goals of price stability and sustainable economic growth and of the information currently available, the Committee believes that the risks are weighted mainly toward conditions that may generate heightened inflation pressures in the foreseeable future.

[FOMC minutes, June 2000, www.federalreserve.gov/FOMC/MINUTES]

Notice four aspects of this directive. First, it begins by stating the Fed's long-term targets—"foster price stability and promote sustainable growth in output." Because the Fed does not directly control either prices or output, the directive must state other variables that the trading desk can affect directly and that impact the Fed's ultimate goals; that is, the directive specifies variables that respond to its policy tools. These variables are the Fed's operating targets. Operating targets include the fed funds rate and reserves. The directive also mentions conditions in the reserve market (the market in which reserves are traded among banks). The fed funds rate and conditions in the reserve market are closely related.

Second, the directive doesn't mention the money multiplier, reserve requirements, discount rate, or open-market operations. All of these variables affect the fed funds rate and the reserve market, and while these variables lie behind changes in operating targets, the Fed focuses on reserves and the fed funds rate. The trading desk is charged with fulfilling the directive, using open-market operations.

Third, the directive says nothing about measures of the money supply (monetary aggregates such as M1, M2, and M3). Before 2000, the Humphrey-Hawkins Act passed by Congress required the Fed to set ranges for growth in the money supply. For a variety of reasons, monetary aggregates have not been reliable measures of monetary policy for the past decade or so. The FOMC agreed in June 2000 to discontinue setting monetary targets but to continue to monitor them for long-term monetary strategies.

Finally, notice that the FOMC also voted to issue an official press release. Economists, bond traders, and others are always waiting to see what the Fed might do in the future. This press release indicated that the directive is negatively asymmetric, which means that, in the future, the Fed will lean toward increasing the fed funds rate. The FOMC believes that the risk of rising inflation is greater than the risk of a recession. This asymmetric directive suggests that the FOMC may meet in a phone conference before its next regularly scheduled meeting to raise the fed funds rate if the threat of inflation becomes significantly higher.

Exhibit 13–3, which shows the operational aspects of monetary policy, is helpful in thinking about the various targets of the Fed and about how the Fed aims at its targets. It divides the targets into operating targets, intermediate targets, and

> Fed policy is specified in terms of operating targets; these affect intermediate targets, which affect ultimate targets.

Exhibit 13–3

Operational Aspects of Monetary Policy

Ultimate Targets

Stable prices
Maximum employment (sustainable growth)
Moderate long-term interest rates

↑

Intermediate Targets

Monetary and Real-Growth Sector Data	*Inflation and Interest Rates*
Monetary and credit aggregates	Employment cost index
Output	Producer and consumer prices
Payroll employment	Interest rates
Purchasing manager's index	Spread between long and short-term interest rates
Inventory/sales ratio	Commodity prices
Resource utilization rates	Exchange rate value of the dollar
Housing starts	Stock prices
Consumer confidence	

↑

Operating Targets

Fed funds rate	Borrowed reserves	Nonborrowed reserves

↑

FOMC

The FOMC's ultimate targets are stable prices, maximum employment, and moderate long-term interest rates. The FOMC uses operating and intermediate targets to assess how well it is achieving its ultimate targets. First, the FOMC aims at an operating target, such as the fed funds rate, which it can affect almost immediately. It then looks at intermediate targets, such as output, employment, various prices, and longer-term interest rates, to see how well it is achieving its ultimate targets of stable prices, maximum employment, and moderate long-term interest rates.

ultimate targets. We've already introduced operating targets and ultimate targets. The Fed's operating targets directly affect intermediate targets such as interest rates. These intermediate targets directly influence the Fed's ultimate targets. Intermediate targets include the money supply, interest rates, and a variety of other variables that indicate the strength of the economy. Intermediate targets give the Fed an early indication of whether the economy is moving toward its ultimate goals, and the time to adjust its actions if the economy is not moving toward those goals. This three-step diagram from the Fed's tools to operating targets, intermediate targets, and ultimate targets is what the video game at the San Francisco Fed is trying to mimic. The Fed's tools are the trigger that releases the dart toward the first moving target (operational targets), which then releases a dart toward the next moving target (intermediate targets), and so on. Let's now look more specifically at each of these targets.

Operating Targets

The FOMC specified its directive in terms of the fed funds rate. However, past directives have targeted the level of reserves based on intermediate targets for M1. Exhibit 13–3 lists the three operating targets the Fed has used: the fed funds rate, borrowed reserves, and nonborrowed reserves.

The Federal Funds Rate. Recall that the fed funds rate is the rate at which banks loan reserves to other banks. Let's see how such a loan might come about. Suppose, at the end of the day, a bank does its books and finds that it has excess reserves. Because reserves earn no interest, it would like to loan any excess reserves. Another bank may find that it has a shortage of reserves. To meet required reserves, it can either borrow at the Fed's discount window, sell some assets, or borrow reserves from other banks. If it can borrow reserves from another bank instead of from other sources, it makes sense to do so.

Assuming that the fed funds rate is competitive, banks will enter the fed funds market—one as a seller, one as a buyer—and one bank will "loan" the reserves to the other overnight. Actually, no paper flows—everything is done as a computer entry. Then, the next day, the process is reversed and the loan is repaid.

The Fed uses the fed funds rate as an operating target for three reasons: This rate is measurable, is controllable, and has a reasonably predictable effect on the intermediate targets. First, the fed funds rate can be measured accurately and quickly. Various news agencies report the fed funds rate throughout each day, and it is never revised. Second, the Fed can control the fed funds rate directly through open-market operations. By adding reserves to the banking system through open-market sales, the Fed increases the supply of reserves. With more reserves in the market, the fed funds rate declines. The Fed sells bonds to increase the fed funds rate. Third, the fed funds rate directly impacts the Fed's intermediate targets—mainly short- and long-term interest rates. Through its effect on intermediate targets, the fed funds rate helps the Fed direct the economy toward its ultimate goals. The Fed raises the fed funds rate when it wants to reduce aggregate spending and slow the economy, and the Fed lowers the fed funds rate when it wants to increase aggregate spending and increase output.

Two points to note about the fed funds market: First, the flow of fed funds is usually from small banks to larger banks, because small banks have smaller reserve requirements and because large banks are usually more aggressive in making loans,

Currently, the fed funds rate—the rate at which banks loan reserves to other banks—is the key operating target.

even when they are close to their legal reserve limits. Second, banks currently have a 2-week period, which expires on alternate Wednesdays, to meet their reserve requirement. This means that on some days, banks can be above their required reserves, and some days, below their required reserves. However, banks often scramble more at the end of each 2-week period as alternate Wednesdays approach. At those times, you can sometimes see the fed funds rate rise significantly as banks borrow to meet their reserve requirements. The New York open market desk (a group of people that buys and sells government securities for the Fed), therefore, targets an average for the fed funds rate.

Reserve Aggregates. Operating targets other than the fed funds rate are reserve aggregates (borrowed reserves and nonborrowed reserves). The Fed reports reserve aggregates daily, and data on these aggregates, like the fed funds rate, are never revised. The Fed can control reserves directly, either through open-market operations or discount window lending. Lastly, reserve aggregates are directly related to monetary aggregates (an intermediate target), which have, at times, been related in a predictable way to output and the price level. As we've stated, although the federal funds rate is the primary target, the Fed watches all operating targets. Let's briefly consider these other targets.

When the Fed is looking at reserve markets, it is gauging reserve pressure. Reserve pressure reflects the market conditions for reserves. When reserve pressure rises (quantity demanded exceeds quantity supplied), the fed funds rate rises. Borrowed reserves are reserves that banks borrow from the Fed at the discount window. When banks borrow more from the discount window (borrowed reserves rise), reserve pressure is rising. Nonborrowed reserves are the reserves in the system, excluding borrowed reserves. When nonborrowed reserves rise, reserve pressure is declining. Excess reserves is another reserve concept the Fed targets.

Generally, the fed funds rate and reserve aggregates provide consistent signals about the direction of monetary policy. A rising fed funds rate and falling reserve aggregates, for the most part, both mean that monetary policy is contractionary. Expansionary monetary policy, similarly, is signaled by a falling fed funds rate and rising reserve aggregates. Although these relationships usually hold, sometimes they do not. When that happens, one must be chosen as the *guiding* operational target.

Intermediate Targets

If you consider Exhibit 13–3 again, you will see a large number of intermediate targets. These could be further divided, but because most policy discussions have concentrated on two of these intermediate targets—the money supply (monetary and credit aggregates) and interest rates—we will concentrate our discussion on those.

The Money Supply. How good the money supply is as an intermediate target depends on how closely it affects its longer-term targets—maximum employment and stable prices. Until the early 1980s, a reasonable connection between the money supply and the price level was predictable, although with a long and variable lag. This is one of the reasons why the Fed concentrated on the relationship between the money supply and stable prices. (In the long-run, the money supply did not appear to affect real output or real interest rates.)

In the 1980s and early 1990s, policy makers relied less on money-supply figures as intermediate targets because institutional changes led people to make significant

Generally, a rising fed funds rate implies falling reserve aggregates.

THE BRIEFING ROOM   Accommodation: The Interface Between Monetary and Fiscal Policy

Governments finance deficit spending by selling bonds. That's why when the IS curve shifts out, the interest rate rises. The Fed can stop that rise by running accommodative monetary policy (shifting the LM curve out), buying bonds the government (in the United States, the Treasury) sells. The Fed holds government securities in its portfolio, and it can influence the interest rate the government pays to borrow funds by buying and selling these securities—that is, by conducting open-market operations.

In times of war, the Fed is able to accommodate the Treasury by buying all of its bonds. For example, in World War II, the Fed and the Treasury reached an accord by which the Fed agreed to buy all of the bonds necessary to keep interest rates fixed. If the Fed had let the interest rate rise, the cost of the war to the government would have risen. In addition, the price of bonds would have fallen and people who had bought war bonds would have felt cheated. The Fed eventually stopped this practice because inflationary pressures grew, and when the government lifted the price controls, the real interest rate was negative.

The degree of accommodation plays an important role in determining the short-run interest rate. When the deficit was rising in the late 1980s and early 1990s, the Fed did not increase the amount of debt being monetized (the purchase of government debt by the Fed), reducing the percentage of deficit monetized. This meant that the interest rate rose more than it otherwise would have.

In the United States, monetary accommodation by the Fed is not the rule. The Treasury generally has no problem selling its bonds. In developing countries, however, that is not often the case. In some developing countries, no market for government securities exists, and the central bank can either accommodate the government deficit by buying the debt or let the government default.

In recent years, the Fed has downplayed monetary aggregates as intermediate targets.

changes in their holdings of financial assets. As discussed in Chapter 7, beginning in the early 1980s, the velocity of money became quite unstable. This caused large fluctuations in M1, M2, and M3, and often these measures of money went in divergent directions, with their definitions subject to so many caveats that the simple measure they once provided disappeared. In 1993, the Fed officially abandoned its targeting of M2. Although in the late 1990s the relationship between M2 growth and the economy appeared to have stabilized, the Fed continues to downplay monetary aggregates. As we saw, the FOMC stopped setting monetary targets as part of its official directive. It remains to be seen whether the money supply returns as a key intermediate target.

The Interest Rate. Some economists have suggested targeting short-term interest rates, such as the interest rate on 1-year or 5-year bonds. In the IS/LM model, the Fed can set interest rates easily. The IS/LM model tells us that to increase interest rates, the Fed should contract the money supply (shifting the LM curve to the left), and to lower interest rates, the Fed should increase the money supply (shifting the LM curve to the right). Interest rates affect expenditure decisions and are a good candidate for influencing output. The interest rate, however, also has its problems as an intermediate target. (For a discussion of a time when the Fed targeted only the interest rate, see The Briefing Room, "Accommodation: The Interface Between Monetary and Fiscal Policy.")

The interest rate can be an ambiguous intermediate target because it has so many dimensions.

First, it is unclear what interest rate the Fed should target. Financial markets are extremely fluid, and interest rates on various bonds fluctuate in response to conditions such as changing fiscal policy, international considerations, and the productivity of capital. The Fed does not know for certain what interest rate in the economy correlates to its ultimate goal, so it could well be targeting the wrong interest rate. The connection between interest rates and the Fed's ultimate goals is loose at best.

Second, real interest rates are what affect expenditure decisions. Although the Fed can set nominal interest rates, it cannot set real interest rates. (Recall that the real interest rate equals the nominal interest rate less inflation.) Even if the Fed targets the right real interest rate, it has no proof that the change in the interest rate it observes means there's a change in the real interest rate, rather than in inflationary expectations. Let's consider an example. A rise in the nominal interest rate could mean either that the real interest rate has risen or that expected inflation has risen. Increases in real interest rates are what will reduce expenditures.

We could discuss these intermediate targets further, but this brief discussion should give you a good idea of the problems, which are substantial. (Appendix A recounts the Fed's use of various targets.)

Dynamic Monetary Policy and Defensive Actions

Open-market operations can be either dynamic or defensive.

Fed actions that are designed to change an operational target, such as the fed funds rate, are called **dynamic open-market operations.** Most open-market operations are not dynamic; they are defensive. **Defensive open-market operations** are Fed actions that are designed to offset temporary deviations of operation targets. For example, say the Fed has chosen the fed funds rate as its operational target, and say that the directive is a symmetrical one, to keep the fed funds rate roughly constant. Does this mean that the trading desk can go fishing? Hardly. Although the Fed has control over some components of the monetary base, it does not have control over other components, such as the amount of currency in circulation. Specifically, how much of the monetary base is in the banking system, and hence is serving as reserves, changes from day to day due to factors beyond the Fed's control. To keep the fed funds rate (and monetary policy) consistent with the FOMC directive, the Fed must offset these factors.

Some of these factors are predictable. One example is the amount of currency in circulation. Because people tend to hold more currency during the December holiday season, reserves decline in December. This decline in reserves tends to increase the fed funds rate. Another fairly predictable factor affecting the monetary base is U.S. Treasury account operations. Deposits of the U.S. Treasury at Federal Reserve banks tend to rise close to tax dates, increasing reserves, and to fall near social security payment dates, reducing reserves. A third factor, float (reserves appearing at two depository institutions simultaneously and, therefore, counted twice for a brief time), is much more random. During severe storms that delay the delivery of checks from one bank to another, float will increase substantially because the Fed will delay debiting the bank on which the check was drawn until after it has already credited the bank to which it was deposited.

To offset increases in float (a defensive open-market operation), the Fed will decrease reserves significantly by selling government bonds with an agreement to repurchase them the next day to offset the float. These are called repurchase agreements, or repos. The next day, when the repos come due, they reverse the process. So, even without taking any dynamic policy action to change the fed funds rate, holding the fed funds rate constant takes active trading by the Federal Reserve trading desk.

To distinguish between defensive and dynamic open-market operations, the Fed trades government securities at different times for different purposes. Trading between 11:30 A.M. and noon is to execute dynamic open-market operations, and buying securities in the afternoon is for defensive purposes. As mentioned, the Fed also announces changes in monetary policy after its FOMC meetings.

Ultimate Targets

Some economists argue that because the relationships among operational, intermediate, and ultimate targets are so elusive, the Fed should simply select an ultimate target. The one that is most often proposed is a *zero inflation rate target*. With this as its target, the Fed's policy would be clear: If there is inflation, the Fed needs to raise the fed funds rate or contract the money supply. One problem with using a zero inflation target is that it could mean giving up using monetary policy to stimulate the economy at all. Say, for example, that this target had been used in the first half of the 1990s. Because inflation had been present throughout that time period, albeit low, this rule would have meant that the Fed should have implemented contractionary monetary policy. The Fed didn't. Instead, it ran expansionary policy for much of the time, and the result was continued economic growth with almost no rise in inflation, at least up to 2001. Another problem is that there are various measures of inflation, and it is unclear what measure the Fed should target.

Supporters of the zero inflation target argue that had the Fed used it, people's expectations about inflation would have changed, and the United States would have had the same economic growth without even the tiny inflation.

Some have proposed that the Fed target zero inflation; recent Fed policy takes a "kitchen-sink" approach—it looks at everything.

Recently, the Fed's position has been to use what some call the kitchen-sink approach—it looks at everything. Of course, in many ways, looking at everything is close to looking at nothing; it is to let judgment, or discretion, guide policy. It is this judgment that concerns many laissez-faire economists, who believe that judgment itself will be guided by short-term political needs and not by the need for long-term price stability.

Several countries and the new European Central Bank have adopted inflation as their primary target. Canada, for example, targets the growth rate of the consumer price index (less food and energy) at 1 percent to 3 percent a year. The true test of these inflation targeting countries will come when their economies enter a large recession (or worse yet, a stagflation) and political pressures are applied to stimulate real output using monetary policy. Many observers believe that when this happens, the inflation target will give way. (In 2001, the ECB cut its lending rate, even as inflation was above target.)

Rules Versus Discretion

To eliminate the discretion policy makers have when targeting more than one variable, a number of economists have proposed rules to guide the choice of policy. The most famous of these rules is Milton Friedman's 3 percent monetary growth rule, which maintains that the Fed should increase the money supply by 3 percent per year. Friedman chose 3 percent to allow for trend growth of real output due to productivity growth. This fixed monetary rule seeks to counter political pressures put on the Fed to expand the economy during election years, leaving the inflationary effects of expansionary monetary policy to arrive much after the election. With monetary growth so unpredictable in the 1990s, however, rules based on a set range for growth of the money supply have lost much of their appeal. The Fed does not follow a rule based on a predetermined money supply growth.

Rules add predictability to policy; when followed, the rule becomes a policy regime.

Feedback Rules. Lately, economists have been proposing what are called *feedback rules*. **Feedback rules** are rules in which the Fed adjusts its operational and intermediate targets on the basis of movements in measures of economic activity that are

Feedback rules involve adjustments to targets based on measures of economic activity.

close to its ultimate goals. Some of the recently proposed rules have made nominal income growth, the unemployment rate, or the actual inflation rate the indicators of economic activity by which the Fed adjusts its operational and intermediate targets. For example, if inflation is higher than targeted, the rule would automatically specify that the fed funds rate target should be raised.

Advocates argue that such rules help reduce the uncertainty associated with monetary policy by making policy more predictable. Opponents of rules argue that the measures the rules specify are highly imperfect. What a rule was meant to achieve in one time period may not be what it is meant to achieve in another. The specification of a particular rule can change the effect of the rule. Ultimately, because of their inherent imperfections, rules will keep the Fed from undertaking beneficial actions.

Time-Inconsistency Problem. Supporters of rules respond that discretionary monetary policy would not be able to achieve its targets as easily as would a rule, because people will build expected changes in the money supply into their actions. Knowing that, ultimately, the increase in the money supply will lead to a higher price level, people will raise their prices whenever the Fed increases the money supply faster than economic growth. Eventually, the economy ends up with a higher price level but no increase in real output. Economists call this the **time inconsistency problem**—the proposition that people will change their behavior in response to expected policy. As they do so, the effect of the policy will be changed.

Let's consider an example that those who support rules rather than discretion have given of this time-inconsistency problem.

> [S]uppose the socially desirable outcome is not to have houses built in a particular flood plain but, given that they are there, to take certain costly flood control measures. If the government's policy were not to build the dams and levees needed for flood protection and people knew this was the case, even if houses were built there, rational people would not live in the flood plains. But the rational person knows that, if he and others build houses there, the government will take the necessary flood control measures. Consequently, in the absence of a law prohibiting the construction of houses in the flood plain, houses are built there, and the army corps of engineers subsequently builds the dams and levees. (Kydland, Finn and Edward Prescott. 1977. Rules rather than discretion: The inconsistency of optimal plans. *Journal of Political Economy* June:473–91.)

When Kydland and Prescott first suggested this argument, they argued that Friedman's fixed monetary rule is similar to the rule against building a dam and is preferable for similar reasons.

However, this suggestion that the time-inconsistency problem can be used to support any specific rule—such as the fixed monetary rule—is incorrect. Time inconsistency only states that some rule is preferable to discretion. It does not state that any specific rule is preferable.

Time inconsistency states that some rule is preferable to discretion; it does not state that any specific rule is preferable to discretion.

Determining what rule is better than discretion is subject to debate. It might be a highly complicated contingency rule that has a different monetary growth rate for every possible event. California's falling into the ocean would be one event that would require a decrease in the money supply in any optimal money-supply rule. So, too, would the changing institutions that led to the Fed's abandoning the monetary aggregates as intermediate targets. Therefore, the rule that is preferable to discretion is likely a highly complicated contingency rule, specifying thousands of exceptions. In fact, the only rule that is always preferable to discretion is a rule that specifies all possible contingencies that might make the rule inappropriate (if *X*, then Z1; if *Y*, then Z2; if *W*, then Z3; etc.). In the preceding example, if a dam were built above the flood plain, and flooding were no longer a problem, then the rule would no longer make sense, so that contingency would have to be built into the rule.

Because an infinite number of contingencies is possible, the optimal contingency rule is inevitably too complicated to institute in practice. Any practical rule has costs, and instead of attempting to define all contingencies, it might be better to follow a discretionary policy that allows the Fed to react to what happens in the economy. Such a discretionary policy does not necessarily imply total discretion. Rules can guide discretionary policies, leaving policy makers to deal with contingencies as they arise.

Law of Diminishing Marginal Control. Regardless of how good a rule seems to be initially, as soon as it is implemented, it is often no longer as good. This is an application of the **law of diminishing marginal control**, which states that whenever an economic variable is singled out for control, individuals will figure out ways to thwart that control. Financial institutions have responded to rules based on the money supply by working out new technological developments, such as the credit card or automatic funds transfer, that avoid the consequences of the rules. (This is one explanation for why money is no longer a good measure of monetary policy.)

The usefulness of a rule tends to erode over time, as individuals figure out ways to exploit the rule.

Who Is Right in the Rules Versus Discretion Debate. The outcome of the rules versus discretion debate is a normal outcome of most economic debates. Both sides are partially right: Rules have advantages as well as costs. We must judge every rule on its merits, and no one answer exists to the rules versus discretion debate. The history of monetary policy in the United States has been one of searching for a workable combination of discretion and rules.

There is no one answer to the rules versus discretion debate.

Measuring the Direction of Monetary Policy

The Federal Reserve has never operated by a strict rule. Instead, it has used discretion, lowering or raising the fed funds rate target based on several indicators. If you read the minutes of the FOMC meetings, you'll see that the decision about what monetary policy stance to take (contractionary, expansionary, or neutral) is based on a complex and careful weighing of many different factors.

Despite this complexity, the Fed aims to achieve two simple objectives with its monetary policy: Keep inflation as low as possible (generally less than 2 percent to 3 percent) and keep output near its potential, as long as doing so doesn't hurt its inflation goal. If the Fed is consistent in its attempt to achieve these goals, we should be able to discern the implicit rule that it uses. The rule that fits recent Fed policy is called the *Taylor rule* (named for Stanford University economist John Taylor). The **Taylor rule** relates the deviation of inflation from its target and the deviation of output from potential to the Fed's fed funds rate target. It states that the Fed tries to keep the fed funds rate at about 2 percent plus current inflation when it wants to have a neutral policy—neither expansionary nor contractionary. If aggregate output rises above potential output, or if inflation rises above the Fed's desired level, the Fed will raise the target for the fed funds rate above 2 percent plus inflation. This will slow the economy down, bringing inflation back to the target and output back to potential. If inflation is below the target or output is below potential, then the Fed will set the fed funds rate target below 2 percent plus the current rate of inflation. This will cause the economy to expand, output will grow to meet potential, and inflation will rise back to its target. The equation for the Taylor rule looks like this:

> **Taylor rule: fed funds rate = 2 + current inflation + one-half the deviation of inflation from desired + one-half the percent deviation of output from potential.**

$$fed\ funds\ rate = 2 + current\ inflation$$
$$+ .5 \times (actual\ inflation\ less\ desired\ inflation)$$
$$+ .5 \times (percent\ deviation\ of\ aggregate\ output\ from\ potential)$$

Percent deviation from potential is positive when actual output is above potential and negative when it is below potential. To see how this equation works, suppose that inflation is 4 percent, the desired inflation rate is 3 percent, and output is 2 percent above potential. The Fed would set the fed funds rate target at 7.5 percent [2 + 4 + .5(1) + .5(2)].

By setting the fed funds rate target at 7.5 percent, assuming short-term interest rates move in tandem, the Fed is targeting the real interest rate at 3.5 percent (7.5 percent fed funds rate minus the inflation rate of 4 percent). The fed funds rate target is more than 2 percentage points above inflation because the Fed wishes to slow the economy and reduce inflation. If the Fed didn't want to change inflation or output, it would set the fed funds rate at 2 percent plus the current rate of inflation. Add .5 percent onto that because inflation is above its target (.5 × 1) and add 1 percent because output is above potential (.5 × 2).

Exhibit 13–4 shows what this equation predicts for the fed funds rate target to keep the inflation rate at 3 percent and output close to potential. Notice that fed funds rate described by the Taylor rule follows the actual fed funds rate.

Exhibit 13-4

Monetary Policy Targets

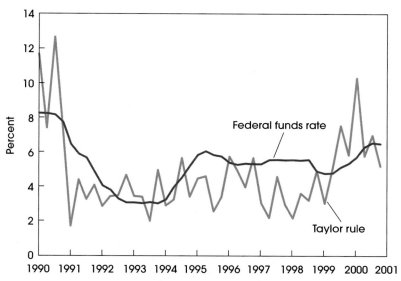

This exhibit shows the fed funds rate and the targeted fed funds rate, as determined by the Taylor rule. If the fed funds rate is above what the Taylor rule suggests, the Fed is expected to ease monetary policy, as was the case in 1998. If the fed funds rate is below what the Taylor rule suggests, the Fed is expected to follow contractionary monetary policy, as was the case in late 1999 and early 2000. Source: The Federal Reserve Bank (www.federalreserve.gov) and author estimates.

In 1997 and 1998, the actual fed funds rate was above the prediction of the Taylor rule. This meant that monetary policy was more contractionary than it had to be to achieve a 3 percent inflation rate, which suggested that the Fed should reduce the fed funds rate target (again, assuming it wants a 3 percent inflation rate), which it did in late 1998. So, we can use the Taylor rule to judge whether monetary policy is currently contractionary or expansionary and whether the Fed is likely to raise the fed funds rate target or lower it, given a particular inflation target.

POLICY PERSPECTIVE: FED POLICY IN THE EARLY 2000s

Throughout the end of the 1990s and into early 2000, the Fed kept a close watch on the inflation rate. The general belief then was that the U.S. economy was operating above potential and the unemployment rate was below the natural rate of unemployment. Both conditions signaled that inflation would soon rise, but it did not. Through 1999, inflation remained below 2.5 percent—low by historical standards. Despite this low inflation, the Fed raised its fed funds interest rate target six times from mid-1999 to mid-2000.

The Fed justified raising the fed funds rate target by pointing to the possibility that inflationary pressures were coming from a new source—the stock market. Gains in the stock market over the past decade had increased consumers' wealth tremendously. Consumers were spending a portion of their increased wealth, which increased the demand for goods and services. If the rise in consumer spending went unchecked, inflation would rise, so the Fed raised interest rates, the economy cooled, and the stock market boom slowed considerably. In late 2000, economic growth slowed, and the Fed feared the economy would go into a recession. It reversed course and reduced interest rates.

Two points in this story relate to this chapter. First, even though stock prices are not an official Fed target, they play a role in policymaking because they affect aggregate spending. They are part of the "kitchen-sink" approach to policymaking. Second, the Fed's concern with stock prices illustrates the flexibility of discretionary monetary policy. It is unlikely that a monetary policy rule would have included stock prices. In this case, however, the Fed used rising stock prices to guide monetary policy.

Executive Summary

- The Fed most directly influences the fed funds rate by varying the amount of reserve pressure in the banking system.

- The Fed's current operating target is the fed funds rate.

- The Fed's ultimate targets are maximum employment, stable price levels, and moderate long-term interest rates. Other countries have recently experimented with having low inflation as their sole ultimate target.

- Some economists advocate conducting monetary policy, using a rule that would specify how the central bank would react to various economic conditions. Proponents suggest that this rule would reduce uncertainty and avoid the time-inconsistency problem. Opponents suggest that the rule would reduce flexibility.

- The Taylor rule is a tool that gauges the stance of monetary policy for a given inflation target.

CONCLUSION

We began this chapter by describing the San Francisco Fed's video game. Now that you have seen the operational context of monetary policy, we hope you can see why the video game is an apt analogy for the Fed's conduct of monetary policy. The FOMC has enormous resources at its disposal, and the fact that it has not yet determined the optimal operating procedure may well suggest that there is no optimal operating procedure.

So, where do economists stand with respect to monetary policy? All economists agree that monetary policy must play a role in stabilizing the economy. They still debate whether that role should be active or passive, and it is doubtful whether any clear answer will be forthcoming. It is unlikely that the Fed will allow a depression like the 1930's Great Depression to occur again from the same causes. But the really difficult issues in monetary policy are new problems that haven't been seen before.

KEY POINTS

- The Federal Reserve Bank is the U.S. central bank. It is a semi-autonomous agency of the federal government, and its IOUs serve as money in the United States.

- The Fed's ultimate targets are stable prices, maximum employment, and moderate long-term interest rates.

- *Fractional reserve banking* means that a small monetary base will create a much larger supply of money through the money multiplier.

- Whenever banks make loans, they create money.

- The simple money multiplier is $1/r$ where r is the reserve requirement.

- The complex money multiplier equals $[(1 + c)/(r + c + e)]$ where c is the currency–deposit ratio, r is the reserve requirement facing banks, and e is the fraction of deposits banks hold as excess reserve.

- The primary tool the Fed uses to control the money supply is open-market operations. The Fed also affects the money supply by changing the reserve requirement and changing the discount rate.

- When pursuing ultimate targets, the Fed watches operating targets and intermediate targets. Operating

targets include the fed funds rate, borrowed reserves, and nonborrowed reserves. Intermediate targets include the money supply and interest rates.

- As intermediate targets, interest rates and the money supply both have their problems. The money supply hasn't affected output predictably for the past decade. Interest rates are affected by other forces in the economy, and the real interest rate is not directly observable.

- The history of monetary policy in the United States has been one of searching for a workable combination of discretion and rules.

- How much discretion should be built into rules is subject to debate.

- The time-inconsistency problem suggests people will change their behavior in response to expected policy, changing the effect of the policy itself.

- The Taylor rule is an equation that relates deviations of inflation from its desired rate and deviations of output from potential to the Fed's fed funds rate target: fed funds rate = 2 + current inflation + .5 × (actual inflation less desired inflation) + .5 × (percent deviation of aggregate output from potential).

KEY TERMS

QUESTIONS FOR THOUGHT AND REVIEW

1. What is the relevance of the quotation that begins this chapter to monetary policy?
2. Why is monetary policy like shooting with a moving weapon at a moving target?
3. Describe the institutional structure of the Federal Reserve. What role does the Federal Open Market Committee play in monetary policy?
4. What are the Fed's three tools for controlling the money supply? Which tool does it use most often? Why?
5. What is the monetary base and how is it related to the money supply?
6. How do banks create money?
7. What are the differences between the simple money multiplier and the complex money multiplier?
8. What are the key differences between *The Beige Book*, *The Green Book*, and *The Blue Book*? What roles do these books play in the conduct of monetary policy?
9. What three operating targets has the Fed used? Which operating target does the Fed currently use?

10. What is the difference between an operational target and an intermediate target?
11. What is the relationship between the fed funds rate and aggregate reserves?
12. Why did the Fed start to place less emphasis on the money supply as an intermediate goal during the 1980s?
13. What is the difference between dynamic and defensive open-market operations?
14. What are the advantages and disadvantages of inflation targeting?
15. What is the time-inconsistency problem associated with discretionary monetary policy and how would a rule overcome that problem?
16. What is the law of diminishing marginal control? What are the implications of this law for monetary policy?
17. State Taylor's rule. For what is it used?
18. What role did the stock market play in the Fed's conduct of monetary policy in the late 1990s and early 2000s?

PROBLEMS AND EXERCISES

1. Suppose people hold no currency, banks hold no excess reserves, and the reserve requirement is 33.33 percent.
   a. What is the money multiplier?
   b. By how much will the money supply increase if the Fed buys $1 billion worth of government bonds?
   c. Redo your answers to items (a) and (b), assuming that the ratio of currency to deposits is 10 percent.
2. Suppose the currency-to-deposit ratio is .3, the reserve requirement is .4 and, excess reserves are initially zero. The total of currency in the economy plus reserves in the banking sector is $200 million.
   a. What is the money multiplier?
   b. What is the money multiplier if the excess reserve ratio is .10?
   c. What is the money supply in items (a) and (b)?
   d. Using an open-market operation, how would the Fed increase the money supply by $93 million in cases (a) and (b)?

   e. By changing the reserve requirement, how would the Fed increase the money supply by $20 million in cases (a) and (b)?
3. Demonstrate the effect on output of a rising currency-to-deposit ratio, using the IS/LM model.
4. Suppose the Fed's current inflation target is estimated to be 3 percent. Current inflation is 8 percent, and the economy is 2 percent above potential.
   a. What is the fed funds rate target implied by the Taylor rule, using the information given?
   b. Suppose the actual fed funds rate is 12 percent. Do you expect the Fed to follow more contractionary or expansionary monetary policy in the near future?
   c. Suppose the actual fed funds rate is 12 percent, but the Fed has announced it is not planning to change its stance on monetary policy, given that inflation is 8 percent and the economy is 2 percent above potential. What is the Fed's implicit inflation rate target?

A Brief History of Monetary Policy

The United States created its Federal Reserve System (the Fed) in 1913 in response to the banking panic in 1907. The creation of the Fed actually marked the third attempt to establish a central bank in the United States. The First Bank of the United States was created in 1791, but its charter was not renewed and it closed in 1811, leaving the government without an adequate means of marketing its securities and storing and transferring its funds. For the next 5 years, a variety of state banks with their own notes emerged, but many of these banks failed. These problems led to the creation of the Second Bank of the United States in 1816, but due to a political fight between rural and urban areas, Congress did not renew this bank's charter, and in 1836, it also died. Between then and 1913, no central bank existed.

The National Banking Act of 1863 authorized the national chartering of private banks, which were the only ones that could issue bank notes. These bank notes served as the currency of the United States, just as Federal Reserve Notes do today. Between 1863 and 1913 three major financial panics—1873, 1884, and 1907—disrupted the system. The creation of the Fed resulted from a compromise effort and reflected the political and economic forces of the early 1900s. The Fed began as a decentralized system of 12 separate districts and regional banks to ensure regional autonomy. That regional autonomy, however, ended with the Federal Reserve Acts of 1933 and 1935, when the Board of Governors was given more power and the system became the centralized system it is today.

THE 1910S AND 1920S: DEVELOPING MONETARY POLICY

Ever since it was established in 1913, the Fed has determined monetary policy. Very early in its development, its primary concern was to "help" the Treasury finance World War I. The Fed did so by supplying funds to private banks so they could buy Treasury bills. So, the Fed, which was a part of the government, loaned money to private banks, which, in turn, loaned money to the government. (If you think this process is a bit like the government making loans to itself through a semi-autonomous intermediary, you're right. Such is the way that the financial system works.)

In January 1920, after the end of World War I, the U.S. economy entered a sharp recession. Wartime inflation ended and wholesale prices fell 45 percent. Despite the fact that commercial banks had emerged from the war owing the Federal Reserve about $2.5 billion and were in no position to extend new loans to consumers and businesses, the Fed did not take any action to help or encourage banks to make new loans or stimulate the economy.

Although a policy of not easing credit conditions during a sharp recession seems almost incomprehensible now, at the time, the duties of the Fed did not include using its powers to promote economic stability. (A good question to ask yourself is, "How might the Fed have avoided a depression?") In response to the recession of 1920–1921, the Fed developed an active monetary policy that focused on three points:

1. Promote price-level stability and high and stable levels of business activities.
2. Prevent excess use of credit for speculative purposes.
3. Promote international monetary stability.

THE 1930S: THE GREAT DEPRESSION

The U.S. economy experienced two mild recessions in the 1920s but recovered quickly. Then, in 1929, the U.S.

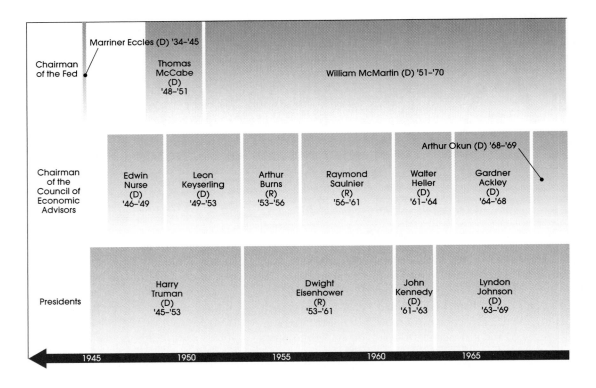

economy went into a depression. Output declined by more than 30 percent from 1929 to 1932, while unemployment rose from 3.2 percent to 23.6 percent. The stock market crash of 1929 and the subsequent severe and persistent decline in output left more and more people unable to repay their bank loans. Increasing loan defaults caused banks to fail. Initial bank failures turned into panic, and depositors began to withdraw more and more of their money from banks, leading to more bank failures. By the spring of 1933, more than one-third of banks had closed their doors.

For the first 3 years of the Depression, the Fed did nothing to stop the bank failures or to offset declining output. One reason the Fed did not act is that, at the time, many policy makers believed that bank failures were, in large part, the result of poor banking practices. (For example, banks had made loans, using stock as collateral.) Another reason involved the gold that the United States required to maintain its commitment to the gold standard, which, in some policy maker's minds, placed a limit on how much currency the Fed could issue. A third reason is that the Fed believed that the economy would recover on its own in the long run, and that the Depression was just another short-run temporary adjustment.

As the Depression continued for years, most policy makers changed their view and began to believe that something had to be done. Beginning in 1932, Congress adopted a number of measures to put people back to work and established the Federal Deposit Insurance Corporation (FDIC) to insure demand deposits and limit bank runs. In 1933, the Fed switched its policy and implemented expansionary monetary policy. In 1935, it changed the controlled price of gold and made it illegal for U.S. citizens to hold gold, eliminating gold reserves as a limit on how much money the Fed could issue.

The Depression officially ended in March 1933, although it took another 9 years for the unemployment rate to fall to a more "normal" rate. From 1933 to 1937, the economy expanded, and many people believed that monetary policy was doing its job. Then, in 1937, the U.S. economy fell into another recession, causing many economists to question the ability of monetary policy to pull an economy out of a recession. This switched the focus of theoretical discussions of policy to fiscal policy and Keynesian economics. After the 1937 recession, output started to grow quickly as the government increased military spending to prepare to enter World War II. This caused many economists

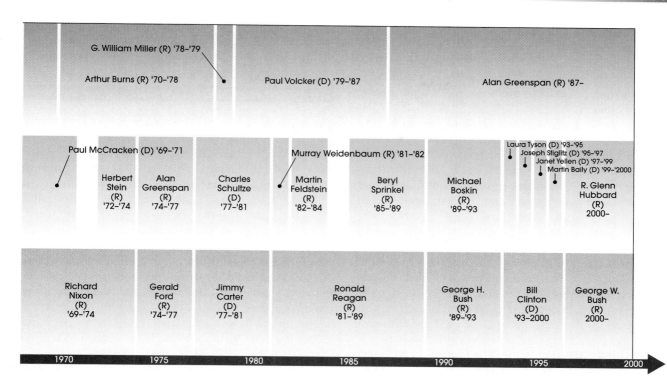

to attribute the end of the recession to government spending.

THE 1940S: ACCOMMODATING WARTIME SPENDING

To keep the cost of government borrowing low during World War II, the Fed and the Treasury agreed to prevent interest rates from rising during the war, which limited any independent monetary policy. To maintain interest rates at a fixed level, the Fed had to buy and sell as many government securities as all other buyers or sellers desired at the predetermined interest rate; as a result, the Fed lost control of the money supply. During this period, prices were held down by direct price controls and selective controls on credit.

At the end of the war, unemployment was at 1 percent, prices had risen about 35 percent above prewar periods, and inflationary pressures, which had been repressed by the controls on prices and savings during the war, were strong. However, the future was unclear. While some policy makers feared inflation and wanted a contractionary monetary policy, other policy makers wanted an expansionary monetary policy, fearing a

return to a depression as government spending levels fell from their wartime highs.

Initially, as Congress dismantled the direct controls, inflation seemed to be winning out, but those predicting a depression kept insisting that one would arrive soon. Monetary policy during this postwar period was like the accommodation policy of the war years—the Fed pegged the interest rates on government bonds, giving up any direct control over the money supply.

The reasons for this policy are many and complicated. One reason is theoretical. Many economists had lost faith in monetary policy after its failure to cure the Great Depression, and the then-in-vogue interpretation of Keynesian economic theory assigned almost no role to monetary policy. (It was against this background that Milton Friedman argued strongly, and, all would now agree, correctly, that money did affect output in the short run.) The theoretical argument was not the deciding factor, however. The Secretary of the Treasury was concerned that increased interest rates would add to the interest the government would have to pay on its debt and that fluctuating yields of government securities would seriously complicate the Treasury's refunding operations. The Treasury stuck fast to the wartime accord. Concern was also expressed for those patriotic citizens and institutions that would suffer a capital loss on their bonds if interest rates were to rise, which would be unfair and could lead to a loss in confidence in financial institutions. In July 1947, the Fed broke the accord on short-term bills, and in 1951, broke the accord on long-term bonds, once again freeing monetary policy.

Often what gets reported in textbooks as a rather dry piece of history was actually marked in real life by bluffs, counter bluffs, and drama. For instance, the Fed had wanted for a long time to end the policy of accommodation but was opposed by the Treasury, the President, and the Council of Economic Advisers. In January 1951, in an attempt to limit Fed actions, the Secretary of the Treasury publicly announced that during the Korean conflict, which had started a few months earlier, all government bonds would pay an interest rate of no more than 2.5 percent. The President met with Fed officials and then announced that the Fed had agreed. The Fed publicly denied any such agreement, and, for months, confrontations between the Fed and the President were front-page news. The confrontation ended on March 4, 1951, with the Treasury losing. The Fed would no longer fix the interest rate. The Fed had won back the freedom of monetary policy. Having won policy independence, the Fed then had to decide what to do with it. Because the post–World War II period was substantially different from the pre–World War II period, there was no adequate guide to policy.

THE 1950S AND 1960S: CHOOSING BETWEEN INFLATION AND UNEMPLOYMENT

In the Employment Act of 1946, the federal government had committed itself to use its monetary and fiscal powers to promote "maximum employment." Precisely what maximum employment was and how it translated into monetary policy was unclear. Initially, the Fed merely attempted to maintain an "orderly" market in government securities, which meant trying to prevent drastic speculative shifts in demand. Following this policy, it allowed interest rates to rise but took no action to reduce the volume of bank reserves. Fear of inflation in 1953 led the Fed to reduce the money supply and raise the discount rate to 2 percent, but the problem changed suddenly from inflation to recession as unemployment increased from 2 percent to 5 percent. To fight the recession, the Fed stimulated the economy with a combination of open-market purchases and a reduction in the discount rate. The recession was a mild one. Throughout the 1950s and 1960s, monetary policy was essentially activist, leaning against the wind and attempting to tread the fine line between inflation and unemployment.

THE 1970S: FIGHTING INFLATION

The 1970s marked a significant change in U.S. monetary policy. In 1971, international considerations became primary as the fixed exchange rate system that had existed since 1944 broke down. Then, in 1971, in response to 6-percent inflation, President Richard Nixon imposed wage and price controls, which remained in effect until 1974. In 1973–1974, the first oil-supply shock occurred. From that point on, the primary concern of monetary policy was inflation and international considerations. However, the threat of unemployment was always present, causing the Fed to expand its monetary policy right before the crunch became too painful, especially if the crunch came near election time.

In all, there were six recessions between 1945 and 1979 (1948–1949, 1953–1954, 1957–1958, 1960–1961, 1969–1970, and 1973–1975), but none was too serious. Inflation, however, increased from about 1960 onward. The Fed reacted by switching, in 1979, to a rule based on a predetermined growth in the supply of money. That rule lasted until October 1982, at which time the Fed took a centrist position, which it continued to follow through the early 1990s. Throughout the 1980s, inflation remained low, but the expectations of inflation continually limited expansionary monetary policy by either an interest rate or a money-supply measure. In 1990, the economy fell into recession and the Fed responded by significantly decreasing interest rates and increasing the money supply, in an attempt to offset that recession.

FED TARGETS: INTEREST RATES OR THE MONEY SUPPLY?

Until the late 1970s, Keynesian ideas dominated monetary policy decisions, and policy makers used interest rates to measure the direction of monetary policy. Using interest rates raised technical questions about which interest rates to use—the fed funds rate, the 3-month Treasury bill rate, the 5-year Treasury bond rate, or the prime rate. However, this question was not the problem that led to the change in using the money supply as the target. Rather, it was inflation and inflationary expectations that did so. For example, in 1974, interest rates were about 9 percent—extremely high by historical standards. However, inflation was 11 percent, which meant that the real interest rate was −2 percent. With the significant fluctuations in inflation rates that occurred during the 1970s, when the Fed was using interest rates to measure monetary policy, it became hard to tell whether monetary policy was contractionary or expansionary. Throughout the 1970s, policy makers paid greater attention to money-supply figures in determining whether monetary policy was expansionary or contractionary.

In 1975, the Fed began presenting 12-month target ranges for monetary growth. The Fed generally reached its targets, but because it was simultaneously trying to control interest rates from 1975 to 1979, it did not always reach them, and sometimes was far off the mark. From September 1976 to September 1977, the Fed's M1 and M2 targets were 4.5 percent to 6.5 percent and 7.5 percent to 10 percent, respectively; and the actual money supply growth was 8 percent for M1 and 11.1 percent for M2. (In the following 3-month period, the Fed brought M2 growth down sufficiently so that it was within the targeted range.)

The Fed's consistent failure to meet its targets led many monetarists to argue that the Fed had lost its credibility. In response to these arguments, in October 1979, the Fed stated publicly that it would place greater emphasis on the money supply and less on interest rates. In doing so, the philosophy behind the Fed's monetary policy shifted from Keynesian to monetarist. Now it was the money supply that was being criticized as a poor measure of monetary policy.

A second but related criticism of using the money supply as a measure of monetary policy concerns the flexibility of the velocity of money. The ultimate goal of monetary policy is to affect the price level and real output, or PY (price times the quantity of real output). From the equation of exchange, $MV = PY$, the Fed affects the price level and real output by affecting MV (money supply times the velocity of money). But the Fed controls only M, not V and shifts in V can offset or exaggerate the effects of the change in M. For example, in 1978, velocity increased at a much higher than expected rate (5.6 percent, rather than 3.7 percent), making the same monetary growth much more expansionary than expected. In 1982, the growth of velocity moved in the opposite direction. The velocity of M1 actually fell 4.9 percent (M2 velocity fell 6 percent), compared with an average annual increase from 1961 to 1981 of 3.2 percent for M1.

Many Keynesians attribute the continuation of the 1981 recession into 1982 to this fall in velocity, arguing that monetary policy was far too contractionary. Another example occurred in the first quarter of 1985, when the Fed was basing its monetary policy on an expected 3 percent increase in velocity. Instead, velocity fell 4.1 percent, leaving monetary policy much more contractionary than desired. According to the Keynesian argument, focusing on a monetary target can cause significant fluctuations in interest rates, and these fluctuations add instability to the economy.

In October 1982, as the economy remained in a major postwar recession after the end of the conflict in Vietnam, the Fed dropped the "rigid monetarism" of its 1979 statement and moved back to an eclectic policy. The money supply was still a key target, but the Fed also began to look at interest rates. The result of this new policy was that the money supply grew substantially in late 1982 and early 1983, and the recession ended. Since that time and into the 2000s, the Fed has followed an eclectic policy, considering interest rates, money supply, and the variety of measures of the state of the economy as its intermediate targets.

B

The Creation of Money Through Fractional Reserve Banking

The text described how fractional reserve banking works by using an example of the Fed buying a $100 bond. In this appendix we describe how fractional reserve banking works again, but this time by showing you how banks' balance sheets change in the multiplier process. Assume, for the moment, that in your travels you suddenly find $100 that had been buried by pirates many years ago.[1] Finding this money increases the money supply and your wealth by $100. Your balance sheet would change as follows:

Assets		Liabilities	
Cash	+$100	Net worth	+$100
Increase in assets	+$100	Increase in net worth	+$100

Having found this money, you decide either to spend it or put it in your checking account at the local bank. To make things easier, assume that your bank is the only bank in the United States (although it may have many branches). Even if you do not put the money into the bank, the business where you spend it will. Either way, the money will eventually be placed in the bank. You decide to deposit the $100 in your checking account. The bank then has the $100 in cash, and you have a checking deposit receipt for $100, which means that a credit for $100 appears on your balance sheet at the bank. Even though this is only an accounting entry, as long as other people are willing to accept your check for $100, it is as good as money; in fact, it is money under the M1 definition of *money*. (Checking account deposits are sometimes considered better than cash because they

cannot be stolen as easily as can cash.) The balance sheets for you and the bank have changed as follows:

Bank			
Assets		Liabilities	
Cash	+$100	IOU to you	+$100
Increase in assets	+$100	Increase in total liabilities	+$100

You			
Assets		Liabilities	
Cash	−$100	Change in total liabilities	$0
IOU from bank	+$100		

The bank now has $100 of cash and a liability to you for $100, while you have transformed the nature of your asset from cash to a checking account deposit.

The bank is in business to earn income. If it sits on the money you deposited, it will have expenses but no revenue, so it is anxious to lend that money out. However, because your demand deposit can be withdrawn at any time, the bank must be careful not to be caught lending long and borrowing short. If this bank were one among many, it would not be able to make a very large loan, because that $100 deposit would likely be spent and transferred to another bank. However, the entire banking system, which is the equivalent of a single bank for the entire country, does not face this constraint. For the banking system as a whole, this is not the end of the process.

If the borrower spends the money, the person who receives it will redeposit it in a branch bank. For the banking system as a whole, the money loaned out is like a boomerang. The system loans the money out and the

---

[1] We choose this far-fetched example to ensure that when your money balances increase, no one else's money balances decrease.

money comes right back in. Transferring cash from one individual to another takes time, so some of the money will be in transit and the bank must keep a reserve to handle fluctuations in the amount of money in transit, but that amount will be relatively small. As discussed, the government requires banks to keep a minimum percentage of total bank deposits in reserve, which, for simplicity, we shall assume is 20 percent. With this assumption, the bank can loan out $80 of the $100.

Assuming the bank was fully loaned out before—that is, it had made loans up to the legal limit—with the addition of the $100, it now has *excess reserves* and can make a loan equal to $100 minus the $20 it must keep on reserve. If it does not loan its excess reserves, it will forgo the profit it could have made on the loan.

Now, in off the street comes Textbook Bill, who has a great idea for a new book but needs $80 to finance the project. Because Bill is a good credit risk, he receives the loan, which the bank credits to his checking account. Now let's see how much money there is in the system. You have $100 in the bank and Bill has $80 in cash, so now there is $180 in the system. This is $80 more than before; $80 in money has been created out of thin air by the fractional reserve process.

Bill takes his $80 and buys a typewriter with it. However, the typewriter company does not want to hold onto the cash, so it deposits the check in the bank. The bank, which thought it had used up its excess reserves with the $80 loan to Bill, discovers that it still has $64 in excess reserves, because its required reserves are $20 to cover your deposit and $16 to cover the typewriter company's deposit. The bank's balance sheet in excess reserves from this transaction is as follows:

Assets		Liabilities	
Cash		Deposit owed to typewriter	$80
Required reserves	$36	company	
Excess reserves	$64	Deposited owed to you	$100
Total owed by Bill	$80		
Total assets	$180	Total liabilities	$180

If you spend the $100, the process does not change as long as the person to whom you pay the money deposits it in the bank. The only change in the balance sheet is the ownership of the deposit. The bank has $64 in excess reserves.

With $64 in excess reserves, the bank is forgoing potential profits from a loan, so when Ms. Student walks in and asks to borrow $64 to buy a textbook, the bank loans it to her. Once again, the bank discovers that even after Ms. Student spends the money, it still has excess

reserves of $51.20. The bank's new balance sheet is as follows:

Assets		Liabilities	
Cash		Deposits owed to	$100
Required reserves		you or to the	
For initial $100 deposit	$20.00	person to whom	
For Bill's loan	$16.00	you paid $100	
For student's loan	$12.80	Deposit owed to	$80
Excess reserves	$51.20	Bill or to the	
Loan owed by Bill	$80.00	person to whom	
Loan owed by student	$64.00	he paid $80	
		Deposit owed to	$64
		Ms. Student or to	
		the person to whom	
		she paid $64	
Total assets	$244.00	Total liabilities	$244

Because of all the assumptions we have made, all the money the bank loans out is going to be redeposited. Depositors know they can go to the bank and change their demand deposits for cash, and if any one person wants so, he or she can. However, if all attempt to do so simultaneously, they cannot. Such concerted action is highly unlikely and is assumed away in this example. Knowing that $100 is 20 percent of $500, the bank could have treated the entire initial deposit of $100 as excess reserves and made loans for $500. Why? Because as long as the cash comes back into the bank, it does not matter how many times it is loaned out. When the entire $100 is in the required reserve accounts, the total money created in the system will equal $500. After the whole process is complete, the bank's balance sheet adjustment is as follows:

Assets		Liabilities	
Cash held for	$100	Initial deposit	$100
required reserves		Deposit owed to typewriter	$80
Loan owed by Bill	$80	company	
Additional loans	$320	Deposit owed to textbook	$64
owed to bank		company	
		Additional deposits owed	$256
		to others	
Total assets	$500	Total liabilities	$500

The important assumptions here are that all of the loaned-out money flows immediately back into the system and that the bank must keep 20 percent on reserve. If the bank had been required to keep only 10 percent on reserve, that $100 would have generated $1,000 in demand deposits. The total expansion of the money supply can be calculated by multiplying reserves by $(1/r)$, where r is the percentage reserve required. When $r = .2$, $1/r = 5$, and the $100 of reserves generates $500 of demand deposits. When individuals hold currency, the process is a bit more difficult, but essentially follows the same type of reasoning.

The Nuts and Bolts of Fiscal Policy

After reading this chapter you should be able to:

1. Explain how U.S. federal government spending and fiscal policy have evolved over the past 70 years

2. Explain how accounting concepts used in the government budget are important for interpreting fiscal policy

3. State the government budget constraint and explain how each method of financing government expenditures affects the economy

4. Outline the U.S. federal government budget process and the legislative timetable

5. List five rhetorical tools politicians use when discussing fiscal policy

6. Describe the real and financial problems that will be associated with the Social Security System over the next 40 years

> Early Keynesians saw fiscal policy as providing a steering wheel for the economy.

Over the past 50 years, policy makers have debated fiscal policy: Should the government use it? Does it work? What are its positive and negative effects? These debates have often been translated into opposing metaphors. The metaphors began in the early 1940s, when economist Abba Lerner, a strong advocate of fiscal policy, said that fiscal policy was a necessary "steering wheel." He described the economy as a car going down the highway—weaving back and forth, bouncing off trees, and running in and out of ditches. As the car passes, you notice something strange—the car has no steering wheel! Lerner argued that an economy without fiscal policy is an economy without a steering wheel. It will bounce from inflation to recession and back. By changing taxes and government spending—and, ultimately, total output—fiscal policy provides the steering wheel that keeps the economy growing smoothly.

This chapter looks at the nuts and bolts of fiscal policy. It shows you that fiscal policy (the government's intentional change in taxes or expenditures to affect the level of activity in the economy) involves a complicated set of choices and political interactions that limit government's ability to steer the economy. Oftentimes, political considerations, instead of economic considerations, determine fiscal policy. An example is the problem of Social Security, which will occur as more Baby Boomers retire. You've probably heard about the financial aspect of this problem—how the Social Security trust fund will run out some time in the future. Politicians focus on this financial problem. A consideration of the real forces underlying the theory of fiscal policy, however, reveals a deeper problem—the mismatch between real aggregate expenditures and real aggregate production that will exist independently of what government does about the financial problem. As Baby Boomers retire, fewer people will be working. Because retirees will have pensions, savings, and Social Security, they, along with current workers, will continue to demand goods. The question involves how the mismatch between real production and the real goods that current workers and retirees demand will be solved.

THE RISE AND FALL OF FISCAL POLICY

Most economists in the 1950s and 1960s accepted the need for a fiscal steering wheel. The debate was not about whether there should be a steering wheel, but how best to connect the steering wheel to the tires. Economists during this period talked about linkages—how the fiscal steering wheel is best connected to aggregate output.

At the time of this debate, the federal government's role in the economy was growing. (This chapter focuses on federal government spending and taxation. State and local governments also tax and spend, but those decisions are not made to steer the macroeconomy.) Exhibit 14–1, which shows U.S. government spending as a percentage of gross domestic product (GDP) over roughly the past 70 years, illustrates that growth. As you can see in Exhibit 14–1, before 1940, government spending was less than 10 percent of GDP. This spending increased enormously, to over 30 percent of GDP during World War II, as it had in most wars. After World War II, government spending remained well above prewar levels and steadily rose until it peaked at about 23 percent of GDP in the early 1990s, when it started on a downward trend.

> After World War II, the role of government in the economy increased dramatically.

The rise in government spending as a proportion of GDP is due mostly to a greater government role in the economy. Regulatory agencies, the Social Security system, agricultural price supports, and a whole host of new programs instituted after World War II rose dramatically. The economy was evolving into a welfare state—a market economy in which the government plays a significant role. For many Keynesian economists, the rise in the welfare state was completely consistent with their macroeconomic policy objectives. Large government spending increased the power of the fiscal steering wheel and gave the government better control over the fluctuations in the economy.

A few economists argued against an expanding government sector. Economist Milton Friedman, for example, argued that even if the economy needed a fiscal steering wheel, directing the economy did not require large amounts of government spending. He argued that most government spending was unproductive, so using spending to steer the economy would be wasteful. Moreover, politics would lead to an ever-expanding government. During downturns, the government would spend to stimulate growth, but it did not have the political will to cut spending during expansions. Every recession would result in an increase in the size of the government. He argued that the best expansionary fiscal policy would be to lower taxes, not increase spending, keeping government small.

Through the beginning of the 1960s, economists and policy makers were optimistic about their ability to **fine-tune** the economy—to make frequent adjustments

Exhibit 14-1

**U.S. Government
Spending Over the
Past 70 Years**

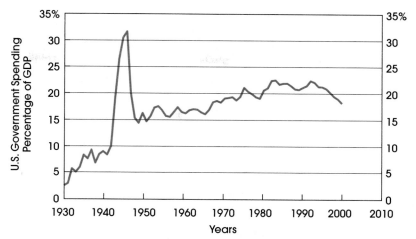

Government spending as a percent of GDP has grown over the past 70 years. The spike in the 1940s was due to U.S. involvement in World War II. Source: U.S. Department of Commerce, Bureau of Economic Analysis. (www.bea.doc.gov)

to keep the economy at desired goals such as full employment. However, attempts to steer the economy in the early 1960s proved difficult and cumbersome. A tax cut that economists argued was needed to bring the economy out of a 1960–1961 recession was not enacted until 1964. By that time, the economy had begun to recover on its own, and the tax cut helped push it beyond potential output. Similarly, in the late 1960s, almost all economists argued that government needed to increase taxes to fund President Lyndon Johnson's war on poverty and fund the military build-up in Vietnam. Johnson resisted because he feared the political ramifications of doing so. Congress and the President did eventually agree to a temporary income tax increase, but it was 2 years too late and insufficient to pay for the large rise in domestic and military spending. In the meantime, increases in government spending exceeded increases in tax revenues, the economy overheated, and inflation began to rise.

By the 1970s, the belief that fiscal policy could steer or fine-tune the economy had faded. During the 1970s, economic growth slowed and high unemployment accompanied high inflation. Concern grew among policy makers that the large government programs of the previous three decades were not cost effective. By the late 1970s, the metaphor had changed. The new metaphor had four people with severe visual impairments sitting in the front seat, fighting over which of them would steer. In this case, maybe no driver was better than the alternative.

This political pressure to move away from an activist view of fiscal policy has been accompanied by a change in the prevailing philosophical view of government throughout many of the Western economies—away from Keynesian-style activism and toward a classical laissez-faire attitude. Rather than seeing the government as trying to do good (a vision that underlies the Keynesian worldview), many economists today have a different vision; they see interest-group politics guiding government action. Because the strong tendency of a government bureaucracy controlled by interest groups is to spend all of the money it collects, one way to limit the size of government is to limit revenue. This led a group of economists who supported supply-side policies, which emphasize the importance of tax incentives on aggregate output, to argue that cutting taxes, whenever possible and regardless of the

Belief in fine-tuning the economy died out in the 1970s.

According to supply-side macroeconomic policy makers, cutting taxes is good regardless of its effect on aggregate demand.

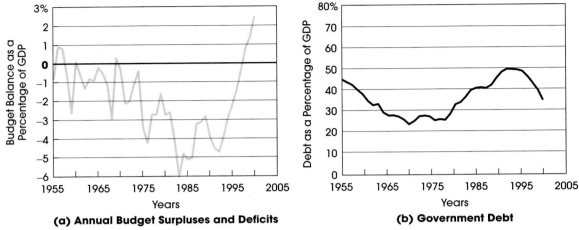

(a) Annual Budget Surpluses and Deficits   **(b) Government Debt**

Exhibit 14–2

**U.S. Government
Deficit, Surplus,
and Debt as a
Percent of GDP**

Panel a shows the government budget balance (deficit and surplus) as a percentage of GDP. The budget balance shown is the unified budget balance. *Panel b* shows the debt as a percentage of GDP. Source: U.S. Department of Commerce, Bureau of Economic Analysis. (www.bea.doc.gov)

fiscal policy consequences, is the best fiscal policy. That view has guided the Republican view of fiscal policy in recent years.

Supply-siders were successful in passing tax cuts. In the early 1980s, top income tax rates were reduced from 70 percent to 50 percent. The Tax Reform Act of 1986 further cut the top income tax rate from 50 percent to 28 percent. Although taxes decreased, government spending did not. Defense spending rose throughout the 1980s. The result was large deficits, as Exhibit 14–2(a) shows. (Recall that the government budget balance is the difference between revenue and expenditures in a year.) When the budget balance is negative (expenses exceed revenues), the government has a budget deficit, and when that balance is positive (revenues exceed expenses), the government has a budget surplus. In the 1980s, spending increases outpaced increases in tax revenue, and the government's budget deficit grew. The rising budget deficits contributed to rapidly rising government **debt**—the total accumulation of past deficits less the total accumulation of past surpluses— throughout the 1980s, as Exhibit 14–2(b) shows.

The rising government debt became a major concern of U.S. citizens. In response, Congress enacted legislation to reduce the deficit. The **Budget Enforcement Act of 1990** established caps on federal government discretionary spending and instituted a **pay-as-you-go requirement**—a law that requires that new expenditures be offset by cutting spending in other programs or by increasing taxes. This Act and two other acts passed in 1993 and 1997, also increased tax rates. These legislative changes, along with higher productivity growth and lower unemployment, caused the deficit to change into a surplus in 1998, with projected surpluses for the near future. These surpluses are reducing the debt. Notice in Exhibit 14–2(b) that, starting in 1998, the debt began to decline. This decline was a result of budget surpluses. The projected surpluses were sufficiently large that politicians talked about the possibility of being able to repay the entire U.S. government debt. The tax cuts in 2001 reduced the likelihood of that happening, but in the early 2000s, the fiscal policy discussion was about surpluses not deficits.

Now that you have an overview of U.S. fiscal policy over the last 70 years, let's look at important issues in fiscal policy. We begin with a discussion of the relationship

The Budget Enforcement Act of 1990 increased government fiscal discipline.

between accounting principles and deficits and surpluses. Then, we look at government's financing options and the mechanics of the budget process. Next, we return to politics in the fiscal policy process. We conclude the chapter by discussing the Social Security problem—a current issue that dominates U.S. fiscal policy debates.

Executive Summary

- As measured by expenditures, the U.S. government has become more involved with the economy since World War II.

- The increase in the size of the welfare state coincided with the fine-tuning objectives of Keynesian economists.

- The government budget balance is the difference between the government's revenues and its expenditures in a year. When that balance is negative, the government has a budget deficit, and when that balance is positive, the government has a budget surplus. The government debt is the total accumulation of past deficits less the total accumulation of past surpluses.

- Using fiscal policy to fine-tune the economy fell out of favor beginning in the 1970s. In the late 1990s, Congress passed laws to limit government spending.

ACCOUNTING AND BUDGETS

The first step in understanding the nuts and bolts of fiscal policy is to understand how the government measures its revenues and expenditures. To make the presentation manageable, we will discuss only surpluses, when revenues exceed expenditures, but the reasoning (reversed) holds for deficits as well. (You can think of a deficit as a negative surplus). So, let's look at the accounting behind the budget numbers.

The United States uses a cash-flow budget.

The U.S. government reports its budget on a **cash-flow basis,** an accounting method that counts revenues when they are collected and expenditures when they are spent. Firms, in contrast, generally divide their expenditures and revenues into two budgets, a capital expenditure budget and a current expenditure budget. When a firm builds a factory, it enters that expense on only the capital expenditure budget, not on the current budget. Therefore, a firm could be borrowing heavily for capital expenditures, but the borrowing would not show up on the current expenditures budget. Only the depreciation of the factory counts as a current account expense.

The U.S. government does not separate its budget into current and capital budgets. It uses only a current expenditure budget, even though not all of its expenditures are "current." Therefore, when the government makes an investment expenditure, it lists that expenditure as an expense on its budget. A firm with a similar investment would not alter its current budget balance at all.

Why the difference? The argument against using a separate capital expenditure budget in government is that determining what is investment for government is difficult. Because government doesn't charge for most of the services it provides, its investments do not earn revenue. Therefore, that which constitutes a productive capital expenditure (purchases that generate income) is unclear. For example, are expenditures on war "an investment in peace," or expenditures on making the income distribution more equal "an investment in the social system?" Such uses, while possible, would make the concept of investment so broad as to be meaningless.

The U.S. government has a unified budget that includes all expenditures and revenues, regardless of their source.

Another feature of the federal government budget is that it is a **unified budget**—a budget that includes all expenditures and revenues regardless of their source. Congress developed the unified budget system in 1969 to avoid what has been called budget

Table 14-1

U.S. Budget Balances, Billions of Dollars

	1980	1985	1990	1995	2000
Unified budget balance	−$72.7	−$212.3	−$221.2	−$163.9	$236.2
On-budget	−73.8	−221.7	−277.8	−226.3	86.4
Off-budget	−1.1	9.4	56.6	62.4	149.8
Social Security	−1.1	9.4	58.2	60.4	151.8
Postal Service			−1.6	2.0	−2.0
Interest Payments	52.5	129.5	184.4	232.2	223.2
Primary Budget Balance	−20.2	−82.8	−36.8	68.3	459.4

The Postal Service was an on-budget item before 1989.

Source: The Congressional Budget Office. **(www.cbo.gov)**

gimmickry. Before 1969, government divided expenditures into sub-budgets, which allowed politicians to choose the budget that supported their position and to ignore their budget's impact on the overall budget balance. The unified budget avoids this practice, because it includes all receipts and expenditures, including those from trust funds. It also "nets out" transactions among government agencies. A unified budget focuses on how specific spending or taxing proposals affect the overall budget balance.

Policy makers often refer to two other accounting measures of the government budget—the structural surplus (discussed in Chapter 9) and the **on-budget surplus.** The structural surplus is the amount the surplus would be if the economy were at potential output. The on-budget surplus is a measure of the surplus that does not count expenditures and revenues that are designated by law as off-budget items—expenditures and revenues resulting from programs established by legislation passed in earlier years. Table 14–1 divides the unified budget into on-budget and off-budget categories. Currently, only Social Security and the Postal Service are off-budget items. Social Security is an off-budget item because current revenues are precommitted to paying for Social Security benefits, which are "promised" by laws governing Social Security. The Postal Service is an off-budget item because its revenue is dedicated solely to supporting the collection and delivery of U.S. mail. Expenditures and revenues for such programs are not part of the annual budget negotiation process between Congress and the President. They are a part of the budget that cannot be cut without amending the original legislation that established them. The on-budget measure of the budget balance recognizes that these programs are really not negotiable.

The on-budget/off-budget distinction is important today, because much of the unified budget surplus is the result of a surplus in an off-budget item—the Social Security trust fund. Because much of that surplus is off-budget, it cannot be used to fund tax cuts or new programs. The on-budget balance gives a truer picture of the budget balance for current tax-and-spend policies.

The on-budget surplus does not include revenues or expenditures designated by law as off-budget programs, such as Social Security and the Postal Service.

Interest Payments and the Primary Budget Balance

The budget becomes more complex when we see that a sizable portion of the government's budgetary outlays are for interest payments on the outstanding debt (accumulated deficits less accumulated surpluses). In 2000, interest payments comprised about 12 percent of total expenditures. These expenditures are the result of past deficits, not expenditures on current programs, and cannot be changed through legislation for budget appropriation. Total tax revenues minus all government outlays except interest payments is called the **primary budget balance.** Current government fiscal policy directly affects the primary budget balance, which is shown in the last row of Table 14–1.

Real and Nominal Budget Deficits and Surpluses

Because the surplus and the debt are stated in nominal terms, we have to adjust them for inflation to get a true picture of how a deficit affects the economy and what it is doing to the U.S. government debt. For example, if annual inflation is 4 percent, inflation reduces the real value of the debt by 4 percent each year. Let's consider the United States in 2000 with a $5.7 trillion debt, a $236 billion nominal surplus, and a 2 percent inflation rate. The 2 percent inflation rate reduces the real value of the debt by 2 percent per year times the total debt, or by $113 billion. This amount must be added to the nominal surplus to get the **real surplus**—the budget surplus adjusted for inflation. So, the real surplus is higher than the nominal surplus. Returning to the example in 2000, the nominal surplus was $236 billion and inflation wiped out $113 billion of the debt so that the real surplus was $349 billion. (Because deficits are negative surpluses, inflation makes nominal deficits smaller.) Considered in more general terms, the larger the inflation rate or the larger the debt, the larger the real surplus relative to the nominal surplus. Following is the equation for calculating the real surplus:

Real surplus = nominal surplus + (inflation × total debt)

$$real\ surplus = nominal\ surplus + (inflation \times total\ debt) \qquad (14\text{-}1)$$

Table 14–2 provides additional examples for you to work through.

Notice that when inflation is high, a nominal deficit might be a real surplus. Expanding the size of the surplus or reducing the size of the deficit by defining the real budget balance may initially sound like sleight of hand, but it is not. To understand why, remember the difference between real and nominal interest rates. Lenders want a real rate of return, so they adjust the interest they charge for expected inflation. They raise the interest rate because they know that the value of dollars with which the debt is repaid will fall with inflation. When inflation is 10 percent, and lenders want a real return of 4 percent, the nominal interest rate will likely be 14 percent, not 4 percent. This means that when government refinances a $1 trillion debt, interest payments will not be $40 billion, they will be $140 billion. Lenders require that borrowers compensate them, through increased interest payments, for the loss in the value of the principal.

Table 14–2						
Real Deficits and Surpluses (in billions of dollars)	**1975**	**1980**	**1985**	**1990**	**1995**	**2000**
Nominal deficit or surplus	−53	−74	−212	−221	−164	+236
Plus inflation × total debt	54	86	66	142	115	113
Government debt	577	930	1946	3,233	5,001	5,665
Inflation (annual percent)	9.4	9.3	3.4	4.4	2.3	2.0
Equals real deficit or surplus	+1	+12	−146	−79	−49	+349

Deficits are shown by a negative sign. Surpluses are shown by a positive sign.

Source: U.S. Department of Commerce, Bureau of Economic Analysis, and author calculations.

Indexed bonds are bonds whose face value rises with inflation.

The differences between the real and the nominal budget balance would be eliminated if the government replaced all current bonds with indexed bonds—bonds whose face value increases to compensate holders for inflation. With the principal indexed to inflation, lenders would no longer require an inflation premium. The interest rate the government would have to pay on bonds would decrease by the difference between the real interest rate and the nominal interest rate, reducing interest payments. When government finances borrowing with indexed bonds, the face value of which increases when there is inflation, the nominal surplus rises because interest payments fall. However, the real surplus stays the same as it was with regular bonds because the value of the debt rises with inflation.

We don't hear the terms *real deficit* or *real surplus* much in today's political rhetoric. One reason is that they are too complicated to fit into a 10-second political sound bite. Most people trust politicians very little and would most likely trust them even less if politicians claimed that the real surplus was higher than reflected by actual revenues less expenditures.

Financial Health and Accounting

This discussion of the accounting of the government budget tells you that actual budget numbers must be used with care. They can mislead you into thinking the government is financially healthy when it's not, and vice versa. A budget deficit or surplus, by itself, does not indicate a government's financial well-being. A budget deficit or surplus is simply a summary measure of a very complicated set of accounts. To determine whether to be worried about a deficit or surplus, you need to understand the accounting procedures used, and ask further questions: Is the government spending money on consumption or investment goods? Is the current-year budget balance hiding future liabilities? What percentage of a budget can the government actually cut in a given year? Is the real debt falling because of inflation?

The choice of budget measure one uses changes with the question being asked. If the issue is what politicians can do during the budget negotiation process, the relevant budget balance is one that includes only on-budget items. If the issue concerns the portion of spending that must be publicly financed, the unified budget is the appropriate budget. If the issue is whether fiscal policy is expansionary or contractionary, the structural budget balance is appropriate. If the issue is how much of a burden a deficit is to an economy, the real budget balance is appropriate.

Executive Summary

- An important first step in understanding the nuts and bolts of fiscal policy is understanding the accounting that underlies the budget balance.

- Unlike private firms, governments do not use separate current and capital account budgets.

- The unified budget includes all expenditures and revenues and avoids the budget gimmickry of "off-budget" accounting.

- The primary budget balance is the budget balance excluding interest payments on the debt.

- Real budget surplus = nominal surplus + inflation × debt

- The real budget surplus rises with inflation. The real budget deficit falls with inflation.

- Budget numbers must be interpreted with care. The government budget surplus or deficit may not be an accurate indicator of the government's financial health.

THE GOVERNMENT BUDGET CONSTRAINT

The government faces the same funding constraint as do individuals—if the government buys something, it has to pay for it. The government's equivalent of your income is its tax revenue. Most of what the government buys, it pays for with tax revenue. The government, like an individual, can also borrow money, which it does by selling bonds. The government, however, has a third financing option that you don't have: It can have its central bank create money, providing seigniorage (government revenue from issuing money). So, the three sources of revenue for the government are (1) taxes, (2) borrowing, and (3) printing money.

We can formally state government's budget constraint in the following way: Total spending must be less than or equal to taxes plus newly issued bonds plus newly printed money, or

> The government budget constraint: Total spending must be less than or equal to taxes plus newly issued bonds plus newly printed money.

$$G \leq T + \Delta B + \Delta M \tag{14-2}$$

where G is government expenditures (including transfer payments and interest payments), T is tax revenue, ΔB is the change in the quantity of new bonds issued, and ΔM is the change in the money supply. Let's consider each of these three sources of funds for the United States.

Taxes

Exhibit 14–3 shows the sources of government financing since 1960 as a percentage of total government expenditures. On average, over the last 30 years government has funded 88 percent of its expenditures with tax revenues. Taxes are clearly the government's largest source of financing. It has funded 11 percent by issuing bonds and 1 percent through money creation.

> Taxes are the primary source of government finance.

Tax revenues move up and down over time because of changes in the tax laws, changes in the total income earned in the economy, and changes in the distribution

Exhibit 14-3

Financing of Government Spending

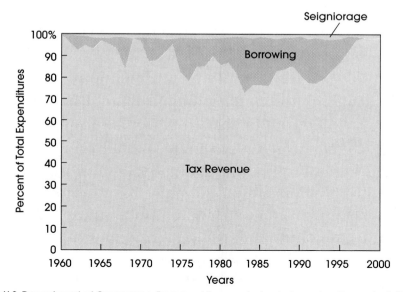

Source: U.S. Department of Commerce, Bureau of Economic Analysis, and author calculations.

of income. Tax revenue financed a lower share of total federal government expenditures after tax rates were cut in 1964, a greater share after the 1968 tax increase and a lower share after the tax cuts in the early 1980s. In the 1990s, a decrease in the growth of government spending, the strong economy, increases in tax rates, and a shift in the distribution of income towards higher income earners who pay higher marginal tax rates, allowed government to finance a higher share of spending through taxes. In 2000 and 2001, it financed nearly all its spending with tax revenues, and had some left over to pay off past debt. (Seigniorage financed a small percent of expenditures.)

Borrowing

Government can also finance expenditures through borrowing. Throughout the 1970s and 1980s, government relied more and more on borrowing to finance annual expenditures. In 1984, borrowing covered 25 percent of the government's spending. Since that time, the government has reduced its annual borrowing, and, in 1998, the government started running surpluses. Instead of borrowing, it began to pay down the debt.

> When the government runs a deficit, it must borrow by selling bonds.

The government borrows by selling bonds, more broadly called securities, to the public, foreigners, and other government agencies. The government has a number of choices about how to borrow, and we look at those choices in the next section. We then look at who buys government securities and how they are sold to the public.

Types of Government Securities. The securities that government sells can be divided into two major categories: marketable and nonmarketable securities. **Nonmarketable securities** are government bonds that do not trade in secondary markets and include savings bonds, bonds held in government accounts such as Social Security, and bonds issued to state and local governments. **Marketable securities** are bonds that the public can buy and sell in secondary markets.

> T-bills have maturities of less than 1 year. T-notes have maturities between 1 and 10 years; T-bonds have maturities between 10 and 30 years.

The majority of publicly held debt consists of three types of securities: Treasury bills, Treasury notes, and Treasury bonds. Table 14–3 shows the amounts of each type outstanding in 2000. The main difference among these three securities is their terms to maturity. Treasury bills (T-bills) are securities sold at a discount that grant the holder one payment at maturity equal to its face value. Maturity can occur at 3 months, 6 months, or 1 year. For example, a 1-year, $100 T-bill that sells for $95

Table 14-3		
Government Securities Outstanding, 2000 (in billions)	**Dollar Amount**	**Percent of Total**
Total interest-bearing public debt	5,647	100
Marketable	3,233	57
T-bills	653	12
T-notes	1,829	32
T-bonds	644	11
Inflation-indexed notes	93	2
Federal financing bank	15	0
Nonmarketable	2,414	43

Source: The United States Treasury. (**www.ustreas.gov**)

yields an annual return of 5 percent. Treasury notes (T-notes) are securities sold at face value that pay interest every 6 months and face value at maturity. Maturity ranges from 2 to 10 years. Treasury bonds (T-bonds) are identical to T-notes, except that their maturity ranges from 10 to 30 years. The Treasury repays maturing securities either with current revenue or by selling new securities.

In addition to these standard T-bills, T-notes and T-bonds, the U.S. Treasury now issues inflation-indexed notes and bonds called *TIPS*. (TIPS stands for "Treasury Inflation Protection Securities." The Treasury started issuing TIPS in 1997.) The interest rate, which the Treasury sets at the time of the sale, remains fixed throughout the term of the security, but the principal amount changes to account for inflation. The inflation-adjusted principal is paid at maturity. In addition, the semiannual interest payments are based on the inflation-adjusted principal at the time the interest is paid. Suppose the interest rate on a 2-year, $1,000 inflation-indexed note is 4 percent. If inflation is 5 percent during the first 6 months, the 4 percent interest payment will be based on a principal of $1,050. If by the end of 2 years (the maturity of the bond) the price level has risen 10 percent, the holder will receive a final interest payment plus $1,100.

How Does the Government Sell Securities? The bond department at the U.S. Treasury Department has two jobs—financing deficit spending and refinancing current debt. When the government runs a surplus, as it has since 1998, the Treasury doesn't need to finance new debt. In this case, it refinances the current debt as it matures. With $3 trillion of government debt held by the public, much of it short-term debt, securities are always coming due. If, however, the Treasury

QUESTION How does the Treasury auction securities?

ANSWER The Treasury auctions securities throughout the year, using single-price bidding.

The Treasury considers the securities market carefully in its auctions. It announces the date, the mix of maturities, and the amount to be issued in advance. Although you might think that the Treasury would look at the yield curve to determine how to best take advantage of interest rate differentials, it doesn't because doing so might disrupt the market. Instead, it decides on a mix of securities to sell, announces it, and sticks to it.

In the 1970s, the average maturity of government debt was 2 years, but the Treasury felt that it entered the bond market too frequently. The Treasury was competing with private borrowers, and coordinating the timing of sales with private firms became complicated. Maturity was lengthened. In the early 1990s, the Treasury made an explicit decision to go the opposite way and reduce the maturity of the debt. The average maturity is currently 5.5 years.

The Treasury auctions securities to investors, using a single-price auction method.* The Treasury announces the auction and accepts bids from the highest price (lowest yield) to the lowest required to sell the amount offered, but requires all individuals to pay only the lowest price. This might, at first, sound odd, but this type of auction has benefited the Treasury. First, it has increased the number of auction participants, because bidders do not have to worry about the winner's curse—the risk that the winning bidder pays more than other bidders at an auction. Second, bidders have raised their prices slightly, resulting in slightly lower borrowing costs for the Treasury.

*Before late 1998, the Treasury used a multiple-price auction method. In a multiple-price auction, the Treasury accepted bids, beginning with the highest price (lowest yield), and continued to award securities to lower bids until it sold all competitive issues. A number of issues were reserved for noncompetitive bidders who paid the weighted-average price of accepted competitive bids.

QUESTION   If the debt is eliminated, what will happen to the Treasury securities market?

ANSWER   The market for T-bills and T-bonds will no longer exist. Too much of a good thing (surpluses) may not be so good.

In 2000 and early 2001, most U.S. politicians thought surpluses were great, but, as some economists point out, we can have "too much of a good thing." The argument is as follows. If surpluses are used to pay down the debt, the market for U.S. government securities will disappear. In current financial markets, government bonds are an important part of many people's portfolios. Government bonds are the quintessential risk-free liquid asset. With a smaller number of new Treasury securities issued, the market for Treasury securities will shrink, making the securities less liquid, harder to trade, and, therefore, less desirable to hold. As this happens, they may lose their "benchmark" status. (Financial market observers have traditionally used the interest rate on Treasury securities as the benchmark risk-free interest rate. Analysts use the spread between interest rates on corporate debt securities and the risk-free Treasuries to measure the premium they'll pay for risk on corporate debt securities.) If Treasury securities disappear altogether—which would happen if the debt is completely paid off—some other security will have to replace Treasury securities as the benchmark.

Without an active Treasury market, the Federal Reserve Bank will have to change the way it conducts monetary policy. This follows because, as we saw in Chapter 13, the Fed conducts monetary policy primarily through open-market operations—the Fed buying and selling government securities. If the debt is totally eliminated, the Fed will have to either find some other type of debt security to buy and sell, or use another tool, such as changing the reserve requirement.

---

redeems more bonds than are maturing, it will have to pay a premium to buy the bonds back. So, refinancing remains important even when government runs a surplus. To carry out this refinancing, the Treasury holds more than 150 auctions throughout the year. These auctions include regular weekly sales of short-term T-bills, monthly sales of 1-year T-bills and 2- to 5-year T-notes, and quarterly sales of 7-year T-bills and 10- to 30-year T-bonds. The frequency and size of each auction depend on the government's financing needs. (See the Q&A feature for a description of Treasury auctions.)

If the government continues to run large surpluses, the privately held debt will shrink and eventually disappear. While this sounds great, it presents some potential problems. (See the Q&A feature, which discusses this issue.)

Who Holds the Government's Debt? About 40 percent of the $5.7 trillion in outstanding U.S. government debt in 2000 was held by the Federal Reserve and government agencies such as the Social Security Administration (SSA). The Federal Reserve holds debt to conduct open-market operations. By tradition, the only asset the Fed has held from past seigniorage is government debt. The Social Security system is currently running a large surplus (Social Security tax revenue exceeds benefit payments). The SSA is compelled by law to purchase nonmarketable government bonds from the Treasury with its annual surplus.

> Government agencies hold almost half of the outstanding government debt.

Subtracting the debt held by the Fed, the Social Security system, and other government agencies, left the total privately held debt at about $3.5 trillion in 2000. Table 14–4 shows who held that private debt.

The largest single holder of private U.S. government debt is foreigners. This category includes foreign individuals, foreign corporations, and foreign governments. Recall from Chapter 7 that foreign purchases of government debt are a capital inflow,

Table 14-4

Who Holds the Government's Debt?

Total outstanding debt, 2000		$5.7 trillion
− Debt held by Federal Reserve, Social Security, and other government agencies		$2.2 trillion
= Total privately held debt		$3.5 trillion

Breakdown of Privately Held Debt

	Dollar Amount	Percent of Privately Held Debt (%)
Depository institutions	0.23 trillion	7.3
U.S. savings bond holders	0.19 trillion	5.8
Pension funds	0.43 trillion	13.5
Insurance companies	0.14 trillion	4.4
Mutual funds	0.34 trillion	11.0
State and local governments	0.26 trillion	8.1
Foreign and international	1.3 trillion	40.0
Other investors	0.3 trillion	10.0

Source: The United States Treasury.

or foreign saving. Foreign inflow of capital has kept past government deficits from reducing private investment and has allowed more domestic saving to finance domestic investment. However, if foreigners withdraw their capital (stop buying, or start selling, U.S. government bonds), there will be pressure for domestic investment to fall, because more saving will have to be used to buy government securities.

Printing Money

The final method by which government can fund spending is by printing money. As stated in Chapter 7, the revenue resulting from the printing of money is called *seigniorage*. The United States, and most other developed economies, finance only a small fraction of expenditures by printing money. The United States typically finances less than 1 percent of its spending with seigniorage. Because printing large quantities of money eventually leads to inflation, seigniorage is used as a last resort to finance expenditures. Even so, for some developing and less developed economies, because other sources are unavailable, money creation is a major source of revenue.

Seigniorage is not an important source of revenue for the United States, but seigniorage can be an important source of revenue for developing countries.

Consider, for example, the developing economies of Peru and Bolivia. During the 1980s, these countries experienced political turmoil, making it nearly impossible to sell government securities. Investors wouldn't buy government bonds because they feared the government would default (not pay back the principal and the interest). These countries (Bolivia especially) also lacked the ability to collect tax revenues, because a large proportion of their economic activity was "underground" or "off the books." Because their primary financing options didn't cover expenses, they had to print money to "finance" their expenditures. During some years of the 1980s, seigniorage accounted for nearly all revenue in Bolivia and two-thirds of revenue in Peru.

Actually, we need to be more precise about how printing money to finance government expenditures works. When governments such as Bolivia or Peru create money to pay for government expenditures, they do it indirectly. Their treasuries issue bonds in the same way as described for bond finance, but their central banks buy up the bonds with newly created money. So, the government finances with bonds, which the central bank (another part of government) buys with the money it creates. Their treasuries then use this newly created money to finance their expenditures.

Choosing a Method of Finance

How does a government choose how to finance its spending? Let's first consider the choice between taxes and borrowing and the political, as well as the economic, consequences of each.

Tax Smoothing. Most governments, for political reasons, cannot continually adjust tax rates to finance their changing spending needs. Instead, they follow a policy of tax smoothing—maintaining a constant tax rate, even if doing so means borrowing or saving—which means they run deficits when expenditures are unusually high or taxes are unusually low, and run surpluses (or smaller deficits) during other years, when expenditures are unusually low or tax revenues are unusually high. For example, during World War II, it didn't make sense, either economically or politically, for the U.S. government to raise taxes high enough to fully fund wartime expenditures. Instead, the government issued bonds with the expectation of raising taxes later to help pay off the bonds. These bonds soaked up the large private savings because there were too few goods for consumers to buy. Paying for spending with bonds is a way to spread a large expenditure over several years. Tax smoothing is consistent with running countercyclical fiscal policy: it increases the surplus in an expansion, and decreases it in a recession.

Incentive Effects of Taxes. Governments also consider the incentive effects of taxes when choosing between taxes and borrowing. High marginal tax rates discourage people from working and firms from investing, lowering potential output. For example, in the late 1990s, Canada's highest income tax rate was over 50 percent and its highest corporate tax rate was about 46 percent. To avoid these high rates, some of Canada's most educated workers and its most highly productive firms moved to the United States, where marginal tax rates were lower. To counter this flow, Canada proposed lowering tax rates by 15 percent. Canadian policy makers hoped that this move would discourage people and firms from leaving and would, therefore, prevent Canada's potential output from falling.

Government can choose among many types of taxes, all of which have different incentive effects. A rule of thumb for many governments is to finance as much current expenditures as is possible with the combination of taxes that has the fewest incentive effects, unless government desires either (1) tax smoothing or (2) a fiscal stimulus.

Tax Equity. Another issue in deciding which tax to use is that of equity. Equity issues played a major role in the debate between Democrats and Republicans about how to structure the tax cut in 2001. Republicans wanted a roughly equal proportional tax cut (each person's tax is cut by 3 percent of their total tax bill). Democrats wanted a roughly equal absolute tax cut (each person gets a $300 tax cut). The final decision was a compromise that leaned toward the Republican approach. Economists, in their role as economists, have little to say about such equity issues, because they involve normative judgments.

Fiscal Stimulus. It is the fiscal stimulus aspect of fiscal policy that is of primary concern to short-run macroeconomic policy. Most economists see some degree of fiscal stimulus occurring along the lines described by the IS/LM model. Some economists, however, argue that government cannot expand the economy with fiscal policy. This argument, called the Ricardian equivalence argument, was introduced in Chapter 9. According to the Ricardian equivalence argument, rational individuals, anticipating that government will raise future taxes, will reduce their current spending, completely offsetting expansionary fiscal policy. Most economists don't see individuals as being that superrational. They see the argument, roughly, as nineteenth-century economist David Ricardo saw it—a neat theoretical notion that is worth keeping in mind, but which generally does not apply to reality.

> According to the Ricardian equivalence argument, individuals will anticipate future taxes from bond financing, and the expansionary effect of fiscal policy will be offset.

Crowding Out Investment. Another consideration when choosing among methods of financing expenditures is the effect that borrowing has on private expenditures. Government borrowing can compete with private borrowing needs and push up interest rates. Higher interest rates crowd out private investment expenditures (as discussed in Chapters 4 and 9), offsetting the expansionary effect of deficit spending and possibly lowering long-run growth by reducing growth in productive capacity. The degree to which crowding out occurs depends on the shape of the LM and IS curves.

Political Considerations. A final consideration is political and is probably the one most on policy makers' minds when they make decisions about how to finance spending. The political reality is that people don't like deficits, and when deficits get large, people want them eliminated. This sentiment guided U.S. macroeconomic policy in the early 1990s. The recent push in most developed Western economies has been toward smaller government and less reliance on deficits to finance expenditures. In the early 2000s, most U.S. politicians were arguing that they would preserve the U.S. budget surplus, although many economists doubted these politicians' commitment to this goal if the economy went into a recession.

For developing and transitional countries, politics also plays a central role. As discussed, generally, these countries have poorly developed fiscal systems and often have difficulty collecting taxes. As a result, they face continual deficits, which they must finance by selling securities. When the private sector won't buy these securities, the central banks of these countries must make a decision—to let their governments default or to buy the bonds, thereby increasing the money supply and inflation. It is in this sense that deficits can be inflationary: They can force a central bank to increase the money supply.

ARE DEFICITS BAD AND SURPLUSES GOOD?

In judging whether a country has its fiscal affairs in order, economists usually look at the size of the deficit relative to GDP. In the European Union, for example, a deficit of less than 3 percent of GDP is required for an economy to be allowed to enter the European Union, and countries are required to keep their deficits below that percentage. Just as in individual finance (borrowing relative to total income indicates a person's capacity to pay), government borrowing relative to taxable capacity, which is determined in large part by GDP, indicates an economy's ability to carry the burden of borrowing.

The negative economic and political effects of deficits are, obviously, reversed when a country starts running surpluses. Most economists supported the U.S. government running surpluses in the late 1990s and early 2000s. They pointed out that the surpluses, by reducing the demand for funds, were accompanied by lower interest rates, which led to higher investment expenditures. In fact, real long-term interest rates were about one-third lower in the late 1990s, when the surplus was growing, compared with the late 1980s, when deficits were growing. Investment spending was a significant contributor to economic growth in the late 1990s and early 2000.

Economists welcomed the surpluses because surpluses were the right short-run fiscal policy for a booming economy; they decreased demand and helped prevent the economy from overheating. Social Security tax receipts were expected to continue to rise, adding to a Social Security trust fund that will be needed to pay retirement benefits when the Baby Boomers begin to retire in 2010.

However, budget surpluses can also create problems. In early 2001, some policy makers feared that if the U.S. government continued to run surpluses, it would eliminate its debt in 10 years. If surpluses continued after the government debt was paid, the government would have to buy private securities, which would create political debate about which securities to buy and whether government ownership of private securities would give government too much control of private companies.

> If the government runs large surpluses for a long enough period, it will eliminate all debt.

Most economists don't expect such issues to arise. In early 2001, both Democrats and Republicans were looking for ways to spend or reduce the surplus. Democrats favored using the surplus to fund a number of new programs, such as expanded health insurance and prescription drug coverage, while Republicans pushed for tax cuts. A $1.35 trillion tax cut over 10 years was passed along with a number of new spending initiatives. These will shrink the surplus from what it otherwise would have been. Even without tax cuts and new spending programs, the surplus will shrink if growth slows and the U.S. economy goes into recession.

Despite the decline in the use of borrowing to finance expenditures in the United States and in many other developed economies, the economic and political costs of deficit financing are not merely of historical interest. Many countries throughout the world, including Brazil and Japan, still rely heavily on deficit financing. In addition, although the United States currently has a surplus, much of that surplus is generated by the large influx of Social Security tax revenue, which is generated from the booming economy and the large number of Baby Boomers in the workforce. Once the Baby Boomers begin to retire, the surplus is expected to disappear and the United States will once again face growing debt and its consequences.

Executive Summary

- The government budget constraint is $G \leq T + \Delta B + \Delta M$. Government must finance spending through taxes, borrowing, and/or printing money.

- Government finances most expenditures through tax revenue.

- The government issues three types of marketable securities to finance its expenditures: Treasury bills, notes, and bonds.

- Seigniorage accounts for less than 1 percent of U.S. revenue. For some developing and less developed economies, seiniorage is a major source of revenue.

- Deficit financing is used to smooth taxes over time and to avoid the negative incentive effects of high taxes.

- Ricardian equivalence argues that people will increase their saving in response to an increase in the deficit, thereby offsetting its stimulative effects.

- In judging whether a country has its fiscal affairs in order, economists usually look at the size of its deficit relative to GDP.

- In the early 2000s, many economists favored using the surplus to pay down the debt, fearing that reversing tax cuts or spending increases would be difficult if the economy slowed and the expected surplus shrunk, or even disappeared.

FORMULATING AND MAKING FISCAL POLICY

So far in this chapter, we have focused on the economic nuts and bolts—the accounting and the terminology of fiscal policy. In this section, we consider the political nuts and bolts of fiscal policy—the process by which budget legislation is introduced, debated, and made into law. To understand how fiscal policy works in the real world, it is important to understand this process.

In Chapter 9, you learned about the legislative lag associated with fiscal policy—the time it takes a fiscal policy proposal to become law. Our discussion of the budget process in this chapter makes it clear that the legislative lag can be substantial, making fiscal policy an inflexible tool for dealing with short-term fluctuations. Attempts have been made throughout the years to shorten or sidestep this lag. For example, automatic stabilizers—built-in changes in government spending or taxes when there are fluctuations in aggregate income—require no new legislative action and avoid the legislative lag. When the economy slows or enters a recession, spending on unemployment insurance, welfare, and food stamps automatically rises. As incomes in the economy fall, people are pushed into lower tax brackets. These automatic increases in spending and decreases in taxes help to reduce the size of the downturn in the economy. When the economy booms, automatic stabilizers work in reverse. Spending on unemployment, welfare, and food stamps falls, and rising incomes push people into higher tax brackets.

Automatic stabilizers help to lessen the severity of the business cycle and overcome the legislative lag associated with fiscal policy. Although automatic stabilizers are by no means large or powerful enough to completely eliminate the business cycle, they do make the U.S. budget balance highly dependent on the state of the economy. The surplus in the early 2000s, for example, was due in large part to tax revenues increasing as the economy boomed; the resulting surplus helped to moderate the boom.

In addition to automatic stabilizers, Congress can sidestep the legislative lag by enacting emergency spending legislation or tax relief. In the early 1960s, Walter Heller, the Chair of the Council of Economic Advisers, proposed giving the President the power to change taxes by small increments and within certain limits, without the approval of Congress. This proposal never passed, but it illustrates policy makers' attempts to adjust the mechanical process of fiscal policymaking, to avoid the legislative lag, and make fiscal policy a more practical tool for managing the economy.

Even if the mechanics of fiscal policy could be adjusted to shorten the legislative lag, there is another major impediment to using fiscal policy to manage short-term fluctuations: politics. In a democratic society, changes in spending and taxes, no matter how automatic, are the outcome of the political process and, therefore, represent a compromise of competing views.

In the process of compromise, fiscal policy actions sometimes run counter to the policy goals of macroeconomics. For example, in the late 1990s and in early 2000, the U.S. economy was booming and the budget surplus was growing. The short-run model (see Chapters 8 through 11) suggested that policy makers should increase the budget surplus even more by cutting spending or increasing taxes to dampen economic growth and lessen inflationary pressures, but that didn't happen. Instead, Congress and the President focused on cutting taxes and increasing spending—both policies tending to exacerbate the cyclical upswing in the economy. The reason for advocating policies that run counter to our aggregate demand management prescription should be

Automatic stabilizers entail automatic counter-cyclical changes in taxes and spending.

Politics, not economic reasoning, generally guides fiscal policy.

obvious—cutting taxes and increasing spending are politically more advantageous (likely to generate more votes) than are increasing taxes and cutting spending. In 2001, as the economy started to slow, politicians started arguing that the reason they needed to cut taxes was to stimulate the economy. However, because they had already advocated doing so, few observers felt that this was their true motivation.

The Budget Process

To better understand the constraints that policy makers face when trying to change taxes or spending we need to look more closely at the budget process. Decisions about the budget are determined both by the executive branch (the President and his advisers) and the Congress. Although Congress is ultimately responsible for the budget, the executive branch prepares and submits the initial budget. Congress then acts on the initial budget. It's important to understand that this budgetary process concerns only **discretionary spending**—expenditures determined through the annual appropriation process—which accounts for about one-third of total federal government spending. Discretionary spending includes expenditures on housing and education, defense spending, and highway construction. Congress must pass annual appropriations bills before it can spend money on discretionary programs. The remaining expenditures are **mandatory spending**—expenditures authorized by permanent laws, including spending on entitlement programs such as Social Security and Medicare, as well as interest payments.

> Federal government spending programs do not contain much flexibility.

Table 14–5 presents a timeline for the budget process. As you can see, the fiscal year runs from October 1 through September 30, but the budget process begins more than a year before, with preparation of a proposed federal budget by the President. The President must submit the proposal to Congress by the first Monday in February, in the year preceding the fiscal year. For example, President George W. Bush presented the budget for fiscal year 2003 (beginning October 1, 2002) to

Table 14–5 **Time Line for the Budget Process**		
	February–December Year 1	• Formulation of the President's budget for Year 2: Executive Branch agencies develop requests and make the final decisions on what goes into the President's budget.
	December Year 1 to February Year 2	• Budget preparation and transmittal: The budget documents are prepared and transmitted to Congress.
	March–September Year 2	• Congressional action on the budget: Congress reviews the President's budget, develops its own budget, and approves spending and revenue bills.
	October 1, Year 2	• The fiscal year begins.
	October 1, Year 2 to September 30, Year 3	• Agency program managers execute the budget provided in law.
	October–November, Year 3	• Data on actual spending and receipts for the completed fiscal year become available.

Congress in February 2002. The actual data for the economy won't be known for another year and a half. Preparation of the proposal begins in the previous spring, more than one and a half years before the fiscal year begins.

The President's budget estimates the costs of continuing the authorized programs for the current fiscal year for another year. These estimates depend on estimates of inflation, unemployment, and the real rate of growth determined by the Council of Economic Advisers (CEA), an advisory panel that formulates and recommends national economic policy to the President. The Joint Economic Committee (an advisory panel of senators and representatives that addresses fiscal policy) reviews and assesses the current service budget and reports to Congress. The Office of Management and Budget (OMB) also assists the President in overseeing the preparation and administration of the federal budget. Its review of the budget begins in March of the previous year, or even earlier.

The budgeting process is highly political.

This initial budgeting process is highly political. Individual agencies are advocates and have a strong interest in justifying their programs. Thus, the President's OMB, which has oversight authority over all agencies, and the agencies themselves often are adversaries. There are, of course, limits to this adversarial process. Agency heads usually take hints from conversations with presidential aides about what the President wants, and they try to tailor their proposals to fit. For example, President George W. Bush pushed for reductions in environmental spending, and his Secretary of Interior went along with it.

The OMB's budget examiners carefully review each part of an agency's proposal and adjust the agency director's letter accordingly. Generally, the OMB "puts a squeeze" on the agency, which must decide to make cuts or appeal its "too-low" budget to the OMB, the President, or Congress. Often, this process can become hectic when new information on the economy becomes available and last-minute adjustments are needed. By about the third week in January, the budget document is sent to the Congress.

Congress' work begins when it examines the President's budget and meets with agencies and lobbyists to decide its position on the budget. Table 14–6 shows the Congressional budget timetable. In February, Congress holds public hearings, with testimony from the President's staff, experts from the business and academic

Table 14–6 **The Congressional Budget Timetable**		
	February	• Congress examines the President's budget, and committees hold hearings.
	April 15	• House and Senate Budget Committees prepare a concurrent resolution.
	April–September	• House and Senate Appropriations Committees make 13 specific appropriations bills, and the House Ways and Means Committee considers revenue measures.
	Early September	• The House and Senate pass final bills for appropriations.
	September 25	• A second concurrent resolution is passed and becomes the budget.

communities, and members of various organizations. Congressional committees also review portions of the President's budget related to their jurisdiction and submit reports to the House and Senate Budget Committees. The Congressional Budget Office (CBO) and the General Accounting Office, Congress's two investigatory and research agencies, also prepare reports on the budget options.

The work on the budget is concentrated in the House and Senate Budget Committees, which have general jurisdiction over the Congressional budget. These committees take their staff reports and the CBO report and present a "concurrent resolution" to their respective houses by April 15. This concurrent resolution is a tentative budget, which sets target goals for budget authority, outlays, receipts, and public debt.

The House and Senate Appropriations Committees then make specific appropriations proposals, and the House Ways and Means Committee considers revenue measures. Congress hears the testimony of the relevant agency and specialists in each area. Although the committees are subject to the general guidelines of the first concurrent resolution, they are not rigidly bound, and the appropriations that come out of these committees can differ from the planned budget.

Finally, both the Senate and the House pass specific bills embodying the individual appropriations, and House–Senate differences are resolved in conference committees. By law, Congress must pass all new appropriations bills by the seventh day after Labor Day, although Congress often misses this deadline.

By September 15, Congress must add up all of the individual appropriations and, by September 25, is required to pass a second concurrent resolution. This second concurrent resolution is reconciled with individual appropriation bills, and, finally, the second concurrent resolution becomes the budget, more than a year and a half after the planning first began. If Congress does not meet the September 25 deadline, it may enact a continuing resolution to fund agencies temporarily. In the late 1990s, the U.S. government often was financed by one continuing resolution after another, mainly because of disagreements between the Democratic President and the Republican Congress.

The second concurrent resolution becomes the budget.

Changing the Budget Process to Reduce Budget Deficits

Beginning in the early 1980s, Congress and the President recognized that, to reduce the budget deficit, they would have to change the budget process. Both realized that they did not have the self-discipline to reduce spending or increase taxes unless required to do so.

The most significant piece of legislation to come out of this realization was the Budget Enforcement Act of 1990, which capped discretionary spending and established the pay-as-you-go (paygo) rule for mandatory programs. The paygo rule stipulates that if Congress wants to increase spending on an existing program or introduce a new spending program that will result in an increased deficit, as estimated by the Congressional Budget Office, it must pay for that program by either raising taxes or cutting spending somewhere else in the budget. Similarly, if Congress wants to cut taxes, it must make up for the cut by reducing expenditures. The paygo stipulation is set on all mandatory spending programs, such as food stamps.

In 1993, the spending caps and paygo rules were extended to 1998, and were again extended to 2002 by the Budget Reconciliation Act of 1998. The Budget Enforcement Act changed the dynamics of the budgetary process, making increasing spending and cutting taxes much more difficult, placing a limit on what government could do. The budget surpluses of the early 2000s removed the force of the Budget Enforcement Act, and both tax cuts and spending increases were again in the news.

The paygo rule helped to change the political dynamics and reduce government deficits.

Discretionary and Mandatory Spending

As mentioned, much of the budget is mandatory, meaning that Congress is pre-committed to funding programs established by past legislation. Consider, for example, the fiscal year 2001 budget. The government proposed spending $1.85 trillion dollars. Roughly 60 percent, or $1.2 trillion, of that spending represented either mandatory spending or interest payments. Mandatory spending, which represent a precommitment on the part of the government, must be paid unless additional legislation changes the program.

You might think that this still leaves a lot of room for maneuvering. After all, this budget leaves nearly $650 billion of discretionary spending that, in a pinch, the government could use to reduce the surplus or increase the deficit. In reality, however, the government also does not have a lot of discretion over much of the remaining spending. For example, expenditures that maintain the Washington monument and the parks around the nation's capital are part of discretionary spending, but they essentially cannot be cut.

A more important component of discretionary spending that is difficult to change is defense spending. Although money for defense has to be appropriated each year, many defense programs are multi-year commitments. Once Congress has approved an order for 10 new fighter jets, those contracts are not likely to be canceled, both because of the political consequences of doing so and because such cancellations would require costly termination payments. In reality, the amount of discretion over defense spending is far smaller than is indicated by the defense budget.

Other examples of discretionary spending that would be difficult to eliminate are the spending by government agencies, such as the Department of Agriculture, the Department of Health and Human Services, the Commerce Department, the Internal Revenue Service, and the Bureau of the Census. Each year, these agencies have to request funds to maintain operations. So, practically speaking, Congress and the President can't cut much spending on these agencies.

As you can see, the government's ability to reduce spending to cut the deficit or increase the surplus is quite limited because of ongoing commitments to government programs. This is why many economists in the late 1990s and early 2000s favored using the surplus to reduce the debt, not to start new spending programs or to reduce taxes.

Executive Summary

- The budget timetable shows that the fiscal policy process is lengthy and has multiple steps.

- The Budget Enforcement Act changed the dynamics of fiscal policy away from deficit spending toward deficit reduction.

- It's difficult for the government to reduce even discretionary spending.

The Importance of Fiscal Regimes

Fiscal policy regimes set the framework within which the economy operates.

Where does all of this budget talk leave us in terms of fiscal policy? It is clear that politics plays a big role in deciding fiscal policy. Policy cannot be changed quickly, which eliminates it as a tool for fine-tuning. Nonetheless, the fiscal policy regime—the general rules that determine the direction of fiscal policy—affects expectations of how government fiscal policy discussions will go in the future. Fiscal policy regimes set the framework within which the economy will operate.

In the late 1990s, the fiscal policy regime was to lower the deficit. Policy discussions centered on reducing the deficit. People came to expect lower government expenditures. During this period, interest rates fell, which tended to stimulate private investment. Higher private investment increased the productive capacity of the economy and contributed to rising worker productivity.

Within the framework of even a balanced-budget fiscal regime, most economists believe that government should have some ability to step in and expand spending in a major recession, and slow spending in a major inflationary expansion. For the long run, however, most economists advocate a regime that keeps the budget balanced, or close to being balanced.

Fiscal Policy as a Process

Policymaking is best viewed as a process that affects expectations.

Recall from Chapter 12 that policy is best viewed as a process. Therefore, we tend to look at a fiscal policy action in the context of what government has done in the past. If, in the past, the government has stepped in with big spending increases or tax cuts to avoid large recessions, people will come to expect that the economy will not be allowed to fall too far into recession. Expectations such as this help keep the economy from falling too far into a recession, and as long as those expectations continue, the government will have an easier time managing the economy. To maintain such expectations, however, policy makers occasionally may have to take action—such as increasing spending or decreasing taxes when the economy goes into a recession—to convince people that they are still operating in the same regime.

Spin Control

What you read in the paper about fiscal policy often contains significant spin and rhetoric.

Despite the political constraints on using fiscal policy, members of Congress and the President continue to talk about using fiscal policy to stimulate or slow the economy. But it is important to look beyond the rhetoric to understand how fiscal policy actually affects the economy. To help you do this, we list five common rhetorical tools that politicians use to talk about fiscal policy. Then we discuss what the proposed policies mean for the economy.

1. *Talk about levels not percentages.*   Politicians like to propose "billions more" for education, "billions more" for defense, or even "billions more" to stimulate the economy. Typically, however, the billions of dollars in proposed spending increases are small relative to the entire budget. For example, when Bill Clinton took office in 1992, the U.S. economy was recovering from the recession of the early 1990s. Clinton proposed increasing spending by about $40 billion to stimulate the economy and increase employment. That amount of money seems like a lot, but for the economy as a whole, it is very little. Clinton's 1992 spending proposal amounted to only two-thirds of 1 percent of the total $6.2 trillion income in the United States. That amount of spending, even with multiplier effects, is rather small. Although the spending or tax changes would be more accurately stated as a percentage of GDP, politicians don't speak in such terms. It is hard to comprehend how big the U.S. economy is, so a "$40 billion spending increase" sounds more impressive than a "two-thirds of 1 percent spending increase."

2. *Front-load spending and back-load taxes.*   Federal budgets are usually multi-year plans for spending and taxes. These plans call for politically easier spending

increases and tax cuts to occur in the near term, and the politically more difficult spending cuts and tax hikes to occur later. In 1998, Congress and the President passed legislation to balance the Federal budget by 2002 through cutting spending and increasing taxes. After passing this legislation, members of Congress could go back home and tell their constituents that they voted to balance the budget, but the legislation really called for no significant spending cuts or tax hikes in the first few years. Those cuts and hikes would come in the later years—2001 and 2002, (and in 2001, taxes were cut). You might be wondering how the budget deficit turned to a surplus in 1998, even though the spending cuts and tax hikes were to come in 2001 and 2002. Strong economic growth raised tax revenues enough to produce a surplus, even before Congress could increase taxes and cut spending. Of course, members of Congress and the President nevertheless took credit for balancing the budget.

3. *Take credit for anything good. Assign blame for anything bad.*   When the economy does well (high growth, low unemployment, and low inflation), politicians take credit for it. In February 2000, the U.S. economy entered its 108th month of continuous expansion, making it the longest U.S. economic expansion in recorded history. Both members of Congress and the President took credit for overseeing this longest expansion. (At the time this book went to press the economy was still in the expansion.) Although it is possible that policies enacted by the sitting president and current members of Congress contributed to the economic situation, it is difficult, if not impossible, to tell by how much and in what direction these policies contributed. Not surprisingly, when the economy is doing poorly, politicians blame predecessors or factors out of their control—OPEC, foreign economies, or the Fed.

4. *Use forecasts that make your policies look good.*   The economy is so complex, no matter how elaborate the economic model, human judgment is part of any forecast. Politicians use the ambiguity inherent in forecasts to choose the forecast that makes their policies look best. Let's consider an example.

In the early 1970s, President Nixon's budget director, George Shultz, hired a young economic forecaster named Arthur Laffer to forecast the U.S. economy. Nixon had proposed a rather large spending increase, much of it going to pay for increased involvement in the Vietnam War, but he didn't want to increase taxes and he didn't want the budget deficit to rise significantly. The only way to get the spending increase was to grow the economy fast enough to automatically generate the tax revenues, given the current tax rates. Coincidentally, Laffer forecasted that the economy would grow enough to do just that, while most other economists came up with much lower estimates. (See The Briefing Room, "How Forecasters Sometimes Impose Their Views on Policy.")

Does this mean Laffer lied about his numbers? No. As we mentioned, forecasting requires judgment. Typically, judgment has enough wiggle room to obtain a politically desirable forecast. Therefore, in the case of Laffer's forecast of GDP, reasonable judgment could have been used to achieve the politically desired number. (Because Laffer refused to show how he came up with his forecasts, however, many economists were skeptical. In actuality, however, Laffer's forecast was closer to being right than were the majority of economists' forecasts.)

5. *Emphasize the positive aspects of data.*   Politicians can put almost any type of spin on any data released by the government. For example, a politician whose constituents include union workers would complain about a high trade deficit, claiming that foreigners are stealing jobs from U.S. workers. A politician from the White House might applaud a trade deficit, saying it shows the robust economic growth of the

THE BRIEFING ROOM   How Forecasters Sometimes Impose Their Views on Policy

Because economic forecasts involve judgment, forecasters can impose their own views on political choices. For example, the Congressional Budget Office (CBO), a nonpartisan government agency that advises Congress about the economy, plays an important role in determining policy options, because paygo requires that Congress use CBO's forecasts in the budget process. The more revenue the CBO projects, given current tax rates, the more Congress can spend or the more it can cut taxes. Although the CBO's judgment is not supposed to be partisan to either Democrats or Republicans, it is judgment nonetheless. The CBO forecasts are primarily determined by economists, and the CBO has a panel of advisers comprised entirely of top U.S. economists.

As discussed in the text, most economists felt that, in the 1990s and early 2000s, the best policy was to maintain the surplus rather than spend it on programs or return it as tax cuts. Based on the advice of economic advisers, throughout the late 1990s, the CBO consistently used an estimate of the natural rate of unemployment that was above the actual rate of unemployment, and an estimate of the rate of growth that was below the

recent economic growth. Both estimates lowered the surplus available to use under paygo. Had the CBO used a lower natural rate and a higher growth rate, it would have increased the tax revenue available to Congress for increased spending and tax cuts.

Some argued that, through its forecast, the CBO imposed the economists' view of fiscal policy over the politicians' view, and it is hard to believe that that is not the case. Even if one agrees that, on economic matters, economists are much better decision makers than are politicians, it is legitimate to question whether economists should use their role within the technical estimation process to impose their views on the political process.

In 2001, the CBO had a change of heart and increased its forecast of economic growth, raising the projected surplus by $1.5 trillion, just about the amount of the tax cut that President Bush had proposed. This change played a role in getting President Bush's tax cut passed by Congress. (*The Wall Street Journal* described this change in the CBO's forecast as Bush's debt to economists at the CBO in the article "President Owes a Lot to Two Economists You Never Heard of" on February 27, 2001.)

United States compared with the rest of the world. A policy maker working for a think tank may point out that the increased trade deficit also means that there is an increase in capital inflows, which could be seen as positive or negative—either the United States is becoming too dependent on foreign saving, or foreign investors see the United States as a safe haven. They'd all be right. The lesson to learn from this is that, when interpreting economists' policy statements, it is important to understand where the economists are coming from (and quite often, whom they are working for).

POLICY PERSPECTIVE: SOCIAL SECURITY AND THE LONG-TERM BUDGET PROBLEM

One of the primary fiscal issues that policy makers will have to deal with in the future is that of Social Security. Social Security is a partially unfunded retirement system, which means that some current expenditures come out of current revenue. In a funded retirement system, all current payments go into a trust fund, from which future benefits are paid. In a partially unfunded system, the trust fund is insufficient to cover future benefit payments.

The Financial Problem

The financial problem of Social Security is that the Social Security system is a partially unfunded system and the ratio of workers to retirees is declining.

As long as a large number of current workers are contributing for each retiree, an unfunded system presents no financial problem; each individual worker will fund only a small fraction of a retiree's benefits. This was the situation when Social Security was started in 1935—there were about 30 workers for every retiree—but this ratio has changed. The first reason why it has changed is that people are living longer. In 1935, a 65-year-old could be expected to live another 12½ years; today, a 65-year-old is expected to live another 17½ years. A second reason it has changed is due to the "Baby Boom." Between 1945 and 1965 (the Baby-Boom years), the fertility rate (the number of children per woman of child-bearing age) was between 3.5 and 4.0. After 1965, the fertility rate dropped to 2.0. So, the United States experienced a population bulge between 1945 and 1965, which has been working its way through the economy. (Many other countries also experienced this pattern of population growth—see The Briefing Room, "Aging Populations Around the World.") The result is that the number of elderly in the United States is expected to double between 2000 and 2030, but the number of workers will increase at a much slower rate. Because of changing demographics, the number of workers per beneficiary has fallen over the years and is expected to continue to fall, as you can see in Exhibit 14–4. In about 2020, the number of workers per beneficiary will drop to below 2.

Congress recognized this problem in the 1980s and in 1983 passed an amendment to the Social Security Act that increased Social Security taxes by about 1.5 percentage points and started to build up a trust fund. The Act also decreased benefits by making them taxable and by increasing the retirement eligibility age to 67 by 2027. These changes improved the financial soundness of Social Security in the short term but did not solve the long-term problem.

These changes have also meant that currently Social Security tax revenues exceed benefit payments (the Social Security trust fund is growing). The trust fund is expected to continue growing until about 2015 or 2020, when many Baby Boomers begin to retire and start collecting. At that point, the tax revenues will fall short of the benefit payments and the trust fund will begin to shrink. Current expectations are that the trust fund will run out of funds by the year 2034, although these projections can change suddenly if economic growth should deviate from what is expected. After 2034, in order to continue paying the same benefits, the government will have to raise taxes, borrow, or print money (recall the three ways that government can finance expenditures).

Exhibit 14–4

Workers Per Social Security Beneficiary

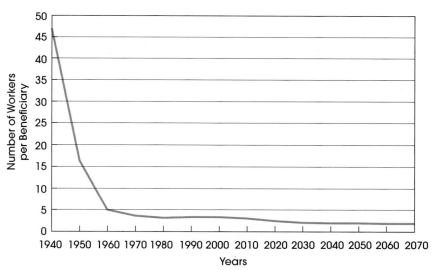

The number of workers per retiree has fallen over the years and is expected to continue to fall. This creates both a financial problem for the Social Security trust fund and a real problem for the economy. Source: The Social Security Administration (www.ssa.gov).

The United States is not the only country facing an aging population. Compared with other countries, the United States is projected to have proportionately fewer elderly. Japan and Italy, for example, are facing serious issues related to the number of people who will retire in the next few decades. The chart shows the percentage of the population age 65 and over for selected countries in 1998 and the percentage projected for 2010. Japan, Germany, and Italy top the list. The United States is actually close to the middle of the pack.

Source: *The Economist*, March 2, 2000.

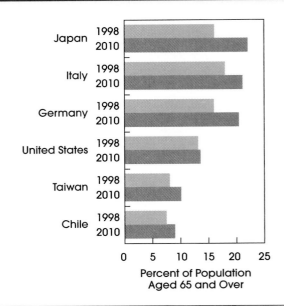

The Real Problem

The financial problem of Social Security is that, under current law, the Social Security trust fund will run out of money. Even if the financial problems are solved, a "real problem" would remain.

What do we mean by a *real problem*? As more and more Baby Boomers retire, the number of people retired will increase. However, given the current birth rate, the supply of labor will rise only slightly, which means that fewer people will be producing goods and more people will be consuming goods. This will be the case independently of how the financial problem is handled. The financial solution will not solve the real problem. That real problem can easily be seen with the AS/AD model. If potential output shifts to the left (production falls as Baby Boomers retire) and aggregate demand remains high, there will be a gap between real production and real expenditures at the given price level, as Exhibit 14–5 shows. The real solution must make the real quantity of aggregate supply equal to the real quantity of aggregate demand.

Financial solutions, such as trust funds, will not solve this problem. They do not increase potential income, or decrease demand in the future. Any real solution must do that. The real solution must eliminate the gap between real aggregate demand and potential output. One way to eliminate the gap is for government to implement policies to reduce aggregate demand in the future to match the reduction in potential output. Cutting benefits in the future would reduce demand and could be accomplished by the government raising the age at which people become eligible for Social Security benefits to 72 or higher, or prorating future Social Security benefits based on income. Either solution would reduce retirees' incomes, meaning that retirees would bear the brunt of the reduction in real expenditures; they would consume less, but the working population would maintain its consumption levels. Politically, neither Democrats nor Republicans have supported these solutions.

Another solution is to increase future taxes on the people who are still working. Thus, in 2030 government could raise income tax rates significantly to cut demand for

> The real problem of Social Security is that fewer people will be producing goods and more people will be consuming goods when the Baby Boomers retire. This will be the case independently of how the financial problem is handled.

> To solve the real problem of the Social Security trust fund, aggregate quantity supplied must be increased or aggregate quantity demanded must be decreased.

Exhibit 14-5

The Real Problem

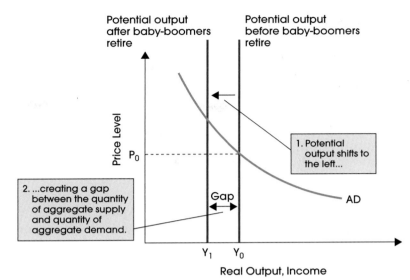

Potential output
after baby-boomers
retire

Potential output
before baby-boomers
retire

Price Level

P_0

1. Potential
output shifts to
the left...

2. ...creating a gap
between the quantity
of aggregate supply
and quantity of
aggregate demand.

Gap

AD

Y_1 Y_0

Real Output, Income

If potential output shifts to the left (production falls as Baby Boomers retire) and aggregate demand remains high, there will be a gap between potential output and aggregate demand: $Y_0 - Y_1$.

goods and services by workers. This would also reduce aggregate demand to match the reduction in potential output. In this case, working people (the younger generation—probably many of you) would bear the brunt of the reduction in real expenditures. Neither Democrats nor Republicans have supported this solution either.

A third solution is immigration, to allow a lot of young workers into the United States, which would increase the ratio of workers to retirees. This, in fact, is currently being done, with immigration at over 1 million persons per year in some years.

A fourth solution is luck—for productivity to grow more rapidly than wages, so that the reduction in output caused by the reduction in the supply of labor is offset by the increase in output caused by the increase in productivity. As you learned in Chapter 6, though, economists do not fully understand what makes productivity growth rise. So, although this solution seems to be the most appealing, all policy makers can do is hope that it happens.

If none of these solutions happens, there is a final solution—inflation will solve the problem. Prices will be pushed up, reducing people's real incomes and the quantity of aggregate demand. If people try to maintain their real incomes by asking for higher wages, inflation will rise by even more. Inflation is the default solution.

> If supply and demand are not adjusted through policy initiatives, prices will be pushed up, and inflation will solve the "real" Social Security problem.

Executive Summary

- Politicians often spin the numbers to make their policies look good. They do this by talking about levels (instead of percentages), front-loading spending increases and back-loading tax cuts, and taking credit for anything good; by assigning blame for anything bad; and by using forecasts that make their policies look good.

- The Social Security trust fund will run out by 2034 unless taxes are raised, benefits are reduced, or the retirement age is increased.

- The "real" Social Security problem is that there will be a smaller fraction of workers producing goods and a larger fraction of retirees demanding those goods once the Baby Boomers retire. Real expenditures will exceed potential output.

- Solving the "real" Social Security problem requires policies that lower consumption and raise output.

CONCLUSION

You should now have a rough idea of the factors that influence the U.S. government's decisions to spend and tax and how those decisions are constrained by politics and institutions. As you can see, economics, when applied to the real world, becomes messy, imprecise, and complicated. This doesn't mean that economics is not useful. It is just that the economist's viewpoint is only one input into the political process that drives fiscal policy. Once you get to this practical level, economics is no longer pure.

At the level of fiscal policy formulation, politicians generally believe that theoretically correct economics are too complicated to explain to the public. Instead, they use oversimplified economic explanations for their policies that seem reasonable, even though they and their economic advisers know that these explanations are, in some ways, wrong. Examples of these oversimplified arguments are that deficits are related to inflation, that large government spending programs will stabilize the economy, and that small tax cuts will create incentives for the economy to grow so fast that the tax cuts will raise tax revenues. We suspect that politicians know that, in their simple form, these arguments are wrong. They make them, nonetheless, because to offer the more complicated, "correct" argument would "lose" 95 percent of the population when the argument is reduced to a sound bite. In such cases, the "end justifying the means" argument often wins out. Such Machiavellian obfuscation would end only by making macroeconomics a required course for all—a pleasant dream for macroeconomics textbook writers, but one that is unlikely to come true.

KEY POINTS

- U.S. Government spending as a percent of GDP was below 10 percent before World War II and remained above 15 percent of GDP after World War II until the early 1990s, when it began to fall.

- The growing welfare state during the 1950s and 1960s coincided with the Keynesian view that fiscal policy was necessary to steer the economy away from large fluctuations in output.

- Fiscal policy fine-tuning fell out of favor in the 1970s after attempts to use it in the 1960s proved to be cumbersome and costly.

- The Budget Enforcement Act of 1990 marked the beginning of the downward trend in the U.S. government's involvement in the economy.

- Unlike most private firms, the U.S. government uses a cash accounting system and does not have separate current and capital accounts.

- The unified budget concept was introduced in 1969 to avoid the gimmickry of putting certain spending items "off-budget."

- The primary budget balance excludes interest payments on the debt.

- The real budget surplus rises with inflation. It equals the nominal surplus + inflation × debt. The real budget deficit falls with inflation. It equals the nominal deficit − inflation × debt.

- The equation for the government budget constraint is $G \leq T + \Delta B + \Delta M$. Total spending must be less than or equal to taxes plus newly issued bonds plus newly printed money.

- Taxes are the major source of revenue in the U.S. economy.

- The Treasury issues three types of marketable securities: bills, notes, and bonds.

- Seigniorage is not an important source of revenue in the United States, but it is sometimes used extensively in developing economies.

- Some economists believe that high marginal tax rates reduce incentives to produce.

- The government sometimes uses deficit financing to smooth the burden of taxes over time.

- Large government spending can lower private investment expenditures (crowding out).
- The budget process begins one and a half years before the beginning of the fiscal year. The President proposes a budget, Congress holds hearings, and laws are passed by Congress, which the President must sign.
- Politicians often "spin" the economic statistics to make their policies look good.
- The Social Security trust fund is expected to be depleted by 2034 unless taxes are increased, benefits are cut, or the retirement age is increased.

- The "real" Social Security problem is that there will be a smaller fraction of workers producing goods and a larger fraction of retirees demanding those goods once the Baby Boomers retire.
- Solutions to the real problem involve lowering consumption or raising output. A default solution is inflation.

KEY TERMS

Budget Enforcement Act of 1990 412
cash-flow basis 413
debt 412
discretionary spending 426
fine-tune 410

mandatory spending 426
marketable securities 418
nonmarketable securities 418
on-budget surplus 414
pay-as-you-go requirement 412

primary budget balance 415
real surplus 415
unified budget 413

QUESTIONS FOR THOUGHT AND REVIEW

1. What factors accounted for the growth in government spending as a percent of GDP during the past 70 years?
2. Why has government spending as a percent of GDP declined since 1990?
3. What caused policy makers and economists to become discouraged about using fiscal policy to fine-tune the economy?
4. Why does the fact that the government uses a cash accounting system matter for evaluating the budget balance?
5. Why was the concept of the unified budget balance introduced in the late 1960s?
6. Why is it important to look at the primary budget balance when evaluating the fiscal health of the economy?
7. What are the three sources of government revenue? Write the government budget constraint.
8. What are the three types of marketable debt that the Treasury issues and how do they differ from each other?
9. Why do some countries use money creation as a major source of revenue, while other countries use it very little?
10. Why do governments sometimes use debt financing instead of taxing during times of heavy spending, such as wartime?

11. Describe how tax policies affect potential output in addition to aggregate demand.
12. Are government deficits necessarily bad and government surpluses necessarily good?
13. Why is the distinction between discretionary and nondiscretionary spending meaningless?
14. Why does it take so long for a spending proposal to work its way through Congress?
15. What changes to the U.S. budget process in the early 1990s shifted the budget dynamics toward deficit reduction?
16. Why do politicians continue to talk about fiscal policy, even though their fiscal policy options are greatly constrained?
17. What can politicians do to make themselves and their policies look more economically important than they really are?
18. Why is the Social Security trust fund expected to be depleted by 2034?
19. What options do policy makers have to address the financial problem of the Social Security trust fund?
20. What is the "real" problem associated with Social Security? What policy options are there to address the "real" economic problem?

PROBLEMS AND EXERCISES

1. Suppose the debt is currently $4 trillion and the budget surplus is $200 billion. Calculate the real budget surplus if the inflation rate is
   a. 10 percent
   b. 4 percent
2. Suppose the debt is $9 trillion, the deficit is $100 billion, the interest rate on all current and past debt is 8 percent, and the inflation rate is 5 percent. Calculate the following:

   a. The real budget balance
   b. The primary budget balance
3. Suppose the debt is $7 trillion, the interest rate on all current and past debt is 8 percent, the inflation rate is 3 percent. The budget deficit is equal to the interest payments on the debt each year.
   a. How fast is the deficit growing each year?
   b. How fast is the real deficit growing each year?

15

One of the most useful roles an economist can perform is to remind policy-makers that the economy is complex.

—*Lee H. Hamilton*

The Art of Macroeconomic Policy

After reading this chapter you should be able to:

1. List the long-run and short-run models of the economy and explain their policy recommendations

2. Discuss how achieving each of the four goals of macroeconomic policy is an art, not a science

3. Explain how the policy implications of short-run and long-run models can conflict

4. State the likely causes of nine macroeconomic problems and recommend a solution for each

5. Describe the challenge facing U.S. policy makers today

John Galsworthy once said, "The beginnings and endings of all human undertakings are untidy." That's definitely true for books. Now that we're at the end of this book, we'll tie up loose ends and provide a summary of what we presented as neatly as possible. Maybe the best way to start is with the quotation that began the book: "Economics is a science of thinking in terms of models, joined to the art of choosing models which are relevant to the contemporary world." That quotation, by John M. Keynes, summarizes the overarching policy theme of this book: Macroeconomics *uses* models, but it is much more than models. Models are logical tautologies whose conclusions depend on their assumptions. As Stanford development economist Anne Krueger has said, "The art of good theory is to choose the simplest possible set of assumptions. . . . The real world never fits the theoretical models exactly. As such, application of theory requires judgment as to which model is appropriate and what, if any, modifications need to be made to bring the model into line with reality."

FOUR BROAD POLICY LESSONS

This book sought to (1) teach you the models, (2) convince you that you cannot use them in a mechanistic way, and (3) discuss the institutions that impact the application of the models. It emphasized four broad policy lessons:

1. *Models do not provide direct policy answers.* The economy is complex, and no model is going to give you mechanistic directions for policy. Economics is a way of thinking, developing models, choosing among them, and applying them. It provides a framework for policy, not policy answers.

2. *Macroeconomic policy inevitably involves trade-offs.* Economics is all about trade-offs. In macroeconomics, these trade-offs include the inflation–unemployment trade-off and the long-run–short-run trade-off. If an aggregate demand policy is too expansionary in the short run, it will lead to inflation in the long run. The term *too expansionary* is defined by potential output and the natural rate of unemployment. In the late 1990s, economists were not too good about predicting either potential output or inflation leading some economists to argue that a new economy had arrived. Most economists say, "Beware of the new economy." Although you can snitch a sandwich once in a while, free lunches are few and far between. Because politicians continually look for free lunches, the best policy is the cautious policy that emphasizes how scarce free lunches are.

3. *Growth requires getting institutions and incentives right.* When thinking about growth policy, it is best to develop institutions and incentives that promote growth, instead of implementing short-run policies. To have growth, an economy needs institutional stability as well as incentives to save, invest, research, and develop new technology. Markets are an institution historically associated with growth. They are a foundation of growth.

4. *Monetary and fiscal policy can help stabilize the economy.* Aggregate output fluctuates in the short run. Well-designed monetary and fiscal policy, built into the economic system and into expectations, can help limit these fluctuations. Because of political pressures, fiscal policy operates mainly through automatic stabilizers, while the Fed can quickly adjust monetary policy. Policy makers must take care to maintain the expectations of a noninflationary policy regime.

A REVIEW

With these four broad policy lessons in mind, let's review the chapters and consider how they fit into this book's grand design. This review will help you study for the final exam and will tie together any loose ends.

Introduction to Intermediate Macroeconomics (Part I)

Part I eased you into the course. It consisted of four chapters.

Chapter 1, "Introduction to Macroeconomics," provided the general argument and overview of the course. It introduced you to the terms and goals of macroeconomics and briefly discussed modeling and applying these models. Chapter 1 pointed out that applying models requires judgment about which model is appropriate to use. Remember the "two faces or urn" picture. You should now be better able to relate that picture to the second theme of this book—models cannot be used in a mechanistic way.

Chapter 2, "The Data of Macroeconomics," presented important terminology. You should remember GDP and its breakdown, know the distinction between real and nominal concepts (real is nominal adjusted for inflation), and have some sense of the dimensions of economic problems.

Chapter 3, "Grappling with Inflation, Unemployment, and Growth," introduced you to policy in a broad way, with a minimal amount of models and theory. It covered costs of both inflation and unemployment, how policy makers at times have faced a trade-off between the two, and some of the policy discussions that occur in macroeconomics.

Chapter 4, "Understanding Policy for the Long Run and the Short Run," served as a transition chapter from the general discussion of macroeconomic problems and issues to that of macroeconomic models. It introduced you to the production function, the circular flow, and the following basic identities of the macroeconomy:

$$AS = AD$$

$$Y = C + I + G + NX$$

$$S^p + S^f + S^g = I$$

In words, the first identity states that aggregate quantity supplied equals aggregate quantity demanded. The second identity is simply a restatement of the first. The third is that saving, which is divided into three components (private saving, foreign saving, and government saving), must equal investment in the long run. This identity tells us the same thing as the first identity but in a different form. Important policy insights come from these identities, although these insights are different depending on whether Y, output, is determined by technology and the supply of inputs, (as it is in the long run) or whether Y depends on expenditures (as it is in the short run). Chapter 4 ended Part I, and you were probably sitting back thinking that this course wouldn't be as bad as you had thought.

> $S^p + S^f + S^g = I$

Growth and the Long Run (Part II)

Part II was a rude awakening. This section of the book is where we switched gears and presented the formal models of macroeconomics. These models simplified relationships in the economy significantly to arrive at aggregate relationships and broad predictions. Models are usually the hardest part of a macroeconomics course.

Chapter 5, "Neoclassical Growth," presented a brief history of growth, showing the connection between markets and growth (caused by division of labor, specialization, and trade), and introduced you to the basic Solow growth model. The Solow growth model begins with the premise that supply creates its own demand, so demand is not an issue. Thus, the Solow growth model focuses exclusively on supply issues. The basic Solow growth model is shown in Exhibit 15–1.

> The Solow growth model focuses solely on supply issues.

As you can see, Exhibit 15–1 consists of an investment function (determined from the production function) and a balanced growth investment line. Equilibrium is where the balanced growth investment line and the investment function intersect. The model answers the question: Given an investment function, what level of capital will put the economy in a steady-state equilibrium? (You should be able to go through that model and show what happens if things change, such as the saving rate decreases or population growth increases.)

Notice how this model directs your thinking toward saving, investment, and capital. In terms of policies that followed from the model, we discussed incentive

Exhibit 15-1

**The Solow
Growth Model**

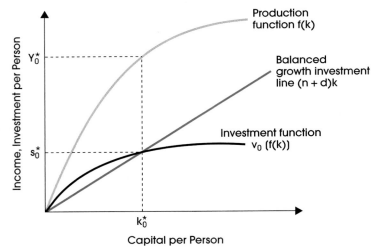

The Solow growth model is composed of a balanced growth investment line and an investment function. The steady-state equilibrium is the intersection of the two curves. At the steady state, the level of capital is k_0^* and investment (saving) is just enough to keep the capital stock growing at the same rate as the growth in the labor force. Additional workers are given the same amount of capital that existing workers have, keeping output per worker constant.

programs for saving and investment. If an economy needs to grow, it has to save and invest, but the models tell us that, even with saving and investment, an economy's growth rate has a limit. The Solow growth model predicted convergence of growth rates for countries with similar attributes, and a decrease in the growth rate over time for all countries as their economies converge to their steady states. You should remember these predictions, as they generally are the source of a question or two on the final exam.

Chapter 6, "Beyond the Solow Growth Model," discussed some of the problems with the basic Solow growth model's predictions; convergence has not taken place, and growth rates have increased, not decreased, over time. It then discussed how the basic Solow growth model can be adjusted to make it consistent with those predictions—allowing for differential qualities of labor and changing institutions. It was here that you saw how a model's predictions are based on its assumptions. If the assumptions are well chosen, the models are useful in shedding light on real-world problems. If the model doesn't seem to fit reality, you can change the assumptions and interpretations of the model. The questions then become the following: If the assumptions need significant modification, should we continue to use that model? Is the model highlighting the right issues? Some economists believe that this model is not highlighting the right issues and have proposed a new growth model that focuses on technology.

New growth theory emphasizes endogenous technology and increasing returns.

We then presented a model of new growth theory that focuses on endogenous technology and increasing returns. This model was presented informally (because the actual models get really complicated), but you should be aware of the general argument of new growth theory and its focus on vicious and virtuous circles, increasing returns, and technology. With endogenous technology, economic growth has no limit and can actually accelerate.

Next we looked at growth more broadly and presented the view of some economists that growth is a process beyond full understanding using simple models—that growth is better understood through case studies and history. Here again, you see this book's central theme: Here are the models. Know them—know them well—but after you know them, use them with common sense.

Chapter 6 concluded with a discussion of the policies that follow from new growth theory. Policies of new growth theory focus on technology and trade, while the basic Solow growth model's policies focus on saving and investment. It is useful to review these policies; they form the basis for current policy debates about economic growth (and they also form the basis for standard final exam questions).

Chapter 7, "Money, Inflation, and Exchange Rates in the Long Run," left the discussion of growth and presented another long-run model—the quantity theory of money model. While growth dealt with only the real economy, Chapter 7 integrated the price level and the nominal economy into a long-run model. To remember the quantity theory, think of the equation of exchange, $MV = PY$, with the direction of causation from money to prices. Output, Y, is determined outside the model, as is velocity, leaving a direct causal connection between money and prices.

> The quantity theory is the equation of exchange, $MV = PY$, read from left to right, assuming velocity is constant and real output is determined outside the model.

The quantity theory model has direct policy relevance. It tells us that the real economy is largely governed by the real forces of production and that the price level is largely governed by the money supply. Inflation occurs only if the money supply is increasing.

The second part of Chapter 7 integrated the quantity theory of money into the international economy, introducing exchange rates and balance of payments issues. A key concept in this part was the real exchange rate, which we used in conjunction with purchasing power parity to determine whether exchange rates are over- or undervalued. Again, the focus of the long-run model is on real forces. Real forces (technology and the factors of production) control the real economy. Monetary forces (demand) influence the price level and nominal exchange rate.

Chapter 7 concluded the presentation of long-run models. From these models, you should have gotten a van de Rohe (a twentieth-century nihilist architect) sense of policy—less is more. Long-run models suggest that policy focus on supply issues rather than on demand. It was these long-run models and the vision underlying them that led classical economists to a laissez-faire policy.

Fluctuations and the Short Run (Part III)

Part III presented a set of models with quite different policy conclusions. These short-run models focused on demand-based policies. The models presented assume that demand creates its own supply.

Chapter 8, "The Determination of Output in the Short Run," introduced you to the IS/LM model and the multiplier. The downward sloping IS curve is the investment/savings (goods market) equilibrium curve. It shows the combinations of real interest rates and incomes where expenditures equal production—or where the goods market is in equilibrium. The upward-sloping LM curve is the liquidity/money (supply and demand for money) equilibrium curve. It shows the combinations of real interest rates and incomes where the quantity of money supplied equals the quantity of money demanded. The IS/LM model is

> The IS/LM model is the basic model of short-run macroeconomic policy.

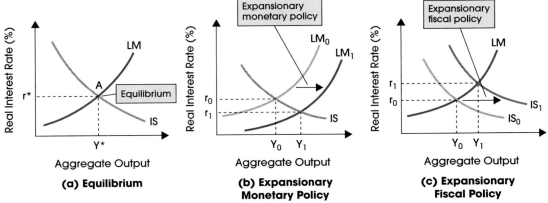

(a) Equilibrium

(b) Expansionary Monetary Policy

(c) Expansionary Fiscal Policy

Exhibit 15-2

Equilibrium in the IS/LM Model

The IS/LM model tells us the level of income and interest rate at which both the goods and money markets are in equilibrium. Equilibrium occurs where the IS and LM curves intersect. A shift in the LM curve to the right increases output and lowers the interest rate. A shift in the IS curve to the right raises output and the interest rate.

shown in Exhibit 15–2(a). Equilibrium occurs where the IS curve intersects the LM curve (point A).

Chapter 8 also went through the various determinants of the shapes of the two curves, and then discussed monetary policy and fiscal policy. Expansionary monetary policy shifts the LM curve out, as in Exhibit 15–2(b), lowering interest rates and raising income. Expansionary fiscal policy shifts the IS curve out, as in Exhibit 15–2(c), raising interest rates and raising income. These are key results and inevitably show up on final exams.

Monetary policy shifts the LM curve; fiscal policy shifts the IS curve.

Chapter 9, "Policy Analysis with the IS/LM Model," continued the discussion of monetary and fiscal policy within the IS/LM model. The first half of the chapter gave you a better sense of the model by considering some examples of fiscal and monetary policies. The second half covered the interpretative and implementation problems of the IS/LM model. Short-run policy is much more complicated than IS/LM analysis makes it look.

The IS/LM/BP model is the basic model of short-run, open-economy macroeconomics.

Chapter 10, "Short-Run Fluctuations in an Open Economy," brought the international sector into the IS/LM model by adding the balance of payments (BP) curve. The upward-sloping BP curve is the combination of interest rates and income levels at which the balance of payments is in equilibrium. The slope of the BP curve depends on the degree to which trade and capital flows respond to changes in income and interest rates. Full internal and external equilibrium occurs where all three curves intersect, such as at point A in Exhibit 15–3(a). If a country has flexible exchange rates, the BP curve shifts to the IS/LM equilibrium, and the external equilibrium always shifts to the internal equilibrium (where IS = LM).

If a country has fixed exchange rates, internal and external equilibrium can differ, which leaves a government with a number of policy options. A government might finance excess supply or demand for its currency by buying or selling its currency. Such transactions appear on the official reserve transactions account of its balance of payments account. A country that buys and sells its currency can maintain an internal equilibrium that is different from its external equilibrium. If a government cannot finance a balance of payments deficit (excess supply of its currency), it must undertake other policies. One possibility is to shift the BP curve

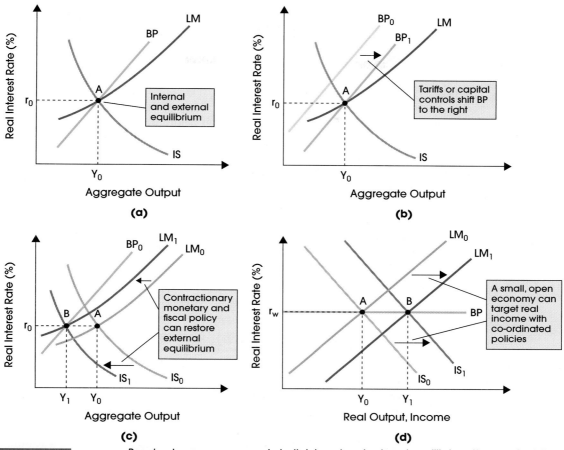

Exhibit 15-3

The BP Curve and Achieving External Balance

Panel a shows an economy in both internal and external equilibrium. If a country follows policies that take it off its balance of payments curve (point *A* in *panel b*), it can institute policies, such as tariffs or capital controls or launching export drives, that directly shift the balance-of-payments constraint from BP_0 to BP_1 as *panel b* shows. Alternatively, it can use monetary and fiscal policies to shift the IS and LM curves back to intersect on the balance-of-payments curve, as *panel c* shows. A small open economy has a limited number of tools with which to expand or contract output. *Panel d* shows that small countries will achieve real output changes with shifts in both IS and LM curves; sterilization is impossible.

through policies such as tariffs and capital controls, to the domestic IS/LM equilibrium, as shown in Exhibit 15–3(b) with the shift from BP_0 to BP_1. Alternatively, a government can undertake contractionary policies to shift the IS/LM equilibrium to the BP curve, as shown in Exhibit 15–3(c) with the shifts from LM_0 to LM_1 and IS_0 to IS_1. Because of expectations, the BP curve can shift suddenly, as happened in some Asian countries in the late 1990s, creating the need for sudden, major policy changes in those countries.

In a small open economy (Mundell Flemming model) the BP curve is horizontal and policy options are more limited.

If the economy is a small open economy, the BP curve is perfectly flat, as Exhibit 15–3(d) shows. In this case, the domestic interest rate must equal the world interest rate, and monetary and fiscal policy—internal balance—must adjust to that reality. In a small open economy monetary and fiscal policy are interdependent and cannot be seen as independent tools: Sterilization is impossible.

Before moving on to the summary of Chapter 11, let's compare the assumptions and conclusions of the short-run IS/LM model and the long-run models. In the long run, supply dominates. All policies designed to change equilibrium center on supply issues. In these long-run models, demand adjusts to supply. Short-run models, however, are dominated by demand issues. Supply adjusts to demand. The reason for the difference is the assumption of flexible prices in the long-run model and fixed prices in the short-run model.

Chapter 11, "Aggregate Supply and Aggregate Demand," summed up the short-run models and integrated them with the long-run model. The AS/AD model is made up of an AD curve and an AS curve, with potential output serving as a long-run anchor. The AD curve shows the combinations of price levels and income levels at which both the goods market (the IS curve) and the money market (the LM curve) are in equilibrium. Chapter 11 showed how IS/LM analysis is modified by an upward-sloping AS curve. The AD curve is derived from the IS/LM model by varying the price level. The AS curve is a curve that shows how the price level responds to changes in aggregate demand. Exhibit 15–4(a) shows short-run AS/AD equilibrium. Exhibit 15–4(b and d) shows the effect of an expansion in autonomous expenditures in both the IS/LM model and the AS/AD model. The expansion in spending shifts both the AD and IS curves out. (The AD curve shifts out to point B by the same distance as the new IS/LM real-income equilibrium.) In the AS/AD model, part of the effect is to increase the price level, which means the equilibrium is point C. Assuming no international effect, the rise in the price level causes the real money supply to decrease and the LM curve to shift back so that it intersects the IS curve at point C. Expansionary fiscal policy leads to a higher price level, higher interest rate and lower equilibrium income than would have been the case if the price level were fixed.

Exhibit 15–4(c) shows the long run adjustment. Because the long run is determined by potential output, we add potential output to the short run AS/AD model to consider long-run equilibrium. Because potential output is independent of the price level, it is represented in the AS/AD model as a vertical line at potential output.

Potential output provides a long-run anchor for real output in the economy. If, in the short-run, the equilibrium (point B) differs from the long-run equilibrium (point C), the economy will be pulled toward a long-run equilibrium through an adjustment that involves changing expectations about the price level and changing wages.

The important factor to remember is that, along the aggregate supply curve, AS_0, workers believe the price level is P_0. Long-run equilibrium requires these expectations to be correct, so AS_0 is only in long-run equilibrium at point A. At point B, the price level is actually P_1, so the economy is not in long-run equilibrium.

Because they misperceive the actual price level, workers are working more than they would work if they realized the true price level and their true real wages. Once workers realize the actual price level, they will require wage increases. These wage increases caused by changes in price-level expectations will shift the AS curve up. The AS curve will continue shifting up until the economy is in both long-run equilibrium and short-run equilibrium at point C.

The policies based on the AS/AD model are similar to those of the IS/LM model but less effective in changing real income in the short run, and ineffective in changing real income in the long run because real output growth gravitates to potential output.

Chapter 12, "Microfoundations of Consumption and Investment," went more deeply into consumption and investment—two components of aggregate demand—and provided a brief introduction into the microeconomic foundations of each. It showed how to modify the short-run model to take into account some of the intertemporal choices that individuals and firms make. Consumption depends

The AS/AD model is an extension of the IS/LM model; the AD curve is derived from the IS/LM model.

The long-run equilibrium in the AS/AD model requires the price level to vary to bring the quantity of aggregate demand into equilibrium with the quantity of aggregate supply.

The degree to which the AS curve shifts depends on how quickly expectations adjust to actual conditions and to institutional constraints on raising wages and prices.

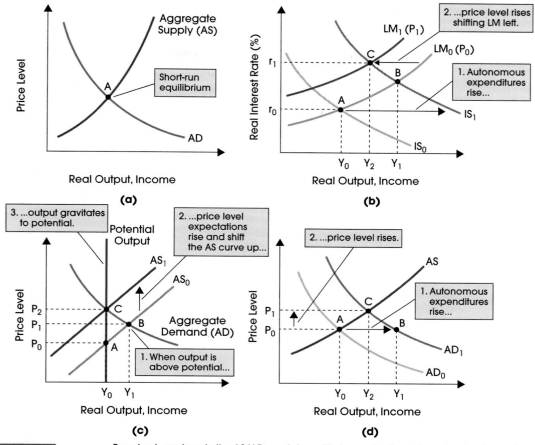

Exhibit 15-4

The AS/AD Model

Panel a shows how in the AS/AD model, equilibrium output and the price level are where the AS and AD curves intersect. *Panels b* and *d* show how the AS/AD model modifies the results of expansionary fiscal policy in the IS/LM model. Expansionary fiscal policy shifts the IS and AD curves to the right. The price level rises, which, through the interest rate effect, shifts the LM curve back, lowering real output. *Panel c* shows how potential output is an anchor for the economy. An economy that is above potential output, such as point *B*, will be pulled back to potential output. This occurs as workers' expectations of the price level increase, shifting the AS curve up until real output returns to potential.

on future income and accumulated wealth, as well as current disposable income. Investment depends on interest rates and expected future profits. Chapter 12 also considered how firms finance investment expenditures by issuing bonds or selling stock.

As a final note to Parts II and III, notice that the discussion of the models in these parts covered the same material as in Part I, but it did so in a more structured way. The discussion in Parts II and III was designed to introduce you to the economist's approach of seeing and understanding the problems of inflation, unemployment, business cycles, and growth within a framework of simple models. These models provide structure to help you understand complex economic reality.

The Nuts and Bolts of Macroeconomic Policy (Part IV)

The chapters in Part IV were designed to introduce you to the institutions in which policy is made and thereby integrated the models into real-world policy discussions. Chapter 13, "The Nuts and Bolts of Monetary Policy," described the Federal

Reserve System, the institution that determines and executes U.S. monetary policy and is responsible for maintaining financial stability. The Fed is charged with maintaining both high employment and price stability—two often-conflicting goals.

Chapter 13 also presented the debate about whether the Fed should follow policy rules or its own discretion. Long-run models recommend that the Fed use monetary rules; short-run models suggest that the Fed needs to maintain some discretion to respond to policy problems. In recent years, the Fed has combined these two views into "feedback rules," which are rules with built-in reactions to the economy. A feedback rule includes, as part of the rule, many of the discretionary policies that previously would have been called *discretionary policy*. A feedback rule, therefore, is a type of predetermined discretion.

Because feedback rules include predetermined discretion, the Fed exercises far less discretion, and people can know what the Fed's reaction to a problem will be. Following a specified feedback rule is called a *policy regime*. The recent Fed policy regime can be described by the Taylor rule, a rule that relates the fed funds rate to the Fed's ultimate targets of inflation and potential output. The Taylor rule looks like this:

> *fed funds rate = 2 + current inflation*
> *+ .5 × (actual inflation less desired inflation)*
> *+ .5 × (percent deviation of aggregate output from potential).*

You should remember the Taylor rule, because it is useful when considering Fed actions and it is often addressed on exams.

Chapter 14, "The Nuts and Bolts of Fiscal Policy," gave you a sense of how fiscal policy works, and why politics rather than economics often guides fiscal policy decisions. It described the U.S. federal government's budget process and the political pressures that guide fiscal policy. It also discussed how government finances expenditures—printing money, taxes, or borrowing—and how government manages the debt.

Summary Tables of Long-Run and Short-Run Models

Tables 15–1 and 15–2 (originally presented in Chapters 7 and 11) summarize the models in the text, along with their key assumptions, predictions, and policy implications. Table 15–1 summarizes the long-run macroeconomic models and theories, and Table 15–2 summarizes the short-run macroeconomic models and theories. The reason that economists separate the long run from the short run is that the economy is assumed to work in fundamentally different ways in each run. In the long run, prices tend toward their market-clearing equilibrium. In the short run, prices and wages tend to be sticky.

The Conflicts Between the Long Run and the Short Run

As you can see from Tables 15–1 and 15–2 the conclusions of different models often conflict. Policy, then, involves deciding which model to use. An important consideration for policy makers in making that decision concerns the immediacy of the problem—does the problem require a short-run policy solution or can it wait for a long-term solution? In reality, of course, some countries face problems that require both, and they must decide which of the often-conflicting policies to pursue.

The Fed uses feedback rules, which are rules with built-in reactions to problems.

Recent Fed policy can be described by the Taylor rule.

Politics, rather than economics, often guides fiscal policy decisions.

The long-term models often lead to different policy prescriptions than do the short-term models.

Table 15-1
Summary of the Long-Run Models

	Key Assumptions	Key Predictions	Key Policy Implications
Solow Growth Model Long-run, steady-state model that focuses on the role of saving and investment in the growth process	• Supply is determined by the factors of production. • Supply creates its own demand. • Technology is exogenous to the model. • Diminishing marginal product • Constant returns to scale	• The economy will grow at the rate the population grows. • Per capita growth will be zero. • Growth rates among countries will converge.	• Government can increase growth in the intermediate run by implementing policies to increase saving and investment. Nothing can be done to affect per capita growth in the long run—the economy always returns to its steady-state growth path.
New Growth Theory Long-run model that focuses on technological advance and trade in the growth process	• Supply creates its own demand. • Technology is affected by policy. • Increasing returns to scale	• Policies can increase per capita growth. • Growth engenders more growth. • Growth rates will accelerate over time. • Rich countries' and poor countries' incomes may not converge.	• Government can increase growth by (1) implementing policies that encourage technological development, (2) reducing protectionism, (3) lowering tax rates, (4) privatizing activities, (5) industrial policy.
Quantity Theory Long-run model of inflation. Real output is determined by aggregate supply, and the price level is determined by aggregate demand—or the quantity of money.	• Based on the equation of exchange: $MV = PY$ • Real output is determined by the factors of production. • Velocity of money is constant. • Direction of causation goes from money to prices.	• Inflation will rise by the same percentage as the rise in the money supply.	• To control inflation, control the growth of the money supply. • Central banks should be independent of politics.
Purchasing-Power Parity Long-run model of exchange rates	• The law of one price holds for internationally traded goods.	• The real exchange rate equals 1. • In the long run, nominal exchange rates are determined by inflation differentials.	• In the long run, the government can control the nominal exchange rate by controlling only the inflation rate.

Table 15-2

Summary of the Short-Run Models

Model and Brief Summary	Key Assumptions	Key Predictions	Key Policy Implications
IS/LM A short-run model of real output. Real output is determined by the level of expenditures (aggregate demand). The two components are the IS curve (goods market equilibrium) and the LM curve (money market equilibrium).	• The price level is fixed. • Equilibrium in the goods market is determined by aggregate expenditures. • Equilibrium in the money market is determined by the demand and supply of money.	• Fiscal policy and monetary policy can directly affect real output. • Expansionary fiscal policy leads to higher interest rates and higher real output. • Expansionary monetary policy leads to lower interest rates and higher real output. • Crowding out can limit the effectiveness of fiscal policy. • A liquidity trap can limit the effectiveness of monetary policy.	• Government can smooth business cycles by using monetary and fiscal policy.
IS/LM/BP (Large Country) A short-run model of real output that includes the international sector. The upward-sloping BP curve shows where the balance of payments is zero.	• The price level is fixed. • Forces constantly push the economy toward IS/LM equilibrium and balance of payments equilibrium.	• If a country has flexible exchange rates, the exchange rate adjusts to domestic IS/LM equilibrium. • A country with fixed exchange rates may have difficulty achieving its domestic goals.	• If exchange rates are flexible, government need not worry about maintaining balance of payments equilibrium. It can focus on domestic goals. • Government can adjust exchange rates, import controls, export drives, and capital controls to achieve domestic goals.
Mundell-Fleming model An IS/LM/BP model for a small open economy. The BP curve is horizontal at the world interest rate.	• The price level is fixed. • Capital will flow in and out of a country to keep domestic interest rates at the world interest rate.	• If exchange rates are fixed, expansionary fiscal policy must be accompanied by expansionary monetary policy. • If exchange rates are fixed, expansionary monetary policy must be accompanied by expansionary fiscal policy. • If exchange rates are flexible, expansionary fiscal policy can affect the economy only if monetary policy is also expansionary.	• Government must accept the world interest rate. • To increase output, an economy should run expansionary fiscal and monetary policies.
AS/AD model A model that integrates the long run and the short run. The AD curve is downward sloping. The AS model determines how changes in aggregate expenditures are split between changes in output and the price level.	• Prices are flexible. • A fall in the price level leads to higher aggregate demand because of the international and interest rate effects. • The more people expect a change in aggregate demand, the less that change will affect real output.	• Increases in aggregate demand lead to increases in real output. • Adverse aggregate supply shocks lead to lower output and higher prices. • Changes in aggregate demand that are perfectly anticipated have a smaller impact on real output and a larger impact in the price level compared to when the changes are anticipated.	• When the economy is below potential output, it should run expansionary monetary or fiscal policy to increase real output. • When the economy is above potential output, it should run contractionary monetary or fiscal policy to reduce real output and avoid inflation. • When the economy is at potential output, policy should be neutral.

Consider an economy in recession that also faces a problem of low long-term growth. Should government implement policies to encourage saving or implement policies to encourage spending? The short-run and long-run models come to different conclusions.

To increase growth (at least in the intermediate run), the Solow growth model recommends policies that encourage saving and investment. These policies include tax incentives for investment and incentives for saving, such as developing 401(k) plans. Investment tax credits (first instituted during the Kennedy Administration) are one example. New growth theories expand the policies to include reducing trade restrictions and adopting policies that encourage technological change, such as maintaining strong intellectual property rights and offering patents. Long-run models downplay fluctuations because, in the long run, supply creates its own demand. These models state "Forget the short run; eventually, the economy will reach potential output."

The short-run model focuses on keeping the economy at potential output. This means using expansionary fiscal and monetary policies that increase consumption and reduce saving during recessions, which is a Keynesian short-run growth strategy. By maintaining high demand, firms will keep producing, and the economy will grow one period at a time. Because the long run is an ongoing sequence of short runs, the economy that grows in the short run will also grow in the long run.

This focus on demand contradicts the long-run prescription for growth. According to the long-run model, high consumption means low saving, and low saving will lead to lower growth. In addition, financing expansionary fiscal policy can lead to higher interest rates and can crowd out private investment. Expansionary monetary policy can lead to inflation, a riskier business environment, and lower investment expenditures, which, according to the long-run model, tend to lower long-term growth. Thus, the trade-off—should policy makers use a long-term growth strategy or short-term growth strategy, or some combination of the two? There is no simple answer.

THE GOALS OF POLICY

Real-world economic problems are much more complex than the models portray. But this does not mean that policy makers should throw up their hands and do nothing. They don't have that luxury. The choice is not between policy and no policy. Even benign neglect is a type of policy.

Perhaps, one day, the policy science of economics will progress to the point that policymaking will be formulaic. In the meantime, policy makers must combine the science of economics with the art of policymaking in order to formulate policy.

To illustrate what we mean, let's consider the four normative goals of macroeconomic policy that are stated in Chapter 1: high growth, low inflation, low unemployment, and smooth growth of output. For each goal, we will briefly review why that goal is important and then explain why achieving that goal requires more than just applying economic models—it requires the art of macroeconomic policymaking.

High Growth

Sustained, high economic growth is in some ways probably the most important of the goals. In the long run, growth determines the wealth of nations. Without growth, standards of living will stagnate or fall. Economic growth expands the economic pie and, by doing so, reduces conflicts. When the pie is fixed in size, people battle over how to share it. When the pie expands, people still battle over the shares of the growing pie, but these battles are less important, because everyone can still end up with more income over time. Macroeconomic theory points to three types of policies to encourage high growth:

1. Policies that maintain stable political, social, and market environments, which give individuals the freedom to operate
2. Policies that save and invest to build up the capital stock
3. Policies that educate the people in a society.

Investment tax credits, tax incentives for individual retirement accounts, or a tax on consumption can be used to encourage saving. These are all standard policies that have been enacted at various times to encourage growth. These policies, however, do not affect the overall growth rate in the Solow growth model and are seen as making minor contributions to growth compared with the development of markets and the creation of institutions to foster technological progress.

When we talk about *developing markets* or *institutions*, we are usually talking about large wholesale changes in the economy, and this is where the application of economic theory becomes an art. Consider the problem the former Soviet-bloc countries faced when they moved from socialism to capitalism. Although economic theory pointed to the types of institutions that those countries should develop to grow (for example, private ownership of business), it gave very little guidance about how to develop those institutions. Some countries, such as Poland, have been successful—its economy grew throughout the 1990s. Other countries, such as Russia, have struggled to make the transition to a market economy. Russia's per capita income fell throughout most of the 1990s.

Low Inflation

Inflation is costly to society because it reduces the information prices provide, diverts resources to avoid the effects of inflation, and erodes people's confidence in their government and institutions. The long-run model of inflation states that, to control inflation, government must control the growth rate of the money supply. However, the fact that experiences of inflation vary widely across countries and over time indicates that this simple policy prescription is sometimes difficult to implement.

Again, the problems are institutional. Some developing countries have poor tax-collection institutions and no market to finance deficit spending. They have to finance spending by printing money and monetizing the debt in order to maintain basic government services (such as law enforcement) that are necessary for a market to function. These countries do so, knowing that such "remedies" will lead to inflation. For these countries, it's better to keep their economies going and risk inflation than risk a total collapse of their economies.

For the United States, such issues are not relevant. The United States has a well-developed market for government bonds and a well-established tax structure to finance spending. These institutions, along with the Fed's independence from political pressure, are important to understanding why the United States has been able to keep inflation relatively low.

The United States uses monetary policy to stabilize its economy in the short run. Given that the U.S. economy is dominated by short-run, quantity-adjusting goods markets, the Fed can increase output in the short run by increasing the money supply. When the economy slows below potential or enters a recession, the Fed can use monetary policy to expand output.

The art of monetary policy involves using expansionary monetary policy to offset recessions while, simultaneously, keeping inflation low. If monetary policy repeatedly expands the economy beyond potential, however, people will come to expect the resulting inflation, and short-run stabilization policy will turn into a long-run inflation problem. These difficulties are compounded by the fact that economists don't know precisely where the economy's potential lies.

The art of monetary policy involves using expansionary monetary policy to offset recessions while simultaneously keeping inflation low.

Low Unemployment

There are two types of unemployment problems: long-run unemployment and short-run unemployment. The long-run unemployment problem focuses on the natural rate of unemployment. Unions, minimum wage laws, search costs, and efficiency wages are all explanations for why unemployment exists in economies during normal times. The short-run unemployment problem (cyclical unemployment) focuses on insufficient aggregate demand. Both types of unemployment are costly in terms of lost income and self-esteem, but each type of unemployment has a different economic cost and a different set of policies to deal with it.

The long-run unemployment problem focuses on the natural rate of unemployment; the short-run unemployment problem focuses on insufficient aggregate demand.

For the natural rate, the issue is whether unemployment can be reduced by modifying institutions. Institutional arrangements, such as welfare and unemployment insurance programs and laws regulating firing in Europe, reduce incentives for workers and firms to find good job matches. Eliminating these policies and programs have costs of their own. Economic theory tells us that eliminating these programs will lower the natural rate of unemployment. Unfortunately, the theory provides very little guidance on whether the benefit of lower unemployment is worth the cost of eliminating the social safety nets and regulations that doing so will entail. Policy makers must use art as well as theory when addressing these issues.

Eliminating cyclical unemployment is also an art. Because the precise natural rate of unemployment is unknown, it is difficult to determine whether or not the unemployment in an economy is cyclical. Most economists, for example, believe the current 9 percent unemployment rate in Europe is not cyclical, while a portion of the 4.7 percent unemployment rate in Japan *is* cyclical. If policy makers use aggregate demand polices to lower unemployment when the economy is already at the natural rate, they risk starting an inflationary spiral.

The difficulty of identifying cyclical unemployment is made clear by considering the United States in the 1990s. In the mid-1990s, most economists believed that the natural unemployment rate was about 6 percent. However, the unemployment rate fell below 6 percent while inflation was falling. Economists revised their estimates to 5 percent. The unemployment rate fell below 5 percent, and inflation continued to fall. In 2000, the unemployment rate fell under 4 percent and inflation did not rise significantly.

Smooth Growth of Output

Recessions result in idle factors of production. However, expansions above potential output eventually result in inflation. For these reasons, policy makers try to avoid fluctuations in output. What do the models suggest? Short-run IS/LM and AS/AD models view the fluctuations as problems that can be remedied by monetary and fiscal policies.

Can government, given political realities, implement these policies effectively? Almost all economists believe that the economy cannot be too finely tuned. Given the political process and the complicated nature of the economy, the government's ability to institute policies that will offset business cycles is limited. It takes a long time for the government to change spending or taxes. By the time policy is enacted, it may be the wrong policy. We saw this with the Kennedy-Johnson tax cuts.

Further, policies must interact with expectations. Expectations can either render policies almost useless, as was the case with the income tax surcharge in the Johnson Administration (it was seen as temporary), or render policies unnecessary. In anticipation of expansionary policy, people may begin to spend more and pull an economy out of recession as a result. Expectations of policy can also be destabilizing by either translating active government policy into larger fluctuations or by creating the fluctuations. If firms expect government to increase spending during a recession, when demand begins to fall, these firms won't lower their prices, and inventories will rise. So, policy makers must take expectations into account, but expectations cannot be measured and are difficult to predict. That is why, in the 1990s, policy makers repeatedly talked about credible, systematic policies. These policy makers were acknowledging the importance of expectations and building them into their policies.

The majority of economists believe that government policies, especially automatic stabilizers, have helped to mute fluctuations in the economy. Those who hold this view point to the decline in the number and severity of fluctuations since 1945, although precisely how significant this decline is and what role government macroeconomic policies played in the decline are in dispute. Most economists accept the argument that automatic stabilizers have reduced fluctuations. Whether discretionary monetary—and especially fiscal—policies have helped to stabilize the economy in the short run is much more controversial.

Some economists argue that fluctuations are not problems at all. These economists—called *real business-cycle economists*—believe that fluctuations in output are, in large part, the efficient response to changes in technology or tastes. Policies to smooth out these fluctuations, then, will only worsen the situation.

International Goals Consistent with Domestic Goals

International economic goals are the hardest to achieve, and for this reason, they require the most *art* of any of the policies we have discussed. This is partly because, generally, domestic goals dominate economic policy. But in some countries, especially small open economies, international goals are equally, or sometimes more, important.

If an economy is in recession, should it use expansionary policy to increase income, even if doing so means accepting a higher trade deficit or a weaker currency? When an economy is booming and has a growing trade deficit, should it use contractionary policy just to deal with the trade deficit? Should a country use contractionary monetary policy to encourage a strong currency and risk a rising trade deficit, or should it use expansionary monetary policy to encourage a weak currency and risk rising inflation? Each question has its own tradeoffs.

> Almost all economists believe that the real-world economy cannot be too finely tuned.

> Real business-cycle economists believe that output fluctuations are the efficient response to changes in technology or tastes and, as a result, do not require government actions.

There is also the issue of what type of exchange-rate regime to adopt. Having flexible exchange rates makes meeting domestic goals easy; policy makers can simply concentrate on domestic goals and the exchange rate will fluctuate to achieve external balance. Currency fluctuations, however, can have real effects on an economy's trade.

Fixed exchange rates limit a country's ability to achieve domestic goals. For example, expansionary fiscal policy to raise domestic output requires either large outflows of foreign currency or contractionary monetary policy. Alternatively, countries can institute import restrictions or capital controls, both of which have problems of their own.

In small open economies, policy makers lose the ability to target interest rates; these economies must accept the world interest rate. For policy, this means that, when exchange rates are fixed, expansionary fiscal policy will be accompanied by an expansion of the money supply as capital floods a country. Similarly, domestic monetary policy used alone becomes ineffective. If exchange rates are flexible and prices are constant, fiscal policy becomes ineffective and expansionary monetary policy is accompanied by a rise in net exports.

In the long run, trade must balance, but, for large countries such as the United States, that period can be a very long time, as evidenced by the U.S. trade deficit that capital markets have been willing to finance for decades. In the interim, both trade deficits and surpluses have advantages and disadvantages. Trade deficits allow a country to consume more than it produces. In many ways, this is desirable; the downside is that countries must finance their trade deficits by selling their assets—either financial or real. As foreigners own more and more assets, a country's firms and citizens will pay out more and more domestic profits and interest without receiving real goods in return. At some point, the country will have to pay back that foreign debt, and when that happens, the country will have to consume less than it produces.

Trade deficits can create short-term problems as well. In 2000, the U.S. trade deficit equaled 3 percent of its GDP, a record high. The U.S. relies heavily on foreign investors to finance that deficit, and if foreign investors suddenly begin to doubt the United States' ability to pay back the foreign debt, they will stop lending, causing the dollar to depreciate and inflation to rise. If policy makers are concerned with the external balance of the economy, they can contract monetary policy and raise interest rates, but this would cause the economy to slow and maybe even enter a recession. The advantage of trade surpluses is that a country is not accumulating foreign debt, but, at the same time, it means that the country is not consuming everything it produces.

The global nature of modern trade requires significant policy coordination among countries and a number of institutions (G-7, the World Bank, the International Monetary Fund) to help bring about that coordination. Domestic politics and the lack of any international control over individual countries' policies makes international coordination difficult.

Conventional Wisdom

Because of conflicting goals and models, economists often disagree about which particular policy to follow in a particular situation. However, they also agree about a wide variety of policies. We call points of agreement *conventional wisdom*. This conventional wisdom does not follow directly from models, but from a combination of models and a knowledge of how policy has worked in the past.

Flexible exchange rates make meeting domestic goals easy; fixed exchange rates limit a country's ability to achieve domestic goals.

In small open economies, policy makers lose the ability to target interest rates.

Table 15-3

Summary of Conventional Wisdom on the Nine Main Macroeconomic Problems

Economic Problem	Likely Cause	Solution
Hyperinflation	• High money growth	• Develop institutions that prevent the central bank from creating high money growth.
Major recession	• Insufficient aggregate demand and possibly a breakdown in institutions	• Use expansionary monetary and fiscal policy; repair institutions.
Minor recession	• Insufficient aggregate demand	• Use expansionary monetary policy to stimulate investment expenditures and aggregate output.
Negative supply shock	• Raw material price, such as for oil, rises suddenly	• Walk a fine line, not letting the supply shock lead to inflationary expectations, but preventing real output from falling too much, with slight, expansionary, short-run policy.
Large trade deficit	• Domestic economy grows faster than foreign economies	• Slow the domestic economy with contractionary monetary policy or depreciate the domestic currency and encourage foreign countries to stimulate their growth.
Exchange rate too low	• Insufficient demand for the domestic currency	• The central bank can buy domestic currency using foreign reserves.
Simultaneous inflation and unemployment	• An adverse supply shock	• The economy must choose one problem to fight. Either reduce unemployment with expansionary policy or reduce inflation with contractionary policy.
Low growth	• Low saving and investment, improper incentives for technological growth	• Change institutions to foster technological innovation. Create tax incentives to save and invest (although this is unlikely to affect the growth rate).
Persistently high unemployment	• Disincentives or institutional barriers to firms and workers finding good employment matches	• Reduce the disincentives and institutional barriers to employment matches.

Table 15–3 summarizes our view of economists' conventional wisdom about various economic problems.

You will notice that this table of conventional wisdom is consistent with, but goes beyond, the four broad policy lessons presented at the beginning of this chapter. The reason is that conventional wisdom is based on more than models. It is based on models combined with a sense of institutions and history. In this book, we haven't had the space to present a lot of history or institutions, but we hope that we have presented enough to give you a good sense of why Table 15–3 represents conventional wisdom. We also hope we have convinced you that conventional wisdom can change. As we discuss in the next section, some economists have been arguing that it is time to change the conventional wisdom.

POLICY FOR THE NEW ECONOMY

In Chapter 1, we told the old joke about how, in economics, the questions remain the same—it's the answers that change. Now that we've covered the conventional wisdom, let's end by turning to the economy with which you are familiar—the U.S. economy from 1992 to 2001, and see how well that conventional wisdom is holding up.

The first thing we find is that the trade-offs that are the centerpiece of economists' conventional wisdom didn't appear. As we wrote this chapter, the U.S. economy was in its longest expansion ever. Even though unemployment had fallen to about 4 percent, close to its lowest point since 1969, inflation remained low. Per capita GDP growth had averaged 2.7 percent per year since 1993. The federal budget had moved from deficit to surplus, and the surplus was predicted to continue. Economists hadn't predicted these good times, and many were suggesting that the good times were temporary—that the trade-offs would soon rear their ugly heads. The trade-offs were just reappearing with a longer-than-usual lag.

Although economists didn't predict the economic events of the late 1990s and early 2000s, we have come up with a variety of explanations for why the economy has enjoyed its recent prosperity. Most economists point to the growth model and focus on factors that have increased the productivity of workers. Productivity growth, which averaged 1.4 percent per year from 1973 to 1995, averaged 2.5 percent per year from 1995 to 2000. Increasing productivity keeps the costs of production and inflation low. A number of factors have contributed to rises in productivity—investment, learning by doing, global competition, and deregulation.

Real investment in plants and equipment (especially in computers and technology) has increased at annual rates of over 10 percent per year since 1993. Spending on research and development increased an estimated 5 percent per year between 1993 and 2000. Investment is a key ingredient to growth in the Solow growth model. Economists also point to learning by doing—workers have learned how to apply new technologies and improve efficiency.

Competition is another factor that has contributed to U.S. economic growth. One source of competition is the increasingly global nature of the U.S. economy. More and more, U.S. firms are competing with foreign corporations in both domestic and foreign markets, and, as a result, these firms are continually having to look for ways to lower their costs and innovate. Government has also continued to deregulate a number of industries—electricity, trucking, and airlines—allowing firms to compete to offer goods and services at lower prices.

Fiscal policy, when viewed just for its direct contribution to aggregate demand, has slowed the economy. Government spending fell from 21 percent of GDP in 1991 to only 18 percent of GDP in 2000 (and is projected to fall to 15 percent by 2010). Viewed in terms of the long-run model, this fiscal restraint has contributed to the rise in investment expenditures because it leads to lower interest rates. Real long-term interest rates are about a third lower than they were during the 1980s expansion, when deficits were rising quickly.

The foundation for the growth spurt was laid during the 1980s, when the Fed established its credibility in fighting inflation and the development of credible feedback rules. So, economists deserve some of the credit.

Many economists don't believe that policy should be designed around the belief that the economy has fundamentally changed. They argue that because contracting the economy is so politically difficult if inflation begins, it is better to be conservative and save now than to be expansive now and sorry later.

CONCLUSION

We began this chapter with a discussion of a quotation, and we end it with another one—from James Meade, a Nobel prize-winning economist. Meade suggested that the following epitaph be put on his tombstone: "I kept trying and trying to be an economist, but common sense kept getting in the way." By this, he meant that he had a habit of going beyond models to understand the economy, when his instincts and educated common sense told him that the models had it wrong. In our view, he's got it wrong; he was a great economist precisely because he went beyond the models, many of which he developed and modified. Good economics is not *anti*–common sense; good economics is *educated* common sense. Good economists know the models, know the assumptions of the models, and use their educated common sense to decide how to apply the models and where to override them.

> Good economists know the models, know the assumptions of the models, and use their educated common sense to decide how to apply the models and where to apply this common sense.

KEY POINTS

- The goals of this text are to (1) teach you the models, (2) convince you that you cannot use the models in a mechanistic way, and (3) give you the institutional background to apply the models in the real world.

- Macroeconomic policy cannot be mechanistically applied to achieve the four goals: low inflation, low unemployment, high growth, and smooth growth of output. Nor can it mechanistically achieve international goals consistent with low inflation, low unemployment, high growth and smooth growth of output.

- The practice of macroeconomic policymaking combines art as well as science.

- Long-run Solow growth and new growth models recommend policies that affect growth in the long run.

- The IS/LM model is a short-run model of goods and money market equilibria. It assumes that the price level is fixed.

- The IS/LM model is combined with the BP curve to create a short-run model of an open economy.

- The AS/AD model integrates the short-run with the long run by allowing prices to fluctuate.

- The points of agreement on macroeconomic policy issues are called "conventional wisdom." Table 15–3 summarizes that conventional wisdom.

- The long-run model says that to grow, an economy must save. The short-run model says that for an economy to get out of a recession, it must consume more (save less). Policy makers must decide when to use which model.

■ The policy challenge facing the U.S. economy today is deciding whether the economy has fundamentally changed or whether the old rules still apply.

A TRIAL FINAL EXAM

At the end of each chapter, we presented several questions and exercises to help you prepare for examinations. At this point you should be ready to take the final examination. Here are some questions that come from past examinations. As is the case with chapters 1–14, you can find the answers to the even-numbered questions at www.prenhall.com/colander. *Good luck!*

1. What are the main determinants of potential output? What are the difficulties associated with estimating potential output? Why is the location of potential output important to policy makers?

2. Suppose the GDP deflator is 1.02 for 1997, 1.03 for 1998, 1.05 for 1999 and 1.07 for 2000 (all are base-year 1996).
   a. Given the following, calculate real GDP for each year:

Year	Nominal GDP (billions of current dollars)
1997	8318.4
1998	8790.2
1999	9299.2
2000	9963.1

   b. Why calculate real GDP? In other words, what does it tell you that nominal GDP does not?
   c. Calculate the inflation rates for 1997–1998, 1998–1999, and 1999–2000.

3. Explain why the CPI inflation rate is biased upward. Explain why this matters for policy.

4. If you bought stock for $10,000 and paid a commission of $30, what would happen to GDP? (Be as specific as possible.)

5. In a make-believe economy there are only two goods: widgets and wadgets. In 1990 the economy produced 20 widgets at a price of $1.00 each and 20 wadgets at a price of $2 each. In 1991 it produced 30 widgets at a price of $1.50 each and 10 wadgets at a price of $3 each. What is a reasonable range of estimates of the change in the price level? Explain your reasoning.

6. Draw a typical Phillips curve. Explain the economic rationale behind its shape. Describe the challenges that policy makers face when trying to use the Phillips curve to guide short-run policy. What is the sacrifice ratio? How is it related to the shape of

the Phillips curve and why is it important to policy makers?

7. Use the Solow growth model to explain what happens to output per capita and per capita output growth in the short run and the long run in each of the following cases:
   a. A one-time increase in saving
   b. A one-time decrease in population growth
   c. A one-time increase in technology
   d. According to the Solow growth model, what is the only possible source of long-term growth?

8. According to the Solow growth model, what causes growth? What policies does the Solow growth theory recommend? According to new growth theory, what causes growth? What policies does new growth theory recommend?

9. In the long run, what causes inflation? Use the quantity theory of money to defend your answer. What are the three key assumptions that lead to this prediction? Why does this prediction hold in the long run but not in the short run? What institutional features of an economy generally lead to inflation?

10. Suppose the United States has a fixed exchange rate and a balance of payments surplus. Explain what actions the Fed has to take to maintain the fixed exchange rate (are they buying or selling foreign exchange?). Now suppose the Fed abandoned their fixed exchange rate target and let the exchange rate float freely. Would the dollar appreciate, depreciate, or not change?

11. Suppose Congress and the President decide to cut taxes. Use the IS/LM diagram to explain what would happen to the economy in each of the following cases:
    a. The Fed accommodates fiscal policy.
    b. The Fed offsets fiscal policy.

12. Suppose the economy is initially in equilibrium. Use the IS/LM diagram to show what would happen to equilibrium income and the interest rate if the payments technology changed so that it was less costly to transfer wealth from interest-bearing financial assets to money.

13. You have been assigned to be the economic advisor to a country almost identical to the United States; it is called Identiland. The president asks you in and tells you he needs to know the economy's current

structural deficit. You ask your research assistant for information and he tells you the country's actual surplus in the federal budget is $70 billion, its GDP is $600 billion, the unemployment rate is 4.5 percent and that the natural rate of uemployment is 5.5 percent, its tax rate is .1, and there are no spending programs that are determined by income. Tell the President what the structural deficit is, giving a specific number and showing your calculations.

14. If the Fed buys bonds, what will likely happen to the short-term interest rate? Why?

15. One of the precocious students asks why when the Fed bought bonds the long-term corporate bond rate rose while the fed funds rate fell. What would be the most likely explanation?

16. Why could the reported budget deficit or surplus be a misleading indicator of whether fiscal policy is expansionary or contractionary?

17. Why does an increase in the money supply lead to an increase in aggregate output?

18. What is *crowding out?* Why does it occur?

19. Congratulations! You've been appointed Chairperson of the Council of Economic Advisors for Strangeland. Luckily, you're assigned a research assistant who tells you the following:

    The marginal propensity to consume is relatively small.

    The marginal propensity to import is large.

    Interest has no effect on investment.

    The interest demand for money is highly elastic.

    The economy is below the target rate of income.

    The trade balance is zero.

    The price level is fixed.

    The president meets you and lets you know that he wants to both *increase* income significantly and *decrease* interest rates. Carefully draw the relevant IS/LM curves and show graphically what policy you would recommend. Explain why you would recommend that policy.

20. Congratulations! You have just been appointed chairperson of the Council of Economic Advisors for the Country of Funlandia. You are assigned a research assistant who provides you with the following information:

    The marginal propensity to save is .3

    The government has a tax rate of 10 percent

    The marginal propensity to import is .1

    Actual income is $800 billion below the government's targeted income

    The country has a trade deficit of $20 billion

    The budget deficit is $30 billion.

The government wants to change the level of exogenous taxes to achieve its targeted income. What change in taxes would you recommend? Show your work.

21. What are two reasons why the AD curve is downward sloping?

22. How does an upward sloping aggregate supply curve modify the results of standard IS/LM analysis?

23. Use the IS/LM model along with the balance of payments line (assuming perfect capital mobility in a small open economy) and words to describe the impact of expansionary fiscal policy in each of the following cases:
    a. Fixed exchange rates
    b. Flexible exchange rates

24. Why do economies experience business cycles? What policies are available to minimize the size of business cycles? Have these policies been successful?

25. How does the impact of a permanent tax cut differ from the impact of a temporary tax cut? Why do these policies have different effects on the economy?

26. What is the present value of $1,000 to be received 10 years from now if the interest rate is 12 percent? How would that present value change if the interest rate rose? How would it change if the payment date were moved closer to the present?

27. If the interest rate in the economy rises from 4 percent to 5 percent, what would you expect would happen to the price of:
    a. a one year $1000 bond with a coupon rate of 4 percent?
    b. a perpetuity bond (a bond that lasts forever) with a face value of $1000 and coupon rate of 5 percent?

28. Why is present value an important concept in the microeconomic foundations of macroeconomics?

29. Describe the institutional structure of the Federal Reserve.

30. At an FMOC meeting a decision has been made to increase income in the economy by $600 million. You are assigned to write the directive for what open market operation to undertake. Your research assistant tells you that the currency to deposit ratio is .4, the reserve requirement is .1, and banks hold no excess reserves. Your research assistant tells you that for each increase in the money supply of $100 million interest rates fall by a percentage point (e.g. from 6 percent to 5 percent) and that for each percentage-point fall in the interest rate, investment rises by $200 million. He also

tells you that the marginal propensity to consume is .7, the marginal propensity to import is .1 and the marginal tax rate is .2. Draft the relevant directive for the open market operation, being as specific as you can be.

31. What are the advantages and disadvantages of conducting monetary policy with a rule versus with discretion? Which type of policy does the Fed currently use?

32. Describe the evolution of fiscal policy since the Great Depression. Are Congress and the President now more or less likely to use fiscal policy to try to steer the economy, compared with the 1960s? Why?

33. What are the three options that governments face to finance their expenditures? Describe the economic impact of each financing method.

34. If the real deficit is 200, the nominal deficit is 500, the real interest rate is 10 percent, and the inflation rate is 12 percent, what is the total government debt?

35. Someone has just suggested that the answer to the Social Security problem is to increase the Social Security trust fund by increasing taxes now. Give a short one or two-sentence response.

36. Describe the rhetorical tools politicians and economists use to describe the impact of fiscal policy. What incentive does each have to overstate the impact of policies they support?

Epilogue

Each chapter of this book began with a quotation that captured either a major theme or a sub-theme of the book. In this epilogue, we consider these quotations and their relevance for policy in relation to the themes they were meant to convey. (Giving you a quote and asking you to comment on its relevance also makes a good examination question.)

CHAPTER 1: INTRODUCTION TO MACROECONOMICS

Economics is a science of thinking in terms of models, joined to the art of choosing models which are relevant to the contemporary world. (John Maynard Keynes, 1883–1946. Famous British economist who revolutionized macroeconomics with the publication of *The General Theory of Employment, Interest and Money*.)

As stated at the beginning of Chapter 1, this is the overarching theme of the book—what you learn in economics is not answers but a set of tools that help you structure your approach to problems.

CHAPTER 2: DATA OF MACROECONOMICS: CONCEPTS, MEASUREMENT, AND PERSPECTIVE

The government is very keen on amassing statistics. . . . They collect them, add them, raise them to the nth power, take the cube root and prepare wonderful diagrams. But you must never forget that every one of these figures comes in the first instance from the village watchman, who just puts down what he damn pleases. (Sir Josiah Stamp, 1880–1941. Head of Britain's revenue department in the late nineteenth century.)

This quotation emphasizes the limitation of data. To talk meaningfully about problems, we must have data, but we must also recognize the limitations these data place on us. We can't run controlled experiments in economics, and we often must use proxies for what we really mean; both limitations require us to keep in mind that the data are always suspect, even as we use them to structure our thinking about a problem.

CHAPTER 3: GRAPPLING WITH INFLATION, UNEMPLOYMENT, AND GROWTH

When more and more people are thrown out of work, unemployment results. (Calvin Coolidge, 1872–1933. Served as the thirtieth President of the United States from 1923–1929.)

This quotation emphasizes that there are tautological truths in economics that you must understand if you are to understand economics.

CHAPTER 4: UNDERSTANDING POLICY FOR THE LONG RUN AND THE SHORT RUN

In the long run we are simply in another short run. (Joan Robinson, 1903–1983. British economist who was a critic of mainstream economics and a proponent of Keynesian economics.)

The short-run–long-run distinction is at the center of many policy debates in macroeconomics. In this quotation, Joan Robinson is expressing the Keynesian view that, by focusing on long-run issues, we can lose sight of the fact that we are always in a short run. When appropriate long-run policy is as unclear as it is, a strong argument can be made that we should focus on short-run policy, as long as we are sure that doing so won't have any definite long-run negative effects. The specific context for the quotation is in aggregate demand policy. High demand causes short-run growth, and a collection of short-run growth spurts is indistinguishable from long-run growth.

CHAPTER 5: NEOCLASSICAL GROWTH

There has been a lot of progress during my lifetime, but I'm afraid it's leading in the wrong direction. (Ogden Nash, 1902–1971. American poet.)

In the book, we assume that growth is desirable. This quotation is to remind you that there are many other issues in addition to economic growth, which the assumption sweeps under the rug. Ultimately, it is not economic output with which we are concerned; it is the well-being of society.

CHAPTER 6: BEYOND THE SOLOW GROWTH MODEL

If I have seen further it is by standing on the shoulders of giants. (Sir Isaac Newton, 1642–1727. British physicist and mathematician, credited for inventing calculus and for discovering many fundamental laws of physics.)

Often, due to space constraints, it looks as though the various models presented are contradicting each other; the reality is more complicated. Models often evolve out of other models, and individuals test the models or develop them further. The later models often embody the insights of the earlier models.

CHAPTER 7: MONEY, INFLATION, AND EXCHANGE RATES IN THE LONG RUN

Inflation is always and everywhere a monetary phenomenon. (Milton Friedman, 1915– . American economist, a proponent of free-market economics, and a Nobel Prize winner in 1976.)

Friedman's quotation simply summarizes the quantity theory's conclusion. Actually, quantity theorists recognize that reality is more complicated than this but, for policy purposes, find that it is best to focus on a single theme.

CHAPTER 8: THE DETERMINATION OF OUTPUT IN THE SHORT RUN

In the long run we are all dead. (John Maynard Keynes, 1883–1946. Famous British economist who played a major role in designing the Bretton Woods system soon before his death.)

As we discussed, the long-run–short-run distinction is central to policy debates, and this quotation by Keynes justifies a short-run focus. What Keynes meant by it is ambiguous, which is why it is so often repeated. It could mean that short-run problems can be so bad that to

ignore them is to eliminate the long run. That's the way Keynesians interpret the quotation. The other interpretation is to "live for today, tomorrow be damned." That's how the Classicals interpret it.

CHAPTER 9: POLICY ANALYSIS WITH THE IS/LM MODEL

The elder grasps the LM with his left hand and the IS with his right and, holding the totem out in front of himself with elbows slightly bent, proceeds in a straight line. . . . The grads of the village skip gaily around him at first, falling silent as the trek grows longer and more wearisome, . . . At long last the totem vibrates, then oscillates more and more; finally, it points, quivering, straight down. The elder waits for the grads to gather round and then pronounces, with great solemnity, "Behold, the Truth and Power of the Model." (Axel Leijonhufvud, 1933– . Swedish economist who spent most of his professional career in the United States. He studied the foundations of Keynesian economics.)

This quotation mocks economists' propensity to reduce everything to a model. (The author is an economist, so he is allowed to do so.) For better or worse, that is the way economists approach problems, and this macroeconomics course introduced you to that approach.

CHAPTER 10: SHORT-RUN FLUCTUATIONS IN AN OPEN ECONOMY

The only thing that has driven more men crazy than love is the currency question. (Benjamin Disraeli, 1804–1881. Conservative statesman and prime minister of Great Britain (1868, 1874–1880).)

One of the sub-themes of this book is the economy's complexity, and that complexity shows up in the exchange rate and open-economy models. These models make the economy seem understandable, but a good economist wouldn't be surprised if the economy doesn't fit the models' predictions.

CHAPTER 11: AGGREGATE SUPPLY AND AGGREGATE DEMAND

Models should be as simple as possible, but not more so. (Albert Einstein, 1879–1955. German physicist who revolutionized physics.)

We used this quotation to emphasize, once again, economists' tendency to reduce economics to models, especially supply–demand models. Economists followed that tendency with the aggregate economy and developed an aggregate demand-and-supply model. This quotation is to remind you that it takes much more than an understanding of the model to make an economist, and that the AS and AD curves are quite different than their microeconomics counterparts.

CHAPTER 12: MICROFOUNDATIONS OF CONSUMPTION AND INVESTMENT

In the long run we're all dead is one of the dumber things that Keynes said. (Robert Lucas, 1937– . A principal founder of the rational expectations approach to macroeconomics and winner of the Nobel Prize in economics in 1995.)

Here we have the other view of the long-run–short-run issue. Lucas, and real business-cycle economists, emphasize long-run policy and the problems that can develop in the long run when policy makers focus on short-run policy. Both views are right, and the reality is that we're never in either the long run or the short run. We are in the present, and the decision to focus our planning horizon on the long or short run is a matter of judgment, for which economics provides no guidance.

CHAPTER 13: THE NUTS AND BOLTS OF MONETARY POLICY

A squirrel in the forest had a particular taste for fish. He finally went to the wise old owl for some guidance and counsel. After listening to his story, the owl advised the squirrel that the way for him to satisfy that desire was to become a kingfisher. So the squirrel happily went away, ran up a tree over a brook, and imagined himself a kingfisher so he could catch some fish.

Of course, imagination was not enough. The squirrel discovered he was still a squirrel. After sitting in the tree for a while, he returned to the owl in a state of some agitation and railed, "You told me the way to satisfy my desire to get some fish was to become a kingfisher, but you haven't told me how to do that. I am still a squirrel" The owl replied, "Look, you came to me

with a problem. I gave you some sound policy advice. The rest is operational detail." (Paul Volcker, 1927– . Chairman of the Federal Reserve Board, 1979–1987.)

This quotation makes fun of economists' propensity to make models with assumptions that give definitive answers. Actual policy is an art, not a science.

CHAPTER 14: THE NUTS AND BOLTS OF FISCAL POLICY

If you don't know what you're doing, for God's sake, do it gently. (William Brainard, 1935– . Monetary economist and Yale University professor.)

This quotation is meant to emphasize that, with the limited guidance that the models actually give you, policy should be used carefully. In many ways, economists' support of laissez-faire is based on a lack of knowledge of, as opposed to understanding of, the economy.

CHAPTER 15: THE ART OF MACROECONOMIC POLICY

One of the most useful roles an economist can perform is to remind policy makers that the economy is complex. (Lee H. Hamilton, 1931– . Democrat and United States Representative from Indiana's ninth district from 1965–1999.)

All too often, people think that economists should have solutions to every policy problem. The quotation emphasizes that this assumption is not true. Many economic problems have no solution other than to run their course. Some policies might be better than others for dealing with the issue, but given institutions, those policies may be impossible to implement. In these cases, models may be insufficient to direct us to the right policy. Models can go only so far in their ability to guide policy in a complex world. Models are the best we can do, but they have to be used with educated common sense, with a full sense of their limitations.

Glossary

Accommodative monetary policy Monetary policy preventing a rise in the interest rates that would otherwise occur when a government increases its deficit.

Agglomeration effects When the concentration of firms producing similar goods in a geographic area increases productivity for all firms in the area.

Aggregate demand (AD) The sum of household consumption expenditures, firms' investment expenditures, government spending, and net exports at various price levels.

Aggregate demand (AD) curve A curve that shows the combinations of price levels and income levels at which both the goods market and the money market are in equilibrium.

Aggregate demand management When policy makers use fiscal *and*/or monetary policy to offset cyclical shocks to the economy.

Aggregate expenditures The sum of consumption expenditures by households (C), investment expenditures by firms (I), government expenditures (G), and net exports ($X − M$).

Aggregate supply (AS) The output produced in an economy at various price levels.

Aggregate supply (AS) curve A curve that shows how the price level responds to changes in aggregate demand.

Appreciate When the value of a currency rises relative to another currency.

Automatic stabilizers Programs that are built into the budget that change expenditures or revenue countercyclically without new legislative action.

Autonomous expenditures Expenditures that are independent of the level of income in the economy.

Average propensity to consume (*apc*) Consumption divided by disposable income.

Balance of payments account The transaction record of goods and assets a country buys from, and sells to, other countries.

Balance of payments constraint The limitation that the need to balance international payments (given fixed exchange rates) places on a country's fiscal policy and monetary policy.

Balance of payments (BP) curve A curve that represents combinations of interest rates and income at which the private balance of payments is in equilibrium.

Balanced growth investment The amount of investment that keeps capital per person constant.

Balanced growth investment line A line in a graph of the Solow Growth model that shows the amount of investment needed to offset depreciation and population growth.

Budget balance The difference between the taxes government collects and the expenditures government makes.

Budget Enforcement Act of 1990 A U.S. law that established caps on federal discretionary spending.

Business cycle The rise and fall of output over time.

Capital The physical goods and raw materials used in the production process.

Capital account balance The difference between capital inflows and capital outflows.

Capital outflow controls Policies that limit the amount of capital that can leave the country.

Cash-flow basis An accounting method that counts revenues when they are collected and expenditures when they are spent.

Cash-flow budget A budget based on an accounting system in which revenues and expenses are counted only when cash is received and spent.

Complex money multiplier The money multiplier when banks hold excess reserves and individuals hold cash. It equals $(1 + c)/(r + c + e)$.

Conditional convergence hypothesis The prediction that incomes per person for economies *with similar attributes* will eventually become equal.

Constant returns to scale The characteristic of the production function in which output rises by the same proportion as the increase in all inputs.

Consumer price index (CPI) A measure of the prices of goods and services consumers pay, stated as an index of base-year prices.

Consumption-based tax A tax on spending.

Consumption function   A mathematical expression of the relationship between consumption and income: $C = C_0 + mpc(Y - T)$.

Convergence hypothesis   The prediction that income per person of poor countries will catch up to that of rich countries.

Convertible currency   A currency that is freely exchangeable for another currency.

Cost-plus-markup rule   A pricing system in which a firm sets prices a percentage above costs, which results in a desirable profit margin and keeps the firm's products competitive.

Credibility   The degree to which people believe that a particular economic policy will be followed.

Crowding out   The amount by which private investment falls when government spending rises.

Current account   A component of the balance of payments account that records the flow of currencies among countries resulting primarily from the trade of goods and services to and from the rest of the world.

Current account balance   The difference between a country's import and export of goods and services, including income from past investment.

Cyclical budget surplus or deficit   The portion of the fiscal budget balance that exists because output is above or below potential output.

Cyclical coordination failures   Problems that develop in an economy because decisions by individuals feed back into the economy, augmenting the effect of the initial decision creating a mismatch between expenditures and production.

Cyclical unemployment   Unemployment that results when real output is below potential output.

Debt   The total accumulation of past deficits less the total accumulation of past surpluses.

Debt financing   Financing investment by the sale of bonds or borrowing from a bank.

Default risk   The possibility that a borrower will not pay back, or will default on, a loan.

Defensive open-market operations   Fed actions that are designed to offset temporary deviations from operating targets.

Deflation   Periods in which the price level falls.

Demand-side policy   Policy that seeks to influence aggregate expenditures.

Depreciate   When the value of a currency falls relative to another currency.

Depreciation   The wear and tear on capital during production.

Devalue   When a country with a fixed exchange rate allows its currency to depreciate.

Diminishing marginal product   The decline in the amount that additional units of an input contribute to output, other inputs held constant.

Discount rate   The interest rate the Fed charges banks that borrow reserves from the Fed.

Discouraged workers   People not in the labor force because they believe they do not have a chance of finding a job.

Discretionary spending   Government expenditures that can be determined in the annual appropriation process.

Disinflation   A decline in the rate of inflation.

Disposable income   The amount of income households have available to spend on consumption.

Division of labor   The splitting up of a task to allow specialization.

Dynamic open-market operations   Fed actions that are designed to change an operational target.

Economic growth   The average percentage change in real GDP in an economy over long periods of time.

Effective LM curve   The LM curve that exists when the money supply is determined by a monetary policy rule.

Efficiency wage   Wages set above equilibrium to attract and retain high-quality workers.

Employed   People who are working for pay for at least 15 hours a week.

Endogenous   Determined within the model.

Equation of exchange   A tautology; $MV = PY$, where M is the money supply, V is the velocity of money, P is average price of goods and services in the economy, and Y is real income.

Equity financing   Financing investment by the sale of stock.

Excess reserves   Reserves that banks hold above what the Fed requires.

Exchange rate   The price at which one currency is traded for another.

Exogenous   Determined outside the model.

Expansion Periods of rising real GDP in an economy.

Export drive A policy that promotes a country's exports, using a combination of subsidies and international appeals to buy its exports.

External balance When the government achieves its goals for its trade balance (given a flexible exchange rate) or for its balance of payments (given a fixed exchange rate), together with its goal for its exchange rate.

Factor market Market in which households supply the factors of production to firms in exchange for income.

Factors of production Resources firms use to produce goods and services, such as labor, capital, and raw materials.

Federal Open Market Committee (FOMC) A group of officials within the Federal Reserve who make key decisions about monetary policy.

Federal Reserve Bank (the Fed) The agency responsible for monetary policy in the United States.

Fed funds rate The interest rate that banks charge each other for overnight loans.

Feedback rules Rules by which the Fed adjusts its operational and intermediate targets in response to movements in economic activity that are related to its ultimate goals.

Financial market Market in which saving flows back into the income stream.

Fine-tuning Making frequent adjustments to policy to keep the economy at desired goals.

Fiscal policy The government's intentional change in taxes or expenditures to affect the level of activity in the economy.

Fixed exchange rate system Government buys and sells its own and other currencies to maintain its exchange rate at a constant level.

Flexible exchange rate system Government lets market forces determine its currency's value.

Flow concept Quantities that are measured over a time interval.

Foreign saving Flow of funds into an economy less the flow of funds out of an economy. Equals the capital account balance.

Fractional reserve banking A banking system in which banks hold only a fraction of their demand deposits in reserve and lend the remaining fraction.

Frictional unemployment The level of unemployment caused by mismatch and search in normal times, when the wage is at the equilibrium level.

GDP price deflator A measure of the market prices of all final goods and services produced in an economy stated as an index of base-year prices.

General-purpose technologies Technologies that affect all aspects of production and have the strongest effect on growth.

Goods market Market in which firms sell goods and services to households.

Government expenditures Government payments for goods and services and investment in equipment and structures.

Government saving The difference between tax revenue and government spending.

Gross domestic product (GDP) The market value of all final goods and services produced within a country within a year.

Gross private investment Business spending on equipment, structures, and inventories and household spending on owner-occupied housing.

Growth The trend rise in output.

Growth accounting formula An equation showing the contribution of each factor of production to growth of total output.

Hansen's Law In the short run, demand creates its own supply.

Human capital The set of skills and the knowledge that enables individuals to produce.

Hyperinflation Very high rates of inflation.

Hysteresis The proposition that an economy's long-run equilibrium is path dependent.

Imperfect information model A model of aggregate supply that bases the upward slope of the AS curve on firms' and workers' lack of information about absolute and relative prices.

Implementation lag The delay between the time policy makers recognize the need for a policy action and when they can institute that policy.

Increasing returns to scale An increase in all inputs leads to a proportionately greater increase in output.

Induced expenditures Expenditures that vary with the level of income in the economy.

Industrial policy Government policy that provides funds, research support, and encouragement to specific industries.

Inflation A continual rise in the average price of goods and services in an economy.

Inflation tax The seigniorage that government receives from money growth as the result of inflation.

Information lag A delay between a change in the economy and knowledge of that change in the economy.

Insider-outsider unemployment The unemployment caused by above-equilibrium wages.

Interest rate effect As the price level rises, the real money supply decreases, causing interest rates to rise and the quantity of aggregate demand to fall.

Internal balance When the government reaches its goals for interest rates and output.

International effect If nominal exchange rates are fixed, as the price level rises, net exports and the quantity of aggregate demand will fall.

Intertemporal choices Choices people make over time.

Inventory investment Goods produced for sale, but not sold.

Investment In the context of the NIPAs, fixed assets used to expand capacity or to replace machines and buildings that are wearing out and expenditures on inventories.

Investment tax credit A government tax rebate to firms for their investment.

IS curve A curve showing all combinations of income levels and real interest rates at which the goods market is in equilibrium.

IS/LM model A model that looks at the combinations of equilibria in the goods and money markets and considers how they interact.

Labor The amount of labor used in production.

Labor force The people who are either unemployed or employed.

Labor force participation rate The labor force as a percent of all the people capable of working.

Labor productivity Output per worker.

Laspeyres index A price index that uses base-year quantities to weight prices.

Law of diminishing marginal control A law that states whenever an economic variable is singled out for control, individuals will figure out ways to thwart that control.

Learning by doing Based on the belief that the more one does something, the more productive one becomes.

Life-cycle hypothesis A theory of consumption that states that people try to even out their consumption expenditures over their lifetimes.

Liquidity The ability to easily exchange one asset for another financial or real asset.

Liquidity trap A situation in which monetary policy doesn't affect the interest rate or investment.

LM curve A curve showing all combinations of income levels and interest rates at which the money market is in equilibrium.

Long-run dichotomy The separation of the real and nominal sectors in the long-run framework.

Maastricht Treaty A 1991 agreement that specified economic conditions that members of the European Union would have to meet for acceptance in the European monetary union.

Macroeconomics The study of issues that affect the economy as a whole, especially unemployment, inflation, and economic growth.

Macro policy question Do current institutions coordinate the decisions of individuals sufficiently well, or should we modify the institutions and adjust the market in some way?

Mandatory spending Government expenditures, authorized by laws, that cannot be changed in the annual appropriation process.

Marginal efficiency of investment (*mei*) The rate of return that makes the present value of a project's cash flow equal to its initial cost.

Marginal product The increase in output when one unit of input is added, holding all other inputs constant.

Marginal propensity to consume The fraction of an increase in disposable income that households spend.

Marginal propensity to expend The fraction of total income that is spent when taxes on income and induced expenditures on imports are taken into account.

Market An institution that coordinates individual decisions to trade goods and services.

Marketable securities Bonds that can be sold in a secondary market.

Microfoundations The study of macroeconomic relationships from an analysis of individual decisions.

Model A simplified representation of relationships within an economy.

Monetary base Total reserves in the banking system and currency in circulation.

Monetary policy Deliberate government action to affect the amount of money available for borrowing.

Money A financial asset that is a unit of account, a store of value, and a medium of exchange.

Money market A financial market in which highly liquid assets are traded.

Money multiplier The relationship between the monetary base and the money supply.

Multiplier The change in output that results from a one-dollar change in autonomous aggregate expenditures.

Multiplier equation An equation that tells us that equilibrium income equals the multiplier times autonomous expenditures.

Multiplier model A model of the economy that shows how changes in expenditures have a multiplied effect on aggregate output.

Mundell-Fleming model A model of an open economy in which capital is perfectly mobile.

National income The total income that a country's businesses and individuals earn in the economy in a year.

National income and product accounts (NIPAs) The U.S. federal government's official report of GDP and related measures.

Natural rate of unemployment The unemployment rate below which inflation tends to accelerate.

Net domestic product Gross domestic product minus depreciation.

Net exports The difference between the value of goods and services a country *sells* (exports) to the rest of the world and the value of goods and services it *purchases* (imports) from the rest of the world.

Net foreign factor income A country's income earned abroad by its domestic factors of production, less income earned in the country by foreign factors of production.

Net investment Gross investment less depreciation.

New growth theory A theory of growth that focuses on the role of technology in growth.

Nominal exchange rate The price at which one currency is exchanged for another currency.

Nominal GDP The production of all final goods and services valued at current market prices.

Nominal interest rate The interest rate lenders charge borrowers for the use of funds.

Nominal wages The actual wages workers receive.

Nonconvertible currency A currency that is not freely exchangeable.

Nonmarketable securities Government bonds that do not trade in a secondary market, such as savings bonds, bonds held in government accounts such as Social Security, and bonds issued to state and local governments.

Normative economics The study of what society's goals for the economy should be.

Obligation budget A budget that includes the expected value of future expenditures and revenues.

Official reserve transactions account The balance of payments account's record of government purchases and sales of currencies.

Okun's rule of thumb Each percentage point rise in the unemployment rate is associated with 2-percentage-point reduction in the annual growth rate of real GDP.

On-budget surplus An accounting measure of the federal budget that does not count expenditures on programs that have been designated by law as off-budget items, such as Social Security and the Postal Service.

Open-market operations The Fed's buying and selling of government securities to manage the money supply.

Optimal currency area A group of countries that is suitable for adopting a common currency without jeopardizing domestic policy goals.

Output gap The difference between actual output and potential output.

Paasche index A price index that uses current-year quantities to weight prices.

Paradox of thrift An increase in saving reduces output in the short run.

Partially flexible exchange rate system Government sometimes buys and sells its currency to influence its exchange rate.

Patent Legal protection that gives the holder the monopoly (sole ownership) rights to an idea or product.

Path dependency   When what happens in one period affects what happens in later periods.

Pay-as-you-go requirement   The requirement in the Budget Enforcement Act of 1990 that forces government to decrease spending in one area, or raise taxes, when spending in another area increases the deficit.

Perfect capital mobility   The ability of investors to buy and sell all of the assets they want across countries with no additional cost and risk.

Permanent income hypothesis   A theory that states that people base their consumption decisions on the present value of their expected future incomes.

Personal consumption expenditure (PCE) deflator   A measure of prices of goods and services that only consumers purchase that allows the basket of goods to change over time as people's buying habits change.

Personal consumption   Payments by households for goods and services.

Phillips curve   A curve that represents the short-run relationship between inflation and unemployment.

Policy regime   A rule that people believe is guiding policy.

Positive economics   The study of the economy and how it works.

Potential output   The amount of goods and services an economy is capable of producing for a sustainable period of time.

Present value   The current value of a future flow of income.

Price level   The average price of goods and services produced in an economy, stated as an index.

Primary budget balance   Total tax revenues less government outlays, excluding interest payments.

Private balance of payments   The sum of the current account and the capital account balances.

Private capital account   A component of the balance of payments account that records the flow of currencies among countries resulting from the purchase and sale of assets between a country and the rest of the world.

Private saving   The difference between disposable income and consumption.

Privatization   Government's sale of government-controlled activities to private, for-profit enterprises, or the transfer of current government activities to the private sector.

Producer price index (PPI)   A measure of the price level that domestic producers pay for intermediate goods and services, stated as an index of base-year prices.

Production function   A simplified description of the relationship between inputs and outputs in an economy.

Profit   Revenue less payments to factors of production.

Public good   A good that, once created, can be used by everyone without diminishing the amount of the good available to others.

Purchasing-power parity   A theory that states that the amount of goods and services a currency can buy should be the same in all countries.

Quantification bias   The tendency to focus on measurable aspects of reality rather than on unmeasurable aspects.

Quantity theory of money   A theory that states that the price level varies in direct proportion to the quantity of money.

Quotas   Quantitative limits on what a country can import.

Rational expectations   Expectations that are based on predictions of the underlying model of the economy.

Real business-cycle economists   Economists who say that technology shocks are the source of output fluctuations.

Real exchange rate   The exchange rate adjusted for price level differences among countries.

Real GDP   The market value of all final goods and services produced in a country within a year, *keeping the market price of those goods and services constant.*

Real interest rate   The nominal interest rate, adjusted for inflation.

Real money supply   The quantity of money in the economy, divided by the price level.

Real surplus   Nominal surplus adjusted for inflation.

Real wages   Nominal wages adjusted for inflation.

Reasonable expectations   Expectations based on relevant information, as processed by "reasonable" people.

Recession   Two or more consecutive quarters of declining real GDP in an economy.

Reserve requirements   The amount of cash that the Fed requires banks to hold either in their vaults or at the Fed, calculated as a percentage of their total demand deposits.

Reserves   Cash in banks' vaults or bank deposits at the Federal Reserve.

Revalue   When a country with a fixed exchange rate allows its currency to appreciate.

Ricardian equivalence A theory which states that financing government spending by borrowing has the same effect on consumption and aggregate output as does financing spending by increasing taxes.

Sacrifice ratio The cumulative percent deviation of GDP from potential divided by the decline in inflation.

Say's Law In the long run, supply creates its own demand.

Secular stagnation A tendency of economic growth to slow over time.

Seigniorage The profit the government earns when it prints money; the difference between the cost of printing the money (almost zero) and the value of that money.

Simple money multiplier The money multiplier when no one holds currency and banks hold no more reserves than the Fed requires. It equals $(1/r)$.

Social capital Institutions of a society, such as trust, customs, civic and government organizations and laws, that positively affect growth.

Solow growth model A model of growth that shows how technological innovation, saving, depreciation and population growth determine steady-state economic growth.

Solow residual The measure of technological progress in the Solow growth model that is derived by determining what part of production is not accounted for by increases in the factors of production.

Specialization The concentration of individuals on the production of a good or on aspects of production.

Speculative bubbles Inflated asset prices that are not based on expected future profits.

Stagflation A simultaneous decrease in output and increase in inflation.

Steady state equilibrium A dynamic equilibrium in which central variables are not changing. In the Solow model, it means that capital and output per person are constant, even though population is increasing and capital is depreciating.

Sticky wage and price model Model of aggregate supply that assumes firms have implicit or explicit contractual relations with their customers not to raise prices, even if demand increases.

Stock concept Quantities that are measured at a particular moment in time.

Structural budget surplus or deficit The fiscal budget balance that would exist when the economy is at potential output.

Substitution bias In the consumer price index, the failure to take into account changes in consumers' buying patterns due to relative price changes.

Supply shocks Changes in the prices of imports or in significant inputs to production.

Supply-side policy Policy that seeks to change incentives and thereby influence the amount an economy is capable of producing.

Tariffs Taxes on imports.

Tax incentives for investment Policies that lower the cost of investment, encouraging investment.

Taylor rule A rule that relates inflation and unemployment to the Fed's federal funds target. It adjusts the federal funds rate with changes in inflation and deviations of inflation from its target and output from potential output.

Technology The recipe for combining labor and capital to produce output in the production process.

The law of one price A law that states that, in competitive markets, the same good (accounting for transportation and other costs) cannot sell for two different prices.

Time-inconsistency problem The proposition that people will change their behaviors in response to a policy announcement, thereby changing the effect of the policy.

Tobin's-q The ratio of the market value of current capital to the cost of replacing that capital.

Trade balance The difference between the value of goods and services a country sells to the rest of the world (exports) and the value of the goods and services it purchases from the world (imports).

Trade policy Government actions to change either imports or exports to affect economic output.

Transfer payments Payments from the government to individuals that are not in exchange for goods and services.

Transition period The time period during which the economy moves from one steady state to another.

Underemployed Part-time workers who desire full-time jobs, and workers whose skills are not fully used.

Unemployed People who are actively seeking work but do not currently have a job.

Unemployment rate The percentage of people who want a paying job but do not have one.

Unified budget   A budget that includes all expenditures and revenues, regardless of their source.

Value added   A firm's revenue minus its purchases of intermediate goods.

Velocity of money   How many times each dollar is spent on average in a given year on final goods and services.

Virtuous circle   Growth creates more growth; growth in technology can increase productivity of capital, which can raise output, which can create more technological progress.

Voluntary restraint agreement   Informal agreement between two countries, in which one country limits its exports to the other.

Wealth effect   The effect that the changing value of wealth has on the economy.

Worker misperception model   A model of aggregate supply that bases the upward slope of the AS curve on workers incorrectly interpreting price-level changes.

Yield curve   A curve showing the relationship between bonds' maturities and interest rates.

Index

T/ one lol
d'm proud!